A CONCISE HISTORY OF THE

MIDDLE EAST

A CONCISE HISTORY OF THE
MIDDLE EAST

ELEVENTH EDITION

ARTHUR GOLDSCHMIDT JR.

Emeritus, Penn State University

WITH

AOMAR BOUM

University of California, Los Angeles

WESTVIEW PRESS

A Member of the Perseus Books Group

Westview Press was founded in 1975 in Boulder, Colorado, by notable publisher and intellectual Fred Praeger. Westview Press continues to publish scholarly titles and high-quality undergraduate- and graduate-level textbooks in core social science disciplines. With books developed, written, and edited with the needs of serious nonfiction readers, professors, and students in mind, Westview Press honors its long history of publishing books that matter.

Published by Westview Press,
A Member of the Perseus Books Group
2465 Central Avenue
Boulder, CO 80301
www.westviewpress.com

Westview Press books are available at special discounts for bulk purchases in the United States by corporations, institutions, and other organizations. For more information, please contact the Special Markets Department at the Perseus Books Group, 2300 Chestnut Street, Suite 200, Philadelphia, PA 19103, or call (800) 810-4145, ext. 5000, or e-mail special.markets@ perseusbooks.com.

Designed by Trish Wilkinson
Set in 10.75 point Minion Pro

A CIP catalog record for the print version of this book is available from the Library of Congress
PB ISBN: 978-0-8133-4962-6
EBOOK ISBN: 978-0-8133-4963-3

10 9 8 7 6 5 4 3 2 1

To the memory of
Agnes Inglis O'Neill,
teacher, counselor, friend.
She taught every subject with a spirit of fun
and each pupil in a spirit of love.

CONTENTS

Illustrations   xiii
Boxes   xv
Preface to the Eleventh Edition   xvii

1   **Introduction**   1
What Is History?   1
Then and Now, There and Here   3
The Physical Setting   5
Some Descriptive Geography   8
Conclusion   11

2   **The Middle East Before Muhammad**   12
Persia and Rome   13
The Arabs   18
Conclusion   22

3   **The First Muslim Revolution**   23
Muhammad's Early Life   23
The Emigration (*Hijra*)   28
Pillars of Faith: What Do Muslims Believe?   35
Pillars of Practice: What Must Muslims Do?   38
Conclusion   42

4   **The Early Arab Conquests**   44
The Succession Issue   44
The Initial Conquests   45
The Beginnings of Islamic Government   48
Dissension in the *Umma*   49
Changes in the Government of Islam   52
Conclusion   59

5   The High Caliphate   60
     Restoration of the Umayyad Order   61
     The Downfall of the Umayyads   64
     The 'Abbasid Caliphate   65
     The Decline of the 'Abbasids   72
     Conclusion   72

6   Shi'ites and Turks, Crusaders and Mongols   74
     Shi'ite Islam in Power   75
     The Turks   80
     The Crusades   84
     The Mongol Invasion   87
     Conclusion   91

7   Islamic Civilization   92
     The Rules and Laws of Islam   92
     Development of Jurisprudence   93
     Islamic Society   98
     Intellectual and Cultural Life   104
     Theology   107
     Conclusion   110

8   Firearms, Slaves, and Empires   112
     The Mamluks   113
     The Mongol Il-Khanids   116
     Gunpowder Technology   119
     The Ottoman Empire   120
     Persia Under the Safavids   132
     Conclusion   135

9   European Interests and Imperialism   137
     Ottoman Weakness   137
     The European Powers and the Eastern Question   139
     Conclusion   147

10   Westernizing Reform in the Nineteenth Century   148
     Egypt's Transformation   149
     Westernization of the Ottoman Empire   154
     Persia Under the Qajars   159
     Conclusion   161

11   The Rise of Nationalism   164
     Egyptian Nationalism   166
     Ottomanism, Pan-Islam, and Turkism   174

Nationalism in Persia   177
Conclusion   180

12   **The Roots of Arab Bitterness   182**
Arab Nationalism   182
World War I   187
The Postwar Peace Settlement   193
Conclusion   198

13   **Modernizing Rulers in the Independent States   199**
Turkey: Phoenix from the Ashes   200
From Persia to Iran   211
The Rise of Saʻudi Arabia   218
Conclusion   224

14   **Egypt and the Fertile Crescent Under European Control   225**
Egypt's Struggle for Independence   226
The Creation of New States in the Fertile Crescent   231
Phony Democracy and False Independence   235
World War II   242
Postwar Egypt   243
Egypt's Era of Political Frustration   244
Independence for Lebanon, Syria, and Iraq   247
Conclusion   248

15   **The Contest for Palestine   249**
Origins   249
Political Zionism   250
The Beginnings of Political Zionism   252
Britain and the Palestine Problem   255
Conclusion   267

16   **Israel's Rebirth and the Rise of Arab Nationalism   269**
Israel's War for Independence   269
The War's Aftermath   272
The Arab Countries   275
Israel's Early Years   281
Middle Eastern Oil   286
The Great Powers and the Arab World   286
Rising Arab-Israeli Tensions   295
Conclusion   298

17   **War and the Quest for Peace   300**
      The June 1967 War   301
      The Palestinians   306
      Abortive Peace Efforts   308
      Political Changes: 1967–1970   309
      Danger Signs in the Middle East   315
      The October (Yom Kippur) War   319
      The War's Aftermath   322
      Lebanon: The Arena for a New Arab Struggle   326
      The Road to Camp David   329
      Conclusion   333

18   **The Reassertion of Islamic Power   335**
      The Changing Role of Religion in Politics   337
      The Iranian Revolution   338
      The Struggle for Gulf Supremacy   347
      The Retreat from Camp David   351
      Western Policy Formation and Islamic Polity   361
      Conclusion   363

19   **The Gulf War and the Peace Process   364**
      The Gulf Crisis   365
      Operation Desert Storm   371
      The Palestinians: Their Struggle and an Elusive Peace   373
      Whither Islam?   383
      Conclusion   385

20   **The War on Terrorism   386**
      Survey of Terrorism   387
      The Iraq War   400
      The Contest for Palestine (Redux)   407
      Conclusion   415

21   **In the Season of Arab Discontent   417**
      Some Background   418
      Rebellions Across the Region   419
      Repercussions in the Non-Arab Middle East   438
      Conclusion   441

22   **Changing Middle Eastern Environments   443**
      Water and Gardens   444
      Environmental Challenges in the Modern Middle East   448
      Water Rights and Potential Political Conflicts   453

Conclusion   455
A Parting Message   455

Chronology   457
Glossary   473
Appendix Figure 1: Basic Statistics for Middle Eastern Countries   505
Appendix Figure 2: Muslim Sects: Major Schools, Notable Branches   507
Index   509

ILLUSTRATIONS

Maps

1.1 Physical features of the Middle East   6
2.1 Byzantine and Sassanid empires, circa 600   17
5.1 The 'Abbasid caliphate, circa 800   67
6.1 The Fatimids and the Seljuks, circa 1090   83
8.1 The Mamluks and the Il-Khanids, circa 1300   114
8.2 The Ottoman Empire in the sixteenth and seventeenth centuries   126
12.1 The Sykes-Picot Agreement, 1916   192
12.2 The Middle Eastern mandates, 1924   197
15.1 The UN Partition Plan for Palestine, 1947   266
17.1 Israel and the occupied territories, 1967–1973   304
17.2 The territorial situation at the end of the October 1973 War   323
18.1 The Persian Gulf area   348
20.1 Iraq   405
20.2 Settlements in the West Bank and Gaza Strip areas, 1967–2010   411
21.1 ISIL activity in Iraq and Syria   427

Figures

4.1 The Hashimite clan, showing Shi'ite imams   57
8.1 The sultans of the Ottoman Empire   121
15.1 Modern day aerial view of the Western Wall, Temple Mount, the Dome of the Rock, and al-Aqsa Mosque   261
20.1 The separation wall   412
22.1 *Qanats*   447

Tables

Appendix 1: Basic Statistics for Middle Eastern Countries   505
Appendix 2: Muslim Sects: Major Schools, Notable Branches   507

BOXES

3.1 'Aisha bint Abi-Bakr   32

4.1 Mu'awiya ibn Abi-Sufyan   55

5.1 Al-Ma'mun   71

6.1 Hulegu Khan   89

7.1 Ahmad ibn Hanbal   109

8.1 Orhan   123

9.1 The Koprulu Family of Viziers   140

10.1 Mustafa Reshid Pasha   158

11.1 Ahmad 'Urabi   171

12.1 Faysal ibn Husayn   195

13.1 Mustafa Kemal (Ataturk)   203

14.1 King Faruq   238

15.1 Hajj Amin al-Husayni   259

16.1 David Ben-Gurion   285

17.1 Anwar al-Sadat   314

18.1 Sayyid Ruhollah Musavi Khomeini   340

19.1 Yasir 'Arafat   378

20.1 Osama bin Laden   388

20.2 Hassan Nasrallah   394

21.1 Abu Bakr al-Baghdadi   429

PREFACE TO THE
ELEVENTH EDITION

The Middle East is significant to the rest of the world for its resources, its current struggles between rulers and peoples, and the rise of various forms of resurgent Islam. Its history helps to explain many of the political and military events that dominate the daily news.

This textbook, sometimes called "classic," is coauthored by Arthur Goldschmidt, Professor Emeritus of Middle East History at the Pennsylvania State University, and Aomar Boum, Assistant Professor of Anthropology at the University of California, Los Angeles, and Faculty Fellow at the Université Internationale de Rabat, Morocco. We facetiously termed an earlier edition *A Decreasingly Concise History of the Middle East*, but the book has to grow as new events and trends emerge. Certain parts of the traditional text, including the annotated bibliographic essay, are transferred to a designated web page constructed by Westview Press. We will add some other relevant photos to the website, as well as some sample test questions for course instructors.

These cuts made room to include coverage of recent significant changes in the region, including a new final chapter describing environmental changes and challenges, and a penultimate chapter that covers and interprets what has been happening since 2012, when the tenth edition was released. We've also made relevant additions to the chronology and glossary.

Teachers and students need a book that reflects current scholarship, does not hide its ideas behind a pseudoscholarly style addressed to pedants, and does not reinforce political or ethnic biases. Students—and members of the wider English-speaking public—deserve clear explanations of the Arab-Israeli conflict, the Middle East's role in the energy crisis, the Islamic resurgence, the Iraq War, and the revolutions in Iran and the Arab countries. The book has gone through ten previous editions and, despite the appearance of other general histories, has become ever more widely used in universities worldwide.

Any work of art or scholarship follows conventions. When writing a book that introduces a recondite subject to students and general readers, its authors must tell the audience what these conventions will be. The English system of weights and measures is giving way to the metric system; this book uses both. Prices expressed in non-American currencies, ancient or modern, are given in 2015 US dollar equivalents. Muslims follow a twelve-month lunar calendar dated from the year Muhammad and his associates moved from Mecca to Medina. Quite naturally, they use this calendar when they teach or learn Islamic history. Conversion between the two systems is cumbersome and prone to error. Therefore, all dates given in this text are based on the Gregorian calendar, though we have also used Muslim dates (and identified them as such in the text). When dates appear in parentheses following a ruler's name, they refer to the span of his or her reign. Personal names in languages using the Arabic script are transliterated according to the *International Journal of Middle East Studies* system, minus the diacritics, except for a few persons and places mentioned often in the press. The same applies to a few technical terms that cannot be translated accurately into English.

Our wives, Louise Goldschmidt and Norma Mendoza-Denton, deserve special acknowledgment for their encouragement, patience, and love. Aomar Boum also thanks his daughter, Majdouline Boum-Mendoza.

The work of a great teacher never perishes—hence we have retained Arthur Goldschmidt's original dedication of this book to an elementary school teacher and principal whose knowledge, ideas, and enthusiasm live on in thousands of her former pupils and in the Georgetown Day School in Washington, DC.

We have likewise retained in this edition many of the contributions made by Lawrence Davidson as coauthor of the eighth, ninth, and tenth editions, and thank him for his generous consent to do so. We would also like to thank the reviewers who sent invaluable feedback and suggestions to Westview Press: Ibrahim al-Marashi (California State University, San Marcos), Sharon Eicher (Friends University), Michael Hinckley (Northern Kentucky University), T. Hunt Tooley (Austin College), and Joan Roland (Pace University).

Finally, we'd like to acknowledge the work our colleagues at Westview—our editor Ada Fung, our project editor Amber Morris, and our copyeditor Carrie Watterson—have done to support the book.

We've enjoyed working together and getting to know each other by e-mail, phone, and Skype. We remain accountable for all errors of fact or interpretation. We welcome readers' comments and advice. You may email Arthur Goldschmidt at axg2@psu.edu and Aomar Boum at aboum@anthro.ucla.edu.

Arthur Goldschmidt Jr.
Aomar Boum

1

Introduction

In this book we introduce the Middle East to English-speaking students and other readers who have not lived in the area or studied its history before. Historical events occur in complex contexts, which everyone must understand in order to act wisely in the future.

Middle East is a rather imprecise term, describing a geographical area that extends from Egypt to Afghanistan or the cultural region in which Islam arose and developed. We plan to make the term clearer in this chapter. First, let us tell you why we think history is the discipline best suited for your introduction to the area. After all, you might look at the Middle East through its systems for allocating power and values using the discipline of political science. An economist would focus on the ways its inhabitants organize themselves to satisfy their material needs. Sociologists and cultural anthropologists would analyze the institutions and group behavior of the various peoples who constitute the Middle East. You could also view its various cultures through their languages, religions, literature, geography, architecture, art, music, dance, and food.

WHAT IS HISTORY?

Why history? Some of you may have picked up a rather dismal picture of history from schools or books. History is supposed to be the study of events that took place in the past. These events have been carefully gathered, checked for accuracy, and written down in chronological order by historians. They are organized according to the reigns of rulers or the life spans of nation-states, divided into manageable chunks of time. Students memorize this "history" in the form of facts, names, and dates. Only an occasional concept, casually communicated and dimly grasped, adds some seasoning to this stew. Some teachers tell their students just to learn the "trends." These are often seen as vague assertions unsupported by evidence from the unheeded lectures or the unread textbook. History, in this all-too-common conception, is a dreary bore, a dead subject. It is not useful. It cannot predict what will happen in the future. It will not get the history student a job.

But let us respond. History belongs to all of us. Whenever you talk about something that happened to you, your friends, your community, or your country, you are relating history through events that occurred in the past. History can cover politics, economics, lifestyles, beliefs, works of literature or art, cities or rural areas, incidents you remember, stories older people told you, or subjects you can only read about. Broadly speaking, everything that has ever happened up to the moment you read these lines is history, or the study of the past.

As an academic discipline, though, history mainly examines those aspects of the past that have been written down or passed on by word of mouth. Historians cannot write or teach about an event that was never recorded. The unrecorded event might be trivial: What did Columbus have for breakfast on 12 October 1492? Or it might be a big question: When Muhammad was dying on 8 June 632, whom did he want as his successor? Historians do not treat all recorded events as being equally important. They evaluate past events, stressing some while downgrading or even omitting others. What historians choose to mention can also change over time or vary from place to place. We will look at this *historiographical* dimension later.

How do historians pick the events they mention or stress? Often, they base their choices on the degree to which those events affected what later happened. Just as chemistry goes beyond spotting the elements on the periodic table, history deals with more than just isolated events. Historians look at cause-and-effect relationships. The Pilgrims sailed to Plymouth in 1620 *because* they wanted to worship God in their own way. Russian intellectuals, workers, and peasants hated the autocratic (and inefficient) rule of Czar Nicholas II; *therefore,* they plotted and rebelled until they overthrew him in 1917. We ask not only *what* occurred but also *why*.

Did the institution of slavery cause the Civil War? Did Roosevelt's New Deal end the Great Depression? Was the creation of Israel in 1948 the result of Hitler's attempt to destroy the European Jews during World War II? When we study cause-and-effect relationships, we are studying processes. What makes individuals or groups act, react, make decisions, or refrain from acting? The answers usually depend on the time and the place.

Now let us raise another issue. What are the most meaningful units of historical study? The West has a strong tradition of studying national history—that of the United States, Britain, France, Russia, or, for that matter, China or Japan. In other parts of the world, including the Middle East, political boundaries have changed so often that nation-states have not existed until recently, let alone served as meaningful units of historical study. In the Islamic and Middle Eastern tradition, historical studies tend to center on dynasties (ruling families), whose time spans and territories vary widely. The Ottoman Empire, for example, was a large state made up of Turks, Arabs, Greeks, and many other ethnic groups. Its rulers, called *sultans*, all belonged to a family descended from a Turkish warrior named Osman. It was not a nation but a dynastic state—one that lasted a long time and affected many other peoples. At some times we will use the old dynastic divisions of time and space; for the modern period, we sometimes use a country-by-country approach, making major wars and crises the points of division. At other times we will examine the history topically, in terms of "Islamic civilization" or "westernizing reform."

From what we now know about Middle East history, we believe that our most meaningful unit of study is not the dynasty or the nation-state but the civilization. Although the term *civilization* is easier to describe than to define, this book, especially in its earlier chapters, focuses on an interlocking complex of rulers and subjects, governments and laws, arts and letters, cultures and customs, cities and villages—in short, on a civilization that has prevailed in most of western Asia and northern Africa since the seventh century, all tied together by the religion of Islam. You will see how Islamic beliefs and practices produced institutions for all aspects of Middle Eastern life. Then you will learn how Muslim patterns of belief and action were disrupted by the impact of the West. You will look at some of the ways in which the peoples of the Middle East have coped with Western domination, accepting some but rejecting much European and US culture. You will also see how they have won back their political independence and tried to regain their autonomy as a civilization. We believe this to be the best way to get started on studying the Middle East.

THEN AND NOW, THERE AND HERE

But why, you may ask, should anyone want to study the Middle East, let alone the history of Islamic civilization? We argue that studying any subject, from philosophy to physics, is potentially an adventure of the mind. Islamic history is a subject worth learning for its own sake. Confronted by distances of time and space, and by differences of thought patterns and lifestyles, we learn more about ourselves—about our era, area, beliefs, and customs. Islam is somewhat like Christianity and Judaism, but not entirely so. The peoples of the Middle East (like those of the West) are partial heirs to the Greeks and the Romans. To a greater degree, however, they are direct successors of the still earlier civilizations of Egypt, Mesopotamia, Persia, and other lands of the ancient Middle East. As a result, they have evolved in ways quite different than we have. They are rather like our cousins, neither siblings nor strangers to us.

In another sense, our culture owes much to the civilizations of the Middle East. Our religious beliefs and observances are derived from those of the Hebrews, Mesopotamians, Egyptians, Persians, and Greeks who lived in the Middle East before Islam. Moreover, many Westerners do not know what they have learned from Islamic culture. A glance at the background of some English words backs up our point.

Let us start with what is closest to ourselves—our clothes. The names of several items we are apt to wear have Middle Eastern backgrounds: cotton (from the Arabic *qutn*), pajamas and sandals (both words taken from Persian), and obviously caftans and turbans. Muslin cloth once came from Mosul (a city in Iraq) and damask from Damascus. The striped cat we call tabby got its name from a type of cloth called *'attabi* once woven in a section of Baghdad by that name. Some Arabs claim that the game of tennis took its name from a medieval Egyptian town, Tinnis, where cotton cloth (used then to cover the balls) was woven. Are we stretching the point? Well, the name for the implement with which you play the game, your racquet, goes back to an Arabic word meaning "palm of the hand." Backgammon, chess, polo, and playing cards came to the West from the Middle East. The rook in chess comes from the Persian *rukh* (castle) and *checkmate* from *shah mat* (the king is dead). As for household furnishings, we have taken *divan, sofa, mattress,* and of course *afghan* and *ottoman* from the Middle East.

You may already know the Middle Eastern origin of such foods as shish kebab, yogurt, tabbouleh, hummus, and pita. Some of our other gastronomic terms have been naturalized over longer periods: *apricot, artichoke, ginger, lemon, lime, orange, saffron, sugar,* and *tangerine. Hashish* is an Arabic word denoting, in addition to cannabis, weeds and grass, depending on the context. Both *sherbet* and *syrup* come from the Arabic word for "drink." Muslims may not use intoxicating liquor, but the very word *alcohol* comes from Arabic. So do words for other familiar beverages: *coffee, soda* (derived from the word for "headache," which the Arabs treated with a plant containing soda), and *julep* (from the Persian word for "rosewater").

Indeed, many words used in the sciences, such as *alembic, azimuth,* and *nadir,* are Arabic. In mathematics algebra can be traced to *al-jabr* (bonesetting) and *algorithm* to a ninth-century mathematician surnamed al-Khwarizmi. The word *guitar* goes back, via Spain, to the Arabs' *qitar.* Other Middle Eastern instruments include the lute, tambourine, and zither. *Mask* and *mascara* both derive from an Arabic word meaning "fool." Let some miscellaneous words round out the digression: *alcove* (from *al-qubba,* a "domed area"), *admiral, arsenal, magazine* (in the sense of a storehouse), *talc, tariff* (from *al-ta'rifah,* a "list of prices"), and *almanac* (from *al-manakh,* meaning "weather"). Middle East history gives us some background to what we have, what we do, and what we are.

Getting back to more practical matters, we must look to the recent history of the Middle East to explain what is happening there now. This area gets more than its share of the news: Arab-Israeli wars (or possibly peace), assassinations, oil, revolutions, terrorism, the Gulf War, the US occupation of Iraq, and the Arab Spring. Current events in the Middle East affect us as individuals, as members of religious or ethnic groups, and as citizens of our countries. Can history give us clues as to how we should respond? We think so. This book will risk relating past events to current ones. As historians, we care about what happened, how it happened, and why it happened. But all of us who live in this world want to know what these events mean for ourselves, here and now.

As this caravan (originally a Persian word) of Middle East history starts off, we wish you *rihla sa'ida, nasi'a tova, safar be-khayr*—and may you have a fruitful intellectual journey.

THE PHYSICAL SETTING

Before we can write anything about its history, we must settle on a definition of the Middle East. Even though historians and journalists throw the term around, not everyone agrees on what it means. It makes little sense geographically. No point on the globe is more "middle" than any other. What is "east" for France and Italy is "west" for India and China. Logically, we could say "southwest Asia," but would that not leave out Egypt and European Turkey? Our conventional view of the "Old World" having three continents—Europe, Asia, and Africa—breaks down once we consider their physical and cultural geography. Do Asia and Africa divide at the Suez Canal, at the border between Egypt and Israel, or somewhere east of Sinai? What differences are there between peoples living east and west of the Ural Mountains or the Bosporus? For us humans, continents are not really logical either.

So let us write about a "Middle East" that the press has made familiar to us. Its geographical limits may be disputed, but this book will treat the

6

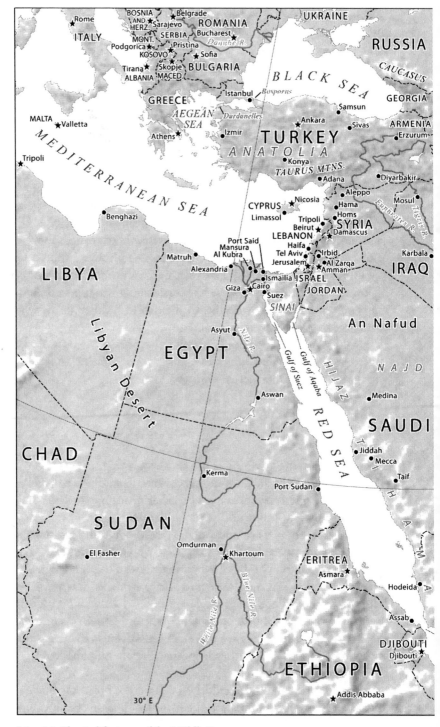

Map 1.1 Physical features of the Middle East

Middle East as running from the Nile Valley to the Muslim lands of Central Asia (roughly, the valley of the Amu Darya, or Oxus, River), from southeast Europe to the Arabian Sea (see Map 1.1). We may stretch or shrink the area when discussing a given historical period in which political realities may have altered the conventional outline. After all, the lands south and east of the Mediterranean were the East to our cultural forebears until they went on to India and China, whereupon the Muslim lands became the Near East. World War II made it the Middle East, and so it has remained, despite UN efforts to rename it "West Asia." For navigation and aviation, peacetime commerce and wartime strategy, and journalism and politics, the area is in the middle, flanked by centers of population and power.

SOME DESCRIPTIVE GEOGRAPHY

History waits upon geography. Before you can have a play, there must be a stage. Perhaps we should spend a lot of time on topography and climate, flora and fauna, and other aspects of descriptive geography. Some textbooks do, but they may remind you of the bad old way of teaching geography by making schoolchildren memorize the names of mountains, rivers, capitals, and principal products of countries. Let us stick to the few essential points you need to master before starting your study of Middle East history. We will elaborate on this topic in Chapter 22.

Climate

The Middle East tends to be hot and dry. Most parts get some rainfall but usually in amounts too small or too irregular to support settled agriculture. Yet the world's oldest farming villages have been unearthed in the highlands of Anatolia (Asiatic Turkey), Persia, and Palestine. Others have been found in the western Sahara. What happened? It seems that as the polar ice caps (from the last, great Ice Age) retreated some 10,000 years ago, rainfall diminished in North Africa and southwest Asia. Hunting and food-gathering peoples, living in lands that could once have been like the Garden of Eden, had to learn how to control their sources of sustenance, as rain-watered areas became farther and farther apart. Some peoples moved into the marshy valleys of the great rivers: the Nile, the Tigris, and the Euphrates. By 4000 BCE (before the Common Era) or so, they had learned how to tame the annual floods to water their fields. Other peoples became nomads; they learned how to move up and down mountains or among desert oases to find forage for their sheep, goats, donkeys, and eventually camels and horses.

The sedentary farmers who tamed the rivers needed governments to organize the building of dams, dikes, and canals for large-scale irrigation that would regulate the distribution of the floodwaters. They also needed protection from wandering animal herders. The latter group, the nomads, sometimes helped the settled peoples as soldiers, merchants, and purveyors of meat and other animal products. But at times they also became a threat to the farmers and their governors when they pillaged the farms and sacked the cities. Farmers and herders often fought, like Cain and Abel, and yet they also needed each other. In arid lands characterized by long, hot summers and cold winter nights, both groups had to coexist to survive.

Location

The Middle East is the natural crossroads of the Afro-Eurasian landmass. It is also the "land of the seven seas." It lies athwart the water route from southern Ukraine to the Mediterranean via the Black Sea, the Bosporus, the Sea of Marmara, the Dardanelles, and the Aegean Sea. In various eras an area between the Nile Delta and the Sinai Peninsula has been adapted to facilitate shipping between the Mediterranean and the Red Sea, which in turn has served as a highway to Asia and East Africa. Ever since the taming of the one-humped camel around 3000 BCE, men and women have crossed the deserts with their merchandise, flocks, and household goods. Even the high mountains of Anatolia and Persia did not bar passage to people with horses, donkeys, or two-humped camels. Invaders and traders have entered the Middle East from Central Asia, Europe, and Africa since prehistoric times. Rarely in the past 4,000 years have Middle Eastern peoples known any respite from outside pressures or influences.

Consider what this accessibility means for the Middle East, compared with other parts of the world. Chinese civilization developed in relative isolation; invading "barbarians" were first tamed and then absorbed into China's political system. British subjects lived for centuries in what they smugly called "splendid isolation" and viewed foreign affairs as "something, usually unpleasant, that happens to someone else." The United States long saw itself separate from the outside world. Writing as Americans to our fellow citizens, who may at times question the political attitudes and actions of Middle Eastern peoples, let us all ask ourselves these questions: When did we last fight a war on US soil? When did we last experience a foreign military occupation? Up to 2001, did we even fear hostile raids from abroad? Middle Easterners have, by contrast, known conquest, outside domination, and a continuing exchange of people and animals (but also of goods and ideas) with both the East and the West throughout their history.

Natural Resources

Nature did not endow the Middle East as lavishly as North America or Europe. There are no more grassy plains. Nearly all the forests have been cut down. Partly as a result of deforestation, drinkable water is scarce almost everywhere and has become so precious that wars have been fought over it. Some coal and lignite are mined in Anatolia. A few mountainous areas harbor deposits of copper, iron, and other metals; in many instances they have been worked since ancient times. These resources are meager. More plentiful are sand and limestone, other building materials, and sunlight (a blessing if solar energy becomes the main source of power).

But what about oil? It is true that some areas, especially those around the Persian Gulf, have huge petroleum deposits, more than half of the world's known reserves. Oil has magnified the Middle East's importance. Its blessings, though, are showered on but few countries, mainly Saudi Arabia, Iran, Kuwait, Iraq, and the United Arab Emirates. Exploitation of Middle Eastern oil did not start until the twentieth century; it became large scale only after 1945. For most of history, crude petroleum was a medicine, a pitch for caulking riverboats, or the cause of mysterious fires that were objects of religious veneration, but not the source of wealth and power that it has now become. And who knows how long it will last?

Human Diversity

The Middle East's geography has contributed to the diversity of its inhabitants. On the one hand, varied landscapes—mountains and plains, river valleys and deserts—require differing lifestyles. Relatively inaccessible mountains, further isolated in winter and spring by fast-flowing streams, have shielded religious and ethnic minorities in such countries as Lebanon, Yemen, and Iran. On the other hand, frequent invasions have brought new races and folkways into the Middle East. The result is a vast mosaic of peoples, a living museum of physical types, belief systems, languages, and cultures.

This diversity may not always show up on statistical tables, such as the one at the end of this book. Even when it does, remember that nine-tenths of the people in the Middle East are Muslims. Half the population of the area speaks Arabic; most of the other half speaks either Turkish or Persian. The mosaic of separate religious and ethnic groups has started to crumble. Widespread primary schooling, satellite television, DVDs, cell phones, and tablets help diffuse a universal culture, mostly among the young. Oil revenues, the proliferation of factories, and the growth of cities have also made the people seem more alike.

But cultural and religious differences persist and promote conflicts. Lebanon's civil wars arose partly because many Muslims felt that they did not enjoy power and prestige equal to that of the Christians, who used to be the country's majority. Syria's current elite comes disproportionately from a minority sect, the Alawites, who used the army officer corps to rise to power in a society otherwise dominated by Sunni Muslims. Christian Arabs, especially the Greek Orthodox, who make up about 5 percent of Syria's population and 8 percent of Lebanon's, were more active than the Muslims in promoting the early spread of Arab nationalism in those countries. Iraq's politics are bedeviled by differences between Sunni and Shi'ite Muslim Arabs, both of whom have resisted attempts by the Kurds (about a fifth of the country's population) to form a separate state. Israel, though mainly Jewish, has 1.7 million Arabs living within its pre-1967 borders and has been ruling 2.6 million additional Arab Muslims and Christians in the West Bank, which it has controlled since the June 1967 war. The Gaza Strip, which Israel occupied from 1967 to 2005 and invaded again in 2006, 2009, and 2014, contains 1.8 million Arabs. Israel's Jews are divided between those of European origin, called *Ashkenazim,* and those who came from Asian or African countries, called *Mizrachim* or Orientals. You may now be confused by these sectarian and ethnic differences, but we will cover them in more detail later. You may also look up the terms in the glossary.

CONCLUSION

The interaction between human beings and their physical surroundings is a fascinating subject, more so than most students realize. As you read through the historical narrative, do not be put off by the names of deserts and mountains, rivers and seas. Think of the challenges they have posed to humanity and the stratagems by which Middle Eastern peoples have overcome them. History is not limited to shaykhs and shahs or to presidents and politicians; it is also the story of traders and teachers, artisans and farmers, herders of goats and warriors on horseback. In the chapters that follow, you will see how they used the mountains, plains, and valleys that appear on Map 1.1 and how they filled the Middle East with cities, dynastic kingdoms, and contending nation-states.

2

❈

The Middle East
Before Muhammad

If history can be defined as humanity's recorded past, then the Middle East has had more history than any other part of the world. Although the human species probably originated in Africa, the main breakthroughs to civilization occurred in the Middle East. It is here that most staple food crops were initially cultivated, most farm animals first domesticated, and the earliest agricultural villages founded. Here, too, arose the world's oldest cities, the first governments, and the earliest religious and legal systems. Writing and the preservation of records were Middle Eastern inventions. Without them, history, as commonly understood, would be inconceivable.

During the last 10,000 years before the birth of Christ, the peoples of the Middle East developed various skills to cope with their challenging environment. They tamed donkeys and cattle to bear their burdens and share their labors. They built ovens hot enough to fire clay pottery. As the uplands grew dry and parched, they learned to harness the great rivers to grow more crops. They fashioned tools and weapons of bronze and, later, of forged iron. They devised alphabets suitable for sending messages and keeping records on tablets of clay or rolls of papyrus. They developed cults and rituals, expressing the beliefs that gave meaning to their lives. They absorbed Medes and Persians coming from the north and various Semitic peoples from Arabia. They submitted to Alexander's Macedonians in the fourth century BCE but soon absorbed them into their own cultures. Finally, in the last century before Christ, the lands east and south of the Mediterranean were themselves absorbed into the Roman Empire.

PERSIA AND ROME

The two great empires existing at the dawn of the Common Era, Persia and Rome, took many pages from the books of their imperial precursors. During the period of the Achaemenid dynasty (550–330 BCE), Persia, the land we now call Iran, ruled over various ethnic and religious groups in an area stretching from the Indus to the Nile. Some, but not all, of the kings and nobles followed the religion of Zoroaster, who lived around the eleventh century BCE. He had taught the existence of a supreme deity, Ahura Mazda (Wise Lord), creator of the material and spiritual worlds, source of both light and darkness, founder of the moral order, lawgiver, and judge of all being. An opposing force, Ahriman, was represented by darkness and disorder. Although Zoroaster predicted that Ahura Mazda would ultimately win the cosmic struggle, all people were free to choose between Good and Evil, Light and Darkness, the Truth and the Lie. The Zoroastrians venerated light, using a network of fire temples tended by a large priestly class. Zoroastrianism appealed mainly to the highborn Persians, not to commoners or to the other peoples under their rule. The Achaemenid kings tolerated the diverse beliefs and practices of their subjects as long as they obeyed the laws, paid their taxes, and sent their sons to the Persian army. Their empire set the pattern followed by most—but not all—of the multicultural dynastic states that have arisen since ancient times. When Alexander the Great humbled the Achaemenids and absorbed their empire into his own, he hoped to fuse Hellenic (Greek) ways with the culture of the Middle East. Many of the ideas, institutions, and administrators of the Egyptians, Syrians, Mesopotamians, and Persians were co-opted into his far-flung but short-lived realm.

Cultural fusion likewise occurred later, when Rome ruled the Middle East. By uniting under its rule all the peoples of the Mediterranean world, the Roman Empire stimulated trade and the interchange of peoples and folkways. Several Middle Eastern religions and mystery cults spread among the Romans, including Mithraism, a cult that had begun in Persia and attracted many Roman soldiers, and Christianity, originally a Jewish sect whose base of support was broadened by Paul and the apostles. Most of the early church fathers lived in Anatolia, Syria, Egypt, and North Africa. These areas—later Islam's heartland—saw the earliest development of most Christian doctrines and institutions. By the late third century, Christianity (still officially banned by the Roman Empire) actually prevailed in the eastern Mediterranean. Its appeal, relative to rival religions, lay partly in its success in adopting the attractive aspects of earlier faiths. For instance, the Egyptians could identify the risen Christ with Osiris, one of their ancient gods who too had died and been resurrected.

When Rome's emperor Constantine (r. 313–337) became a nominal Christian, he redirected the course of history, both Middle Eastern and Western. Rome became a Christian empire. The emperor ordered the construction of a new capital, strategically situated on the Straits linking the Black Sea to the Aegean. He called it *Nova Roma* (New Rome), but its inhabitants named it Constantinople. Its older name, Byzantium, survives in the parlance of historians who call his "new" state the Byzantine Empire. Actually, you may get away with calling it Rome, just as people did in the fourth century and long afterward. Even now, when Arabs, Persians, and Turks speak of "Rum," they mean what we term the Byzantine Empire, its lands (especially Anatolia), or the believers in its religion, Greek Orthodox Christianity. Rum was far from the Italian city on the banks of the Tiber, but the old Roman idea of the universal and multicultural empire lived on in this Christian and Byzantine form. Later, Arabs and other Muslims would adopt this idea and adapt it to their own empires.

Roman rule benefited some Middle Eastern peoples. Their trading and manufacturing cities flourished, just as before. Greek, Syrian, and Egyptian merchants grew rich from the trade among Europe, Asia, and East Africa. Arab camel nomads, or Bedouin, carried cloth and spices (as well as the proverbial gold, frankincense, and myrrh) across the deserts. Other Middle Easterners sailed through the Red Sea, the Gulf, and the Indian Ocean to lands farther east. Surviving remains of buildings at Leptis Magna (Libya), Jerash (Jordan), and Ba'albek (Lebanon) give us a hint of the grandeur of Rome in the Middle East.

But Roman dominion had its darker side. Syria and Egypt, the granaries of the ancient world, were taxed heavily to support large occupying armies and a top-heavy bureaucracy in Rome and Constantinople. Peasants, fleeing to the big cities to escape taxes, could find no work there. Instead, they joined rootless mobs that often rioted over social or religious issues. In principle, an urbane tolerance of other people's beliefs and customs was the hallmark of a Roman aristocrat. But we know that long before Rome adopted Christianity, its soldiers tried to put down a Jewish rebellion by destroying the Second Temple in Jerusalem. Many of Jesus's early followers were tortured or killed for refusing to worship the Roman emperor.

Christian Rome proved even less tolerant. The spread and triumph of Christianity brought it into the mainstream of Hellenistic (Greek-influenced) philosophy. Major doctrinal crises ensued, as Christians disputed the precise nature of Christ. The debated points are hard to grasp nowadays and may puzzle even Christians, as well as everyone else. Let us simplify the issues. The essence of Christianity—what distinguishes it from Judaism and Islam, the other monotheistic (one god) religions—is its teaching that God, acting out of love for an often sinful humanity, sent his son, Jesus, to live on earth among men and women and to redeem them from their sins by suffering and dying on the cross. If you hope, after your death, to be reunited with God in the next world, you must accept Jesus as Christ (Greek for "anointed one" or "messiah") as your personal savior. Christ's central role as mediator between God and humanity led the early Christians into many disputes over his nature.

Dissident Christian Sects

One Christian group, the Arians, which arose in the early fourth century, taught that Christ, though divinely inspired and sired, was still a man not equivalent to God. The Arians' foes argued that if Christ were merely a man, his crucifixion, death, and resurrection could not redeem humankind. They won the church's acceptance of Christ's divinity at a council held in Nicaea in 325 CE (the Common Era). Arianism became a heresy (a belief contrary to church doctrine), and its followers were persecuted as if they had betrayed the Roman Empire. Most Christians, though, accepted the divine Trinity: God as Father, Son, and Holy Spirit. Was Christ really God? If so, do Christians accept the Gospel stories of his mother's pregnancy and of his birth, baptism, mission, and suffering—all essentially human attributes?

In Antioch arose a school of theologians called the Nestorians. They saw Christ as two distinct persons, divine and human, closely and inseparably joined. A church council at Ephesus condemned this view in 430, after which the emperor and the Orthodox Church tried to suppress Nestorianism throughout the Byzantine Empire. Many Nestorians found refuge in Persia and sent out missionaries to Central Asia, India, China, and even southern France. Some of their opponents, called Monophysites, went to the opposite extreme, claiming that Christ contained within his person a single, wholly divine nature. Though centered in Alexandria, this Monophysite idea won followers throughout Egypt, Syria, and Armenia (an independent kingdom in eastern Anatolia). The Egyptian Monophysites called themselves Copts, the Syrians Jacobites; their churches (plus the Armenian one) still survive today. The majority of Orthodox bishops, meeting at Chalcedon in 451, declared that the Monophysites were heretics, like the Arians and the Nestorians. The Orthodox Church found a compromise formula: Christ the savior was both perfect

God and perfect man. His two natures, though separate, were combined within the single person of Jesus Christ. Whenever the Byzantine emperor upheld the Chalcedon formula, the Orthodox bishops would use their political power to oppress Egyptians and Syrians who would not recant their Monophysite (or Nestorian) heresy. This policy turned dissenters against Constantinople and would later facilitate the Arab conquests and the process by which Islam displaced Christianity as the majority religion in the Middle East.

Rome's Persian Rival

The Roman Empire never monopolized the Middle East. There was always a rival state in Persia that covered not just today's Iran but also what we now call Iraq (Mesopotamia), in addition to lands farther east, such as present-day Afghanistan, Pakistan, and Central Asia. Mountain ranges, such as the Zagros in lands north of the Gulf, the Elburz just south of the Caspian, and the Khurasan highlands, got enough rain and snow to support hundreds of hillside agricultural villages. Some Persian farmers shrewdly channeled groundwater through underground *qanat*s, a sophisticated irrigation system that sustained farms and homes in otherwise parched lowlands. The Persians were better than the Romans at bronze casting and iron working. Both East and West adopted Persian architectural motifs, such as domes mounted on squinches (reinforced corners), shaded courtyards, and huge bas-relief murals.

From 250 BCE to 226 CE, Persia was ruled by the Parthians, a poorly understood dynasty. Their written histories have come from the Romans, who could never subdue them, and the Sassanids, the Persian dynasty that supplanted them. We can hardly expect these sources to be sympathetic. But archaeological excavations have proved that the Parthians, who were proficient hunters on horseback, engaged architects and artisans. They preserved Persian culture and the Zoroastrian religion, yet they welcomed Buddhists and Jews into their country to live.

Their successors, the Sassanid dynasty, usually get credit for Persia's revival. Between the third and seventh centuries, they amassed an extensive empire (shown on Map 2.1), established Zoroastrianism as the state religion, and set up a strong and centralized administration. The early Sassanids sent out scholars to many other countries to collect books, which were translated into the Pahlavi (Middle Persian) language, to trade, and to collect scientific and technical lore. Many foreign scholars were attracted to Persia, a tolerant kingdom in which Nestorian Christians, Jews, and Buddhists could worship and proselytize freely. Driven from a bigoted

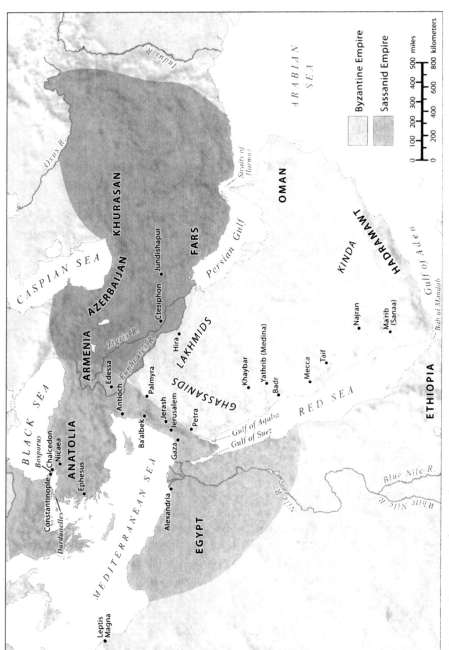

Map 2.1 Byzantine and Sassanid empires, circa 600

Byzantine Empire in the fifth century, Nestorian savants found refuge at the legendary Persian academy of Jundishapur, a center for the preservation of Hellenistic culture—indeed, the humanistic heritage of the whole ancient world. Scholars and students came from all parts of Europe and Asia to teach and study there, unhindered by racial prejudice, religious dogma, or political restrictions.

Persia's influence spread far. Although Zoroastrianism's appeal was limited mainly to Persians, it spawned a more popular dualistic faith called Manichaeism, which spread throughout Europe and Asia during the Sassanid era. Meanwhile, Persian art influenced architecture, sculpture, painting, and even jewelry and textile design, from Western Europe to China. Ctesiphon, the Sassanid capital just south of what is now Baghdad, featured vaulted buildings higher and wider than any to be found in the Roman Empire. Small wonder that this highly cultured kingdom defied the Romans and their Byzantine successors. With the help of their Bedouin allies in Arabia, Persian soldiers managed to overrun Syria, Palestine, and Egypt early in the seventh century. This climax, however, would be brief.

THE ARABS

It was not the Persians who ended the Hellenistic age in the Middle East but their Arab allies. How did the Arabs begin? The domestication of the camel, a slow process that began around 3000 BCE, enabled bands of people to cross the vast deserts of Arabia, eastern Persia, and eventually North Africa. The Arabian dromedary, or one-humped camel, is famous for its ability to go for days across great distances without needing water, owing to its drinking capacity of 53 gallons (200 liters) in three minutes, its retention of liquids once consumed, and its memory for desert water holes. Relative to other animals, the camel loses little water through perspiration, skin evaporation, and urination. Padded feet, short hair, and a high ratio of skin surface to body mass all help it withstand the heat. Camels can subsist on thorny plants and dry grasses that other animals cannot digest. They store fat—not water—in their humps as a reserve against scarcity.

The people who tamed the camel, probably first for food and only later for transportation, were Arabs. No one is sure where the Arabs came from. Popular legends identify them as descendants of Ishmael, Abraham's son by his Egyptian maid, Hagar. Scholars think the Arabs are kin to the ancestors of other peoples who speak Semitic languages, such as the Hebrews, the Assyrians, and the Arameans, all of whom settled in the Fertile Crescent (Syria and Mesopotamia). In ancient times, as the population outstripped the means of subsistence in such well-endowed areas as the Fertile Crescent, some groups took to herding sheep and goats in lands where no crops could grow. A few ventured farther away and migrated from one desert oasis to another (or up and down mountains) to find seasonal water and vegetation for their flocks. Those who had mastered the camel could move even farther away from the lands of the peasant, the shepherd, and the tax collector.

Conditions in Arabia

The Arabian Peninsula was just such a place: desolate, bereft of rivers and lakes, cut off by land and sea from all but the bravest invader. The sole exception is its mountainous southern region, Yemen, which we will discuss later. The prevailing west winds from the Mediterranean, which carry winter rain to Syria and Anatolia, rarely bring moisture as far south as Arabia. Now and then a freak storm can send floods coursing down the dry valleys, but most of the water runs off because the ground is too hard to absorb it. Fortunately, underground water does reach the surface in springs, water holes, and oases, where date palms flourish. The Arabs learned to move around constantly, following the seasonal availability of groundwater and forage for their animals. Milk and dates—occasionally meat and bread—made up their staple diet.

It would have been hard for an individual or even a small band of people to survive in such a harsh environment. Great military empires or mercantile city-states would not have arisen there. The Arabs were organized into clans and tribes, extended families that migrated together and held their property in common. Significantly, the tribes protected their members against other nomads and the settled peoples. The Arabs were belligerent and zealous in defending their honor, on which their freedom depended. Tests of strength, such as raids and skirmishes, were common. Each tribe was governed by a council of adult men who represented the various clans or smaller family groupings. The council chose a *shaykh* (elder), usually the member of the tribe most respected for his bravery and generosity, except in a few tribes where the leadership was hereditary. The council decided on questions of waging war or making peace, inasmuch as the tribe increased its meager income by raiding other tribes and "protecting" the caravans that carried goods between Syria and the Indian Ocean. Some members of tribes served as auxiliaries in the Persian or Roman armies; one of the third-century Roman emperors was named Philip the Arab. Others built trading cities on the fringes of the settled areas, such as Palmyra in Syria, Petra in Jordan, and Najran in Yemen. Still others took up farming land, as in the region around Yathrib (now called Medina). But camel breeding and raiding remained the Arabs' favorite and most respected activities.

Arabian Culture

The Bedouin Arabs, having adapted to desert life, may have lacked the refinement of the Romans or the Persians, but they were not barbarians. They were warlike; hunger or habit led them to prey on one another or on outsiders. Their constant movement gave them no chance to develop architecture, sculpture, or painting. But they did possess a highly porta- ble form of artistic expression—poetry. Pre-Islamic poetry embodied the Arab code of virtue, the *muruwwa:* bravery in battle, patience in misfor- tune, persistence in revenge (the only justice possible where there was no government), protection of the weak, defiance toward the strong, hospi- tality to the visitor (even a total stranger), generosity to the poor, loyalty to the tribe, and fidelity in keeping promises. These were the moral prin- ciples people needed to survive in the desert, and the verses helped to fix the *muruwwa* in their minds. Recited from memory by the tribal Arabs and their descendants, these poems expressed the joys and tribulations of nomadic life, extolled the bravery of their own tribes, and lampooned the faults of their rivals. Some Arabs loved poetry so much that they used to stop wars and raids yearly for a month in which poets might recite their new verses and match wits with one another. Pre-Islamic poetry helped to shape the Arabic language, the literature and culture of the Arabs, and hence the thoughts and actions of Arabic-speaking peoples even now.

Southern Arabia

During the time when Rome and Persia seemed to dominate the Middle East, there was actually a third power, far off and almost ignored. South- ern Arabia, with its monsoonal rain and lush vegetation, seemed a world apart, but it fostered the growth of several city-states. Saba (whence came that mythic queen of Sheba to call on Solomon) is the best known. Even before the time of Christ, its people, the Sabaeans, had developed a thriv- ing trade between their base in Yemen and the far shores of the Indian Ocean. They were the first people to make India and its products known to the Roman world and to colonize East Africa. The Sabaeans dammed mountain streams and terraced the Yemeni hillsides to support an elab- orate agriculture. Their main export crop was frankincense, used by the pagan Romans to mask the offensive odor when they cremated their dead. The spread of Christianity, which replaced cremation with burial, hurt the frankincense trade. When Ethiopia turned Christian and became allied with the Byzantines, the Yemeni Arabs, whose kings had adopted Judaism by then, got caught in the middle. Several dam breaks, an Ethiopian invasion, and a commercial depression combined in the sixth century to weaken southern Arabia.

Arabia's political situation ranged from complex to chaotic. Three outside powers contended for control: the Byzantine Empire, champion of Orthodox Christianity; Sassanid Persia, ruled by Zoroastrians but harboring Nestorian Christians, Jews, Buddhists, dissident Manichaeans, and other sects; and Ethiopia, which espoused the same Monophysite Christianity as the Byzantines' rebellious Egyptian subjects, the Copts. Each empire had a client Arab tribe that it paid handsomely and furnished with the trappings of monarchy in return for military service. The peninsula was often ravaged by wars among these three tribes: the pro-Byzantine Ghassanids of the northwest; the pro-Sassanid Lakhmids, with their capital at Hira, near the Euphrates; and the Christian tribe of Kinda, situated in central Arabia and friendly to Ethiopia. Other Arab tribes, some still animist (ascribing spiritual power to natural objects), others partly Zoroastrian, Jewish, or Christian, would mix in their quarrels. Southern Arabia was occupied by the Ethiopians from 525 until 570, when the Jewish kings were restored to power with Sassanid help.

Mecca

Most of central and northern Arabia kept a precarious independence. In times of peace the area was crossed by the camel caravans plying the overland trade route from Syria to Yemen. Despite the falling demand for frankincense, overland trade was gaining in importance as the shoals and pirates of the Red Sea made sailing comparatively risky. The Byzantine-Sassanid wars also tended to divert trade toward western Arabia. One Arabian town, formerly tied to the Sabaean kingdom as a religious shrine, emerged in the sixth century as a major caravan station. This was Mecca, set inland from the Red Sea among the mountains of the Hijaz. Hot and dry, Mecca was useless for farming. It gained some of its wealth and power from trade. But its primacy among Arab towns stemmed from three additional assets: a yearly poets' fair at nearby 'Ukaz; Mount 'Arafat, already a pilgrimage site; and its Ka'ba, a cube-shaped structure of unknown antiquity that housed idols (reportedly 360) standing for the various deities venerated by the tribal Arabs. Also nearby were lesser shrines honoring individual goddesses, notably al-Lat, al-'Uzza, and al-Manat, who were worshiped by the pagan Meccans themselves.

Mecca's rulers belonged to a sedentarized Arab tribe called the Quraysh. Every Muslim caliph for more than six centuries could trace his ancestry back to this family of traders, shrine keepers, and politicians. Under their leadership, the centers of Middle Eastern power would shift from the Mediterranean Sea and the Persian plateau to the Arabian Desert and the Fertile Crescent. Historians usually say that this change marked the transition from the ancient to the medieval era. The prime cause of this transition will soon become clear: Muhammad, the last and the greatest of Islam's prophets, was a Meccan of the Quraysh.

Conclusion

Historians of Southwest Asia divide themselves according to their specialization into those of the ancient world, those of medieval Islam, and those of the modern Middle East. Although this practice reflects our training (especially the languages we learn), you, as a student first learning about the Middle East, should not dismiss as irrelevant the history of the area before Islam. The achievements of the ancient Egyptians and Mesopotamians in hydraulic engineering have lasted (with periodic renovations) up to now. The world's first law code was proclaimed in Mesopotamia by Hammurabi. The development of monotheism by the Egyptians and especially by the Jews was a necessary precursor to both Christianity and Islam. Greek philosophy and Roman law are part of the heritage of the Middle East as well as the West. The doctrinal disputes in early Christianity eventually set the direction of Catholic and, hence, of Protestant theology, although they also undermined Christian resistance to Islam's expansion. Sassanid Persia's imperial kingship, bureaucratic traditions, and tolerance of dissident faiths set a pattern for later Muslim-ruled, multicultural, dynastic states. The experience of the Arabs before Islam formed the matrix for the rise of Muhammad and his mission as a prophet. Ancient institutions and customs lived on in medieval Europe and the early Muslim world. Some, indeed, still do.

3

The First Muslim Revolution

Around 570 an Ethiopian army marched northward from Yemen with a baggage train of elephants and tried to take Mecca. It failed. Legend has it that some birds flew over the Ethiopians and pelted them with stones. Smallpox broke out among the troops, and they withdrew to Yemen. Soon afterward they were driven out of Arabia entirely. From then on, the "Year of the Elephant" was remembered by the Arabs—especially Meccans—as a lucky one. Most people think that Muhammad was born in that year, a few months after his father's death. Before Muhammad was six, his mother also died. His grandfather, taking responsibility for the boy, sent him out to live with Arab Bedouin. Meccans often farmed out their children so that they might learn to speak more grammatical Arabic and get a healthier start in life than they could have in the city. When his grandfather died, Muhammad's upbringing was taken over by his uncle, a caravan merchant named Abu-Talib, from whom he learned the business of buying, selling, and transporting goods. Muhammad's family was called the clan of Banu (sons) Hashim, or Hashimites. They were a reputable, if relatively poor, branch of the ruling Quraysh tribe.

MUHAMMAD'S EARLY LIFE

Despite the handicaps of being orphaned and without property in a materialistic society, Muhammad grew up to be a capable and honest merchant. When he was a young man, a merchant widow named Khadija entrusted him with the care of her caravan. When he had done his job well, she broke with Arab custom and proposed marriage to him. Although she was said to be forty, fifteen years older than Muhammad, the marriage proved to be happy. She bore six children, and Muhammad took no other wives during her lifetime. The business (hence his reputation) did well. In the normal course of events, Muhammad should have become one of Mecca's leading citizens, even though the Umayyads and Banu Makhzum, the strongest clans in Quraysh, looked down on the Hashimite family, to which he belonged.

Confrontation with Pagan Arab Values

Muhammad was not wholly content. The *muruwwa* code of ideal Arab behavior, which upheld bravery in battle and generosity to the poor as noble ideals, was no longer a priority for Mecca's leaders, who now strove to get rich as merchants and shrine keepers. The Arabs' polytheistic animism and ancestor worship were no longer a living faith, even though pilgrimages to the Ka'ba and other shrines continued and provided much of Mecca's income. The clan of Hashim was entrusted with *siqaya*, taking care of the Ka'ba and providing food and water to the pilgrims, the most honorable task in Mecca. The nomads believed in their gods only so long as they did what the nomads wanted. They were more apt to fear the *jinns* (genies), invisible creatures who could do both nice and nasty things to people. A few Christians lived in Mecca, and whole tribes and cities elsewhere in Arabia had converted to Judaism or to some sect of Christianity. There were other pious folk, neither Christian nor Jewish but leaning toward monotheism, known as Hanifs. But Mecca's merchants, profoundly practical, scoffed at such notions as the bodily resurrection or Judgment Day and at holy laws that might interfere with their pursuit of money. To Muhammad, though, the Jews, Christians, and Hanifs just might have answers to the problems that were gnawing at the core of pagan Meccan society. On many evenings he went to a nearby cave to meditate.

First Revelation

One night in 610, during the Arabic month of Ramadan, Muhammad was visited by an angel, who exhorted him to read aloud. In awe and terror, he cried out, "I cannot read" (for Muhammad, Muslims believe, was illiterate). Hugging him until he almost choked, the angel again ordered:

> Read: in the name of thy Lord who created,
> created mankind from a blood-clot.
> Read: for thy Lord the most generous;
> He has taught by the pen
> taught man what he knew not.
> (QUR'AN, 96:1–5)

Wherever he looked, he saw the same angel looking back at him and saying, "O Muhammad, thou art the messenger of God, and I am Gabriel." Fearing that he had gone mad, Muhammad hurried home and asked Khadija to cover him with a warm coat. His quaking subsided, but then he saw Gabriel again, and the angel said:

> O thou who art shrouded in thy mantle,
> rise and warn!
> Thy Lord magnify,
> Thy robes purify,
> And from iniquity flee!
> (QUR'AN, 74:1–5)

Khadija, as it happened, had a cousin who was a Hanif (or, some say, a Christian). She went to see him, and he assured her that Muhammad, far from being mad, was God's long-awaited messenger to the Arabs. She returned to her husband and gave him the backing that he needed. Hesitantly, Muhammad realized that what he had heard was God's exhortation to make the divine presence known to the Arabs. Also, he had to warn them (just as God had sent earlier prophets to warn the Jews and the Christians) of a Judgment Day when all would be called to account:

> When the earth shall quake with a predestined quaking,
> When the earth shall bring forth her burdens,
> and men shall ask, "What ails her?"
> Upon that day shall she tell her news
> with which thy Lord has inspired her,
> Upon that day shall men come out in scattered groups
> to be shown what they have done.
> Then he who has done one atom's weight of good shall see it
> And he who has done one atom's weight of evil shall see it.
> (QUR'AN, 109:1–8)

Being God's messenger to the Arabs was an awesome task for an unlettered, middle-aged merchant, an orphan who had gained a precarious hold on a little wealth and status. Muhammad was tempted to shirk the responsibility, and yet when he received no messages for a while, he feared that God had abandoned him. During this time, he kept asking himself whether he really was a prophet, but his wife never doubted him. A few of his friends and relatives believed in him, too. Once new revelations reached Muhammad, he came to know that his mission was real.

The Early Muslims

The first believers, although they came from every class and many of Mecca's clans, were mainly young men from the upper-middle stratum—that of the "nearly haves" from which so many revolutions elsewhere have sprung—rather like Muhammad himself. Some converts were sons or younger brothers of the leading merchants; others were notables who had somehow lost (or failed to attain) the status they wanted within pagan Mecca. A few were "weak," meaning that they came from outside the system, that they had no clan to protect them against harm from other Arabs, or that their families lacked the political clout of the Umayyads or the Hashimites. Even though Muhammad's uncle, Abu-Talib, never embraced Islam, he went on protecting his nephew. Abu-Talib's son, 'Ali, raised in Muhammad's home, was probably his first male convert. Later, he would marry the Prophet's daughter, Fatima, and become a leader of early Islam. Other early converts were Abu-Bakr, Muhammad's best friend and a man of wealth and social standing; Al-Arqam, a young member of the strong clan of Makhzum, who let the Muslims meet at his home; 'Umar, an imposing figure from a weak clan; 'Uthman, an elegant but quiet youth of the powerful Umayyad family; Bilal, an Ethiopian slave set free by Abu-Bakr; and Zayd ibn Haritha, a captured Christian Arab whom Muhammad adopted.

Let us make a few points on terminology. During Muhammad's mission, those who believed in him as God's messenger came to be known as Muslims. The Arabic word *muslim* means "one who submits"—to God's will. The act of submission is *islam*, which became the name of the religion. You may see *Mohammedanism* used in place of *Islam* in old books, but Muslims detest the term because Muhammad is only a prophet through whom Islam was revealed. *Moslem* is a variant spelling of *Muslim*.

Often pagans and Muslims were related to one another. Muhammad's message disrupted families and threatened the established order. W. Montgomery Watt, whose books on the life of the Prophet have won wide acceptance, summarized his early message in five main points:

1. God is good and all-powerful.
2. God will call all men and women back to himself on the Last Day and will judge and reward them on the basis of how they acted on earth.
3. People should thank God, through worship, for the blessings he has given the earth.
4. God expects people to share their worldly goods with others needier than themselves.

5. Muhammad is God's designated messenger to his own people, the Arabs.

Later revelations taught that Muhammad was a prophet for all humanity.

Meccan Opposition

The Meccans who rejected this message feared that Muhammad might try to take away their wealth and power. Even if the early Muslims had kept a low profile, they would have attracted the notice—and hostility—of Mecca's leaders. If the pagan tribes accepted Islam, would they stop making their annual *hajj* (pilgrimage) to the Ka'ba and Mecca's other shrines? We now know that Muhammad respected the Ka'ba and never wanted to displace it as a center for pilgrims. Nor was he trying to undermine Mecca's economy. A few accounts depict Muhammad as having been so eager to win the Meccan leaders' acceptance that he even conceded that the three pagan goddesses, al-Lat, al-'Uzza, and al-Manat, were "sacred swans" worthy of veneration. This accommodation shocked many Muslims. When Muhammad realized what he had done, he denounced what he had mistaken for a divine revelation, and the Qur'an addressed the Quraysh regarding those goddesses:

> What, would you have males and He females?
> That would indeed be an unjust division.
> They are nothing but names you and your fathers have named,
> God has sent down no authority touching them.
> (QUR'AN, 53:21–23)

When Muhammad disowned the goddesses, the Meccan leaders became angry, for the keepers of the nearby shrines were Mecca's allies. Unable to attack Muhammad while he had Abu-Talib's protection, the Meccans tried a boycott of the whole Hashimite clan. It failed. Still, they could torment the most vulnerable Muslims, some of whom took refuge in Christian Ethiopia. Then Muhammad made what, to the pagan Meccans, was a still more incredible claim. Following a Qur'anic revelation, he said that he had journeyed in one night upon a winged horse, first to Jerusalem, then up through the seven levels of heaven, where he saw the celestial Ka'ba and received from God the fundamentals of the Islamic creed, and that he had talked to Moses during his return to earth. Although the Qur'an confirmed Muhammad's claims, the pagans mocked them. They averred that he had slept that whole night in his own bed.

In 619 Muhammad lost the two people who had most helped him in his early mission: Khadija and Abu-Talib. Muhammad would later marry many women, but none could match the loyalty and support of his first wife. And without his uncle, Muhammad had no protector within the Hashimite clan, and so the persecution grew worse. The Muslims realized that they would have to leave Mecca, but where else could they go?

THE EMIGRATION (*HIJRA*)

During the pagan pilgrimage month in 620, Muhammad was visited by six Arabs from an agricultural oasis town called Yathrib (now Medina), located about 270 miles (430 kilometers) north of Mecca, just after they had completed their *hajj* rites at the Ka'ba. They told him that fighting between Yathrib's two pagan tribes had grown so bad that they could no longer protect themselves against the three Jewish tribes with which they shared the oasis. They asked Muhammad to come and, because of his reputation as an honest man, arbitrate their quarrels. The next year more pilgrims came from Yathrib, and some embraced Islam. In return for Muhammad's services as an arbiter, they agreed to give sanctuary to the Meccan Muslims.

This was a great opportunity for Muhammad. He quickly grasped that his mission as God's spokesman would be enhanced once he became the chief judge of a city rather than the spiritual leader of a persecuted band of rebels. Besides, the Jewish presence in Yathrib made him hope that he might be accepted as a prophet by people who were already worshiping the one God—his God—revealed to the Jews by earlier scriptures. In the following months, he arranged a gradual transfer of his Muslim followers from Mecca to Yathrib. At last, he and Abu-Bakr departed in September 622.

This emigration, called the *hijra* in Arabic, was a major event in Islamic history. Rather than a "flight," as some call it, the *hijra* was a carefully planned maneuver by Muhammad in response to his invitation by the citizens of Yathrib. It enabled him to unite his followers as a community, as a nation, or (to use an Arabic word with no direct English translation) as an *umma*. From then on, Muhammad was both a prophet and a lawgiver, both a religious and a political leader. Islam was both a faith in one God as revealed to Muhammad (and the earlier prophets) and a sociopolitical system. Muhammad and his followers drew up the Constitution of Medina as a concrete expression of their *umma*. No wonder the Muslims, when they later set up their own calendar, made the first year the one in which the *hijra* had occurred.

The Struggle for Survival

Once the *umma* was set up in Yathrib, renamed Medina (or *madinat al-nabi,* "the city of the Prophet"), Muhammad faced new challenges. Medina's Arabs did not become Muslims at once, their quarrels proved hard to settle, and it was harder still for him to win the allegiance of the city as a whole. If the Jews of Medina had ever harbored any belief in Muhammad as the Messiah, or the messenger of God, they were soon disillusioned. His revelations differed from what they knew from the Bible. Muhammad's divine revelations, which now were becoming known as the Qur'an, repeatedly called Abraham a Muslim, a man who submitted to God's will. Muhammad had brought into Islam some Jewish practices (as he understood them), such as fasting on Yom Kippur (the Day of Atonement) and leading Muslim worship while he and his followers faced Jerusalem. The Jews were not convinced, and they rejected his religious authority. Even the Medinans who converted to Islam, called *ansar* (supporters), grew tired of supporting the Meccan emigrants, who showed no aptitude for farming, the economic basis of their oasis. The emigrants were cut off from commerce so long as pagan Mecca controlled the caravan routes.

If Muhammad was ever to lead Medina's Jews and *ansar,* the emigrants would have to find ways to support themselves. The Qur'an suggested that they might raid the Meccan caravans:

> To those against whom war is made
> Permission is given [to those who fight] because they are wronged;
> and surely God is able to help them.
> (QUR'AN, 22:39)

Perhaps, in time, they would control enough of the trade route between Syria and Mecca to compete with the Meccans. This challenged the Muslims, for the Meccans' caravans were armed and had the support of many of the Bedouin tribes. But raid they did, and, after a few fiascoes, Muhammad and his men hit the Meccans hard enough to hurt. They attacked even during the month in which pagan Arabs were forbidden to raid because of their traditional pilgrimage to Mecca. This shocked many Arabs, but a Qur'anic revelation stated:

> They will question you about the holy month and fighting in it,
> Say "Fighting in it is wrong, but to bar from God's way,
> and disbelief in Him,
> and the sacred Ka'ba, and to expel its people from it—

that is more wicked in God's sight;
and persecution is more wicked than killing.
(QUR'AN, 2:213)

The pagan Meccans did not agree. In the second year after the *hijra*—March 624, to be exact—the Muslims were zeroing in on a rich Umayyad caravan returning from Syria, just as Mecca was dispatching a retaliatory army of almost a thousand men. They met Muhammad's forces (86 emigrants, 238 *ansar*) at an oasis called Badr, southwest of Medina. Clever tactics helped the Muslims win, but nothing succeeds like success. To Muhammad's people, victory was a tangible sign of God's favor, a chance to gain captives and booty. The latter was divided among the warriors, except for a fifth that the Prophet took to support poor members of the *umma*.

In addition, the victory at Badr enhanced the prestige of Islam—and of Medina—among the tribal Arabs. Even though the Meccans avenged themselves on the Muslims in 625 at Uhud, just north of Medina, they could not take the city itself. The *umma* survived. Islam was taking root and could not be wiped out. In 627 Mecca sent a larger force to capture Medina, but the Muslims foiled the army by digging a trench around the city's vulnerable parts. The ditch was too broad for the Meccans' horses and camels to cross, so they turned back in disgust. Meanwhile, Muslim raids from Medina were endangering the Meccan caravan trade. The Arab tribes began to break with Mecca and make treaties with Muhammad to join in these lucrative attacks.

Muslim Life in Medina

Muhammad was becoming the head of both a large household and a small state. God's revelations now laid down laws about marriage and divorce, inheritance, theft and other crimes, and interpersonal relations more than they told of God's power and the impending Judgment Day. Moreover, Muhammad's own sayings and actions concerning practical matters unaddressed by the Qur'an or traditional Arab customs were becoming an authoritative guide for Muslim behavior. For the most part, a non-Muslim can readily admire the humane common sense that underlay Muhammad's conduct of his public and private life and thus respect his role as a model for Muslims. But non-Muslims often note two accusations that have been made against him: his lust for women and his mistreatment of the Jews. If we raise these issues now, are we not judging a seventh-century Arab by the standards of our own time and place? Is this fair? All we can do is present some facts and let you draw your own conclusions.

Muhammad's Marriages

Before Islam, Arab men commonly took as many wives as they could afford. Various forms of extramarital sexual relations were also accepted. Seeking to limit this license, the Qur'an allowed Muslim men to marry as many as four wives, provided that they treated them all equally, but this permission was granted in the context of a revelation concerning the welfare of widows and orphans—a natural concern, given Muhammad's own background and the heavy loss of young men in raids and battles. After Khadija died, he gradually took other wives, possibly as many as ten. Several were widows of his slain followers, for whom he offered to provide support. Other marriages involved the daughters of tribal chieftains whom Muhammad wanted as allies. 'Aisha, who became his favorite wife, was the daughter of Abu-Bakr, his best friend, and she was nine when she came to live with him (see Box 3.1). Muhammad's critics pointed to his marriage to Zaynab, whom he came to know while she was married to his adopted son, Zayd. A new Qur'anic revelation allowed Zayd to divorce her, but even 'Aisha was quick to attack Muhammad for marrying her. Muhammad believed that his marriages were prescribed for him by God, and he always enjoyed the company of women. One can find other inconsistencies in his behavior: He forbade wailing at funerals until his infant son died. He forgave many of the foes he faced in battle, but not the poets who made fun of his mission. Prophets were human beings, not plaster saints.

Muhammad and the Jews

Muhammad's relations with the Jews of Medina deteriorated as his own power grew. Islam viewed many biblical figures as prophets, or as men to whom God had spoken. He respected Jews and Christians as "People of the Book," because they worshiped God as revealed by sacred scriptures. Why could he not have been more magnanimous in Medina? In part, he expected the Jews to recognize him as God's messenger, just as he had accepted their prophets; but they could not reconcile his Qur'an with their sacred scriptures. There were too many discrepancies. They opposed the Constitution of Medina, and they were turning some of the less sincere *ansar* against him, publicly mocking him and his followers. The split widened. Following a Qur'anic revelation, Muhammad changed the direction of prayer—south toward Mecca instead of north toward Jerusalem. The one-day fast of Yom Kippur ceased to be obligatory, and Muslims started fasting instead during the daylight hours of Ramadan, the month in which Muhammad's first Qur'anic revelations occurred. Sabbath observance was

---

BOX 3.1   'Aisha bint Abi-Bakr

'Aisha, Muhammad the Prophet's third, and reportedly his favorite, wife is one of the heroines of early Islam. She was born in 614 CE, the daughter of Abu-Bakr, who was Muhammad's closest companion. He would eventually become Islam's first caliph.

The marriage between 'Aisha and Muhammad, a political one, was contracted to seal the bond between the Prophet and the family of Abu-Bakr. Little attention was paid, therefore, to the age difference between bride and groom. When the contract was made, 'Aisha was six years old. She was nine when she moved to Muhammad's home (623 CE). The Prophet was fifty. Such marriages were common in the seventh century and, for that matter, in biblical times.

The historical records, mostly based on *hadiths*, of which many are attributed to 'Aisha herself, tell of a basically happy marriage ended by the Prophet's death in 632 CE. 'Aisha remained an active leader of the Muslim community for some fifty years following her husband's passing.

'Aisha was one of the foremost authorities on the Prophet's life, which made her an important contributor to the early compilation of an authentic version of the Qur'an and the *sunna* (Muhammad's own words, habits, practices, and silent approvals). In other words, much of the early basis for Islamic religious law (the Shari'a) comes through the memory and accounts of 'Aisha. An assertive, self-confident, and politically active person, she clashed with at least one of the Prophet's early companions, 'Ali.

There is a story that early in 'Aisha's marriage, while on a trip through the Arabian Desert, she became separated from Muhammad and the rest of their caravan. Muhammad ordered a search for her. She was eventually located and brought back to the main group by a young male Muslim. 'Aisha and her young escort probably spent several hours alone together. Soon gossip started, and 'Aisha's reputation and Muhammad's and Abu-Bakr's honor were in danger. It was at this point that 'Ali, Muhammad's son-in-law and cousin, recommended that Muhammad divorce her. As it happened, Muhammad received a revelation from God condemning all such gossip and setting strict requirements for proving adultery. But 'Aisha never forgave 'Ali, and many years later she would seek revenge by participating in a rebellion against 'Ali, who had become the fourth caliph. 'Aisha helped lead a famous military engagement, the Battle of the Camel, so named because she exhorted the rebel troops from the back of a camel.

For Sunni Muslim women through the ages, 'Aisha has been, and continues to be, a role model. The memory of her actions encourages active and independent-minded women to challenge some of the patriarchal customs often used to justify gender inequality in the Muslim world. The current struggle for Muslim women's rights to an active public life has a strong precedent in the role played by the Prophet's favorite wife so long ago.

replaced by Friday congregational worship with a sermon. Dietary laws were eased. Islam was becoming more distinct and also more Arabian.

After winning at Badr, Muhammad expelled one of the Jewish tribes for conspiring with his Meccan foes but let its members keep their property. The Muslims expelled another Jewish tribe after their defeat at Uhud, seizing the tribe's groves of date palms. According to traditional accounts, the last of the three tribes suffered the worst fate: the men were killed, and the women and children were sold into slavery. Muhammad believed that this tribe, despite an outward show of loyalty, had backed the Meccans in 627 during their siege of Medina's trench. He sought the advice of an associate who seemed neutral but who in fact coveted the Jews' property. His advice led to a slaughter that enriched some Muslims and raised Muhammad's prestige among the Arab tribes, for it showed that he had no fear of tribal blood reprisals.

We should understand the situation as people then saw it. The Jews were not defenseless. The Muslims could have lost their grip on Medina and fallen prey to the Meccans and their tribal allies. Neutralizing their enemies was essential to their security, if not to their survival. Partly because of these confrontations, the Qur'an contains some harsh words about the Jews. These events did not poison later Muslim-Jewish relations, nor did Muhammad's policies cause what we now call the Arab-Israeli conflict.

The Winning of Mecca

It is a historical irony that Mecca's pagans who persecuted Muhammad later embraced Islam and then prospered under the new order, whereas the Jews of Arabia, whose beliefs were closer to his, rejected him as a prophet and then suffered severely. The story of Mecca's final capitulation seems almost anticlimactic. The emigrants in Medina missed their homes, their families (many were the sons and daughters of leading Meccan merchants), and the Ka'ba, so in 628 Muhammad led a band of would-be pilgrims toward Mecca. They encountered Meccan troops at Hudaybiyya, slightly north of Mecca, and the two sides worked out a truce that ended their state of war. The Muslims had to return to Medina then but would be admitted into Mecca the next year as pilgrims. In effect, the Meccans accepted the Muslims as equals. Three months after the Hudaybiyya truce, two of the best Arab fighters, Khalid ibn al-Walid and 'Amr ibn al-'As, embraced Islam and eventually went on to greater glory as warriors for the *umma*. Muhammad won more key Meccan converts during that pilgrimage in 629. The next year, claiming that some clans had breached the terms of Hudaybiyya, he led 10,000 troops and marched on Mecca. The Meccan leaders, overawed, quickly gave in, letting the Muslims occupy the city peacefully. Soon almost everyone in Mecca became Muslim.

Bolstered by Meccan troops, the Muslims defeated a large coalition of Arab tribes from around Taif. The Hijaz was now united under Islam. From then on, other tribes and clans, recognizing Muhammad's power, began sending delegations to Medina, which remained the capital of the new state. As a condition for his support, Muhammad required the tribes to accept Islam and even to pay taxes, a condition that the Quraysh tribe had never been able to impose. Traditional accounts maintain that by 632 nearly all the Arab tribes were Muslim. More probably, though, only some clans, factions, or persons within each tribe embraced Islam. We will discuss this more later.

Muhammad's Death

The Prophet's final years were clouded by worries about would-be rivals in Arabia, heavy political responsibilities, marital problems, the death of his infant son and several daughters, and failing health. He did manage to lead a final pilgrimage to Mecca in March 632. Thus he finished incorporating into Islam the rituals of the *hajj*, which he had cleansed of its pagan features. In his final sermon he exhorted his followers, "O ye men, listen to my words and take them to heart: Every Muslim is a brother to every other Muslim and you are now one brotherhood." Soon after his return to Medina, Muhammad retired to 'Aisha's room. He appointed her father, Abu-Bakr, to lead public worship in his place. Then, on 8 June 632, he died.

How can we evaluate Muhammad and what he did? For Muslims he has always been the exemplar of Muslim virtues, such as piety, patience, humor, kindness, generosity, and sobriety. Non-Muslim Westerners, recalling Christian battles and disputations with Islam, have often judged him harshly. These different assessments remind us that observant Jews and sincere Christians do not believe, as Muslims must, that Muhammad was obeying God's commands as revealed to him by the Angel Gabriel.

The life of any famous person becomes a lens or mirror by which other people, as individuals or in groups, view themselves and the world. The biographer or the historian stresses some facts and omits or downplays others. The reader seizes upon a few points and expands them to fit a preconceived image. How, then, to judge Muhammad? Surely he was a kind and sincere man who came to have an overwhelming faith in God and in himself as God's final messenger. As such, he had to warn the Arabs and other people about the impending Judgment Day and to form the *umma,* a religious community, within which Muslim believers could best prepare themselves for that dread occasion. Yet he had a sense of humor, saying, "Let a man answer to me for what waggeth between his jaws, and what between his legs, and I'll answer to him for Paradise." He let his grandsons climb on his back even while prostrating himself in worship. He must have been a skilled political and military tactician, for who else has ever managed to unite the Arabs? He took terrible chances when he accepted his prophetic mission and forsook his home city for an unknown future. But what you can conclude about Muhammad's life will depend on how well you know Islam, the religion for which he did so much.

PILLARS OF FAITH: WHAT DO MUSLIMS BELIEVE?

When we write about Islam—or any religion that has lasted for a long time—we should remember that it has evolved through history and will continue to do so. It has varied from time to time, from place to place, and even from one person to another. As personal belief systems, religions are hard to describe, for each person's truest and deepest thoughts are unique. Nevertheless, Muslims tend to abide by some general pillars of faith (*arkan al-iman*).

In Islam, faith (*iman*) is the act of submission to the will of God (*Allah* in Arabic). *Iman* is a prerequisite to *islam* and implies belief beyond reason. It must conform to God's rules, or to what atheists might call nature's laws. Rocks and trees, birds and beasts all submit to God's will because they were created to do so. Human beings, creatures capable of reason, have been made free to choose whether and how to do what God wills. Many refuse out of ignorance or because they have forgotten the divine commandments they once knew. Some Christians and Jews may have been misled by their scriptures or by the way they have interpreted them. But anyone who submits to God's will, worships him, and expects his reward or punishment in the next world is, broadly speaking, a *mu'min* (believer). Muslims believe in the following principles:

Unity of God (Tawhid)

In common usage, though, a Muslim is one who believes that God's will for all humanity was last revealed through the Qur'an to Muhammad. What is God? To Muslims, God is all-powerful and all-knowing, the Creator of all that was and is and will be, the righteous Judge of good and evil, and the generous Guide to men and women through inspired messengers and divine scriptures. God has no peer, no partner, no offspring, no human attributes, no beginning, and no end. Anyone professing Judaism or Christianity agrees that there is only one God, but monotheism entails more than rejecting a pantheon of gods and goddesses. There can be no other Absolute Good; all material blessings—our houses, furniture, cars, clothing, and food—are worth less than the one true God. The pleasures we pursue are (if lawful) fine, but finer yet is the satisfaction of God's commands. Spouses and consorts, parents and children, friends and teammates may be dear, but they must remain second to God in our hearts. God is the giver of life and death. Some Muslims think that God has predestined all human actions. Others argue that God has given us free will, making us strictly accountable for what we choose to do. God wants willing worshipers, not human robots.

Angels (Mala'ika)

Muslims believe that God works in a universe in which dwell various creatures, not all of whom can be seen, heard, or felt by human beings. Jinns, for instance, do much good and evil here on earth and are addressed in some Qur'anic revelations. But more powerful in God's scheme of things are angels, the heavenly servants who obey the divine will. God did not reveal the Qur'an directly to Muhammad but sent the Angel Gabriel to do so. Angels taught him how to pray. An angel will blow a horn to herald the Judgment Day. When each of us dies, we will be questioned by a pair of angels. Satan, called Iblis or al-Shaytan in Arabic, was a jinn who flouted God's command to bow down to Adam. Having fallen from grace, he now tries to corrupt men and women. He seems to be doing well.

Revealed Books (al-Kutub Assamawiya)

How was God's existence made known to humanity? How does the Infinite reveal itself to finite minds? Christians say that the Word became flesh and dwelt among us: God became a man. But Muslims argue that God is revealed by the words placed in the mouths of righteous people called prophets or messengers. These words have been turned into books: the Torah of the Jews (consisting of the first five books of the Bible), the Gospels of the Christians, and the Qur'an of the Muslims.

Muslims also believe that God's earlier revelations, in the form we know them, were corrupted and had to be corrected by the Qur'an. Modern scholarship has shown that the books of the Bible were written down only after some time had passed since they were revealed. Muslims ask, therefore, whether Jews changed some passages of the Torah to depict themselves as God's chosen people (a concept rejected by Islam) or whether Christians rewrote the Gospels to prove the divinity of Jesus of Nazareth (for Muslims maintain that no human can be God). The Qur'an, by contrast, is God's perfect revelation. It has existed in heaven since time began. It will never be superseded. After Muhammad's death it was carefully compiled ("from scraps of parchment, from thin white stones, from palm leaves, and from the breasts of men," wrote an early Muslim) by his followers. Some parts had actually been written down while Muhammad was still alive. If any passage had been misread, a Muslim who had heard Muhammad give the passage would surely have put it right. Seventh-century Arabs had prodigious memories.

The Qur'an is not easy reading. It is the record of God's revelations, via the Angel Gabriel, to Muhammad. It contains laws, stories from the past, and devotional pieces intended for guidance and recitation, not for literary entertainment. Most of its 114 chapters bring together passages revealed at different times. The chapters, except for the first, are arranged in order of length. Those revealed in Medina, filled with injunctions and prohibitions, tend to precede the Meccan chapters, which stress God's power and warn of the coming Judgment Day. Because the Qur'an was revealed in Arabic, most Muslims do not think it can or should be translated into any other language. As its usage reflects that of seventh-century Meccans, even Arab Muslims may now need help to understand parts of what they read. The Qur'an's language is rhymed prose (not metrical like poetry), but it can sound lyrical when chanted by a trained reciter. Try to hear one. Muslims venerate the Qur'an for many reasons: its Arabic language and style are inimitable, the book sets Islam apart from all other religions, and its teachings have stood the test of time. The speech and writing of pious Muslims are studded with Qur'anic expressions. No other book has affected so many minds so powerfully for so long.

Messengers (Rusul)

Although Islam stresses that Muhammad was the last of the prophets, Muslims recognize and venerate many others, including Adam, Noah, Abraham, Moses, Jonah, and Job. Biblical personages (such as King Solomon) reappear in the Qur'an as prophets. Christians may be astonished that Muslims count Jesus as one of God's messengers. The Qur'an affirms that he was born of the Virgin Mary, that he is a "word" of God, and that someday he will return, but it denies that he was crucified or that he was the son of God. All prophets must be revered; no one prophet, not even Muhammad, may be exalted above the others.

Many people nowadays do not know what prophets can do. They do not predict what will happen or perform miracles unless God enables them to do so; they are just good people chosen to bring God's message to other men and women. According to Islam, no more prophets will come before Judgment Day.

Judgment Day (al-Qiyama or al-Akhira)

Among Islam's basic tenets, none was preached more fervently by Muhammad than belief in a final Judgment Day, from which no one can escape. On this day of doom, all living people will die, joining those who have gone before them. All will be summoned before the heavenly throne to be judged for the good and the bad things they have done. Later Muslims built up the imagery: a tightrope will stretch across the fires of hell, and only the righteous will cross over safely into heaven. The Qur'an depicts paradise as a shaded garden with cooling fountains, abundant food and drink, and beautiful maidens for the eternal bliss of righteous men. Righteous women, too, will enter heaven, but the Qur'an is less specific on what they will find. Popular Islam teaches that they will go back to the age at which they were most beautiful. Both men and women will know peace, live in harmony, and see God.

Hell is everything that is horrible in the Arab mind: fearsome beasts, fiery tortures, noxious vapors, foul-tasting food to eat, and boiling water to drink. There will be no peace and no harmony. God will not be present, and for the worst sinners the torments will never end.

PILLARS OF PRACTICE: WHAT MUST MUSLIMS DO?

How can the believer obey God? What are the divine commands? The Qur'an and Muhammad's teachings are full of dos and don'ts, for Islam (like Judaism) is a religion of right actions, rules, and laws. We cannot cover all of the Islamic rules, but they are symbolized by five obligatory acts: the five pillars of practice (*arkan al-iman*) in Islam.

Witness (Shahada)

This is the first of the famous five pillars of practice in Islam. "I witness that there is no god whatever but Allah, and that Muhammad is the messenger of God" (Ashhadu an la ilaha illa Allah, Muhammad rasulu Allah). Anyone who says these words—and really means them—is a Muslim. It can be found in the muezzin's call to worship; it is emblazoned in white letters on the green flag of Sa'udi Arabia. Any Muslim who associates other beings with God or denies believing in Muhammad or any of the other prophets is no longer a Muslim but an apostate. Apostasy may be punished by death.

Worship (Salat)

The second pillar of Islam is worship, or ritual prayer—a set sequence of motions and prostrations performed facing in the direction of the Ka'ba in Mecca and accompanied by brief Qur'anic recitations. Worship reminds men and women of their relationship to God and takes their minds off worldly matters. It occurs five times each day, at fixed hours announced by the muezzin's call from the minaret (tower) of a mosque, a building constructed for congregational worship. Muslims may worship anywhere, but men are encouraged to do so publicly as a group; women usually worship at home. All adult men should go to a mosque on Friday at noon, as congregational worship at that time is followed by a sermon (*khutba*) and sometimes by major announcements. Before any act of worship, Muslims wash their hands, arms, feet, and faces. Worship may include individual prayers (that is, Muslims may call on God to bring good to, or avert evil from, them and their loved ones); but such invocations, called *du'a* in Arabic, are distinct from *salat*.

Fasting (Sawm)

Muslims must fast during the month of Ramadan. From daybreak until sunset they refrain from eating, drinking, smoking, and sexual intercourse. Devout Muslims spend extra time during Ramadan praying, reciting from the Qur'an, and thinking about religion; lax ones are apt to sleep in the daytime, for the nights are filled with festivities, bright lights, and merrymaking. The discipline of abstinence teaches the rich what it is like to be poor, trains all observant Muslims to master their appetites, and through the shared experience of daytime fasting and nighttime feasting creates common bonds among Muslims. The Muslim calendar has exactly twelve lunar months in each year. With no month occasionally added, as in the Jewish calendar, the Muslim year consists of only 354 days. Thus Ramadan advances eleven or twelve days each year in relation to our calendar and to the seasons. In the Northern Hemisphere the fast is relatively easy to keep when Ramadan falls in December, but great self-discipline is needed when it falls in June (as it will between 2014 and 2019). A Muslim who gets sick or makes a long trip during Ramadan may put off all or part of the fast until a more suitable time. Growing children, pregnant women and nursing mothers, soldiers on duty, and chronically ill Muslims are exempt. Yet nearly all Muslims who can fast do so, even those who have given up other outward observances of the faith.

Tithing (Zakat)

All Muslims must give a specified share of their income or property to help provide for the needy. This payment is called zakat, often translated as "alms," although it began as a tax levied on all adult members of the umma. In modern times many Muslim countries stopped collecting the zakat as a tax, but their citizens still have to make equivalent charitable donations. Lately, though, some Muslim governments have gone back to exacting the tithe. In either case, wealthy and pious Muslims make additional gifts or bequests to feed the hungry, cure the sick, educate the young, or shelter the traveler. Many fountains, mosques, schools, and hospitals have been founded and maintained by a type of endowment called a waqf (plural: awqaf), about which you will read later. In essence, the fourth pillar of Islam is sharing.

Pilgrimage (Hajj)

The fifth duty is the hajj, or pilgrimage to Mecca, during the twelfth month of the Muslim year. All adult Muslims should perform the hajj at least once in their lives if they are well enough and can afford to make the journey. Each year, from all parts of the world, observant Muslims, their bodies clad in identical unsewn strips of cloth, converge on Mecca to perform rites hallowed by the Prophet Muhammad, although some are taken from earlier Arab practices. These rites include circling the Ka'ba; kissing the Black Stone set in one of its walls; running between the nearby hills of Safa and Marwa; stoning a pillar near Mina representing the devil, sacrificing sheep there; and assembling on the plain of 'Arafat. Some of the rites may have begun as pagan practices, but Muhammad reinterpreted them in monotheistic terms. Thus Muslims believe that Abraham and Ishmael found the Black Stone and erected the Ka'ba around it.

Running seven times between Safa and Marwa commemorates Hagar's frantic quest for water after Abraham had expelled her and Ishmael from his tent. The sacrifice of a sheep recalls Abraham's binding of Ishmael (Muslims do not believe it was Isaac) at God's command and the last-minute substitute of a sacrificial lamb provided by an angel. The day of sacrifice is a high point of the *hajj* and the occasion for a major feast throughout the Muslim world. The pilgrimage rites have served throughout history to bring Muslims together and to break down racial, linguistic, and political barriers among them.

Other Duties and Prohibitions

The five pillars do not cover all Muslim duties. There is another, which some name the "sixth pillar of Islam," called *jihad,* or "struggle in the way of God." Non-Muslims think of the *jihad* as Islam's holy war against all other religions. This is not wholly true. To be sure, the Qur'an calls on Muslims to "fight in the way of God . . . against those . . . who start a fight against you, but do not aggress against them by initiating the fighting; God does not love the aggressors" (2:190). Another Qur'anic passage commands Muslims to "fight against those who do not believe in God or the Judgment Day, who permit what God and His messenger have forbidden, and who refuse allegiance to the true faith from those who have received scriptures, until they humbly pay tribute" (9:29). This would mean fighting Christians and Jews in some situations and pagans in any case (for the passage was revealed when the Muslims were at war with Mecca before its conversion). But Islam also decreed tolerance toward the earlier monotheistic faiths.

Just how militant should Muslims be? We can give part of the answer now and the rest later on. Muslims tried to expand the territory controlled by their *umma,* not to convert conquered Christians or Jews. Those who agreed to live in peace and to pay tribute were entitled to Islam's protection; those who resisted or rebelled against Muslim rule were crushed. Some modern Muslims interpret *jihad* to mean defending Islam against attacks, whether military or verbal, from non-Muslims.

To protect the *umma,* Muslims must first cleanse their souls of error, pride, and forgetfulness. Islam is a religion of community: every Muslim is a brother or a sister to every other Muslim. If some err or forget their duties to God or to other Muslims, the others, like good brothers or sisters, must correct them. Prohibited to Muslims are all intoxicating liquors, all mind-altering drugs, gambling, and usury. Muslims may not eat the flesh of pigs or of any animal not slaughtered in the name of God. Men may not wear silk clothes or gold jewelry. The Qur'an lays down harsh penalties for murder, theft, and certain other crimes. There are also punishments for Muslims who make or worship idols, but this does not mean a total prohibition against artistic depictions of living creatures, as some people suppose. But Muslims have not, until modern times, sculpted statues, and pictures of living creatures rarely appear in mosques.

Muslims believe that sexual relations are meant to beget children and thus should not occur outside marriage. Most marriages are arranged by the parents of the bride and groom; in bygone days the young couple often met for the first time on their wedding day. Strict rules are used to separate the sexes in order to ward off inappropriate romantic relationships. These rules led in practice to the seclusion of women from the mainstream of political and social life and subjected them to the command of their fathers, brothers, and husbands. Wearing a veil has been customary for urban women in many ancient Middle Eastern societies. A late Qur'anic revelation required Muhammad's wives to do so when they went outside, so eventually most Muslim women veiled their faces, at least in the cities. Nowadays, most cover their hair and some cover their faces in public. Adults of both sexes dress modestly and shun situations requiring nudity. Homosexual acts and masturbation are included in the prohibition against extramarital sex. Even if a few Muslims privately flout some of these rules, public acceptance of the prohibitions remains the norm.

Cleanliness is close to godliness. In addition to ritual ablutions before worship, Muslims must wash themselves after performing an act of nature, before eating, upon awakening, and after handling certain objects considered unclean. Total immersion in running water is required after sexual intercourse and, for women, after menstruation and childbirth as well. Traditionally, Muslim men shaved or cropped their heads and body hair but let their beards grow. Women remove their body hair.

CONCLUSION

Muhammad was a great religious leader. Muslims do not call him "the founder of Islam." But his words and actions did much to shape what Muslims believe and do. This chapter has barely scratched the surface of Muhammad's life and faith. Hundreds of books have been written and thousands of speeches made trying to answer the question "What is Islam?" Every life lived by a Muslim is a statement about Islam, which now has more than 1.6 billion adherents living in every part of the world, though they are most heavily concentrated in the southern third of Asia and the northern two-thirds of Africa.

The religion prescribes a complete lifestyle. In later chapters you will learn about the Shari'a, or the sacred law of Islam, which was developed and assembled during the first three centuries after Muhammad's death. Let us say for now that the Qur'an, combined with the teachings and practices of Muhammad, provides a comprehensive and coherent pattern for Muslim daily practices and thoughts (*sunna*). Islam has no bishops or priests. Even the '*ulama,* the learned men well versed in Islamic doctrines and practices, are not set apart from other Muslims. All Muslims are equal except in their obedience to God's will. Men and women, young and old, friends and neighbors—all have mutual rights and duties within Islam. All can find freedom, without giving up security, in this world and the next. It is more than a faith; it is a complete way of life.

4

✦

The Early Arab Conquests

Muhammad's death left a great void in his followers' community, the Islamic *umma*. As long as he was alive, he had been prophet, arbiter, law-giver, and military commander. In fact, just about any issue that arose among Muslims had been referred to him. How could they make decisions without his guidance? This posed a crisis for the *umma*, but Muhammad's survivors found new leaders. They overcame the challenge of an Arab tribal rebellion and went on to expand the area under their control. The mightiest empires of the Middle East—Byzantium and Persia—were humbled by the Arab warriors of Islam. Success bred dissension and later caused sectarian rifts that have never completely healed, but the momentum of expansion was only briefly broken. The early Muslims' ability to surmount these crises ensured that Islam would survive, that its civilization would flourish, and that its legacy would endure.

THE SUCCESSION ISSUE

During his lifetime Muhammad never chose a successor. He probably did not expect to die as soon as he did. He would not have thought of designating another divine messenger, for he viewed himself as the seal of the prophets. No one after his death could receive revelations. Perhaps no more were needed, for Judgment Day was supposed to come at any time. Yet even if the *umma* sought no successor-as-prophet, it still needed some sort of leader, comparable to a tribal shaykh, who could direct its affairs until the hour of doom.

Indeed, a leader was needed at once. To avert a tribal war, the best hope would be to elect a leader from the prestigious Quraysh tribe—not one of the ex-pagans who had harassed the Prophet but one of the early converts who had moved with him to Medina. 'Umar, the most decisive of Muhammad's companions, carried the day by naming Abu-Bakr, who belonged (as did 'Umar) to a clan of the Quraysh that was neither Umayyad, Makhzum, nor Hashimite. Abu-Bakr was a modest man, but he knew the Arab tribes and their relationships thoroughly. He had been Muhammad's closest friend, the first person the Prophet had converted outside his own family, the father of Muhammad's beloved wife 'Aisha, and the designated worship leader during the Prophet's final illness.

Later, some Muslims would claim that a member of Muhammad's family should have been chosen. As Muhammad had no surviving sons, they argued that his successor should have been his cousin and son-in-law, 'Ali, the son of Abu-Talib. Later, you will learn about some Muslims, called Shi'ites, who argue that Muhammad had indeed named 'Ali as his successor and that his associates concealed this designation.

Abu-Bakr (r. 632–634) called himself *khalifat rasul Allah* (successor of the messenger of God), soon shortened to *khalifa,* or caliph in English. His Muslim followers called the caliph *amir al-muminin* (commander of the faithful). Abu-Bakr surely earned the title. As soon as the Arab tribes heard of Muhammad's death, most of them broke with the *umma.* Later Muslims would call this event *ridda* (apostasy), seeing the break as a renunciation of Islam. To the tribes, however, the leader's death had ended all treaties that would have required them to pay *zakat*—which they viewed as a form of tribute—to Medina. Abu-Bakr realized that if they could evade paying the required tithe, the unity of the Arabs would be sundered, and the *umma* would lose revenue. Islam might vanish entirely. To avert these dangers, he sent his best generals, Khalid ibn al-Walid and 'Amr ibn al-'As, to force the tribes to rejoin the *umma.* Although the *ridda* wars were costly, the tribes capitulated one by one and were then forgiven. But what, beyond a superficial adherence to Islam or a fear of the caliph's army, could hold the Arab tribes together?

THE INITIAL CONQUESTS

The caliphs' brilliant answer was to turn the Bedouin's combative energies away from one another and toward conquering the settled lands to the north, the territories of the Byzantine (Roman) and Sassanid (Persian) empires. Abu-Bakr's successor, 'Umar I (r. 634–644), forgave the tribal rebels and enlisted them in the service of the caliphate, in a jihad to expand the *umma*'s lands. This momentous decision would lead to the capture of

Rome's Middle Eastern possessions (Palestine, Syria, Egypt, and Cyrenaica) in little more than a decade. It took a generation to absorb the whole Sassanid Empire. Within a century Muslim soldiers would be stationed from Spain in the west, across North Africa and the Middle East, to the borders of China in the east.

Western historians once viewed the Arab victories as the main events separating the ancient world from the Middle Ages. Europeans were almost cut off from the rest of the world. Christianity was set back, notably in the lands of its origin. But we must add that those conquests brought together the diverse cultures of North Africa, Egypt, Syria, Iraq, and Persia. Out of this combination would grow a new civilization matching those of Greece and Rome.

If you had asked someone in the streets of Damascus (or anyplace else) around 625 to predict who would be ruling the Middle East a generation later, he or she might have named the Byzantine emperor, the Sassanid shah, or perhaps some new Roman or Persian dynasty. No one would have expected the rulers to be Meccan Arabs. The speed of the Arab conquests amazed everyone, then and now. People still ask why they succeeded. As you try to come up with an answer, here are some points to keep in mind:

- The Arab armies were small, usually under a thousand men, thus fewer in number and less well equipped—but more cohesive—than their Roman or Persian foes. They fought few engagements and chose them carefully. Their decisive victories enabled them to gain vast expanses of territory. Their horses were the essential ingredient in their speed, but their camels gave them endurance and mobility in the desert. Arab victories took place in or sufficiently close to the desert to enable the troops to get away from Roman or Persian legions if they needed to. A common Arab tactic was to draw enemy forces into a valley and then use the terrain to trap them. One of the Arabs' triumphs, the Battle of the Yarmuk River in 636, resulted from a dust storm that concealed Khalid's troops from the Romans. This victory gave the Arabs control over Syria. Another dust storm helped the Arabs to defeat the Persians in 637 at al-Qadisiyya and hence to overrun Iraq. The Arabs later conquered western Persia after trapping the Sassanid army in a ravine.

- Contrary to their image in popular histories, not all Arab warriors were fired up with Muslim zeal. A few were, but others belonged to Christian tribes estranged from the Byzantine Empire. Being Christian did not bar an Arab from fighting for the caliphate. Some Muslim leaders and tribes may have believed in predestination and martyrdom as their passport to paradise. Most tribal Arabs believed in taking booty. Economic hardship in Arabia had cast many of them into deep poverty. In fact, the Arab conquests facilitated a Semitic emigration from Arabia comparable to those of the earlier Akkadians and the Arameans, for the Arabian Peninsula often became overpopulated. Meanwhile, some of the settled lands of Egypt and Syria had been depopulated by outbreaks of plague in the sixth and seventh centuries.

- Years of warfare between the Sassanid and Byzantine Empires had depleted the resources and manpower of both. Each side hired mercenaries, mainly Arabs. But both pro-Byzantine and pro-Sassanid Arabs had become unreliable by 632, and some converted to Islam.

- The subject peoples, especially those under Byzantine rule in Syria and Egypt, were discontented. Their main grievance was theological or, rather, Christological. The Orthodox view of the Byzantine Empire, as explained in Chapter 2, was that Jesus Christ combined in his person both a divine and a human nature. However, the Egyptian Copts and the Syrian Jacobites followed the Monophysite doctrine that described Christ's nature as wholly divine, causing them to suffer religious persecution at the hands of the Byzantines. Emperor Heraclius, hoping to win the support of both sides, proposed a compromise: Christ contained two natures within one will. Almost no one (except Lebanon's Maronites, whom we will mention later) liked that solution. Disgruntled Syrian and Egyptian Christians viewed the Muslim Arabs as liberators from the Byzantine yoke and often welcomed them. The Copts, for example, turned Egypt over in 640 to 'Amr's Arab force, which, even with reinforcements, numbered fewer than 10,000. Likewise, the Jews, numerous in Palestine and Syria, chose Muslim indifference over Byzantine persecution.

- The sudden collapse of Sassanid Persia, after having been master of Egypt, Syria, and much of Arabia as recently as 625, created a vacuum that the Arabs were quick to fill. Persia was falling back because of political chaos in Ctesiphon, its capital. Power struggles sapped the central administration, which was needed to supervise the irrigation system on the Tigris and Euphrates rivers. Farm production fell and discontent rose. Besides, Iraq's Christian, Jewish, and Manichaean peasants resented both the Zoroastrian priests and the Sassanid absentee landlords who lived in the Persian highlands. As soon as Iraq fell, following the Battle of al-Qadisiyya (637), the Sassanid state began to fall apart. The Arabs picked up one Persian province after another, until the last Sassanid shah died, a fugitive, in 651.

To recapitulate, during Muhammad's lifetime the lands of the *umma* were limited to western Arabia as far north as the Gulf of 'Aqaba, in addition to parts of the rest of the peninsula in which the Arab tribes supposedly embraced Islam. Under Abu-Bakr, the government at Medina overcame the challenge of a tribal revolt. The conquest of the adjacent lands in Syria and Iraq began under Abu-Bakr while he was suppressing the *ridda*. Upon Abu-Bakr's death in 634, 'Umar became the new caliph. Granting a blanket pardon to the rebellious tribes, 'Umar turned what had been a few forays into a systematic policy of territorial acquisition. During his caliphate and that of his successor, 'Uthman, all of Syria, Iraq, Persia, Egypt, and Cyrenaica (what is now eastern Libya) were added to the lands of the *umma*. You can readily imagine the strain this put on the primitive government in Medina, where Muhammad and Abu-Bakr used to buy their own food in the market, mend their own clothes, cobble their own shoes, and dispense justice and money in the courtyards of their own homes. A more sophisticated government was needed.

THE BEGINNINGS OF ISLAMIC GOVERNMENT

'Umar was shrewd enough to see that the Arab tribes, easily led into battle by the lure of booty far richer than they had ever known, might rebel when they were not fighting. What would happen when civilization's centers fell under the sway of these Bedouin? Would they wreck the palaces and libraries first, or would the wine shops and dancing girls sap their martial skills and religious zeal? For centuries, nomads and foreign armies had overrun the settled parts of the Middle East, only to fall under the influence of their own captives. 'Umar did not want his Muslims to become corrupted in this way. It was no mere quirk of character that made him stride through the streets and bazaars of Medina, whip in hand, ready to scourge any Muslim who missed the prayers or violated the Ramadan fast. 'Umar may have admired the military leader Khalid's skill at beating the Romans and Persians in battle, but he resented his illegally contracted marriages. That and Khalid's hiring of poets (the publicity agents of the time) to sing his praises led 'Umar to dismiss him, the "sword of Islam," as an example to other Arabs.

When the troops were not fighting, they had to be kept under strict discipline. 'Umar's policy was to settle them on the fringe between the desert and the cultivated lands in special garrison towns (*amsar*), notably Basra and Kufa, both in Iraq, and Fustat, just south of what is now known as Cairo, Egypt. He aimed to separate the Arabs from the settled peoples.

The Arab soldiers were forbidden to acquire lands outside Arabia. Their right to seize buildings and other immovable war booty was restricted. One-fifth of the movable prizes of war had to be sent back to Medina, where 'Umar set up a register that carefully divided the spoils into shares for members of the *umma,* ranging from Muhammad's widows and associates to the humblest Arab soldier.

Although Arab generals and Meccan merchants usually took the top posts of the newly won provinces, their civil administration was left almost untouched. That hypothetical person in the streets of Damascus would not have found life in 650 much different from what it had been in 625. Local administrators went on running affairs just as before. For those towns and provinces that had not resisted the Arab conquests, land and house taxes were lighter than before, but they now went to Medina rather than to Ctesiphon or Constantinople. Governmental languages did not change: Greek and Coptic were used in Egypt, Greek and Aramaic in Syria, Persian and Syriac in Iraq and Persia. Conquered peoples went on speaking the languages they were used to. Few Jews or Christians rushed to convert to Islam, for they were protected as People of the Book. Zoroastrians and Manichaeans in Iraq and Persia were less tolerated and more apt to become Muslim, albeit gradually.

Early Muslims conferred honorary Arab status on any non-Arab male convert by making him a client member (*mawla;* plural *mawali*) of an Arab tribe. Persians and Arameans who flocked to the garrison towns were especially apt to turn Muslim. Soon the *mawali* outnumbered the Arabs living in such towns as Basra and Kufa. How ironic, considering that those cities had been set up to keep the Arabs from being corrupted by Persian civilization! They soon became melting pots and centers of cultural interchange.

DISSENSION IN THE UMMA

The garrison towns also became hotbeds of dissension and intrigue, especially after 'Umar's guiding hand was removed by assassination. Before he died of his wounds, 'Umar appointed a *shura,* or electoral committee, to choose the third caliph. Some modern writers cite the *shura* to prove that early Islam was democratic. In fact, it consisted of six Meccan associates of Muhammad, all caravan traders who belonged to the Quraysh tribe. Owing perhaps to personal rivalries, they ended up choosing the only man in the *shura* who belonged to the prestigious Umayyads, the clan that had long opposed Muhammad.

Their choice to succeed 'Umar, 'Uthman (r. 644–656), has come down in history as a weak caliph, eager to please the rich Meccan merchants and to put his Umayyad kinsmen into positions of power. But such an interpretation is unfair to 'Uthman, who had defied his clan to become one of Muhammad's earliest converts. He also defied many of Muhammad's companions when, as caliph, he established a single authoritative version of the Qur'an and ordered the burning of all copies that contained variant readings. Many reciters were appalled when their cherished versions of the Qur'an went up in smoke, but would Islam have fared better with seven competing readings of its sacred scriptures?

As for 'Uthman's relatives, it is true that some lusted after power and that others did not know how to govern. But 'Uthman used his family ties to assert greater control over the government. His cousin Mu'awiya (already appointed by 'Umar) administered Syria well. 'Uthman and his foster brother in Egypt built Islam's first navy to conquer Cyprus in 655. 'Uthman's mistake was to continue 'Umar's policies in a more complex time, without having 'Umar's forceful character. Perceiving this, the Muslims in Iraq's garrison towns began plotting against him.

'Uthman's Troubled Caliphate

Traditional accounts contrast the second and third caliphs. "The luck of Islam was shrouded in 'Umar's winding-sheet," remarked a survivor. 'Uthman complained to the Medinans from the pulpit of Muhammad's mosque: "You took it from 'Umar, even when he whipped you. Why then do you not take it from one who is gentle and does not punish you?" Perhaps this is why: 'Umar, during his caliphate, slept on a bed of palm leaves and wore the same wool shirt until it was covered with patches, while 'Uthman, as caliph, amassed estates worth more than $100 million.

Modern scholars play down the personality contrast, however, and stress changing conditions in the *umma*. The influx of money and treasure enriched Medina and Mecca far beyond anything Muhammad could have anticipated and eventually beyond what his associates could assimilate. Greed and vice proliferated. Once the early conquests had reached their limits (Cyrenaica in the west, Anatolia's Taurus Mountains in the north, Khurasan in the east, and the Indian Ocean and upper Nile in the south), the Arab tribesmen could not change from border warriors into military police. They sat idly in their garrison towns, bewailed the lost opportunities for booty, and plotted against the caliphate in far-off Medina.

From about 650, 'Uthman's rule was threatened by a mixture of people: pious old Muslims, mostly Medinans, who resented the way the Umayyads were taking over the same *umma* they once had tried to destroy; Qur'an reciters who had lost power because of 'Uthman's authorization of a single version; and tribal Arabs who chafed at having no new lands to seize and plunder. Of all the garrison towns, Kufa was the most restive. An open revolt started there in 655, spread to Arabia, and reached Medina in 656. The insurgents besieged the house of 'Uthman, who got no protection from any of Muhammad's associates. A group of rebels from Egypt broke in and killed the aged caliph as he sat with his wife, reciting from the Qur'an. Five days later, 'Ali (r. 656–661) agreed, reluctantly, to become the fourth caliph.

'Ali's Caliphate

Thus began Islam's first time of troubles, which the Arabs call their *fitna* (temptation). It seems unfair, for 'Ali appeared highly qualified for the caliphate. He was the son of Muhammad's uncle and protector, the Prophet's first male convert, the husband of the Prophet's daughter Fatima, and hence the father of his only grandsons, Hasan and Husayn. 'Ali had risked his life so that Muhammad could safely leave Mecca during the *hijra*. He had fought against the pagan Meccans, accompanied the Prophet on most of his expeditions, and advised the earlier caliphs on questions of dogma and policy. He was pious and generous. Regrettably, he proved to be a weak caliph. Either 'Ali came too late to do the office any good, or the caliphate came too late to do him any good.

Challenges to 'Ali

Soon after his accession, 'Ali left Medina, never to return; Kufa would serve as his capital. But when he reached Basra, he was challenged by two of Muhammad's associates, Talha and Zubayr; 'Aisha joined in, branding 'Ali unfit to rule because he had not tried to protect 'Uthman. This was a strange accusation, as none of the challengers had liked or defended the third caliph. Their real motives were political and personal. 'Ali had allegedly denied government posts to Talha and Zubayr, and 'Aisha had never forgiven him for having accused her of infidelity to Muhammad. 'Ali and his troops defeated the challengers in a bloody clash, the Battle of the Camel, so called because it raged around 'Aisha's camel-borne litter. Talha and Zubayr died in battle (as, it is said, did 13,000 others), and 'Aisha was sent back to Medina. The Battle of the Camel was the first instance in which two Muslim armies fought against each other. It set an unhappy precedent.

A more dangerous challenge came from Mu'awiya, 'Uthman's cousin and governor of Syria, whom 'Ali tried to dismiss. The Umayyad clan was understandably outraged when 'Uthman was murdered and replaced by 'Ali, a Hashimite, who seemed reluctant to find and punish the assassins. Mu'awiya had a loyal garrison of Arab troops, and they challenged 'Ali. The two sides met in a series of skirmishes at Siffin (in northern Syria) in 657. Finally, when 'Ali's side seemed to be winning, wily old General 'Amr ibn al-'As advised Mu'awiya's men to stick pages of the Qur'an on the tips of their spears, appealing for a peaceful arbitration of the quarrel. 'Ali suspected a trick, but his troops persuaded him to accept the appeal.

'Ali and Mu'awiya each chose a representative and agreed to let them decide whether the Umayyads were justified in seeking revenge for 'Uthman's murder. Soon afterward, some of 'Ali's men turned against him for agreeing to the arbitration. Called Kharijites (Seceders), these rebels harassed 'Ali for the rest of his caliphate, even after he defeated them in battle in 659. Meanwhile, the appointed arbiters of 'Ali and Mu'awiya met. Emboldened by the Kharijite revolt against 'Ali, Mu'awiya's representative, 'Amr, convinced 'Ali's arbiter to agree to his master's deposition from the caliphate. 'Ali did not resign, but the arbitration sapped his authority. His followers faded away. One province after another defected to Mu'awiya, who had himself proclaimed caliph in Jerusalem in 660. Finally, in 661, 'Ali was murdered by a Kharijite seeking revenge for his sect's defeat.

CHANGES IN THE GOVERNMENT OF ISLAM

'Ali's death ended the period known to Muslims as the era of the al-Khulafa' al-Rashidun (meaning "rightly guided") caliphs. All four were men related to Muhammad by marriage and chosen by his companions. Later Muslims would look back on this period as a golden ideal age to which many longed to return. They contrasted the simple governments in Medina and Kufa with the swollen bureaucracies of Damascus and Baghdad, headed by kingly caliphs who succeeded by heredity. But three of the four Rashidun caliphs were assassinated. Theirs was an era of political strife, crises of adjustment to changing conditions, and much improvisation. Even the caliphate itself had begun as a stopgap measure, shaped by 'Umar into a lasting institution. It became the linchpin for a state that was doubling and redoubling in area, population, and wealth. Now, upon 'Ali's death, it seemed to be in peril.

Mu'awiya

The man who saved the *umma* and the caliphate from anarchy was the Umayyad governor of Syria, Mu'awiya. He possessed a virtue prized among Arabs—the ability to refrain from using force unless absolutely necessary. As Mu'awiya put it, "I never use my sword when my whip will do, nor my whip when my tongue will do. Let a single hair bind me to my people, and I will not let it snap; when they pull I loosen, and if they loosen I pull."

It is interesting that Mu'awiya first claimed the caliphate in Jerusalem, the city sacred to Jews, Christians, and Muslims. What if he had made it his capital, something no Arab or Muslim ruler has ever done? But Mu'awiya had started his career as a Meccan merchant, and he chose to stay in Damascus, his provincial capital, because it was on the main trade route between Syria and Yemen. He seems to have viewed Syria as a stepping-stone toward taking over all the Byzantine Empire. Each summer the caliph's armies penetrated Anatolia. Meanwhile, his navy drove the Byzantine fleet from the southeastern Mediterranean and twice during his reign besieged the very capital of the empire. But Byzantium withstood the onslaught. The Arabs consoled themselves by pushing westward across Tunisia and eastward through Khurasan.

Administrative Changes

Mu'awiya, once called the "Caesar of the Arabs" by none other than Caliph 'Umar himself, was more worldly than his precursors; but the changes that took place after 661 could not be ascribed to personality differences. Patriarchal government—namely, what had grown up in Medina on the model of the Arab tribal system, modified somewhat by the Qur'an and the Prophet's practices—could not meet the needs of a sprawling empire encompassing many peoples and religions. Mu'awiya adopted some of the Byzantine imperial customs and the bureaucratic practices familiar to Egypt and Syria. Many of his administrators and some of his warriors were Syrians or Christian Arabs, often survivors or sons of the old Byzantine bureaucracy and soldiery.

Mu'awiya depended on the Arab tribes for most of his military manpower. He kept them loyal by flattering their sense of racial superiority and requiring tribal representatives (really hostages) to reside at his court in Damascus. Troublesome areas like Iraq were cowed by ruthless local governors such as Ziyad, Mu'awiya's alleged half brother. Upon taking charge in Basra, Ziyad warned the people from the pulpit of its main mosque:

You are putting family ties before religion. You are excusing and shelter-
ing your criminals and tearing down the protecting laws sanctified by Islam. Beware of prowling by night; I will kill everyone who is found at night
in the streets. Beware of the arbitrary call to obey family ties; I will cut
out the tongue of everyone who raises the cry. Whoever pushes anyone
into the water, whoever sets fire to another's home, whoever breaks into a
house, whoever opens a grave, him will I punish. Hatred against myself I
do not punish, but only crime. Many who are terrified of my coming will
be glad of my presence, and many who are building their hopes upon it
will be undeceived. I rule you with the authority of God and will maintain
you from the wealth of God's *umma*. From you I demand obedience, and
you can demand from me justice. Though I may fall short, there are three
things in which I shall not be lacking: I will be ready to listen to anyone at
any time, I will pay you your pension when it is due, and I will not send
you to war too far away or for too long a time. Do not let yourselves be carried away by your hatred and wrath against me; you will suffer if you do.
Many heads do I see tottering; let each man see to it that his own remains
on his shoulders!

When Muʿawiya realized that he would die soon, he obtained in advance his followers' consent for the succession of his son Yazid to the caliphate. It was this act that later earned Muʿawiya the condemnation of
Muslim historians, because from that time until the caliphate was abolished in 1924, the highest political office in Islam was hereditary, even if it
remained elective in principle (see Box 4.1).

But would Islam have fared better if Muʿawiya had not founded the
Umayyad dynasty? Most tribal Arabs, if given a choice, would have gravitated to the Kharijite view—that any adult male Muslim could become
caliph, no matter his race or lineage, and that any caliph who sinned
should be overthrown in favor of another. The Kharijite idea would recur throughout Islamic history, especially among the nomads in Arabia
and North Africa. In fact, some modern Muslims seek to revive the caliphate without restricting the office to descendants of the Quraysh tribe.
But a popular election of the Muslim ruler, based on Kharijite principles,
would have caused anarchy in the seventh century—or even now. Yes, the
Umayyads were lax Muslims. Muʿawiya had resisted Muhammad until all
Mecca surrendered to Islam, but he then turned 180 degrees and became
the Prophet's secretary. Some of his descendants' drinking and sexual exploits shocked the pious Muslims of their day. However, the Umayyads
maintained the caravan trade between Syria and Yemen, and their business acumen helped them to choose policies, reconcile differences, and

Box 4.1   Mu'awiya ibn Abi-Sufyan

Mu'awiya (602–680) was the founder of the Umayyad dynasty. The Umayyads were the dominant clan in Mecca; they did not associate with Muhammad's followers. In fact, Mu'awiya did not accept Islam until the city surrendered to the Prophet in 630. The second caliph, 'Umar, appointed him governor of Syria, a position at which he excelled.

In June 656 the third caliph, 'Uthman, was murdered in Medina. His successor was 'Ali, the Prophet's cousin and son-in-law. After suppressing the rebellion led by 'Aisha and two other early companions of the Prophet, 'Ali decided that, to maintain loyalty in the provinces, he would have to replace the governors appointed by his predecessors. This led to a confrontation with Mu'awiya, who refused to resign from his post. Their confrontation was intensified by the fact that 'Uthman was Mu'awiya's first cousin; the latter demanded that Caliph 'Ali produce the assassins or he himself would be suspected as an accomplice in the crime.

This struggle between the two men followed a convoluted path that at times saw their respective armies fighting on the battlefield and sometimes led them to attempt arbitration. In the end, 'Ali was assassinated by a disgruntled Kharijite in 661. Mu'awiya then became Islam's next caliph.

Mu'awiya's success rested on the base he had laid in Syria, where he proved a shrewd and strong governor. He had ruled there successfully for twenty years and made that land prosperous. Its people repaid him with loyalty. In Syria he had also molded the local Arab tribes into the best-trained, best-equipped, and best-organized provincial army in the Muslim world. Reversing 'Umar's insistence that all conquests take place on land, he also built Islam's first navy. He would stay in Syria even after successfully taking over the caliphate. Thus, Damascus replaced Medina as the capital of the growing Islamic empire.

Mu'awiya's reign broke with the past in other ways as well. The empire was still rapidly expanding, and now the caliph faced serious internal dissension that sometimes challenged his rule. Thus, Mu'awiya's ability to innovate, with less dependence on tradition than had occurred under 'Umar, became another reason for his success. Through his innovations, the nature of Muslim rule quickly changed from the more immediate, personal, and collaborative styles of the first four caliphs to a more imperial, bureaucratic art that reflected the practices of the Byzantine and Persian states the Muslims had defeated. The resulting government and court life were alien to the ways of those who cherished the political practices of the Prophet and his companions.

All this harmed Mu'awiya's reputation with later Muslim historians. Many of them favored the cause of 'Ali (i.e., Shi'ism) or were influenced by the very negative accounts written for the 'Abbasid rulers who later overthrew the Umayyads. Nonetheless, it is clear that Mu'awiya was a great innovator and a shrewd wielder of power. He probably saved the young Muslim state from chaos following 'Ali's death and set it on a stable administrative path to greater empire.

neutralize opposition. The Umayyad dynasty, though condemned by most Muslim historians on moral grounds, built up the great Arab empire.

Mu'awiya's Successors

What Mu'awiya achieved was almost buried with him in 680. Yazid, his designated successor, was hated by Muhammad's old Meccan companions and by some of the Arab tribes, despite his victories in earlier battles against Byzantium. This animosity could linked back to Yazid's childhood. His mother, one of Mu'awiya's favorite wives, had detested the settled life of the Umayyad court and pined for the Bedouin camps of her youth. She wrote a poem to this effect, grossly insulting to Mu'awiya, that convinced him that she and her young son belonged in the desert. Yazid grew up with his mother's tribe, the Kalb. Upon his accession to the caliphate, he favored his tribe over its great rival, the Qays. During the early conquests, the tribes had formed two large confederations involving most of the Arab soldiers: one "southern" and including the Kalb, the other "northern" and including the Qays. During Yazid's reign, their rivalries escalated into a full-scale civil war, part of Islam's second *fitna*.

Husayn's Rebellion: The Beginning of Shi'ism

Some Muslims still abhorred the very idea of an Umayyad caliphate and wanted the *umma*'s leadership restored to the Hashimite clan, preferably in the person of a direct descendant of the Prophet. Muhammad had no sons. His son-in-law, 'Ali, had been killed, as had Hasan, leaving the Prophet's other grandson, Husayn, as the only possible claimant. Husayn was a pious man who had lived most of his fifty-four years quietly in Medina. But when Yazid succeeded Mu'awiya in 680, Husayn refused to recognize the new caliph as legitimate. Some Kufan foes of the Umayyads, thus encouraged, talked Husayn into rebelling against them. Intimidated by their governor, though, most Kufans withheld their support in Husayn's hour of need. When the Prophet's grandson reached Karbala, Iraq, he found he had only 72 warriors pitted against 10,000 Umayyad soldiers. Husayn's tiny band fought as bravely as they could, but they all fell in battle on 10 Muharram 61 *Anno Hegirae* (10 October 680). Husayn's severed head was laid at the feet of Yazid in Damascus. The Umayyads seemingly had triumphed once more.

The significance of these events was that the partisans of the Prophet's "martyred" descendants, 'Ali and now Husayn, vowed never to recognize the Umayyads as legitimate caliphs. They came to be called *Shi'at 'Ali* (the Party of 'Ali), from which came the name Shi'ites. From Iraq they spread throughout the empire, wherever Muslims sought a pretext to defy Umayyad rule. Today, the Shi'ites make up the second-largest Muslim sect, as contrasted with the majority group, called Sunnis, who accepted (often reluctantly) the ruling caliphs. Religious differences do exist between Sunnis and Shi'ites, due mainly to the latter's conviction that only 'Ali and his descendants (see Figure 4.1) had any right to lead the *umma*. To Shi'ite Muslims, even Abu-Bakr, 'Umar, and 'Uthman, let alone Mu'awiya and his heirs, were usurpers, whereas 'Ali was the first *imam* (leader), and he

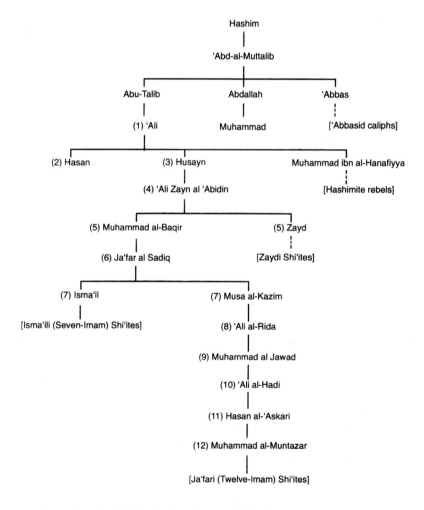

Figure 4.1   The Hashimite clan, showing Shi'ite *imams*

bequeathed special powers and esoteric knowledge to his sons, his sons' sons, and so on.

As time passed, disputes arose among various brothers claiming the imamate, causing splits among their Shi'ite followers. As you will soon see, some Shi'ites later managed to form states in opposition to the Sunni caliphate. Since about 1500, as you will learn in Chapter 6, the rulers of Persia (called Iran in modern times) have been Shi'ite Muslims. But do not identify Shi'ism with Persian nationalism, for the former began as a polit-ical protest movement couched in religious terms, appealing to Arabs as well as Persians. It found expression in pilgrimages to Najaf and Karbala (the burial sites of 'Ali and Husayn, respectively), in annual processions mourning the martyrdom of Husayn, and in the passion play re-enacting his tragic end.

Other Challengers

The other challenges to the Umayyads, although they seemed more threat-ening then, are now largely forgotten. Abdallah ibn al-Zubayr, son of the Zubayr killed in the Battle of the Camel, also refused allegiance to Yazid. When Yazid died in 683, he left the caliphate to his sickly young son, but Abdallah, who lived in Mecca, claimed the office for himself. Muslims in all the provinces, even some in Syria, promised to back him. The Arab tribes favoring the Qays, the northern confederation, rose up against the Umayyads, who were linked to the Kalb and hence to the southern Arabs. When the teenage caliph died, leaving the Umayyads with no plausible candidate, Abdallah could easily have come to Damascus to seize the ca-liphate there. But he was allied with the pious descendants of Muham-mad's associates living in Medina and Mecca. They hated Damascus and everything that smacked of Umayyad rule, so Abdallah stayed in Mecca. The oldest and most respected member of the Umayyad clan, Marwan, reluctantly agreed to oppose Abdallah's partisans, and in July 684 the Umayyad supporters defeated the opposing Arab tribes and drove them out of Syria.

Rebellions went on for almost a decade. In 685 a group of penitent Shi'ites in Kufa started a two-year revolt that was notable for its appeal to non-Arab converts. There were several Kharijite uprisings—one could generally expect them whenever there was trouble. It took years for the Umayyads to crush the rival caliphate of Abdallah ibn al-Zubayr, but we must leave that story for Chapter 5. Never again would a large group try to make Mecca the capital city of Islam.

CONCLUSION

Between Muhammad's death and the second *fitna*, the *umma* had grown so large that Arabia could no longer be its political center. The Arabian tribes that had carried out the conquests had formed a powerful aristocracy that spread throughout the empire, but their effectiveness as a police force was fatally weakened by their rivalries. The *umma*'s government had ceased to be an extension of either Arab tribal democracy or Muhammad's religious prestige; now it was firmly grasped by a Meccan mercantile clan based in Syria. Its administrative arm was a team of Arabs and Syrians, some of them Christian, who carried on the ruling practices of the Byzantines. Many of the Arabs, whether nomads, sedentarized Meccan traders, Medinan farmers, or tribal warriors living in garrison towns, felt alienated from this neo-Roman kingdom. Some of the non-Arab subjects had become Muslims, but these *mawali*, especially in Iraq, were second-class citizens who resented Arab claims to superiority. Shi'ite and Kharijite movements reflected these various tensions. Meanwhile, most of the caliphs' subjects remained Jews, Christians, or Zoroastrians, not Muslims who could be counted on to support the *umma* whenever it was in danger. In sum, we should marvel that Islam survived Muhammad's death, that it gained new lands and adherents so quickly, and that it assimilated mighty empires and civilized societies. Yet, despite these achievements spanning half a century, Muslims were not yet secure.

5

The High Caliphate

For about a thousand years, history has been playing mean tricks on the Arabs. They have been wracked with internal factionalism and strife, external invasion, subordination to outside rulers, natural disasters, and exaggerated hopes and fears. But, in their history's bleakest moments, the Arabic-speaking peoples of the Middle East have comforted themselves with the memory of a time when their ancestors ruled most of the Eastern Hemisphere, when the Europeans and the Chinese feared and courted them, and when theirs was the language in which humanity's highest literary and scientific achievements were expressed. This was the time of the two great caliphal dynasties, the Umayyads and the 'Abbasids. We call this era, the years from 685 to 945, the High Caliphate.

During this period, the Islamic *umma* was initially headed by the Marwanid branch of the Umayyad family, ruling in Damascus, and then by the 'Abbasids of Baghdad. Both dynasties belonged to the Quraysh tribe and were backed by those Muslims who came to be called Sunnis. The caliphal state was militarily strong, relative to Western Europe, the Byzantine Empire, India, and China. Territorial conquests continued until about 750, when the 'Abbasids took over from the Umayyads. After that time some land was lost to local rulers, and the empire began to break up.

As long as any semblance of unity remained, though, the old Roman, Syrian, and Persian political practices and cultural traditions went on combining in new ways. Economic prosperity, based mainly on agriculture, was enhanced by commerce and manufacturing. The relative power of the various peoples shifted gradually during the High Caliphate. Under the 'Abbasids, if not earlier, Arab dominance waned, as many non-Arabs became Muslims and, in most instances, adopted the Arabic language as well. These factors facilitated the movement of people and the spread of ideas and hence the growth of an Islamic civilization.

The name Arab denoted more and more people. Originally, it meant the Bedouin living in Arabia who, as Muslims, would conquer vast lands. That conquest spread the Arabic language and combined Arab culture with the lifestyles of the conquered. Over time many of those who partook of that culture and spoke Arabic would also be viewed by others, and themselves, as Arabs. During the High Caliphate, tribal soldiers from Arabia would gradually be replaced by salaried troops, notably Persians from Khurasan, then by Turkish tribal horse soldiers paid with land grants. Persians and Turks were not Arabs.

As the caliphal state grew larger and more complex, it needed more people to run it. The early Umayyads had inherited Roman bureaucratic traditions, but now Persian administrators took over and introduced Sassanid practices. At the same time, there grew up a class of pious Muslims who could recite and interpret the Qur'an, relate and record *hadiths* (authenticated accounts of Muhammad's sayings and actions), systematize Arabic grammar, and develop the science of law (called *fiqh* in Arabic). Eventually they became known as *'ulama*, which means "those who know," or experts on Muslim doctrines, laws, and history. Muslims also became interested in classical philosophy, science, and medicine, as Greek works were translated into Arabic. One result was the evolution of systematic Islamic theology. Muslims also developed more esoteric ideas and rituals, leading to the rise of Sufism (organized Islamic mysticism), which you will read about later.

The caliphate faced ongoing opposition from the Kharijites, who rejected any type of hereditary rule, and from Shi'ite movements backing various descendants of 'Ali. Late in this era, most of the Muslim world came under the rule of Shi'ite dynasties. Until about 1000, non-Muslims predominated in the lands of the *umma*, but their relative power and influence were waning.

RESTORATION OF THE UMAYYAD ORDER

Most scholars list 'Umar, Mu'awiya, and 'Abd al-Malik among the caliphs regarded as the founding fathers of Islamic government. You have already learned about 'Umar, who presided over the early conquests, and about Mu'awiya, who bequeathed the caliphate to his Umayyad heirs. 'Abd al-Malik took over the caliphate on the death of his aged father, Marwan, who had ruled briefly during what was (for the Umayyads) the worst year of the second *fitna*. When 'Abd al-Malik took charge, the northern Arab tribal confederation was rebelling against his family, in league with

Abdallah ibn al-Zubayr, who was in Mecca claiming the caliphate. Every province except Syria had turned against Umayyad rule. The martyrdom of the Prophet's grandson, Husayn, had further antagonized many Muslims, especially the Shi'ites.

'Abd al-Malik's Triumph

Although he took office in 685, 'Abd al-Malik waited until 691 to take Iraq from Abdallah's forces. The next year al-Hajjaj, an Umayyad general famed for his harsh government in Iraq and Iran, captured Arabia. His men had to bombard Mecca (even damaging the Ka'ba) before Abdallah's army surrendered. Al-Hajjaj spent two years wiping out Kharijite rebels in Arabia before he went into Kufa. Wearing a disguise, he entered the main mosque, mounted the pulpit, tore the veil from his face, and addressed the rebellious Kufans: "I see heads ripe for the cutting. People of Iraq, I will not let myself be crushed like a soft fig. . . . The commander of the believers ['Abd al-Malik] has drawn arrows from his quiver and tested the wood, and has found that I am the hardest. . . . And so, by God, I will strip you as men strip the bark from trees. . . . I will beat you as stray camels are beaten." The Kufans, thus intimidated, gave no more trouble, and al-Hajjaj restored prosperity to the Umayyads' eastern provinces.

'Abd al-Malik laid the basis for an absolutist caliphate, one patterned after the traditions of the divine kings of the ancient Middle East instead of the patriarchal shaykhs of the Arab tribes. You can see the change not only in the policies of such authoritarian governors as al-Hajjaj but also in 'Abd al-Malik's decree making Arabic the administrative language. Before then, some parts of the empire had used Greek, others Persian, Aramaic, or Coptic, depending on what the local officials and people happened to speak. Many bureaucrats, especially the Persians, did not want to give up a language rich in administrative vocabulary for one used until recently only by camel nomads and merchants. But it is these Persians who systematized Arabic grammar, for they soon realized that no Persian could get or keep a government job without learning to read and write this complicated new language.

Following the old Roman imperial tradition of erecting fine buildings, 'Abd al-Malik had the magnificent Dome of the Rock built atop what had been Jerusalem's Temple Mount. It was a shrine erected around what local tradition said was the rock of Abraham's attempted sacrifice and what Muslims believe to be the site of Muhammad's departure on his miraculous night journey to heaven. With the Dome of the Rock set almost directly above the Western Wall, the sole remnant of the Jewish Second Temple, you can see why Arabs and Jews now dispute who should control Jerusalem's Old City, holy to all three monotheistic faiths.

Another symbolic act by 'Abd al-Malik was the minting of Muslim coins, which ended the Muslims' dependence on Byzantine and Persian currency. The use of Arabic-language inscriptions (often Qur'anic quotations) made it easier for Arabs to sort out the various values of the coins. Eventually, Muslim rulers came to view the right to issue coins in their own names as the symbol of their sovereignty.

Resumption of the Conquests

The caliphal state was becoming an empire. The Arab conquests resumed after the second *fitna* ended. One army headed west across North Africa, while a Muslim navy drove the Byzantines from the western Mediterranean. The North African Berbers, after surrendering to the Arabs, converted to Islam and joined their armies. Under 'Abd al-Malik's successor, a Muslim force crossed the Strait of Gibraltar and took most of what is now Spain and Portugal. It was not until 732—exactly a century after the Prophet's death—that a European Christian army stemmed the Muslim tide in central France. The greatest Arab thrust, though, was eastward from Persia. Muslim armies attacked the Turks, first in what is now Afghanistan, then in Transoxiana (the land beyond the Oxus River, or the Amu Darya), including Bukhara and Samarqand. They eventually reached China's northwest border, which became the eastern limit of the Arab conquests. Another force pushed north to the Aral Sea, adding Khwarizm to the lands of Islam. Yet another moved south, taking Baluchistan, Sind, and Punjab, roughly what is now Pakistan.

There was one nut too tough to crack—the Byzantine Empire. The Byzantines, though weakened by the loss of their Syrian and North African lands and shorn of their naval supremacy in the western Mediterranean, reorganized their army and the administration of Anatolia, making that highland area impregnable to Arab forces. Constantinople, guarded by thick walls, withstood three Umayyad sieges, the last of which involved an Arab fleet of a thousand ships and lasted from 716 to 718. Using "Greek fire," probably a naphtha derivative, that ignited upon hitting the water and (with favorable winds) set fire to enemy ships, the Byzantines wiped out most of the Arab fleet. After that, the caliphs concluded that Byzantium was too hard to take. Gradually they stopped claiming to be the new "Roman" empire and adopted a neo-Persian aura instead.

Fiscal Reforms

Whether the caliphs took on the trappings of Roman emperors or Persian shahs, their government favored the Arabs and depended on their backing. But most of their subjects were not Arabs, and they paid most of the taxes. Even those non-Arabs who became Muslims still had to pay the Umayyads the same rates as those who did not convert. The terminology and administration of these taxes were confusing, for they were rigged against the *mawali*, the non-Arab converts to Islam who had become as numerous as the tribal Arabs themselves.

This problem was tackled by 'Umar II (r. 717–720), who alone among all the Umayyad caliphs is praised for his piety by later Muslim historians. 'Umar wanted to stop all fiscal practices that favored the Arabs and to treat all Muslims equally and fairly. When his advisers warned him that exempting the *mawali* from the taxes paid by non-Muslims would cause numerous conversions to Islam and deplete his treasury, 'Umar retorted that he had not become commander of the believers to collect taxes and imposed his reforms anyway. As he also cut military expenditures, his treasury did not suffer, and he did gain Muslim converts. He must have wanted conversions, because he also placed humiliating restrictions on non-Muslims: they could not ride horses or camels, only mules and donkeys; they had to wear special clothing that identified them as Jews or Christians; and they were forbidden to build new synagogues or churches without permission. These rules, collectively called the *Covenant of 'Umar,* were enforced by some of his successors and ignored by many others.

We cannot generalize about the conditions of Jews and Christians under Muslim rule—they varied so greatly—but conversion to Islam was usually socially or economically motivated, not forced. It was Hisham (r. 724–743) who finally set the taxes into a system that would be upheld for the next thousand years: Muslims paid the *zakat,* property owners (with a few exceptions) paid on their land or buildings a tax called the *kharaj,* and Christian and Jewish men paid a per capita tax called the *jizya.*

THE DOWNFALL OF THE UMAYYADS

Despite the fiscal reforms of 'Umar II and Hisham, the Umayyad caliphate remained an Arab kingdom. Muslims could endure this as long as the conquests continued. But, as they slowed down in the 740s, the Arab tribes that supplied most of the warriors became worthless because of their constant quarrels. A few of the later caliphs also seemed useless, with their hunting palaces, dancing girls, and swimming pools filled with wine.

Some of them sided with one or the other of the tribal confederations, raising the danger that the slighted tribes would stir up bitter Shi'ite or Kharijite revolts. Hisham faced these problems bravely; his less able successors did not.

Meanwhile, the *mawali* had become the intellectual leaders, the bureaucrats, and even the commercial elite of the *umma,* but the political and social discrimination they had to endure dulled their support for the existing system. The best way for them to speak out was to back dissident Muslim movements that might overthrow the Umayyads. Especially popular among the *mawali* was a Shi'ite revolutionary movement called—ambiguously— the Hashimites. As you can see from Figure 4.1 (on page 57), the name denotes Muhammad's family. The Hashimites, as a conspiratorial group, concealed from outsiders just which branch of Shi'ism they were backing. In fact, their leaders descended from a son born to 'Ali by a woman other than Muhammad's daughter. In the early eighth century, some of the Hashimites conferred their support on one branch of their clan, the 'Abbasids, so called because they had descended from Muhammad's uncle 'Abbas. The 'Abbasids exploited these Shi'ite revolutionaries and disgruntled *mawali* to gain power. Their power center was Khurasan, in eastern Persia.

The Umayyads' weakness was the 'Abbasids' opportunity. The Arab tribes were bitterly divided, the army was demoralized, river irrigation had raised Iraq's importance relative to Syria, popular opinion called for Muslim equality in place of Arab supremacy, and Khurasan was a province in which thousands of Arab colonists mixed with the native Persian landowners. There, in 747, a Persian named Abu-Muslim declared a revolution to support the 'Abbasids. Despite the heroic resistance of the last Umayyad caliph and his governor in Khurasan, the revolt spread. The 'Abbasids reached Kufa in 749 and claimed that an 'Abbasid named Abu al-'Abbas was the new caliph. Abu-Muslim's troops crushed the Umayyads' army in January 750, pursued their last caliph to Egypt, and killed him. Then they went on to wipe out all the living Umayyads and to scourge the corpses of the dead ones. The only member of the family who escaped was 'Abd al-Rahman I. After a harrowing journey across North Africa, he safely reached Spain, where he established in Cordoba a separate state that would later become a rival caliphate that lasted until 1031.

THE 'ABBASID CALIPHATE

The 'Abbasid revolution is generally viewed as a turning point in Islamic history. People used to think that it marked the overthrow of the Arabs by the Persians. However, the ʿAbbasids were Arabs, proud of their descent from the Prophet's uncle. Their partisans included Arabs and Persians, and Sunni and Shiʿite Muslims, all united by a desire to replace an Arab tribal aristocracy with a more egalitarian form of government based on the principles of Islam. Like other historic revolutions, the overthrow of the Umayyads reinforced trends that had already begun: the shift of the power center from Syria to Iraq, the rise of Persian influence in place of the Byzantine-Arab synthesis of Muʿawiya and ʿAbd al-Malik, the waning drive to take over all the Christian lands of Europe, and the growing interest in cultivating the arts of civilization.

The Building of Baghdad

When Abu al-ʿAbbas was acclaimed as the first ʿAbbasid caliph in 749, Baghdad was just a tiny Persian village a few miles up the Tigris River from the ruined Sassanid capital, Ctesiphon. The early ʿAbbasids wanted to move the government to Iraq, but they tried a few other cities before Abu al-Abbas's brother and successor, Abu Jaʿfar al-Mansur, chose that site in 762 for his capital. It was located at exactly the point where the Tigris and Euphrates come closest together (see Map 5.1). A series of canals linking the rivers there made it easier to defend the site and also put Baghdad on the main trade route between the Mediterranean (hence Europe) and the Persian Gulf (hence Asia). River irrigation in Iraq was raising agricultural output. It was also an area in which Persian and Aramean culture remained strong. Finally, it was closer to the political center of gravity for an empire still stretching east toward India and China.

Al-Mansur wanted a planned capital, not a city that, like Kufa or Damascus, had long served other purposes. His architects gave him a round city. The caliphal palace and the main mosque fronted on a central square. Around them stood army barracks, government offices, and the homes of the chief administrators. A double wall with four gates girdled the city, and soon hundreds of houses and shops surrounded the wall. Across the Tigris rose the palace of the caliph's son, with a smaller entourage. The later caliphs built more palaces along the Tigris, which was spanned by a bridge of boats. The building of Baghdad was part of a public works policy by which the ʿAbbasids kept thousands of their subjects employed and their immense wealth circulating. It was a popular policy, for it led to the construction of mosques, schools, and hospitals throughout the empire, but its success depended on general prosperity, for the people paid high taxes to support it.

67

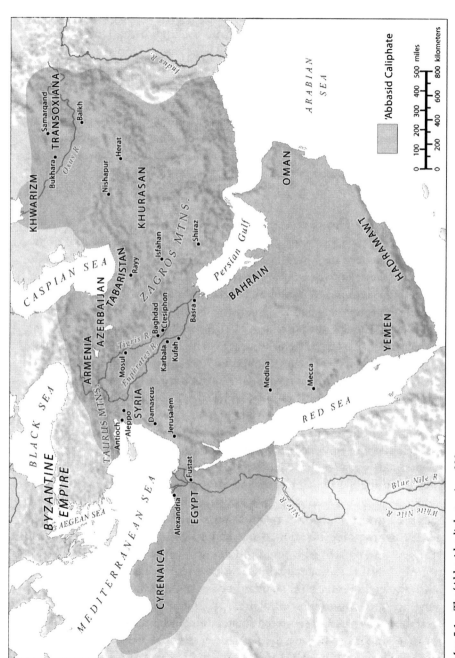

Map 5.1   The 'Abbasid caliphate, circa 800

Public Piety

The 'Abbasids made a public display of their piety, which had been their main justification for seizing power from the high-living Umayyads. Al-Mahdi, the third 'Abbasid caliph, loved wine, music, and perfumed slave girls, but he also paid handsomely to expand the courtyard surrounding the Ka'ba and to set up guard posts and wells along the pilgrimage routes in Arabia. The fifth caliph, Harun al-Rashid, performed the *hajj* every few years throughout his life, hoping to earn divine merit. Harun personally led his army in a Muslim jihad across Anatolia that almost reached Constantinople before the Byzantines paid enough tribute to persuade the 'Abbasids to withdraw.

Anti-'Abbasid Revolts

With so much public piety, you might think the 'Abbasids could have avoided religious uprisings like the ones that had troubled the Umayyads. Not so. The revolts became more frequent and varied than ever before, reflecting economic hardships and social discontent in the lands of Islam. Kharijite groups rebelled in Oman and North Africa, forming states of their own. The Shi'ites posed a greater threat, for they soon saw that the 'Abbasids had tricked them by using their help to oust the Umayyads. Two descendants of Hasan revolted in 762, one in Mecca and the other in Basra. To crush their revolts, al-Mansur's troops killed thousands of Shi'ite dissidents. In 788 another Shi'ite led a Berber rebellion that permanently severed Morocco from 'Abbasid rule.

Some of the revolts against 'Abbasid rule were anti-Islamic in spirit, especially those in which Persians took part. Why were they so restive? A dark curtain had shrouded Persia's history after the Arab conquests destroyed the Sassanid Empire, and for a century the Persians sank into shocked despair. Gradually, they became Muslims, learned Arabic, and adjusted to the new power relationships. The Umayyads' fall in 750, followed by Iraq's regeneration, drew the Persians out of their shock. Many would back any hero who could restore their lost prestige.

Abu-Muslim was popular in Khurasan, where the Persians viewed him as their leader, not merely the standard-bearer of the 'Abbasid revolution. The first two 'Abbasid caliphs, Abu al-'Abbas and al-Mansur, used him to defeat the Umayyads and crush the Shi'ites. But al-Mansur feared that the Persians might turn on his own dynasty. The Persians later charged that Mansur treacherously summoned Abu-Muslim to his court and had him put to death. Some Arabs called Abu-Muslim a Zindiq (heretic), meaning that he practiced a pre-Islamic Persian religion. He remains a controversial figure.

Abu-Muslim's execution brought the 'Abbasids no peace. Revolts soon broke out in Khurasan. These uprisings were inspired by Persia's pre-Islamic religions, such as Zoroastrianism (practiced by the Sassanid rulers) and a peasant movement called Mazdakism. Moreover, the Manichaeans' philosophical dualism survived or revived in Persia among the Zindiqs, but this group is hard to define, as pious Muslims used that name for most dissidents. If you study this period further, you will find that these religious revolts often had economic motives, too.

Persians in Power

The resurrection of Persian influence did not always take dissident forms. Hundreds of Persians, mainly from Iraq and Khurasan, rose to high posts in the army and the civil administration, replacing the Arabs and Syrians favored by the Umayyads. These men may have been more interested in the Sanskrit and Persian classics than their Arab colleagues would have liked them to be, but they also learned Arabic and carefully toed the 'Abbasid line on religious matters. Some Persians became *'ulama* and helped to shape Islam. Loyal to their 'Abbasid masters, they helped them suppress dissenting ideas and movements, but in fact they Persianized the state from within.

As the central administration grew more complex, Persian bureaucratic families rose to power. The greatest of these was the Barmakids, of whom three generations served the 'Abbasids from al-Mansur to Harun al-Rashid as bursars, tax collectors, provincial governors, military commanders, tutors, companions, and chief ministers. The title they bore, pronounced *wazir* in Arabic and *vizier* in Persian, came to be applied to any high-ranking official. Originally meaning "burden-bearer," it now is used to mean "cabinet minister" in most Middle Eastern languages. Harun unloaded many of his burdens onto his Barmakid viziers, until he realized that he had let them take too much of his power and wealth. Then he dramatically killed the one to whom he was most attached. The Barmakids' power and prestige were eclipsing Harun's own position. Either he or they had to go. How could Harun claim to be God's representative on earth and the fountainhead of justice if everyone looked to the Barmakids for patronage?

A less spectacular ladder for upwardly mobile Persians was a literary movement called the Shu'ubiya. The Persians, especially in the bureaucratic class, used their knowledge of literature to prove their equality with (or superiority over) the Arabs. After all, they reasoned, Persians had built and ruled mighty empires, prospered, and created a high culture for centuries while the Arabs were riding camels in the desert. The Arabs were quick to accuse the Shu'ubiya of attacking Islam and the Prophet, but its scholars and bureaucrats really sought equality within the system.

The greatest threat to the 'Abbasids came from those Persians who broke away to form separate dynastic states in Persia. These included a general who founded the Tahirids (r. 820–873) and a coppersmith who started the durable Saffarids (r. 861–1465). Indeed, the 'Abbasids themselves were being Persianized by their harems. The caliphs had so many Persian wives or concubines that the genetic mix of the ninth-century 'Abbasids was more Persian than Arab. Harun's Persian mother pushed him into becoming caliph. The succession struggle between his two sons was intensified by the fact that the mother of Amin (r. 809–813) was Harun's Arab wife, whereas al-Ma'mun (the challenger and ultimate victor) was born of a Persian concubine.

Al-Ma'mun's Caliphate

Al-Ma'mun (r. 813–833) deserves a high rank among the 'Abbasid caliphs, even though his rise to power resulted from a bloody civil war that almost wiped out Baghdad. A patron of scholarship, al-Ma'mun founded a major Islamic intellectual center called *Bayt al-Hikma* (House of Wisdom). It included several schools, astronomical observatories in Baghdad and Damascus, an immense library, and facilities for the translation of scientific and philosophical works from Greek, Aramaic, and Persian into Arabic.

Al-Ma'mun's penchant for philosophical and theological debate led him to espouse a set of Muslim doctrines known collectively as the *Mu'tazila*. Although this theological system undertook at first to refute Persian Zindiqs and the Shu'ubiya, it became a rationalist formulation of Islam, stressing free will over divine predestination. Under al-Ma'mun and his two successors, each high-ranking Muslim official or judge was tested by being asked whether he believed that God had created all things, including the Qur'an. A yes answer meant that he was a Mu'tazilite, one who opposed the popular idea that the Qur'an had eternally existed, even before it was revealed to Muhammad. (We will revisit this issue in Chapter 7.) The extreme rationalism of the Mu'tazila antagonized the later 'Abbasids, who ended the test, and it offended ordinary Muslims, who revered the Qur'an and believed that God had decreed all human acts. Al-Ma'mun also tried to reconcile Sunni and Shi'ite Muslims by naming the latter's imam as his successor. The plan backfired. Iraq's people resisted al-Ma'mun's concession to a descendant of 'Ali, and the imam died, probably of poison. (See Box 5.1).

Box 5.1	Al-Ma'mun

Al-Ma'mun (786–833) was the son of Caliph Harun al-Rashid by a Persian slave girl named Marajil. At this time Persia was still a land of heterodox beliefs within the growing Muslim empire. Thanks to his mother and a host of non-Arab tutors, al-Ma'mun grew up with a wide interest in a variety of philosophical and scientific approaches to knowledge.

Al-Ma'mun had to fight for the throne against his slightly older half brother Amin, whose mother, an Arab, was a descendant of the Quraysh tribe. The struggle between the two half brothers reflected the last stage of an old battle between the traditional culture of the conquering Arabs and the ways of the non-Arab (mostly Persian) Muslim converts who demanded equality and acceptance of their own cultural and artistic heritage within Muslim society. Al-Ma'mun's followers came mostly from this latter group.

In 813 al-Ma'mun's forces prevailed. The fighting had destroyed a good part of Baghdad and left much of Iraq in anarchy. Al-Ma'mun lived for six years in Marw, the provincial capital of Khurasan, while his armies suppressed several revolts and workmen rebuilt Baghdad. Only then would he move to the capital city.

Al-Ma'mun, the seventh caliph of the 'Abbasid dynasty, proved to be an energetic patron of the arts and sciences, but also one of Islam's most intellectually eccentric rulers. Apparently a rationalist at heart, he was troubled by the paradoxes and contradictions inherent in some of the more popular Muslim beliefs. For instance, most Muslims adhered to the orthodox view that the Qur'an was an eternal work that had existed even before it was revealed to Muhammad. They also believed that God foreordained all human actions. These beliefs made little sense to the caliph and the Mu'tazila movement he espoused. If God is all-merciful and the Lord of Justice, how could he create a universe where one may be punished for a foreordained act? Al-Ma'mun imposed his views on his judges and administrators in the year 827. His decree and its enforcement against those who adhered to the orthodox view turned many Muslims against the caliph.

Even as he tried to impose his theological views on the people he ruled, al-Ma'mun sponsored the search for new knowledge by supporting translations of Greek works of philosophy and science. He sent envoys as far afield as Sicily and Constantinople to find manuscripts for his translation and research center, the House of Wisdom (which also housed the world's first astronomical observatory). Through such efforts, much of ancient Greek thought was preserved. Later it would be transmitted to the West via Muslim Spain. This may well be his most important legacy.

In addition to being an intellectual, al-Ma'mun was a conqueror, as a Muslim caliph was expected to be. In 830 and 833 the caliph led his armies against the Byzantine Empire. During the latter campaign, he was unexpectedly stricken by a "burning fever" after eating some local dates. He died soon thereafter, at age forty-eight, having reigned for more than twenty-two years.

THE DECLINE OF THE 'ABBASIDS

Given so many dissident sects, revolts, secessions, and intellectual disputes going on between 750 and 945, you may wonder how the 'Abbasids managed to rule their empire. Well, as time passed, they no longer could. In addition to those aforementioned Shi'ite and Kharijite states in the remote areas of their empire, the 'Abbasids appointed some governors who managed to pass down their provinces to their heirs. An 'Abbasid governor, sent by Harun in 800 to Tunis, founded his own dynasty, collectively known as the Aghlabids. Intermittent Arab and Berber revolts did not stop the Aghlabids from raiding nearby Sicily, Italy, and southern France. These raids enhanced their prestige among Muslims at a time when Harun's successors were no longer taking Christian lands. Rather, Egypt's Christians overthrew their 'Abbasid governor in 832, and a Byzantine navy invaded the Nile Delta some twenty years later. Ahmad ibn Tulun, sent by the 'Abbasids in 868 to put Egypt in order, made the country virtually independent. As the 'Abbasids declined, the Byzantine Empire revived. Under its tenth-century Macedonian rulers, that Christian state would briefly retake southern Anatolia and even Syria.

Ahmad ibn Tulun was a Turk. In the ninth century some Turkish tribes from Central Asia entered the Middle East, seeking grazing lands for their horses and employment for their warriors. Moreover, individual Turks were incorporated into the 'Abbasid ruling system. Some captured in war became slaves of the caliphs. But under al-Mu'tasim (r. 833–842), the induction of Turks into the service of the caliphate became more systematic and pervasive. Hundreds of boys were bought from traders in Central Asia, taken to Baghdad, converted to Islam, and trained to be soldiers, administrators, or domestic servants for the 'Abbasids. Taught from childhood to view the caliphs as their benefactors, these Turkic slaves seemed more trustworthy than the Persian mercenaries. Soon they became the strongest element in the 'Abbasid army. Then they were able to manipulate the caliphs and murder anyone they disliked. Hardy and disciplined, the Turks took over the caliphal state—both the capital and some of its provinces—from within.

CONCLUSION

The High Caliphate was the zenith of Arab political power. The Umayyads and 'Abbasids have come to be seen collectively as great Arab leaders, yet only a few of these caliphs merit such a tribute. Some were brave, generous, and farsighted; most are now forgotten. Naturally, Arab chroniclers praised wise and magnanimous rulers, slighting the work that was really done by viziers and *'ulama,* traders and sailors, let alone artisans and peasants. Improved river irrigation and long-distance trade enriched Muslim lands. The Arab conquests brought together people of diverse languages, religions, cultures, and ideas. Artistic and intellectual creativity flourished as a result.

The political history, as you now know, was turbulent—a chronicle of palace coups, bureaucratic rivalries, and rural uprisings. Islam did not efface ethnic differences. Indeed, Muslim unity was turning into a façade, a polite fiction. No dramatic revolt toppled the 'Abbasids. Though their power ebbed away in the ninth and tenth centuries, their accumulated prestige and wealth enabled them to outlast most of the usurper dynasties. They went on producing caliphs in Baghdad until 1258, then in Cairo up to 1517. But dry rot had set in during the Golden Age of Harun al-Rashid and al-Ma'mun, if not before; for the political unity of the *umma* had ended when the Umayyads had held on to Spain after 750. During the late ninth and tenth centuries, a welter of Muslim dynasties took control of the various parts of North Africa, Syria, and Persia. Finally Baghdad was captured in 945 by a Shi'ite dynasty called the Buyids, and the 'Abbasids ceased to be masters even in their own house.

The decline of the 'Abbasids mattered less than you might think. As the caliphate declined, other types of political leadership emerged to maintain and even increase the collective power of the Muslim world. New institutions sustained the feeling of community among Muslim peoples, now that the caliphate could no longer fulfill that function. Our next two chapters will treat these trends in greater depth.

6

※

Shi'ites and Turks,
Crusaders and Mongols

The period of Middle East history from the tenth through the thirteenth centuries challenges us. There is no one dynasty or country on which to focus our attention; our story jumps around. The Arabs were no longer dominant everywhere; they had given way to the Berbers in North Africa and to the Persians and Kurds in the lands east of the Euphrates River. Various Central Asian peoples, Iranian or Turkish in culture, took over the successor states to the 'Abbasid caliphate, which lingered on in Baghdad but now had to obey other dynasties. Most of the Central Asians came in as slaves or hired troops for the 'Abbasids or their successors. Gradually they adopted Islam, learned Arabic and Persian, and adapted to Middle Eastern culture. By the late tenth century, numerous Turks on horseback entered the eastern lands. Some, notably the Ghaznavids and the Seljuks, formed large empires.

During this time, the Byzantines briefly retook northern Syria, Spanish Christians began to win back the Iberian Peninsula, and (most notoriously) Christians from various European lands launched a series of crusades to recapture the "Holy Land" from the Muslims. The general effect of the Christian onslaught was to make Islam more militant by the twelfth century than it had ever been before. Declining Byzantine power in the eleventh century enabled the Muslim Turks to enter Anatolia, which until then had been a land of Greek-speaking, Orthodox Christians. Thus Christians were gaining in some areas and Muslims in others. Two centuries later, however, Islam's heartland was hit by a dreadful disaster—the invasion of the Mongols, who had built up a great empire under Genghis Khan and his heirs. Nearly every Muslim state in Asia was conquered or forced to pay tribute to the Mongols. Only an unexpected victory by the Mamluks of Egypt saved Muslim Africa from the same fate.

You may be tempted to call this chapter "One Damned Dynasty After Another," because so many ruling families came and went, but you will soon see that Islamic civilization overcame sectarian disputes, thrived despite Turkish infiltration and domination, drove out the Christian Crusaders, and subverted the Mongol vision of a universal empire. Some of the greatest Muslim dynasties of this era were Shi'ite, but not all from the same sect. Although these sectarian splits affected what people thought and did, geopolitical and economic interests mattered more. The concept of being a Sunni or a Shi'ite Muslim had just begun to form. Once people started to think in these terms, though, leaders often rose to power by exploiting the sectarian leanings of influential groups in a given area. As soon as these rulers were securely entrenched, they tended to adopt policies that maintained a Muslim consensus. Muslim civilization survived because a growing majority of the people wanted to keep the coherent and comprehensive way of life made possible by Islam.

SHI'ITE ISLAM IN POWER

Periodization is a problem in any historical account, and certainly in Islamic history. How do we decide when one period ends and another begins? Once scholars used the dates of caliphal and dynastic reigns; now we will look to broader trends, social as well as political, to spot the turning points. This chapter's first theme is the rise of Shi'ism as a political force in the Middle East, during roughly the tenth and eleventh Christian centuries.

The Major Sects of Islam

As you know, we tend to identify Muslims as being Sunni, Shi'ite, or Kharijite. Sunni Islam is often misidentified as the "orthodox" version. Some Muslims call anyone "Sunni" who follows the recorded practices (*sunna*) of Muhammad. But most people identify a Muslim as a Sunni if he or she acknowledged the Rashidun, Umayyad, and 'Abbasid caliphs as legitimate leaders of the *umma* because most other Muslims accepted their rule. The person in question might have been a mystic, a rationalist freethinker, or a rebel against Islam's laws; the "Sunni" designation is more political than theological. But it usually indicates that the particular Muslim adhered to one of the four standard "rites" of Islamic law, which we will explain in Chapter 7, though these rites were not clearly established until the ninth or tenth century.

A Shi'ite Muslim, in contrast, is a partisan of 'Ali as Muhammad's true successor, at least as imam (leader) or spiritual guide of the *umma*, and of one of the several lines of 'Ali's descendants, shown in Figure 4.1 (see page 57). Shi'ites reject all other caliphs and all of 'Ali's successors not in the "correct" line, whose members supposedly inherited from him perfect knowledge of the Qur'an's inner meaning and Muhammad's whole message. Given its essentially genealogical differences, Shi'ism split into many sects. Some grew up and died out early, such as the Hashimites, who supported a son of 'Ali born of a wife other than Fatima—Muhammad ibn al-Hanafiyyah. Others stayed underground until the 'Abbasid caliphate grew weak, then surfaced in revolutionary movements.

The three Shi'ite sects you are most likely to read about are the Twelve-Imam (or Ja'fari) Shi'ites (sometimes called Twelvers), the Isma'ilis (sometimes called Seveners), and the Zaydis (sometimes called Fivers), all shown in Figure 4.1. The first group believed in a line of infallible imams extending from 'Ali to Muhammad al-Muntazar, who is thought to have vanished in 874 but will someday return to restore peace and justice on earth. The Isma'ilis had by then broken with the Twelve-Imam Shi'ites over the designation of the seventh imam, maintaining that Isma'il was wrongly passed over in favor of his brother. The Zaydis had broken off even earlier. Zayd, who rebelled against Umayyad Caliph Hisham (r. 724–743), was to his followers the legitimate imam. By 900 Zayd's descendants were leading independent states in the mountains of Yemen and Tabaristan. Under the Zaydi system, each imam named his own successor from among his family members. The Zaydi imams of Yemen ruled up to 1962, when an army coup ousted them and set off a long civil war. The Zaydis are believed to be the closest to Sunnis in terms of Islamic beliefs and practices. Although the majority of the Shi'a belongs to the three major groups outlined above, there were other small splinter Shi'ite groups known as Ghulat "extremes" including Kaysanites, Ghurabiyya, and the Hurufiyya.

To round out this overview, let us remind you that the Kharijites were the Muslims who had turned against 'Ali in 657. They believed that neither he nor his descendants nor the Umayyads nor the 'Abbasids had any special claim to lead the *umma*. The Kharijites were prepared to obey any adult male Muslim who would uphold the laws of Islam. But if he failed to do so, they would depose him. Even though their doctrines seemed anarchistic, some Kharijites did form dynastic states, notably in Algeria and Oman, where they are known today as the Ibadis.

As political unity broke down during the ninth and tenth centuries, various dynastic states emerged in the Middle East and North Africa in response to local economic or social needs. Most are little known, but two

Shi'ite dynasties threatened the Sunni 'Abbasids in Baghdad: the Fatimids, who challenged their legitimacy, and the Buyids, who ended their autonomy.

The Fatimid Caliphate

The Fatimids appeared first. You may note that their name looks like that of Fatima, Muhammad's daughter who married 'Ali and bore Hasan and Husayn. This choice of name was deliberate. The dynasty's founder, called Ubaydallah (Little Abdallah) by the Sunnis and al-Mahdi (Rightly Guided One) by his own followers, claimed descent from Fatima and 'Ali. Hoping for Shi'ite—specifically Isma'ili—support, he proposed overthrowing the 'Abbasid caliphate and restoring the leadership of Islam to the house of 'Ali. The Isma'ilis had become an underground revolutionary movement, based in Syria. During the late eighth and ninth centuries, Isma'ili Shi'ism slowly won support from disgruntled classes or clans throughout the Muslim world. Toward this end, it formed a network of propagandists and a set of esoteric beliefs, the gist of which had allegedly been passed down from Muhammad, via 'Ali and his successors, to Isma'il, who had enlightened a few followers before his death.

Ubaydallah overthrew the Aghlabids, Muslim Arabs tied to the 'Abbasid caliphate, and seized their North African empire in 909 by allying themselves with Berber nomads. These spirited rebels embraced Shi'ism in rejecting their Sunni Aghlabid overlords. To the Fatimids, however, Tunisia seemed too remote a base from which to build a new universal Muslim empire to replace the faltering 'Abbasids. Initially, they hoped to capture Baghdad. Instead, they found Egypt, which had played a surprisingly minor role in early Islamic history. It had been ruled by various dynasties since Ahmad ibn Tulun had broken away from Baghdad in 868. While fighting the Byzantine navy in the Mediterranean, the Fatimid general Jawhar saw that Egypt was in political chaos and gripped by famine. In 969 Jawhar entered Egypt unopposed and declared it a bastion of Isma'ili Shi'ism. Then the Fatimid caliph, al-Mu'izz, brought his family and government from Tunis to Egypt. It is said that a welcoming deputation of *'ulama* challenged him to prove his descent from 'Ali. Al-Mu'izz unsheathed his sword, exclaiming, "Here is my pedigree!" Then he scattered gold coins among the crowd and shouted, "Here is my proof." They were easily convinced.

The Fatimid caliphs built a new city as the capital of what they hoped would be the new Islamic empire. They called their city *al-Qahira* (meaning "the conqueror," referring to the planet Mars); we know it as Cairo. It soon rivaled Baghdad as the Middle East's leading city. Its primacy as an intellectual center was ensured by the founding of a mosque-university called al-Azhar, where for two centuries the Fatimids trained Ismaʻili propagandists. Cairo and al-Azhar outlasted the Fatimids and remained, respectively, the largest city and the most advanced university in the Muslim world up to the Ottoman conquest in 1517. Today Cairo, with its 12 million inhabitants, is again Islam's largest city, and al-Azhar remains a major university, drawing Muslim scholars from many lands.

The Fatimid government in Egypt was centralized and hierarchical. It promoted long-distance trade but not agriculture, for it neglected the Nile irrigation works. Like many Muslim states then and later, the Fatimids set up an army of slave-soldiers imported from various parts of Asia. Their strong navy helped them to take Palestine, Syria, and the Hijaz, but they lost control over their North African lands.

Surprisingly, the Fatimids did not try to convert their Sunni Muslim subjects to Ismaʻili Shiʻism. They respected the religious freedom of the many Christians and Jews over whom they ruled. The exception was Caliph al-Hakim (r. 996–1021), who has been depicted as a madman who persecuted Christians, destroyed their churches, killed stray dogs, outlawed certain foods, and finally proclaimed himself divine. Modern scholars think al-Hakim's hostility was aimed mainly against Orthodox Christians; he accused them of backing the Byzantines, who had just retaken part of Syria. He issued sumptuary laws to fight a famine caused by his predecessors' neglect of Nile irrigation. Far from claiming to be God, he ended distinctions between Ismaʻilis and other Muslims. One day he vanished in the hills east of Cairo; his body was never found.

Possibly al-Hakim's bad name among Muslims is due to the preaching done on his behalf by an Ismaʻili propagandist, Shaykh Darazi, who convinced some Syrian mountain folk that al-Hakim was divine. These Syrians built up a religion around the propaganda of Darazi, from whom they got the collective name of Duruz, hence Druze. The Druze faith is a secret one that combines esoteric aspects of Ismaʻili Shiʻism with the beliefs and practices of other Middle Eastern religions. As mountaineers, the Druze people could not be controlled by Muslim rulers in the low-lying areas. Muslim historians therefore called them troublemakers and heretics. The Druze survive today and take part in the tangled politics of modern Syria and Lebanon and the Palestinian-Israeli conflict. A proud and hardy people, they share the language and culture of the Arabs, but their desire to retain their religious identity has kept them distinct politically.

The Fatimids ruled Egypt for two centuries, a long time for a Muslim dynasty, but they seem to have done better at building a strong navy and a rich trading center than at spreading their domains or their doctrines. Could they have won more converts? Sunni Islam seemed to be waning in the tenth and early eleventh centuries. The 'Abbasid caliphs were no longer credible claimants to universal sovereignty, for they had become captives of the Buyids, who were Persian and Shi'ite. In fact, the strongest states resisting Fatimid expansion were already Shi'ite and not impressed by these self-styled caliphs, with their propagandists and their fake genealogies.

The Buyid Dynasty

Best known for having captured Baghdad and the 'Abbasids in 945, the Buyids were one of several dynasties that helped revive Persian sovereignty and culture. By this time Persia had fully recovered from the Arab conquest. During the tenth century, all Persia came to be ruled by such families: the Shi'ite Buyids in the west and the Sunni Samanids in the east. Both consciously revived the symbols and practices of Persia's pre-Islamic rulers, the Sassanids. Persian language, literature, and culture made a major comeback at this time, but attempts to revive Zoroastrianism failed.

The Buyid family consisted of several branches concurrently ruling different parts of Iraq and western Persia; indeed, the dynasty was founded by three brothers, each with his own capital. The most important was Isfahan, in the prospering province of Fars, rather than Baghdad, whose politics were turbulent and whose agricultural lands were declining. All Buyids were Twelve-Imam Shi'ites, but they tolerated other Muslim sects. Although they allowed the 'Abbasids to retain the caliphate, they confined them to their Baghdad palace and took away their means of support. One 'Abbasid caliph was blinded, and another was reduced to begging in the street; but the institution of the caliphate was a useful fiction because it stood for the unity of the *umma*. The Buyids' foreign policy was friendly to Christian Byzantium, to whoever was ruling Egypt, and to the Isma'ili Qarmatians. They were hostile to their Twelve-Imam Shi'ite neighbors, the Hamdanids of Mosul, and to their fellow Persians, the Samanids of Khurasan. In short, when making alliances, the Buyids heeded their economic interests more than any racial or religious affinities.

Domestically, the Buyids let their viziers govern for them, promoted trade and manufacturing, and expanded a practice begun by the 'Abbasids of making land grants (*iqta'*) to their chief soldiers and bureaucrats instead of paying them salaries. The *iqta'* was supposed to be a short-term delegation of the right to use a piece of state-owned land or other property. Under the Buyids, though, it came to include the right to collect the land tax (*kharaj*) and to pass on the property to one's heirs. The *iqta'* system often caused landowners to gouge the peasants and neglect the irrigation works so necessary to Middle Eastern agriculture. More harmful to Buyid interests was the shifting of trade routes from Iraq toward Egypt and also toward lands farther east.

THE TURKS

Before we can learn the fate of the Buyids, we must turn to Central Asia. Both the century of Shi'ism and the Persian revival were cut short by events taking place there, notably the rise of the Turks. The origin of the Turkic peoples has been lost in the mists of legend; we will know little until archaeologists have excavated more of Central Asia and Mongolia, where the Turks probably began. We do know that they started as nomadic shepherds who rode horses and transported their goods on two-humped camels, although some became settled farmers and traders. Their original religion revolved around shamans, who were wizards supposedly capable of healing the sick and communicating with the world beyond. They also served as guardians of the tribal lore.

Early Turkic Civilization

Around 550 the Turks set up a tribal confederation called Gokturk, which Chinese sources call the Tujueh. Its vast domains extended from Mongolia to Ukraine. But soon the Tujueh Empire split into an eastern branch, which later fell under the sway of China's Tang dynasty, and a western one, which became allied with Byzantium against the Sassanids and later fell back before the Arab conquests. This early empire exposed the Turks to the main sixth-century civilizations: Byzantium, Persia, China, and India. It also led some Turks to espouse such religions as Nestorian Christianity, Manichaeism, and Buddhism. Some had even developed a writing system.

The transmission of cultures among the various Eurasian regions seems incredible until you stop to think that people and horses have crossed the steppes and deserts for ages, forming one of the world's oldest highways, the Great Silk Route. In the eighth century a group of eastern Turks, the Uighurs, formed an empire on China's northwestern border. Its official religion was Manichaeism, and its records were kept in a script resembling Aramaic. This shows how far the Turks could take some of the ideas and customs they had picked up in the Middle East. Meanwhile, one of the western Turkic tribes, the Khazars, adopted Judaism, hoping to get along with its Christian and Muslim trading partners, while distancing itself from both sides.

The Islamization of the Turks

Eventually, though, most Turkic peoples became Muslim. The Islamization process was gradual, and it varied from one tribe to another. Once the Arab armies crossed the Oxus River—if not long before then—they encountered Turks. Even in Umayyad times, some Turks became Muslims and served in the Arab armies in Transoxiana and Khurasan. Under the 'Abbasids, you may recall, the Turks became numerous and powerful in the government. The first Turkic soldiers for Islam were probably prisoners of war who were prized for their skill as mounted archers but were viewed as slaves. Most historians think that the institution of slavery grew in 'Abbasid lands to the point where some tribes would sell their boys (or turn them over as tribute) to the caliphs, who would have them trained as disciplined soldiers or skilled bureaucrats. These slaves became so imbued with Islamic culture that they no longer identified with their original tribes. In addition, whole Turkic tribes, after they had embraced Islam, were hired by the 'Abbasids or their successors (notably the Samanids) as *ghazi*s (Muslim border warriors) to guard their northeastern boundaries against the non-Muslim Turks. As for Sunnism versus Shi'ism, those Turks who served a particular Muslim dynasty usually took on its political coloring. The *ghazi*s cared little about such political or doctrinal disputes. Their Islam reflected what had been taught to them by Muslim merchants, mendicants, and mystics, combined with some of their own pre-Islamic beliefs and practices.

The Ghaznavids

Two Turkish dynasties, both Sunni and both founded by *ghazi* warriors for the Samanid dynasty, stand out during this era: the Ghaznavids and the Seljuks. The Ghaznavids got their name from Ghazna, a town located 90 miles (145 kilometers) southwest of Kabul (the capital of modern Afghanistan), because their leader received that region as an *iqta'* from the Samanids in return for his services as a general and a local governor. The first Ghaznavid rulers, Sebuktegin (r. 977–997) and his son Mahmud (r. 998–1030), parlayed this *iqta'* into an immense empire, covering at its height (around 1035) what would now be eastern Iran, all of Afghanistan and Pakistan, and parts of northern India. It was the Ghaznavids who extended Muslim rule into the Indian subcontinent, although their efforts to force Hindus to adopt Islam have discredited them among some Indians.

The Seljuk Empire

The other major dynasty, the Seljuks, takes its name from a pagan Turkic chieftain who converted to Islam about 956. Later Seljuk enrolled his clan as warriors for the Samanids. His descendants became one of the ablest ruling families in Islamic history (see Map 6.1), making themselves indispensable first to the Samanids and then to the Ghaznavids as *ghazis* in Transoxiana against the pagan Turks. In return, they received *iqta's,* which they used to graze their horses and to attract other Islamized Turkic tribes, who would occupy the grazing lands with their sheep and goats, horses and camels. As more Turkic tribes joined the Seljuks, they increased their military strength as well as their land hunger. The trickle became a flood; in 1040 the Seljuks and their allies defeated the Ghaznavids and occupied Khurasan. The Buyids had grown weak, leaving western Persia and Iraq open to these military adventurers who had the encouragement of the 'Abbasid caliph himself, eager to welcome Sunni Muslims.

When the Turks, thus encouraged, entered Baghdad in 1055, it was not to wipe out Arab sovereignty but to restore caliphal authority, at least in name. The Turco-'Abbasid alliance was cemented by the marriage of the Seljuk leader to the caliph's sister, and the caliph recognized him as regent of the empire and *sultan* (which may be translated as "authority") in both the East and the West. Soon the title was real, as the Seljuks went on to take Azerbaijan, Armenia, and, finally, most of Anatolia following a major victory over the Byzantines at Manzikert in 1071. You would have to go back to the ninth century, when the Aghlabids took Sicily and raided the coasts of France and Italy, to find a time when a Muslim ruler had so successfully waged a war against Christendom. Not since the early 'Abbasids had so much land been held by one Muslim dynasty. Malikshah, the sultan at the height of Seljuk power, ruled over Palestine, Syria, part of Anatolia, the Caucasus Mountains, all of Iraq and Persia, plus parts of Central Asia up to the Aral Sea and beyond the Oxus River. The Seljuk Turks claimed to be the saviors of Islam.

The Seljuks' success story was too good to last. Soon after Malikshah's death in 1092, the empire began to crumble. By the end of the twelfth century, nothing was left except a part of Anatolia ruled by a branch called the Rum Seljuks. Rum meant Anatolia, which historically was part of the Byzantine Empire. That empire, in turn, called itself Rome, which is why the

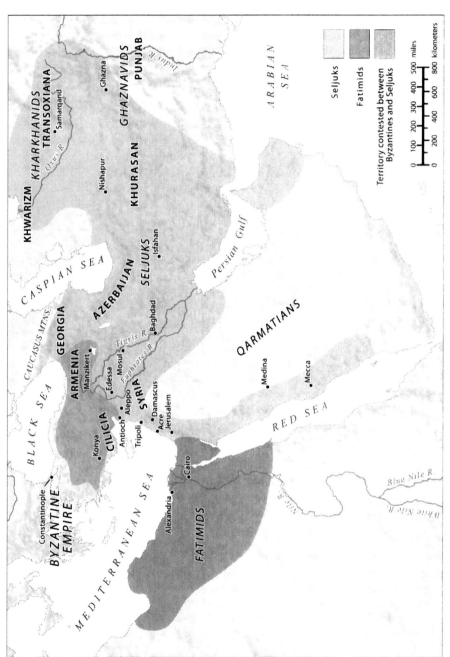

Map 6.1   The Fatimids and the Seljuks, circa 1090

Arabs, Persians, and Turks all called the area *Rum*. The Turkish "Rome," with its capital at Konya, lasted until about 1300.

The Seljuk legacies helped transform the Middle East. Let us summarize them: (1) the influx of Turkic tribes from Central Asia; (2) the Turkification of eastern Persia and northern Iraq, most of Azerbaijan, and later Anatolia (the land we now call Turkey); (3) the restoration of Sunni rule in southwest Asia; (4) the spread of Persian institutions and culture (which the Seljuks greatly admired); (5) the development of the *madrasa* (mosque-school) for training *'ulama* in Islamic law; (6) the regularization of the *iqta'* system for paying the tribal troops; and (7) the weakening of the Byzantine Empire in Anatolia, long its main power center.

THE CRUSADES

The last of these enumerated results of Seljuk rule opened a new chapter in the history of Christian-Muslim relations. The Byzantines worried about the encroachment of Muslim Turkic nomads and were alarmed by the Seljuks' rise to power during the eleventh century—so alarmed, in fact, that the Byzantine Emperor Alexios I begged the Roman pope, with whom the Greek Orthodox Church had broken definitively forty years earlier, to save his realm from the Muslim menace. Pope Urban II, hardly a friend of the Byzantine Empire, responded to the call for help—but for his own reasons. Eager to prove the papacy's power in relation to the secular rulers of Christendom, Urban in 1095 made a speech inviting all Christians to join in a war to regain Jerusalem's Holy Sepulcher from "the wicked race." This call to arms inaugurated the first of a series of Christian wars, known to history as the Crusades.

As the Crusades have inspired so many popular novels, films, and television programs, you may know something about what seems a romantic episode in the history of medieval Europe. Many Catholics and Protestants have learned a positive view of the Crusaders from their religious education. You will soon see why this early confrontation between the Middle East and the West is less fondly recalled by Muslims in general and by Syrians and Palestinians in particular.

Their Beginning
The success of Christian armies in pushing back the Muslims in Spain and Sicily encouraged travel overland or across the Mediterranean to the Middle East for trade or pilgrimage. One of the telling points in Pope Urban's

speech was his accusation that the Muslims (probably the Seljuks) were disrupting the Christian pilgrimage to Jerusalem. Thousands of volunteers, mighty and lowly, rich and poor, northern and southern Europeans, left their homes and fields in response to the papal call. Younger sons from large noble families, unable to inherit their fathers' lands, wanted to win new estates for themselves. Led by the ablest European generals of the day (but not by kings), the soldiers of the cross joined up with the Byzantines in 1097. They took Antioch after a nine-month siege, progressed southward along the Syrian coast, and reached the walls of Jerusalem in June 1099. Only 1,000 Fatimid troops guarded the city. After six weeks of fighting, the 15,000 Crusaders managed to breach the walls. Both Muslim and Christian accounts attest to the bloodbath that followed, as thousands of noncombatant Jews, Muslims, and even native Christians were beheaded, shot with arrows, thrown from towers, tortured, or burned at the stake. Human blood flowed knee-deep in the streets of Jerusalem. The Dome of the Rock was stripped of hundreds of silver and gold candelabra and turned into a church.

Once the Holy Sepulcher was back in Christian hands, some of the European and Byzantine soldiers went home, but many stayed to colonize the conquered lands. Four Crusader states were set up: the kingdom of Jerusalem, the principality of Antioch, and the counties of Tripoli and Edessa. The Crusaders also shored up a tiny state called Little Armenia, formed in southwest Anatolia by Armenian Christians who had fled from the conquering Seljuks. The Armenians would remain the Crusaders' staunchest allies.

Muslim Reactions

You may ask how Islam, supposedly reinvigorated by the Turks' influx, stood by and let the Crusaders in. To some extent, the Crusaders were lucky. By the end of the eleventh century, Seljuk rule in Syria and Palestine had broken up. The successor states were fighting one another. The Shi'ite Fatimids farther south cared little about stopping an invasion that, until it reached Jerusalem, took lands from Sunni rulers. The 'Abbasid caliph in Baghdad was helpless; it is wrong to suppose that he was an Islamic pope who could command all Muslims to wage jihad against the Crusaders. Besides, the lands taken by the Crusaders were inhabited mainly by Christians of various sects, some of whom did not mind Catholic rule, or by Jews, Druze, or dissident Muslims. The Crusaders never took a city that really mattered to the political or economic life of Islam, such as Aleppo, Damascus, Mosul, Baghdad, or Cairo. Relative to the Muslim world in 1100 as a whole, the First Crusade was only a sideshow.

Why, then, did it take the Muslims so long to expel the Crusaders? Part of the reason is that then, as now, they were divided into many quarreling states. Some Muslim rulers even formed alliances with the Crusaders against their own coreligionists. Fatimid Egypt usually had close ties with the Crusader states because of the lucrative trade going on between Alexandria and such Italian ports as Venice and Genoa.

The first turning point came in 1144, when Mosul's governor, Zengi, who had carved himself a kingdom from the decaying Seljuk Empire in eastern Syria, captured Edessa from the Crusaders. The Second Crusade, led by the Holy Roman emperor and the king of France, tried to take Damascus and thus the Syrian hinterland, including Edessa. The Crusaders botched the attack, however, and Islam resumed the offensive. Zengi had meanwhile been killed by one of his slaves, but his son, Nur al-Din, proved to be a worthy successor. Soon he controlled all of Syria, except for the narrow coastal strip still held by the Crusaders.

The Rise of Salah al-Din

The scene then shifted to Egypt, still under the Fatimid caliphs, who were by then declining. They had gradually given their powers over to their viziers, who commanded the army and directed the bureaucracy. Both Nur al-Din in Damascus and the Crusader king of Jerusalem coveted the rich Nile Valley and Delta. But Nur al-Din got the upper hand through the political acumen of his best general, a Kurd named Shirkuh. Now Shirkuh had a nephew aiding him, Salah al-Din, known to the West as Saladin. Serving their patron, Shirkuh and Salah al-Din fended off a Crusader invasion of Egypt and won for themselves the Fatimid vizierate. As the last Fatimid caliph lay dying, Salah al-Din quietly arranged to replace mention of his name in the Friday mosque prayers with that of the 'Abbasid caliph. In effect, Egypt rejected Shi'ism, a change hailed by the country's Sunni majority. In practical terms, it meant that Egypt was now led by a lieutenant of Nur al-Din, Syria's ruler, for Salah al-Din proclaimed himself sultan as soon as the Fatimid caliph died in 1171.

Salah al-Din seized power in Syria after Nur al-Din died three years later, but he needed at least a decade to overcome challenges by the Shi'ites. Then he managed to take Jerusalem and most of Palestine from the Crusaders between 1187 and 1192. Salah al-Din was a master at perceiving his enemies' weaknesses and his own opportunities in time to exploit them. Both Muslim and Christian historians portray him as a paragon of bravery and magnanimity (what we call chivalry and the Arabs call *muruwwa*), unlike some of his Christian foes. For example, Reginald of Chatillon, one of the Crusader princes, raided caravans of Muslim pilgrims going to Mecca. When Salah al-Din sought revenge, he held off attacking Reginald's castle when told that a wedding feast was going on inside. Yet he could be vindictive toward Muslims who disagreed with him; he had many of the Fatimid courtiers and poets publicly crucified in Cairo.

Most Europeans thought Salah al-Din had a master plan to drive the Crusaders out of the Middle East. If so, he did not wholly succeed, for he failed to dislodge them from much of what we now call Lebanon. The Third Crusade, which lured France's King Philip and England's Richard the Lionheart to Palestine, took Acre from Salah al-Din in 1191. Some scholars think he wanted to restore Muslim unity under the 'Abbasid caliphate, but his aims were less grandiose. Salah al-Din did manage to unite Egypt and Syria under his own family, which became the Ayyubid dynasty. The Ayyubids went on ruling these lands, though not always wisely or well, for almost two generations after Salah al-Din's death. Although the 'Abbasid caliphate did revive at this time, the lands it recovered were in Iraq and Persia. Stranger still, in 1229 the Ayyubid sultan in Cairo chose to lease Jerusalem back to the Crusaders, who also held the coast of Syria and Palestine. Twice they raided the Egyptian Delta. Egypt's Ayyubids resisted the Christian raiders, using their Turkic slave soldiers, called Mamluks, who then took over the country for themselves.

In general, Muslim militancy and intolerance grew in response to the Crusader challenge. The Ayyubid dynasty's founder, Salah al-Din, is still revered as a hero of Muslim resistance to the Christian West. Because he took Jerusalem back from the Crusaders, Muslims regained their self-confidence—just in time to face a far fiercer challenge from the East.

THE MONGOL INVASION

The unwelcome interlopers from Asia were the Turks' cousins: the Mongols. For centuries these hardy nomads had inhabited the windswept plateau north of the Gobi Desert, occasionally swooping down on China or on the caravans that plied the Great Silk Route linking China, India, and Persia. Most Mongols had kept aloof from the civilizations and religions surrounding them, worshiping their own deity, Tengri (Eternal Blue Sky). But in the late twelfth century, a warrior chieftain known as Genghis Khan united the eastern Mongol tribes into a great confederation. He made forays into northern China but then turned abruptly toward Central Asia in response to a call for help from Turks who were being oppressed by a rival Mongol confederation called the Kara-Khitay. After he annexed their lands, Genghis faced the ambitious but foolhardy Prince Muhammad of the Khwarizm-Shah Turks.

From 1218 to 1221 the Mongols chased Muhammad's army, laying waste to the great cities and some of the farmlands of Transoxiana, Khwarizm, and Khurasan. The atrocities perpetrated by the Mongol armies defy description: they slaughtered 700,000 inhabitants of Merv; their engineers broke the dams near Gurganj to flood the city after it had been taken; they poured molten gold down the throat of a Muslim governor; they carried off thousands of Muslim artisans to Mongolia as slaves, most of them dying on the way; they stacked the heads of Nishapur's men, women, and children in pyramids; and they even killed dogs and cats in the streets. The Mongols hoped to paralyze the Muslims with such fear that they would never dare to fight back.

Genghis Khan's death in 1227 gave Islam a respite, during which his successors ravaged China, Russia, and Eastern Europe. But one of his sons sent a large army into Azerbaijan, from which the Mongols could threaten both the Christian kingdoms of the Caucasus Mountains and the Muslims of Iraq and Anatolia. One result of this incursion was the defeat of the Rum Seljuks in 1243. The Mongols reduced them to vassal (subordinate) status and let the Turkish tribes carve up Anatolia into dozens of principalities. Another result was a lasting alliance between the Mongols and the kingdom of Little Armenia (which had earlier backed the Crusaders against Islam). This led many Europeans to hope that a greater alliance between the Mongol East and the Christian West would crush the Muslim world forever.

Destruction of the Caliphate

But the Mongols needed no help. In 1256, Hulegu, Genghis's grandson, renewed the attack. He may have been spurred into action by the envoys sent by the kings of Europe to the Mongol court, but he spurned their alliance offers. Although Hulegu was a pagan, his wife was a Nestorian Christian who might have inspired his hatred of Islam. The continued existence of the 'Abbasid caliph, with even a shadowy claim to the obedience of millions of Muslims, offended Hulegu, who could brook no rivals. The Mongols crossed the Zagros Mountains into Iraq and proceeded to bombard Baghdad with heavy rocks flung from catapults until the caliph surrendered in February 1258. Then the Mongols pillaged the city, burned its

Box 6.1	Hulegu Khan

Hulegu Khan (c. 1216–1265) was the grandson of Genghis Khan and the younger brother of Mongke Khan. In 1255 Mongke, as ruler of the great Mongol khanate, dispatched Hulegu at the head of a large army to conquer the Muslim lands of Persia, Iraq, and greater Syria. As a young man Hulegu was interested in philosophy and science, but he gave them up when summoned to command a great Mongol horde. Although by religion he was a lifelong pantheist, both his mother and favorite wife were Nestorian Christians.

Hulegu moved slowly southwest with his army and crossed the Oxus River, the frontier between Mongol-ruled lands and Persia, only in 1256. Then he rapidly subdued the Isma'ilis and put an end to their infamous Assassins headquartered at Alamut. In 1257 he sent emissaries to Caliph Mustasim in Baghdad, calling on him to accept Mongol suzerainty, as his predecessors had submitted to the Seljuk Turks. Mustasim, the thirty-seventh 'Abbasid caliph, was sure that any attack on Baghdad would unite the Muslim world behind him and rejected the Mongol demands. Hulegu then replied as follows:

> When I lead my army against Baghdad in anger, whether you hide in heaven or in earth I will bring you down from the spinning spheres; I will toss you in the air like a lion. I will leave no one alive in your realm. I will burn your city, your land and yourself. If you wish to spare yourself and your venerable family, give heed to my advice with the ear of intelligence. If you do not, you will see what God has willed.

Hulegu carried out his threats in January and February 1258. He destroyed Baghdad, killing at least 90,000 of its inhabitants, including the caliph. He then withdrew his forces into Azerbaijan, which became the center for the Mongol Il-Khanid dynasty, which would rule the eastern Muslim lands. Later in 1258, he once more set out to conquer Syria, taking Aleppo and Damascus with ease. By 1260 the Mongols had reached southern Palestine and Egypt's Sinai frontier.

At this point Hulegu received news that his brother Mongke Khan had died. This made him return home with most of his army to take part in the ensuing succession struggle. This turn of events enabled the Mamluk forces from Egypt to defeat a diminished Mongol army at 'Ayn Jalut in 1260.

Even if the Mongols had maintained their forces at full strength, they probably could not have conquered Egypt. The Mongol armies traveled with thousands of horses and tens of thousands of sheep and cattle. A pastoral society on the move needs plenty of land to support its animals. The Sinai and Arabian deserts would have posed an impenetrable barrier to Hulegu's hordes.

schools and libraries, destroyed its mosques and palaces, murdered possibly a million Muslims (the Christians and Jews were spared), and finally
executed all the 'Abbasids by wrapping them in carpets and having them
trampled beneath their horses' hooves. Until the stench of the dead forced
Hulegu and his men out of Baghdad, they loaded their horses, packed the
scabbards of their discarded swords, and even stuffed some gutted corpses
with gold, pearls, and precious stones, to be hauled back to the Mongol
capital. It was a melancholy end to the independent 'Abbasid caliphate,
to the prosperity and intellectual glory of Baghdad, and, some historians
think, to Arabic civilization itself. (See Box 6.1.)

Mamluk Resistance
The world of Islam did not vanish. Its salvation came from the Mamluks (their name literally means "owned men"), who in 1250 had seized
Egypt from their Ayyubid masters, the descendants of Salah al-Din. In
1259–1260, Hulegu's forces pushed westward, supported by Georgian and
Armenian Christians eager to help destroy their Muslim enemies. They
besieged and took Aleppo, massacring its inhabitants. Damascus, abandoned by its Ayyubid ruler, gave up without a fight. Then Hulegu sent
envoys to Cairo with this message:

> You have heard how we have conquered a vast empire and have purified
> the earth of the disorders that tainted it. It is for you to fly and for us to
> pursue, but whither will you flee, and by what road will you escape us?
> Our horses are swift, our arrows sharp, our swords like thunderbolts, our
> hearts as hard as the mountains, our soldiers as numerous as the sand.
> Fortresses will not detain us. We mean well by our warning, for now you
> are the only enemy against whom we have to march.

But then Hulegu learned that his brother, the Mongol emperor, had
died. Grief stricken (or perhaps power hungry), he headed home from
Syria, taking most of his men with him. In the meantime, the Mamluks
murdered his envoys and entered Palestine, where they defeated the Mongols at 'Ayn Jalut (Goliath's Spring) in September 1260. This battle was
doubtless a climactic moment in history, as it marked the high point of
Mongol expansion against Islam. Thus the Muslim world survived its Mongol ordeal. But it was hardly an Arab victory, for the Mamluks were mainly
Turks at most one generation removed from the Central Asian steppes.

CONCLUSION

Hulegu and his descendants did settle down in Iraq and Persia, calling themselves the Il-Khanid dynasty. Eventually they adopted Persian culture, including Islam, and repaired some of the damage they had done. The Mamluks survived for centuries, driving the last Crusaders out of Palestine in 1293. The kingdom they founded in Egypt and Syria became the major Muslim center of power, wealth, and learning for two centuries.

What can we learn from this mournful chronicle of invasions, conquest, and destruction and from the bewildering succession of dynasties, few of which are known outside the Middle East? The rise and fall of Shi'ite power and the Turkish influx benefited the area; however, the Crusaders and the Mongols did the Middle East more harm than good. But people cannot wish away the bad things that happen in their lives, nor can a country efface the sad events of its history. People learn from their misfortunes and overcome them. The religion and culture of Islam survived and grew stronger. The sources of its resilience will be the subject of Chapter 7.

7

❈

Islamic Civilization

Now that we have covered almost seven centuries of political history, let us look at the civilization as a whole. But what should we call it? Scholars argue between using Islamic and Arabic. Some say the civilization was *Islamic* because the religion of Islam brought together the various peoples—mainly Arabs, Persians, and Turks—who took part in it. Islam also affected politics, commerce, lifestyle, ideas, and many forms of artistic expression. But up to about 1000 CE, Muslims were a minority within the lands of Islam. Inasmuch as they were relatively unlettered at first, many scholars and scientists active within the civilization were understandably Jews, Christians, Zoroastrians, or recent Muslim converts whose ideas still bore the stamp of their former religions. The evolving Middle Eastern civilization drew on many religious and philosophical traditions.

The alternative term, *Arabic*, highlights Arabic's role in the development of the culture. Not only because of its prestige as the language of the Qur'an and of the conquering elite but also because of its capacity for absorbing new things and ideas, Arabic became the almost universal language of arts, sciences, and letters between 750 and 1250. But do not assume that all the artists, scholars, and writers were Arabs. The builders of the civilization came from every ethnic group within the *umma*. Although many were Arabized North African Berbers (Amazigh), Egyptians, Syrians, and Iraqis whose present-day descendants would call themselves Arabs, only a few were wholly descended from tribal Arabs. Because *Islamic* is a more comprehensive term than *Arabic*, we have chosen "Islamic Civilization" for this chapter's title.

THE RULES AND LAWS OF ISLAM

Islam begins with a profession of faith but is manifested and elaborated by what Muslims do and what they condemn. Ever mindful of the impending

Judgment Day, Muslims wish to know and obey the rules of behavior that will please God and maintain a harmonious society. These rules have been carefully put together into a religious law and moral code called the Shari'a (an Arabic word meaning "pathway"). It is somewhat likened to the Halacha (Talmudic law) in Orthodox Judaism; nothing comparable exists in Christianity. The Shari'a tries to describe all possible human acts, classifying them as obligatory, recommended, neutral, objectionable, or forbidden by God, the Supreme Legislator. In addition to some commercial and criminal law, the Shari'a includes rules about marriage, divorce, child rearing, other interpersonal relationships, property, food, clothing, hygiene, and the manifold aspects of worship. At least up to the Mongol era, there was very little a Muslim might experience or observe that was not covered in the Shari'a.

DEVELOPMENT OF JURISPRUDENCE

The first Muslims based their ideas of right and wrong on the norms of the society they knew, that of western Arabia. Caravan traders had worked out elaborate rules about commercial transactions and property rights, but criminal law still held to the principles of retribution based on the tribal virtues (*muruwwa*). Muhammad's mission broadened and strengthened the realm of rights and responsibilities. The Qur'an spelled out many points. Muhammad's precepts and practices (what later Muslims would call his *sunna*) set some of the laws for the nascent *umma*. After the Prophet died, his successors tried to pattern their lives on what he had said or done and on what he had told them to do or not to do. Muhammad's companions, especially the first four caliphs, became role models for Muslims who came later; indeed, their practices were the *sunna* for succeeding caliphs and governors. Gradually, Arabia's traditional norms took on a Muslim pattern, as the companions taught their children the values of the Qur'an and the *sunna* and instructed the new converts to Islam. Even after the men and women who had known Muhammad died out, the dos and don'ts of Islam were passed down by word of mouth for another century.

Because of the Arab conquests, the early Muslims picked up many concepts and institutions from Roman and Persian law. Qur'an reciters and Muhammad's companions gradually gave way to arbiters and judges who knew the laws and procedures of older, established empires. As the *umma* grew and more disputes arose about people's rights and duties within this hybrid society, both the leaders and the public realized that the laws of

Islam had to be made clear, uniform, organized, acceptable to most Muslims, and enforceable. By the time the 'Abbasids took power in 750, Muslims were studying the meaning of the Qur'an, the life of Muhammad, and the words and deeds ascribed to him by those who had known him. Thus evolved a specifically Islamic science of right versus wrong, or jurisprudence. Its Arabic name, *fiqh*, originally meant "learning," and even now Muslims see a close connection between the *fuqaha* (experts on the Shari'a) and the *'ulama* (Muslim religious scholars, or literally "those who know").

Sources of the Law

Historians of Islam see in the Shari'a elements taken from many ancient legal systems, but Muslims customarily view their law as having four, or at most five, main sources: the Qur'an, the *sunna* of Muhammad, interpretation by analogy, consensus of the *umma*, and (for some) judicial opinion. Strictly speaking, only the first two are tangible sources. The Qur'an, as you know, is the record of God's revealed words to Muhammad. It contains many commandments and prohibitions, as well as value judgments on the actions of various people in history. For example, the Qur'an lays down explicit rules, obeyed by all Muslims up to modern times, about instituting divorce (2:226–238), contracting debts (2:281–283), and inheriting property (4:11–17). But the variety of human actions far exceeds what the Qur'an could cover. It might command people to pray, but only Muhammad's example taught Muslims how to do so.

The Prophet's *sunna* was broader than the Qur'an, but Muslims had to avoid certain pitfalls to use it as a source for the Shari'a. How could they be sure the Prophet had committed or enjoined a certain act? There had to be a *hadith* (oral report) that specified that he had done it or said it. The *hadith* would have to be validated by a chain of reporters (*isnad*). The recorder of the *hadith* would have to say who had reported this new information and who had told his informant and who had told him and so on, back to the person who had witnessed the action or saying in question. The *isnad* served the function of a source footnote in a term paper; it authenticated the information by linking it to an established authority. As the *hadith*s were not written down until more than a century had passed, the *isnad*s helped eliminate those falsely ascribed to Muhammad, but what if the *isnad*s, too, were fabrications? To weed out *hadith*s with false *isnad*s, the early *'ulama* became experts on the life of the Prophet, his family, his companions, and the first generation of Muslims. If it could be proved that one link in the chain of transmitters was weak because the person at issue was a liar or could not have known the previous transmitter, then the *hadith* itself was suspect. After many scholars labored for about a century, there emerged several authoritative collections of *hadiths*—six for Sunni Muslims and several others for the Shi'ite sects. They are still being used by Muslims today.

Meanwhile, some scholars formulated the Shari'a itself. This they did by writing books that compiled the laws of Islam for reference and guidance. Because of the many changes that had occurred in the *umma* since the Prophet's lifetime, most '*ulama* conceded that the Qur'an and *hadith* compilations could not cover every conceivable problem. Thus they adopted reasoning by analogy, or comparing a new situation with one for which legislation already existed. Because the Qur'an forbids Muslims to drink wine, the '*ulama* reasoned that all liquors having the same effect as wine should also be banned. Frequently, too, Muslim scholars relied on the consensus of the *umma* to settle hard legal points. This does not mean that they polled every Muslim from Cordoba to Samarqand. Rather, consensus meant that which could be agreed upon by those who had studied the law. Thanks to this practice, many rules from older societies were incorporated into the Shari'a. Accordingly, the laws of Islam applied to the lives of people far removed from conditions known to Muhammad: a sailor in the Indian Ocean, a rice farmer in the marshes of lower Iraq, or a Turkish horse nomad in Transoxiana. In addition, the Shari'a incorporated decisions that had been made by reputable judges in difficult or contested cases, much as legal precedents helped to shape Anglo-Saxon law. Resorting to judicial opinion, frequent during the Arab conquests, later became rare. Whenever they could, Muslim legists relied on the Qur'an and the *sunna*.

Sunni Legal Systems

The compilation of the Shari'a into authoritative books was, at least for the Sunni majority, completed by the late ninth century. Several "rites" or systems of Sunni legal thought resulted, of which four have survived: Hanafi, Maliki, Shafi'i, and Hanbali. The Hanafi rite is the largest of the four. It grew up in Iraq under 'Abbasid patronage and drew heavily on consensus and judicial reasoning (in addition, of course, to the Qur'an and the *sunna*) as sources. Today it predominates in Muslim India, Pakistan, and most of the lands formerly under the Ottoman Empire. The Maliki rite developed in Medina and drew heavily on the Prophetic *hadiths* that circulated there. It now prevails in Upper Egypt and in northern and western Africa. The Shafi'i rite grew up in ninth-century Egypt as a synthesis of the Hanafi and Maliki systems but with greater stress on analogy. It was strong in Egypt and Syria at the time of Salah al-Din; it now prevails in the Muslim lands around the Indian Ocean and in Indonesia. The fourth canonical rite, that of the great jurist and theologian Ahmad ibn Hanbal (d. 855), rejected analogy, consensus, and judicial opinion as sources. Because of its strictness, the Hanbali rite has a smaller following, although its adherents have included the thinkers who inspired the modern reform movement within Islam. It is also the official legal system in present-day Saʻudi Arabia. Other Sunni rites that used to exist have died out. The substantive differences among the four rites are minor except in ritual matters. Each (except at times the Hanbali rite) has regarded the others as legitimate.

Shiʻite Legal Systems

Shiʻite jurisprudence also relies on the Qurʼan, the *sunna,* analogy, and consensus. Some differences do exist between Shiʻite and Sunni Muslims regarding the authenticity of certain statements by the Prophet, notably one concerning whether he wanted ʻAli as his successor. In some matters Shiʻite law is more permissive: it allows temporary marriage, the female line receives a slightly larger share of the inheritance, and some sects let Shiʻite Muslims conceal their religious identity (*taqiya*) if their safety is at stake. The major difference is that, whereas most Sunni rites no longer allow reinterpretation of the Shariʻa, in Shiʻism the imams can interpret the law. The imams are regarded as being, in principle, alive. Among Twelve-Imam Shiʻites, whose last imam is hidden, qualified legists called *mujtahids* may interpret the Shariʻa until the twelfth imam returns. This "interpretation" (*ijtihad*) does not mean changing the law to suit one's temporary convenience; rather, it is the right to re-examine the Qurʼan and the *hadith* compilations without being bound by consensus. In this sense, Shiʻism has kept a flexibility long since lost by the Sunni majority, and the Shiʻite ʻulama, especially the *mujtahids,* have remained influential up to now in such countries as Iran. Indeed, the main issue for Sunni Muslim ʻulama committed to Islamic reform has been to regain the right of *ijtihad.*

Administration of the Law

At the dawn of Islamic history, administering and enforcing the law were handled by the caliphs or their provincial governors. As society grew more complex, they began to appoint Muslims who knew the Qurʼan and the *sunna* (as practiced by the early caliphs as well as by Muhammad) to serve as *qadis* (judges). As the judicial system evolved, an aspiring *qadi* got his legal training by reading the law books and commentaries under the guidance of one or several masters in his chosen legal rite or sect. When he had mastered enough information to serve as a *qadi*, he would be certified to practice on his own.

Various other judicial offices also evolved: the *mufti* (jurisconsult), who gives authoritative answers to technical questions about the law for a court and sometimes for individuals; the *shahid* (witness), who certifies that a certain act took place, such as the signing of a contract; and the *muhtasib* (market inspector), who enforces Muslim commercial laws and maintains local order. Islam's legal system has never had lawyers to represent opposing parties in court cases. Muslims maintain that advocates or attorneys might enrich themselves at the expense of the litigant or criminal defendant. There were also no prosecutors or district attorneys. In most cases the *qadi* had to decide from the evidence presented by the litigants and the witnesses, guided by relevant sections of the Shari'a and sometimes by advice from a mufti.

The caliph had to ensure that justice prevailed in the *umma*, not by interpreting the Shari'a but by appointing the wisest and most honest *qadis* to administer it. True, some Umayyad caliphs might have flouted the Shari'a in their personal lives, but its rules remained valid for the *umma* as a whole. No Umayyad or 'Abbasid caliph could abolish the Shari'a or claim that it did not apply to him as to all other Muslims.

When the caliphate ceased to symbolize Muslim unity, widespread acceptance of the Shari'a bridged the barriers of contending sects and dynasties. Even when the Crusaders and Mongols entered the lands of Islam and tried to enforce other codes of conduct, Muslims continued to follow the Shari'a in their daily lives. And to a degree that surprises some Westerners, they do so now. You can go into a bazaar or *suq* (marketplace) in Morocco and feel that it is, in ways you can sense even if you cannot express them, like the bazaars in Turkey, Pakistan, or fifty other Muslim countries. The performance of worship, observance of the Ramadan fast, and, of course, the pilgrimage to Mecca all serve to unify Muslims from all parts of the world.

Applicability of the Law

But is the Shari'a relevant today? Its laws are fixed forever, and critics claim that they cannot set the norms for human behavior in a rapidly changing world. Even in the times we have studied so far, strong rulers tried to bypass some aspects of the Shari'a, perhaps by using a clever dodge but more often by issuing secular laws, or *qanuns*. The *'ulama*, as guardians of the Shari'a, had no police force with which to punish such a ruler. But they could stir up public opinion, sometimes even to the point of rebellion. No ruler ever dared to change the five pillars of Islam. Until recently, none interfered with laws governing marriage, inheritance, and other aspects of personal status (except in a few cases such as Tunisia). Islam today must deal with the same issue facing Orthodox Judaism: How can a religion based on adherence to a divinely sanctioned code of conduct survive in a world in which many of its nation-states and leading minds no longer believe in God—or at any rate act as if they do not? Someday, perhaps, practicing Muslims, Christians, and Jews will settle their differences to combat their common enemies: secularism, hedonism, positivism, and the various ideologies that have arisen in modern times.

What parts of the Shari'a are irrelevant? Are the marriages contracted by young people for themselves more stable than those that their parents would have arranged for them? Has the growing frequency of fornication and adultery in the West strengthened or weakened the family? If the family is not to be maintained, in what environment will boys and girls be nurtured and taught how to act like men and women? Has the blurring of sex roles in modern society made men and women happier and more secure? Should drinking intoxicating beverages be allowed when alcoholism has become a public health problem in most industrialized countries? Does lending money at interest promote or inhibit capital formation? Do games of chance enrich or impoverish the people who engage in them? If the appeal to jihad in defense of Islam sounds aggressive, on behalf of what beliefs were the most destructive wars of the twentieth century fought? Would Muslims lead better lives if they ceased to pray, fast in Ramadan, pay *zakat,* and make the *hajj* to Mecca? Let those who claim that Islam and its laws are anachronistic try to answer these questions.

ISLAMIC SOCIETY

In early Muslim times, social life was far more formalized than it is today. Every class had certain rights and duties, as did each religion, sex, and age group. The rulers were expected to preserve order and promote justice among their subjects, to defend the *umma* against non-Muslim powers, and to ensure maximum production and exploitation of the wealth of their realm. Over time, Sunni Muslims developed an elaborate political theory. It stated that the legitimate head of state was the caliph, who had to be an adult male, sound in body and mind, and descended from the Quraysh tribe. His appointment was to be publicly approved by other Muslims. In practice, though, the assent given to a man's becoming caliph might be no more than his own. Some of the caliphs were young boys. A few were insane. Eventually, the caliphal powers were taken over by viziers, provincial governors, or military adventurers. But the fiction was maintained, for the Sunni legists agreed that it was better to be governed by a usurper or a despot than to have no ruler at all. The common saying was that a thousand years of tyranny was preferable to one day of anarchy.

Abuses of power were often checked by the moral authority of the *'ulama*. The rulers had to work with the classes commonly called the "men of the pen" and the "men of the sword." The men of the pen were the administrators who collected and disbursed state revenues and carried out the rulers' orders, plus the *'ulama* who provided justice, education, and welfare services to Muslims. The Christian clergy and the Jewish rabbinate served their religious communities in ways similar to those of the *'ulama*. The men of the sword expanded and defended the lands of Islam and also, especially after the ninth century, managed land grants and maintained local order.

Social Groupings

Strictly speaking, Muslims reject class distinctions, but the concept of ruler and subject was taken over from the Sassanid political order of pre-Islamic Persia. The great majority of the people belonged to the subject class, which was expected to produce the wealth of the *umma*. The most basic division of subjects was between nomads and settled peoples, with the former group further divided into countless tribes and clans and the latter broken down into many occupational groups. Urban merchants and artisans formed trade guilds, often tied to specific religious sects or Sufi orders (brotherhoods of Muslim mystics also known as *zawayas* [sing. *zawiya*] or *turuq* [sing. *tariqa*]), which promoted their common interests. The largest group consisted of farmers, generally lower in status and usually not full owners of the lands they farmed. There were also slaves. Some served in the army or the bureaucracy, others worked for merchants or manufacturers, and still others were household servants. Islam did not proscribe slavery, but it urged masters to treat their slaves kindly and encouraged their liberation. Slaves could be prisoners of war, children who had been sold by their families, or captives taken from their homes by slave dealers. These concepts of class structure did not originate in Islam, which stressed the equality of all believers; they went back to ancient times and existed in most agrarian societies.

Crossing these horizontal social divisions were vertical ones based on ancestry, race, religion, and sex. Although some *hadiths* showed that Muhammad and his companions wanted to play down distinctions based on family origins, early Islam did accord higher status to descendants of the first Muslims, or of Arabs generally, than to later converts to the religion. As you have read in previous chapters, Persians and then Turks gradually rose to equal status with Arabs. Other ethnic groups, such as Berbers, Indians, and Africans, kept a distinct identity and often a lower status even after they converted to Islam. Racial discrimination, however, was less acute than it has been in Christian lands even in modern times.

The divisions based on religion, though, were deep and fundamental. Religion was a corporate experience—a community of believers bound together by adherence to a common set of laws and beliefs—rather than a private and personal relationship between people and their maker. Religion and politics were inextricably intertwined. Christians and Jews did not have the same rights and duties as Muslims; they were protected communities living within the realm of Islam, where the Shari'a prevailed. Though exempt from military duty, they were forbidden to bear arms. They did not have to pay *zakat,* but they were assessed the head tax (*jizya*) plus whatever levies they needed to support their own religious institutions. They were sometimes not allowed to testify in a Shari'a court against a Muslim or to ring bells, blow shofars (rams' horns used in some Jewish holidays), or hold noisy processions that might disrupt Muslim worship. At times they found the limitations even more humiliating, and in a few cases their lives and property were threatened. But for centuries they managed to keep their identity as Christians or Jews and to follow their own laws and beliefs. The treatment of religious minorities in Muslim countries that upheld the Shari'a was better than in those that watered it down or abandoned it totally and much, much better than the treatment of Jews in medieval Christendom, czarist Russia, or Nazi Germany.

As for social divisions based on gender, Islam (like most religions that grew up in the agrarian age) is patriarchal and hence gives certain rights and responsibilities to men that it denies women. Muslims believe that biology has dictated different roles for the two sexes. Men are supposed to govern states, wage war, and support their families; women, to bear and rear children, manage their households, and obey their husbands. Traditional history tells little about women; a few took part in wars and governments, wrote poems, or had profound mystical experiences, but most played second fiddle to their husbands, fathers, brothers, or sons. Often they had more influence than the traditional histories admit.

Family Life

The family played a central role in early Islamic society. Marriages were arranged by the parents or by the oldest living relatives of the potential couple, for it was understood that a marriage would tie two families together or tighten the bonds between two branches of the same house. Marriages between cousins were preferred because they helped keep the family's property intact. Muslims assumed that love between a man and a woman would develop once they were married and had to share the cares of maintaining a household and rearing children. Romantic love did arise between unmarried persons, but it rarely led to marriage. The freedom of Muslim men to take additional wives (up to a total of four) caused some domestic strife, but many an older wife rejoiced when her husband took a younger one who could better bear the strains of frequent pregnancy and heavy housework. The "harem" of the Western imagination was rare. Only the rich and powerful man could afford to support the four wives allowed him by the Qur'an (provided he treated them equally); many poor men could not afford any, as the groom had to pay a large dowry. Islamic law made divorce easy for husbands and difficult for wives, but in practice divorce was rare, because the wife was permitted to keep the dowry.

Parents expected (and got) the unquestioning obedience of their sons and daughters, even after they had grown up. Once a woman married, she also had to defer to her husband's parents. Women naturally wanted to bear sons, who would eventually give them daughters-in-law to boss around. Parents disciplined their children harshly but loved them deeply and, if those children were among the few to survive the rigors of growing up, took great pride in their later achievements. Although a boy usually learned his father's trade, the gifted son of a peasant or merchant could get an education and move into the ranks of the 'ulama or the bureaucracy. Girls rarely were able to go to school, but certain occupations were limited to women. Wives often worked beside their husbands in the fields or in domestic industries, such as spinning. Ties among brothers, sisters, and cousins had an intensity (usually love, sometimes hate) that is rare in the Western experience, because Muslim youths spent so much of their time within the family circle.

Personal Relationships

The individual in early Islamic society knew fewer people than in our more mobile world, but his or her friendships (and enmities) tended to be stronger and more lasting. Physical as well as verbal expressions of endearment between same-sex friends were more common than in the West and did not have to mean homosexuality (although such relationships did exist). Men's friendships were usually based on childhood ties or common membership in a mystic brotherhood, trade guild, or athletic club. Women's associations were limited by custom to kinfolk and neighbors, but they had mystic sisterhoods, too.

Both men and women entertained their friends, segregated by sex, at home. Mutual visiting, at which food and drink were shared and news exchanged, was the most common pastime for every class in Islamic society. The customary time for these visits was late afternoon or early evening as the weather cooled off, or at night during the month of Ramadan. Large groups of men (or women) liked to gather at someone's house to listen to poetry recitations or, less often, musical performances. Egypt and Persia retained pre-Islamic holidays that involved a spring trip into the countryside for a family picnic. The two great Muslim festivals, 'Id al-Adha (Feast of Abraham's Sacrifice) during the *hajj* month and 'Id al-Fitr (Feast of Fast-Breaking) that follows Ramadan, were major social occasions everywhere. People often gave lavish parties to celebrate births, circumcisions, and weddings. Funeral processions, burials, and postburial receptions also played a big part in the social life of Muslims. Men used to meet in mosques, bazaars, public baths, and restaurants. Women often saw their friends at the women's baths, at the public well where they drew their water, or at the stream where they did their laundry. Compared with our society, early Muslims had less freedom and privacy but more security and less loneliness.

Food, Clothing, and Shelter

The foods early Muslims ate, the clothes they wore, and the houses in which they lived varied according to their economic condition, locality, and the era in question, so it is hard to generalize about how they met their basic needs. Wheat was the chief cereal grain. It was usually ground at a mill, kneaded at home, and baked in small flat loaves in large communal or commercial ovens. Bulgur or parched wheat was used in cooking, especially in Syria and Palestine. Bedouin ate wheat gruel or porridge. Rice was rarer than now; corn and potatoes were not grown in the Middle East until the seventeenth century. Many fruits and vegetables were eaten fresh; others were dried, pickled in vinegar, or preserved in sugar. Milk from sheep, goats, camels, water buffaloes, and cows was turned into cheese, butter (clarified for use in cooking), and yogurt. The meat

Muslims ate most often was lamb or mutton, commonly roasted, baked, or stewed. Various animal organs not highly prized by Westerners, such as eyes, brains, hearts, and testicles, were considered delicacies. Pork was forbidden to Muslims, as were fermented beverages. Lax Muslims drank wine made from grapes and other fruits, beer, and *araq* (fermented liquor from date-palm sap, molasses, or rice). The observant majority drank fruit juices in season, sherbet (originally snow mixed with rosewater or fruit syrup), and diluted yogurt. Coffee and tea did not come into widespread use until the seventeenth century. Middle Eastern food was moderately spiced, usually with salt, pepper, olive oil, and lemon juice. Saffron was used for its yellow coloring more than for its flavor, because Muslim cooks liked to enhance the appearance of their dishes. Honey served as a sweetener, but sugar cultivation gradually spread through the Muslim world from India.

Clothing had to be both modest and durable. Linen or cotton clothes were worn in hot weather and woolen ones in the winter—or throughout the year by some mystics and nomads. Loose-fitting robes were preferred to trousers, except by horseback riders, who wore baggy pants. Both sexes shunned clothing that might reveal their bodily contours to strangers. Early Muslim men covered their heads in all formal situations, with either turbans or various types of brimless caps. Different-colored turbans served to identify status; for instance, green singled out a man who had made the *hajj* to Mecca. Arab nomads wore flowing *kufiya*s (headcloths) bound by headbands. Muslims never wore hats with brims or caps with visors, as they would have impeded prostration during worship. Women used some type of long cloth to cover their hair, if not also to veil their faces, whenever male strangers might be present. Jews, Christians, and other minorities wore distinctive articles of clothing and headgear. Because the ways in which people dressed showed their religion and status, strangers knew how to act toward one another.

Houses were constructed from the materials that were most plentiful locally: stone, mud brick, or, sometimes, wood. High ceilings and windows provided ventilation in hot weather. In the winter, only warm clothing, hot food, and possibly a charcoal brazier made indoor life bearable. Many houses were built around courtyards that had gardens, fountains, and small pools. Rooms were not filled with furniture; people were used to sitting cross-legged on carpets or low platforms. Mattresses and other bedding would be rolled out when people were ready to sleep and put away after they got up. In rich people's houses, cooking facilities were often in separate enclosures. Privies always were.

Intellectual and Cultural Life

We do not have enough time and space to give the intellectual life of early Islam the attention it deserves. Regrettably, many Westerners still believe the Arab conquest of the Middle East stifled its artistic, literary, and scientific creativity. On the contrary, it was the Arabs who saved many of the works of Plato, Aristotle, and other Greek thinkers for later transmission to the West. In fact, no field of intellectual endeavor was closed to Muslim scholars. Aristotle's encyclopedic writings, translated by Syrian Christians into Arabic, inspired such Muslim thinkers as al-Kindi, al-Farabi, ibn Sina, and ibn Rushd.

As "Philosopher of the Arabs," al-Kindi (d. 873) rated the search for truth above all human occupations except religion, exalted logic and mathematics, and wrote or edited works on science, psychology, medicine, and music. He was adept at taking complex Greek concepts, paraphrasing them, and simplifying them for students, a skill any textbook writer can appreciate. Everything al-Kindi did was done even better by Abu Nasr al-Farabi (d. 950), a Baghdad-educated Turk who won such renown that later philosophers called him the "second teacher," the first having been Aristotle. Al-Farabi was the first to integrate Neoplatonic philosophy with Islamic concepts of God, angels, prophecy, and community. A prolific writer on logic, he was also a skilled musician.

Ibn Sina (d. 1037) also combined philosophy with medicine. His theological writings are unusually lucid and logical, though his devout contemporaries shunned them because he separated the body from the soul and argued that every person has free will. He stated that the highest form of human happiness is not physical but spiritual, aiming at communion with God. His scientific writings include an encyclopedia of medical lore. Translated into Latin, this work remained a textbook in European medical schools up to the seventeenth century. Like al-Kindi, he wrote on logic, mathematics, and music. The greatest Muslim writer of commentaries lived in twelfth-century Spain. Ibn Rushd (d. 1198) is noted for his works on the philosophy of Aristotle and on Muslim theologians. Because of his unorthodox religious views, many of his writings were burned, and some of his original contributions to knowledge may have been forever lost.

Mathematics and Science

Muslims tended to treat mathematics, science, and medicine as branches of philosophy, as they did not split up the areas of human knowledge as finely as we do now. Westerners tend to appreciate Muslim thinkers, if at all, for preserving classical learning until the Europeans could relearn it during the Renaissance. Our debt is really much greater. Muslim mathematicians made advances in algebra, plane and spherical trigonometry, and the geometry of planes, spheres, cones, and cylinders. Our "Arabic numerals" were a Hindu invention, but Arabs transmitted them to Europe. Muslims were using decimal fractions at least two centuries before Westerners knew about them. They applied mathematics to business accounting, land surveying, astronomical calculations, mechanical devices, and military engineering.

We already mentioned Europe's use of ibn Sina's work as a medical textbook. In medicine the Muslims built on the work of the ancient Greeks, but they were especially indebted to Nestorian Christians. One of these was Hunayn ibn Ishaq (d. 873), who translated many Greek and Aramaic texts into Arabic but did his greatest work in optics. Muslim physicians studied botany and chemistry to discover curative drugs as well as antidotes to various poisons.

Scientific and pseudoscientific methods of observation could be linked. Chemistry was mixed with alchemy and astronomy with astrology. A knowledge of the movements of stars and planets aided navigation and overland travel by night. But early Muslims, like most other peoples, thought that heavenly bodies affected the lives of individuals, cities, and states, and thus many of the caliphs kept court astrologers as advisers. Muslims also used astrolabes (devices for measuring the height of stars in the sky) and built primitive versions of the telescope. One astronomer is said to have built a planetarium that reproduced not only the movements of stars but also peals of thunder and flashes of lightning. Long before Copernicus or Galileo expounded their theories, Muslim scientists knew that the earth was round and that it revolved around the sun.

Descriptive geography was a favorite subject of the early Muslims. Thanks to the Arab conquests and the expansion of trade throughout the Eastern Hemisphere, they liked to read books describing far-off lands and their inhabitants, especially if they could become trading partners or converts to Islam. Much of what we know about Africa south of the Sahara from the ninth to the fifteenth centuries comes from the writings of Arab travelers and geographers. History was also a major discipline. Nearly all Muslim scientists wrote accounts of the development of their specialties. Rulers demanded chronicles to publicize what they had done or to learn from their predecessors' successes and failures. Many Muslims read accounts of the early caliphs and conquests. Muslim historians were the first to try to structure history by seeking patterns in the rise and fall of dynasties, peoples, and civilizations. These efforts culminated in the fourteenth century with ibn Khaldun's monumental *al-Muqaddima,* which linked the rise of states to strong group feeling (*'asabiya*) between the leaders and their followers.

Literature

Every subject we have discussed so far is part of the Muslims' prose literature. Although Arabic remained the major language of both prose and poetry, Persian revived during the 'Abbasid era, and Turkish literature emerged a little later. Poetry facilitated artistic expression, instruction, and popular entertainment. Some poems praised a tribe, a religion, or a potential patron; some poked fun at the poet's rivals; others evoked God's power or the exaltation of a mystical experience; and still others extolled love, wine, and God, or perhaps all three (you cannot always be sure which).

Prose works guided Muslims in the performance of worship, instructed princes in the art of ruling, refuted claims of rival political or theological movements, and taught any of the manifold aspects of life, from cooking to lovemaking. Animal fables scored points against despotic rulers, ambitious courtiers, naive *'ulama,* and greedy merchants. You may know the popular stories that we call *The Arabian Nights,* some of which are set in Harun al-Rashid's Baghdad but actually composed by many ancient peoples, passed down by word of mouth to the Arabs, and written in the late Middle Ages. But you may not have heard of a literary figure beloved by many Middle Eastern peoples. The Egyptians call him Goha (*Juha*), the Persians say he is Mollah Nasroddin, and the Turks refer to him as Nasroddin Hoja. One brief story must suffice. A man once complained to Goha that there was no sunlight in his house. "Is there sunlight in your garden?" asked Goha. "Yes," the other replied. "Well," said Goha, "then move your house into your garden."

Art

Muslims do not neglect the visual arts. Some of the best-proportioned and most lavishly decorated buildings ever erected were the large congregational mosques in Islam's greatest cities. The city of Yathrib, later renamed Medina, exemplified the prototype Islamic city with the mosque of the Prophet at its center. Congregational mosques had to be monumental to accommodate all their adult male worshipers on Fridays. Some have not survived the ravages of either time or the Mongols, but the congregational mosques of al-Qayrawan, Cairo, Damascus, and Isfahan are impressive. Muslim architects also devoted some of their time and talents to palaces, schools, hospitals, caravanserais (inns where caravans stopped), and other buildings, as well as to gardens, reflecting pools, and fountains.

Artists worked in many different media. Although painting and sculpture were rare until modern times, early Muslim artists did illustrate manuscripts with abstract designs, beautiful pictures of plants and animals, and depictions of the everyday and ceremonial activities of men and women. Calligraphy (handwriting) was the most important art form, used for walls of public buildings as well as for manuscripts. Calligraphic styles included Kufi, Naskh, Riqa, Taliq, Deewani, and Thuluth. These styles were incorporated with a set of geometric designs that combined squares, rectangles, circles, stars, and hexagons. Many artistic creations were in media we usually regard as crafts: glazed pottery and tile work; enameled glass; objects carved from wood, stone, and ivory; incised metal trays; elaborate jeweled rings, pendants, and daggers; embroidered silk cloths; and tooled-leather book bindings. You have doubtless seen some "oriental" carpets. Most genuine ones were woven or knotted in Middle Eastern countries.

THEOLOGY

Like medieval Christianity, Islam had to settle some burning issues: Does divine revelation take precedence over human reason? Is God the Creator of all the evil as well as all the good in the universe? If God is all-powerful, why are people allowed to deny God's existence and disobey divine laws? If God has predestined all human acts, what moral responsibility do people have for what they do? Philosophical questions led Muslims into theology, as did disputations with their Jewish and Christian subjects, who were often more sophisticated than they.

Islam developed several systems of scholastic theology, climaxing with the Mu'tazila (mentioned in Chapter 5), the system of the self-styled "people of unity and justice." Their main tenets are (1) God is one, so his attributes have no independent existence; (2) God is just, rewarding the righteous and punishing the wicked; (3) God does not cause evil; (4) people, responsible for their own acts, are not a tool in God's hand; (5) only reason that agrees with revelation can guide people to know God; (6) one should try to justify God's ways to humanity; and (7) the Qur'an was created. If such tenets seem reasonable, you may wonder why some Muslims rejected them. For example, was the Qur'an really created? It must have been known to God before Gabriel revealed it to Muhammad. How could God exist without divine knowledge? If God has always existed, then his speech (the Qur'an) must also have been around since time began, not having been created like all other things. Muslims have always revered the Qur'an as the means by which to know God; its place in Islam resembles that of Jesus in Christianity. As for free will, if all people will be rewarded or punished for what they do, what will happen to babies and small children who die before they have learned to obey or to flout God's will? If the innocents automatically go to heaven, is this fair to those who obeyed Islam's laws all their lives? Despite these doubts, the Mu'tazila was briefly the 'Abbasids' official theology. As its adherents attacked dissident Muslims, though, a reaction set in, new ideas arose, and the movement declined.

The reaction against the Mu'tazilites was spearheaded by Ahmad ibn Hanbal, founder of the Sunni legal system that bears his name, for he opposed their application of rigid logic to the Qur'an and the laws of Islam (see Box 7.1). His writings influenced a major theologian named al-Ash'ari (d. 935), who concluded that divine revelation was a better guide than reason for human action. The Qur'an, he argued, was an attribute of God—eternally existent yet separate from God's existence. Faith was absolute. If the Qur'an mentioned God's hand (or other human features), this allusion had to be accepted as is—"without specifying how" or even interpreting the words allegorically, as the Mu'tazilites and some later theologians tried to do. Finally, al-Ash'ari and his disciples accepted God's complete omnipotence: everything people do is predestined, for God created all persons and all their actions, yet God assigned these actions to them in such a way that individuals remain accountable for what they do. The capstone of early Muslim theology was the work of Abu Hamid al-Ghazali (d. 1111), one of Baghdad's finest law teachers. His greatest theological achievement was to apply Aristotelian logic to prove Islam's main tenets, but he also wrote a stinging attack on Muslim philosophers. Muslims honor him for harmonizing law, theology, and Sufism.

Mysticism

Sufism is an experience, a path into the real nature of things and, ultimately, to God. Defining it (as we did) as "organized Muslim mysticism" may be too prosaic. Some Muslims scorn Sufism as a nonrational perversion of Islam; others make it the essence of their faith. Some Sufis regard their beliefs and practices as universal, hence no more (or less) Islamic than they are Buddhist, Christian, or Zoroastrian. Sufis seek to uncover meaning that is veiled from our senses and impenetrable to human reason. In monotheistic religions such as Islam, finding ultimate truth is called communion with God. This communion can be achieved through

---

Box 7.1   Ahmad ibn Hanbal

Historians differ on Ahmad ibn Hanbal's (780–855) place of birth—some report he was born in Baghdad, while others say he was born in Central Asia. Anyway, it is certain that he grew up in Baghdad, where he excelled in the study of religion. After receiving his basic education, he became an itinerant traveling scholar in Iraq, Syria, Arabia, and elsewhere. As he traveled, he collected *hadiths* and became an expert in this field. He became committed to the literal textual meanings of the *hadiths* and the Qur'an as guides to Muslim belief and behavior. Thus he came to adamantly oppose innovation of any kind.

This devotion to tradition brought Ahmad ibn Hanbal into conflict with the more logic-driven Mu'tazila school, which taught that the Qur'an was created by Allah when it was revealed to Muhammad, and had not existed for all eternity, and that mankind possessed free will. Such ideas suited the mentality of the reigning caliphs of the day, al-Ma'mun and al-Mu'tasim, but ran counter to the long-standing popular interpretations that the Qur'an was indeed eternal and that everyone's actions were foreordained. All this would have remained an esoteric disagreement except that Caliphs al-Ma'mun and al-Mu'tasim commanded the *'ulama* to adhere to Mu'tazila doctrines. To ensure this, they maintained a court to investigate *'ulama* beliefs.

Ahmad ibn Hanbal became the leader of those opposed to Mu'tazila ideas. When he was arrested and brought to court, he refused to recant. He was imprisoned and reportedly suffered greatly and may have been tortured. His steadfastness made him a popular hero among Muslim believers. Eventually, he was released by a new caliph, Mutawakkil, who opposed the proponents of Mu'tazila. Instead of being a suffering prisoner, ibn Hanbal became an honored teacher, even a living legend.

During this stage of his life, he founded one of the four canonical schools of Muslim legal thought, the Hanbali rite. It was and is the strictest, rejecting such sources as analogy and consensus in favor of strict adherence to the Qur'an and *hadith*. The Hanbali legal rite prevails in today's Sa'udi Arabia. Ahmad ibn Hanbal died in Baghdad at age seventy-five. Hundreds of thousands escorted his coffin to the grave.

---

meditation or such rites as fasting, night vigils, controlled breathing, repetition of words, or whirling for hours in one spot.

Islam always contained elements of mystical spirituality, but Sufism became a distinct movement during the second century after the *hijra*. At first it was a movement of ascetics, people who sought to exalt their souls by denying themselves the comforts of the flesh. Their driving force was a strong fear of God, but this fear later evolved into belief in God's love. Sufism could cut through the intellectualism of theology and soften the legalism of "formal" Sunni or Shi'ite Islam. It also enabled Islam to absorb some of the customs of converts from other religions without damaging its own essential doctrines—a capacity that facilitated Islam's spread to Central Asia, Anatolia, southeastern Europe, India, Indonesia, and Africa south of the Sahara. From the eleventh century to the nineteenth, Sufism dominated the spiritual life of most Muslims. Brotherhoods and sisterhoods of mystics, also called Sufi orders, arose throughout the *umma,* providing a new basis for social cohesion. The Safavid dynasty, which ruled Persia from 1501 to 1736, began as a Sufi order. Sufism also held together the warrior *ghazis* who founded the Safavid dynasty's better-known rival, the Ottoman Empire. The Safavid rulers were Shi'ites and the Ottomans, Sunnis; indeed, both of the main branches of Islam could accommodate Sufism.

Review of Muslim Divisions

Let us review the bases of division in Islam. The first is political: After Muhammad died, should the leaders have been chosen by the *umma* (the Sunni view) or taken from the male members of his household (the Shi'ite position)? The second, overlapping somewhat with the first, is legal: Which rite or system of jurisprudence can best guide the conduct of individual and communal Muslim life? The third raises theological issues: How much can people apply reason to expressing or debating Islamic beliefs? Does God ordain all human actions, or is each person accountable for what he or she does? The fourth can be termed spiritual: To what degree should Islamic practice include mysticism, or the search for hidden meanings not evident in religion's outwardly tangible aspects? These sectarian divisions were not watertight compartments. For instance, an eleventh-century Egyptian could be a Sunni Muslim adhering to the Maliki rite and to al-Ash'ari's theology and practicing Sufism within a mystic brotherhood, even while being ruled by the Shi'ite Fatimids.

CONCLUSION

The social, cultural, and intellectual life of early Islam was too rich and varied to be quickly summarized. The Muslim peoples of the Middle East drew on their own pre-Islamic traditions and those of the various civilizations that they encountered, many of which had been flourishing for centuries. They absorbed the customs and ideas that fit in with their basic belief in the unity of God and the mission of Muhammad and rejected the others. Over many centuries and under many dynasties, they went on developing and enriching this multifaceted civilization, through trade and manufacturing, the spoken and written word, the erection of imposing mosques and the design of refreshing gardens, and the formulation of lofty theological and philosophical ideas. Even the destruction of Baghdad during the Mongol invasions did not stop these processes. Nor did centuries of Muslim-Christian warfare prevent Europeans from learning the arts and sciences of Islam at the dawn of the Renaissance. In fact, the apogee of Muslim power and artistic expression was not reached until the sixteenth century, the gunpowder era that will be the subject of Chapter 8.

8

Firearms, Slaves, and Empires

Because we tend to equate the history of the Middle East with that of the Arabs, we assume that Muslim military might, political power, and artistic elegance all peaked sometime before the Mongol conquests. This is wrong. To be sure, the Mongols attacked Muslims in thirteenth-century Transoxiana and Khwarizm, Khurasan and Persia, Iraq and Syria. Their record for mass murder and destruction stood unbroken until the time of Hitler and Stalin. Their champion wrecker, Hulegu, hated Islam generally and its political claims specifically. Yet his descendants, the Il-Khanid dynasty, converted to Islam within half a century and adopted Persian culture. Indirectly, Hulegu and his heirs laid the groundwork for a succession of Muslim military states: the Mamluks in Egypt and Syria, the Safavids in Persia and Iraq, the Timurids in Central Asia and later in India (where they became known as the Mughals), and, most notably, the Ottoman Empire, which ruled the Balkans, Anatolia, and most of the Arab lands up to modern times.

What do firearms have to do with Muslim empires? None of the states we have just listed started out using them. We chose this title for the chapter because the harnessing of gunpowder, used in fireworks since ancient times, transformed the nature of European and Middle Eastern politics and society. Once this change occurred, around the fourteenth century, any army or navy that failed to adapt to using firearms in sieges and later in battles got crushed. The states that successfully made the transition to the gunpowder age were those that strengthened their administrative and commercial classes at the expense of the landowning aristocracy. No Middle Eastern country succeeded as well in this as England and the Netherlands. The one that came closest was the Ottoman Empire.

We open this chapter with a Muslim victory, that of the Mamluks over the Mongols at 'Ayn Jalut in 1260, and close it in 1699, the date of a widely recognized Muslim defeat, when the Ottoman Empire ceded Hungary to Habsburg Austria. Between these two dates, the Muslims recovered from the Mongol shock, formed new political institutions, expanded the lands of Islam by taking the Balkans and parts of India and by peacefully penetrating West Africa and Southeast Asia, reached new heights of prosperity, and built monumental works of art—such as the Taj Mahal—that still set the standard for created beauty.

THE MAMLUKS

You may recall from Chapter 6 that the Mamluks who saved Egypt from the Mongol menace in 1260 were Turkish ex-slaves who had recently seized power from the Ayyubids, the descendants of Salah al-Din. This illustrious ruler had adopted the practice of many Muslim dynasties, going back to the ʿAbbasids, of importing Turkish boys (*mamluks*, or "owned men") from Central Asia and training them to be soldiers. Under Salah al-Din's descendants, the Mamluks came to dominate the Ayyubid army. In the thirteenth century, Egypt, not Jerusalem, bore the brunt of the Crusader attacks. The Seventh Crusade, led by France's King Louis IX (later Saint Louis), occupied the coastal town of Damietta in 1249 and was about to take Mansura when the Ayyubids sent the Mamluks to stop his forces. In the process, the Mamluks captured Louis and his army. Back in Cairo, meanwhile, the Ayyubid sultan died, with his son and heir presumptive far away. For six months, his widow, Shajar al-Durr, concealed his death and ruled in his name. When the son returned to Cairo, the dominant Mamluk faction, seeing that he favored a rival group, killed him before he could ascend the throne. The murderers proceeded to make Shajar al-Durr the new sultan—one of the few times in Islamic history that a woman has ruled in her own name—but in reality the Mamluks took over (see Map 8.1). Their commander made this clear when he married Shajar al-Durr a few months later.

The Mamluk Ruling System

The Mamluks developed a succession pattern unique in Middle East history. Although a son would often succeed his father as sultan, he usually (especially after 1382) had only a brief reign during which the major factions would fight for power. As soon as one Mamluk party had defeated the others, its leader would seize the sultanate. It should have been the

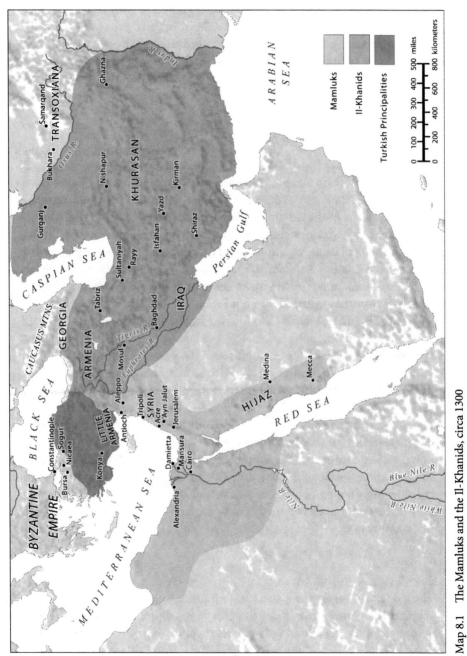

Map 8.1   The Mamluks and the Il-Khanids, circa 1300

worst governmental system in history; oddly enough, it worked for more than 250 years.

One reason was that it enabled several gifted leaders to rise to the top and stay there. One example is Baybars (r. 1260–1277), who had served his predecessor as one of his generals at 'Ayn Jalut. Soon after this victory, he killed his master and conned the other Mamluks into accepting him as their new sultan. Ever mindful of the Mongol threat to the east, Baybars tried to bring much of Syria under Mamluk control. This meant absorbing a few lands still under Ayyubid princes, reducing the Crusaders' territories to a coastal strip (they held Acre until 1291), and ravaging the kingdom of Little Armenia, the Mongols' most faithful ally. But Baybars did not let religion or nationality stop him from making useful alliances. He courted the Byzantines and the Christian rulers of Aragon, Sicily, and several Italian city-states, all of which became Egypt's trading partners. He sided with the Mongols in Russia—the Golden Horde (which had become Muslim)—against their Il-Khanid cousins in Persia. Baybars made Egypt the richest Muslim state. He also took in a fugitive 'Abbasid prince from Baghdad and proclaimed him caliph, thereby gaining some prestige. But Muslims cared more that Baybars earned the title of "Servant of the Two Holy Cities," when Mecca and Medina accepted Mamluk sovereignty. What this title meant was that until those cities were taken by the Ottoman Empire in 1517, any Muslim making the *hajj* passed through Mamluk lands.

Only lately have scholars learned the secrets of Mamluk power and endurance. A mamluk, as you know, is a slave. Slavery in early Islam was not as bad as we might think, for it often enabled gifted young men to rise to power through the army or the bureaucracy. In remote Middle Eastern areas—the Central Asian steppes (home of the Turks and the Mongols), the eastern shore of the Black Sea (inhabited by Circassians), the northern Zagros Mountains (Kurdistan), and even the Mediterranean islands—lived families that were willing to let their sons go, via slave traders, to serve Muslim rulers. In the thirteenth and fourteenth centuries, the greatest source of new mamluks was the Kipchak Turkic tribe. Then, after 1382, the Circassians took the lead, sending their sons to the barracks and their daughters to the harems of Muslim sultans and *amirs* (princes).

A boy usually became a mamluk when he was between ten and twelve, not yet adolescent but old enough to take care of himself and to learn to ride a horse, if indeed he had not been riding ever since he knew how to walk. He would be sold into the service of the reigning sultan (if he was lucky), or to one of the amirs, and put into a barrack or dormitory with other mamluks his own age. All the boys would receive basic instruction in Islam and Arabic. They would be drilled in the care and riding of horses, taught to fight with lances and swords, and trained in archery. This rigorous education lasted eight to ten years, during which the youths were kept under the strictest discipline (a visit to the public baths was the high point of their week), but cohorts developed a feeling of unity that lasted the rest of their lives. Each mamluk, upon completing his military training, received his liberation paper, a horse, and his fighting equipment.

Even as a freed soldier of fortune, though, the mamluk stayed loyal to the sultan or amir who had trained and liberated him. Each cohort of trainees tended to become a faction within the army, rather like a pledge class in a fraternity. Sometimes mamluk leaders took power for themselves. Their ability to reach the top depended on their military skills and political acumen. Upon taking power, they, in their turn, became the owners and trainers of new mamluks, forming strong, almost familial, bonds with their troops. The natural sons of mamluk soldiers rarely entered this relatively closed establishment; they usually became 'ulama or administrators. This system proved durable. No Muslim dynasty you have studied so far managed to rule Egypt and Syria for as long as the Mamluks did.

The Decline of the Mamluks

In time, however, favoritism replaced advancement by ability, the rigor of the mamluks' training declined, and the quality of Mamluk rule (especially under the fifteenth-century Circassian sultans) deteriorated. The system caused the mamluks to crave wealth and power. Mamluk attempts to monopolize commerce in luxury goods so offended both European Christians and Asian Muslims that the lucrative trade routes began shifting away from Egypt during the fifteenth century. At a time when other armies were adopting cannons and muskets, the Mamluks relegated the use of firearms to minor corps of mercenary foot soldiers and continued to fight on horseback, wielding their accustomed swords and spears, and shooting with bows and arrows. This failure to keep up with developments in military technology caused their dramatic defeat by the disciplined Ottoman army in 1516 and 1517.

THE MONGOL IL-KHANIDS

The Mamluks' first rivals were the Il-Khanids, descendants of the Mongol conquerors of Iraq and Persia. Their founder, Hulegu (d. 1265), established his capital at Tabriz. He had good reasons for this choice: Tabriz was in the Azerbaijan highlands, it was close to the Great Silk Route leading to China and to southeast Europe, and it was also near large concentrations of Christians then remaining in Anatolia and northern Iraq. You will see that this proximity to other ethnic and religious groups raises an interesting issue.

The Religious Issue

The history-shaping question for Hulegu and his successors was which religion they would adopt now that they were living among sedentarized peoples. They might well have become Christian. The popes of this era sent missions to make contact with the Mongol empires, open trade with them, and, if possible, convert them. The Roman Church could offer little at the time to the Mongols, but some did adopt a form of Christianity already common in Iraq, Persia, and Central Asia—namely, Nestorianism. The Mongols also allied themselves with Georgians, Armenians, and other Middle Eastern Christians during their assault on Islam. The late thirteenth century was the last golden age for such Christian sects as the Nestorians and the Jacobites (Syrian Monophysites). Later, their political power and culture declined, and most of the world forgot about them.

Most of the early Il-Khanids preferred Buddhism, with which the Mongols had long been familiar. Buddhist temples were erected in many Persian towns, and saffron-robed priests contended with turbaned *'ulama*. But the Il-Khanids tolerated all faiths and did not try to convert Muslims, clearly the majority of their subjects. In time, tribal Mongols intermarried with Turkish or Persian Muslims, adopted their language, and then took on their religion. Eventually, one Il-Khanid ruler, Ghazan Khan (r. 1295–1304), formally embraced Islam. Persian Buddhism, an exotic growth, soon shriveled and died.

Ghazan and his successors converted temples into mosques and repaired much of the damage done to Persia by their ancestors. Ghazan's successors proved to be weaker, and conflicts broke out between Sunni and Shi'ite factions. By 1335 Il-Khanid rule had fragmented and vanished.

Effects of Il-Khanid Rule on Persia

Despite the massacres and destruction that you have read about, the Mongol era was not a tragic one for Persia. Even before they became Muslims, the Il-Khanids encouraged and supported architects, artists, poets, and scholars. Some of the great mosques, such as those of Yazd and Kerman, date from the Il-Khanid period. Several of the Il-Khanids commissioned great new complexes, with mosques, public baths, bazaars, hostels for travelers and Sufi mystics, schools, libraries, hospitals, and monumental tombs for themselves, in or near Tabriz. Regrettably, most of the monuments of Mongol architecture, however, have not survived the ravages of time, earthquakes, and later invaders.

The Mongol conquests introduced Persian artists and craftsmen to the achievements of Chinese civilization, and so they produced some beautiful manuscript illustrations, glazed tile walls, and other ceramic creations. Hulegu, contrite at the damage he had wrought, patronized the great Persian scholar Nasiruddin Tusi (d. 1274), who saved the lives of many other scientists and artists, accumulated a library of 400,000 volumes, and built an astronomical observatory that became the model for later ones in both the Middle East and Europe. Some Persian Muslims became viziers to the Il-Khanids and other Mongol dynasties. Two of these men, Ata Malik Juvaini (d. 1284) and Rashid al-Din (d. 1318), wrote universal histories—a rare achievement in any culture; these are chronicles from which we learn much about the Mongol empire and its accomplishments. The late thirteenth and fourteenth centuries were a time of economic revival and intellectual brilliance for Persia, as Islamic civilization east of the Tigris took on a distinct Persian character. Once again, as in the days of the Arabs and the Seljuk Turks, the Mongol era proved the old adage that captive Persia always subdues its conquerors.

Timur (Tamerlane) and the Timurids

Just as the Il-Khanid state was fading, a new military star rose in the east. A petty prince, Timur Leng, often called "Tamerlane," was born in 1336 in Transoxiana, an area often disputed between Turkic and Mongol tribes. As a young man, Timur gathered an army of Muslim Turks (or Turkish-speaking descendants of the old Mongol tribes), with which he hoped to build a universal empire like that of Genghis Khan. Even before he could subdue his turbulent homeland, Timur crossed the Oxus in 1369 and proceeded to plunder Khurasan. When Russia's Mongols, the Golden Horde, tried to align the principalities of eastern Anatolia and western Persia against him, Timur led his troops through Azerbaijan, Georgia, Armenia, northern Iraq, and parts of southern Russia. Everywhere they went, thousands of men, women, and children were killed, cities were razed, and farms were destroyed. Posing as a devout Muslim, Timur inflicted special torments on Middle Eastern Christians.

After a brief rest, during which he embellished his capital at Samarqand, he invaded Persia a second time, crossed Iraq and Syria, and brought his empire to the eastern shore of the Mediterranean. Then, leaving the

Middle East, he turned against India. He defeated its Muslim amirs, sacked Delhi, and filled his coffers with Indian booty, using its proceeds to march westward once more. Between 1400 and 1403, he took Aleppo and Damascus from the Mamluks and almost wiped out the rising Ottoman Empire at Ankara. But even when his Middle Eastern realm matched his Asian empire at Samarqand, Timur pined for a vaster domain to match that of Genghis Khan. Only his sudden death in 1405 stopped Timur's soldiers from setting out to conquer China itself.

Some people may admire the ambition of an Alexander, a Napoleon, or a Genghis Khan to build by war a universal empire under which all peoples would live together in peace. A world full of contending tribes and kingdoms seems anarchic, and the conquerors we have named were visionaries. They esteemed scholars, artists, and artisans and left legacies in the fields of political or military organization. If we focus on social history, though, we cannot praise Timur, whose main legacies were pyramids of human heads and smoking ruins where cities had once stood, but he did erect monumental *madrasas* (schools), mosques, and mausoleums in Samarqand. His Timurid descendants patronized scholars, manuscript illustrators, and jewelers. His great-great-grandson, Babur (r. 1483–1530), would found a Muslim state in India. We call it the Mughal Empire, though it began as a Timurid offshoot. It would last until 1858, when Britain took full control of India.

Except for Central Asia, Afghanistan, and some parts of Persia, Timur's conquests broke away soon after he died. The Mamluks recovered Syria, the Turkish amirs of Anatolia won back their independence, and various dynasties took over in Persia. Most memorable of these dynastic states were those of the Shi'ite Black Sheep and the Sunni White Sheep Turcomans, who fought each other for most of the fifteenth century. Out of this chaos would come a new dynasty, the Safavids (1501–1736), to spur yet another Persian cultural revival.

GUNPOWDER TECHNOLOGY

The spread of gunpowder and firearms was as momentous a technological change at that time as the proliferation of nuclear weapons has been since 1945. Gunpowder had been used in China for fireworks since before the Common Era. It was used as an incendiary device during the Mongol era, spreading from northern China to Europe. By 1330 both Christian and Muslim armies in Spain were loading gunpowder into cannons to fire huge projectiles against enemy fortifications. The big guns were too clumsy to hurt an enemy soldier, but by injuring or frightening horses, they could block a cavalry charge. During the fourteenth and fifteenth centuries, Italian and German gunsmiths were refining these weapons. Bronze (easy to cast but very costly) gave way to iron, the diameters of the barrels were slowly standardized, and the weapons were made easier to load and to transport. Simultaneous improvements were being made in the related areas of mining, metallurgy, designing and assembling the component parts, harnessing draft animals, and building roads.

New methods of recruitment and training were devised to produce disciplined corps of foot soldiers and sailors who could maintain and fire these gunpowder weapons. Any European ruler who wanted to keep his territory—or even to survive—had to obtain these new implements. Those Muslim states that opposed Europe also had to get firearms. The amir of Granada had them by 1330 and the Mamluks (although they used them reluctantly) by 1365, but the greatest Muslim gunpowder state was the Ottoman Empire.

THE OTTOMAN EMPIRE

Our tale begins with a humble Turkish principality located near Sogut, a mountain village in northwest Anatolia. At the end of the thirteenth century, it was one of several dozen such petty states, fragments of the once-mighty Rum Seljuk sultanate. The growth of this principality into a sprawling empire, perhaps the greatest power of the sixteenth century, is an amazing success story. An ancient legend traced the empire's origins to the Turkic Kayi tribe, whose members fled westward from their ancestral lands in Khurasan to escape from the thirteenth-century Mongol invaders. The Rum Seljuk sultan was fighting the Byzantines when one of the Kayi chieftains, Ertugrul, showed up. Ertugrul's offer of his 444 horse soldiers turned the tide of battle in favor of the Seljuks, who rewarded him with an *iqta'* (land grant) at Sogut. Upon Ertugrul's death, the leadership passed on to his son, Osman, who was girded by a Sufi leader with a special sword and commanded to wage jihad against his Christian neighbors, the Byzantines. He took the title of *ghazi* (frontier warrior for Islam). From that time until the empire's end in 1923, Osman's descendants—the Ottomans—would upon accession be girded with his sword and (according to legend) ordered to fight for Islam against Europe's Christian rulers. You can still see that sword, among the Ottoman Empire's many treasures, at the Topkapi Palace Museum in Istanbul.

We do not know whether Ertugrul really lived, but we historians need to know what people believe to have happened as we also seek the literal truth. The legend stresses the Ottoman opposition to the Mongols and to the Byzantines (neither of whom were Turkish or Muslim) as well as Ottoman loyalty to the Seljuks and to the tradition of militant Islam. If you keep these attitudes in mind, you will understand the spirit of the Ottoman state. (The succession of Ottoman sultans is diagrammed in Figure 8.1.)

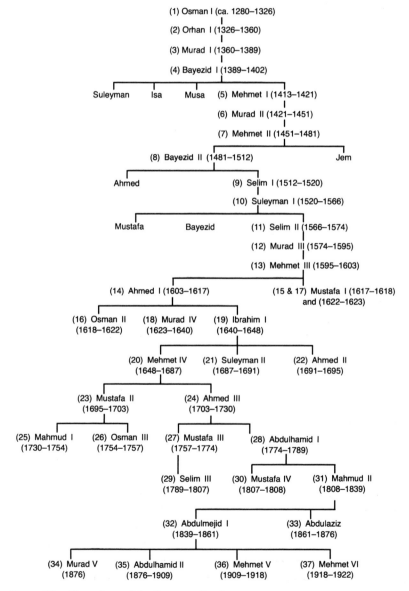

Figure 8.1   The sultans of the Ottoman Empire

Beginnings
The thirteenth century was a time of weakness for both the rump Byzantine Empire and the Rum Seljuks. The Byzantines had suffered defeat at the hands of the Venetians in 1204 (during the Fourth Crusade) and had not regained Constantinople until 1262. The Seljuk sultanate had been defeated by the Mongols in 1243 and reduced to a tributary of their empire. The border between these two enfeebled powers, known as marches, was a zone controlled by neither power, one where a strong and resourceful *ghazi* might rise to prominence. The local settled population was Greek speaking and Orthodox Christian. The hillside nomads were Turkish speaking and Muslim, either Sunni or Shi'ite but almost always Sufi. The nomads often raided the settled peoples, seeking land and booty.

Osman's *iqta'* at Sogut, though tiny, was well situated on a hill overlooking Byzantine lands. Osman I (r. ca. 1280–1326) was a warrior chief who led a band of pastoral nomads and cavalry adventurers on raids into Byzantium to win new territories for other Turkic tribes from the east, who constantly sought more grazing lands for their flocks. Recently, historians have found that although Osman's followers called themselves *ghazi*s and adopted Islamic titles that had been used by their Seljuk and even 'Abbasid precursors, they welcomed alliances with local Christian warlords, including some who did not convert to Islam. Land-hungry Turkic nomads from the east were joined by sedentary Turks, drawn by Osman's ties with the militant trade guilds, and they set up his rudimentary government. For nine years the Turks besieged the Byzantine stronghold at Bursa; as Osman lay dying, they finally took the city. It became the first real capital of the Ottomans (the name Europeans would give to Osman's descendants).

Expansion
Orhan (r. 1326–1360) was the first Ottoman to have coins minted in his name, a traditional attribute of Muslim sovereignty, as he expanded his realm northwest to the Dardanelles and east to Ankara (see Box 8.1). Twice his armies were invited to cross the Straits into Europe by Byzantine emperors seeking Ottoman support against internal rivals and external foes. In 1354 Orhan's men crossed over a third time, took Gallipoli, and refused to go back to Anatolia. Orhan's son, Murad I (r. 1360–1389), took many parts of the Balkans, including Thrace, Macedonia, and Bulgaria. The Byzantine Empire became a mere enclave on the European side of the Bosporus, a shriveled husk that survived on Ottoman awe and protection. Southeastern Europe's great Christian power was Serbia. Its king, Lazar,

Box 8.1	Orhan

Orhan (1288–1360) was the son of Osman, founder of the Ottoman dynasty. He took over the young *ghazi* principality when his father died in 1326 and ruled until his own death. During these years Orhan laid the foundations for the future Ottoman Empire.

Details on his life before he became ruler are few, though we know that he sometimes led his father's warriors on raids into Christian territory. When he succeeded his father as ruler, therefore, he had acquired the respect and experience necessary to retain the loyalty of the *ghazis*.

Upon his accession, Orhan began the process of transforming a warlord principality into an expanding empire. He incorporated administrative procedures and financial practices characteristic of the Byzantines. He built mosques and subsidized such municipal services as public baths and hostelries, thus winning the support of the city dwellers. Orhan also expanded his military capacity by supplementing his *ghazi* horsemen with mercenary troops, some of whom may have been Christians.

Orhan's forces managed to conquer most of the Byzantine cities and villages in northwestern Anatolia. Bursa, its main metropolis, became the first Ottoman capital. Orhan also got involved in the frequent civil strife within the Byzantine lands across the Dardanelles. Between 1341 and 1347 he contracted himself and his forces out as mercenary troops fighting for John VI Cantacuzene, a rival for the Byzantine throne. He made a political marriage with Cantacuzene's daughter, Theodora, and established a permanent Ottoman outpost on the European side of the Strait. Soon Orhan began fighting for his own cause in Europe, taking Gallipoli in 1354 (the city's walls had just collapsed in an earthquake). The wealth gained from his freewheeling plundering of Thrace helped strengthen the evolving Ottoman state.

Orhan's expansionist ambitions were not restricted to Byzantine territory. He also wanted to take control of his local Muslim rivals. At this stage the Ottomans used less violent methods, such as waiting until a local *bey* (or leader) died and then absorbing his *ghazi*s and lands. This is how they took over Karasi in 1345, a move that brought them to the southern shore of the Dardanelles.

An ambitious and exceedingly shrewd leader, Orhan proved to be very successful. Because of his success, the number of *ghazi*s who rallied around him constantly grew. The Ottomans had uncanny luck, as one early leader after another proved administratively and militarily capable.

amassed a force of Serbs, Albanians, Bosnians, Bulgars, and Wallachians (totaling possibly 50,000 men) to defend his bastion against the Ottoman menace. Murad, leading perhaps 40,000 troops, defeated Lazar's coalition at Kosovo in 1389. Both rulers lost their lives, but Serbia also lost its independence. The new Ottoman ruler, Bayezid I (r. 1389–1402) started to besiege Constantinople in 1395. The Europeans perceived this new threat to Christendom, and Hungary's king led English, French, German, and Balkan knights in a crusade against the Ottomans. The Christians were defeated at Nicopolis, though, and the Ottoman Empire emerged as master of the Balkans. In an action that symbolized the Ottomans' focus on Europe, they moved their capital from Bursa (in Anatolia) to Edirne (in Thrace) and waited for nearby Constantinople to fall.

If Bayezid had maintained his father's policy of attacking mainly Christians in Europe, the Ottomans might have taken Constantinople and expanded farther into the Balkans, but he began conquering nearby Turkish principalities in Anatolia. His eastward push angered Timur, who was invited into Anatolia by dispossessed Turkish amirs. The armies of Bayezid and Timur clashed near Ankara in 1402. The Ottoman sultan, deserted by his Turkish vassals, was defeated and taken prisoner. Bayezid died in captivity, and four of his sons started quarreling over what was left of the Ottoman Empire.

After an eleven-year interregnum, Mehmet I (r. 1413–1421) overcame his brothers and started to rebuild the empire. Toward that end, he had to fight new wars against the Turkish amirs in Anatolia, the Venetian navy in the Aegean Sea, and a Christian ex-vassal in the Balkans. He also suppressed revolts by a popular Sufi leader and by a Byzantine hostage who claimed to be his lost brother and the true sultan. Murad II (r. 1421–1451) pressed farther into Europe but was stymied by the Hungarians. After several Ottoman setbacks between 1441 and 1444, the king of Hungary was encouraged to call a crusade, just when Murad had turned over his throne to his twelve-year-old son, Mehmet. The Christians reached the Black Sea port of Varna, whereupon Murad came out of retirement to take charge of the Ottoman army and defeat the latter-day Crusaders. Having resumed the sultanate, Murad led expeditions against John Hunyadi of Transylvania and Skanderbeg of Albania, two Christian warriors whose resistance to the Ottomans would make them legendary among their people.

The Ottoman Zenith
When Mehmet II (r. 1451–1481) regained his throne, he built a castle on the European side of the Bosporus, facilitating Ottoman movement

between Anatolia and the Balkans while cutting the Byzantines off from any aid they might have gotten from their Christian allies at Trebizond, a Black Sea port city (see Map 8.2). In 1453 Mehmet did what so many Muslim rulers since Mu'awiya had tried: he laid siege to the walled city of Constantinople. But this time the Ottoman ships and guns succeeded where earlier Arab and Turkish attacks had failed. Constantinople was taken, pillaged for three days, and converted into the new Ottoman capital. The city, which gradually came to be called Istanbul, was repopulated with Turks, Greeks, Armenians, and Jews. Soon it grew as rich as it had ever been under the Byzantines. The Greek patriarch gained civil and religious authority over all Orthodox Christians in the Ottoman Empire. Monophysite Christians and Jews later received similar confessional autonomy under what would come to be called the *millet* system. This live-and-let-live policy contrasted sharply with the fanatical bigotry of Christian states at the time. Some of the Greek Orthodox Christians used to say, "Better the turban of the Turk than the tiara of the pope." By the end of Mehmet's reign, they had gotten what they called for, as his troops took the Morea (southern Greece), most of Albania, and the coast of what is now Croatia. In 1480 the Ottomans landed on the heel of Italy and threatened to march on Rome, but Mehmet's death saved the Roman Church from the fate of Greek Orthodoxy. What might have happened to the West if Mehmet the Conqueror had lived longer?

Mehmet's son, Bayezid II (r. 1481–1512), conquered little, but he brought rival factions into balance, restored lands confiscated by his father to their rightful owners, and ended debasement of the currency. He also sent his troops against the Mamluks to take Cilicia and against Venice for some of the Aegean islands. More threatening was the Shi'ite challenge from the Turks of Anatolia, spurred by the rise of the Safavids in Azerbaijan. Anatolian peasants and nomads often adopted Shi'ism to voice their opposition to Ottoman rule. When a Turkish nomad rebellion spread as far west as Bursa in 1511, Bayezid's son Selim decided to seize control.

Selim I the Inexorable (r. 1512–1520) transformed the Ottoman Empire from a *ghazi* state on the western fringe of the Muslim world into the greatest empire since the early caliphate. Equipped with firearms and highly disciplined, Selim's forces routed the Safavids at Chaldiran in 1514 and even entered their capital, Tabriz, before withdrawing from Azerbaijan. Two years later they defeated the Mamluks and took over their vast empire. As the new masters of Syria, Egypt, and the Hijaz, the Ottomans now ruled the heartland of Arab Islam. The Ottoman capture of Cairo made Selim the most respected ruler in the Muslim world as he took over the caliphate from the Mamluks' puppet 'Abbasid caliph—or so the

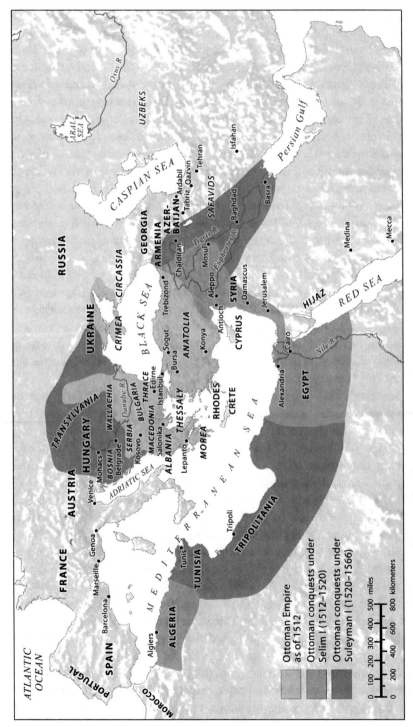

Map 8.2 The Ottoman Empire in the sixteenth and seventeenth centuries

Ottomans would later claim. Islam's holy cities, Mecca, Medina, and Jerusalem, also came under Ottoman rule.

Suleyman the Lawgiver, or the Magnificent (r. 1520–1566), had no living brothers to challenge his succession to Selim. Seen as the greatest of the Ottoman sultans by Turks and Westerners alike, Suleyman headed the forces that took Rhodes and Belgrade, defeated the Hungarians, besieged Vienna, took most of the North African coast, drove Portugal's navy from the Red Sea, and twice defeated the Safavids. He revamped the Ottoman Empire's government and laws. Regrettably, though, he delegated too many of his functions to his viziers. Late in life he fell under the influence of his favorite wife, who caused him to have one of his sons (by another wife) killed and another exiled, thus leaving the throne to her son, Selim II the Sot (r. 1566–1574). Few of the remaining sultans would match the quality of the first ten.

Causes of Ottoman Success

You may have inferred that the power and the glory of the Ottoman Empire stemmed from the personalities and policies of those first ten sultans. Rarely in history has one state enjoyed such a succession of just and brave rulers for almost three centuries. No doubt the Ottoman Empire owed some of its strength to these capable sultans, who learned the principles of government from their fathers during their on-the-job training in the provinces. They gained power by competing against their brothers, and usually the best man won. To avoid costly power struggles, they established a rule that the man who succeeded to the sultanate had to put all his brothers to death. They let no religious prejudices stop them from using the administrative, military, and naval skills of their Anatolian and Balkan Christian subjects to benefit the Ottoman Empire. When rival factions arose in the army and the bureaucracy, they kept them balanced and thus under control. "No distinction is attached to birth among the Turks," wrote a sixteenth-century envoy from the Habsburg Empire:

> The deference to be paid to a man is measured by the position he holds in the public service. There is no fighting for precedence; a man's place is marked out by the duties he discharges. In making his appointments the sultan pays no regard to any pretensions . . . of wealth or rank, nor does he take into consideration recommendations of popularity; he considers each case on its own merits, and looks carefully into the character, ability, and disposition of the man whose promotion is in question. . . . Among the Turks, therefore, honors, high posts, and judgeships are the rewards of great ability and good services.

Political Institutions

The strength and efficiency that awed the sixteenth-century Europeans were made possible by the ruling class, the so-called *Osmanlilar* (Ottomans). The main competing groups in the ruling class were the landowning aristocracy, made up of conquered Christian princes in the Balkans and Turkish amirs in Anatolia, and a group of slaves taken by force from their families as boys, converted to Islam, and trained for military or administrative service. The system of recruiting and training this group was called the *devshirme* (boy levy). The same word can also mean the group of soldiers and bureaucrats produced by this system. As in the Mamluk system, special schools were set up in the capital and the main provincial centers to train youths for Ottoman government service. Nearly all of these boys were taken from Christian families under the *devshirme* system. Although some families resisted this apparent theft of their preadolescent sons, others brought them to the recruiters, for the *devshirme* enabled the lads to rise as high in the government as their talents and aspirations might take them.

The ruling class contained four branches: administrative, military, scribal, and cultural. The administrative branch was the palace; it included the sultan's wives, children, and household servants (sometimes called the inner service) and the cabinet (*divan*), which supervised all the other branches of the Ottoman government (and hence was called the outer service). Its chief administrator was the grand vizier, who was authorized to replace the sultan on military campaigns or in the *divan*. By Suleyman's time, the viziers often did both and were second in power and prestige only to the sultan himself. The early viziers were usually Turkish princes or administrators from older Muslim states; Christian converts to Islam first became chief ministers under Mehmet the Conqueror and almost monopolized the post by Suleyman's reign.

The military branch was important, too, for the Ottoman Empire often resembled an army camp. Many subdivisions, both administrative and functional, existed, but we limit ourselves here to the horse soldiers (*sipahi*s) armed with lances or bows and arrows, and the foot soldiers (notably the janissaries), who were trained to use firearms. Although the *sipahi*s played the lead role in the early conquests, it was the well-armed, disciplined janissary corps that enabled the sixteenth-century Ottomans to defeat the Safavids, Mamluks, and Habsburgs. The janissaries, whose origins are shrouded in legend, were by far the most numerous and important product of the *devshirme* system. In the sixteenth century their training and discipline were extremely strict. Confined to barracks except during campaigns, the janissaries were forbidden to marry or to own land so that their whole loyalty could be focused on the sultan and his state. The *sipahis*, in contrast, received estates, called *timars*, which they were entitled to exploit only as long as they reported for duty and outfitted a specified number of horse soldiers whenever the sultan needed them. As armies used more siege cannons and other firearms during the sixteenth century, the *sipahis* declined in power relative to the janissaries, whose cohesion was reinforced by their belonging to a Sufi brotherhood called the Bektashis.

The janissaries and other foot soldiers had to get their food, clothing, and shelter from the government, and by the sixteenth century they also received salaries, plus accession money each time a new sultan took power. The Ottoman Empire needed a well-run treasury to meet these demands. This function was performed by the scribal branch, which took in the revenues and paid salaries and other government obligations. Tax collection was not usually done by salaried officials, as in our system; rather, it was farmed out to Ottomans known as *multezims*. A *multezim* (tax farmer) was entitled to collect all the taxes he could from a given area of land (or block of houses or shops in a bazaar) on the condition that a fixed amount or specified percentage of his take be remitted to the treasury. The *multezim* pocketed the rest. On the same principle, many officials were authorized to collect fees, called *bakhshish* (a word that has come to mean "bribe" or "handout" in the modern Middle East), for services rendered not from the state treasury but rather from the public. As long as the Ottoman government was strong, this delegation of the right to collect taxes or fees ensured that officials would carry out their duties efficiently. Later on, as the state needed more money than it could collect from the *multezims*, clerks had to buy their posts in the scribal branch and then recoup their investment by levying exorbitant taxes and fees on the public. Thus the system came to exploit and oppress Ottoman subjects.

The cultural branch of the ruling class was what you know as the *'ulama*. These Muslim scholars administered justice, managed *waqfs* (Islamic endowments) to support schools and hospitals, educated most Muslim youths, and performed other religious tasks. Sometimes they also served as a buffer between the subject peoples and the other branches of the ruling class. What was new in the Ottoman system was that the higher *'ulama* became a recognized governmental branch headed by an official called the *shaykh al-Islam*, appointed by the sultan.

The subject class (*ra'iya*) included everyone in the Ottoman Empire who did not belong to the ruling class. Its function was to produce the wealth of the empire. Herders and peasants, miners and builders, artisans and merchants, were all *ra'iya*. Their cohesion was strengthened by trade guilds, Sufi orders, and athletic clubs (groups of men who did calisthenic exercises together). Their political and social organization was the *millet,* or religious community. The Greek Orthodox Church was headed by a patriarch who served at the pleasure of the sultan. He was responsible for all ecclesiastical, judicial, educational, and other benevolent activities involving Orthodox Christians in the Ottoman Empire, from Bosnia to Basra. The Armenian patriarch performed similar functions for Armenians (and, in theory, other Monophysite Christians) wherever in the empire they lived. Later on, the Ottoman sultan appointed a chief rabbi to exercise similar jurisdiction over Ottoman Jews. The Muslim *ra'iya,* who made up less than half the population of the Ottoman Empire at its height, were considered members of the Islamic *umma.* The cultural branch of the ruling class served as their religious organization.

Europeans living or doing business in the Ottoman Empire, being Catholic or (from the sixteenth century) Protestant, were not a part of this system. Nor did they have to be. The Ottoman government adopted a practice, dating back to the Ayyubids, of issuing "Capitulations" that gave autonomy to foreigners living in a Muslim territory. In effect, European nationals were freed from having to obey Ottoman laws or pay local taxes. The deal was reciprocal: Muslim merchants received the same concessions when living in foreign states. It may seem odd that the Ottoman sultans would accept a system that kept them from prosecuting criminals within their empire if they had the protection of a foreign power. Indeed, when the European states grew stronger and the Ottomans weaker in the eighteenth and nineteenth centuries, many Westerners did abuse the privileges they enjoyed under the Capitulations. Muslims conceive of the law as binding on people who espouse the religion from which it stems, not on those who happen to be living in a particular place. The Capitulations also attracted European traders and technicians to reside in the empire, while sparing the Ottomans the trouble of settling their quarrels.

Ottoman Decline: Signs and Causes

The accession of Selim II in 1566 and the defeat of the Ottoman navy at Lepanto in 1571 are commonly identified as the first signs of decline. Some of its root causes go back earlier, though, and the outward signs were not visible until later. Well into the seventeenth century, Ottoman armies went on attacking European Christians and Persian Shi'ites almost at will.

Why did the Ottoman Empire begin to decline in the sixteenth century? One reason was its insistence on having only one army, for the experience of previous Muslim states had taught that dividing their forces led to breaking up their realms. Besides, the army was, in principle, led by the sultan himself or by his authorized deputy, the grand vizier. Under these conditions, the army could fight only one campaign at a time, and never farther from Istanbul than it could march during the campaign season (April to October), because the *sipahis* went home in the autumn to supervise their *timars* and the janissaries wintered in Istanbul. Occasional border setbacks, however, showed that the janissaries were no longer keeping up their high training standards of yore or using the latest weapons and techniques of war. In fact, they used their dominance within the military branch of the ruling class to extract privileges for themselves from the sultans. They now lived outside their barracks, got married, enrolled their sons in the corps, rioted to gain more privileges, and took up trades more lucrative than soldiering. By the end of the sixteenth century, the Ottomans lagged behind the West in weaponry and fighting techniques. Officers and troops did not care to learn new ways that would require more work and might undermine their power. The Ottoman navy was still using oar-driven galleys when rival powers had converted to sailing ships and could blockade the Turks in the Mediterranean, the Black Sea, and even the Persian Gulf. When the Ottoman army besieged Vienna in 1683, the superior arms and tactics of the Europeans saved the Habsburg capital and repelled the Turks, despite their greater numbers. By 1699, when the Ottomans signed the Treaty of Karlowitz, ceding control of Hungary to the Habsburg Empire, they were clearly on the defensive. The Ottoman Empire had ceased to be the scourge of Christendom.

Economic conditions, too, deteriorated. Europe's discovery and exploitation of the New World and of sea routes around Africa to Asia's riches weakened the role of the Muslim countries as intermediaries controlling the main trade routes. Cheap Latin American silver flooded Europe and the Middle East, inflating prices generally in the late sixteenth century. Some states, such as England and the Netherlands, had ambitious merchants and manufacturers who were ready to expand their business activities; other countries, including Spain as well as the Ottoman Empire, suffered severe economic disruption because of the inflation. Many Ottoman merchants and artisans were ruined by foreign competitors sheltered by the Capitulations. Extortionate taxation by the *multezims* and rural overpopulation caused many peasants to leave their farms and flock to the cities. When they found no work, they became vagabonds and brigands, further impoverishing the economy.

Many Westerners think that Islam engenders fatalism and dampens individual initiative. If this were universally true of Muslims, it would be hard to account for their successes under the High Caliphate, the early Mamluks, or the Ottomans up to 1566. But the Ottoman *'ulama* became too conservative. To uphold Muslim law, the Shari'a, they guarded against innovations (*bida'*) deemed harmful to Islam. They carried this caution to absurd lengths when they forbade the importation of Arabic and Turkish printing presses into the empire until the eighteenth century, lest a printed Qur'an violate the principle that God's word was written and, in more practical terms, lest Muslim scribes be thrown out of work. The *'ulama* also wielded power as interpreters of the laws, *waqf* managers, and local administrators, and resisted any threat to their position.

The basic reason for the Ottoman loss of power, though, was the disappearance of the balance among the various forces within the ruling class. The early sultans had encouraged competition between the traditional leaders (the landowners and *'ulama*) and the men who had been recruited and trained under the *devshirme* system. When Suleyman the Magnificent appointed a succession of viziers all taken from the *devshirme,* he tilted the balance in favor of that group. By the end of his reign, neither the old aristocracy nor anyone else could check the *devshirme* bureaucrats' power. By the late seventeenth century, they were no longer effective defenders of the empire. The Ottoman government took no more levies of Christian boys, and it phased out the rigorous training schools for janissaries and administrators. Appointment and promotion came to be based on family ties and favoritism in place of merit.

PERSIA UNDER THE SAFAVIDS

Let us compare the Ottoman Empire with a contemporary Muslim state less known or feared in the West, Safavid Persia. The Safavid dynasty grew out of a militant Sufi order in Ardabil, a city in Azerbaijan. Initially Sunni, the Safavids became ardently Shi'ite after the Mongol conquest. The collapse of Timur's empire after his death in 1405 led in Persia to many small dynastic states, most of them ruled by quarrelsome nomadic tribes such as the Black Sheep and White Sheep Turcomans mentioned earlier. Led by Shaykh Junayd (d. 1460) and protected by the Black Sheep Turcomans, the Safavids began converting large numbers of Turks in Azerbaijan and Anatolia to Shi'ism. These Shi'ite Turks came to be called *kizilbash* (red heads) because of their distinctive headgear. When the Black Sheep Turcomans betrayed Junayd and drove him out of Ardabil, he allied himself with their White Sheep rivals, even though they were Sunni.

The Safavids grew in strength and numbers, even after Junayd's death, until they challenged their new patrons. The White Sheep Turcomans proceeded to kill or imprison almost the whole Safavid family. By 1494 no leader of the *kizilbash* revolutionaries remained free except a seven-year-old grandson of Junayd, Isma'il, who eluded his pursuers during a house-to-house search of Ardabil and escaped to another part of Persia. During the summer of 1500, young Isma'il and his *kizilbash* followers began a revolt in Anatolia against their oppressors. Turkish Shi'ite tribal warriors came in droves, and in early 1501 the White Sheep Turcomans were decisively defeated.

Rise of Safavid Power

The Safavid state began in Azerbaijan when Isma'il, now thirteen, entered Tabriz, proclaimed himself shah, and declared that Twelve-Imam Shi'ism would become the state's sole religion. This stance amounted to a declaration of war against the Ottoman Empire, which, as you know, was Sunni and not securely in control of the Shi'ite-leaning Anatolian Turks. In fact, just about every Muslim dynasty in 1501 was Sunni, which made the Safavids quite distinctive. It was hard for them even to find books expounding the fundamentals of Shi'ite Islam, and they had to import their *'ulama* from what is now southern Lebanon. Nevertheless, supported by his faithful *kizilbash* warriors, Isma'il aspired to conquer the whole Muslim world for Shi'ism. Even though most Turkish nomads and Persian peasants under Safavid rule were Sunni, Isma'il was determined to unite the country politically and religiously. Within a decade the Safavids, though Turkish by race, had taken control of all Persia. It took longer to win over the local inhabitants to Shi'ism, especially in the eastern provinces, but once converted the Persians came to view their sect as a badge of national identity. Likewise, they thought of the Safavids as a Persian dynasty. Indeed, the Safavid era was one of the most glorious for the history of Persian art and political power.

But the Safavids could not match the might of the Ottoman Empire. In the Battle of Chaldiran (1514), the janissaries with their firearms defeated the *kizilbash* fighting on horseback. The Ottomans entered Tabriz but left after a week, for the janissaries would spend the winter only in Istanbul; thus Persia was saved from Ottoman rule. However, the devotion of the *kizilbash* to Isma'il was shaken by the Chaldiran defeat, and the impetus to spread Safavid rule to other lands under Sunni Islam was lost. So unhinged was Isma'il that he spent the last decade of his short life hunting and drinking. Why did the Safavids lag behind the Ottomans in adopting gunpowder weapons? Like the Mamluks, the *kizilbash* knew about firearms but viewed them as unmanly and awkward to carry on horseback.

The Safavid Zenith

The Safavids' drive to conquer the rest of the Muslim world shifted to creating a good life for themselves. Tabriz, Qazvin, and finally Isfahan became their imperial capitals. Each in turn became a center for artists, artisans, and (most conspicuously) architects. Isfahan was a dazzling and beautiful city. Even now, its mosques, bazaars, *madrasas*, and palaces are eloquent testimony to the opulent lifestyle of the Safavid shahs. But Isfahan is better seen, even in a website, than read about in a textbook. As the Persians say, *Isfahan nisf-i-jehan,* or "Isfahan is half the world."

The reign of Shah 'Abbas I (1587–1629) was the zenith of Safavid wealth and power. Earlier shahs had been manipulated by the *kizilbash* tribal chiefs, but 'Abbas brought them to heel by executing anyone he suspected of plotting against him and by seizing much of their agricultural land. Like many earlier Muslim rulers, 'Abbas brought in slave boys (called *ghulams* in Persian) to be indoctrinated and trained as salaried warriors and administrators. In the Safavid case, they were mainly Armenian and Georgian Christians, not all of whom converted to Shi'ism. 'Abbas hoped to set up a balance between his aristocracy (the *kizilbash*) and this new corps of *ghulams*, each competing to serve the Safavid state. Like the Ottoman sultans, the Safavids divided their government into branches: the royal household, the state administration, the military corps, and the religious-judicial system. Each branch contained two or more dignitaries competing for the shah's favor, giving him more leverage. This governmental system was not unique to this era; you can trace Persia's hierarchy back to the early caliphs, the Sassanids, and even the Achaemenids.

The Europeans courted 'Abbas. He brought in English advisers to train his *ghulams* to use cannons and pistols, strengthening the Safavid army against the Ottomans. Because of the hostility between the Christian West and the Ottoman Empire, every European country that hoped to be a naval and commercial power sent envoys and merchants to Isfahan, seeking Abbas's help against Istanbul. Spain, Portugal, France, England, and the Netherlands had representatives at his court. Even Catholic missionaries entered Safavid Persia.

'Abbas was a great Muslim ruler, like Harun al-Rashid or Suleyman the Magnificent. His reign marked a turning point in the history of his dynasty (as had theirs). Significant changes were taking place within the Shi'ite religious establishment as the Sufis who had formerly led the rulers and people lost their power and influence to the *'ulama*. Among the *'ulama*, too, the earlier school, which had based its doctrinal and legal decisions heavily on the Qur'an and the prophetic *sunna*, gave way to one that accorded far-reaching authority to the *mujtahids* (legists) to interpret the Shari'a. This led in time to an ever more powerful Shi'ite *'ulama*, who would spearhead the 1979 Iranian revolution. Shah 'Abbas, troubled early in his reign by the *kizilbash*, suspected anyone else who had power. This category included his own sons, all of whom he had blinded or put to death, and thus his ultimate successor was a weak grandson. The later Safavids continued Abbas's policy of putting more and more land under state control at the expense of the *kizilbash* chieftains. They may have needed money to pay the *ghulams*, but the Safavids took so much land that they impoverished the countryside. Like the *devshirme* groups in the Ottoman Empire, the *ghulams* kept increasing their numbers and internal power—though not their strength as a fighting force—until they could manipulate and strangle the Safavid dynasty.

The Aftermath of the Safavids

By the eighteenth century, Safavid Persia was ripe for the plucking. In 1722, a group of tribal Afghans seized Isfahan, and the Safavids took to the hills of Azerbaijan, their first home. The Ottoman Empire, breaking a ninety-year truce, invaded the region. No match for the janissaries on the field, the Afghans skillfully negotiated a peace, ceding large areas of western Persia to the Ottoman Empire. This appalled the Persian people. Under the inspiring leadership of a warrior named Nadir Afshar, Persian and Turkish tribes united to drive out the Afghan usurpers and then, more gradually, the dissolute Safavids. The victorious leader crowned himself Nadir Shah in 1736. His reign was traditional Persia's "last hurrah." Within a decade he had driven back the Ottomans and had taken most of India. He might have become a world conqueror had he not tried to convert the Persians from Shi'ite to Sunni Islam, thus weakening his domestic support. Upon his assassination in 1747, Nadir Shah's empire collapsed. Successive minor dynasties led Persia into 160 years of political breakdown and social decay from which it would be slow to recover.

CONCLUSION

In this chapter, or perhaps earlier, you may have seen a pattern emerging that will help you chart the rise and fall of dynastic states. An area is divided among many states or nomadic tribes. In its midst a ruler emerges with a mission, usually related in some way to Islam, that inspires his followers to do great deeds and to mobilize others like them to overcome rival states. The conquerors cut taxes or improve public order, thus gaining peasant favor, increasing food production, and promoting economic well-being. As the empire expands, it builds up a large army and bureaucracy that it must then support, increasing the burden on its subjects. The ruling class and the 'ulama become rich, powerful, and conservative. The rulers' descendants prove to be less and less capable of ruling, and their subjects become more and more prone to rebel, until the empire falls and the cycle repeats itself.

All of the empires covered in this chapter—the Mamluks and the Il-Khanids, the Timurids and their Mughal descendants (slighted here, because India is not in the Middle East), the Ottomans and the Safavids—were Muslim military states in an era when possession and mastery of firearms became prevalent, then essential, for survival. But some of these states lasted a long time because they also set up institutions that harnessed their subjects' talents as soldiers and bureaucrats while keeping a power balance among their competing factions. When even this was lost, the Ottoman Empire and other Muslim states found another type of equilibrium that saved their independence—the European balance of power.

9

European Interests
and Imperialism

In the eighteenth century, the West achieved and then maintained military, political, and economic superiority over the Middle East. This had not been the usual power relationship before. It may not be so in the future. Neither the rulers nor the subjects of the Ottoman Empire—or any other Muslim country—wanted this subordination to the European Christians, whom they had formerly looked down upon. But what could they do? Whereas once the Muslims had controlled the commercial routes between Europe and Asia and had dictated the terms of trade to both, now Europeans were selling their manufactures to the Middle East in exchange for raw materials and agricultural products. Europeans living or trading in Muslim lands dwelled in special quarters of the big cities and did not have to pay local taxes or obey local laws and regulations. Whereas once the Mediterranean Sea and the Indian Ocean had been dominated by Muslim navies (or pirates), now European sailing ships—military and merchant— controlled the high seas. Earlier, the Ottoman sultan could choose the time and place to attack Christian Europe and then dictate peace terms; now his armies were at the mercy of Austria's Habsburgs and Russia's czars. To the Muslims, accustomed to victory on the battlefield, these changes seemed a cosmic error. Was God punishing Muslims who had lost their purity of intention and strayed from his plan for their community?

OTTOMAN WEAKNESS

We can trace the changing relationship between the Middle East and the West by a series of dated events: in 1683 the Ottomans failed to take

Vienna, the capital of the Habsburg Empire; in 1699 they signed a treaty at Karlowitz, ceding Hungary to the Habsburgs and the Aegean coast to the Venetians; in 1718 they gave up more of their European lands; in 1774 they lost the Crimea and allowed Russia to protect *their* Orthodox Christian subjects; and in 1798 Napoleon Bonaparte occupied Egypt and invaded Palestine. Meanwhile, other Muslim dynasties, such as the Mughals of India, the Safavids and their Persian successors, the Central Asian Uzbeks, and the Sharifian rulers of Morocco, were also fading before the mounting might of eighteenth-century Europe. But the Ottomans were closest to the new powers, viewed themselves as *ghazis* fighting for Islam, and stood to lose the most if the Europeans partitioned their lands.

Some Symptoms and Causes

Some popular histories may tell you that the Ottoman rulers cared nothing for their empire's fate. Enchanted by the charms of the harem, dulled by wine or hashish, hamstrung by janissary revolts or quarreling court factions, the sultans lost interest in maintaining their regime or defending their lands. By the same token, the venal viziers tried to keep the sultans out of their way, in order to profit from the corruption of the system. Bureaucrats bought their offices and sold subordinate posts to others, while everyone in power gouged the poor peasants and workers on taxes and fees (which were really assessed bribes). The janissaries, who should have been the backbone of the Ottoman army, became a hereditary caste of merchants and artisans who failed to keep in training or to learn how to use such modern weapons as muskets and bayonets. Worse, they overturned their soup pots and went on a rampage if anyone dared to call for reforms. As long as the state fed and paid them, they saw no need to reform or to let other troops take their place. The *'ulama* became *juhala* (ignoramuses) steeped in superstition and untouched by the growth of knowledge taking place in Europe. Landowners and merchants were robbed by brigands, against whom they had no protection. Peasants suffered from greedy landlords and tax farmers; many ran away to become brigands themselves. So turned the sad cycle. The easy answer is to blame incompetent or impotent sultans. As the Turks used to say, "The fish stinks from the head."

The Reforming Sultans and Viziers

There is, as usual in such popular accounts, a germ of truth in all this. The sultans were getting worse. No one denies the insanity of Sultan Ibrahim (r. 1640–1648), who allegedly had his 280 concubines tied up in sacks and drowned in the Bosporus. Mustafa II (r. 1695–1703) insisted on leading his troops into battle and was decisively beaten by Prince Eugen of Savoy, the military genius of the age, costing the Ottomans the province of Hungary and their military prestige. Alcohol abuse and harem intrigues afflicted the later sultans far more than they had the first ten. Some members of the ruling class milked the Ottoman system to enrich themselves while failing to perform their duties. But one of the secrets of Ottoman longevity was that the system went on producing capable sultans and viziers who saw the corruption and introduced reforms. Among the reforming sultans were Osman II (r. 1618–1622), whose attempt to form a new militia led to his being killed by revolting janissaries; Murad IV (r. 1623–1640), who executed 25,000 rebellious subjects in a single year; Mahmud I (r. 1730–1754), the first to bring in Europeans to teach new fighting techniques; and Selim III (r. 1789–1807), who introduced a comprehensive reform scheme, the *nizam-i-jedid*, which we will soon describe.

What about the reforming viziers? The Koprulu family produced six grand viziers who enhanced Ottoman security abroad and imposed political, social, and aesthetic changes at home (see Box 9.1). The first, Mehmet (d. 1661), was taken from his Albanian Christian parents by the *devshirme* and started his career working in the imperial kitchen. As grand vizier to Sultan Mehmet IV (r. 1648–1687), he defeated the Venetians and quashed revolts in Transylvania and Anatolia, executing thousands in the process. His son, Ahmet, strengthened the vizierate, checked the Habsburgs, and took Crete as well as parts of Poland. His brother led the Ottoman troops to the gates of Vienna in 1683 but failed to capture the city. A nephew of Mehmet Koprulu, serving Mustafa II, reduced taxes on consumer goods, set up factories, and hoped to restore farm production to its earlier level.

Another vizier was Damad Ibrahim, best known for diverting Sultan Ahmed III (r. 1703–1730) into building pleasure palaces and tulip gardens. But he also brought in European artists, commissioned Turkish translations of Western scientific works, and introduced the first Ottoman printing press. Even in this dark age of Ottoman history, some sultans and viziers tried to bring in some light. More westernizing reformers would arise in the nineteenth century; you will read about them later. However, reforms alone could not save the Ottoman Empire.

THE EUROPEAN POWERS AND THE EASTERN QUESTION

We think the key to the Ottomans' predicament—but also, paradoxically, their salvation—lay in Europe. Without the Renaissance, the Reformation,

Box 9.1   The Koprulu Family of Viziers

For most of its existence, Ottoman rule mixed a hereditary succession with the promotion of administrators and military officers on the basis of merit. The empire did have a long run of luck with its hereditary sultanate, but that could not last forever. After the reign of Suleyman I, the Ottomans' luck turned bad. Weak and incompetent rulers inherited power. This was not the only problem facing the empire, but without strong and capable leaders, other problems—military, economic, and governmental—could not be solved. Problems in the sultanate affected the rest of society.

The Ottoman decline lasted more than three hundred years, allowing time for people within the ruling class to try repeatedly to solve problems. These efforts were usually undertaken by strong viziers who would appear now and then to reverse the empire's fortunes. The most famous of these men came from one family of Albanian heritage, the Koprulus.

There is a pattern in the behavior of the Koprulu viziers. Each was given dictatorial or near-dictatorial powers by sultans or their regents (often their mothers) who could not or would not rule directly. Each vizier ruled brutally when needed to root out corruption, rebellion, or incompetence. Most of them used the stick far more often than the carrot to achieve their ends. The Koprulus, each one learning from his predecessor in an informal apprenticeship, were very successful. A key fact, though, is that none of their reforms endured. This ultimate failure had many reasons, but one of them lies in the very definition of Ottoman success.

Among other things, the people expected the Ottoman government to expand its borders. They wanted a strong government not only to maintain stability and tradition, or to defend the faith, but also to enlarge the Dar al-Islam (land of Islam). Thus, ending corruption, suppressing rebellion, dismissing the incompetent, and instituting discipline—all of which the Koprulus did well—were not enough. They needed to wage war. Almost all of the Koprulus, having stabilized the empire, quickly directed its renewed energies toward waging war. And, most of the time, the newly reformed institutions proved too fragile to withstand eventual defeat by a powerful Western foe. Finally, the fifth Koprulu vizier, Huseyin (r. 1697–1702), recognized the futility of these efforts and negotiated the Treaty of Karlowitz (1699), in which the sultan ceded Hungary to the Austrians, marking the beginning of the end, militarily and diplomatically, for the Ottoman Empire.

Custom and tradition are hard to alter. They usually change only over long periods or under extreme circumstances. The first four Koprulus used the fruits of their labors to promote the age-old custom of expansive war. Only when the empire's state of exhaustion became obvious did the fifth Koprulu change this pattern of behavior. By then he had very little choice.

the age of exploration and discovery, the expansion of trade, the Enlightenment, and the Industrial Revolution, the West would not have surpassed the Muslim world in the eighteenth century. The Ottoman Empire had not experienced all the changes these movements brought to Western culture. But neither had such traditional Ottoman foes as Venice, Poland, and Spain; by 1750 they no longer menaced Ottoman security. Habsburg Austria still played its customary role as Christendom's chief defender against Islam. But Austria's leadership was paling before a new star rising in the north, czarist Russia. Many Westerners believed that Russia would have taken over all Ottoman lands but for the firm opposition of the other European states. To test this belief, let us look at the Middle East policies of the most important European countries of the nineteenth-century—the Great Powers: Russia, Austria, Britain, and France.

Czarist Russia

Unlike the other Great Powers involved in the Ottoman Empire, Russia had experienced Muslim rule under the Mongol Golden Horde. Russia had emerged in the fifteenth century as a small but independent state, centered on Moscow and close to the sources of central Eurasia's main rivers and portage routes. Some historians argue that the expansionist policy of Muscovite rulers was made possible by their control of these rivers and dictated by their ceaseless quest for outlets to the high seas. Rivers flowing into the Baltic Sea or the Arctic Ocean are apt to be icebound for half the year; therefore, Russia needed the Black Sea as a warm-water outlet for trade. In the seventeenth century this body of water was almost completely surrounded by Ottoman lands. As a result, Peter the Great and his successors fought several wars against the empire in the eighteenth century to ensure Russian access to the Black Sea. By the middle of the nineteenth century, the Russians could regard the Black Sea as mainly theirs, but their ships still had to pass through the Ottoman-ruled Bosporus and Dardanelles (the Straits) to reach the Aegean and hence the Mediterranean. So Russia sought control of the Straits, or at least assurances that the Ottomans would not bar passage to its warships and merchant vessels. Russia also wanted to rule the Straits to better defend its Black Sea ports against naval attacks from invaders.

Some Russians had an additional motive to seize the Straits: they wanted to rule that great city on the Bosporus—Istanbul. You know that, up to the Ottoman conquest, it had been Constantinople, capital of the Byzantine Empire, hence the "Second Rome," and chief jewel of the Greek

Orthodox Church. When Constantinople fell, Russia became the leading Greek Orthodox country and declared Moscow the "Third Rome." A Muscovite prince married the niece of the last Byzantine emperor. Their descendants, Russia's czars, sometimes sought to gain control of Constantinople (which they called Czargrad) and restore the power and prestige of Greek Orthodoxy to the level of Roman Catholicism. Besides, many Orthodox Christians lived under Ottoman rule, mainly in the Balkans. Austria captured some of them in the early eighteenth century, but the Habsburgs, being Catholic, were unsympathetic. Mother Russia would be a better protector for the Serbs, Bulgars, Albanians, Romanians, and Greeks seeking freedom from Muslim rule, for they were nearly all Orthodox. So, when Catherine the Great defeated the Ottomans in 1769–1774 and thus could set the terms of the peace treaty, she secured Ottoman recognition of Russia's right to intervene diplomatically on behalf of Orthodox Christians living within the Ottoman Empire. The wording of this Treaty of Kuchuk-Kainarji is ambiguous, but Russians claimed later that it set a precedent for relations between Russia and Turkey (as the Ottoman Empire came to be called by the Europeans).

Later on, the Russians maintained that they had something else in common with many of the sultan's Balkan subjects—namely, that they were Slavs. The term *Slav* denotes membership in a language group. Russian and Ukrainian are Slavic languages; so, too, are Bulgarian, Polish, Serbian, and Croatian. During the nineteenth century, some Balkan peoples espoused a kind of nationalism called pan-Slavism that aimed to unite within a single state all peoples speaking Slavic languages. Russia, the largest Slavic country, claimed to be its leader. Ottoman Turkey feared the divisive effect of pan-Slavism as much as it had Russia's earlier sponsorship of the Orthodox Christians. But pan-Slavism threatened such European neighbors as Prussia and Austria with their many Polish subjects; thus Russia had to mute its pan-Slavism when it wanted to placate those powers. Indeed, many Russian officials preferred upholding Ottoman integrity and friendly ties with the other European powers over unity with Orthodox Christians or their Slavic cousins.

In the nineteenth century, Russia's drive toward the sea, leadership of the Orthodox Christians, and encouragement of pan-Slavism combined at times to produce an aggressive Middle East policy. Russian troops entered the Balkans during the 1806–1812 conflict, the Greek war for independence in the 1820s, the 1848 Romanian uprising, the 1853–1856 Crimean War, and the 1877–1878 Russo-Turkish War. In the last of these struggles, Russian troops came within 10 miles (15 kilometers) of Istanbul and dictated the peace terms at San Stefano in February 1878. Because all the other Great Powers opposed Russia's military and political gains from that war, the sultan regained some of the Balkan lands in the comprehensive Treaty of Berlin, signed later that same year. Russian encouragement of pan-Slavism even helped cause the Balkan Wars of 1912–1913 and the outbreak of World War I in 1914. Although you (like us) may feel overwhelmed by all the twists and turns of the "Eastern Question" from 1774 to 1917, you may assume that the Ottomans viewed Russia as their main enemy for most (but not all) of that time.

The Eastern Question centered on whether Russia would gobble up Turkey's European possessions, especially the Straits, or be stopped from doing so by the other Great Powers. Although other countries at times accepted or even welcomed Russia's growing might (for example, when Russian forces helped defeat Napoleon in 1812–1814, or Hitler in 1942–1945, to jump ahead a bit), they usually tried to prevent a Russian capture of the Balkans and the Straits, lest it endanger the European balance of power.

Now, here is a concept you may want us to explain. No one could decree that each state would have as much power as all the others. After all, Britain had industrialized first, built up the strongest navy, and acquired a large overseas empire. France derived more of its wealth from farming than manufacturing, but it, too, had a big empire and a very strategic location. Austria and Russia each controlled vast areas with large and diverse populations, necessitating big standing armies. Prussia (which became Germany only in 1871) had a well-armed and disciplined army. The balance of power did not, therefore, ensure that each state had equal power; it did mean that no state or coalition could become strong enough to dominate all the other European countries. Failure to maintain that equilibrium had enabled Louis XIV and later Napoleon to impose French power over the rest of the continent, hardly an experience that the British or the Germans (or any other country) cared to relive. By the same logic, many people in the nineteenth century feared that if Russia ruled the Balkans and controlled the Straits, all Europe would be at the mercy of the czars. The West felt a similar dread of Soviet influence over Turkey (and over Central Asia and Afghanistan) during the Cold War of 1945–1991. Even now, the realist theory of international relations stresses the need to keep a power balance among the world's countries.

Remember also that Russia was, like the United States, a continental power and an expanding one, except that the direction of its growth was eastward and southward. The Ottomans saw how the Islamized descendants of the Mongols, Tatars, and Turks who had occupied Central Asia fell under Russian control in the nineteenth century. While the West feared that Russian rule in the Balkans would upset the European balance of power, the czars were also building an Asian empire that menaced Persia, Afghanistan, and British India.

Habsburg Austria

Russia's rivals had positive reasons to get involved in Ottoman Turkey. The Habsburg Empire, for instance, bordered directly on Ottoman lands in southeastern Europe from the fifteenth to the nineteenth centuries. Having whetted its appetite by taking Hungary in 1699, Austria hoped to move down the Danube River toward the Black Sea. It also wanted to control lands south of the Danube, especially Croatia, Bosnia, and Serbia. The Habsburg emperors may have pursued commercial interests, but they also saw themselves as carrying on the old crusading traditions against the Muslim Turks. During the nineteenth century, as each of the Balkan states wrested its independence from the Ottoman Empire, Austria would step forward as its patron, protector, and trading partner. Some seemingly traded one master for another. Bosnia and Herzegovina, two regions culturally and geographically close to Serbia (but with large Muslim populations), were placed under Habsburg military occupation as part of the 1878 Berlin treaty. Thirty years later, with no prior consent from Ottoman Turkey (and to Russia's dismay), Austria annexed Bosnia and Herzegovina. But their acceptance of Habsburg rule was undermined by propaganda from nearby Serbia, leading to the 1914 assassination at Sarajevo of the heir to Austria's throne. You may know that this event ignited World War I. Some historians see Austria's Balkan policy as a cause of that great conflict once facetiously named "the War of the Turkish Succession."

Britain and the Middle East

Britain was a naval and imperial power in India. Safe sea transport to India became a primary British concern once it had consolidated its Asian empire by defeating France in the Seven Years' War (French and Indian War) of 1756–1763. As long as most maritime transport between Europe and Asia went around South Africa, Britain hardly worried about the Ottoman Empire and at times even backed Russian expansionism in the Balkans. It did not, however, favor French control of Egypt and Syria, as we shall soon see. From about 1820, the growth of steamship transport and the improvement of overland communications made it faster and safer to transship people and goods across Egypt or the Fertile Crescent, both nominally Ottoman lands, instead of taking the long route around Africa.

Britain decided in the 1830s that the Ottoman Empire would be the best guardian of its routes to India and soon committed itself firmly to the empire's defense. It also had a commercial motive, for, as you will learn in the next chapter, Britain and the Ottoman Empire signed a treaty lowering their import duties on each other's goods. By 1850 the empire had become a leading buyer of British manufactures and a major supplier of foodstuffs and raw materials to Britain. The British also came to share Austria's suspicions of Russia's Balkan aims.

The largest European conflict between Napoleon's defeat and the outbreak of World War I was the Crimean War. Although many people think the war was sparked by a fight between Catholic and Orthodox priests in Jerusalem, the real cause was the fear of most European countries that Russia's growing strength in the Balkans in 1853 would threaten the balance of power in Europe. By leading the anti-Russian coalition, Britain proved that it would go to great trouble and expense to defend Turkey against Russian expansionism and thus to preserve the balance of power. On the same logic, Britain sent part of its fleet into the Dardanelles in 1878 as a warning, after Russia had occupied most of the Balkan lands. In Chapter 10 you will see how Britain's commitment extended to pressing westernizing reforms on the Ottoman rulers at these critical times. In a further attempt to secure its routes to India, Britain also took Aden in 1839, Cyprus in 1878, and Egypt in 1882 and made treaties with Arab rulers along the Gulf from Oman to Kuwait. Several times Britain sent troops to Afghanistan or Persia to deter the advancing Russians, whose hope of reaching the Gulf nearly equaled their drive to the Straits. Britain feared that the czars' land hunger might extend to the Himalayas, India, and even China. These nineteenth-century events foreshadowed Britain's attempt to dominate the Middle East after World War I.

France: Protector and Civilizer

The Ottoman Turks' best friend was usually France. Its strategic location, with ports on both the Atlantic and the Mediterranean, made France a contender for mastery in Europe. Until the nineteenth century its greatest Mediterranean rival was the Habsburg Empire, making France the ally of the Ottomans. France claimed to have the first Capitulations, and French merchants and investors usually led the Europeans doing business in the Ottoman Empire. When it needed military or naval experts, engineers, or teachers, the Ottoman government usually sought French ones. Young Ottomans were more apt to choose France than any other foreign country for higher education or advanced vocational training.

Religion, too, strengthened the French connection. When Russia tried to protect Orthodox Christians under Ottoman rule, France advanced similar claims on behalf of the Catholics. Because they were less numerous, the Turks minded them less. One fateful result was the special bond between France and Syria. And one key to this tie was a Christian sect, the Maronites, who predominated in what is now northern Lebanon. In the seventh century, the Maronites had stood for a position between Orthodox and Monophysite Christianity, giving them a unique identity. They later entered into communion with Rome during the Crusades but retained their traditional practices (e.g., having prayers in Syriac and married priests). From the seventeenth century, they had access to Western learning through a papal seminary for Maronites in Rome. When France emerged as the leading Catholic power, the Maronites welcomed French missionaries and merchants to Syria, where they built up a network of schools, churches, factories, and trading posts. France's primacy in Syria also rested on ties with other Christians. Some Christians were leaving their native churches, usually Orthodox but some Jacobite (Monophysite) and Nestorian, and entering into communion with Rome as Uniates. These Catholic converts, like the Maronites, studied in the French schools and traded with French merchants. Some adopted other aspects of French culture and viewed France as their patron and protector. When fighting erupted in 1860 between Syria's Muslims and Christians, Paris intervened to rescue the latter.

Strategically speaking, Egypt mattered more to France than Syria did. This concern was not widely felt in the eighteenth century, when Egypt's economy and society reached a low point, owing to Ottoman neglect and Mamluk misrule, for the Mamluks, as will be explained later, retained their power in Egypt. But Napoleon Bonaparte, who called Egypt the world's most important country, occupied it in 1798. For three years Britain and Turkey engaged in military and diplomatic maneuvers to get the French troops out of Egypt. Following France's departure, a military adventurer named Mehmet 'Ali (the Arabs call him Muhammad 'Ali) seized power in Cairo. Using French advisers, he started an ambitious reform program, built up a strong army and navy, and took Syria from the Ottomans in 1831. France abetted and applauded Mehmet 'Ali's gains. Not so the other Great Powers, who saw these gains as a threat to the European balance of power and viewed Mehmet 'Ali as a French agent. It took British naval intervention to get his troops out of Syria in 1840, but Mehmet 'Ali stayed in power and founded a dynasty that would rule Egypt until 1952.

France played the lead role in yet another Egyptian drama. Mehmet 'Ali's son, Sa'id, granted a concession in 1854 to a French entrepreneur to build a ship canal across the Isthmus of Suez. The British tried to block the project, fearing that it would put the French in control of a major route to India. But once the Suez Canal was opened in 1869, Britain became its main user. Soon it bought the Egyptian government's shares in the controlling company, then it sent troops into Egypt (France was supposed to send troops, too, but failed to act at the critical moment) to quell a nationalist uprising in 1882. France's economic and cultural ties with Egypt remained strong, but by the end of the nineteenth century, despite French opposition, Britain dominated the Nile Valley. France did, however, take control of most of the rest of North Africa. After World War I it would seek further compensation in Syria and Lebanon.

CONCLUSION

This brings to a close our rapid survey of Middle Eastern interests and policies of the major European powers. We went beyond the eighteenth century, hoping to give you a context for events occurring later on. You may ask why we focused on Russia, Austria, England, and France, to the exclusion of all other countries. Admittedly, we have oversimplified the scenario somewhat. The complete cast of characters in the Eastern Question would include Swiss archaeologists, Belgian bankers, German military advisers, American Protestant and Italian Catholic missionaries, Greek grocers, and Armenian photographers. By 1900 the German, Italian, and US governments had also acquired bit parts in the political drama. Persia was becoming more important as well, especially as an object of Anglo-Russian commercial and military rivalry.

This chapter also treats the Middle East not as an area acting but as one acted upon. This, too, is a distortion. Even if it did lose lands in the Balkans and North Africa, the Ottoman Empire (increasingly called Turkey by the Europeans) remained independent throughout this time. Even though Western ambassadors and advisers tended to direct sultans and viziers too much, the scope of their actions was limited by Muslim conservatism and their need to block other countries from intervening. Likewise, Persia staved off the Russians and the British until both agreed to split the country into zones of influence in 1907. Most Middle Eastern peoples went on living their lives as if Europe were on another planet. The changes affecting them were the westernizing reform policies of their own rulers. It is to these reforms that we must now turn.

10

⊠

Westernizing Reform in the Nineteenth Century

Europe's power rose so dramatically between the sixteenth and nineteenth centuries that every other part of the world had to adapt or go under. Some human groups, such as the Fuegian Indians at the southern tip of South America and the natives of Tasmania, were totally wiped out by white people's diseases, alcohol, or deportation. Others, such as the North American Indians and the Australian aborigines, lost nearly all their lands and liberties to the English colonists. Some peoples mixed with the European settlers, creating a hybrid culture, as in Brazil. Many Africans were uprooted, enslaved, and shipped to strange and distant lands. Such ancient countries as India, Java, and Vietnam were absorbed into European empires. Japan kept its independence but copied Western ways on a large scale. Several other Asian states tried to stay independent by grafting onto their traditional societies those Western customs and institutions that they believed to be sources of power. China, Thailand, Persia, and the Ottoman Empire followed this path, which seemed moderate, logical, and appropriate for countries with deeply ingrained norms and values. Islam, for instance, was both a faith and a way of life. Muslim countries wanted to strengthen their armies and navies, their governments and economies, but not to cast off a lifestyle they had built up and followed for centuries. Reformers had to choose with care the systems they borrowed from Europe. They soon learned that a westernizing program in, say, defense could not be blocked off from the rest of society. Military, political, and economic reforms sparked reactions in seemingly remote areas, often catching the reformers off guard.

What is reform? In a Western country, reformers often come from outside the power elite, challenge the system, and, if successful, change it. They may resort to violent revolution, but most successful reforms are achieved through the ballot box, the legislature, or the forum of public opinion. They may well reflect social and economic changes that have already occurred. When we speak of the Reform Bills in English history, we mean the acts of Parliament that extended voting rights to more people in the nineteenth century. A reform party in US politics usually is an out-group fighting against corrupt or unjust practices in a city, state, or national government.

You might suppose that reformers come from below. In a few cases they have, even in the Middle East. You learned earlier about the Kharijite and Hashimite rebels against the Umayyad caliphate. In the seventeenth and eighteenth centuries, farmers rebelled in Anatolia and the Balkans, but they hoped to break away from, not reform, the Ottoman government. A better example would be the Wahhabis, a puritanical Muslim group growing out of the Hanbali rite of Sunni Islam, that seized power in central Arabia during the eighteenth century. Led by a family named Sa'ud (hence the modern state named Sa'udi Arabia), these Wahhabis wanted to conquer the Arabian Peninsula (if not more) and to purify Islam from practices they deemed corrupt. They built up a fairly strong state in the late eighteenth century, then they were checked by the Ottomans and Mehmet 'Ali in the nineteenth but made a strong comeback early in the twentieth century (see Chapter 13). Many of their ideas have won acceptance from Muslim thinkers outside Sa'udi Arabia. Call them reformers if you wish. Many other movements within Islam in the past two centuries have aimed to restore Islamic civilization's grandeur or to bring Muslim institutions into harmony with modernity. They have come not from below but from the intellectual elite. At times they have been started by the rulers themselves.

In Middle East history, you should assume that significant and effective reforms usually come from above. They are instituted by the rulers or by their viziers, generals, or local governors. Seldom are they demanded by the poor or do this class much good once put into effect. In particular, we will look at those governmentally imposed reforms that imitated the ways of the West, often at the expense of Islam as the people understood it. Westernization was—and still is—often confused with modernization. This chapter will focus on reform in Egypt, the rest of the Ottoman Empire, and Persia.

EGYPT'S TRANSFORMATION

If Rip Van Winkle had nodded off in Cairo around 1795 and roused seventy-five years later, he would have been amazed—if not bewildered—by the changes that occurred during his nap. Egypt made the fastest and most dramatic transformation of any Middle Eastern country in the nineteenth century. Since 1517 the country had been ruled by the Ottoman Empire, but an early rebellion had taught Istanbul to leave local control to the Mamluks, the aristocracy of ex-slave soldiers who had ruled Egypt since 1250. During Ottoman times, the Mamluks continued to import Circassian boy slaves and to train them as soldiers and administrators. It had been a good system once, but by the eighteenth century the Mamluks had become rapacious tax farmers and cruel governors. Caught up in factional struggles, they failed to provide the irrigation works and security needed by the peasants, whose well-being and population declined. Starved for revenue, the *madrasas*, including the ancient university of al-Azhar, declined in intellectual caliber. Most *'ulama* became incompetent, lazy, and corrupt. Their Christian and Jewish counterparts were no better. The Ottoman governors could do nothing. Soldiers and peasants revolted, sometimes successfully, but they could not reform the system either. Egypt was becoming run-down. It took two extraordinary foreigners to get the country moving again: Napoleon Bonaparte and Mehmet 'Ali.

Napoleon's Occupation

Napoleon was sent by France's revolutionary government in 1798 to conquer Egypt and, if possible, Syria and Iraq. That regime wanted to get the ambitious young general out of Paris and may have hoped to retake India, where France had lost its colonies to the British in 1763. Napoleon aspired to emulate the conquests of Alexander the Great. To do this, he would have had to lead his army from Egypt via the Fertile Crescent to Persia, Afghanistan, and what is now Pakistan. It was a fantasy never realized, but Napoleon did defeat the Mamluks easily and occupied Cairo. Seeking to win over the Egyptians, he posted manifestos, like this excerpt:

> Peoples of Egypt, you will be told that I have come to destroy your religion. This is an obvious lie; do not believe it! Tell the slanderers that I have come to you to restore your rights from the hands of the oppressors and that I, more than the Mamluks, serve God . . . and revere His Prophet Muhammad and the glorious Qur'an. . . . Formerly in the land of Egypt there were great cities, wide canals, and a prosperous trade. What has ruined all this, if not the greed and tyranny of the Mamluks? . . . Tell your nation that the French are also faithful Muslims. The truth is that they invaded Rome and have destroyed the throne of the Pope, who always incited the Christians to make war on the Muslims. . . . Furthermore,

the French have at all times declared themselves to be the most sincere friends of the Ottoman sultan and the enemy of his enemies. The Mamluks, on the contrary, have always refused to obey him. . . . Blessing upon blessing to the Egyptians who side with us. They shall prosper in fortune and rank. Happy, too, are those who stay in their dwellings, not siding with either of the parties now at war; when they know us better, they will hasten to join us. . . . But woe upon woe to those who side with the Mamluks and help them to make war on us. They will find no escape, and their memory shall be wiped out.

The Egyptians had little love for the Mamluks, but they soon loved the French even less. Napoleon and his men were not Muslims, nor did they restore Ottoman sovereignty. France's occupation of Egypt was harsh, heavy handed, and hated. Taxes and government fees, high but sporadic under the Mamluks, were now collected regularly from everyone, making them seem more oppressive. Ignorant of local mores and customs, the French troops shocked pious Muslims by their lewd conduct, public drinking, and blasphemous acts, which included firing on al-Azhar to quell a local uprising. When the British navy sank most of Napoleon's ships at Abu-Kir, then when the French army invaded Palestine but failed to take Acre from the Turks, and when Napoleon himself slipped through the British blockade to return to France, the Egyptians became even more hostile. Yet the French occupation lasted until 1801. The Egyptian people were sullen but unarmed. Their Mamluk ex-rulers were divided and weakened. It took a joint Anglo-Ottoman landing at Alexandria, followed by a general European treaty, to get the French forces out of Egypt. The British navy left soon afterward.

Popular histories stress the French occupation because Napoleon was so colorful and because France would later form strong cultural ties with Egypt. More important, its expeditionary force included 167 scholars, scientists, and artists, who went around Cairo and the countryside studying almost every aspect of Egypt. The published results of their studies give us a surprisingly thorough and fairly accurate description of the country's condition and culture. The French brought in a printing press and set up a research institute, which attracted the notice of a few inquisitive *'ulama*. Few historians now think, as they once did, that these events caused the intellectual awakening of Egypt. It had not been asleep, but Napoleon's invasion did (1) spark ongoing Anglo-French competition for Egypt; (2) destroy any notions Ottoman Muslims still cherished about their superiority over Europe; and (3) weaken the Mamluks, creating a leadership vacuum once the last British troops left in 1802.

Mehmet 'Ali and His Reforms

The man who eventually filled that vacuum was a soldier of fortune named Mehmet 'Ali. He had come to Egypt as second in command of the Albanian regiment in the Ottoman expeditionary force that tried, unsuccessfully in 1799 but victoriously two years later, to dislodge the French. Mehmet 'Ali underscored his personal ambitions by remarking, "I was born in the same year as Napoleon in the land of Alexander." He patterned his career after both men: by 1805 he had emerged from the pack of contenders for power and won recognition from a group of *'ulama* and local notables. Later that year he incited a revolt against the Ottoman governor and secured the sultan's consent to take his place. Like many of the Ottoman reformers, Mehmet 'Ali realized that losses on the battlefield showed the glaring weakness of the existing army and the government behind it. Unlike the others, though, he saw that adopting European uniforms, arms, and tactics, or even importing foreign instructors and technicians, could not solve their military problems. Wholehearted and far-reaching reforms were a must. When those Western ways angered Muslims, Mehmet 'Ali became ruthless and dictatorial.

The Nile Valley made Egypt a proverbially easy land to govern, once all rival power centers were wiped out. The Mamluks posed the major obstacle; in 1811 Mehmet 'Ali had them all massacred. Because the *'ulama* enjoyed great power and prestige, he exploited their internecine rivalries, then weakened them by seizing most of the land they had managed as *waqfs*. He also put most privately owned land under state control, thereby wiping out the tax farmers and the rural aristocracy. His government thus gained a monopoly over Egypt's most valuable resource, its agricultural land. The state now decided which crops the peasants might grow; supplied them with seeds, tools, and fertilizer; purchased all their crops; and sold them at a profit. To make it easier to move goods from one part of the country to another, Mehmet 'Ali drafted farmers to build roads and dig barge canals. New irrigation works enabled them to raise three crops a year in fields that used to produce just one. Egypt became the first Middle Eastern country to make the shift from subsistence agriculture (in which farmers raised the crops they consumed, plus what they had to pay in rent and taxes) to cash-crop farming (in which they raised crops to sell for money). Tobacco, sugar, indigo, and cotton became major Egyptian crops. Using the revenues they produced, Mehmet 'Ali financed his schemes for industrial and military development.

Mehmet 'Ali was the first non-Western ruler to grasp the significance of the Industrial Revolution. He realized that a modernized army would need textile factories to make its tents and uniforms, dockyards to build its ships, and munitions plants to turn out guns and bayonets. French advisers helped the Egyptian government build and equip them. Hundreds of Turkish- and Arabic-speaking Egyptians were sent to Europe for technical and military training. Western instructors were imported to found schools in Egypt for medicine, engineering, and military training. Finally, a new Arabic press was set up to print translated textbooks and a government journal.

Mehmet 'Ali's Military Empire

Mehmet 'Ali was also the first ruler since the Ptolemies to use Egyptian farmers as soldiers. They hated military service. Few of the conscripts ever saw their homes again. Despite their ingenious attempts at draft dodging, they got dragged into the army. Turkish, Circassian, and European officers whipped this new Egyptian army into a potent fighting force that served Mehmet 'Ali (at the Ottoman sultan's request) against the Wahhabis, who had occupied Mecca and Medina. He also put together an Egyptian navy, with which he helped the Ottomans against the Greeks, who were fighting for their independence. After the Great Powers stepped in to help the Greeks defeat the Ottoman Turks, however, Mehmet 'Ali turned against the sultan himself. He sent his son Ibrahim to lead an expeditionary force that marched into Palestine and Syria. By the end of 1832 he ruled most of the Fertile Crescent and the Hijaz. Ibrahim tried to impose his father's westernizing reforms in Syria, but the Syrians proved less docile than the Egyptians. Revolts broke out in the mountains as Syrian peasants resisted agricultural controls and the confiscation of their firearms. Taking advantage of Ibrahim's troubles, the Ottoman government tried to regain some of his land. Mehmet 'Ali and Ibrahim struck back, penetrating Anatolia. By 1839 it looked as if Egypt was poised to take over the whole Ottoman Empire as the whole imperial fleet deserted to Alexandria and a sixteen-year-old prince was girded with the sword of Osman. Only intervention by the Great Powers (mainly Britain) made Mehmet 'Ali withdraw from Syria and settle for autonomy in Egypt.

Mehmet 'Ali cared little for the Egyptians. After his diplomatic defeat, he abandoned his economic and military reforms. Most of the schools and nearly all the state-run factories were closed. The state monopolies and other controls on agriculture lapsed. Most of the lands were parceled out to his friends and relatives. Nevertheless, upon his death Mehmet 'Ali could bequeath to his children and grandchildren a nearly independent Egypt with memories of military might. Also, his empire had been built on agricultural and industrial development, using no money borrowed from Western governments, banks, or investors. Few of his heirs matched this boast.

WESTERNIZATION OF THE OTTOMAN EMPIRE

Less impressive results came from efforts by Mehmet 'Ali's contemporaries to reform the Ottoman Empire. The first was Sultan Selim III (r. 1789–1807), a transitional figure among the westernizing reformers. The Ottoman government's reform efforts can be divided into three phases. In the first, such reformers as the Koprulu viziers tried to restore the administrative and military system to what it had been when the empire was at its height. When this effort failed, some eighteenth-century sultans and viziers adopted a selective westernizing policy, chiefly in the army and navy, but failed to check Russia's advance into the Balkans or Napoleon's occupation of Egypt. In the third phase of Ottoman reform, mainly in the nineteenth century, the state tried to westernize many imperial institutions in an effort (only partly successful) to halt the secession or annexation of its territories.

The Nizam-i-Jedid

Selim III feared European designs on his country; he was also aware of its internal problems, with some provinces in open revolt, a war with Austria and Russia in progress, and a serious shortfall in tax revenues. In response, he planned a full-scale housecleaning, a *nizam-i-jedid* (new order) that would reform the whole Ottoman government. But with the military threat so imminent, Selim concentrated on creating the westernized elite army, to which that name is usually applied. The *nizam* soldiers, some recruited from Istanbul street gangs, had to be trained secretly. Selim knew that the janissaries—and their friends—would object once they found out. He was right. The janissaries feared that an effective fighting force, trained by European instructors and using modern arms, would unmask them as parasites of the state. They would not give up their privileges for military reform, however necessary. They revolted, killed the new troops, locked up Selim, and started a bloody civil war. Selim could have built his army and stopped the Russians if he had implemented the comprehensive reform scheme he had originally proposed. But his plan was bolder than he. Selim therefore seems to stand between the phase of selective westernization and the nineteenth-century effort to reshape the entire Ottoman Empire along European lines.

Mahmud II

An ill-fated attempt by Selim's successor to revive the *nizam* sent the janissaries on such a rampage that they killed all male members of the Ottoman family but one, a cousin of Selim named Mahmud II (r. 1808–1839). Understandably, Mahmud mounted his throne with fear and trembling. Not only could the janissaries stir up the city mobs, trade guilds, and *madrasa* students to defend their privileges, but the whole empire was in danger. Some of the North African and Balkan provinces had become virtually independent under local warlords. A Serbian nationalist uprising threatened to influence other subject peoples. Local landowners in parts of Anatolia were taking the government into their own hands. Garrisons in such Arab cities as Aleppo and Mosul were held by dissident mamluk or janissary factions. Worse yet, Russia had again gone to war against the empire and had invaded its Danubian principalities (now called Romania), while Napoleon's forces were battling the British navy for control of the eastern Mediterranean. The Ottoman outlook was bleak, but Mahmud surprised everyone. Like his late cousin, he wanted to reform and strengthen the Ottoman state. But Mahmud also saw that (1) westernizing reforms must include every aspect of Ottoman government and society, not just the military; (2) reformed institutions would work only if the ones they replaced were destroyed; and (3) any reform program must be planned in advance and accepted by the country's leaders.

At first Mahmud kept a low profile, quietly cultivated groups that favored centralization of Ottoman power, and slowly built up a loyal and well-trained palace guard, to be used when it was strong enough against the janissaries and their backers. Only in 1826 did Mahmud strike. In a move reminiscent of Mehmet 'Ali's fifteen years earlier, he ordered a general attack on the janissaries. This time the sultan had an army, the *'ulama,* the students, and most of the people on his side. The janissaries were killed, their supporting groups (including the Bektashi Sufi order) abolished, and their properties redistributed among Mahmud's backers. So glad were the people to be rid of the janissaries that the massacre in Turkish history is called the "Auspicious Event." It cleared the way for a large-scale reform program during the last thirteen years of Mahmud's reign.

Highest priority went, predictably, to forming a new military organization to replace the janissaries and other outmoded units, for the Greeks, backed by the Great Powers, were rebelling against Ottoman rule. Mahmud gathered into his new army soldiers from all units of the old system, to be issued European uniforms and weapons and subjected to Western drillmasters and instructors. Ottoman youths were also trained in technical fields that served the military. Existing schools of military and naval engineering were expanded, a medical college was founded, and other schools were set up to teach European marching music and military sciences. A secondary school system was formed to help boys to transition from the mosques that provided most primary education to these new technical colleges and military academies.

It was hard to create schools in Istanbul based on French, German, or Italian models. The first teachers were all European. So, too, were the books they assigned. As a result, the boys had to master French or German before they could study medicine, engineering, or science. Even now this situation persists in the Middle East, due to the rapid growth of human knowledge. University students in Turkey, Iran, Israel, and (to a lesser extent) the Arab countries still use European or US textbooks for specialized courses in engineering, medicine, business, and even the humanities. But the problem was more acute 175 years ago in the Ottoman Empire. Printed books in any language were rare, and Turkish books on the European sciences were yet to be written. Some French and German textbooks were translated, but never enough of them. Special courses were set up to train Turkish Muslims to become government interpreters, replacing the Greeks who could no longer be trusted, now that there was an independent Greece. Like Mehmet 'Ali, Mahmud started a journal to print government announcements. He also sent some of his subjects to study in European universities, military academies, and technical institutes.

The main aim of the Ottoman reforms was to transfer power from the traditional ruling class to the sultan and his cabinet. Government ministries were reorganized to end overlapping jurisdictions and superfluous posts. Mahmud abolished the system of military land grants (*timars*) that had sustained the *sipahis* throughout Ottoman history. He could not imitate Mehmet 'Ali by putting all farmland under state control—the Ottoman Empire was larger and more diverse than Egypt—but he could at least tax the rural landlords. Building better roads helped to centralize power. Mahmud had to overcome opposition from local and provincial officials, feudal *sipahis*, conservative government clerks, and 'ulama. Too few Ottomans shared Mahmud's dream of an empire reformed and invigorated, like Peter the Great's Russia. It would not benefit them enough.

Military Defeat and European Protection
Westernizing reform in the Ottoman Empire had another grave fault: it did not stop its army from losing wars. In 1829 the Greeks won their independence, although their tiny kingdom in the Morea held less than half of all Greek-speaking people. Their success was due mainly to intervention

by Russia, which fought the Ottomans again between 1827 and 1829 and also took land east of the Black Sea. Ibrahim's advances into Syria were another blow to the Ottoman Empire, especially when Mahmud's new army failed to dislodge them. Outside help would be needed if the empire were to survive. The first choice should have been France, but it was backing Mehmet 'Ali and Ibrahim, so Mahmud turned instead to his mighty northern neighbor. In a treaty bearing the euphonious name of Hunkar-Iskelesi, Russia agreed in 1833 to defend the territorial integrity of the Ottoman Empire. It meant the fox would guard the henhouse!

This pact between two states that had fought four wars in sixty years shocked the West. Britain believed that the Hunkar-Iskelesi Treaty gave Russian warships the right to pass through the Straits, from which Western naval vessels were barred, and it railed against the threat of Russian control of Istanbul. How could the British outbid the Russians? Luckily, the Ottomans wanted more trade with Britain. In a commercial treaty signed in 1838, the Ottoman government increased Britain's Capitulatory privileges and limited to 9 percent its import tariffs on British manufactures. This low rate stimulated British exports to the empire, thus wiping out many Ottoman merchants and artisans who could not compete against the West's more mechanized factories. One unexpected result of the 1838 treaty was to increase Britain's economic interest in the Ottoman Empire and hence its desire to keep it alive. That outcome soon benefited the Ottoman Turks.

The Tanzimat Era

Mahmud II died while Ibrahim's army was invading Anatolia, whereupon his navy, laboriously rebuilt with British and US help after the Greek war for independence, defected to Alexandria. Mahmud was succeeded by his young son, Abdulmejid (r. 1839–1861). Although he seemed ill prepared to rule, Abdulmejid reigned during the greatest Ottoman reform period, the era of the Tanzimat (reorganizations). The Tanzimat's guiding genius was Mahmud's foreign minister, Mustafa Reshid, who happened to be in London seeking British aid against Mehmet 'Ali when Abdulmejid took over (see Box 10.1). Advised by the British and Reshid, the new sultan issued a decree (which had been written by Mahmud before his death) called the Noble Rescript of the Rose Chamber (or *Hatt-i-Sherif* of Gulhane), authorizing the creation of new institutions to safeguard his subjects' basic rights, to assess and levy taxes fairly, and to conscript and train soldiers. Tax farming, bribery, and favoritism would end.

But how would these promises, revolutionary for the Ottoman Empire, be fulfilled? Well, Reshid led some young and able officials who believed

---

Box 10.1   Mustafa Reshid Pasha

By the nineteenth century, the Ottoman Empire was obviously declining relative to an increasingly modern and powerful West. This situation had long divided the empire's peoples into two groups. One remained bound to the past. For reasons of custom or religion, they resisted reform and looked for salvation in adherence to traditional ways. The other group consisted of reformers who were convinced that if the empire were to survive, it would have to adopt Western ways, at least in terms of administrative and military practices. In the first half of the nineteenth century, one of the ablest of these reformers was a statesman and diplomat named Mustafa Reshid Pasha (1800–1858).

Born in Constantinople, Reshid began training for government service at an early age. He was essentially apprenticed to become a state administrator. He proved adept in this profession and rose rapidly through the ranks of the civil service. From 1834 to 1836 he was Ottoman ambassador in Paris and then London. In this capacity he observed those practices he believed made the West strong. In 1837 he was appointed minister for foreign affairs. Throughout his career he would serve six times as grand vizier. Thoroughly familiar with European methods of government, he became convinced that the empire had to westernize to survive: "only through reforms that will bring Turkey closer to the norms of European life can we get over the enduring political and economic crisis."

In 1839 Reshid got his opportunity to turn theory into practice. In that year Sultan Abdulmejid called on him to help implement the *Tanzimat* (reorganization) of the governmental practices of the empire. These reforms were designed to strengthen the state through administrative reform, but many were actively resisted by officials who had a vested interest in maintaining tradition. This eventually stymied the reform effort and got Reshid demoted to his old post as ambassador to France. However, at the insistence of the British, the reform movement would be renewed in 1856 following the Crimean War.

After the Ottoman Empire was defeated in World War I, Turkey, independent and divested of its empire, thoroughly westernized its society. The man who would accomplish this task, Mustafa Kemal Ataturk, stood at the end of a long line of westernizers, one of whom was Mustafa Reshid Pasha.

---

that liberal reforms would save the Ottoman Empire. Most aspects of Ottoman public life were restructured: a state school system was set up to train government clerks; the provinces were reorganized so that each governor would have specified duties and an advisory council; the network of roads, canals, and now rail lines was extended; and a modern financial system was set up featuring a central bank, treasury bonds, and a decimal currency.

The Tanzimat was not a total success. Some Ottoman aristocrats lost the power and prestige they had customarily enjoyed. The subject nationalities expected more from the 1839 rescript than the actual reforms could deliver. Balkan Christians did not want centralization of power; they demanded autonomy. Some now sought independence. The Romanians were among the many European peoples who rebelled in 1848; it took a Russian invasion to quell their revolt. Without firm British backing, the Ottoman reform movement would have failed. Unfortunately, Britain's support of Ottoman territorial integrity was on a collision course with Russia's attempt to spread its influence in the Balkans. The crash was the Crimean War of 1853–1856. The Ottoman Empire, aided by British and French troops, defeated Russia and regained some lands in the Balkans and the Caucasus.

However, the price for Western support was a second official proclamation, Abdulmejid's 1856 Imperial Rescript (*Hatt-i-Humayun*). Its gist was that all Ottoman subjects, whether Muslim or not, would now enjoy equal rights under the law. This was a revolutionary statement. Most Ottoman Muslims opposed giving Christians and Jews the same rights and status as themselves, defying the basic principles of the Shari'a. Some of the *millet* leaders feared losing their religious autonomy. Discontented Christian subjects still rebelled, but now there were also uprisings by Muslims who opposed the new Ottoman policy.

The Tanzimat reforms continued, though, in such areas as landownership, codification of the laws, and reorganization of the *millet*s (those of the Armenians and the Jews, who did not yet seek separate states). The 1858 Land Reform tried to regulate landownership throughout the empire, but its long-term effect would be to create a new landowning aristocracy, especially in the Arab lands. The Ottoman Empire was admitted to full membership in the European Concert of Powers, and no one dared—until later—to speak of its imminent collapse or partition.

PERSIA UNDER THE QAJARS

Persia was the only Middle Eastern country outside the Arabian Peninsula that was never fully absorbed by the Ottoman Empire. Even if the Safavid shahs had often fallen back before the might of the janissaries in the sixteenth and seventeenth centuries, they had always retained control at home. After the Safavids' fall in the early eighteenth century, a succession of dynasties (most of them Turkic in origin but Persian in culture) ruled over that sprawling and heterogeneous country, in either uneasy alliance or open contention with the nomadic tribes, rural landlords, urban merchants, and Shi'ite *'ulama*. Following the meteoric career of Nider Shah (d. 1747), the country went into a long decline. The Qajar dynasty (1794–1925) ineffectually resisted dissolution from within and encroachments from without. Russia was pushing into the Caucasus region and into such Central Asian lands as Transoxiana, Khwarizm, and Khurasan. The czars' ultimate goal was to conquer the Gulf region. Britain, concerned with the defense of India, vacillated between a policy of backing Persia's government and one of seizing parts of its southern territory. The Qajars designated Tehran, hitherto an obscure mountain town, their capital. Their rule rarely reached the countryside, which was controlled by absentee landlords and nomadic tribes. For the most part, the shahs seemed intent on enriching themselves and enlarging their families. One example is Fath 'Ali Shah (r. 1797–1834), who was survived by 158 wives, 57 sons, 46 daughters, and almost 600 grandchildren. Persians joked that "camels, lice, and princes are everywhere."

Persia had no Mehmet 'Ali, no Mahmud II, and precious little Tanzimat. Let us make a grudging exception for Nasiruddin Shah (r. 1848–1896). He had gained some on-the-job experience as crown prince ruling in Tabriz, but, because his father, the ruling shah, disliked him, young Nasiruddin received no funds with which to feed and clothe his soldiers and officials or even to heat his palace. When he succeeded his father at the age of eighteen, his progress from Tabriz to Tehran was impeded by tribal and village leaders who importuned him for accession gifts he could not provide. Nasiruddin never forgot his humiliation. He began his reign with a program of military, economic, and educational reforms. Some factories were opened, and Tehran got its first bank and its first technical school. But the credit for these reforms goes to his energetic prime minister, who antagonized Nasiruddin's mother, a powerful figure in the Qajar court. The prime minister was suddenly executed in 1851. After that, Persia got embroiled in a war with Britain over control of port cities in the Persian Gulf and mired in tribal and religious uprisings, many of which were fueled by social and economic discontent against the government. Even women joined in urban riots when bread and other foodstuffs became scarce and expensive.

One religious movement that would have fateful consequences was the revolt of a Shi'ite Muslim who proclaimed himself the Bab, or precursor to the hidden Twelfth Imam. Although the Bab was put to death in 1850, he was succeeded by Baha'ullah, who was exiled to Baghdad, then a part of the Ottoman Empire. Later he proclaimed himself a prophet and founded the Baha'i faith, a universal religion of peace and unity that has won support in the West but is now seen as a heresy in Iran, where since 1979 its adherents have been persecuted by the Islamic Republic.

Persia's state treasury never had enough money to pay for the things Nasiruddin wanted to do, like building palaces and traveling to Europe. To supplement revenues from taxes, which were hard to collect, the government set up monopolies over such economic activities as mining and manufacturing. The shah began selling these monopolies as concessions to British and other European investors. He also hired Russian Cossack officers to train his army. Instead of using reform to protect Persia from foreigners, the shah encouraged them to take over his country.

CONCLUSION

Westernizing reforms seemed a cure-all for the ills of the nineteenth-century Middle East, but seldom did they work as well in practice as they had looked on paper. What went wrong? First, the reforms threatened Muslim culture and values. Second, they were costly. Modern armies and westernized bureaucracies could not subsist on the traditional Islamic taxes: the *kharaj* paid on land and other fixed property, the *jizya* paid by Jewish and Christian subjects, and the canonical *zakat*. Each of the countries we have studied would, in later years, come to grief on finance, having run up a foreign debt so high (by nineteenth-century standards) that it had to accept European control over its governmental receipts and expenditures.

A related problem for all reformers was a shortage of trained personnel to run the westernized institutions they had set up. True, Europeans could do the work. Some were talented, dedicated to their jobs, and cooperative with native officials. Others were incompetents who could not have held a job back home, fugitives from an unhappy past, alcoholics, or snobs who hated the local leaders. Turks, Arabs, and Persians could also be trained to administer the reforms. If they were sent abroad for their training, though, they often picked up some of the less admirable aspects of Western civilization: drinking, gambling, dueling, and even worse habits. Some resisted such temptations and came home well trained, only to be stymied by conservative bureaucrats. If the native reformers attended the newly formed local schools, subject to steadying influences from home and mosque, they could turn into half-baked Europeans unable to grasp either the values of the West or the real needs of their own societies. Such "Levantines" should have been a bridge between Europe and the Middle East. Most were not.

The best members of the generation that got its education from the reforms of Mehmet ʿAli, the Tanzimat, or Nasiruddin's vizier embraced ideas that were in a sense opposed to those of the early reformers themselves. Instead of hoping to centralize power in the hands of the ruler, they called for constitutions that would protect the individual's rights against a powerful government. Some rulers even encouraged this idea. Mehmet 'Ali's grandson, Isma'il, the *khedive* (viceroy) of Egypt from 1863 to 1879, was as ambitious a reformer as his illustrious ancestor. During his reign, parts of Alexandria and Cairo were modeled on Paris, railroads crisscrossed the Nile Valley and Delta, and Egypt adopted such modern attributes as law codes, schools, factories, and even an African empire. Isma'il also set up a representative assembly and a newspaper press, both of which started out tame yet turned later into noisy critics of his regime. He may have fostered a nationalist party in his army, but let us save that story for Chapter 11.

The Ottoman reaction to the reforms was more complex. Some officials and *'ulama* resisted them. They were encouraged to do so by Sultan Abdulaziz (r. 1861–1876), who patronized pan-Islam—an ideology that called on all Muslims, no matter where they lived, to unite behind Ottoman leadership and to uphold their traditional institutions and culture against Western influences. There were also bureaucrats, army officers, and intellectuals who reacted against the Tanzimat in the opposite direction, demanding more individual freedom, local autonomy, and decentralization of power. They called themselves New Ottomans, not to be confused with the Young Turks of the next generation.

Great Power policies, briefly discussed in Chapter 9, often hindered reforms more than they helped. Britain and France stepped up their competition for control of Egypt after the Suez Canal became a major waterway. When Khedive Isma'il ran up a debt of nearly £100 million ($1.5 billion), Britain and France first set up a financial commission in 1876, then made him appoint foreigners to key cabinet posts, then ordered the sultan to depose him, and finally threatened to suppress the Egyptian nationalist movement, all to guard their financial and strategic interests. Russia's zeal for protecting Orthodox Christians, gaining control of the Straits, and promoting pan-Slavism led in 1875 to revolts against Ottoman rule in several parts of the Balkans. In that same year, the Ottoman government admitted that it could no longer repay its debts, and the Europeans set up a financial commission to make sure their creditors got whatever Istanbul owed them. The next year the New Ottomans seized control of the government, drew up a liberal constitution for the empire, and asked the Great Powers to let them settle their internal affairs in peace. Some countries agreed, but Russia distrusted the Ottoman promises, invaded the Balkans, and set off the Russo-Turkish War. Turkey's humiliating defeat put an end to the Tanzimat, the New Ottomans, and their constitution.

Persia, too, suffered from foreign imperialism. Its northern part, especially the key province of Azerbaijan, was often occupied by Russian troops. European entrepreneurs (usually backed by their governments) went about gaining concessions—for which they paid Nasiruddin Shah handsomely—to run Persia's mines, banks, railroads, and public utilities. The sale of its assets reached the point where a concession to process and market all the tobacco raised in the country was sold to a British firm. This event touched off a nationwide tobacco boycott in 1892. It worked so well that the shah himself could not smoke his water pipe in his palace! The boycott was led by Shi'ite *ulama,* who would remain politically active thereafter. Its success was a warning to the West, little heeded at the time, that the patience of Middle Eastern peoples had limits and that someday they would strike back. This brings us to the rise of nationalism, a subject we cover in the next chapter.

11

⬧

The Rise of Nationalism

Among the ideas the Middle East has imported from the West, none has been more popular and durable than nationalism. Often called the religion of the modern world, this ideology or belief system is hard to pin down. Drawing on the Western historical experience, we define nationalism as the desire of a large group of people to create or maintain a common statehood, to have their own rulers, laws, and other governmental institutions. This desired political community, or nation, is the object of that group's supreme loyalty. Shared characteristics among the peoples of Egypt and also among those of Persia stimulated the growth of nationalism in those two countries in the late nineteenth century. Other nationalist movements have grown up in the Middle East around shared resistance to governments, institutions, and even individuals regarded as foreign.

Nationalism was itself foreign to the world of Islam. In traditional Islamic thought, the *umma*, or community of believers, was for Muslims the sole object of political loyalty. Loyalty meant defending the land of Islam against rulers or peoples of other faiths. All true Muslims were meant to be brothers and sisters, regardless of race, language, and culture. Although distinctions existed between Arabs and Persians, or between them and the Turks, common adherence to Islam was supposed to transcend all differences. Nationalism should not exist in Islam.

Yet it does, though religion has deeply influenced nationalism in the Middle East. Arab nationalism at its start included Christians and even Jews, but its clearest expressions since World War II have been opposition to Christian control in Lebanon and to Jewish colonization in Palestine (Israel since 1948). The rhetoric of nationalism often confuses the Arab nation with the Islamic *umma*, as when an Arab nationalist cause is termed a jihad. Other Middle Eastern nationalist movements were based even more firmly on religion and called on their people to resist oppression by others having a different faith. These include Greeks and Armenians among the Christians of the Middle East, as well as Turks and Persians among its Muslims. Political Zionism, which called for Israel's creation as the Jewish state, drew its inspiration from Judaism, even if many of its advocates were not themselves observant. In all three monotheistic faiths, the rise of nationalism has meant substituting collective self-love for the love of God, enhancing life on this earth instead of preparing for what is to come after death, and promoting the community's welfare instead of obeying God's revealed laws.

During the forty years before World War I, the peoples of the Arab world, Turkey, and Persia began to develop nationalist feelings. As this was the high-water mark of European imperialism, we can see rising nationalism as a natural reaction to Western power. But it was also the end result of a century of westernizing reform, with its enlarged armies and bureaucracies, modern schools, printing presses, roads and rail lines, and centralized state power. One could not learn Europe's techniques, most often taught in French, without absorbing some of its ideas. Middle Eastern students at French or German universities had ample exposure to Western ideas, even if they never heard lectures on political theory. There were newspapers and magazines being hawked in the streets, lively discussions in cafes, demonstrations, and encounters with Western orientalists (the nineteenth-century counterpart of our Middle East historians) who could explain what was happening in Europe to a Turkish, Egyptian, or Persian sojourner. Even the students who learned their technical skills in Istanbul, Cairo, or Tehran were apt to be exposed to Western ideas by their European instructors. Besides, their schools usually had reading rooms. A Middle Easterner studying engineering could read works by Rousseau or other Western writers.

In short, as Middle Easterners learned how to work like Europeans, some also started to think like them. They learned that bad governments did not have to be endured (indeed, many earlier Muslims had defied tyrannical rulers), that individuals had rights and freedoms that should be protected against official coercion, and that people could belong to political communities based on race, language, culture, and shared historical experience—in short, they form nations. In the 1870s these liberal and nationalist ideas became current among many educated young Muslims of the Middle East, especially in the capital cities. While they faced the frustrations of these years and those that followed, their ideas crystallized into nationalist movements.

Many religious and ethnic groups formed nationalist movements in the Middle East before World War I. We will limit this chapter, however, to three that arose within existing states that had governments and some experience with westernizing reform: those of the Egyptians, the Turks in the Ottoman Empire, and the Persians under the Qajar shahs. Arab nationalism and Zionism will be covered later. Nationalism among such Christian peoples of the Ottoman Empire as the Greeks and Armenians will be treated only as they spurred the rise of Turkish nationalism.

EGYPTIAN NATIONALISM

Western writers used to call Egypt "the land of paradox." Almost all its inhabitants were crowded into the valley and delta of the great River Nile, without which Egypt would have been only a desert supporting a few Bedouin nomads. To European tourists of a century ago, Egypt was filled with ancient relics—temples, obelisks, pyramids, sphinxes, and buried treasures—and haunted by pharaohs whose tombs had been violated by Bedouin robbers or Western archaeologists. To most Muslims, however, Egypt was the very heart and soul of Islam, with its mosque-university of al-Azhar, its festive observance of Muslim holy days and saints' birthdays, and its annual procession bearing a new cloth that would be sent to cover the Ka'ba in Mecca. Egypt meant Cairo, with its hundreds of mosques and *madrasas*, ornate villas and bazaars—survivals of a time when the Mamluks really ruled and the city stood out as an economic and intellectual center. To a student who has just been exposed to Mehmet 'Ali's reforms and the building of the Suez Canal, Egypt was the most westernized country in the nineteenth-century Middle East.

Imagine one of the newer quarters of Cairo or Alexandria in 1875, or the new towns of Port Said and Ismailia, their wide, straight avenues lined with European-style houses, hotels, banks, shops, schools, and churches. Horse-drawn carriages whiz past the donkeys and camels of a more leisurely age. Restaurants serve coq au vin or veal scallopini instead of *kufta* (ground meat) or kebab; their customers smoke cigars instead of water pipes. The signs are in French, not Arabic. The passersby converse in Italian, Greek, Armenian, Turkish, Yiddish, Ladino (a language derived from Spanish and spoken by Mizrahi Jews), or several dialects of Arabic. Top hats have replaced turbans, and frock coats have supplanted the caftans of yore. Each of these images fits a part of Egypt 140 years ago—but not all of it.

Khedive Isma'il
The ruler of this land of paradox was Mehmet 'Ali's grandson, Isma'il (r. 1863–1879), a complex and controversial figure. Was he a man of vision,

as his admirers claimed, or a spendthrift who would ultimately bring Egypt into British bondage? His admirers cited the railroads, bridges, docks, canals, factories, and sugar refineries built during his reign. It was also the time when the Egyptian government paid explorers and military expeditions to penetrate the Sudan and East Africa and tried to abolish slavery and slave trading within its empire. The Egyptian Mixed Courts were set up to hear civil cases involving Europeans protected by the Capitulations. Public and missionary schools—for girls as well as boys—proliferated in the cities. The Egyptian Museum, National Library, Geographical Society, and many professional schools began under Isma'il.

But Isma'il's detractors point out that he squandered money to impress Europe with his munificence and power. Building the Suez Canal cost the Egyptian government much, for the state treasury had to reimburse the Suez Canal Company when it was forced to pay wages to the construction workers (the company had expected to get the peasants' labor for free). This was the fault of Isma'il's predecessor, Sa'id. But it was Isma'il who turned the canal's inauguration into an extravaganza, inviting the crowned heads and leaders of Europe to come—at Egypt's expense. Costing at least 2 million Egyptian pounds (worth $300 million in today's prices), it must have been the bash of the century, with enormous receptions, all-night parties, balls, parades, firework displays, horse races, excursions to ancient monuments, and cities festooned with flags and illuminated by lanterns. New villas and palaces sprouted up, streets were widened and straightened, old neighborhoods were demolished, and even an opera house was erected in Cairo. Giuseppe Verdi, the Italian composer, was commissioned to write *Aida* for the inauguration of that opera house. Isma'il also paid huge bribes in Istanbul to lessen his ties to the Ottoman government, changing his title from *pasha* (governor) to *khedive* (viceroy) of Egypt and obtaining the right to pass down his position to his son in Cairo rather than to a brother living in Istanbul. He also won a fateful privilege: to take out foreign loans without Ottoman permission.

Financial Problems
But where could the money have come from? Egyptian taxpayers could not cover Isma'il's extravagance. His reign had begun during the American Civil War, which caused a cotton boom in Egypt. The British, cut off by the Northern blockade from their usual cotton supply, would pay any price for other countries' crops to supply the textile mills of Lancashire. The high demand for Egypt's cotton stimulated output and enriched both the Egyptian growers and the government. During this cotton boom, European

investment bankers offered Isma'il loans on attractive terms. When the boom ended after the Civil War, Egypt's need for money was greater than ever, but now he could get credit only at high interest rates. In 1866 Isma'il called together an assembly representing the landowners to seek their consent to raise taxes. Soon they were taxing date palms, flour mills, oil presses, boats, shops, houses, and even burials.

Isma'il adopted still other stratagems to postpone the day of reckoning. He offered tax abatements to landowners who could pay three years' taxes in advance. He sold Egypt's shares in the Suez Canal Company—44 percent of the stock—to the British government in 1875. When a British delegation came to investigate rumors of Egypt's impending bankruptcy, the khedive agreed to set up a Dual Financial Control to manage the public debt. But a low Nile in 1877, high military expenses incurred in the Russo-Turkish War, and an invasion of Ethiopia put the Egyptian government deeper in debt. In August 1878 Isma'il, pressed by his European creditors, agreed to admit an Englishman and a Frenchman to his cabinet; he also promised to turn his powers over to his ministers. At the same time, he secretly stirred up antiforeign elements in his army. This was easy, for the Dual Control had cut the Egyptian officers' pay in half. A military riot in February 1879 enabled Isma'il to dismiss the foreign ministers and later to appoint a cabinet of liberals who began drafting a constitution, much as the Ottoman Empire had done in 1876. Britain and France, guarding their investors' interests, asked the Ottoman sultan to dismiss Isma'il. He did. When Isma'il turned over the khedivate to his son, Tawfiq, and left Egypt in July 1879, the state debt stood at 93 million Egyptian pounds (about $1.4 billion). It had been 3 million when he came to power in 1863.

The Beginnings of Nationalism

Isma'il's successes and failures made him the father of Egypt's first nationalist movement. His new schools, law courts, railroads, and telegraph lines drew Egyptians closer together and helped to foster nationalist feeling. So did the newspapers he patronized in hope of creating a positive public image. The Suez Canal and related projects drew thousands of Europeans into Egypt; they became models for modernization and at the same time targets of native resentment.

Muslim feeling, always strong but usually quiescent, was aroused at this time under the influence of a fiery pan-Islamic agitator, Jamal al-Din, called al-Afghani (despite his claim of being an Afghan, he really was from Persia), who came to teach at al-Azhar. Afghani would pop up in almost every political movement that stirred in the late nineteenth-century Middle East. He soon clashed with the *'ulama* and quit al-Azhar to form a sort of independent academy that attracted many young Egyptians who would later become political leaders or Islamic reformers. Two of them were Muhammad Abduh, the greatest Muslim thinker of the late nineteenth century, and Sa'd Zaghlul, leader of Egypt's independence struggle after World War I. Afghani, like Isma'il, encouraged journalists; but his protégés were bolder ones, often Jews or Christians who turned more readily to secular nationalism than did the Muslims whom Afghani wanted to stir up.

Isma'il's financial crisis, which tied Egypt to Western creditors and to their governments, shamed Egyptians, especially members of his representative assembly. Once a subservient group of frightened rural landlords, it had now turned into a vociferous body of antigovernment critics. But the key breeding ground for nationalism was the army. Sa'id had started admitting Egyptian farmers' sons into the officer corps and had promoted some of them rapidly, whereas Isma'il withheld their promotions and pay raises in favor of the traditional elite, the Turks and Circassians. Frustrated, the Egyptian officers formed a secret society to plot against their oppressors. It later would become the nucleus of the first National Party.

Isma'il's deposition set back the nascent nationalists. During his last months in power, the Egyptian officers had joined with government workers, assembly representatives, journalists, and *'ulama* to back the drafters of a constitution that would give to Egyptians some of the rights and freedoms Europeans enjoyed in their own countries. But Tawfiq, the new khedive, thought it safer to back the European creditors than the Egyptian nationalists. He dismissed the liberal cabinet, restored the Dual Control, banned newspapers, and exiled Afghani and other agitators.

Ahmad 'Urabi

The nationalists seemed to be in eclipse, but we suspect that Khedive Tawfiq secretly encouraged them. Sa'd Zaghlul and Muhammad Abduh could still demand constitutional rule in the official journal they edited. The disgruntled Egyptian officers continued to meet. In February 1881 these men, led by Colonel Ahmad 'Urabi, mutinied and "forced" Tawfiq to replace his Circassian war minister with a nationalist, Mahmud Sami al-Barudi. Seven months later, 2,500 Egyptian officers and soldiers surrounded the khedive's palace and "made" him appoint a liberal cabinet. Moreover, they demanded a constitution, parliamentary government, and an enlarged army. The same demands were sought by the civilian nationalists; they were also feared by the European creditors, who wondered how Tawfiq or 'Urabi would ever find money to pay for these reforms.

During the next year Egypt came as close as it ever would to democratic government (if you take the Egyptian nationalist view of history) or anarchy (if you buy the British interpretation of what happened). A liberal cabinet drafted a constitution and held elections as Egypt's debts rose further. In January 1882 Britain and France sent a joint note, threatening to intervene to support Tawfiq (they really meant to restore the Dual Control). The nationalists called their bluff, declaring that Egypt's new parliament, not the British and French debt commissioners, would control the state budget. Barudi took over the premiership and 'Urabi became war minister, threatening the Turkish and Circassian officers in Egypt's army. The nationalists even thought of ousting Tawfiq and declaring Egypt a republic. More likely, though, they would have replaced him with one of his exiled relatives, a strange treatment for their secret patron.

As nationalism was new in Egypt, could an outsider have inspired these moves? A few English liberals helped the movement, and France's consul in Cairo may have encouraged 'Urabi; however, the outside supporters were probably the Ottoman sultan and a dispossessed uncle of Tawfiq living in Istanbul. This fact may make the movement seem less than wholly nationalist. One scholar argues that what we call the National Party was really a constellation of several groups with various political, economic, and religious interests. Still, the movement had become popular by June 1882. What destroyed it was Britain's determination to dispatch troops to protect European lives and investments in Egypt and to defend the Suez Canal, which had become vital to British shipping.

Riots in Alexandria caused a general exodus of Europeans, and both British and French gunboats dropped anchor near the harbor. Then the British fired on Alexandria's fortifications, somehow much of the city caught fire, and British marines landed to restore order (as the French ships sailed away). 'Urabi declared war on Britain, but Tawfiq declared him a traitor and threw in his lot with the British in Alexandria. Other British Empire troops entered the canal and landed at Ismailia. Defeating 'Urabi's army was easy, and the British occupied Cairo in September 1882. Barudi's cabinet was dismissed, the nationalists were tried for rebellion, 'Urabi was exiled, the constitution suspended, the nationalist newspapers banned, and the army broken up by Tawfiq and his British advisers. The early nationalists had proved a weak force. Their party had been divided among Egyptian officers resenting privileged Turks and Circassians in the army, civilians seeking parliamentary rule, and reformers like Afghani and Abduh who wanted an Islamic revival. (See Box 11.1.)

Box 11.1	Ahmad 'Urabi

'Urabi (1841–1911) was an Egyptian military officer and national hero. 'Urabi was born to a relatively well-to-do peasant family in the village of Qaryat Rizqa, the son of a village shaykh who made sure Ahmad received a strong traditional Islamic education. He entered the Egyptian army as a teenager and moved up through the ranks quickly, reaching the rank of lieutenant colonel by age twenty. He had a charismatic personality and was an excellent public speaker. His gifts would be borne out by his eventual achievements.

Several problems afflicted Egypt during 'Urabi's time. The Egyptian army was more a patronage bureaucracy than a true fighting force, and its officer corps was divided into competing ethnic groups. Native Egyptians faced discriminatory treatment in the army by officers of Circassian and Turkish origin. In addition, the indebtedness of the khedives and the strategic location of Egypt and the Suez Canal combined to make that country matter greatly to Europe's imperial powers, particularly Great Britain. Finances and strategy would encourage European intervention in Egypt.

'Urabi acted out of both personal interests and patriotism. For instance, when Khedive Tawfiq, acting under the influence of Turkish officers in the army, passed a law barring peasants from becoming officers, 'Urabi, reacting out of self-interest, organized resistance among the Egyptian soldiers and forced the law's repeal. He also forged an alliance between the army officers and Egyptian nationalists seeking to limit the growing influence of Europeans in Egyptian affairs. Additional pressure on the khedive (who may have encouraged the nationalists) brought 'Urabi into the government as war minister. From this position, he and other nationalists contested the Egyptian budget, with its Anglo-French Dual Financial Control.

In the end Europe's power overwhelmed 'Urabi and those who sought real independence for Egypt. The British were not willing to risk their investments or control of the Suez Canal by supporting Egyptian nationalism. When they invaded Egypt in 1882, 'Urabi's charismatic leadership was no match for Britain's Gatling guns. 'Urabi's forces were defeated in the Battle of Tel al-Kebir. 'Urabi fled to Cairo, where he finally surrendered. By this time the khedive had switched sides, thrown in his lot with the British, declared 'Urabi a rebel, and wanted to have him sentenced to death. The British high commissioner in Cairo, Lord Dufferin, recognizing that 'Urabi's death would make him a martyr, had the sentence commuted to permanent exile in Ceylon.

Long disdained by civilian nationalists, Colonel 'Urabi has now become a national hero in Egypt. His resistance against foreign invasion was an important milestone in Egyptian national history.

Lord Cromer and the British Occupation

The British government that sent troops to Egypt in 1882 expected a brief military occupation. As soon as order was restored, Britain's troops were supposed to leave, and Egypt was to resume being an autonomous Ottoman province. But the longer the British stayed, the more disorder they found to clean up and the less they wanted to leave Egypt. The financial situation in particular required drastic economic and administrative reforms. The British agent and consul general in Cairo from 1883 to 1907, Lord Cromer, was a talented financial administrator. With a small (but growing) staff of British advisers to Egypt's various ministries, Cromer managed to expand the Nile irrigation system to raise agricultural output, increase state revenues, lower taxes, and reduce the public debt burden. His officials were competent, devoted to the Egyptians' welfare, and honest. Cromer's epitaph in Westminster Abbey would call him the "regenerator of Egypt."

He may have been so, but Cromer is not well remembered in Egypt today. Egyptians living in his era believed their own advancement in government jobs or the professions was blocked by the numerous foreigners holding high posts in Cairo. Besides, they objected to Cromer's policy of limiting the growth of education. Some were angry that the Egyptian army, despite its British officers, lost the Sudan in 1885 to a rebellion led by the self-styled *mahdi* (rightly guided one). After British and Egyptian troops regained the Sudan in 1898, it was placed under joint sovereignty, with Britain effectively in control. Opposition to the continuing British occupation of Egypt came from a few British anti-imperialists; the French, who (despite their large economic stake in Egypt) had failed to intervene in 1882; and the Ottoman Turks, who resented losing another province of their empire. As long as there was no internal opposition, though, these groups could do little to thwart British rule.

The Revival of Egyptian Nationalism

Major resistance began when 'Abbas, Khedive Tawfiq's seventeen-year-old son, succeeded him in 1892. High spirited and proudly guarding what he considered his khedivial prerogatives, 'Abbas fought with Cromer over the right to appoint and dismiss his ministers and over control of the Egyptian army. Although the British consul won the battles by bullying the ministers and asking his own government to send more troops to Egypt, he lost the trust of the youthful khedive. Seeking to undermine Cromer, 'Abbas created a clique of European and native supporters. Among the latter was an articulate law student named Mustafa Kamil, who emerged as a potent palace propagandist in Europe and Egypt. In the ensuing years, he converted what had been Abbas's secret society into a large-scale movement, the (revived) National Party. He founded a boys' school and a daily newspaper to spread nationalist ideas. As his popularity grew, Mustafa came to care more about obtaining a democratic constitution and less about the khedive's prerogatives. He and his followers always demanded the evacuation of British troops from Egypt.

In 1906 an incident occurred that spread Mustafa Kamil's fame. A group of British officers entered a village called Dinshaway to shoot pigeons. Because of some misunderstandings between the villagers and the officers, a fracas broke out. A gun went off, setting a threshing floor on fire. Another bullet wounded a peasant woman. The villagers began to beat the officers with clubs. One of the latter escaped, fainted after running several miles, and died of sunstroke. The British authorities, suspecting a premeditated assault, tried fifty-seven farmers before a special military court, which found many of them guilty of murder. Four were hanged and several others flogged in the presence of their families as an object lesson to the Dinshaway villagers. These barbarous sentences appalled Mustafa Kamil, most Egyptians, and even many Europeans, for at that time people were shocked by atrocities that now seem tame. Mustafa exploited this reaction to win new followers and hasten Cromer's retirement. He publicly established the National Party in December 1907 but tragically died two months later.

Mustafa's successors disagreed about their tactics and aims. Was the National Party for Muslims against Christian rulers or for all Egyptian people opposed to the British occupation? If the latter, could Egypt expect support from its nominal overlord, the Ottoman Empire? Should the party seek national independence by peaceful or revolutionary means? If the latter, would it oppose Khedive 'Abbas and other large landowners? Should it seek economic and social reform, or stress ejecting the British from Egypt? How could a party mainly of lawyers and students, with few backers in the Egyptian army, persuade Britain to leave?

More moderate leaders argued that constitutional government should precede independence. Muhammad Abduh, who had backed 'Urabi in 1882, later worked for the regeneration of Islam and the reform of al-Azhar University, encouraged by Lord Cromer. Abduh's followers, together with some secular intellectuals and large landowners, formed the Umma Party in 1907 to counter the Nationalists. The British consul who replaced Cromer in 1907 neutralized the Nationalist threat by wooing Khedive 'Abbas and the more conservative landowners to Britain's side. The next consul won peasant support through his agrarian policies. By 1914 the Nationalist leaders were in exile. Only after World War I would the Egyptians build up enough resentment against British rule to form a truly national and revolutionary movement.

OTTOMANISM, PAN-ISLAM, AND TURKISM

The rise of Turkish nationalism was hampered by the fact that until the twentieth century no educated Ottoman, even if Turkish was his native tongue, cared to be called a Turk. The Ottoman Empire, though Westerners called it Turkey, was definitely not a Turkish nation-state. It contained many ethnic and religious groups: Turks, Greeks, Serbs, Croats, Albanians, Bulgarians, Arabs, Syrians, Armenians, and Kurds, to name but a few. Its rulers were Sunni Muslims, but it included Greek Orthodox, Armenian, and Jewish subjects organized into *millet*s (which functioned like nations within the state), as well as many smaller religious groups. Its inhabitants were either Osmanlilar, who belonged to the ruling class, or *ra'iya*, who did not, with nothing in between.

Early Nationalism in the Ottoman Empire

Nationalism in the modern sense first arose among the Greeks and the Serbs (peoples exposed to Western or Russian influences), then spread to other subject Christians. As independence movements proliferated in the Balkans, the Ottoman rulers worried more and more over how to hold their empire together and counter the Russians, who openly encouraged Balkan revolts. Westernizing reforms were their first solution, but these raised more hopes than could be met and did not create a new basis of loyalty. The reformers espoused the idea of Ottomanism (loyalty to the Ottoman state) as a framework within which racial, linguistic, and religious groups could develop autonomously but harmoniously. To this the New Ottomans of the 1870s had added the idea of a constitution that would set up an assembly representing all the empire's peoples. The constitution was drafted in 1876—the worst possible time, with several nationalist rebellions going on in the Balkans, war raging against Serbia and Montenegro (two Balkan states that had already won their independence), the Ottoman treasury nearly bankrupt, Russia threatening to send in troops, and Britain preparing to fight against the Turks to protect the Balkan Christians and against the Russians to defend the Ottoman Empire (a policy as weird to people then as it sounds now). Moreover, the New Ottomans had seized power in a coup, put on the throne a sultan who turned out to be crazy, and then replaced him with his brother, Abdulhamid II (r. 1876–1909), whose promises to uphold the new constitution were suspect.

Well, they should have been. The ensuing Russo-Turkish War put the empire in such peril that no one could have governed under the Ottoman constitution. Sultan Abdulhamid soon suspended it and dissolved parliament. For thirty years he ruled as a dictator, appointing and dismissing his own ministers, holding his creditors at bay, fomenting quarrels among the Great Powers to keep them from partitioning the empire, and suppressing all dissident movements within his realm. Europeans and Ottoman Christians viewed him as a cruel sultan, reactionary in his attitudes toward westernizing reforms and devoted to the doctrine of pan-Islam. This movement alarmed Russia, Britain, and France, with their millions of Muslim subjects in Asia and Africa. It is interesting that Istanbul, seat of the sultan-caliph, became the final home of that wandering pan-Islamic agitator, Jamal al-Din al-Afghani.

Abdulhamid is remembered for his censors and spies, his morbid fear of assassination, and his massacres of Armenians (some of whom were plotting against his regime). Scholars trying to rehabilitate his image have claimed he furthered the centralizing policies of the earlier Tanzimat reformers, noting that the Ottoman Empire lost no European lands between 1878 and 1908. Even though Muslims at home and abroad hailed him as their caliph, Sultan Abdulhamid was incompetent, paranoid, and cruel. The empire's finances were controlled by a European debt commission, freedoms of speech and assembly vanished, the army came to a standstill, and the navy deteriorated. The ablest reformers went into exile. Midhat, leader of the New Ottomans, was lured back with false promises, tried for attempted murder, locked up in the Arabian town of Taif, and secretly strangled there.

Many Ottomans, especially if they had attended Western schools, felt that the only way to save the Ottoman Empire was to restore the 1876 constitution, even if they had to overthrow Abdulhamid first. A number of opposition groups were formed. All of them tend to get lumped together as the Young Turks, a term possibly derived from the New Ottomans. Many were not Turks, and some were not even young, but the term has stuck. The key society was a secret one formed by four cadets—all Muslims but of several nationalities. It became known as the Committee of Union and Progress (CUP). Its history was long and tortuous, with moments of hope interspersed with years of gloom, centering at times on exiled Turkish writers living in Paris or Geneva, at others on cells of Ottoman army officers in Salonika and Damascus. Gradually, many Ottomans adopted the CUP's goals: the empire must be militarily and morally strengthened, all

religious and ethnic groups must have equal rights, the constitution must
be restored, and Sultan Abdulhamid must be shorn of power. Otherwise,
Russia would take what was left of the empire in Europe, including Istanbul and the Straits. The Western powers would carve up Asiatic Turkey, as
they had partitioned Africa and divided China into spheres of influence.

The Young Turks in Power
The CUP was Ottomanist, not Turkish nationalist, as long as it was out of
power. Fearful of the reconciliation between Britain and Russia in 1907,
the CUP inspired an army coup that forced Abdulhamid to restore the
Ottoman constitution in 1908. Every religious and ethnic group in the empire rejoiced; the committee, even if its leaders were Turks, was backed by
many loyal Balkan Christians, Armenians, Arabs, and Jews. Most wanted
to be Ottoman citizens under the 1876 constitution. Western well-wishers
expected Turkey to revive. Elections were held for the new Parliament,
the tide of democracy seemed to be sweeping into Istanbul, and the CUP
started so many changes that we still call vigorous reformers Young Turks.
Indeed, their rise to power portended the many revolutions that have
changed the face of Middle Eastern politics since 1908.

But if we examine what really happened to the Ottoman Empire under the Young Turks, we must give them lower marks for their achievements than for their stated intentions. They did not halt disintegration, as
Austria annexed Bosnia, Bulgaria declared its independence, and Crete rebelled, all in late 1908. Their hopes for rapid economic development were
dashed when France withdrew a loan offer in 1910. The next year Italy
invaded the Ottoman province of Tripolitania. Russia incited Bulgaria and
Serbia to join forces in 1912 and attack the empire in Macedonia. In four
months the Turks lost almost all their European lands. Even Albania, a
mainly Muslim part of the Balkans, rebelled in 1910 and declared its independence in 1913. And the Arabs, as you will see in Chapter 13, were
getting restless.

How could Istanbul's government, as set up under the restored 1876
constitution, weather these problems? After the CUP won the 1912 election
by large-scale bribery and intimidation, the army forced its ministers to resign in favor of its rival, the Liberal Entente. It took another military coup
and a timely assassination in 1913 to restore the CUP to power. By the outbreak of World War I, the Ottoman government was a virtual triumvirate:
Enver as war minister, Talat as minister of the interior, and Jemal in charge
of the navy. Though these men had led the 1908 revolution to restore the
1876 constitution, democracy was dead in the Ottoman Empire.

Turkish Nationalism

Amid these crises, the CUP leaders became more and more Turkish in their political orientation. Their early hope that the Great Powers and the empire's minorities would back their Ottomanist reforms had been dashed. The Great Powers grabbed land and withheld aid. The minorities grumbled, plotted, or rebelled. What could the Young Turks do? Some stuck to their Ottomanist guns. Others argued for pan-Islam, which would have held the loyalty of most Arabs and won needed support from Egypt, India, and other Muslim lands. But the new wave was pan-Turanism. This was the attempt to bring together all speakers of Turkic languages under Ottoman leadership, just as pan-Slavism meant uniting all speakers of Slavic languages behind Russia. Indeed, as most speakers of Turkic languages were then under czarist rule or military occupation, pan-Turanism seemed a good way to pay back the Russians for the trouble they had caused the Ottoman Empire. Some of the leading pan-Turanian advocates were refugees from Russian Central Asia or Azerbaijan, but it was hard for the Ottoman Turks to forget their traditional ties to Islam or their own empire. Few believed in a distinct Turanian culture. The CUP's efforts to impose Turkish in the schools and offices of their Arabic-speaking provinces stirred up Arab nationalism, further weakening the empire. The committee could not influence Central Asian Turks. The Turks' ethnic and linguistic nationalism caused more problems than it solved, until they limited their national idea to fellow Turks within the Ottoman Empire. The idea was not unknown. A Turkish sociologist named Ziya Gokalp was writing newspaper articles to promote what he called Turkism, but this idea would become popular only after World War I. By then it was too late to save the Ottoman Empire.

NATIONALISM IN PERSIA

Persia did not westernize as early as Egypt and the Ottoman Empire, but it had a compensating advantage when it came to developing Persian nationalism. Let us look at what historians and political scientists usually cite as nationalism's components: (1) previously existing state, (2) religion, (3) language, (4) race, (5) lifestyle, (6) shared economic interests, (7) common enemies, and (8) shared historical consciousness. If you test Egyptian or Turkish nationalism against these criteria, you will find that it falls short on several counts. Not so Persian nationalism. The Qajar dynasty may have governed ineptly, but it was heir to a Persian political tradition traceable to the ancient Achaemenids, interrupted by Greek,

Arab, Turkish, and Mongol invasions. Persia was predominantly Muslim; but its uniqueness was ensured by its general adherence to Twelve-Imam Shi'ism, whereas its Muslim neighbors were mainly Sunni. Its chief written and spoken language was Persian, although many of the country's inhabitants spoke Turkish while numerous Muslims in India and the Ottoman Empire read and wrote Persian well. Race is a treacherous term to use in a land so often invaded and settled by outsiders, but certainly the Persians viewed their personal appearance as distinctive. Their culture had withstood the tests of time, invasions, and political change. Both visitors and natives hailed the Persian way of life: its poetry, architecture, costumes, cuisine, social relationships—and even its jokes. The economic interests of nineteenth-century Persia seem to have been, if not homogeneous, at least complementary among city dwellers, farmers, and nomads. No other Middle Easterners could match the Persians' strong historical consciousness, expressed in their monumental architecture, painting, epic poetry, written history, and music, glorifying twenty-five centuries as a distinctive people.

Early Resistance to Foreign Power

It should not surprise you, therefore, to learn that a Persian nationalist movement arose between 1870 and 1914. Basically, it was a reaction against the threat of a Russian military takeover, against growing dependence on the West, and against the divisive effects of tribalism in the rural areas. It was facilitated by the spread of roads, telegraphs, and both public and private schools. Nasiruddin Shah's policy of selling to foreign investors the rights to develop Persia's resources alienated his own subjects. In 1873 he offered a concession to one Baron de Reuter, a British subject, to form a monopoly that would build railways, operate mines, and establish Persia's national bank. Russian objections and domestic opposition forced the shah to cancel the concession, although the baron was later authorized to start the Imperial Bank of Persia. In 1890 Nasiruddin sold a concession to an English company to control the production, sale, and export of all tobacco in Persia. As we wrote in Chapter 10, a nationwide tobacco boycott, inspired by the same Afghani you saw earlier in Egypt, forced the cancellation of this concession. The boycott gave westernized Persians, Shi'ite 'ulama, and bazaar merchants enough confidence in their political power to spur the growth of a constitutionalist movement in the ensuing years.

Many observers noted the mounting problems of the Qajar shahs, their economic concessions to foreigners, the widening disparities between rich landowners and poor peasants (owing to the shift from subsistence to cash-crop agriculture), and Persia's growing dependence on Russian military advisers. Well might they have wondered how long it would take for Russia to occupy Persia. Persians knew about the British occupation of Egypt, Sultan Abdulhamid's weakness, and the foreign penetration of China. If the Russian troops did not come, some asked, would British investors take over Persia more subtly? Russia was Persia's main enemy, but Britain was a close second. The shah, surrounded by corrupt courtiers, had sold most of his inherited treasures and spent the proceeds of his foreign loans on palaces, trips abroad, and gifts to his family and friends.

The Constitutionalist Movement
Patriotic Persians believed the remedy to these ills was a constitution that would limit their rulers' arbitrary acts. The idea spread among bazaar merchants, landlords, *'ulama,* army officers, and even some government officials and tribal leaders. Secret societies sprang up in various cities, notably Tabriz (Azerbaijan's main city) and Tehran (Persia's capital). The spark that set off the revolution was an arbitrary act by the shah's prime minister, 'Ayn al-Dowleh, who had several merchants flogged for allegedly plotting to drive up the price of sugar in the Tehran bazaar. The merchants took refuge in the royal mosque (which, by a time-honored Persian custom called *bast,* gave them sanctuary from arrest), but 'Ayn al-Dowleh had them expelled. This move enraged Tehran's *'ulama* and swelled the number of protestors, who moved to another mosque. Desiring peace, the shah offered to dismiss his minister and to convene a "house of justice" to redress their grievances. But he failed to act on his promises. When the shah was incapacitated by a stroke, 'Ayn al-Dowleh attacked the protestors, who organized a larger *bast* in Tehran. Meanwhile, the *mujtahids,* or Shi'ite legal experts, sought *bast* in nearby Qom and threatened to leave Persia en masse—an act that would have paralyzed the country's courts—unless their demands were met. Tehran's shops closed. When 'Ayn al-Dowleh tried to force them to open, 15,000 Persians took refuge in the British legation, camping on its lawn for several weeks during July 1906. Finally the shah bowed to popular pressure. He fired 'Ayn al-Dowleh and accepted a Western-style constitution in which the government would be controlled by a Majlis, or representative assembly. So great was his aversion to the Persian nationalists, however, that only pressure from Britain and Russia (plus the fact that he was dying) kept him from blocking the constitution before it could take effect.

The Persian nationalists achieved too much too soon. In 1907 Britain and Russia reached an agreement recognizing each other's spheres of influence in Persia. Britain was to have primary influence over the southeast, close to its Indian empire. Russia acquired the right to send troops and advisers to the heavily populated north, including the key provinces of Azerbaijan and Khurasan, plus Tehran itself. Russia backed the new shah enough to enable him to close the Majlis in 1908. Though one of the main tribes helped the constitutionalists to regain control of Tehran and then to reopen the Majlis in 1909, Persian nationalism now lacked the fervent popular support it had enjoyed three years earlier. The Majlis got bogged down in debates and achieved nothing.

Oil Discoveries

Persians might have welcomed news from Khuzistan, located in the southwest, where a British company had begun oil exploration in 1901. In 1908 it made its first strike. By 1914 thousands of barrels were being piped to a refinery on the Gulf island port of Abadan. When Britain's navy switched from coal to petroleum just before World War I, the future of Persian oil looked even brighter. But to the nationalists this growing industry was cold comfort. It was far from Tehran, in lands controlled by tribal shaykhs. The revenues were going mainly to British stockholders— not to the Persian government, let alone its impoverished subjects. In the last years before World War I, Persia as a whole seemed to be drifting toward becoming a Russian protectorate.

CONCLUSION

Nationalism in the West earned a bad name in the twentieth century, partly due to the destruction caused by two world wars, partly because of the excesses of such dictators as Mussolini and Hitler, and maybe also because our intellectual leaders have become more cosmopolitan. Even in the Middle East, people now attack secular nationalism and exalt Islamic unity. Nearly everyone recognizes the artificial character of most of the so-called nations set up by foreign imperialism.

Generally speaking, Middle Eastern nationalist movements fared badly before World War I. They did not increase the power, the lands, or the freedom of the Muslim states in which they arose. Except for a few successful moments, which now seem like lightning flashes within a general gloom, these movements did not win any wide popular support. There is no nationalism in Islam, said the critics, so these movements could appeal only to youths who had lost their religion because of Western education.

Even when they reached a wider public, their success was due to popular misunderstandings. The uneducated majority often mistook the nationalist triumphs for Muslim victories. And these were few indeed.

You may wonder why we told you so much about these unsuccessful nationalist movements. Why learn about them? History is not just the story of winners; sometimes we study losers whose grandchildren would be winners. History is more than a collection of mere facts, names, and dates; we must also learn how the peoples whom we care about view their own past. Ahmad 'Urabi and Mustafa Kamil are heroes to the Egyptian people today; Khedive Isma'il and Lord Cromer are not. In Istanbul, you can buy postcards with pictures of the leading New Ottomans. Every Turkish student sees the Young Turks as a link in the chain of national regenerators going from Selim III to Kemal Ataturk. The 1906 constitution remained the legal basis of Iran's government until 1979, and the Islamic Republic still honors the Shi'ite leaders and bazaar merchants who joined forces against the shah to make the older constitution a reality. For the peoples of the Middle East, these early nationalist movements were the prologue for the revolutionary changes yet to come.

12

⬛

The Roots of Arab Bitterness

Few topics in Middle East history have generated as much heat—and as little light—as Arab nationalism. Few people are as poorly understood as today's Arabs. Even deciding who is an Arab or defining what is meant by Arab nationalism can easily get scholars and students into trouble, with both the Arabs and their detractors. Nevertheless, Arabs are becoming more politically active in the twenty-first century. In our analysis we may find that what is called Arab nationalism has been dissolving into many different movements, whose common feature is that they pertain to various Arabic-speaking peoples who seek to control their own political destinies. We must study these various manifestations of Arab feeling. And let us not fool ourselves: Arab feeling is strong and is likely to get stronger. It is also sometimes bitter, owing to the Arabs' unhappy experiences in the early twentieth century. Let us see what happened, and why.

ARAB NATIONALISM

What is Arab nationalism? Simply put, it is the belief that the Arabs constitute a single political community (or nation) and should have a common government. Right away we can see problems. There is no general agreement on who is an Arab. The current definition is that an Arab is anyone who speaks Arabic as his or her native language. This is not enough. Many speakers of Arabic do not think of themselves as Arabs, nor do other Arabs so regard them: take, for example, the Lebanese Maronites, the Egyptian Copts, and of course the Jews born in Arab countries who went to live in Israel. A more eloquent definition is the one adopted by a conference of Arab leaders years ago: "whoever lives in our country, speaks our language, is reared in our culture, and takes pride in our glory is one of us."

Historical Background

As we review the history of the Arabic-speaking peoples, we must remember that they have not been united since the era of the High Caliphate, if indeed then. Moreover, except for the Bedouin, they did not rule themselves from the time the Turks came in until quite recently. The very idea of people ruling themselves would not have made sense to Middle Easterners before the rise of nationalism. Settled peoples cared that a Muslim government rule over them, defend them from nomads and other invaders, preserve order, and promote peace in accordance with the Shari'a. It did not matter whether the head of that Muslim government was an Arab like the Umayyad caliphs, a Persian like the Buyid amirs, a Turk like the Seljuk and Ottoman sultans, or a Kurd like Salah al-Din and his Ayyubid heirs. Almost all rulers succeeded by either heredity or nomination; no one thought of letting the people elect them.

The Arabs Under Ottoman Rule

From the sixteenth to the twentieth centuries most Arabs—all of them, really, except in parts of Arabia and Morocco—belonged to the Ottoman Empire. Even in periods of Ottoman weakness, the local officials and landlords were usually Turks, Circassians, or other non-Arabs. Since World War I, Arab nationalists and their sympathizers have denounced the horrors of Ottoman rule, blaming the Turks for the Arabs' backwardness, political ineptitude, disunity, or whatever else was amiss in their society. What went wrong? Were the Arabs under Ottoman rule better or worse off than they had been earlier? In fact, the Arabs' decline cannot be blamed on Istanbul. You can even argue that early Ottoman rule benefited the Arabs by promoting local security and trade between their merchants and those of Anatolia and the Balkans. If the eighteenth-century Ottoman decline and overly zealous nineteenth-century reforms hurt the Arabs, the Turks within the empire suffered too. If Ottoman rule was so oppressive, why did the Arabs not rebel?

Well, at times they did. We have mentioned the Wahhabi revolt in eighteenth-century Arabia, but that group wanted to purify Islam, not create an Arab state. Some peasant and military revolts broke out in Egypt, but for economic rather than national reasons. Some historians find an anti-Ottoman angle in the policies of Mehmet 'Ali and Ibrahim. The latter, as governor of Syria, supposedly said, "I am not a Turk. I came to Egypt as a child, and since that time, the sun of Egypt has changed my blood and made it all Arab." But Mehmet 'Ali and his heirs spoke Turkish, thought they belonged to the Ottoman ruling class, and treated Egyptians like servants. 'Urabi's name implied an Arab identity, and he did oppose Turk-ish and Circassian officers in the Egyptian army, but his revolution was an Egyptian one directed mainly against the Anglo-French Dual Control. Up-risings in Syria were frequent, but their cause was usually religious. Tribes in Iraq and the Hijaz often revolted against Ottoman governors, but over local—not national—grievances.

Most historians, therefore, have concluded that Arab identity played no great part in Middle East politics up to the twentieth century. Muslim Arabs feared that any attempt to weaken the Ottoman Empire would hurt Islam. Even under Sultan Abdulhamid, despite his faults, most Arabs went on upholding the status quo. Many served in the army or civil adminis-tration. A few were prominent advisers. They might have been proud of belonging to the same "race" as Muhammad, but this did not inspire them to rebel against the Turks, who were Muslims too.

Christian Arab Nationalists

Not all Arabs are Muslim. In the nineteenth century, as many as one-fourth of the Arabs under Ottoman rule belonged to protected minori-ties. Most of these were Christians, who were less likely than the Muslims to feel a strong loyalty to the empire. But we must pin down the time, the place, and the sect before we can discuss the politics of the Arabic-speaking Christians. The ones whose role mattered most in the birth of Arab nationalism lived in greater Syria, which then included most of what we now call Israel, Jordan, Lebanon, the Republic of Syria, and even parts of southern Turkey. Until they came under the rule of Ibrahim in 1831, or under the Tanzimat reformers, Arabic-speaking Christians cared little about who governed them. The *millet* system gave virtual autonomy to both Orthodox and Monophysite Christians. Most of the others were usually so well protected by deserts, mountains, or river gorges that they hardly felt the Ottoman yoke. The Maronites (and other Catholics) en-joyed French protection by the nineteenth century. Russia took a growing interest in the welfare of the Greek Orthodox Syrians. From the 1820s on, American and French missionaries founded schools in Syria, as did the British, Russians, and other Westerners, though to a lesser extent. Inas-much as Syrian Christians naturally sent their children to mission schools closest to their own religious affiliation, Maronites and Uniate Catholics tended to go to French Catholic schools and to identify with France. How could the Orthodox compete? Alienated by the low educational level of their clergy, some were converting to Catholicism or Protestantism and sending their children to the relevant mission schools.

The Americans helped solve their problem, but they also aided the rise of Arab nationalism, quite by accident. US mission schools, especially their crowning institution, the Syrian Protestant College (now the American University of Beirut), admitted students of every religion. But most of them hoped also to convert young people to Protestant Christianity. Because Protestantism has traditionally stressed the reading and understanding of its sacred scriptures, the Bible was soon translated into Arabic for local converts. Many of the early American missionaries learned the language well enough to teach in it and even to translate English-language textbooks into Arabic. Until they realized that they could not recruit enough teachers and translate enough books under this system, the US mission schools and colleges used Arabic as their language of instruction. Reluctantly they switched to English in the late nineteenth century. Given this relative acceptance of their culture, many Arabs sent their children to American schools despite their Protestant orientation. The Orthodox Christians were especially apt to do so. This led to a higher standard of Arabic reading and writing among Syrian Orthodox youth, many of whom went into journalism, law, or teaching. Some became scholars and writers. Before long they were leading the Arabic literary revival, which turned into a nationalist movement, just as happened to literary movements in some European nations.

The growth of nationalism was also fostered by such American ideas as using the schools to develop moral character, promoting benevolent activities, and teaching students to create new institutions to fit changing conditions. The commitment of students and alumni of the American University of Beirut, in both the nineteenth and the twentieth centuries, nurtured the ideas of Arab nationalism and spread them among both Muslim and Christian speakers of Arabic. The American missionaries hoped to convert Arab youths to Protestantism through exposure to the Arabic Bible; the unintended outcome was to make them cherish more their heritage of Arabic literature and history. Their secular colleagues taught them to respect Western ideals of liberalism and democracy, but the students applied them to building an Arab nationalist ideology. Teachers sow their seed in unknown soil; their pupils decide what they will cultivate and determine what posterity will reap.

Muslim Arab Nationalists
But Arab nationalism could not have won Muslim acceptance if all its advocates had been westernized Christians. The centralizing Ottoman reforms, covered in Chapter 10, alienated some Arabs, high-ranking officials as well as local landlords, from what they were coming to view as a Turkish

empire. The first truly Muslim strain within Arab nationalism was a campaign during the 1890s, popularized by a writer named 'Abd al-Rahman al-Kawakibi, to revive the Arab caliphate, preferably in Mecca. Pan-Islam, strong among Muslims since the 1860s, had urged them to unite behind the Ottoman sultans. By juggling a few historical facts, their backers had claimed that the caliphate, maintained in Cairo by the Mamluks after the Mongol capture of Baghdad in 1258, had been transferred to the Ottoman sultans upon their conquest of Egypt in 1517. But Sunni political theory states that the caliph must belong to Muhammad's tribe, the Quraysh. The Ottomans were not Arabs, let alone members of the Quraysh tribe. Actually, they had seldom used the title of caliph before Sultan Abdulaziz (r. 1861–1876) did so to garner support from Ottoman Muslims and to counter the harmful effects of Russian pan-Slavism. Sultan Abdulhamid exploited the caliphate even more, trying to win the backing of Egyptian and Indian Muslims ruled by Britain—one of the reasons for his bad reputation in Western history books. Britain's rising hostility to the Ottoman sultan may have stimulated Kawakibi's nationalism. Whatever the cause, his idea of an Arab caliphate did gain support from some Arabian amirs as well as Egypt's Khedive 'Abbas. Although the khedives were descendants of Mehmet 'Ali, originally an Albanian, they often tried to win away Arab support from the Ottoman sultans. In short, Kawakibi's campaign to free the Arabs from Turkish rule mattered more as a power ploy for diplomats, khedives, and amirs than for its popular following at the time.

The Arabs and the Young Turks

The first breakthrough for Arab nationalism was the 1908 Young Turk revolution, which restored the long-suspended Ottoman constitution. Suddenly, men living in Beirut and Damascus, Baghdad and Aleppo, Jaffa and Jerusalem were choosing representatives to an assembly in Istanbul. Hopes were raised for Arab-Turkish friendship and for progress toward liberal democracy in the Ottoman state. Arab hopes soon faded, though. Representation in Parliament favored Turks against the empire's many ethnic, linguistic, and religious minorities. Moreover, the elections were rigged to ensure that most of the deputies belonged to the CUP. The Young Turk regime, imperiled by European imperialism and Balkan nationalism, resumed the centralizing policies of earlier Ottoman reformers. Consequently, the Arabs began to fear these threats to their liberties, preserved by the weakness or indifference of earlier governments. The imposition of Turkish as the language of administration and education especially angered the Arabs.

But how could they react? Not since Muhammad's day had large numbers of Arabic-speaking peoples mobilized politically to gain unity and freedom. How could they oppose a government headed, at least in name, by a sultan-caliph? What good would it do Syria's Arabs to overthrow Turkish rule, only to become, like Egypt, a dependency of a Christian power? Few Syrians (other than some Maronites) sought French rule. Nor did Iraqi Arabs want their port city of Basra to become, like Suez, a link in Britain's imperial communications.

The result of these deliberations was a low-profile movement of a few educated Arabs aimed not at separation but at greater local autonomy. It included three groups: (1) the Ottoman Decentralization Party, founded in 1912 by Syrians living in Cairo and seeking Arab support for more local autonomy instead of strong central control by the Ottoman government; (2) *al-Fatat* (Youth), a secret society of young Arabs who were students in European universities and who convoked an Arab Congress, held in Paris in 1913, to demand equal rights and cultural autonomy for Arabs within the Ottoman Empire; and (3) *al-'Ahd* (Covenant), a secret society of Arab officers in the Ottoman army, who proposed turning the Ottoman Empire into a Turco-Arab dual monarchy on the pattern of Austria-Hungary. Each of these groups found backers among educated Arabs living in Istanbul, Beirut, Damascus, and abroad.

But do not overestimate the appeal of Arab nationalism before World War I. Most Arabs remained loyal to the CUP, the Ottoman constitution that gave them parliamentary representation, and a government in which some Arabs served as ministers, ambassadors, officials, or army officers. If Arab nationalism had led to their separation from the Ottoman Empire, Egypt's khedive or the British might have gained more of Syria or Iraq than the Arabs. Even if Egypt was prospering, Arabs elsewhere did not crave British rule, let alone a French imperialism like that already ruling in Algeria. The Jewish settlers in Palestine, as yet too few to threaten the Arab majority, might later aspire to separate statehood (see Chapter 15), and Arab nationalists opposed this potential threat even more strenuously than Turkish rule.

World War I

The next turning point in the rise of Arab nationalism occurred when the Ottoman Empire decided in August 1914 to enter World War I on the German side. The CUP leaders, especially War Minister Enver, may have been influenced by their exposure to German military advisers, but their main motives were to regain Egypt from the British and the Caucasus Mountains from Russia. In 1914 Germany was respected for its economic and military might. The Germans were building a railway from Istanbul to Baghdad that would hold together what was left of the Ottoman Empire. A German military mission in Istanbul was training officers and soldiers to use modern weapons. Two German warships, caught in the Mediterranean when the war started and pursued by the British navy, took refuge in the Straits, whereupon they were handed over by the German ambassador as gifts to the Ottoman government (complete with their German crews, who donned fezzes and called themselves instructors). They replaced two ships being built for the Ottoman navy in British shipyards and already paid for by public subscription that the British navy had commandeered when the war began. So strongly did the Ottoman government and people support the German cause that after the new "Turkish" ships had drawn the empire into the war by bombarding the port of Odessa, the sultan proclaimed a jihad against Britain, France, and Russia. All three had millions of Muslim subjects who, if they had heeded the message, would have had to rebel on behalf of their Ottoman sultan-caliph.

Britain and the Arabs

The British, especially those serving in Egypt and the Sudan, sought to counter this pan-Islamic proclamation serving the Turks and Germans, who invaded the Sinai in late 1914, as Britain declared its official protectorate over Egypt. Some Ottoman army units reached the Suez Canal in February 1915, and one even crossed to the western side under cover of darkness. For three years, Britain had to station more than 100,000 imperial troops in Egypt—partly to intimidate the Egyptian nationalists, but mainly to stop any new Ottoman effort to take the canal, which the British now viewed as their imperial lifeline.

Britain responded by approaching an Arab leader in the Hijaz—namely, Husayn, the *sharif* and amir of Mecca. Let us explain these titles. A sharif is a descendant of Muhammad, of which there were many in the Hijaz, especially in the Muslim holy cities. Being protectors of Mecca and Medina conferred prestige on the Ottoman sultans; they lavished honors on the sharifs but also exploited their rivalries to control them. The various clans of sharifs competed for the position of amir (prince), which carried some temporal authority. During the nineteenth century, however, the Ottoman government had tried to assert direct rule over the Hijaz by appointing a local governor. Sharif Husayn, the leader of one of the contending clans (which he called the Hashimites, the clan of the Prophet himself), had long struggled with the Ottoman sultan and his governors. Although loyal to the Ottomanist ideal when he became amir in 1908, Husayn hated the CUP's centralizing policies.

One of Husayn's sons, Abdallah, had ties with Arab nationalist societies in Syria before World War I. Just before the war began, Abdallah went to Cairo to seek support from the British consul, Lord Kitchener. The British government hesitated to plot against the Ottoman Empire, which it had long tried to preserve, but Kitchener remembered the meeting later. When he went home to help plan Britain's war effort, London thought of forming an anti-Ottoman alliance with these Hashimite sharifs in Mecca. The British government instructed its Cairo representative to contact Husayn, hoping to dissuade him from endorsing the jihad or, better yet, to persuade him to lead an Arab rebellion against Ottoman rule.

The Husayn-McMahon Correspondence
In Cairo, Britain's high commissioner (the new title resulted from the declaration of the British protectorate over Egypt), Sir Henry McMahon, wrote to the sharif of Mecca, hoping he would rebel against Ottoman rule in the Hijaz. Husayn in turn asked for a pledge that the British would support the rebellion financially and politically against his Arab rivals as well as against the Ottoman Empire. If he called for an Arab revolt, it was not for the sake of changing masters. The British in Egypt and the Sudan knew from talking with Arab local nationalists that the Hashimites could not rally other Arabs to their cause—given the power and prestige of rival families living elsewhere in Arabia—unless the Arabs were assured that they would gain their independence in the lands in which they predominated: Arabia, Iraq, and Syria, including Palestine and Lebanon.

Keeping these considerations in mind, the amir of Mecca and the British high commissioner for Egypt and the Sudan exchanged some letters in 1915–1916 that have since become famous and highly controversial. In the course of what we now call the Husayn-McMahon Correspondence, Britain pledged that, if Husayn proclaimed an Arab revolt against Ottoman rule, it would provide military and financial aid during the war and would then help to create independent Arab governments in the Arabian Peninsula and most parts of the Fertile Crescent.

Britain did, however, exclude some parts, such as the port areas of Mersin and Alexandretta (which now are in southern Turkey), Basra (now in Iraq), and "portions of Syria lying to the west of the areas [districts] of Damascus, Homs, Hama, and Aleppo." One of the toughest issues in modern Middle East history is to figure out whether McMahon meant to exclude only what is now Lebanon, a partly Christian region coveted by France, or also Palestine, in which some Jews hoped to rebuild their ancient homeland. Lebanon is more clearly west of Damascus and those other Syrian cities than is what we now call Israel. The Arabs argue, therefore, that Britain promised Palestine to them. But if the letter referred to the province of Syria (of which Damascus was the capital), what is now Israel and was then partly under a governor in Jerusalem may have been what McMahon meant to exclude from Arab rule. Not only the Zionists but also the British government after 1918, even McMahon himself, believed that he had never promised Palestine to the Arabs. However, because Britain cared more in 1915 about its French alliance than about reserving Palestine for the Jews, we think that Lebanon was the area excluded from Arab rule in the negotiations. Only later would Jewish claims to Palestine become the main issue.

The exclusion of these ambiguously described lands angered Husayn; he refused to accept the deal, and his correspondence with the British in Cairo ended inconclusively in early 1916. The Ottomans could have averted any major Arab revolt, but for its authoritarian governor in Syria, Jemal, who needlessly antagonized the Arabs there. As former naval minister and one of the three Young Turks who controlled the Ottoman government when it entered World War I, Jemal had led the Turkish expedition to seize the Suez Canal and free Egypt from British rule. Although his first attempt failed, Jemal planned to try again. He settled down as governor of Syria while he rebuilt his forces, but he did little for the province. Many areas were struck by famine, locusts, or labor shortages caused by the conscription of local farmers into the Ottoman army. Fuel shortages led to the cutting down of olive trees and hindered the transport of food to the stricken areas. One-fourth of all Syrians died during the famine. Meanwhile, the Arab nationalist societies met and pondered which side to take in the war. One of Husayn's sons, Faysal, came to Syria to confer with both the Arab nationalists and Jemal in 1915, but in vain. Then in the spring of 1916 Jemal's police seized some Arabs, including scholars who were not nationalists, tried them for treason, and had twenty-two of them publicly hanged in Beirut and Damascus. The executions aroused so much anger in Syria—and among Arabs in general—that Faysal returned to Mecca a convert to Arab nationalism, and convinced his father that the time for revolt had come.

The Arab Revolt

On 5 June 1916 Husayn declared the Arabs independent and unfurled the standard of their revolt against Turkish rule. The Ottoman Empire did not fall at once, but numerous Arabs in the Hijaz, plus some in Palestine and Syria, began to fight the Turks. But were the Arabs in these areas truly nationalists? Most probably did not care whether they were ruled from Istanbul or Mecca, so long as the war's outcome was in doubt.

The Arab Revolt raged for the next two years. Guided by European advisers, notably T. E. Lawrence, Amir Husayn's Arab backers fought on the Allied side against the Ottoman Empire. Working in tandem with the British Empire troops advancing from the Suez Canal, they moved north into Palestine. While the British took Jaffa and Jerusalem, the Arabs were blowing up railways and capturing 'Aqaba and Amman. When Britain's forces drew near Damascus in late September 1918, they waited to let Lawrence and the Arabs occupy the city, which then became the seat of a provisional Arab government headed by Faysal. Meanwhile, the Ottoman army, now led by Mustafa Kemal (later Ataturk), withdrew from Syria. The Turks were also retreating in Iraq before an Anglo-Indian army. Late in October the Ottoman Empire signed an armistice with the Allies at Mudros. The Arabs, promised the right of self-determination by the British and the French, were jubilant. Surely their independence was at hand.

The Sykes-Picot Agreement

But this was not to be. The British government during the war had promised Ottoman-ruled Arab lands to other interested parties. Russia had already demanded Allied recognition of its right to control the Turkish Straits. In a secret treaty signed in London in 1915, Britain and France promised to back Russia's claim. Italy and Greece also claimed portions of Anatolia. France, while fighting the Germans on the Western Front, could not send many troops to the Middle East, but it wanted all of Syria, including Lebanon and Palestine. So Britain, France, and Russia drew up a secret pact called the Sykes-Picot Agreement (see Map 12.1). Signed in May 1916, it provided for direct French rule in much of northern and western Syria, plus a sphere of influence in the Syrian hinterland, including Damascus, Aleppo, and Mosul. Britain would rule lower Iraq directly. It would also advise an Arab government to be given lands between the Egyptian border and eastern Arabia, thus ensuring indirect British control from the Mediterranean to the Gulf. An enclave around Jaffa and Jerusalem would be under international rule because Russia wanted a part in administering the Christian holy places. The only area left for the Arabs to govern without foreign rulers or advisers was the Arabian desert.

Arab apologists claim that Amir Husayn knew nothing about the Sykes-Picot Agreement until after the war. T. E. Lawrence was wracked by guilt

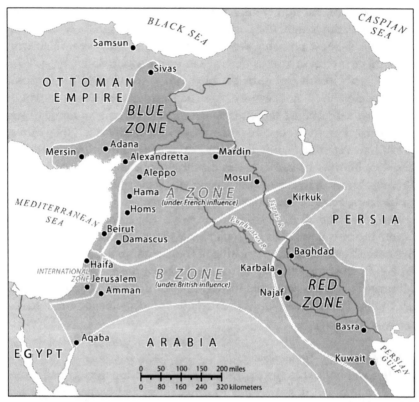

Map 12.1   The Sykes-Picot Agreement, 1916

because he had encouraged the Arabs on Britain's behalf, thinking that they would get their independence after the war, when in fact they were being manipulated by British diplomacy, if not duplicity. Lawrence's *Seven Pillars of Wisdom* is a readable book and *Lawrence of Arabia* is a great film, but neither one is history. Amir Husayn did know about the Sykes-Picot Agreement. Not only had the Allied secret treaties been published by the Communists after they had seized control of Russia in 1917, but Husayn learned about the agreement from Turkish agents trying to draw him out of the war and, indeed, from the British and French themselves. To Husayn, the advantages of directing an Arab revolt against the Turks, who had kept him in detention before the war, outweighed the perils of Sykes-Picot, which the British claimed would not involve the lands he hoped to rule. To other Arab nationalists, this Anglo-French agreement betrayed their cause; worse, it was kept secret until after World War I.

The Balfour Declaration

More public was a decision by the British cabinet to help establish a Jewish national home in Palestine, formally announced on 2 November 1917. This was the famous Balfour Declaration, so called because it appeared as a letter from the foreign secretary, Lord Balfour, to Lord Rothschild, titular president of Britain's Zionist Federation. The letter will be analyzed in Chapter 15, but we can note here its salient points: (1) the British government would help set up a national home in Palestine for the Jews, (2) it would not undermine the rights or status of Jews choosing not to live there, and (3) it would not harm the civil and religious rights of Palestine's "existing non-Jewish communities." The Arabs' main objection to the Balfour Declaration was that they made up over nine-tenths of what would later become Palestine. How could anyone create a home for one group of people in a land inhabited by another? Worse still, the inhabitants had never been asked whether they wanted their land to become the national home for a people who would be coming from far away. Moreover, the Balfour Declaration never mentioned the political rights of non-Jewish Palestinians, a point that still stirs deep Arab resentment because the Declaration does not allow them the right to form an independent nation-state. If Britain tried to realize the Zionist dream of a Jewish state, what would be the political status of Palestine's Arabic-speaking Christians and Muslims? Did this document not contradict the Husayn-McMahon Correspondence and other statements meant to reassure Arabs who had thrown themselves into the revolt against the Turks?

THE POSTWAR PEACE SETTLEMENT

How would these conflicting commitments be reconciled, once the war was over? In November 1918 the guns in Europe fell silent. Everyone hoped the diplomats would make a lasting peace. During the war, President Woodrow Wilson, the greatest statesman of the day, had proposed a set of principles called the Fourteen Points, upon which he wanted the Allies to build the peace once the war was won. He denounced secret treaties, urged self-determination for all peoples (specifically including those who had been under Ottoman rule), and proposed creating the League of Nations to avert future wars. When he came to Europe to represent the United States at the Paris Peace Conference, Wilson was hailed everywhere as a hero and savior.

But Britain and France, the Allies that had borne the brunt of the fighting and the casualties, were determined to dictate the peace. The defeated powers—Germany, Austria-Hungary, and the Ottoman Empire—could not attend the peace conference until it was time to sign the treaties. Russia (now a Communist state that had signed a separate peace treaty with Germany) was also excluded. Georges Clemenceau, who headed France's delegation, expressed the popular mood when he demanded that Germany be punished and that France get control over all of geographical Syria. David Lloyd George, heading the British delegation, agreed that Germany should be punished, but he also sought a formula to bring peace to the Middle East without harming the British Empire. The Zionist (or Jewish nationalist) movement was ably represented by Chaim Weizmann. The Arabs had Faysal, assisted by Lawrence (see Box 12.1).

The King-Crane Commission

No one could reconcile the Middle Eastern claims of the Arabs, the Zionists, the British, and the French, but the conferees did try. Wilson wanted to send a commission of inquiry to Syria and Palestine to find out what their people wanted. Lloyd George accepted Wilson's idea, until the French said that unless the commission also went to Iraq (whose inhabitants were resisting Britain's military occupation), they would boycott it. The British then lost interest, so the US team, called the King-Crane Commission, went alone. It found that the local people wanted complete independence under Faysal, who had already set up a provisional Arab government in Damascus. If they had to accept foreign tutelage, they would choose the Americans, who had no history of imperialism in the Middle East, or at least the British, whose army was already there, but never the French.

The King-Crane Commission also examined the Zionist claims, which its members had initially favored, and concluded that their realization would provoke serious Jewish-Arab conflict. Its report proposed to scale back the Zionist program, limit Jewish immigration into Palestine, and end any plan to turn the country into a Jewish national home. The Arabs hoped the King-Crane Commission would win Wilson to their side, but he suffered a paralytic stroke before he could read the commissioners' report, which was not even published for several years.

Allied Arrangements: San Remo and Sèvres

Contrary to Arab hopes, Britain and France agreed to settle their differences. France gave up its claims to Mosul and Palestine in exchange for a free hand in the rest of Syria. As a sop to Wilson's idealism, the Allies set up a mandate system, under which Asian and African lands taken from

Box 12.1	Faysal ibn Husayn

Faysal (1883–1933) was the third son of Husayn ibn 'Ali, sharif and amir of Mecca. Following a local custom, Faysal was sent to spend his early childhood among the Bedouin of Arabia. From 1891 to 1909 he lived with his father in Istanbul. Upon returning to Mecca in 1909, he gained military experience by participating in his father's wars against rival Arab tribes. As a military commander, if not as a politician, Faysal would prove quite successful.

In early 1916, while on a visit to Damascus, Faysal was drawn into a secret Arab society called al-Fatat. This society wanted to liberate Arab lands from Ottoman rule and believed the best way to do this was to encourage the British and the Turks to compete for Arab loyalty. Faysal returned to Mecca with a document known as the Damascus Protocol, which outlined which Arab lands should be independent after the war. His father, Amir Husayn, was to use this document to bargain with the British. Believing he had Britain's commitment to support an independent Arab state, Husayn declared the Arab Revolt in June 1916. Faysal would lead his northern legions in this effort.

Although aided in this task by the famous Lawrence of Arabia (T. E. Lawrence), Faysal was the one who united and effectively led an army made up of independent-minded Bedouin irregulars, Arab regulars, and a few European auxiliaries. He served as the mobile right wing of General Edmund Allenby's Egyptian Expeditionary Force as it invaded Palestine and Syria. On 3 October 1918 Faysal's forces occupied Damascus, where he took charge of the Arab occupation forces holding Syria. At this point Arab plans started to go downhill because of circumstances outside of Faysal's control.

When Faysal, again advised by Lawrence, attended the Paris Peace Conference, he demanded that the British fulfill their promises made to his father, Husayn: they should create an independent state that would include the Arab lands of the Middle East. However, the British decided to honor contradictory Middle East deals made to their fellow Europeans: the French (the Sykes-Picot Agreement) and the Zionists (the Balfour Declaration). To accommodate the French and the Zionists, the British abandoned most of their promises to the Arabs.

The Arabs considered this an act of betrayal, and they have never forgotten it. The British sought to compensate Husayn with rule in the Hijaz. Faysal ruled in Syria until 1920 when, abetted by the British, French forces occupied the country and forced Faysal to flee. In 1921, the British made him king of Iraq. Despite his dependence on the British, Faysal was seen as a leader by the Arab nationalists in the interwar period. He was the only Arab leader who was able to deal with all sides. His sudden death of a heart attack in 1933 came as a shock to the Arabs, who mourned his passing as a devastating loss to the cause of Arab nationalism.

Turkey and Germany were put in a tutelary relationship to a Great Power (called the mandatory), which would teach the people how to govern themselves. Each mandatory power had to report periodically to a League of Nations body called the Permanent Mandates Commission, to prevent exploitation. Meeting in San Remo, Italy, in 1920, British and French representatives agreed to divide the Middle Eastern mandates: Syria (and Lebanon) to France, and Iraq and Palestine (including what is now Jordan) to Britain. The Hijaz would be independent. The Ottoman government had to accept these arrangements when it signed the Treaty of Sèvres in August 1920. By then the French army had already marched eastward from Beirut, crushed the Arabs, and driven Faysal's provisional government out of Damascus. The Arab dream had been shattered.

The Result: Four Mandates and an Emirate

What happened then to the Arabs of the Fertile Crescent? The French had absolutely no sympathy for Arab nationalism and ruled their Syrian mandate as if it were a colony. Hoping to weaken the nationalists, the French split Syria into smaller units, including what would eventually become Lebanon, plus Alexandretta (which would be given to Turkey in 1939), states for the Alawites in the north and the Druze in the south, and even Aleppo and Damascus as city-states. Lebanon's separation from Syria lasted because it had a Christian majority (as of 1921) that was determined to keep its dominant position. The other divisions of Syria soon ended, but the Syrians rebelled often against French rule, which in the 1920s and 1930s seemed likely to last (see Map 12.2).

The British were inconsistent backers of Arab nationalism, working with the Hashimite family. Husayn still ruled in the Hijaz, but the prestige he had gained from the Arab Revolt made him a troublesome ally for the British. He refused to sign the Versailles and Sèvres treaties, proclaimed himself "king of the Arabs," and later claimed to be the caliph of Islam. These actions so offended the British that, as the Sa'ud family rose to power in eastern Arabia (see Chapter 13), they did nothing to stop the Sa'udis from marching into the Hijaz and toppling his regime in 1924. As for Iraq, British control led to a general insurrection in 1920. Needing a strongman to pacify the Iraqis, the British brought in Faysal to become their king, and peace was restored.

What would become of Abdallah, who had planned to rule in Baghdad? After Faysal was ousted from Damascus in 1920, Abdallah gathered about 500 tribal Arabs, occupied Amman, and threatened to attack the French

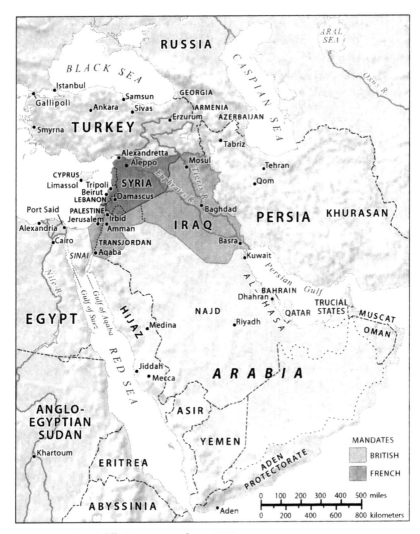

Map 12.2   The Middle Eastern mandates, 1924

in Syria. Although he could not have expelled them, the British wanted to keep him quiet. Colonial Secretary Winston Churchill met Abdallah in Jerusalem and persuaded him to accept—temporarily—the part of Palestine east of the Jordan River, until the French left Syria. This provisional deal was opposed by the Zionists, who wanted all of Palestine, as defined by the 1920 peace treaties, to be open to Jewish settlement and eventual statehood. France feared that Abdallah's new principality would become a staging area for Hashimite raids on Syria. No one expected this Emirate of Transjordan to last long, but it did. While the western part of the Palestine mandate seethed with Jewish-Arab strife, Transjordan became an oasis of tranquil politics. The sad story of Britain's mandate in the rest of Palestine must be saved for Chapter 15.

CONCLUSION

The Arabs had been roused from centuries of political lethargy, first by American teachers and missionaries, then by the revolution of the Young Turks, and finally by the blandishments of Britain and France during World War I. They recalled their ancient greatness and longed to recover it. From the West they learned about rights and freedoms, democratic governments, and national self-determination. Led by descendants of the Prophet Muhammad, a few Arabs had dared to rebel against the greatest Muslim state left in the world, the Ottoman Empire. In its place they hoped to set up one or more states that would have the same sovereign rights as all other independent countries. They helped the British and French defeat the Ottoman Turks in World War I, but later on the Allies failed to keep the pledges they had made to the Arabs. In the Fertile Crescent, where Arabs were clearly the majority, where they hoped to form independent states, where someday the Arab nation might revive its former power and glory, the victorious Allies set up mandates that were disguised colonies. Instead of being united, the Arabs found themselves being pulled farther apart. One area, Palestine, was declared the Jewish national home, leaving in doubt the future of its Arab inhabitants. These were the roots of Arab bitterness, put down almost a century ago. In the chapters to come, we shall see how this Arab anger bore bitter fruit.

13

Modernizing Rulers in the
Independent States

In the previous four chapters we have written about Middle Eastern peoples and countries that fell under European control. In fact, there was no area, except for the inaccessible deserts of Arabia and the remote mountains of Anatolia and Persia, that did not feel the West's impact by 1914. As you now know, Egypt and the Fertile Crescent came under Western rule, direct or indirect, before or during World War I. Even the regions that escaped—Anatolia, central Persia, and most of Arabia—were being eyed as potential colonies. The Allied secret agreements during the war would have awarded Istanbul and the Straits to czarist Russia and parts of western and southern Anatolia to Italy and France. Meanwhile, British agents were contacting the tribes of Arabia and Persia. Treaties were drafted that would have made their lands virtual British protectorates, as indeed Kuwait, Bahrain, the Trucial States (now called the United Arab Emirates), and Oman had become by 1914. Aden remained a settlement of the Indian government; only in 1937 would it become a Crown colony. In 1917 the Bolshevik Revolution pulled Russia out of the war and out of the contest for influence over its Middle Eastern neighbors, briefly at least. Once the Ottoman Empire and Germany surrendered in 1918, there seemed to be no one left to stem the spread of Western—especially British—power throughout the whole Middle East.

But the tide did turn. At least three areas of the Middle East did manage to salvage their independence after the war. The Turks in Anatolia drove off the Western invaders, terminated the moribund Ottoman Empire, and set up the Republic of Turkey. A group of soldiers and civilian nationalists blocked British and Bolshevik attempts to take over Persia, reorganized the country, and then replaced the weak Qajar shah with a strong ruler. In a remote part of east-central Arabia called Najd, a young man from an old ruling family combined a Muslim reform movement with a tribal warrior confederation to unite most of the peninsula as the Kingdom of Sa'udi Arabia.

Because most of the Middle East maps we see on television and in classrooms show political borders, we tend to think of Turkey, Iran, and Sa'udi Arabia as entities that have always existed. In reality, Turkey and Sa'udi Arabia got their present names and boundaries only between the world wars. Although its modern borders differ little from those of the 1890s, Iran (as Persia came to be called in 1935) is a far cry from the Persia that was divided in 1907 into Russian and British spheres of influence. In each of these states, these changes resulted from the inspiration, ingenuity, and industry of a military commander who became a political leader: Mustafa Kemal Ataturk in Turkey, Reza Shah Pahlavi in Iran, and 'Abd al-'Aziz ibn 'Abd al-Rahman (Ibn Sa'ud) in Sa'udi Arabia.

TURKEY: PHOENIX FROM THE ASHES

When the Ottoman naval minister signed the Mudros Armistice in October 1918, ending his country's active role in World War I, the empire was nearly prostrate. Its armed forces had suffered some 325,000 deaths (more than the total number of US casualties), 400,000 wounded, and 250,000 imprisoned or missing in action. High government spending had led to crushing taxes, deficit financing, and a severe price inflation that ruined many families.

Turkey's commerce, finance, and administration had already been disrupted by a fateful government policy: the deportation of the Armenians. Although they were Christians, most of these industrious people were loyal Ottoman subjects. Some had served in the army or the civil administration before the war. Others had made their mark in medicine, teaching, business, or skilled trades such as goldsmithing and photography. Only a few Armenians wanted a separate nation-state, for there was no Ottoman province in which they could have formed the majority of the population. But because some had earlier turned nationalist and rebelled against Sultan Abdulhamid, many Turks suspected them of treason. Once World War I broke out, the Ottoman government, abetted by its German advisers and fearing the Armenians as a potential fifth column, decided to clear them out of areas in eastern Anatolia near their coreligionists in enemy Russia. Many Armenians resisted deportation from their ancestral farms and pastures, villages and towns, so the Ottoman army allowed local Turkish and Kurdish brigands to loot and kill them. Only the hardiest and luckiest escaped. Even Armenians in southwestern Anatolia and Constantinople, far from Russia, were uprooted. About 1.5 million Armenians died. The survivors, having lost all they had, were bitter and vengeful. Those living east of the lands under Turkish control formed an independent Republic of Armenia in 1918. Some hoped to enlarge this state and put it under a US mandate. The American public was strongly pro-Armenian and anti-Turkish at the time, but later the US government refused any direct responsibility for rehabilitating what we now call eastern Turkey. Part of Armenia was absorbed by Turkey in 1920; the rest became a Soviet republic. The Armenians, generally pro-Ottoman up to World War I, became Turkey's most implacable foes.

Turkey had other problems. Mass conscription and prolonged fighting had deprived many areas of the country of their young men. Farms and villages fell into neglect, and weeds choked once-fertile fields. Whole forests had been cut down to fuel the trains and run the factories when coal grew scarce. Demoralized by defeats, disease, arrears in pay, and poor food, many soldiers deserted their units and roamed the countryside as armed brigands. British Empire troops, aided by the Arab Revolt, had driven the Ottomans from the Fertile Crescent. Meanwhile, in 1918, the Young Turk triumvirs, Enver, Talat, and Jemal, sent troops deep into the Caucasus. They hoped to build a new Turanian empire among the Muslims of what had been czarist Russia, now torn by civil war between the Whites (anti-Communists) and the Reds (Bolsheviks). One of the ironies of World War I is that Germany and the Ottoman Empire surrendered while some of their troops still occupied foreign lands.

Challenges to the Nationalists

The Mudros Armistice terminated the Young Turk regime; Enver, Talat, and Jemal fled from Istanbul on a German warship just before the British and the French occupied the Straits. So anxious was the Ottoman sultan to keep his power that he aligned himself totally with the Western powers and was ready to do whatever they demanded. Soon his brother-in-law, Damad Ferid, took over the government, started dismantling the Ottoman army, and tried to pacify the country. French troops entered the area of southern Anatolia known as Cilicia (authorized by the Sykes-Picot Agreement), while the Italians laid claim to Antalya, in the southwest. Although the Bolsheviks renounced claims made on Istanbul and the Straits by previous Russian governments, Britain and France now occupied these areas on the pretext of aiding the White Russians against the Communists. The winter of 1918–1919 was a nightmare for Istanbul's Turks. Influenza was rife, coal and wood were scarce, youth gangs roamed the darkened streets and robbed shopkeepers and passersby, food prices skyrocketed, and the Greek inhabitants flew their national flag openly. The victors even gave the French commander a white horse, on which he triumphantly entered the city, just as Mehmet the Conqueror had done in 1453.

By the time the Allies opened their postwar conference in Paris, they were prepared to divide Thrace and Anatolia—as well as the Arab lands discussed in Chapter 12—into spheres of influence. Some proposed a US mandate over Anatolia as well as Armenia. The Turks, weary from wars that had taken their young men and drained their treasury since the 1911 Libyan War, might have accepted foreign tutelage and military occupation, but for an unforeseen challenge. Eleftherios Venizelos, the Greek prime minister, argued before the Paris Peace Conference that the west Anatolian city of Smyrna (now Izmir) should be awarded to Greece. Greek nationalists in Athens wanted a reconstituted Byzantine Empire that would include Istanbul, Thrace, and western Anatolia, areas in which many Greek Christians still lived under Ottoman rule. Egged on by the Allies, especially Lloyd George, Venizelos acted to realize these ambitions. On 15 May 1919 some 25,000 Greek troops landed at Smyrna, welcomed by its mainly Greek and foreign inhabitants. No resistance came from the Ottoman government, which was trying to pacify a country that was close to anarchy. Yet this landing of the Greeks, long the most rebellious subjects of the Ottoman Empire, was the spark that ignited Turkish nationalism in Anatolia. Four days later another landing, equally fateful for Turkish history, occurred at the Black Sea port of Samsun.

Mustafa Kemal Ataturk

Commanding the force that landed at Samsun was Mustafa Kemal, a general who had been sent by the sultan's government to disarm the people and restore order to eastern Anatolia's turbulent provinces. Mustafa Kemal, later surnamed Ataturk, had already won fame for his military exploits in World War I. He had commanded the Turks' successful Dardanelles defense against the Western Allies in 1915. The following year his troops drove back the Russians in the east. He also directed the Turks' orderly retreat from Syria in 1918, gaining the respect of his British adversaries. His frank hostility toward the Young Turks had kept him from getting the positions or the power he craved. His ambitions thwarted by the CUP and the sultan's clique, Kemal had personal as well as patriotic reasons to oppose Istanbul's subservience to the Allies (see Box 13.1).

Box 13.1 Mustafa Kemal (Ataturk)

Mustafa Kemal (1881–1938) was born into a middle-class family in the Ottoman city of Salonika (now the Greek Thessaloniki). His father, a lumber merchant, died when Mustafa was still a child but left his family well off. Mustafa was first educated in a traditional Muslim *madrasa* and then transferred to a European-style school. When he was twelve, he entered a military high school, where a teacher gave him the nickname Kemal (meaning "perfection") in recognition of his superior work. The name stuck, and he was thereafter known as Mustafa Kemal.

By 1905 Mustafa Kemal had graduated from the War Academy in Istanbul with the rank of captain and was posted to Damascus. Already disenchanted with the Ottoman government, he started a clandestine society called Homeland and Freedom. In 1908 he participated in the Young Turk revolution that seized power from the sultan.

Mustafa Kemal then served as a field officer in a number of campaigns, including actions in Albania and Libya. When World War I broke out, he was given command of the forces resisting the British assault on the Dardanelles. This action made him a war hero among the Turks, and the next year, at the age of thirty-five, he was promoted to general. As the war turned bad for the Turks, Kemal kept their Syrian retreat from turning into a rout, thus coming out of the war with his reputation intact.

The victorious Allies soon found cooperative elements within the Ottoman elite. But Mustafa refused to acquiesce to a Turkey run by an occupation force that would serve the interests only of its former enemies. Once again he rallied Turkish forces to resist invading foes. Kemal proved charismatic enough to lead the resistance, and he took full advantage of the situation. When in 1923 Turkey became independent of any Allied occupation, Kemal was proclaimed the leader of his country. For the next fifteen years, he utterly transformed the nation by following nationalist, reformist, and secular principles. As a testament to his forcefulness, Turkey's Grand National Assembly bestowed on Kemal the honorary title of Ataturk, "Father of the Turks."

Kemal was convinced that, to remain independent of Western control, Turkey had to become ever more like the West. The defeat suffered in World War I discredited the old Ottoman regime based on Islamic traditions and laws. This gave Kemal the chance to force the Turks to rapidly adopt a complete program of westernizing reforms that affected all aspects of life, from clothing to language to gender relations to law codes. It gave the Turks the ultimate "culture shock." While all acquiesced in the process, some did so more enthusiastically than others. Westernization took root most securely in Turkey's urban cosmopolitan regions and less deeply in the rural villages. When Kemal Ataturk died in 1938, the country's Western orientation seemed assured. Today, however, after decades of westernization, many remain who contest Kemal's road to Turkish national salvation.

That Kemal alone gave life to Turkish nationalism in May 1919 is a myth. In reality, many groups in Thrace and Anatolia resisted the Greeks, the Armenians, their foreign backers, and the hapless Ottoman government. The driving spirit was Muslim as much as Turkish; *'ulama* and Sufi leaders commanded great respect in the countryside. What Kemal did was to energize these "defense of rights associations" by publicly resigning from the Ottoman army and convoking a national congress in the central Anatolian town of Sivas. But leaders of the Eastern Provinces Society for the Defense of National Rights had already called a congress at Erzurum. Invited to the Erzurum conference, Kemal was elected its chairman. It was here that the Turks first drew up their National Pact, calling for the preservation of Turkey's existing borders (the Ottoman Empire minus the Arab lands lost in the war), opposition to any future changes in those borders, formation of an elected government, and denial of special privileges to non-Turkish minorities. This set the stage for the September 1919 Sivas Congress, which rejected any foreign mandate over Turkey and demanded that the weak Ottoman government be replaced by an elected one willing to uphold Turkish interests.

Such was the general mood that the grand vizier did resign—pushed by a nationwide telegraph operators' strike (Turkey's westernizing reforms had given the country an extensive communications network). A coalition cabinet including several of Kemal's men took over. New parliamentary elections gave the Turkish nationalists a whopping majority, but the popular government did not last. In ratifying the National Pact, the Turkish deputies antagonized the Allies, who formally occupied Istanbul and forced the coalition ministry to resign. Damad Ferid resumed power, and the *shaykh al-Islam* (as appointed head of the Muslim community) branded the nationalists rebels against the sultan. Parliament was dissolved, and many of its deputies escaped to Ankara, safely beyond the range of Allied gunboats and occupation forces. There, in central Anatolia, Kemal convoked what he called the Grand National Assembly in April 1920.

The Kemalist movement now found itself at war with the Ottoman government in Istanbul, the (British-backed) Greek invaders around Smyrna, the Republic of Armenia in the east, the French in the south, and the British on the Straits. Poorly armed and half-starved Turkish irregulars were ranged against the well-supplied forces of the Allies and their Christian protégés. Underestimating the will of Kemal's nationalist following, the Allies in August 1920 made the Ottoman government sign the Treaty of Sèvres. This pact would later become the empire's death warrant.

Among its terms, the Sèvres treaty provided that (1) the Straits would be managed by a permanent Allied commission; (2) Istanbul could be removed from Turkish administration if it infringed on minority rights; (3) eastern Anatolia would belong to an independent Armenia and an autonomous Kurdistan; (4) Greece would have Smyrna as well as Thrace; (5) Italy and France would each get parts of southwestern Anatolia; (6) the Arab lands would be divided into British and French mandates (as described in Chapter 12); and (7) the Capitulations, abolished by the Ottomans in September 1914, would be restored and extended. Turkish nationalists resented the whole treaty, but even this humiliation did not satisfy Venizelos. Encouraged by Lloyd George, the Greek forces pushed eastward, taking Turkish lands never awarded to the Greeks at Sèvres.

What saved Turkey was the aid it got from Soviet Russia. Both countries were embroiled in civil war and in fending off foreign attackers. Together, they occupied the infant Republic of Armenia in late 1920. No longer challenged from the east, Kemal's forces managed to slow the Greek advance early in 1921. It gradually became clear that some Western countries would not back the Greeks either, once they claimed lands beyond what the Sèvres treaty had given them. France settled with the Kemalists after they had fought the Greeks to a standstill in a bitter battle near Ankara in August and September 1921. Both France and Italy renounced their territorial claims in Anatolia. Only Britain continued to occupy the Straits, control the sultan, and cheer on the Greeks. In the next summer the Turks launched a fierce offensive that drove the Greek armies completely out of Anatolia. Then, at last, the British government decided to cut its losses by calling for another Allied conference to negotiate a new peace treaty with Turkey. The Ottoman sultan, deprived of foreign support, fled from Istanbul, whereupon the Grand National Assembly in Ankara abolished the sultanate altogether. On 29 October 1923 Turkey became the first republic in the modern Middle East.

The Turkish nationalists may have shown the world that they could wear down their opponents militarily, but Britain still had to learn that they could also withstand political pressure. The British expected that the new peace conference, to be held in Lausanne, would be quick, letting them keep by diplomacy part of what their protégés had lost by war. General Ismet, chosen by Kemal to represent Turkey, stood firm and wore down his British counterpart, Lord Curzon, by feigning deafness and delaying the talks to get instructions from his government. When the Lausanne peacemakers finished replacing the Sèvres treaty, the Turks had freed their country of the hated Capitulations, all foreign armies, and any threat of an Armenian state or an autonomous Kurdistan. Most Greek Orthodox Christians living in Anatolia were deported to Greece as part of a population exchange that sent many Muslims from Bulgaria and Greek-ruled parts of Macedonia to a Turkey they had never known. The only setbacks for Turkey in the Lausanne treaty were an international commission to supervise shipping through the Straits (which were demilitarized) and the failure to obtain Mosul (which the League of Nations would later award to Iraq).

Thanks to the 1923 Lausanne Conference, Turkey became the only country defeated in World War I that could negotiate its own peace terms. Except for the 1936 Montreux Convention, which gave Turkey the right to fortify the Straits, and the annexation of Alexandretta in 1939, the Lausanne treaty remains the basis of Turkey's place among the nations of the world. By contrast, the Versailles treaty and all other postwar peace arrangements have long since been scrapped. Well might the Arabs, who had rebelled against the Turks to back the World War I victors, envy their erstwhile masters who had tied their fate to that of the vanquished!

Kemal's Domestic Reforms

Mustafa Kemal devoted the last fifteen years of his life to changing Turkey from the bastion of Islam into a secular nation-state. Islam, the lifestyle and basis of government for the Turks since their conversion a thousand years earlier, was now to be replaced by Western ways of behavior, administration, and justice. If persuasion failed, then the changes would be imposed by force. Twice opposition parties arose within the Grand National Assembly, but in both cases Kemal suppressed them. A Kurdish uprising in 1925 was crushed, and an attempt on Kemal's life led to the public hanging of most of his political opponents. As president of the republic, Kemal was authoritarian; yet he also detested fascism, opposed Marxist communism (although he took Soviet aid and was the first Middle Eastern leader to adopt state economic planning), and allowed free debate in the elected assembly. Kemal admired democracy in theory, but he ruled as a stern father and teacher to his people, who he believed were not yet ready to govern themselves.

Was Kemal a Muslim? He certainly flouted the Shari'a in his card playing, drinking, and sexual escapades. Yet he also relied on Islamic symbols and joined with Muslim leaders to defend Turkey against the Greeks. Even if he kept some of the attitudes and practices of his Muslim forebears, he was determined to destroy Islam's power to block Turkey's modernization. He let a member of the Ottoman family retain the caliphate briefly, but abolished the position in 1924. Angry protests from Muslims in Egypt and India could not save the caliphate, and the Turks themselves were indifferent. After all, the caliphs had been powerless for a thousand years.

From 1924 on, the Grand National Assembly passed laws closing the Sufi orders and *madrasas*, abolishing the *waqfs* and the position of *shaykh al-Islam,* and replacing the Shari'a, even in the hitherto untouchable realm of family law, with a modified version of the Swiss Civil Code. Women were assured of equal rights with men in marriage, divorce, and property inheritance, and they also started to enter the higher schools and professions, as well as shops, offices, and factories. Given the vote for the first time in 1934, Turkish women elected seventeen of their sex to the Assembly the next year. The veil, which had begun to disappear in Istanbul and Smyrna before and during the war, was discarded (with Kemal's encouragement) during the 1920s.

Of great symbolic importance was a law forbidding Turkish men to wear the fez or any other brimless headgear. Muslim males had always worn turbans, skullcaps, *kufiyas,* or other head coverings that would not hinder prostrations during formal worship. In common speech, "putting on a hat" meant apostasy from Islam. But Kemal, addressing a crowd in one of Anatolia's most conservative towns, wore a panama hat, mocked the traditional clothing of Turkish men and women, and announced that henceforth all males would have to wear the costume of "civilized" peoples, including the hat. It is ironic that Turkish men fought harder to go on wearing the fez, imposed by Sultan Mahmud a mere century earlier, than to save the caliphate, begun by Abu-Bakr in 632. What people wear often reflects how they live, the way they think, and what they value most. Soon, Turkish men and women dressed like Europeans.

Turkey faced west in other ways. The Ottoman financial calendar was replaced by the Gregorian one, and clocks were set to European time, a change from the Muslim system by which the date changed at sunset. Metric weights and measures replaced the Turkish ones, and the adoption of a formal day of rest (initially Friday, later Sunday) showed how Western the country had become. The call to worship and even Qur'an recitations were given in Turkish instead of Arabic. In 1928 the Turkish constitution's reference to Islam as the state religion was expunged.

Turkish culture experienced an even more drastic change at this time. Kemal announced that the Turkish language, hitherto written in an Arabic script ill-suited to its sounds and syntax, would thenceforth use a modified Roman alphabet. Within three months all books, newspapers, street signs, school papers, and public documents had to be written in the new letters. Only a tenth of the people had been literate under the old system; now it was their national duty to learn the new one and teach it to their children, their neighbors, even to porters and boatmen (to use Kemal's own expression). The new alphabet, which was easier to learn and more phonetic, accelerated the education of the Turks. The number of school pupils doubled between 1923 and 1938. The literacy rate would reach 95 percent in 2015. It was now easier for Turks to learn English, French, or other Western languages but harder to study Arabic or Persian, or even to read classics of Ottoman Turkish prose and poetry. The new Turkish Language Academy began replacing Arabic and Persian loanwords with neologisms based on Turkish roots. As in other Middle Eastern countries, English and French words entered the language, producing such new terms as *dizel* (diesel), *frak* (frock coat), *gol* (goal, as in soccer), *kuvafür* (coiffeur), *kovboy* (cowboy), and *taksi* (taxi).

Another westernizing step was the law passed by the Grand National Assembly requiring all Turks to take family names. As society became more mobile and the need grew for accurate record keeping, the customary use of a person's given name—sometimes combined with a patronymic (Mehmet son of 'Ali), military title, physical features, occupation, or place of origin—caused widespread confusion. Under the new law, Ismet, Kemal's representative at Lausanne, took the surname Inonu, the site of two of his victories over the Greeks. Mustafa Kemal became Ataturk (Father Turk) by a unanimous vote of the Grand National Assembly. Old titles, such as *pasha, bey,* and *efendi,* were dropped. Kemal Ataturk even gave up the title of *ghazi* used by Ottoman sultans and given to him earlier by a grateful Assembly following his victory over the Greeks. Henceforth men had to prefix their names with *Bay,* comparable to Mr. Women were to use *Bayan* in place of the traditional *hanum.* But old practices die hard: it took years to alphabetize the Istanbul phone book by the new family names.

Because Ataturk launched a comprehensive westernization program, he should have stressed economic growth. Actually, he took little interest in economics. But Turkey did move toward industrialization, as factories sprang up in the large cities and around the coal-mining region near where the Black Sea meets the Bosporus. Kemal was among Asia's first non-Communist leaders to call for state ownership and control of the main means of production. Hoping to speed up modernization, he brought in Soviet economists to draft Turkey's first five-year plan. During the 1930s the Turkish government set up a textile spinning and weaving complex, a steel mill, and various factories for producing cement, glass, and paper. Agrarian reform limped in this land of 50,000 villages, some linked by just a donkey path to the rest of the world, but agricultural training institutes, extension agents, rural health and adult education centers, and model farms did lead to some improvement.

Ataturk summed up his program in six principles, which were later incorporated into the Turkish constitution. Often called the Six Arrows, from the symbol of Ataturk's Republican People's Party (RPP), they are republicanism, nationalism, populism, statism, secularism, and reformism. Republicanism entails the selection of a leader from the citizenry, in contrast to the hereditary system of the Ottoman Empire and other dynastic states. Nationalism calls on the Turks to devote themselves to the needs of the Turkish nation, rejecting special ties to other Muslims or to foreign ideologies. Populism means that the government belongs to the Turkish people, working together for the common good, without distinction of rank, class, or sex. Statism is state capitalism: the government must direct and take part in the country's economic development. Secularism amounts to the removal of religious controls over Turkey's politics, society, and culture. Reformism (originally called revolutionism) refers to the ongoing commitment of the Turkish people and government to rapid but peaceful modernization.

Kemal Ataturk was a westernizing reformer, but above all he was a Turkish nationalist. The linguistic reforms simplified Turkish, bringing the written language closer to what the Turkish people spoke. Moving the capital from Istanbul to Ankara meant rejecting the cosmopolitan Byzantine and Ottoman past in favor of an Anatolian Turkish future. The study of history now stressed the Turks, from their misty origins on the Asiatic steppes up to their triumph over the Greeks, instead of the Islamic caliphate rooted in the Arabic and Persian cultures. Even westernization was defended in terms of Turkish nationalism: cultural borrowing was all right, considering how much Western civilization owed to the Turks. According to the sun language theory, once a popular idea that is now discredited, all languages could be traced back to Turkish, whose word for *sun* was the sound uttered in awe by the first articulate cave dweller. If the Turks had created the first language, anything they now took from other cultures was only a fair exchange. In addition, the schools, armed forces, rail and motor roads, newspapers, and radio broadcasting all reinforced the Turkish sense of nationhood.

The Legacy of Kemalism

The greatest tribute paid by the Turkish nation to Kemal since his death in November 1938 is its continuation of the Kemalist program. To be sure, some of the extremes have been moderated. The Qur'an and the call to worship are now chanted in Arabic, the Sufi orders have been allowed to resume their activities, and many Turks flock to the mosques on Fridays. But industrial and agricultural growth has moved ahead even faster than during Kemal's lifetime. To many Turks, their country is European, not Middle Eastern. Turkey has joined the North Atlantic Treaty Organization

(NATO), the Organization for Economic Cooperation and Development, and the Council of Europe. It hopes to become a full member of the European Union, having revised its taxes and tariff duties, improved its rights policies with regard to its Kurdish citizens, and even agreed to recognize Greek-ruled Cyprus, but protracted negotiations have not yet led to Turkey's admission into the EU, and it probably won't be admitted soon. Many Turks work in Europe, and those who have returned have pressed for strong Western ties. Although Turkey stayed out of World War II, it has since then built up its military might under US tutelage and acquitted itself well in the war against the Communists in Korea. Because of communal strife between the Greeks and Turks living in Cyprus, Turkey's armed forces intervened there in 1974; from that time on, the Turks have controlled the northern third of the island. Military experts rate Turkey's armed power second only to that of Israel among the countries of the Middle East.

Ataturk's methods and achievements were impressive, but let us put them into broader perspective. Keep in mind that his program was a link in the chain of westernizing reforms from Selim's *nizam-i-jedid* to Mahmud II, the Tanzimat era, Abdulhamid, the Young Turks, and Ziya Gokalp. His ambivalent position between dictatorship and democracy may remind you of Turkey's brief attempts at constitutional government in 1877 and 1908 or of its ongoing search for a political system that is both popular and orderly. After Ataturk's death, Turkey evolved toward a two-party system, as the new Demokrat Party rose to challenge the Kemalist RPP. After a free election in 1950, the Demokrats took power peacefully, a rare occurrence in a Middle Eastern country. Basing its power on the support of entrepreneurs, peasants, and pious Muslims, the Demokrat Party grew so strong that it alarmed the army officers, who overthrew the government in 1960. Under the army's watchful eye, civilian politicians in 1961 drew up a constitution for what would be called the Second Turkish Republic. They also outlawed the Demokrat Party and hanged its leader.

Yet the social forces that had made them popular soon created a new challenge for the Kemalists in the army and the RPP. This challenge took the form of the Justice Party, which won enough votes in the first election to enter into a coalition with the RPP and later was able to gain complete control of the government. The army intervened in 1971 to check what it deemed the excesses of the Justice Party. The RPP made a comeback, but small Marxist and neo-Muslim parties also grew up during the 1970s. Soon every Turkish cabinet was a coalition of several diverse parties, making government impossible. In 1980, after recurrent clashes between left- and right-wing extremists killed hundreds of Turks, the army again took control of the government. General Kenan Evren banned all political parties, detained their leaders, and set up a caretaker cabinet.

For the next three years, it looked as if the Turks had traded their liberties for security. The caretaker cabinet convoked a consultative assembly that drew up a constitution giving vast powers to the president and curtailing the rights of academics, labor unions, journalists, and anyone who had been active in party politics before 1980. Nevertheless, a nationwide referendum approved the new document in 1982, and general elections were held in 1983. Turgut Ozal, who as deputy prime minister for economic affairs had taken heroic measures to stop inflation, led the new Motherland Party to an electoral victory, becoming Turkey's first prime minister under its new constitution. Pressed by the Western European governments, Turkey hesitantly lifted its ban on political freedoms, and the Ozal administration helped the country achieve greater political stability and economic growth. Ozal himself moved from being prime minister to president in 1989, just as new economic problems beset the country, and he died in 1993, to be replaced by Suleyman Demirel. Tansu Ciller became Turkey's first female prime minister in the same year.

The resurgence of Islam (to be discussed in Chapter 18) has not spared Turkey, though, as an Islamist group, the Welfare Party, won a slight plurality in the 1995 election and briefly headed the government (until the army intervened to remove its prime minister and bring back the secularists). An Islamist government was elected again in 2002, headed by Recep Tayyip Erdogan of the Freedom and Justice Party. He served as prime minister for twelve years and was elected president in 2014. The country remains divided on religious issues, as many women agitate for the right to wear the Islamic head scarf in schools and universities and as Erdogan's government has given aid to Islamist fighters in Syria and Iraq. Ataturk's westernizing reforms split the mind of Turkey between acceptance of secular values and a desire to uphold Muslim principles and institutions.

FROM PERSIA TO IRAN

Persia is unique among the countries or cultures we have studied so far. Deserts and mountains give the land distinct boundaries, yet it has been invaded many times. Usually it has absorbed its invaders, but the absorption process has led to a mosaic of tribal nomads and sedentary peasants with distinctive folkways. Persian is the national language, but many of the people speak variants of Turkish, Kurdish, or Arabic. Its religion is Islam, but Persians adhere to the Twelve-Imam Shi'ite branch. More often than not in its history, Persia has been a distinct political entity, but historians commonly describe it by the name of its ruling family during the time in question—and Persia has had numerous dynasties.

Historical Recapitulation

Starting in the late eighteenth century, Persia's ruling family was the Qajar dynasty. It was under the Qajars that the country shrank to its currently recognized borders, losing to Russia the Caucasus Mountains and parts of Central Asia, and renouncing all claims to Afghanistan and what is now Pakistan. Tehran, a village near the Elburz Mountains, became Persia's capital under the Qajars, as it has remained ever since. Most Persians take no pride in the Qajar dynasty. Its westernization lagged behind that of the Ottoman Empire. Its resistance to Russian expansion was feeble. It invited commercial penetration and exploitation by British and other foreign merchants. Its subjects, led by their 'ulama (whom they call mollahs) and bazaar merchants, resisted political and economic subjection to these outsiders. This resistance was called Muslim fanaticism (by nineteenth-century imperialists) or Persian nationalism (by twentieth-century writers); no doubt political and religious feelings coexisted. One result was the 1906 constitution, which set up a representative assembly, the Majlis, to limit the shah's power.

Constitutionalism alone could not build a great nation. Unable to weld the diverse military units into one army, hamstrung by strong and lawless tribes, lacking the power to collect the taxes to pay for its expenses, Qajar rule was weak. Besides, Britain and Russia agreed in 1907 to set up spheres of influence in Persia. Russian troops occupied the northern third of the country before and during World War I. Several armies vied to control the British-held parts of the south, protecting the new wells, pipelines, and refinery of the Anglo-Persian Oil Company. During the war, a German colonel formed a rebel army in lands just north of the Gulf. Elsewhere in central Persia, German agents incited acts of murder and sabotage against British or Russian consuls and merchants. The 1917 Bolshevik Revolution briefly reduced Russian pressure on Persia, as the new Soviet Communist regime gave up all the czarist claims. Germany's defeat in 1918 left Britain as the sole foreign contender for control.

The Apogee of British Power

In 1919 Britain seemed ready to absorb Persia as it had most of the Arab lands. British imperial troops occupied Iraq; guarded most of the Arab sultanates, emirates, and shaykhdoms along the Gulf; invaded the Caucasus republics that were formed as the Turks pulled out; and aided White Russian forces against the Bolsheviks. Britain offered the Qajars a treaty that would have turned Persia into a veiled protectorate. But popular opposition to the proposed treaty was so fierce that the Majlis never ratified it, and it became a dead letter.

As we have shown elsewhere, 1919–1920 marked the high tide of British power in the Muslim world. The Kemalist revolt in Turkey, nationalist uprisings in Egypt and Iraq, Arab riots in Palestine, Britain's reluctance to defend the Caucasian republics (Azerbaijan, Armenia, and Georgia), its mediocre performance in its third Afghan War (1919), and the failure of Allied efforts to crush the Bolsheviks elsewhere, all taken together, marked a turning point in British policy. The public was clamoring to bring the troops home. Parliament would not commit funds to a long occupation. London, therefore, had to cut back its presence in the Middle East.

But Persia's territorial integrity was still threatened. Separatist revolts, aided by the Bolsheviks, broke out in 1920 in the northern provinces of Gilan and Azerbaijan. British officers remained in many areas as trainers for various Persian army units, but they were widely disliked. Trying to make both sides withdraw, Tehran negotiated a treaty with Moscow early in 1921. The Soviets removed their troops, renounced all extraterritorial privileges, canceled debts, and turned over all Russian properties in Persia. But the treaty had an article allowing the Soviet Union to send in troops whenever it felt menaced by another foreign army occupying Iranian soil. Although the Soviets would invoke this clause later, it helped Persia in 1921 to free its land from both Russian and British troops.

The Rise of Reza Shah

Five days before the Soviet-Persian pact was actually signed, an officer in the Persian Cossack Brigade (a local police force trained by Russians) toppled the regime in Tehran. This officer, Reza Khan, born in 1878 in Mazandaran, rose to prominence within the brigade during the tumultuous period after the war. Having helped to oust the brigade's pro-Bolshevik commander, Reza took charge of its infantry regiment and organized a secret society of Persian officers opposed to both British and Russian control. A general mutiny of the Persian Cossacks resulted in the dismissal of all Russian officers left in the brigade. Reza, seeing how easily he had gained control of his country's strongest force, was encouraged to enter the political arena. Working with an idealistic young journalist, Sayyid Ziya ud-Din Tabatabai, Reza led his Cossacks into Tehran and ousted the existing ministry on 21 February 1921. Ziya became the new premier and Reza the commander in chief of the Persian army. A vigorous and comprehensive reform program began, but Ziya held power for only three months. Opposed by many of his own ministers and probably by Reza, he resigned and went into exile.

Persia's political culture lapsed into its customary anarchy. The Majlis opened a new session with demands from the deputies for financial and bureaucratic reform. The last of the Qajars, Ahmad Shah, kept trying to leave the country. The old politicians were divided and dispirited. Reza, who by now was war minister, became the real power behind the throne. He concentrated on uniting Persia by restoring public security, consolidating the various armies, and suppressing tribal rebels, communists, and other dissidents. After an attempt on his life in 1923, Reza arrested the premier and made Ahmad Shah appoint him instead. The shah left for Europe, never to return.

Reza now intended to declare Persia a republic, following Kemal's example in Turkey, but the Shi'ite 'ulama, fearing a secular regime, mobilized nationwide opposition. After threatening to resign, Reza finally gave in. He evened the score by replacing the cabinet, putting in ministers who, though more competent, were also more compliant with his own wishes. He then set out to quash a tribal revolt in Khuzistan, followed by a pilgrimage to the Shi'ite shrines at Najaf and Karbala to mollify the mollahs. He returned to Tehran determined to strengthen his hold on the government. As the Majlis dithered, he acted alone to forge major reforms. One of these now stands as his greatest achievement—the Trans-Iranian Railway, which connects the Caspian Sea to the Gulf. This railway is notable because it was financed without foreign loans. Its costs were met by taxes on sugar and tea, two staples of the Persian diet.

In a nationalistic spirit, the Majlis in 1925 adopted the old Persian solar calendar in place of the Muslim lunar one and required everyone to take a family name. Reza took the surname Pahlavi, the name of the pre-Islamic Persian language. The Majlis proceeded to depose Ahmad Shah, abolish the Qajar dynasty, and proclaim Reza Khan Persia's new ruler. He officially became Reza Shah in December 1925 and then crowned his own head in a formal ceremony.

Reza's Reforms

Reza Shah was the regenerator of Persia just as Kemal, whom he admired, was the father of modern Turkey. The two leaders have often been compared, usually to Reza's disadvantage. But these nationalist reformers faced different conditions. Kemal had won fame as a successful general of a losing army, whereas Reza was known to just a few officers when he led the 1921 coup. Turkey was heir to more than a century of westernizing reforms; it had a cadre of trained officials and officers to carry out Kemal's programs. Persia had been less exposed than Turkey to the West, except for the dubious blessing of bordering on Russia. Kemal expressed the disillusionment toward Islam felt by many Turks and equated westernization with "civilization." Few Turks cared about their own pre-Islamic heritage in the far-off Asian steppes. Reza could make no such break with the Persian past. His people remained loyal to Shi'ite *mujtahids* and *mollahs*. Although he fought this Muslim influence, Reza also saw that Persia's pre-Islamic heritage was alive and meaningful to his subjects. This historic tie could promote his reform program, too, as Sassanid monuments were spruced up, Zoroastrianism won official toleration, and the Persian language was purged of some of its Arabic words. In a more drastic break with the past, Reza changed his country's name from Persia to Iran (the land of the Aryans) in 1935. The post office was even ordered to return any letters addressed to the country's old name. These symbolic changes strengthened national pride and distanced Iran from Islam and the Arab world.

One of Reza's ablest subordinates summarized his reforms under four convenient headings: (1) liberation from foreign political and economic domination, (2) establishment of internal security and centralized government, (3) administrative reforms and economic progress, and (4) social reforms and cultural progress. Let us examine each in more depth.

Liberation from foreign domination entailed more than ousting British and Russian troops. It also meant replacing British with Iranian control along the Gulf coast; taking charge of banks, currency, telephones, and telegraphs; and gaining the right to try foreigners accused of crimes and to fix and collect customs duties on imports. Reza succeeded in implementing every reform until he tried to annul the Anglo-Persian (soon to be renamed Anglo-Iranian) Oil Company's concession. Britain took the issue to the League of Nations. The company finally agreed to pay higher royalties to the Iranian government, which in turn extended the concession by thirty years. Later on, many Iranians would accuse Reza of being corrupted by British bribes.

Strengthening Iran's national government necessitated weakening the nomadic tribes. Many were forced to settle down, their chiefs in some cases being put under house arrest. Those allowed to remain nomadic often moved their flocks under police escort. The army was reorganized, with improved munitions, weapons, training, barracks, and health-care facilities. All security forces came under central control. A rudimentary political police was instituted.

Iran gradually acquired a civil service, European-style law codes and courts, a state budget, and a national system for registering births, land transfers, marriages, and deaths. Roads paved for cars and trucks, almost nonexistent in 1921, crisscrossed the country by 1941. Often accused of stealing peasants' lands to augment his own holdings, Reza claimed he wanted his estates to serve as model farms to discover and teach new methods. His modern factories and imposing public buildings probably boosted morale more than they really benefited the nation.

To Reza, social reform meant education. Schooling increased drastically at all levels, for girls as well as boys. Although Reza's opening of the University of Tehran in 1935 is well known, he cared most about the basic education of farmers and workers. Night schools proliferated, and the army became a vast training program. Officers were held responsible for teaching their troops to read, write, and do basic arithmetic. If any soldier did not gain these skills by the end of his two-year stint, then his unit commander would not get promoted. Sports and games had long been a part of Iran's culture, although many *mollahs* frowned on them; Reza made a cult out of physical fitness and athletic contests. He did not attack organized Islam directly (as Ataturk had done), but he sometimes nettled the *mollahs* by drinking beer or wine in public, and he did insist that all men who wore the garb of *'ulama* pass examinations proving their right to do so. He followed Ataturk's example by requiring Iranian men to wear European-style clothes and surpassed him by forbidding women to veil their faces. This reform deeply offended conservative Muslims, who argued that Westerners would be just as shocked if women of all ages had to go topless in public. Muslims did block what might have been a useful reform: romanizing the Persian alphabet.

Reza's Downfall

Although Reza Shah tried in many ways to transform Iran, the results often disappointed him. An impatient man, he never could delegate tasks. Trying to reduce Iran's dependence on Britain, he brought in foreigners from other lands to advise him on reforms. When a US mission improved Iran's fiscal administration in the 1920s but failed to attract American investors, Reza made the director resign and phased out his subordinates. The US government did not step in, much to the Iranians' astonishment. Germany was more active. An able German director built up the National Bank of Iran in the early 1930s. After Hitler took power, German entrepreneurs and advisers flocked to Iran. Reza and many of his subjects were flattered by Nazi racial theories, because they viewed Iran as the original

Aryan nation. When Nazi forces overran most of Europe early in World War II, the British had reason to fear Germany's presence in Iran. In 1941 a group of Arab nationalist officers briefly seized control of neighboring Iraq. Suspecting them of backing the Nazis, Britain intervened to install a pro-British regime. When Hitler suddenly invaded the Soviet Union that June, both the British and the Soviets sent troops into Iran. Once again Iran's independence was violated. Unwilling to rule under a military occupation that could undo his reforms, Reza abdicated in favor of his son, Mohammad, went into exile, and died three years later.

Epilogue

When he succeeded his father, Mohammad Reza Shah Pahlavi seemed a mere Western protégé. The tribes hastened to regain their lost power and lands. The Majlis asserted its constitutional right to govern. The World War II Allies treated Iran as a supply line, a source of oil, a convenient meeting place, and a subordinate ally. Once the war ended, the Soviet Union tried to set up Communist republics in northern Iran but withdrew its troops in 1946 under UN pressure. The Communists then exploited the rising discontent of the workers in the Anglo-Iranian Oil Company (AIOC). Iranian nationalists won control of the Majlis, electing Mohammad Mosaddiq as prime minister. Because it nationalized the AIOC, Mosaddiq's government became popular at home but angered Britain and the United States, so it was toppled in 1953 by a CIA-backed military coup. For the next quarter century, Mohammad Reza Shah ruled Iran as a dictator. Skyrocketing oil revenues enabled his government to build up its schools, industries, and armed forces. The shah's White Revolution promised changes in landownership, rural development, education, and women's rights beyond his father's wildest dreams. It also alienated the 'ulama.

The shah inherited his father's authoritarian streak. When his reforms failed to meet his subjects' expectations, he fell back on propaganda, censorship, and his secret police (SAVAK) to stay in power. Though successive US governments backed him as a bulwark against communism, many Americans questioned his commitment to human rights. Iranian students abroad and 'ulama at home stirred up opposition to the shah. They decried the erosion of Muslim values, the widening gap between rich and poor, the huge sums spent on arms, the failure of agrarian reform, and the shah's oppressive regime. A nationwide revolution, led by Shi'ite 'ulama, sapped the shah's authority. He left Iran in January 1979, giving way to an Islamic republic. Iran's vaunted "modernization" was only superficial. Billions of petrodollars could not solve Iran's problems or sustain a ruler whose people had turned against him. We will resume this story in Chapter 18.

The Rise of Sa'udi Arabia

Nowadays people think of Sa'udi Arabia as a rich, modern, and very influential country. Yet as late as 1945 it was poor and viewed as backward. The homeland of Islam and Arabism had been a backwater of history since the High Caliphate. If Istanbul was in the vanguard of westernizing reform movements up to this century, few parts of the Middle East could have opposed them more than central Arabia, especially the area known as Najd. It was isolated. Situated among barren hills, lacking an outlet to any sea, Najd attracted no foreign traders or Western imperialists. Most of its people were Bedouin; a few small towns contained Arab merchants and 'ulama. So far we have hardly mentioned the area, except in connection with the rise of a puritanical Muslim sect called the Wahhabis, whose beliefs still prevail in today's Kingdom of Sa'udi Arabia.

Historical Background

The story starts in the mid-eighteenth century, when a wandering young scholar, Muhammad ibn (son of) 'Abd al-Wahhab, became a Hanbali—an adherent to the strictest of the four canonical rites of Sunni Muslim law. The latter-day Hanbalis came to oppose certain practices associated with popular Islam, such as venerating saints and their tombs, trees, and wells. When this Muhammad began preaching and writing in his hometown about cleansing Islam of these practices, his own relatives drove him out. Taking refuge in a nearby village, he converted his protector, Muhammad ibn Sa'ud, to his strict doctrines. Thus leagued together, the two Muhammads set out to convert the nearby Arab tribes, with the son of 'Abd al-Wahhab as spiritual guide (hence the name *Wahhabi* for the sect) and the son of Sa'ud as military and political leader (which is why we speak of the Sa'udi dynasty). In the late eighteenth and early nineteenth centuries, the Sa'udis managed to spread their rule and Wahhabi doctrines to most of Arabia, using methods like those of the Kharijites centuries earlier. They even took Mecca and Medina, destroying or damaging many of the tombs and other shrines that are part of the Muslim *hajj*. You may remember that the Ottoman sultan sent Mehmet 'Ali's army to the Hijaz to expel these Wahhabis, whose threat to the Ottomans in this sensitive area could undermine their legitimacy in other Muslim lands as well. After years of desert warfare, the

Sa'udi-Wahhabi combine was defeated, and the Turks garrisoned the Hijaz. Although Wahhabi doctrines continued to spread to the Gulf region and even to India, the Sa'udi family was confined to central and eastern Arabia. It struggled against the Rashid dynasty, which enjoyed Ottoman backing and seemed by 1900 to have triumphed over the house of Sa'ud.

The man we call Ibn Sa'ud (Sa'udis call him 'Abd al-'Aziz ibn 'Abd al-Rahman) was born in Riyadh, the Sa'udis' home base, in 1880. When he was ten, the Rashids drove his family out. The Sa'udis took refuge near the Rub' al-Khali (the Empty Quarter, in the eastern part of the Arabian Peninsula) among the Bani Murrah, a tribe so poor and primitive that its people are called the Bedouin's bedouin. Among these desert desperadoes, Ibn Sa'ud learned to ride and shoot expertly and to deal with other tribal Arabs. Later the Sa'udis were given asylum by the shaykh of Kuwait, a fishing port near the head of the Gulf. There Ibn Sa'ud began learning about the outsiders who now coveted the Arabian Peninsula, one of the few lands not already carved up by the great European empires. Actually, Arabia in 1900 had a complicated patchwork of local and foreign rulers. Sultan Abdulhamid was extending Ottoman control into formerly autonomous lands, such as the coastal region east of Najd called al-Hasa. Some of the Arab shaykhs along the Gulf had made treaties letting the British manage their defense and foreign relations. But young Ibn Sa'ud craved neither protection by foreign Christians nor dependency on the Ottomans, scorned by the Wahhabis as backsliders from Islam; he wanted to retake Riyadh from the Rashid dynasty. Heading a small band of loyal Wahhabis on a night raid, he won back his ancestral capital in 1902. Thus began an epic that has been told time and again by Sa'udi and foreign chroniclers.

The Emergence of the Sa'udi Kingdom

This epic is the story of how, over the span of thirty years, most of the tribes and emirates of the Arabian Peninsula became united under Ibn Sa'ud. The process involved many Bedouin raids, battles, and wars between the Sa'udi-Wahhabi combine and other contenders for power. Having subdued the Ottoman-backed Rashid dynasty by 1906, the combine began to win control over the central and eastern Arabian tribes. Few outsiders noticed until Ibn Sa'ud's warriors attacked the kingdom of the Hijaz, the state headed by Amir Husayn (see Chapter 12). When he conquered the Hijaz and took over Islam's holy cities in 1924, Ibn Sa'ud became the most respected leader in Arabia—indeed, the whole Arab world. How different history would have been if Britain had heeded its India Office during World War I and backed Ibn Sa'ud instead of the Hashimites!

Ibn Sa'ud won because he believed in Wahhabi Islam and enforced its rules among his followers, using religious belief to temper the Bedouin love of battle and booty. His convictions, along with his physical courage and personal magnetism, led thousands of Arabs to love and obey him. His skills were marital as well as martial; both his victories and his marriages were countless. Most of Ibn Sa'ud's nuptials served to cement peace with the tribes he had subdued. In case you wonder how he stayed within the Qur'anic limit of four, he divorced most of his wives and returned them to their guardians. Yet people said that any woman who married Ibn Sa'ud, however briefly, loved him for the rest of her life. We wonder who could verify this—or how!

Another way Ibn Sa'ud controlled the tribes was to unite them in a religious organization called the *Ikhwan* (Brothers). He persuaded these Bedouin to give up camel nomadism for settled agriculture. Although many of them never learned how to push a plow, their settlement in farming villages made them more tractable, more willing to heed the teachings of Wahhabi *'ulama* from Riyadh, and better disciplined when Ibn Sa'ud needed them in battle. Without the Ikhwan, the Sa'udis could not have united most of Arabia within a generation.

But some parts of Arabia never fell under their control. Like Ataturk, Ibn Sa'ud knew his political limits. Once he had taken Asir, the kingdom between the Hijaz and the Yemen, and had formally created the Kingdom of Sa'udi Arabia in 1932, his conquests ceased. After a brief war two years later, Ibn Sa'ud gave up all claims to the imamate of Yemen. This magnanimity was wise, for the Yemeni highlanders were Zaydi Shi'ites who would have bitterly resisted Wahhabi (that is, Hanbali Sunni) rule by the Sa'udis. He also disbanded the Ikhwan in 1930 after it took to raiding tribes in Iraq, then a British mandate. Rarely did the Sa'udis attack Arab rulers under British protection, such as Abdallah of Transjordan, the shaykh (later amir) of Kuwait, other shaykhs on the Gulf coast, the sultan of Muscat and Oman, or the rulers of southern Arabia east of Aden. By the 1940s Ibn Sa'ud was the Arabs' elder statesman. Even his Hashimite rivals in Transjordan and Iraq, although they resented his driving their father from the Hijaz, came to respect Ibn Sa'ud.

Oil Discoveries and Their Effects on the Sa'udi Kingdom

Considering how the world is now, it is easy to forget that Ibn Sa'ud and his kingdom were extremely poor for most of his life. Najd was a sun-parched, mountainous land far from any sea, the Gulf provided only pearls and scanty trade to al-Hasa, Asir had some upland areas suitable for farming, and the Hijaz provided a meager income from the annual *hajj*. About 150,000 pilgrims came to Mecca each year; less than one-twelfth the number that would make the pilgrimage annually in the early twenty-first century. Sa'udi Arabia's economy depended on the date palm and the camel until the late 1930s. Several British companies had unsuccessfully prospected for oil in a few provinces of the kingdom. There were abandoned gold mines, and it was widely thought that Arabia contained other valuable minerals; but its harsh climate, rapacious Bedouin, and Wahhabi fanaticism discouraged outside explorers. Ibn Sa'ud was once heard to say, "If anyone were to offer a million pounds, he would be welcome to all the concessions he wanted in my country."

The man of the hour was an American whose surname you may recall from Chapter 12—Charles Crane, a plumbing manufacturer and philanthropist involved in the 1919 King-Crane Commission. After a sojourn in Yemen, where he financed a successful search for minerals, Crane visited Ibn Sa'ud in 1931. They discussed a similar quest in the Hijaz, hoping to find enough underground water to pipe it into Jidda (Mecca's port). But Crane's mining engineer, Karl Twitchell, soon found that neither water nor oil existed in economic quantities beneath the largely barren Hijaz. Two years later, though, Twitchell returned, this time in the service of Standard Oil of California (Chevron), which outbid a British representative of the Iraq Petroleum Company (now BP) for exploration rights in eastern Arabia. For a cash loan amounting to 50,000 gold sovereigns (about $300,000, now worth $3 million), plus an annual rent of 5,000 more, Ibn Sa'ud gave the Americans a sixty-year concession to search for oil in Hasa, with preferential exploration rights in other parts of his kingdom. They agreed that more loans would be made later if oil were found in marketable quantities, plus a royalty of a gold sovereign ($60 today) for every five long tons (a long ton equals 2,240 pounds, slightly more than a metric ton) of oil taken from Sa'udi territory.

Five years of exploration and drilling ensued before the Americans struck oil in 1938 at Dhahran and began sending barrels to the British refinery on the nearby island of Bahrain, already an oil-exporting country. Soon they were building their own refinery, storage tanks, and a loading dock on the Gulf. Petroleum technicians, construction foremen, and equipment poured into Dhahran, which became a "Little America" replete with lawns, swimming pools, air-conditioned buildings, and a commissary where the Americans could buy the canned goods, chewing gum, and cigarettes they had known back home. By this time, the Texas Oil Company had joined Standard Oil of California in setting up a subsidiary officially called the Arabian American Oil Company, nicknamed Aramco. Tanker shortages during World War II delayed its operations, but eventually Aramco began selling to US forces in the Pacific. After the war, new oil exploration and discoveries raised Sa'udi output to 1.3 million barrels per day in 1960, 3.8 million in 1970, and more than 10 million in 1981, when the kingdom's annual oil revenue reached $113 billion. Over a quarter of the world's proven petroleum reserves are thought to lie in Sa'udi territory.

The exploitation of Middle East oil was the most revolutionary change of that time. Karl Twitchell was surely no Karl Marx, but the result of his labors—amplified by Aramco's later geologists and explorers—transformed the economic, social, cultural, and moral life of the Sa'udi Arabs. No Middle Eastern people or country has been untouched by the shower of Sa'udi wealth. Its effects on the world economy will be discussed later, but let us say for now that oil wealth made the Sa'udi government the most influential in the Arab world.

What is less well known is that Sa'udi Arabia had very little government while Ibn Sa'ud ruled. For most of this period, Sa'udi Arabia was "governed" insofar as Ibn Sa'ud had the personal charm and, if needed, the force to subdue (and collect tribute from) the Bedouin tribes within his realm. Any money he got from the tribal shaykhs, the pilgrims, or Aramco went into his private treasury. It was used to maintain his palace, support his harem, increase his herds of Arabian horses and camels, or bestow sumptuous gifts on his foreign visitors or on his subjects, each of whom had the right to go directly to Ibn Sa'ud to vent his grievances and obtain justice. There was no formal cabinet; Ibn Sa'ud talked with his relatives and a few foreign advisers, but he made his own decisions. There was no state bank; the gold sovereigns were stored in wooden chests. The laws were those of the Qur'an and the *sunna,* administered by Hanbali *'ulama.* Thieves got their hands chopped off. Murderers were beheaded. Disobedient tribes were fined or banished from their grazing lands. The Wahhabis forced all Sa'udi Muslims to pray five times a day, going from house to house to ensure compliance. Alcohol and tobacco were strictly forbidden to Muslims, as were Western clothes, movies, music, dancing, and even (for a while) radios and telephones.

Imagine the effect of Little America in Dhahran, where the foreign Aramco employees lived in ranch houses with their wives (who wore no veils), built stills in their back rooms, threw parties, did not pray five times daily, and opened their clinic and hospital to Sa'udi Arabs, many of whom had never seen a doctor before. How could God bless these alien Christians more than the Muslims who feared and worshipped him? Imagine what happened when Ibn Sa'ud's sons and grandsons went abroad on diplomatic or educational missions. Palaces sprang up around Riyadh in imitation of what the Sa'udis had seen in Paris, London, and Hollywood. And camels gave way to Cadillacs, although it took time to train a cadre of local mechanics to maintain and repair them.

Ibn Sa'ud was unprepared for the sudden wealth that oil brought to his kingdom. Aging, lame, blind in one eye, he lived to see corruption and licentiousness spread among his courtiers and even some of his sons, wounding his conscience and affronting his morals. He did not understand economics. When told that his subjects could not afford to buy food, he ordered Aramco to double the wages it paid to Sa'udi employees, only to see inflation get worse. Politics also bewildered him. He worried about the divisions among his fellow Arab rulers during and after World War II. He felt betrayed by the Palestine policies of the countries he had trusted, Britain and the United States. When he met President Franklin D. Roosevelt in 1945, Ibn Sa'ud asked him why the Allies could not seize the Germans' homes and lands to house survivors of Hitler's atrocities, instead of punishing Palestine's Arabs by calling for a Jewish state. Roosevelt promised not to act on the Palestine question (see Chapter 15) without consulting both Arabs and Jews. Six weeks later he died, and the next president, Harry Truman, ignored his promise. But Ibn Sa'ud could not really attack the Americans for supporting Israel when their company was pumping his oil, filling his coffers, and building a railroad from Riyadh to the Gulf. Besides, he loathed Soviet communism more.

Ibn Sa'ud's Successors

Ibn Sa'ud died in 1953. The ablest of his sons was Faysal, but the princes and the 'ulama agreed that the succession should go to the oldest surviving son, Sa'ud, a weaker figure. Within a few years Sa'ud managed to run up a $300 million debt despite his government's rising income. Then a sensational press story alleged that Sa'ud had bribed a Syrian minister to kill Egyptian president Gamal 'Abd al-Nasir, who was at the peak of his popularity in the Arab world. In 1958, a turbulent year in Arab politics, the Sa'udi princes agreed to turn over all executive powers to Faysal as premier. Six years later Sa'ud was deposed and Faysal became king. Under Faysal the Sa'udi government became much better organized, with regular ministries, an annual budget, development plans, new roads, schools, and hospitals. As Sa'udi Arabia plunged headlong into modernity, King Faysal became as influential among Arab rulers and Muslim activists as his father had been. His oil policies and eventual fate will be covered in Chapter 17.

Conclusion

Three Middle Eastern countries weathered the period between the two world wars—the apogee of Western control over the area—without becoming colonies, protectorates, or mandates. Each country established the borders it has had ever since. Each government tightened its hold over groups that had checked the power of previous rulers. Personal income rose, more children (and adults) went to school, and public health improved.

These were not democratic regimes. In each case, the agent for change was a military leader whose successes in war won him the respect and obedience of his subjects. Other Middle Eastern countries soon learned from them. Army officers became the main force for modernization in the area. As efficiency is essential in military operations, commanders apply the same standards and employ similar methods to modernize their countries. Nationalist leaders can persuade otherwise recalcitrant subjects to make sacrifices for the common good. But how much will they give up? And what if conditions change, as has happened (thanks to oil) in Iran and Sa'udi Arabia?

These reformers raise other issues. Can modernization be sustained without a set of shared values between those who order and those who obey? Kemal Ataturk saw Islam as a barrier to progress and tried to reduce its influence, but Turkish nationalism has not replaced Islam in the hearts and minds of many Turks. Reza Shah was ambivalent about Islam, but his reform program empowered a westernized elite at the expense of Iran's Muslim leaders, who took their revenge after the 1979 revolution. Ibn Sa'ud's devotion to Islam united a disparate band of tribes under his rule, but his puritanical values clashed with the innovations that flooded his country because of its oil revenues. He died a bitterly disillusioned man. None of these leaders, however hard they tried to forge their people into nation-states, managed to establish a set of values to guide their successors. All equated westernization with modernization. You will see later in our history that the two processes are not the same, that authoritarian leaders continued to wield power, and that the people sometimes found ways to challenge them.

14

※

Egypt and the Fertile Crescent Under European Control

When World War I ended and the victorious Allies met in Paris to determine the fate of their defeated foes, both the Egyptian people and the Fertile Crescent Arabs thought they would soon become independent. President Wilson had stated in the twelfth of his Fourteen Points in January 1918 that "the Turkish portion of the present Ottoman Empire should be assured a secure sovereignty, but the other nationalities which are now under Turkish rule should be assured an undoubted security of life and an absolutely unmolested opportunity of autonomous development." The previous chapter showed that after the war the Turks had to fight against the Greeks and the Allies to preserve their independence, but what about the Arabic-speaking peoples who predominated in the Fertile Crescent? We also noted that the Kurds and the Armenians formerly under Ottoman rule were offered independence by the 1920 Sèvres treaty but did not attain it. Although Egypt was no longer ruled by the Ottoman Empire, the Allies had not yet recognized Britain's protectorate, proclaimed in December 1914. Egyptians and Arabs thought the US government wanted self-determination for all peoples, not only Europeans.

They were wrong. For Egypt, Iraq, and Syria from 1918 until after World War II (and sometimes later), the promise of independence was a receding mirage, always on the horizon, longed for but not attained. The Arabic expression is *Bukra fi al-mishmish,* which means "Tomorrow in the apricot [season]." You say this when someone promises to do something tomorrow, but you doubt he or she will ever get around to it. In Egypt, the British granted "complete independence" in 1922 but maintained their troops' presence in the Suez Canal Zone, Cairo, and Alexandria. They also reserved the right to override the king or the popularly elected government when they needed to ensure Egypt's obedience to British imperial interests. The British did not care about the Egyptians themselves but only about Egypt's strategic position. Iraq, too, mattered to the strategic needs of the British Empire, because it controlled the Euphrates and Tigris rivers, basing facilities important to the Royal Air Force, and increasingly oil in Mosul and Kirkuk. British control of Iraq was backed by a League of Nations mandate and by a succession of Anglo-Iraqi treaties, even though frequent uprisings showed that the Iraqi people did not want British troops in their midst. The Syrians constantly resisted the French mandate, which they had never wanted despite France's long-standing claims of cultural and commercial ties with the lands east of the Mediterranean.

EGYPT'S STRUGGLE FOR INDEPENDENCE

For more than a century Egypt has loomed large in any discussion of Middle East politics, whether the country was acting or acted upon. One reason for this is the Suez Canal, so strategically and economically important to any state that wanted to be a great power. Another is Egypt's position in the vanguard of westernizing reform, going back to Napoleon and Mehmet 'Ali. In modern times Egypt has usually been the leader of the Arab countries, yet it underwent a long and complicated struggle for independence. For centuries, Egypt was valued by foreign powers as an object to be seized and held, as a symbol of imperial might, as a means of influencing the rest of the Arab world, or as a stepping-stone to Asia or to the Mediterranean Sea—but never as Egypt.

What about the Egyptians themselves? Rather than being actors, they had long been acted upon. With centuries of experience as a doormat for outside invaders, oppressors, and explorers, many Egyptians, not surprisingly, distrusted the foreigners who lived or traveled within their country. After all, no Egyptian ruled Egypt from the time of the pharaohs to the fall of King Faruq in 1952. Even its aristocrats were mainly foreign—hence the popular proverb *Fi bilad Misr khayruha lighayriha* (In the land of Egypt, what is good belongs to others). In Egypt's independence struggle, the main antagonist for seventy-five years was Britain. By rights, Egypt was an autonomous province of the Ottoman Empire from 1841 to 1914. In reality, it was a land under British military occupation from 1882. Major decisions about how to run Egypt were made in London, not Istanbul, or (if locally) in the British Agency and not in the khedive's palace. The ministers were puppets in the hands of their British advisers. Both the occupier and the occupied knew that theirs was a power relationship, with

Britain dominant and Egypt either passive or protesting, although all sides observed diplomatic niceties up to World War I.

When the Ottoman Empire went to war against the Allies in November 1914, Britain had to act. Hundreds of troop ships were carrying Australians, New Zealanders, and Indians through the Suez Canal to reinforce British forces against the Germans. Britain ended Egypt's vestigial Turkish ties decisively in December, and Egypt became a British protectorate. Khedive 'Abbas, already living in Switzerland, was deposed. The British replaced 'Abbas with a pliable uncle, Husayn Kamil (r. 1914–1917), who was given the title of sultan to highlight the break with the Ottoman Empire. Prime Minister Husayn Rushdi stayed in office, hoping Egypt would become independent after the war. Britain's representative became the high commissioner for Egypt and the Sudan. A few Egyptians rebelled, but most accepted these changes, hoping the Turks and Germans would win the war anyway.

The period from 1914 to 1956 has been called "Britain's moment in the Middle East." As long as the British dominated the area, the main drama was their relationship, rarely an easy one, with Egypt. "Egypt and England are bound together in a Catholic marriage," said a cabinet minister in the 1940s. They might quarrel from time to time, but they would always make up in the end. Well, they eventually did get a divorce, but the comparison remains apt. A marriage can be built on many forces besides love. One common basis is power. One partner makes the decisions; the other goes along, out of self-abnegation or stark necessity. Eventually, Britain's power waned, and Egypt, never willingly obedient, found ways to sap that country's authority. It was a miserable marriage.

The British stayed in Egypt because it was a stepping-stone to India and the oil wells of Arabia or Iran and because it was a base in their struggles against Kaiser Wilhelm II of Germany, the Nazis, or the communists. The Egyptians knew this and resented it deeply. The British did not even like them, to judge from their diplomatic reports, social arrangements, and even the fiction of the age. The Egyptian, as viewed by the British, was a portly parody of a petty French official, a boastful coward, a turbaned Muslim fanatic, a noisy agitator blind to the benefits that British rule had given his country, or a "wog" (for "wily Oriental gentleman") selling dirty postcards in a dark alley. The Egyptians saw the British as coldhearted, exclusive (for many years, the only Egyptians allowed to enter Cairo's posh Gezira Sporting Club were servants), mercenary, and power hungry. Egyptians preferred the French or the Americans when they competed with Britain for Egypt's favor. The British related well to almost everyone else in the Arab world, especially the Bedouin, for desert Arabs excelled at horseback riding, hunting, and other sports enjoyed by upper-class British males.

World War I

The quality of British administration in Egypt, superb up to 1914, declined during the war. Many of the best Englishmen either left or were called home for military service, never to return. Hordes of new officials and officers poured into Egypt, making the country a vast Allied camp. The new men, inexperienced and less sensitive than their precursors toward Muslims, often gave offense and ignored the country's real needs. So much attention had to be paid to the war against Ottoman Turkey that the British neglected vital problems in Egypt, which was under martial law throughout the war.

Cairo and Alexandria were becoming overpopulated. Food shortages drove up prices in the cities and other places in which troops were concentrated. Egypt's government, hoping to increase wheat harvests, limited the acreage for raising cotton, a more lucrative wartime crop for rural landlords and peasants. After having promised not to demand any wartime sacrifices from the Egyptian people, the British ended up requisitioning grain, draft animals, and even peasant labor for their Palestine campaign.

The 1919 Revolution

As the British grew in numbers, they lost touch with the Egyptians. No Englishman foresaw a revival of Egyptian nationalism after the war. The National Party had declined. Just before the war began, the British had helped to found the Legislative Assembly, led by landowners and intellectuals. One was Sa'd Zaghlul, the elected vice president of that representative body, who then emerged as a prominent critic of the government and its British advisers. The son of a prosperous farmer, Sa'd was educated in the 1870s at al-Azhar University, where he came under the influence of Jamal al-Din al-Afghani. He then edited the government journal and backed the 1882 'Urabi revolution. Shortly after the British occupied Egypt, he was arrested for plotting to kill Khedive Tawfiq. Upon getting out of jail, Sa'd studied law in France, returned to Egypt, became a judge, and married the prime minister's daughter. His wife's family introduced him to Lord Cromer, who proposed him as education minister. In a public speech just before Cromer left Egypt in 1907, he described Sa'd: "He is honest, he is capable, he has the courage of his convictions, he has been abused by many of the less worthy of his own countrymen. These are high qualifications. He should go far."

Sa'd did go far, but not in the way Cromer had hoped. He quit the cabinet in 1912 after quarreling with both the khedive and the British. During the war, when the legislature was closed, Sa'd had ample time to plot against the government. He often played poker with Husayn Kamil's successor, Sultan Fu'ad (r. 1917–1936), who aspired to take power away from the British once the war ended and thus supported Sa'd. Fu'ad's ambitions were matched by those of many Egyptian politicians, who wanted parliamentary government, liberal democracy, and Egyptian control over the Sudan, untrammeled by the British protectorate. They looked to Sa'd, well educated, honest, and devoid of religious fanaticism, as their spokesman, as he had been in the Assembly.

On 13 November 1918, two days after the European armistice, Sa'd and two of his friends called on the British high commissioner, Sir Reginald Wingate. In a cordial conversation, they announced their plan to form a delegation (Wafd) to go to London to argue for Egypt's independence. Wingate counseled patience but agreed to wire home for instructions. The Foreign Office, busy preparing for the impending Paris Peace Conference, refused to meet this delegation of "disappointed and disgraced" politicians or even to receive Husayn Rushdi, who had stayed on as premier through the war, expecting Britain to end its protectorate as soon as peace returned.

During the winter Sa'd announced that he would head a six-man delegation to present Egypt's case for independence before the Paris Peace Conference. Though made up of landowning moderates, this Wafd circulated throughout Egypt a petition whose signers authorized Sa'd's delegation to represent them in demanding complete independence, meaning an end to the British protectorate and evacuation of all foreign troops from Egypt and the Sudan. In March 1919 the Rushdi cabinet resigned and the British exiled Sa'd and his friends to Malta, whereupon the movement to support the Wafd became a popular revolution, the largest of all that have occurred in modern Egypt. Students and teachers, lawyers and judges, government employees and transport workers went on strike. Villagers rioted, attacked railroad stations, and cut telegraph lines. Every class demonstrated against the British protectorate; even women from wealthy families took to the streets. Muslim *'ulama* preached in Christian churches, and Christian priests gave Friday mosque sermons, as Copts and Muslims walked hand in hand, demanding "Egypt for the Egyptians." Only when Britain's government recalled Wingate, appointed as its new high commissioner General Edmund Allenby (who had commanded the Egyptian Expeditionary Force that had taken Palestine), and freed Sa'd to go to Paris did the Egyptians go back to work.

When the Wafd went to Paris to present its case to the peace conference, Egyptians had high hopes. Would President Wilson, champion of subject nations' political rights, ignore those of the world's oldest one? Was Egypt not as entitled as the Arabs of the Hijaz to a hearing in Paris?

Did it not have as much right to independence as, say, Yugoslavia or Albania? Apparently not. On the day the Wafd arrived in Paris, the US government formally recognized what Egypt's nationalists were fighting against—the British protectorate. The Wafd was never invited to address the peace conference. Sa'd and his colleagues could only make speeches that were unheeded and draft letters that went unanswered by those with the power to redraw the political map of the Middle East.

British Efforts at a Solution

As unrest continued in Egypt, the British government decided to send a commission, headed by Lord Milner, to "inquire into the causes of the late disorders, and to report on the existing situation in the country, and on the form of constitution which, *under the protectorate* [emphasis added], will be best calculated to promote its peace and prosperity, the progressive development of self-governing institutions, and the protection of foreign interests." Egyptians might desire peace, prosperity, and the progressive development of self-rule, but they did not want the protectorate. They organized a general boycott of the Milner mission, and some even attacked British soldiers and Egyptian ministers. Milner's mission saw that Britain had to somehow come to terms with Egyptian nationalism, but its leaders were in Paris, not Cairo.

The Egyptian government persuaded Sa'd Zaghlul to talk informally with Milner, but neither man wanted to compromise. The British called Sa'd a demagogue trapped by his own propaganda. The Wafd thought that Britain, anxious to protect its imperial communications, would never let the Egyptians rule themselves. A Zaghlul-Milner memorandum, which would have replaced the protectorate by an Anglo-Egyptian treaty, failed to gain the support of the Egyptian government or its people when Sa'd himself refused to endorse it. But Britain had now openly admitted that it might give up the protectorate. An official Egyptian delegation, headed by the new prime minister, 'Adli Yakan, went to London in 1921 to negotiate, but Sa'd exploited his popularity in Egypt to undermine support for 'Adli's parleys with the Foreign Office.

Having thus failed to negotiate a new relationship with the Egyptians, either officially with 'Adli or unofficially with Sa'd, Britain was stymied on the Egyptian question. Strikes and assassinations made action imperative. Continued control over the Suez Canal and Alexandria's port, the radio and telegraph stations, the railroads and the airports—all communication links vital to the British Empire—could have been endangered by a nationwide revolution backed by Sultan Fu'ad and his ministers and led by

Sa'd Zaghlul and his Wafd. Britain's dilemma in 1921–1922 would become common in a later era of decolonization: How much should a strong country defer to the national pride of a weaker one and yet preserve its own interests? High Commissioner Allenby devised a solution. He persuaded the British government to declare unilaterally an end to its protectorate over Egypt on 28 February 1922. The declaration limited this independence by reserving for Britain, pending future Anglo-Egyptian agreement, (1) protection of British imperial communications in Egypt, (2) defense of Egypt against foreign aggression, (3) protection of foreign interests and minorities in the country, and (4) administration of the Sudan.

Despite these limits on Egypt's sovereignty, which became known as the Four Reserved Points, the Egyptians took the half loaf and began to set up their new government. Fu'ad changed his title from sultan to king and watched nervously while a committee of Egyptian lawyers prepared a constitution modeled on that of Belgium. The British residency (Allenby kept his title as high commissioner) encouraged this democratic experiment. It was a time when Britain, weary of war and especially of negotiating Middle East postwar arrangements, was willing to make concessions. Elsewhere, this policy meant accepting nationalist leaders in Turkey and Persia and promoting the movement toward self-rule in Iraq and Palestine. Late in 1923 Egypt finally held free elections. The Wafd, reorganized as a political party, won an overwhelming majority of seats in the Parliament. King Fu'ad accordingly invited Sa'd to form a cabinet made up of Wafdist ministers. Sa'd hoped to make a deal with the British government to reconcile Egyptian nationalist and British imperialist interests. We shall see later what happened.

THE CREATION OF NEW STATES IN THE FERTILE CRESCENT

Egypt has existed since the dawn of history, and you probably know that river valley civilizations began on the Tigris and Euphrates at least as early as those on the Nile. But no country called Iraq existed before the twentieth century. Authorities differ on what the name means, but the most likely translation is "the land along the river banks." In earlier centuries Arabs, Persians, and Turks had sometimes used the term in a geographical sense, as Americans speak of the Midwest or Britons of the Lake Country, but Iraq never denoted a nation. Europeans and Americans called the land Mesopotamia. It had contained many city-states and empires in ancient times. It was disputed between the Roman and Parthian Empires and between the Byzantines and the Sassanids. After the Arab conquests, the region prospered agriculturally and commercially; its largest city, Baghdad, was the seat of the 'Abbasid caliphate. The Mongol conquests destroyed Baghdad in 1258 and laid waste to the region's river irrigation system, which was slow to recover. Ruled by the Il-Khanids and in the fifteenth century by the Black Sheep and White Sheep Turcomans, Iraq became heavily tribal. The Safavids of Persia controlled it briefly, but for four centuries it belonged to the Ottoman Empire and was divided into three provinces: Mosul, Baghdad, and Basra.

Iraq: From Three Provinces to One Country

Britain became interested in Iraq, especially Basra, during the nineteenth century, as the growth of steam navigation made the Euphrates and Tigris Rivers, as well as the Persian Gulf, major trade routes to India. Just after the Ottoman Empire entered World War I, British imperial troops (mainly Indians) invaded Basra to forestall a German drive toward the Persian Gulf. Soon they reached the outskirts of Baghdad, but the Turks drove them back down the Tigris to Kut. Following a six-month siege, the British troops surrendered. Less than a year later, though, a new and larger British imperial force captured Baghdad. The occupied Mesopotamian lands, basically the Baghdad and Basra provinces, were administered from India, whose British governors opposed Arab nationalism, unlike the British in Cairo, who backed the Arab Revolt and the Hashimites. No one could be sure whether there would be an Iraq, or who would rule over it, when the Ottoman government signed the Mudros Armistice in 1918. The Ottoman Empire still ruled Mosul, which under the Sykes-Picot Agreement was to have gone to France, but the British made the Turkish governor surrender control of the province three days later. French premier Georges Clemenceau gave up France's claim in return for British support for French control over the rest of Syria in the postwar negotiations. A British company had signed an agreement with the Ottoman government shortly before World War I to exploit the oil resources in Mosul. France and Britain agreed to share whatever oil might be discovered there.

The combination of Mosul with Baghdad and Basra (although not definitive until 1926) created a territory that had some economic coherence as the valley of the Euphrates and Tigris Rivers. Once the League of Nations was formed and the system of mandates was created, the major powers agreed that Iraq should be mandated to the British, who would prepare the new country for self-government. The downside was that its population (roughly 3 million in 1920) was about 55 percent Shi'ite and 40 percent Sunni Muslim. About half of the latter spoke Kurdish or Turkish rather than Arabic. The remaining 5 percent included Assyrians (Nestorian Christians and Chaldean Catholics), Jews, and small religious groups such as the Yazidis and the Mandeans. Most of the Muslims belonged to tribes and clans to which they owed their main allegiance. How could these disparate groups be welded into a single nationality? The British themselves disagreed on whether to rule this new possession directly as a colony (like India) or indirectly through tribal shaykhs, Sunni muftis, and Shi'ite *mujtahid*s. The government in London was preoccupied with other domestic and foreign problems in 1919–1920 and failed to decide on an Iraq policy.

Indecisive rulers create rebellious subjects. In retrospect, the outbreak of a nationwide revolt in 1920 seems inevitable. Britain's Arab allies were a group of officers who had deserted the Ottoman army to fight for the amir of Mecca in the Arab Revolt of 1916–1918 and had aided the British against the Turks in the conquest of Baghdad. By May 1920 they were disillusioned with the British in Iraq and with the French, who were ousting the Arab rulers from Syria. The officers called for an Iraqi rebellion against the British mandatory regime, with strong backing from *mujtahid*s in the Shi'ite holy cities of Najaf and Karbala. Many tribal shaykhs in the Euphrates Valley joined the uprising, which peaked in June and July 1920. By the time the British had suppressed the rebellion in late October, roughly 6,000 Iraqis and 500 British and Indian soldiers had lost their lives.

The British government concluded that indirect rule would work best in its Iraqi mandate and proceeded to form a government dominated by Sunni urban notables, army officers, and tribal leaders, the same groups that the Ottomans had relied on until 1914. These arrangements were to be ratified in the Cairo Conference of March 1921, presided over by none other than Winston Churchill, then Britain's colonial secretary. As mentioned in Chapter 12, Faysal had expected to rule in Damascus, and the British envisioned a throne for his brother Abdallah in Baghdad. After the French drove Faysal and his supporters out of Syria, he became the obvious candidate for a new Hashimite kingdom in Iraq, and so Churchill created the Emirate of Transjordan for Abdallah. Thus supported by the conference, Faysal came to Baghdad to rule following a nationwide plebiscite, but rumors of bribery and corruption abounded. With Britain eager to reduce the size of its garrisons in Iraq and with a king who had never lived in the country, it was decidedly unclear in 1921 how well the Iraqis would learn to view themselves as a nation capable of self-rule.

Syria: From One Nation to Many Fragmented States

Up to 1914, it was customary for outsiders to call the varied inhabitants of the Levant Syrians. The area was a patchwork of coastal plains, mountains, rivers, fast-moving streams, fertile valleys, swamps, and deserts. Although inhabited since ancient times, Syria's cultivable lands had shrunk since the era of the Mamluks and the Mongols and did not suffice to feed their inhabitants even before 1914. So Syrians—especially unmarried young men—frequently went abroad, to Egypt, Europe, and the Americas, to seek their fortunes. Those who prospered often returned to buy land, marry, and live out their lives in relative comfort. Some brought with them ideas of democracy, industrialization, and progress. Their ideas and money helped to fuel the growth of Syrian patriotism and Arab nationalism. Syrians, both at home and abroad, condemned French imperialism and its effect on their political development.

At the end of World War I, France envisioned Syria as the linchpin for its projected domination of the Mediterranean area. France hoped to develop its new mandate as it had Algeria, Tunisia, and Morocco—as an agricultural powerhouse producing food and fiber for export to France and as a market for French manufactures. Syria would be crisscrossed by rail lines and roads, dotted with French settlements, and served by schools and hospitals. France originally hoped to administer all of Syria, from the Sinai to Mosul. Indeed, many people living in what we now call Israel, Jordan, Lebanon, southern Turkey, and western Iraq then viewed themselves as Syrians. Because British troops clearly dominated the postwar Levant, the French had conceded to Britain control over Palestine and Mosul, as they would also concede their Anatolian claims to Kemal and the Turks, but they held on to Syria.

The French stressed Syria's religious and ethnic diversity, for indeed Sunni Muslim Arabs made up only 65 percent of the country's 2.2 million inhabitants in 1920. There were also Orthodox and Maronite Christians, Shi'ites, Alawites and Druze, Kurds and Circassians, Yazidis and Isma'ilis. Cities (and even villages) were often rivals. The French claimed to uphold this diversity when they created separate administrations for Aleppo and Damascus, for the Alawites in the northwest and for the Druze in the mountainous southwest (including what we now know as the Golan Heights), and especially for the diverse religious minorities in Lebanon. There had been a semiautonomous governorate for Mount Lebanon from 1860 to 1914, four-fifths of its inhabitants being Maronites. When they took over Syria in 1920, the French enlarged Mount Lebanon by adding the coastal cities of Tripoli, Beirut, and Sidon, and the mainly Druze and Shi'ite mountain and valley lands to create a "Greater Lebanon," which was 55 percent Christian (it is now 60 percent Muslim). Aleppo and Damascus were soon reunited, but the Alawite and Druze areas remained separate until 1936. By 1922 Greater Lebanon was evolving into an independent republic, one whose separate existence Syrian nationalists were (and still are) loath to accept.

Although the French allowed the Syrians and Lebanese to form ministries and elect parliaments, the actual administration of the mandate was firmly grasped by a high commissioner headquartered in Beirut, with governors general in the provincial centers. State power was enforced by France, many of whose troops were drawn from its other colonies, notoriously Senegalese and Algerian soldiers. Despite glowing reports submitted by the French authorities to the League of Nations Permanent Mandates Commission in Geneva, they did little to prepare the Syrians to rule themselves. Syrian political leadership was drawn mainly from landowners who had consolidated their estates following the Ottoman land reforms of 1858 and had few ties with the tenant farmers whom they claimed to represent. The high hopes the French expressed in 1918 that they would develop Syria economically were never realized. France's own economy had been harmed by the German occupation of its northeast and by the death or disability of a million young men in World War I. Postwar Syria's economy suffered from the loss of many of its traditional markets in areas now under British control and from the tying of its own currency to the declining French franc.

Popular dissent was rife, sometimes boiling over into peasant or urban uprisings. The greatest of these was the Syrian revolution of 1925–1927, which broke out in the Druze area and spread to Hama, Damascus, and some of the tribal regions. The rebels formed the People's Party, Syria's first mass nationalist movement. The revolution was suppressed by invading French troops, aerial bombardment, and the destruction of many homes and historic sites. France's mandate was meant to be brief; during the 1920s, however, it became clear that Syria would be ruled by the French for a long, long time.

PHONY DEMOCRACY AND FALSE INDEPENDENCE

Although the British had conceded that Egypt would become independent, and the leading Egyptian moderates had drawn up the 1923 constitution and held parliamentary elections that brought the popular Wafd, headed by Sa'd Zaghlul, to power, the path to independence was far from easy. Sa'd appointed a cabinet of Wafdists, including two Copts, and expected to negotiate with Britain's first Labour Party government on those Four Reserved Points that had to be settled before Egypt could be free. The high hopes of Egypt's liberal nationalists lasted only a few months. The 1919 revolution had unleashed violent forces that its leaders could no longer contain. Even Sa'd was wounded by a would-be assassin in June 1924. The attempt presaged the assassination that November of the British commander of the Egyptian army. Later investigations revealed that a secret society backed by some of Egypt's leading politicians was perpetrating these and other terrorist acts.

Meanwhile, High Commissioner Allenby handed Sa'd an ultimatum stating that the murder "holds up Egypt as at present governed to the contempt of civilized peoples" and demanding an indemnity to the British government, the withdrawal of all Egyptian officers from the Sudan, and an undefined increase in the Nile waters to be diverted—at Egypt's expense—to irrigate the Sudan. Rejecting this humiliating ultimatum, Sa'd's cabinet resigned. King Fu'ad named a caretaker cabinet of palace politicians, who called for new parliamentary elections and tried to rig their outcome. When they failed to keep the Wafd out of power, the king dissolved parliament and suspended the constitution. A sterner imperialist replaced Allenby.

The following decade of Anglo-Egyptian relations can be summed up as an emerging power triangle. The first party was the British, anxious to protect its position in Egypt with respect to India and the rest of the Middle East. The second party to the struggle was the Wafd, the popular Egyptian nationalist movement, led by Sa'd Zaghlul until his death in 1927, then less ably by Mustafa al-Nahhas until the 1952 revolution. Its insistence on Egypt's complete independence enabled the Wafd to win any free election in which it chose to run candidates for Parliament. It might have held power longer had it been supported by the third party in the power triangle, King Fu'ad, who wanted more power for himself. He could count on the cooperation of rival parties and politicians to form governments more amenable than the Wafd to his wishes. The king could also make appointments within the Egyptian army, civil administration, and 'ulama. In 1930, when the contest between the Wafd and the British grew too intense, Fu'ad and his prime minister declared a state of emergency, replaced the 1923 constitution with a more authoritarian one, and turned Egypt's government into a royal dictatorship.

Even though Egyptian politics were chaotic during the 1920s and 1930s, Arab culture underwent a remarkable renaissance in Egypt. The proliferation of political parties led to soaring numbers of newspapers, magazines, and publishing houses. Egyptian authors, often educated in France, began to publish novels, short stories, poems in meters never before used in Arabic, and essays about the country's problems. Taha Husayn, a gifted writer trained at al-Azhar and the newly formed Cairo University, published many essays, one of which argued that most pre-Islamic Arabic poetry, long seen by Muslims as the formative influence on the Arabic language and hence on the Qur'an, had not in fact been composed until after the time of Muhammad. Another writer argued that Ataturk's controversial abolition of the caliphate in 1924 would do Islam no harm, for the religion did not require a caliph. These essays stirred up widespread controversy, as educated Egyptians had to decide how much they were willing to renounce hallowed Muslim traditions. Taha Husayn and some other Egyptians glorified the pharaonic past at the expense of their Arab-Muslim heritage. This was an era of intellectual ferment. Egypt's film and recording studios began, and Cairo University was reorganized and expanded. Egypt was emerging as the intellectual capital of the Arabic-speaking world, a role model for Iraq and Syria. Yet it was not politically independent.

A series of fortuitous events in 1935–1936 seemed to resolve the Egyptian question. Mussolini's Italy, already ruling Libya, menaced both British and Egyptian interests by invading Ethiopia, a move that brought the two sides together. Ever more frequent student riots in Cairo showed how the people hated the existing royal dictatorship under the 1930 constitution. The British, seeking better relations with Egypt, called for a return to the 1923 constitution and free elections. The death of King Fu'ad in 1936 and the succession of his teenage son Faruq (under a regency) gave new hope to believers in Egyptian democracy (see Box 14.1). In accordance with the 1923 constitution, new elections were held in 1936, and the Wafd Party predictably won. Mustafa al-Nahhas formed a Wafdist ministry, which successfully negotiated a treaty with Britain's foreign secretary, Sir Anthony Eden.

Because it replaced the reserved points that had left Egypt's independence in doubt for fourteen years, this new Anglo-Egyptian Treaty was initially popular in both countries. For Britain it guaranteed for at least twenty years a large military base from which to defend the Suez Canal, plus bases in Cairo and Alexandria, as well as in other Egyptian cities in case a war broke out. The question of the Sudan, ruled in fact by Britain, was put on the back burner. Egypt now had a constitutional monarchy with ministers responsible to Parliament, ambassadors in other countries' capitals, membership in the League of Nations, and the trappings of independence so long deferred. Faruq was hailed with ovations wherever he went, and Sir Anthony Eden became the first foreigner ever to have his picture on an Egyptian postage stamp.

Box 14.1   King Faruq

Faruq (1920–1965) was modern Egypt's second and last king. He was born in Cairo, the only son of Egypt's first king, Fu'ad. He received his education in Cairo and later at the Royal Military Academy at Woolwich in England. This was cut short, however, when in 1936 he was recalled to Egypt upon his father's death. He was formally crowned king the next year when he was only seventeen.

Faruq has acquired a very bad reputation. Though at first he was looked upon as a promising ruler, devoutly Muslim and dedicated to his people, he soon became distracted by petty palace intrigues and immoral indulgences. In 1937 the British high commissioner in Egypt seemingly predicted Faruq's future when he described him as an "untruthful, capricious, irresponsible and vain" young man of "superficial intelligence and charm of manner." Is this, however, the whole story?

When Faruq assumed the throne, he had an understandable ambition to really rule Egypt. He also envisaged reforms that might well have benefited the average Egyptian. But these plans soon foundered upon the resistance of an entrenched establishment made up of political parties (the king frequently quarreled with the Wafd, Egypt's largest party), bureaucrats, and large landowners. More important, Faruq could never reconcile himself to the fact that the real power behind the throne was held by the British high commissioner. Thus, a battle of wills often played itself out between the indigenous leader and his unwanted imperial overlord. It turned out to be a battle that Faruq could not win.

The power imbalance between the Egyptian monarch and the British high commissioner limited Faruq's expression of his resentment of imperial control to petty acts. For instance, Britain dragged Egypt into World War II because of its strategic bases in the country. Though Egypt became a staging area for Allied operations in North Africa and the Middle East, most of the Egyptian people, including the king, did not support the cause of a power they regarded as an unwanted occupier. Thus, when High Commissioner Sir Miles Lampson ordered Faruq to intern, for the duration of the war, his Italian servants, the king replied, "I'll get rid of my Italians when you get rid of yours," referring to Lampson's Italian wife.

King Faruq could have made his life much easier and his reign longer if he had gone along with the powers that confronted him. However, he chose instead to act as an independent leader—for instance, in strongly advocating the creation of the Arab League and later in backing the Arabs in Palestine. It was ultimately Faruq's realization that he could not win this competition with the British or with Egyptian politicians that led him into cynicism and a life of self-indulgence—a decline that began in 1942. In 1952 he was finally overthrown by Egyptian military officers. He ended up in European exile, dying in a Rome nightclub when he was only forty-five.

Again the high hopes of Egypt's liberal nationalists were dashed. The Wafdist government lasted only eighteen months. King Faruq proved as adept as his father in locating anti-Wafd politicians willing to form cabinets he liked better than those led by Mustafa al-Nahhas. Even some of the Wafd Party leaders disliked Nahhas so much that they bolted in 1937 to form a rival party. Meanwhile, the government was doing little to solve Egypt's pressing economic and social problems. The extremes of wealth and poverty were grotesque, all the more so in a country where nearly all of Egypt's 16 million people lived on 3 percent of the land, an area roughly equal to that of the entire state of New Jersey. Egypt was becoming much more urbanized and somewhat industrialized. Although foreigners continued to dominate the ranks of the owner and managerial classes, some Egyptian industrial capitalists were emerging. In addition, there was a growing middle class of Egyptian professionals, shopkeepers, clerks, and civil servants. The Capitulations, long a drag on Egypt's independence, were abolished in 1937, and even the Mixed Courts, special tribunals for civil cases involving foreign nationals, were phased out over the next twelve years. No longer would Egypt's large foreign (and minority) communities get special privileges and protection.

Still, most Egyptian people remained as poor after independence as they had been under the British, for the landowners and capitalists who dominated Parliament opposed social reform. Poverty, illiteracy, and disease stalked the lives of most Egyptian workers and farmers to a degree unparalleled in Europe or elsewhere in the Middle East. The failure of nationalism and liberal democracy to solve these problems led many Egyptians to turn to other ideologies. A few intellectuals embraced Marxist communism, but the communists' militant atheism made their doctrine abhorrent to the Muslim masses. Mussolini's Italy and Hitler's Germany provided models more attractive to Egyptians disillusioned with liberal democracy, and a right-wing authoritarian party, Young Egypt, arose.

But the most popular Egyptian movement of the 1930s was one wholly indigenous to the country, the Society of the Muslim Brothers. This group wanted Egypt to restore the Islamic customs and institutions established by Muhammad and his followers. Though notorious for attacking Christians and Jews, not to mention demonstrating against movies, bars, modern women's fashions, and other "Western innovations," the Muslim Brothers had a point. They were reacting against westernizing reforms that had brought little benefit and much harm to the average Egyptian. The Brothers' slogan, "The Qur'an is our constitution," appealed more to most Egyptians than the demands for independence and democratic government set forth by the Wafd and the other parties. The parliamentary system, unable to solve Egypt's social problems or to confront Young Egypt and the Muslim Brothers, stumbled from one cabinet to the next as the king kept the Wafd out of power.

Independence and democracy fared no better in Iraq than in Egypt. The British government in London and the administrators on the scene hoped they could establish a democratic government; the principle of the mandate system was that Iraqis should be trained to rule themselves. The 1920 revolution, although brief, was intense. It convinced the British that they had to seemingly cooperate with King Faysal and the local leaders. These included religious notables, Arab soldiers who came to Baghdad with Faysal, bazaar merchants, and tribal shaykhs. When it came time to elect a constituent assembly to prepare a democratic constitution for Iraq, all these groups took part, but the British adviser to Iraq's Interior Ministry secretly picked the candidates. Because the nomadic tribes still controlled much of Iraq and often challenged its government, the British also retained small garrisons of British and Indian soldiers and, more importantly, Royal Air Force planes to bombard rebellious nomads into submission. Aerial bombardment made the very concept of the mandate unacceptable to Faysal and local politicians; instead, the British and Iraqi governments drew up a succession of treaties defining their rights and duties toward each other. As was the case with Egypt, these treaties were not between governments as equals, for the Iraqis had no power to intervene in Britain as the British could and did in Iraq. Not even the handpicked Iraqi delegates could be counted on to ratify these treaties, but the British managed to secure Faysal's cooperation by promising that Iraq would soon become independent and Britain would sponsor the country for membership in the League of Nations.

In accordance with the Anglo-Iraqi Treaty signed in June 1930, the British recommended to the League of Nations that their mandate be officially terminated in 1932, although some members of the League's Permanent Mandates Commission were concerned about discrimination against Shi'ites, Kurds, and, especially, Assyrian Christians. The fear regarding the Assyrians was justified. This minority had played a prominent role in manning a special police force recruited by the British at a time when the Iraqi army, officered mainly by Sunni Muslims, was deemed inadequate to maintain order in the country. Iraq's new government disbanded (and disarmed) the Assyrian militia, and in August 1933 Iraqi army units entered many Assyrian villages, burned their houses, and massacred their inhabitants—clearly an act of revenge.

Soon afterward, Faysal died, depressed (it was said) by his subjects' failure to adopt a nationalist spirit. "In Iraq," he said shortly before his death, "there is still . . . no Iraqi people, but unimaginable masses of human beings, devoid of any patriotic ideal, imbued with religious traditions and absurdities, connected by no common tie, giving ear to evil, prone to anarchy, and perpetually ready to rise against any government whatsoever." The despairing views Faysal expressed seem almost prophetic. When his handsome and popular son Ghazi mounted the throne, he was only twenty-one and preferred driving fast cars to running the country.

Iraq's Parliament had come to be dominated by large landowners, who cared mainly about protecting their own interests. Most were tribal shaykhs who had been induced to settle on reclaimed lands on condition that the other members of their tribes became their tenants—in reality their serfs. In 1936 a popular army officer seized control of the government, beginning a series of military coups—some fifteen altogether—that punctuated Iraq's political history between 1936 and 1958. British troops and planes remained in Iraq. The oil fields and installations developing around Kirkuk, built up by the Iraq Petroleum Company (mainly British owned, though the French also held shares), were starting to augment Iraq's national income. Even after 1932, "independent" Iraq was almost as subordinate to Britain as it had been as a mandate.

Syria made no progress toward independence as a result of its great revolution of 1925–1927. Meanwhile, the Maronites of Lebanon, well aware that their dominance was resented by Sunnis and Shi'ites under their control, drew up with France a new and separate constitution in 1926 to reinforce their confessional, or religious, system. Lebanon functioned under local Christian leadership and French protection quite apart from Syria. The French also drew up a Syrian constitution in 1930 and governed under its terms for six years. Not satisfied, the Syrians became ever more determined to become independent from France. The existing People's Party, consisting mainly of town-dwelling landowners, was eclipsed after 1931 by a larger movement, more representative of the population as a whole, called the National Bloc, patterned after Egypt's Wafd Party. Its leaders, inspired by the progress of Egypt and Iraq toward independence from Britain, focused on uniting the Syrians against the French mandate. Some hoped to promote the unification of Syria with Lebanon and even with British-mandated Palestine and the Emirate of Transjordan, but such ambitions for a greater Syria were becoming unrealistic.

Syrian nationalism received two severe setbacks from France during the 1930s. France offered Syria a treaty in November 1933 that proposed less independence than the nationalists wanted, and it was shelved. In 1936 France's liberal Popular Front government drew up a pact with Syria that would have granted independence, on the pattern of Britain's 1930 treaty with Iraq and the Anglo-Egyptian Treaty then under consideration. The French and Syrian prime ministers actually signed their treaty, but after the Front fell from power, France's Parliament never ratified the document. Then in 1938 the French separated from Syria its province of Alexandretta, which after a year of autonomy voted to join Turkey. Syrians have never recognized this detachment of a portion of their territory. French high commissioners and their staffs continued to decide the key issues, while the National Bloc felt marginalized and angry.

WORLD WAR II

Britain and France declared war on Nazi Germany in 1939. Hitler's troops overran most of Europe in 1940, and those parts of France not occupied by German troops came under a collaborationist regime headquartered in Vichy. Many Arabs expected Britain to fall and hoped to free their countries from Western imperialism. Egypt, however, became a vast army camp for the Western Allies, although popular feeling was hostile. Even King Faruq and his ministers tried to wriggle out of the 1936 Anglo-Egyptian Treaty, as German general Erwin Rommel's crack Afrikakorps swept across Libya into Egypt's Western Desert in early 1942. With demonstrators filling Cairo's streets and calling for a German victory, the British ambassador, Sir Miles Lampson, sent tanks to surround the royal palace and handed an ultimatum to King Faruq: he had to either appoint a Wafdist cabinet that would uphold the Anglo-Egyptian Treaty or sign his own abdication. After some hesitation, Faruq caved in; he decided to keep his throne and give in to British demands. Mustafa al-Nahhas, the Wafdist leader and hence the standard-bearer for Egypt's independence struggle, came to power at the point of British bayonets. Neither the king nor the Wafd ever recovered from this national humiliation.

In Iraq, a group of four army officers, all of them originally trained in the Ottoman Military Academy before World War I and hostile to Britain, took power in 1940. Led by Rashid 'Ali al-Gaylani, they hoped to oust the British from their military and air bases and move Iraq's government toward an Arab nationalist policy and closer ties with the Axis powers. Germany started to send troops and supplies to Rashid 'Ali through Syria, but not enough. The Arab nationalist government was ousted in May 1941 by the British troops remaining in Iraq, backed by Transjordan's British-officered Arab Legion, and Iraq's subsequent wartime cabinets reverted to a policy of close collaboration with Britain and its allies.

After Nazi Germany occupied Paris in June 1940, the collaborationist Vichy government ruled in Syria and Lebanon. The Vichy leaders tried briefly to conciliate the nationalists but reverted to repressive policies because of wartime conditions. After Rashid 'Ali's regime in Iraq fell, the British and the Free French, led by General Charles de Gaulle, invaded Syria and Lebanon in June 1941. After a week of fierce fighting between the Vichy French and the Allies, causing much damage to Beirut from aerial bombardment, the Allied side triumphed. De Gaulle and the British both promised independence for Lebanon and Syria after the war.

For the duration of World War II, the Middle East (except for neutral Turkey) was an area controlled by the Allies, meaning Britain and its dominions, the Free French, and, from 1941, the Soviet Union and the United States. Because European manufactured goods became unavailable as a result of German and Italian submarine warfare, the region moved toward economic self-sufficiency, due in large part to the creation of the Middle East Supply Centre, headquartered in Cairo, which promoted the growth of local manufacturing industries and cash-crop agriculture. The British also encouraged political unification, especially among Arabic-speaking peoples, leading to the Iraqi government's 1943 proposal to create a Fertile Crescent union. Because this union would have excluded Egypt, Sa'udi Arabia, and Yemen, the Arab states eventually chose instead to form the Arab League, which came into formal existence in March 1945. If the Arab League had been willing to absorb the Middle East Supply Centre following World War II, the subsequent integration of the Arab countries might have advanced faster, and the modern history of the Middle East would have been much different.

POSTWAR EGYPT

Egypt emerged from World War II as the leading country in the Arab world. It had the largest population, the leading universities, and the most powerful radio stations. Its films were shown wherever there were theaters frequented by Arabs. Its books, newspapers, and magazines circulated throughout the Arab world. It had completely paid off its foreign debts and had become a creditor nation. Yet, paradoxically, Egypt was not yet independent. British troops would withdraw from Cairo and Alexandria in 1946, but they still patrolled the Suez Canal Zone. Britain's 1942 intervention, forcing King Faruq to appoint Wafdist leader Mustafa al-Nahhas as prime minister, was a national humiliation for the Egyptians.

Neither Nahhas nor the king ever recovered. Faruq, a handsome and popular youth with high political ideals, turned into the monstrous, dissolute playboy older Egyptians and Westerners remember today. The Wafd was tainted as the standard-bearer of Egypt's struggle for independence, but no other parliamentary party could match its popular appeal. The Muslim Brothers were gaining strength, but their resort to terrorism rendered them suspect. The war years enhanced the importance of Egypt as an economic hub, as Allied soldiers and statesmen flooded the country. Industrial and agricultural employment and output boomed. So did price inflation, urban congestion, disruption, and crime. Would the end of World War II lead to popular uprisings as massive as the 1919 revolution?

EGYPT'S ERA OF POLITICAL FRUSTRATION

Between 1945 and 1951 Egypt experienced much unrest, but no revolution. Britain no longer intervened in Egypt's domestic politics. Many people hoped the new United Nations (UN), of which Egypt was one of the founders, would rid the world of war and colonialism. The communists, who might have had the discipline to lead a revolution, were not as strong in Egypt as their counterparts were in Europe. Finally, Egypt's government managed to distract the people with a novel enthusiasm for Arab nationalism. Although few Egyptians had viewed themselves as Arabs before, King Faruq and the Wafd both aligned Egypt more with the rest of the Arab world, partly because of the rising Arab-Jewish contest for Palestine. More important was Iraq's attempt to unite the Fertile Crescent states, to which Nahhas responded by promoting the Arab League. Formally set up in 1945, it preserved the sovereignty of each Arab country while coordinating their policies on key Arab issues. Hoping to uphold its own influence at France's expense, Britain encouraged this trend toward Arab cooperation.

The drawback was that the Arab states could agree on only one issue: they did not want the Jews to form a state in Palestine. Egypt, with many domestic problems, plus the unresolved issues of British rule in the Sudan and British troops within its own borders, diverted its attention and energies to the Palestine issue. Egypt set its policies less to block any Zionist threat to Arab interests than to counter what the other Arab governments might do. Transjordan's Amir Abdallah, backed by Iraq, was Egypt's main rival. If he fought against any Jewish attempt to form a state in Palestine, he could annex much (or all) of the country to his desert kingdom. If he made peace with the Zionists, they might divide Palestine between them. Either outcome would strengthen Amir Abdallah at Faruq's expense. The UN General Assembly voted in 1947 to partition Palestine into a Jewish state and an Arab one. Egypt and the other Arab governments resolved to fight the decision and to crush the Jewish state if it came into being. The Arabs had valid objections to a partition plan that assigned over half of Palestine to a third of its 1947 population, but the Egyptian government cared mainly about what other Arab governments thought and did.

Many Egyptians, notably the Muslim Brothers, called for a jihad to free Palestine from Zionist colonialism. Faruq, sensing an easy victory in a popular war, decided (without consulting his cabinet or his generals) to commit his army to fight in Palestine in May 1948. The army was unprepared. Logistical bottlenecks, inept commanders, politicians who bilked the government on arms purchases, an ill-timed UN ceasefire, and general demoralization of the Egyptian troops led to a crushing defeat. Some Egyptian units fought bravely in Palestine, but the victories heralded in Egypt's newspapers and radio broadcasts were imaginary. Early in 1949 Egypt had to sign an armistice agreement with the new State of Israel, as did Jordan, Lebanon, and Syria. But even then there was no peace.

The Egyptian Revolution

Defeat in Palestine discredited Egypt's old regime—the king, the ministers, the high-ranking army officers, and the democratic experiment itself. The government clamped down on the Muslim Brothers after they assassinated the prime minister, but the unrest continued. Free elections in 1950 brought back the Wafd Party, this time with plans for social reform plus a commitment to drive the remaining British troops from the Nile Valley. Premier Nahhas repudiated the 1936 Anglo-Egyptian Treaty he himself had signed and sent Egyptian commandos to attack British troops in the Suez Canal Zone. The British struck back, killing fifty Egyptian policemen in January 1952. Now the rumble of popular anger turned into an explosion. On a Saturday morning hundreds of Egyptians, better organized than any mob of demonstrators had ever been before, fanned across central Cairo and set fire to such European landmarks as Shepherd's Hotel, Groppi's Restaurant, the Turf Club, the Ford Motor Company showroom, and many bars and nightclubs. Only after much of Cairo had burned to the ground did Faruq and Nahhas try to stop the rioting, looting, and killing. "Black Saturday" proved the old regime could no longer govern Egypt. Who would? Some people thought the Muslim Brothers had set the fires and were about to seize power. Others looked to the communists. Few suspected that the army, humiliated in Palestine and generally assumed to be under palace control, would take over Egypt and kick out the king.

However, in July 1952 the army did just that. An officers' secret society, using a popular general named Muhammad Nagib as its front man, seized control of the government in a bloodless coup d'état. Three days later Faruq abdicated and went into exile. Sweeping reforms followed as the patriotic young officers, like their counterparts in Turkey a generation earlier, took over the powers of the old regime. Political parties were abolished, and the Parliament was dissolved. The military junta would rule until a new political system could replace the discredited 1923 constitution. Land reform was instituted. New schools and factories were opened. In 1954, the figurehead leader, General Nagib, admired abroad as a moderate, was ousted from power by the real mastermind of the young officers, Colonel Gamal 'Abd al-Nasir (often written as Gamal Abdel Nasser).

The Final Chapter

The early Nasir regime wanted to complete Egypt's independence from any foreign military presence. With pressure put on Britain by the United States, which hoped to bring Egypt into a Middle Eastern anti-Communist alliance, Anglo-Egyptian talks resumed. Britain finally agreed to leave its Suez Canal base, but on condition that British troops might reoccupy the canal in case of an attack on any Arab League country or on Turkey, presumably by the Soviet Union. British civilian technicians might also stay in the Canal Zone. Some Egyptian nationalists balked at Nasir's conditions, just as they had opposed Nagib's concession that the Sudanese people might decide by a plebiscite between union with Egypt and complete independence (they voted for the latter). On 18 June 1956 the last British soldier was out of the Suez Canal base. For the first time since 1882, no British troops remained in Egypt.

Egypt's independence struggle should have ended then, but it did not. In October 1956 British and French paratroopers landed at Port Said and reoccupied the Suez Canal, while Israel's army pushed westward across the Sinai Peninsula. The world's two superpowers, the United States and the Soviet Union, joined forces to pressure the British, French, and Israelis to stop their attack and to pull out of Egypt's territory. Meanwhile, the Nasir government expelled thousands of British subjects and French citizens from Egypt and seized their property, thus ending much of what remained of Western economic power within the country. Nasir had finished the struggle for Egypt's independence, but at a cost of much Western anger against his regime and his country.

INDEPENDENCE FOR LEBANON, SYRIA, AND IRAQ

There are some interesting parallels with the Egyptian saga. France and Britain willingly announced that they recognized the independence of their former mandates but were reluctant to pull out their occupying armies. In the case of Lebanon, the Free French agreed to let the Lebanese hold elections in the summer of 1943, and the result was a strong majority in favor of independence. The Free French balked at accepting the Lebanese nationalists, and a rebellion broke out in November. Pressured by the British, France formally recognized Lebanon as an independent republic on 22 November, but not until 1945 did the last French troops leave the country. Because the Lebanese had themselves reached an unwritten "gentlemen's agreement" that their president would always be a Maronite (and the Maronites tended to be pro-French), France should have left sooner. Syria was a tougher issue, as it was perfectly clear that its Sunni Muslim majority wanted the French to leave. A Sunni landowning politician named Shukri al-Quwatli managed to obtain France's formal recognition of Syria's independence by siding with the British and the Americans. Even so, French troops remained in Syria in 1945, sparking a nationalist revolt in the major cities that was suppressed after heavy loss of life and property, and it took action by the newly formed UN Security Council to pressure France to withdraw its forces in April 1946.

Although Iraq had been formally independent since 1932, it still housed British military bases. Postwar Britain still had an interest in Iraqi oil and wanted to maintain its control over the Persian Gulf. Britain opened negotiations with Iraq in 1947 over its remaining bases in the country, and the two sides reached an agreement in January 1948 in the British city of Portsmouth to share in controlling those bases. By this time Iraqi public opinion, because of rising tensions in Palestine, was so inflamed that a nationwide rebellion broke out against the government for signing the Portsmouth Agreement, which was never ratified. Its nullification, however, left the British troops in control of those bases. The Iraqi government imposed martial law, due in part to the Palestine War, and tried to distract its people's resentment against the British with policies championing Arab nationalism and sponsoring large-scale development projects. Iraq even promoted a military alliance with Britain, Turkey, Iran, and Pakistan, the so-called Baghdad Pact, to oppose "international Communism." Only in July 1958 did a group of Iraqi army officers stage a coup, modeled on the Egyptian one of 1952, that ousted the Hashimite monarchy, pulled Iraq out of the Baghdad Pact, and ended Britain's military and political influence in the country.

CONCLUSION

Egypt, Iraq, and Syria all chafed under European imperialism. Understandably, they believed they had kicked the Turks out their front door in World War I, only to find the British and the French had entered through the windows and were sitting in the living room. The European powers during the war had entertained idealistic plans to develop these countries and had repeatedly made promises of independence then and afterward. The people of these countries thought they were being valued not as heirs of a great Islamic civilization or as participants in an Arab awakening but as inconvenient inhabitants of lands that possessed strategic value for Britain and France (or oil). Some historians argue that these states were not nations, that they could not have defended themselves or even remained united had they been free of British or French control, that they were fractured by religious and ethnic differences, and that they were agrarian societies controlled by landowning elites who lacked any ties with their tenant farmers. We cannot tell you what would have happened if Egypt had become a liberal democracy under Sa'd Zaghlul; if the Allies had created a greater Syria including Palestine (now Israel), Transjordan (now Jordan), Lebanon, and the district of Alexandretta; or if Iraq had been created as a loose federation of Basra, Baghdad, and Mosul. We can say that what these countries did experience under Western imperialism left a lasting legacy of anger that helped to poison the politics of the contemporary Middle East.

15

The Contest for Palestine

Palestine, the "twice-promised land," as British wags used to call it, has caused more ink to spill than any other Middle Eastern issue in modern times—even more ink than blood. Although the Palestine question or the Arab-Israeli conflict is not the only dilemma to beset the region, it is hard to name any problem in today's Middle East that has not somehow been affected by it. Certainly the attention the major powers, the United Nations, and legions of propagandists for both sides have paid to the conflict should show how large it looms in the world today.

ORIGINS

How did the Arab-Israeli conflict begin? Is it a religious war between Judaism and Islam that can be traced back to the rivalry between Abraham's sons, Isaac and Ishmael? The Arabs say that it is not and that the Jews were always welcome to settle and prosper in Muslim lands. The Zionists reply that the Jews under Muslim rule were usually second-class citizens (as were all other non-Muslims). Both sides agree that Christian anti-Semitism (a regrettable term for prejudice against Jews, for Arabs are Semites, too) was worse but that historic prejudice sets a poor standard for religious toleration.

Many may claim that these arguments stretch back far in time, but this really is not true. Although Jews and Arabs have claims to Palestine going back hundreds of years, the real contest was just starting when World War I broke out. At that time, few foresaw how strong it would be. The duration and intensity of what we now call the Arab-Israeli, or Palestinian-Israeli, conflict were due to the rise of nationalism in modern times. We have already studied the Arab nationalist movement in Chapter 12; now it is time to look at the history of Zionism. This chapter will carry the contest for Palestine (itself a debatable and ill-defined geographical term) up to the creation of Israel as the Jewish state.

POLITICAL ZIONISM

Let us first define *political Zionism*. Zionism is the belief that the Jews constitute a nation (or, to use a less loaded term, a *people*) and that they deserve the rights of other such groups, including the freedom to return to what they consider their ancestral homeland, the land of Israel (or Palestine). Political Zionism is the belief that the Jews should form and maintain a state for themselves there.

Not every Jew is a Zionist. Some Jews identify solely with the countries in which they are citizens, reject altogether the idea of nationalism, or believe that the only meaningful affirmation of Jewishness is observance of their religion, its laws, and its traditions. Not every Zionist is a Jew. Some Christians believe that the restoration of the Jews to Palestine or the creation of Israel must precede the Second Coming of Christ. Many Gentiles (non-Jews) back Israel out of admiration for Jews or Israelis or out of guilt for past wrongs committed against European Jews. Some Gentiles who dislike Jews support Israel because it opposes the assimilation of Jews into Gentile society.

Likewise, anti-Zionists are not necessarily anti-Semites. Some may be pro-Arab out of sincere conviction. Some people who favor Jews and Judaism still think that Zionism and the creation of Israel have done Jews more harm than good. This is a point that Jews should keep in mind. For their part, non-Jews must recognize that expressions of opposition—or even skepticism—toward Zionism and Israel do sound anti-Semitic to many Jews. We all must discuss Zionism with care if Jews and Gentiles, or Arabs and non-Arabs, are to understand each other and reach peace in the Middle East.

It may seem odd to Americans that Zionist Jews should call themselves a "nation." No one speaks of a Catholic or a Methodist nation in the United States. Nevertheless, most Jews believe that they do constitute one people and that their collective survival depends on mutual support and cooperation. Even persons of Jewish ancestry who do not practice Judaism—even those who have converted to another faith—are still apt to be regarded as Jews unless they make strenuous efforts to prove they are not.

The idea that the Jews are a single and united people is deeply rooted in the Torah and in the Christian Bible: a nomadic tribe, the Hebrews, came to regard their deity as in fact the one true God, YHWH (Jehovah in English). He had chosen them for his love and protection because they had chosen him; he had commanded them to keep his covenant and obey his laws from generation to generation; he had led them out of Egyptian bondage and brought them safely to Canaan, which they called the land of Israel, for he had promised it to the seed of Abraham. Because Arabs as well as Jews claim descent from Abraham, the term *land of Israel* restricts its possession to the descendants of Jacob (i.e., the Israelites). Jerusalem is featured in prayers and common expressions and is a symbol of the Jewish people's hopes and fears. *Jew* originally meant "one from Judea," the region in which Jerusalem is the main city; only later did it take on a religious significance.

The Jews in Dispersion

For at least two millennia, most Jews have not been Judeans. Only recently could it be said that they possessed Jerusalem or even that they spoke Hebrew (although they did read the Torah in that language). Jews kept their identity as a people by their observance of the faith and laws of Judaism and by their wish to survive as one people, even without having land, a common tongue, a state, or most of the other attributes of nationhood. No matter how tenuous the ties between the Jews and their ancestral land might seem, they never forgot them. There were always some Jews living in Palestine, and many thought that only those who lived there could feel wholly Jewish. The common anti-Semitic attitude of European Christians enhanced Jewish solidarity and identification with the land. Jews in Muslim lands were better treated and knew they were free to live in Palestine, but only a few actually did so.

The European Enlightenment and the rise of liberal democracy freed many Western Jews from discrimination and isolation. A Jewish enlightenment (*Haskala* in Hebrew) grew up in the late eighteenth century, leading in Germany and the United States to what is called Reform Judaism and to greater Jewish assimilation into Western society. This assimilation caused a few people to deny their Jewishness and convert to Christianity (e.g., writer Heinrich Heine and the parents of such famous men as Karl Marx, Felix Mendelssohn, and Benjamin Disraeli).

If most Jews had resided in Germany, England, or America and actively assimilated then, Zionism might never have arisen. But the majority lived in czarist Russia (mainly Poland) and in parts of the declining multinational empires of the Habsburgs and the Ottomans. Here liberal democracy had not taken hold. When the peoples of Eastern Europe began to embrace nationalist ideas, they had to fight against despotic monarchs or nobles to gain their freedom. The local Jews got caught in the middle. Although law abiding and usually loyal to their rulers, they often were viewed by the nationalists as enemies in their midst. Some rulers also tried to deflect popular anger from themselves by using the Jews as scapegoats, stirring up pogroms (organized attacks) against Jewish ghettos and villages. A few Jews—and more than a few Christians—said that the only way for the Jews to escape persecution was to move to Palestine and rebuild their state in the land of Israel. The idea that Jews constitute a nation (Zionism by our definition) is nothing new, but saying that the Jewish nation should revive its ancient state in Palestine (the idea we call political Zionism) was indeed revolutionary for the nineteenth century.

THE BEGINNINGS OF POLITICAL ZIONISM

Like most revolutionary doctrines, political Zionism started with very few supporters. Most rabbis said the Jews could not be restored to the land of Israel until after God had sent the Messiah. Some called nationalism a form of collective self-love that ran counter to Judaism's basic commandment: "you shall love the Lord your God with all your heart, and with all your soul, and with all your might" (Deut. 6:5). However, Moses Hess, one of the first German socialists, argued in *Rome and Jerusalem* (1862) that Jews could form a truly socialistic nation-state in the land of Israel. Hess's book was little read (until much later), but another early Zionist work, Leon Pinsker's *Auto-Emancipation* (1882), had immense influence in Russia. Official persecution was reaching new heights at this time as the czarist regime implemented a series of so-called May Laws that restricted Russian areas in which Jews might live and set artificially low quotas on admitting Jews to the universities and the professions. Pinsker's book was the first systematic attempt to prove that Jews were vulnerable to anti-Semitism because they lacked a country of their own. It inspired Russian Jews to form Zionist clubs and study groups in Russia. Their federation, *Chovevei Tzion* (Lovers of Zion), spread from Russia to other countries where Jews lived. A more activist movement, BILU (*Beit Ya'cov lchu Vnelcha* in Hebrew; "To the house of Jacob go and we will follow"), sent groups of young Russian Jews to Palestine. Immigrants in these two organizations made up what historians of Zionism call the "first *aliya*." *Aliya* really means "going up," the term Jews had long used for going to Jerusalem, set among the Judean hills, but it came to mean "going to the land of Israel." Jewish immigrants were called *olim* (ascenders).

Early Jewish Settlers

The Zionist *olim* found other Jewish newcomers in Palestine. There were always mystics and scholars going to Jerusalem and the other main centers of Jewish culture: Tiberias, Safed, and Hebron. Moreover, there were already immigrants buying land and trying to farm it. In the late nineteenth century, the total number of Jewish settlers in Palestine was less than 20,000; the local inhabitants, numbering about 570,000, spoke Arabic. The land was governed by the Ottoman Empire—inefficient, corrupt, and suspicious of the Zionists. Not a few Jewish settlers quit in disgust and went home—or to the United States.

Theodor Herzl

Zionism based solely on Russian resources—mainly youthful enthusiasm—probably would not have lasted. What gave the movement endurance and wider appeal was the work of an assimilated Jewish journalist living in Vienna, Theodor Herzl, who in 1896 wrote *Der Judenstaat* (The Jews' state), an eloquent plea for political Zionism. Because Herzl was a popular writer, his book carried the ideas of Pinsker and other early Zionists to thousands of German-speaking Jews. Their conversion to Zionism enabled Herzl to bring together the first International Zionist Congress in Basel, Switzerland, in 1897. At its conclusion, the conferees adopted the following resolution:

> The goal of Zionism is the establishment for the Jewish people of a home in Palestine guaranteed by public law. The Congress anticipates the following means to reach that goal:
>
> 1. The promotion, in suitable ways, of the colonization of Palestine by Jewish agricultural and industrial workers
> 2. The organizing and uniting of all Jews by means of suitable institutions, local and international, in compliance with the laws of all countries
> 3. The strengthening and encouraging of Jewish national sentiment and awareness
> 4. Introducing moves toward receiving governmental approval where needed for the realization of Zionism's goal

Herzl proceeded to work unremittingly toward the formation of the Jewish state by writing more books, making speeches, and courting support from rich Jews and various European governments as well as from the Jewish middle class. At one time he even got an offer from the British government (often misnamed the Uganda Scheme) that would have let the Zionists settle in what later would be called Kenya's White Highlands. But most of Herzl's followers, especially the Russian Jews, refused to form a state anywhere outside the land of Israel, saying, "There can be no Zionism without Zion." The movement split on this issue and others. When Herzl died in 1904, it seemed likely that the high hopes of early Zionism would never be realized.

The Second Aliya

If Herzl's life and teachings constituted the first event that saved political Zionism, the second was the large-scale emigration of Jews from Russia following its abortive 1905 revolution. Even though most decided to seek freedom and opportunity in that *goldene medina* (a Yiddish term meaning "land of gold") overseas, the United States, a small number of idealistic men and women chose Palestine instead. With intense fervor and dedication, these Jewish settlers of the second *aliya* (1905–1914) built up the fledgling institutions of their community in Palestine: schools, newspapers, theaters, sports clubs, trade unions, worker-owned factories, and political parties. No Arabs were allowed to join these organizations—and none tried to. Because the Jews entering Palestine had spoken so many different languages in the countries from which they had come, the *olim* made a concerted effort to revive Hebrew as a spoken and written language that all could share.

Their most famous achievement was a novel experiment in agricultural settlement called the *kibbutz* (collective farm), in which all houses, animals, and farming equipment belonged to the group as a whole, all decisions were made democratically, and all jobs (including cooking, cleaning, and child rearing) were shared by the members. Although most *olim* settled in the cities, including what became the first all-Jewish city in modern history, Tel Aviv, those who chose the kibbutzim have come to typify Israel's "pioneer spirit": idealistic, self-reliant, and rather contemptuous of outsiders. The kibbutzniks were determined to develop their lands (bought for them by the Jewish National Fund at high prices from absentee Arab and Turkish landlords) without resorting to cheap Arab peasant labor, a step toward Jewish self-reliance but also toward the exclusion of Arab Palestinians from their homeland.

Because the pioneers of the second *aliya* were brave and resourceful people, we may forget that most of the *olim* soon lost their zeal for this risky and unrewarding adventure. Hot summers, windy and rainy winters, malarial swamps, rocky hills, sandy desert soil, and frequent crop failures dimmed the fervor of many young pioneers. Arab nomads and peasants raided the kibbutzim. Their cousins in Jaffa and Jerusalem eyed Zionism with suspicion. As their own nationalist feelings grew, the Arabs understandably opposed a colonization scheme that seemed likely to dispossess them, reduce them to second-class status, or break up Syria. Already they were protesting in their press and in the Ottoman Parliament against these foreign settlers and their plans to build up a Jewish state in Palestine. The Ottoman government, both before and after the 1908 Young Turk revolution, obstructed Jewish colonization for fear of adding yet another nationality problem to those in the Balkans and the Arab lands that were already tearing its empire apart. No European government would risk offending Istanbul by supporting Jewish settlement in Palestine.

BRITAIN AND THE PALESTINE PROBLEM

World War I was the third event that saved political Zionism. Both sides thought they needed Jewish backing. In 1914 Berlin was the main center of the Zionist movement. Most politically articulate Jews lived in (and supported) the countries that made up the Central Powers: Germany, Austria-Hungary, and the Ottoman Empire. Up to 1917, when the United States entered World War I on the side of the Allies, American Jews tended to favor the Central Powers because they hated the tyranny of czarist Russia, from which so many Jews had barely managed to escape. The overthrow of the regime in March 1917 made Russia easier to support, but now the issue facing its new government (which most Russian Jews favored) was whether to stay in the war at all. Germany, too, wanted Jewish support but could not espouse Zionism owing to its ties with the Ottoman Empire, which still held Palestine. This is when the British government stepped in.

The Balfour Declaration

Britain, though it had relatively few Jewish subjects, could speak out most forcefully for Zionism. There the leading Zionist advocate was Chaim Weizmann, a chemist who won fame early in the war by synthesizing acetone, a chemical used in making explosives. Weizmann's discoveries made him known to leading journalists and thus to members of Britain's wartime cabinet. The prime minister, David Lloyd George, had come to favor Zionism from reading the Bible. Weizmann also won the backing of the foreign secretary, Lord Balfour. It was he who informed British Zionists of the cabinet's decision to support their cause in a letter that became known as the Balfour Declaration. The letter stated:

> His Majesty's Government view with favor the establishment in Palestine of a national home for the Jewish people, and will use their best endeavors to facilitate the achievement of this object, it being clearly understood that nothing shall be done which may prejudice the civil and religious rights of the existing non-Jewish communities in Palestine, or the rights and political status enjoyed by Jews in any other country.

Because this declaration has come to be seen as the founding document of political Zionism, it deserves our careful scrutiny. It does not say that Britain would turn Palestine into a Jewish state. The British government promised only to work for the creation of a Jewish national home in Palestine. Moreover, it pledged not to harm the civil and religious (but not political) rights of Palestine's "existing non-Jewish communities"—namely, the 93 percent of its inhabitants, Muslim and Christian, who spoke Arabic and dreaded being cut off from other Arabs as second-class citizens within a Jewish national home. Both Britain and the Zionist movement would have to find a way to assuage these people's fears and to guarantee their rights. They never did. Here, in short, is what Arabs see as the nub of the contest for Palestine. Even now its toughest issue is to define and uphold the legitimate rights of the Palestinians.

The Balfour Declaration also had to take into account the fears of Jews who chose to remain outside Palestine and who would not want to lose the rights and status they had won in such liberal democracies as Britain, France, and the United States. Up to the rise of Hitler, Zionism had the backing of only a minority of these Jews. What the Balfour Declaration seemed to ensure was that the British government, upon gaining control of Palestine, would be committed to build the Jewish national home there. Let us see what really happened.

The British Occupation

When World War I ended, the British imperial forces and Faysal's Arab army jointly occupied the area that would become Palestine. The British set up in Jerusalem a provisional military government that soon became embroiled in a struggle between Jewish settlers, who were entering Palestine in large numbers and organizing their state, and the Arab inhabitants, who were resisting their efforts.

Zionist writers often accuse British officers and officials of having stirred up Arab resentment. This is unfair if they mean the period from 1918 to 1922, although later British administrators did favor the Palestinian Arabs. True, some British troops who came from Egypt or the Sudan knew better how to treat Arabs, who were usually polite, than to deal with Eastern European Jewish immigrants, who could be intransigent because of their past suffering under czars and sultans. Some British officials assumed that, because of the Communist takeover in Russia, Jews from that country favored the Bolsheviks. In fact, only a few did. There were ample grounds for suspicion between British imperialists and Zionist colonists.

As early as April 1920, the Palestinians revolted, venting their frustrations and fears in attacks on the Jewish community. It was an opening salvo in the Arab nationalist revolution in Palestine, a struggle still going on today. This was also the time when the Allies met at San Remo to assign the mandates in the Arab world, putting Palestine under British control. Once the Colonial Office took over the administration of Palestine from the army, Britain should have devised a clearer and fairer policy toward both Jews and Arabs. But this was not to be.

The Palestine Mandate

In the ensuing years, Britain's Palestine policy went in two opposite directions. In the international arena it tended to back Zionist aims because of Jewish political pressure on London and the League of Nations. In Palestine British officials favored the Arabs, often influenced by concern for Muslim opinion in neighboring countries and in India. Remember that these were general tendencies, not hard-and-fast rules. When the League of Nations awarded the Palestine mandate in 1922, it specifically charged Britain with carrying out the Balfour Declaration. In other words, Britain had to encourage Jews to migrate to Palestine and to settle there, to help create the Jewish "national home," and even to set up a "Jewish agency" to assist the British authorities in developing that national home, which none dared call a state.

The Palestine mandate could not be the same as the League's mandates for Syria and Iraq, which were to help them evolve into independent states. In Palestine, however, although most of its inhabitants were Arabs, it was the Jewish national home that was to be created, a publicly declared intention to create a Western colonial entity. The Arabs suspected that the British mandate would hold them in colonial bondage until the Jews achieved a majority in Palestine and could set up their state.

Beginnings of the Anglo-Zionist Rift
In reality, though, the British started effacing the mandate's pro-Zionist features before the ink was even dry. In 1922 Colonial Secretary Winston Churchill issued a white paper denying that the British government meant to make Palestine as Jewish as England was English (Weizmann's expression) or to give preference to Jews over Arabs. Its fateful provision was to restrict Jewish immigration to fit Palestine's "absorptive capacity." This restriction did not hurt Anglo-Zionist relations in the 1920s, when quotas exceeded the number of Jews who came, but after the rise of Hitler the question of Palestine's ability to absorb Jews would become a major issue.

Another British action that seemed to violate the mandate was the creation of the Emirate of Transjordan, removing the two-thirds of Palestine that lay east of the Jordan River from the area in which the Jews could develop their national home. Zionists viewed Britain's attempt to give Abdallah a kingdom as a needless concession to Arab nationalism. The British predicted that this first partition of Palestine would last only until Syria could become an independent Arab kingdom. But as the French did not leave Syria and as Abdallah built up a bureaucracy and an army (the British-officered Arab Legion) in Amman, the separation of Transjordan became more and more set in stone. Most Jewish leaders in Palestine still chose to work with the British, but some turned to direct and even violent resistance. The most notorious of these leaders was Vladimir Jabotinsky, founder of a group called the Revisionists, which advocated a Jewish state that would include both Palestine and Transjordan, cleansed of any Arab inhabitants who opposed it. Revisionist ideas have influenced such recent Israeli leaders as Menachem Begin, Yitzhak Shamir, Benjamin Netanyahu, and Ariel Sharon.

The Jewish Governor and the Nationalist Mufti
Britain's first civilian governor in Palestine was Sir Herbert Samuel. Although he was a prominent Zionist, he tried hard to be fair to all sides. For instance, he named an ardent young nationalist, Hajj Amin al-Husayni, to be the chief *mufti* (Muslim legal officer) of Jerusalem. Samuel probably hoped to tame Hajj Amin with a small taste of power, but he used his control of the *waqfs* and appointments to key Muslim posts to become the leader of Palestinian Arab nationalism. Although his flamboyant personality won him enemies as well as friends among the Arabs, he became so influential as a spokesman and revolutionary leader that the British would later try to deport him (see Box 15.1).

Box 15.1   Hajj Amin al-Husayni

Amin al-Husayni (1893–1974) is a hero to many Palestinian Arabs and a villain to Zionists. Born into a prominent Jerusalem family, he got his education in Jerusalem, at al-Azhar in Cairo, and at the Istanbul Military Academy, and he served briefly as an artillery officer in the Ottoman army. He became interested in the Arab nationalist cause and became active after World War I in Palestinian national politics. Britain's high commissioner in Jerusalem decided the best way to tame this rising local leader was to give him some responsibility. Thus, in 1922 he was named grand mufti of Jerusalem and president of the newly formed Supreme Muslim Council. The British would later regret these appointments.

Using these positions to his advantage, Husayni came to dominate the Palestinian Arab drive for independence. His goal of an independent Arab Palestine put him at odds with the British mandate government, which backed the Zionist movement for a Jewish homeland in Palestine. As ever-growing numbers of Jewish immigrants arrived from Europe, Palestinian factions united in 1936 to form the Arab Higher Committee under Husayni's leadership. Demanding independence and an end to Jewish immigration into Palestine, the committee declared a general strike and refused to pay taxes. The strike evolved into an open rebellion that lasted until 1939. The British removed Husayni from his position as grand mufti and declared the Higher Committee illegal. Husayni had to flee to Lebanon in 1937. Two years later he was forced to flee again, this time to Iraq, where he took part in the 1941 uprising against the British, and eventually to seek refuge in Nazi Germany.

His alliance of convenience with the Germans during World War II made Husayni a controversial and hated figure in the West. Yet it is historically incorrect to regard him as a Nazi. He was the leader of a nationalist movement fighting against British imperialism and Zionist colonialism. Declared an outlaw by the British, he could either surrender to his oppressors or seek refuge with Britain's enemies. He chose the latter path. While living in Germany, he did make radio appeals to his fellow Arabs, asking them not to support the Allies, but there is no convincing evidence that he took part in the Nazi genocide against the Jews.

After the war Husayni made his way to Cairo, where he continued his struggle for an independent Palestine, but now it was the Egyptian government (which had its own ambitions in Palestine) that tried to restrain and manipulate him. At this time, the Zionists launched a concerted smear campaign against Husayni to connect the entire Palestinian nationalist movement with the Holocaust. Thus thwarted both by internal Arab and Zionist opposition, his efforts came to naught. He died in Beirut at the age of eighty-one, discredited in the West but still a hero to many Palestinians.

Samuel encouraged both Jews and Arabs to form their own institutions. The Jews in Palestine went on developing organizations covering nearly every aspect of their lives, including the Jewish Agency for Palestine, a body representing world Jewry and designated by the British as the official representative of the Jewish people in its mandate, and the *Vaad Le'umi* (Jewish National Council), a consultative national council for the Jewish settlers. Political parties mushroomed, each having its own unique blend of socialism, nationalism, and religion. The general labor federation, called *Histadrut* (a shortened form for General Federation of Labor for Workers in the Land of Israel), set up factories, food-processing plants, and even a construction company. It also organized an underground defense organization, *Haganah* (Defense), formed after the 1920 rebellion. Some Palestinian Arabs continued to call for unity with Syria. Others, divided by family and religious loyalties, could not create comparable organizations or even a united nationalist party. Instead, they pursued obstructionist policies that hindered their cause outside the country. In 1923 Britain tried to set up a legislative council that would have given the Arabs ten out of twenty-two seats, but the Arabs refused, accurately noting that the two seats designated for the Jews and the ten for the British were disproportionately high for their numbers. Arab and Muslim leaders in other countries encouraged Palestinian Arab resistance. Because they were outside Palestine and had their own problems, though, they gave little material aid.

In the days of Samuel and his immediate successor, it looked as if Jewish-Arab differences could be resolved. The number of Jewish *olim* shrank; in 1926–1928 more Jews left Palestine than entered it. There was also a complementary relationship—ill concealed by each side's propaganda—between settlers and natives, between Jewish technical expertise and Arab knowledge of local conditions, and between Jewish capital and Arab labor. Wise British administration might have moderated their differences. There were always Jews who advocated friendly relations with Arabs, as well as Arabs who quietly welcomed Jewish immigration and investment. Could they have taken the lead if both sides had toned down their most extreme claims?

A New Arab-Jewish Clash

Any such hopes were dashed by the 1929 Wailing Wall incident. The issues were complex. The Wailing Wall (more properly called the Western Wall) is a remnant of the Jewish Second Temple and an object of veneration to most Jews (see Figure 15.1). To some it symbolizes the hope that someday the temple will be rebuilt and the ancient Jewish rituals revived.

Figure 15.1   Modern day aerial view of the Western Wall, Temple Mount, the Dome of the Rock, and al-Aqsa Mosque

However, the Western Wall also forms part of the enclosure surrounding the historic Temple Mount or Sacred Enclosure (al-Haram al-Sharif in Arabic), on which stand the Dome of the Rock and al-Aqsa Mosque, pilgrimage centers almost as important for Muslims as Mecca and Medina. Legally, it had been a *waqf* since the time of Salah al-Din. Muslims feared that Jewish actions before the Western Wall could lead to their pressing a claim to the Temple Mount.

In 1928 Jewish worshippers brought benches to sit on and a screen to separate men from women. Muslims viewed this activity as an attempt by the Jews to strengthen their claims to the Wall. These actions violated mutually accepted regulations that maintained traditional practices. Positioning the screen blocked the narrow public thoroughfare used by the local Arab residents. Unable to persuade the Jews to remove the benches and screen, the police seized them, inciting provocative Zionist protests. Several fights broke out between Arabs and Jews. During the following year, these escalated into a small civil war, causing hundreds of casualties on both sides. Arabs perpetrated massacres elsewhere in Palestine, notably Hebron, where they killed most of the Jewish inhabitants and expelled the others. British police could not protect innocent civilians.

When the Jews complained, Britain sent a commission of inquiry, which later issued a report that recognized the Arabs' grievances. Then the colonial secretary, Lord Passfield, issued a white paper blaming the Jewish Agency and Zionist land purchases from Arabs (which had rendered some peasants homeless) for the 1929 disturbances. The British also tightened restrictions on Jewish immigration. Weizmann was so incensed by this report that he resigned as the Jewish Agency's leader. Chagrined, the British government issued a letter explaining away the Passfield White Paper, thus alienating the Arabs and showing them that Zionist influence was strong enough to sway the British government whenever it favored Arab interests. The letter hardly mollified the Zionists either. This incident shows just how weak Britain's Palestine policy had become. Indeed, it doomed the mandate to failure by exposing evolving conditions that the British could no longer control.

Jewish Immigration and Arab Resistance
During the 1930s, Jewish-Arab relations worsened. The rise to power of Hitler and his Nazi party in Germany put its Jews—numbering about half a million—in peril. Many stayed in Germany despite discriminatory laws, official harassment, and hooliganism against Jews, but other German Jews (not to mention Jews from nearby countries such as Poland) began trying to get out. Even the Nazis tried, at least for a while, to help them leave. But which country would take them in? Most European countries during the worldwide depression had rising unemployment. They did not want to admit many German Jews. Neither did the United States, which since 1921 had strictly limited foreign immigration. This left Palestine. From 1933 on, the trickle of Jewish immigrants into that country turned into a flood. Naturally, the Arabs wondered how long it would be before they became the minority. They had not brought Hitler to power, they reasoned, so why should their rights be sacrificed for the sins of the Germans?

As Arab feelings of anger and helplessness mounted, Hajj Amin al-Husayni took charge of the new Arab Higher Committee, which represented nearly all Palestinian Muslim and Christian factions. The committee called a general Arab strike in 1936. The strike turned into a large-scale rebellion that almost paralyzed Palestine for several months. Again, the British government sent a commission of inquiry, this one headed by Lord Peel. The Arabs tried to impress the Peel Commission with their power by boycotting it until just before it departed in January 1937. Consequently, the Zionists got a better hearing. The Peel Commission report, issued later that year, recommended partition. It would give part of northern and central Palestine to the Jews to form their own state and leave most of the rest to the Arabs. The Arab state was expected to join Abdallah's Transjordan. The Palestine Arabs, backed by other Arab states, opposed partition, as they feared that Britain's acceptance of the Peel Commission's plan would be a step toward their loss of Palestine. As often happened in this struggle, Britain soon scaled down the offer and finally retracted it.

Seeking a peace formula that would satisfy all parties, Britain called a roundtable conference of Jewish and Arab leaders (including Arabs from other countries) in London in early 1939. By then the differences between Palestinian Jews and Arabs had become so great that they would not even sit around the same table. No agreement was reached, and the conference ended inconclusively. By then a new war with Germany was imminent, and Britain needed Arab support. It issued a policy statement, the White Paper, announcing that the mandate would end in ten years, whereupon Palestine would become fully independent. Until then, Jewish immigration would be limited to 15,000 each year up to 1944, after which it could continue only with Arab consent (which hardly seemed forthcoming). The sale of Arab land to Jews was restricted in some areas and prohibited in others.

Like the Arabs earlier, the Jews now felt angry but helpless. The White Paper seemed to sell out Britain's commitment to help build the Jewish national home pledged in the Balfour Declaration and the mandate itself. Remember that this happened after Hitler's troops had marched into Austria, after the Western democracies had consented to dismembering Czechoslovakia at the Munich conference, and when Poland was being menaced by a German attack. Europe's Jews were in peril. Owing to the strict immigration policies of the Western democracies, they had nowhere to go but Palestine. Now Britain, bowing to Arab pressure, had nearly shut Palestine's gates to the Jews. The Arabs, too, spurned the White Paper, because it postponed their independence and did not stop Jewish immigration and land purchases altogether.

During World War II, most of the Arab countries remained neutral. Some of their leaders (including the exiled mufti of Jerusalem) sought out the Nazis, hoping they would free the Arab world from both British imperialism and Zionism. But the Jews in Palestine had no choice. The threat of annihilation by the Nazis outweighed the evils of British appeasement to the Arabs, so they committed themselves to the Allied cause. On the advice of the Jewish Agency's chairman, David Ben-Gurion, the Zionists agreed that "we must assist the British in the war as if there were no White Paper and we must resist the White Paper as if there were no war." Thousands of

Palestinian Jews volunteered for the British armed services, taking high-risk assignments in various theaters of war. Some also undertook dangerous missions to rescue Jews from European areas controlled by Hitler and his allies. As the Nazi threat receded, a few frustrated Zionists turned to terrorist acts, such as assassinating the British minister-resident in Cairo.

The Growing US Role

As it became clear that Britain would not lift its restrictions on Jewish immigration into Palestine or relent in its opposition to a Jewish state, the Zionists increasingly looked to the United States for support. Zionism had not attracted many American Jews earlier, but the rise of Hitler had alerted them to the dangers of anti-Semitism running rampant. If Germany, once among the safest countries for Jews, now persecuted them, was there any country in which Jews could always live as a minority? Maybe a Jewish state would not be such a bad idea after all, American Jews reasoned, even if few of them planned to settle there.

In 1942 American Zionists adopted what was called the Biltmore Program, calling on Britain to rescind the White Paper and to make Palestine a Jewish state. Soon the World Zionist Organization endorsed this resolution. US politicians, aware of the feelings of their voters but not those of the Arab majority living in Palestine, began clamoring for a Jewish state. This was not just a knee-jerk response to the "Jewish vote," as many Christians hoped that the formation of a Jewish state would atone for Hitler's vile deeds and for the past persecution committed by so many others. Why were more Jewish survivors not admitted into the United States? Although it might have alleviated the Palestine problem, it also would have undermined what the Zionists wanted, a Jewish state. Besides, anti-Semitism remained strong in the United States; most Christians and even some Jews did not want to raise the immigration quotas for Jewish refugees from Europe.

As World War II was winding down, violence in Palestine mounted. Zionist terrorist groups, such as the *Irgun Tzvei Le'umi* (National Military Organization) and the Stern Gang, blew up buildings and British installations in Palestine. The US government began to pressure Britain to end restrictions on Jewish immigration and to accommodate demands for Jewish statehood. The Anglo-American Committee of Inquiry went to Palestine in 1946 and interviewed both mandate officials and nationalist leaders. Its most publicized recommendation was to admit 100,000 European Jewish refugees at once and to end all restrictions on Jewish land purchases. The new Labour government in Britain rejected this advice and advocated instead a federated Arab-Jewish Palestine. This satisfied no one, and the fighting worsened. Finally, Britain went before the UN General Assembly in February 1947 and admitted that it could no longer keep the mandate. Its Palestine policy was bankrupt.

The UN Partition Plan

It was up to the new world organization—the United Nations—to settle the issue. The General Assembly responded to the challenge by creating yet another investigatory body, the UN Special Committee on Palestine. This group of ten member states toured Palestine during the summer of 1947 but could not come up with a policy on which they could all agree. Some favored a binational Palestinian state, shared by Arabs and Jews. The Arabs still made up two-thirds of the country's population, though, and they were expected to resist admitting any Jewish refugees from Europe. The majority of the special committee members recommended partitioning Palestine into seven sections, of which three would be controlled by Arabs and three by Jews. The seventh, including Jerusalem and Bethlehem, would be administered by the United Nations (Map 15.1). Neither the Palestinian Arabs nor the governments of neighboring Arab countries welcomed a plan to set up an alien state in their midst, against the wishes of the land's Arab majority. But the Communist countries, the United States, and nearly all the Latin American republics favored it. The partition plan passed in the General Assembly by a 33 to 13 vote. All five Arab member states opposed it.

The Zionists did not like all aspects of this plan, but they accepted it as a step toward forming the Jewish state for which they had waited and worked so long. The Arabs threatened to go to war to block its implementation. Jewish paramilitary groups in Palestine soon seized lands not allotted to their side, and Arab commandos often struck back at Jewish targets. Although Arab League members met to coordinate their strategy, their public threats masked private quarrels and a lack of military preparedness. Amir Abdallah of Transjordan negotiated with the Zionists, hoping to annex Arab Palestine. Most other Arab countries opposed him, calling for volunteers to fight in Palestine. At the end of 1947, it was not yet clear whether these nations would commit their regular armies to action.

The Creation of Israel

The 1947 partition plan was certainly no peaceful resolution to the contest for Palestine. Both Jewish and Arab armies lined up volunteers and

Map 15.1   The UN partition plan for Palestine, 1947

equipped themselves as well as they could. Both sides committed terrorist acts against innocent civilians. For example, the Irgun raided Dayr Yasin, an Arab village near Jerusalem, and massacred 254 men, women, and children. A few days later, an Arab group ambushed a bus going to the Hadassah Medical Center on Mount Scopus, killing 75 Jewish professors, doctors, and nurses. The British stayed aloof, as they were preparing to withdraw totally from Palestine.

Mindful of the mounting violence in Palestine, the US representative in the United Nations suggested in March 1948 that the partition plan be postponed for a ten-year cooling-off period under a UN trusteeship. This compromise might have satisfied the Arabs but certainly not the Zionists, with the Jewish state now almost in their grasp. They pressured President Harry Truman, who finally reaffirmed his support for a Jewish state, over the objections of the State Department and his own secretary of defense. That spring the Zionists began to implement their Plan Dalet to drive the Arab population from Jewish-designated and adjacent areas, many Palestinian Arabs panicked and fled for safety to nearby countries (creating a refugee problem that still exists), and finally the British troops pulled out of Jerusalem.

On 14 May 1948 the Jewish Agency Executive Committee, meeting in Tel Aviv, formally declared that those parts of Palestine under Jewish control were now the independent State of Israel. It also announced that the provisions of the 1939 White Paper limiting Jewish immigration and land purchases were null and void. The Zionists urged the Arab inhabitants of Israel "to preserve the ways of peace and play their part in the development of the state, on the basis of full and equal citizenship and due representation in all its bodies and institutions." They also called on the neighboring Arab states to cooperate with them for the common good. Even if these statements were sincere, they came too late. Many Palestinian Arabs, having already fled from their homes during the early stages of the fighting, distrusted the Zionists and called on their Arab neighbors for help. The next day five Arab governments sent their armies into Palestine to fight against the new State of Israel.

CONCLUSION

The contest for Palestine entered a new phase. Arab nationalists and political Zionists had for years inflamed each other's worst fears under the bungling British mandate. Now they could fight each other openly.

The Arab-Israeli conflict, as it came to be called for the next thirty-five years, would become one of the most intractable problems of modern diplomacy. American journalist I. F. Stone quipped that if God is dead, he died trying to solve the Arab-Israeli conflict. Before 1948 a compromise might have been found between the extremes of Arab nationalism and political Zionism. But no attempt at accommodation worked, and the world continues to pay a high price for that failure.

16

Israel's Rebirth and the
Rise of Arab Nationalism

The 1948 war between the new State of Israel and its Arab neighbors was a revolutionary event, setting in motion many drastic changes in the Middle East. To the Israelis and their admirers, the war was a struggle for Jewish independence, fought first against the resistance of the indigenous Palestinians, later against British imperialism, and finally against the armies of the Arab states. They called Israel's victory revolutionary because for the first time in modern history the citizens of a Middle Eastern country managed to oust a colonial regime and set up a democratic government. From the Arabs' point of view, their defeat in Palestine was revolutionary because it humiliated their armies and discredited their regimes. It also established a colonial settler state in their midst. The Palestine disaster uprooted about 725,000 Arabs, who sought refuge in the Gaza Strip (a small part of Palestine occupied by Egypt in 1948), Jordan, Syria, or Lebanon. These Palestinian refugees emerged as a potent force. Some became ardent Arab nationalists. Others espoused any ideology or backed any leader who promised to restore their dignity and their homes. The Palestinians' bitter opposition to Israel was matched only by their hostility to Arab governments that might seek peace with the Jewish state. They became the revolutionaries of the Arab world. From 1948 to 1967, all sides had to adjust to the new conditions created by the war.

Israel's War for Independence

How and why did Israel win the war? The Arab states were bigger and more populous. Some had large standing armies and ample military equipment. On 14 May 1948, when the Jewish Agency leaders declared Israel independent, the armies of Egypt, Transjordan, and several other Arab countries proceeded to invade Israel. If for them the war was just starting, for the Israelis (as the Jews of Palestine now called themselves), it had been going on for years. Consequently, there were already many experienced Jewish fighters. But they had not all belonged to the same force. Aside from Haganah, which had become the military arm of the Jewish Agency, several of the political parties had their own militias. The best known was the Irgun Tzvei Le'umi, attached to the party that hoped to set up the Jewish state on both sides of the river Jordan. Under Menachem Begin, the Irgun conducted many terrorist attacks, of which the most notorious were the bombing of Jerusalem's King David Hotel in 1946 and the Dayr Yasin massacre of 1948.

The Israelis were divided at first, for the Irgun and the even more extreme Stern Gang resisted absorption into Haganah (renamed the Israel Defense Force [IDF] soon after independence). However, the Arab invasion and what the Israelis viewed as the dire consequences of an Arab victory welded the people together. The IDF quickly grew in numbers, equipment, and experience. Also, having anticipated an attack, the Israelis' Plan Dalet called for extending Israel's borders beyond the UN partition lines and removing as many Palestinian Arabs as possible. They began implementing this plan even before the Arab armies attacked.

The Contending Forces

The opposing Arab armies turned out to be smaller than expected. Countries such as Egypt held back most of their troops to preserve order at home. The best-equipped and best-trained army was Transjordan's Arab Legion, but its field strength of 10,000 could hardly match the IDF, which grew to 100,000 men and women. The Israelis committed more troops to battle than all the Arab armies combined. At the beginning of the war, small bands of poorly armed Israelis had to ward off large Arab armies. However, it mattered less that Jewish soldiers outnumbered Arab ones in Palestine than that the Arabs came to think it did. Ill informed about the character and abilities of Palestinian Jews, Arab leaders tended to underestimate them at first. Then, when the IDF gradually brought more force to bear, the Arabs overreacted and overestimated the Jews' strength. Poor morale was a major reason for the Arab defeat.

The Outside Powers

The attitudes and policies of the Great Powers confused both sides, but this confusion hurt the Arabs more than the Israelis. The United States and the

Soviet Union both rushed to recognize Israel. Although most countries cut off arms to both sides, Communist Czechoslovakia sold large quantities of weapons to Israel. Communist countries backed Israel in 1948 for several reasons. First, they desired to weaken British influence in the Middle East. Second, they hoped that the new Jewish state might adopt socialism or even communism. Third, they wanted to discredit "feudal" and "bourgeois" Arab regimes. The US government equivocated. Public opinion favored Israel. With a presidential election approaching, Truman, an incumbent in deep trouble, vied with his Republican opponent in supporting the Jewish state. However, State Department and Pentagon officials feared that an anti-Arab policy would harm the growing US oil interests in the Middle East. Entrepreneurs, educators, and missionaries who had spent years in the area argued cogently against policies that would antagonize the whole Arab world. But Israel's supporters, especially in Congress, had more clout.

The Arabs expected more support from Britain, which had been estranged from the Zionists since the 1939 White Paper. It had treaties with Iraq and Egypt permitting British troops to guard airfields and strategic waterways. The commander of Transjordan's Arab Legion, Sir John Bagot Glubb, and many of his officers were British subjects. But although the Foreign Office and many senior diplomats did favor the Arabs, the British government depended too heavily on US military and economic support to openly challenge US Middle East policies. Europe was recovering from World War II, and most liberals sympathized with the Jewish state, partly to atone for the Holocaust.

UN Mediation Efforts

The United Nations, overtaken by events in May 1948, tried to settle the Arab-Israeli conflict. Its mediator, Sweden's Count Folke Bernadotte, managed to get both sides to accept a month-long ceasefire in early June. Both sides were exhausted from four weeks of intense fighting, but only the Israelis used this respite to obtain and distribute arms to its troops. Bernadotte published a plan that would have given the Negev Desert (assigned mainly to the Jews under the 1947 Partition Plan) and Jerusalem to Transjordan. In return, Israel would get parts of western Galilee that had been allotted to the Arabs. On 8 July fighting resumed on all fronts. During the next ten days, the Israelis took part of Galilee and the strategic towns of Lydda and Ramleh. But the United Nations secured another ceasefire ten days later, before the Jewish forces could capture Jerusalem's Old City (containing the revered Western Wall).

As both sides prepared for yet another round of fighting, the UN mediator made a new appeal for Arab support. Bernadotte added to his plan a stipulation that the Arab refugees would be allowed to return to their homes in cities and villages now under Israeli control. But the Israelis wanted the Arabs' homes, lands, and crops for the Jewish immigrants they hoped to attract. Bernadotte was murdered in September by Stern Gang extremists who believed that he favored Arab interests. Ralph Bunche, an American, became the new UN mediator. What Israel most wanted was Judea, where Brigadier General Moshe Dayan attacked Arab Legion positions around Hebron and Bethlehem until the United Nations obtained a new ceasefire. Meanwhile, Israeli forces in Galilee drove the Syrian-backed Arab Liberation Army northward into Lebanon. While UN members debated Bernadotte's plan in late 1948, Israel tried to push Egyptian and Arab Legion forces out of the Gaza area and the southern Negev. By year's end the main fighting front had crossed the old border into the Egyptian Sinai. When Egypt still would not sue for peace, Britain invoked the 1936 Anglo-Egyptian Treaty to thwart the Israelis. Although embarrassing the Egyptian government, which no longer wanted British protection, no Arab country was prepared to rescue Egypt.

The United Nations now began a bizarre exercise in diplomacy. No Arab state was willing to confer directly with Israel, giving it de facto recognition, but in January 1949 Bunche opened what he called "proximity talks" on the island of Rhodes. Egyptian and Israeli delegations, in separate suites of the same hotel, haggled over terms while Bunche carried proposals from one side to the other, finally securing an armistice agreement. Three months later, after the Arab Legion had lost the Negev areas it had occupied, Transjordan signed at Rhodes a separate agreement to ratify a secret pact that King (formerly Amir) Abdallah had made with Israel's army commanders. Israel thus gained access to the Gulf of 'Aqaba. No longer would Egypt and Transjordan have direct overland contact. Israel proceeded to build a port at Eilat. Lebanon signed an armistice with Israel in March, and Syria followed suit in July 1949. Iraq, which had also sent forces into Palestine, never signed an armistice and opposed any Arab peace with Israel.

The War's Aftermath

Would these agreements lead to a comprehensive Arab-Israeli peace? The UN Conciliation Commission for Palestine called a conference in Lausanne, where Israeli and Arab delegations were to settle their outstanding differences. But negotiations dragged on for four months and ended inconclusively. Israel wanted a comprehensive peace settlement, but the Arabs demanded that Israel first withdraw from all lands not allotted to the Jewish state by the 1947 Partition Plan and to also readmit the Palestinian refugees. The Arabs argued that these stipulations were contained in the General Assembly resolutions and that Israel had been admitted to the United Nations on condition that it comply with them. Israel replied that it was the Arabs who had first defied the General Assembly's Partition Plan. Hopes for a settlement dissipated amid these arguments. Once most UN members recognized the Jewish state, Western observers thought the Arab governments would soon admit that Israel was in the Middle East to stay. We will show later why they did not.

Arab Divisions

The Arabs failed to defeat Israel in 1948 because of political divisions. All the Arab states were opposed to the 1947 Partition Plan and to the creation of a Jewish state in Palestine. As Arab League members, they had vowed to fight and put their armies under the nominal command of an Iraqi general. Some, however, refused to appropriate funds or to commit troops as long as the British governed Palestine. Transjordan's Hashimite king Abdallah, supported by Hashimite-ruled Iraq, still wanted a "Greater Syria." Even in 1948 he was willing to make a deal with the Israelis to annex parts of Palestine to his own kingdom, a first step toward annexing Lebanon and Syria, few of whose citizens still backed the Greater Syria idea. Both Egypt's Faruq and Sa'udi Arabia's Ibn Sa'ud opposed Abdallah's plan. Egypt aspired to be the leading Arab country; it had the largest population, universities, newspapers, and broadcasting stations in the Arab world. The Arab League headquarters was in Cairo, and its energetic secretary general was an Egyptian. Egypt did not want a Hashimite king ruling in neighboring Palestine who might later try to annex Syria and Lebanon. Ibn Sa'ud, having ousted the Hashimites from Arabia, agreed with Faruq.

The Arabs claimed to be united and were threatening the Zionists with invasion if they dared to set up a state in Palestine, but their leaders were actually trying to outbluff one another. Once the fighting started, the Egyptian army and the Arab Legion undercut each other. The Palestinians had the Arab Liberation Army, led by a Syrian; it, too, would not work with the Arab Legion. Abdallah also hated the best-known Palestinian Arab nationalist, Hajj Amin al-Husayni, Jerusalem's ex-mufti, who was now working for Faruq. As long as the Arabs had a chance of winning, their leaders and armies competed to pick up the most land and glory in Palestine. Once Israel drove the Arabs back, they began bickering over who was to blame.

The Palestinian Arabs

No Arab government heeded the needs or the interests of the Palestinian Arabs, who up to 1948 had formed the majority of Palestine's population. About 150,000 Palestinians managed to stay in their homes within lands controlled by Israel and became Israeli citizens. These Arabic-speaking Muslim and Christian citizens were a restricted minority within the Jewish state. In time, though, Israeli Arabs came to enjoy political rights, economic benefits, and educational opportunities unmatched by most of their Arab neighbors. The 400,000 Arabs who lived in those parts of Palestine not taken by Israel (including the Old City of Jerusalem) came under the military occupation of the Arab Legion. Abdallah soon annexed this region, now usually termed the West Bank, to the state he renamed the Hashimite Kingdom of Jordan. Although Israel opposed "Jordanian" rule over Jerusalem's Old City, its emissaries had secretly agreed to let Abdallah keep the West Bank, as they hoped to make a comprehensive peace settlement with Jordan later. There were also 200,000 Palestinians, many of them refugees, in the Gaza region, where Egypt set up an "all-Palestine government" under the former mufti. However, this political ploy against Abdallah's hegemonic claim to Palestine foundered. The Gaza Strip fell under Egypt's military administration.

At the end of 1948, Palestinian refugees numbered around 725,000. Some had voluntarily left their homes even before the struggle started, while most had had to flee during the fighting. Who forced their flight? Israel's supporters claim that Arab governments broadcast orders to Palestinian civilians to get out so that their armies could more easily move in against the Israelis, but no evidence documents this claim. The Palestinians argue (with some support from Israeli scholars) that they were terrorized by Zionist paramilitary groups up to 14 May 1948 and that the IDF drove out others during the later phases of the war. However, the debate is likely to go on because both sides committed terrorist acts. In the end, the Palestinians got no state of their own.

The Arab countries (except for Jordan) would not absorb the refugees, mainly for political reasons, but some would have found it challenging to do so. The Palestinians themselves rejected assimilation because they wanted to go back to their homes. Israel, busy absorbing European

Jewish survivors and unwilling to take in a "fifth column" of implacable foes, would not readmit the Palestinian refugees. The United Nations set up the UN Relief and Works Agency (UNRWA) as a stopgap measure. The UNRWA housed Palestinians in camps, gave them enough food and clothing to survive, and educated their children in hopes that the problem would, someday and somehow, be solved. A few refugees did manage to go back to Israel, and many younger Palestinians gradually became absorbed in the economies of the Arab countries; but many others stayed in the camps, growing ever more bitter against Israel, its Western backers, and the Arab leaders who had betrayed them. We will further discuss the Palestinians later.

THE ARAB COUNTRIES

In the wake of what was soon termed the *Nakba* ([Palestine] disaster), what happened in the Arab world? Some Arab states were stable, and a few were popular, but most were neither. Would-be Arab leaders espoused pan-Arabism. If only the Arabs had been united, they claimed, they would not have lost the war to Israel. No matter what claims to unity may have been made by Arab nationalists, there were several Arab states, many leaders, and various policies.

Jordan

The country most directly affected by the war was Jordan. What had been a desert emirate called Transjordan became the Hashimite Kingdom of Jordan. A half million Transjordanians, most of Bedouin origin, were joined by about 900,000 Palestinians, half of them local farmers or city dwellers in the newly annexed West Bank and the other half refugees in UNRWA camps. The Palestinians, all of whom were offered Jordanian nationality, tended to be more westernized and politically articulate than the Transjordanians over whom Abdallah had long ruled as a father figure. Most of the Palestinians were farmers, but some were lawyers, teachers, merchants, or bureaucrats. Few were monarchists. For King Abdallah, controlling Jerusalem's Old City, with its Muslim shrines such as the Dome of the Rock, made up for his father's loss of Mecca and Medina to Ibn Sa'ud a generation earlier. Content with his new lands and the tripled number of subjects, he secretly offered Israel diplomatic recognition in exchange for rail access to Haifa. Angry Palestinians, especially supporters of the ex-mufti, denounced Abdallah as a traitor. In 1951 a young Palestinian murdered him in Jerusalem. His son was soon eased off the Jordanian throne because of alleged mental instability in favor of Abdallah's seventeen-year-old grandson, Husayn, who took charge officially in 1952.

During this time, Britain continued to subsidize Jordan's government, and Sir John Bagot Glubb commanded the Arab Legion. Although Jordan had become nominally independent in 1946, the Soviets did not agree to its admission to UN membership until 1955. There followed a brief period during which King Husayn supported Arab nationalism and the Palestinian left. The lesson of Abdallah's assassination was clear. The Palestinians might have lost their homes and accepted refuge in Jordan, but they could block any attempt to bury their claims by a peace settlement. Husayn would never be the first to settle with Israel. As for Abdallah's Greater Syria ambition, it faded like a desert mirage.

Syria and Lebanon

What did happen to the rest of Greater Syria? The war's impact on Syria and Lebanon was different but no less disruptive. What was now the Republic of Syria had grown embittered during a generation of unwanted French rule. The Syrians resented not only France's amputation of Alexandretta and the creation of Lebanon during the mandate era but also the Western powers' decision to take Palestine and Transjordan from Syria in 1920. Why not reunite what the West had divided? Now that the British and French had given up their mandates, why not turn what had once been Faysal's Arab kingdom into a republic of Greater Syria?

But there were two flies in the ointment. One was the creation of Israel, which the Syrians saw as an imperialist plot to keep the area divided and under Western control. The other was Abdallah and his family. Indeed, there was a group of Syrians, the People's Party (which went back to the Great Syrian Revolution of 1925), who wanted Arab unity restored, under Hashimite rule, in the form of an organic union of all Fertile Crescent states, including Iraq. But the Syrians in power from 1945 (the National Bloc, formed in 1931), wanted to keep the Hashimites from ruling Syria. They, too, desired Arab unity, but under the aegis of the Arab League; they favored closer ties with Egypt and Sa'udi Arabia than with Iraq and Jordan. Accordingly, Syria fought against Israel in 1948 in alliance with Egypt and in competition with Jordan's Arab Legion. The poor showing of Syria's troops led to scandals in Damascus. The discredited civilian government was ousted by army coups in 1949, and Colonel Adib Shishakli took power. His populist dictatorship became the prototype for those of Egypt's Nasir and other Arab army officers in the 1950s.

Deeply split by religious and local differences, Syria became notorious for instability and disunity; yet its leaders hoped to unite all Arabs against Zionism and imperialism. Shishakli's overthrow in 1954 led to another attempt at civilian government, but its bureaucracy ignored the country's need for economic and social reforms. It was Syria that hosted the founding of the first popular Arab socialist movement, the Ba'ath (Renaissance) Party, which appealed to young people, army officers, workers, and Palestinians throughout the Arab world. It demanded land reform, nationalization of basic industries, unification of all Arabic-speaking peoples, and militant resistance to Israel and all vestiges of imperialism in the area. No patriotic Syrian wanted peace with Israel or the absorption of the Palestinian refugees. Syria's ethnic and religious minorities, such as the Armenians, other Christian sects, Shi'ite Muslims, Alawites (an offshoot of Shi'ite Islam), Druze, and Jews, generally fared badly in this era of rising Arab nationalism.

As for Lebanon, with seventeen recognized religious sects, it had been ruled since 1943 under an unwritten "gentlemen's agreement" that specified that its president would always be a Maronite Christian, its prime minister a Sunni, and the speaker of its National Assembly a Shi'ite Muslim. Its government was "democratic" in the sense that its legislators were popularly elected, but it functioned as a constitutional oligarchy, for wealth and power were concentrated in the leading families, now mainly commercial industrial leaders. Lebanon's system was also discriminatory: Christian sects were allocated six parliamentary seats and administrative posts for every five assigned to Muslims. This apportionment was based on a census taken by the French in 1932, but no census has been taken since then, as the Maronites and several other sects fear that any head count would show their relative decline. The influx in 1948 of some 150,000 Palestinian refugees upset the population balance. Lebanon quickly absorbed those who were Christian, but the Muslim majority was denied citizenship and confined in large refugee camps. In this way the system of proportional representation by religious sects continued to reflect Lebanon's situation under the French mandate. The leaders also agreed to cooperate, despite their religious differences, to preserve Lebanon's independence and territorial integrity. This National Pact (as it is always called) meant that the Christians would not keep Lebanon tied to France or re-create an autonomous Mount Lebanon under their control, while the Muslims would not seek to unite the country with Syria or any possible pan-Arab state.

The National Pact, endorsed by all Christian and Muslim leaders sub-scribed in 1943, guided Lebanon through a coup d'état in 1952 and a civil war in 1958, up to the catastrophic breakdown of 1975 through 1991. Lebanon seemed to thrive under this system, but a few families retained most of the wealth and power, the government and army were too weak to protect the country or even to preserve order, and Beirut's free press became an arena for competing liberal, pan-Arab, and socialist ideologies. The influx of Palestinians, whom the Christian elite refused to assimilate, would undermine the system, but so, too, did urbanization, education, and growing awareness of the gap between rich and poor.

Iraq

Of all the Arab states in southwest Asia, the most populous is Iraq. With its two great rivers and rising oil revenues, it might have become the stron-gest Arab country. There are several reasons that it did not. First, it was pasted together from three Ottoman provinces by the British after World War I. Although its rivers appear to unite these parts, the Euphrates and the Tigris both start in Turkey and the former also flows through Syria. In addition, most of Iraq's arable land came under the control of the shaykhs of various quasi-independent Bedouin tribes. The Muslim population was divided between Sunnis and Shi'ites, the latter having ties with neighbor-ing Iran. Religious minorities included Jews and Assyrians. One-fifth of Iraq's population was Kurdish. A smaller share was Turkish. What these disparate groups had in common were four centuries of Ottoman rule, followed by a British military occupation in 1917, a nationwide revolt in 1920, and the selection of Amir Faysal as their first king in 1921. In 1932 Iraq was the first Arab mandate to become nominally independent, but British troops remained. Iraq viewed itself as the real leader of Arab na-tionalism, a rival to Egypt.

Iraq's army fought in the 1948 Palestine War, but the country suffered less from the defeat than did Israel's neighbors. Its rising oil revenues were being invested in river irrigation and other projects that promised future prosperity. Its cabinets changed with alarming frequency, the various mi-nority problems festered (nearly all Jews were allowed to emigrate, minus their property, to Israel), the socioeconomic gap between the landowning shaykhs and the peasant masses widened, and the pro-Western monarchy lost popular support. But the West did not notice. Britain's remaining mil-itary presence was camouflaged politically in 1955 when Iraq joined with Turkey, Iran, Pakistan, and Britain to form an anti-Communist alliance commonly called the Baghdad Pact. To Westerners, Iraq was a model modernizing nation—that is, until its monarchy was felled by an army coup in 1958, one that Westerners blamed on Egypt's press and radio attacks.

Egypt's Nasir and His Policies

The 1952 revolution that led to Nasir's rise to power can be viewed as the result of mounting frustration over either Britain's prolonged occupation of the Nile Valley or Egypt's defeat by Israel. Most historians favor the latter interpretation because from 1948 to 1977 Egypt's energies were mobilized toward fighting against Israel and competing for the leadership of the Arab world. US and Soviet pressure persuaded the British to give up their Suez Canal base in 1954, and Egypt recognized Sudanese independence in 1956. Nile Valley unity gave way to Arab nationalism.

Let us put Egypt's role as an Arab country into historical perspective. Even though the Arabs have not been politically united since the 'Abbasid revolution in 750—if indeed they were ever really united—the idea arose in the twentieth century that all people who speak Arabic do constitute one nation. They should unite in a single state, as the Germans tried to do under Bismarck and Hitler or the Italians under Mazzini and Mussolini. A united Arab state, hypothetically, must include Egypt, the largest Arab country and the one linking North Africa's Arabs with those of southwest Asia. The Egyptians believed that only a strong and united Arab world could withstand the domination of the Western powers. They viewed Israel's creation as a colonial imposition on the Arabs. They did not want to become communists, as some British and American observers thought in the 1950s, but because Moscow had not ruled the Arab world in the past, the Arabs did not resent the Soviets. Their leaders seized this chance to weaken the West's influence: the Soviet Union turned away from Israel and began to back the Arabs.

The rise of pan-Arabism in Egypt coincided with the overthrow of General Nagib, the titular leader of the 1952 revolution that ousted King Faruq, by Colonel Gamal 'Abd al-Nasir in 1954. For the next sixteen years, he would, as Egypt's president, loom larger than life in the words and imaginations of both those who loved him and those who hated him. He could be dictatorial or deferential, charismatic or suspicious, ingenuous or crafty. He reacted more than he acted. The son of an Alexandrian postal clerk and grandson of an Upper Egypt peasant, Nasir had known poverty and humiliation in his youth. Moody and withdrawn, young Nasir read widely, especially history books and biographies of such leaders as Julius Caesar, Napoleon, and (closer to home) Mustafa Kamil. He embraced Egyptian nationalism, but not the parties of the 1930s. Unable to afford law school and yet eager to lead his country's fight for independence, Nasir managed to enter the Egyptian military academy in 1937, the first year that young men without palace or aristocratic ties could be admitted into the officer corps.

After being commissioned, Nasir served in various army posts and slowly gathered a group of young officers from equally modest backgrounds. Intensely patriotic, these men chafed at Britain's power and their own army's weakness, shown by the unopposed British ultimatum to King Faruq in 1942 and Egypt's defeat by Israel in 1948. The bonding of these officers led to a conspiratorial cabal, for they saw that only by ousting the discredited regime could Egypt be liberated and redeemed.

Nasir started out leading from behind the scenes, but he engineered Nagib's overthrow in 1954 because the latter seemed to have become too popular. A ponderous speaker at first, Nasir did not win public support until he openly defied the West. An Israeli raid on the Gaza Strip early in 1955, allegedly in retaliation for Palestinian raids into Israel, proved to Nasir that Egypt needed more arms. His officers wanted to get them from Britain or the United States, but neither country would sell any to Egypt unless it promised to join an anti-Communist alliance and refrain from attacking Israel. Nasir rejected these strings on Western aid. He assailed Iraq for joining the anti-Soviet Baghdad Pact in the spring of 1955. Egypt spoke out against any Arab alliance with the West.

Instead, as Nasir emerged as the leader of Arab nationalism, he adopted a policy he called "positive neutralism" after his exposure to nationalist and communist leaders at the 1955 Bandung Conference of Asian and Middle Eastern states opposed to Western domination. Defying the West, he agreed to buy $200 million (then a huge sum) in arms from the Communist countries. Arab nationalists outside Egypt, especially the Palestinians, hailed Nasir as their champion. Egypt started arming bands of *fida'iyin* (Arabic for "those who sacrifice themselves"), made up mainly of Gaza Strip Palestinians, to make incursions into Israel.

The US government tried to deflect Nasir from his anti-Western drift by adopting a policy that now seems confused. Secretary of State John Foster Dulles wanted Nasir to leave the other Arab states and Israel alone, so he offered technical and economic assistance, notably a large loan to finance the construction of a new dam at Aswan. However, Dulles denounced Nasir's "positive neutralism" between communism and the West, his threats against Israel and pro-Western Arab regimes, and his recognition of the People's Republic of China. In July 1956, just after Egypt had decided to accept the Aswan Dam loan offer, Dulles, hoping to humiliate Nasir, yanked it away. The Egyptian leader responded by nationalizing the Suez Canal Company, pledging to use its profits, most of which had gone to European investors since its opening in 1869, to finance the dam. "O Americans," he shouted before a vast crowd, "may you choke to death in your fury!"

It was not the Americans who choked. After all, the British and French were the canal's main users, largely for oil imports from the Gulf. They began planning diplomatic and military measures to get it back. That summer and fall witnessed international conferences, trips to Cairo, and other Western stratagems aimed at prying the canal from Nasir's grip. Meanwhile, the Arabs hailed Nasir's defiance as just retribution for all they had suffered from Western imperialism. When diplomatic attempts to subject the canal to international control failed, the British and French resolved to regain it by force—and to overthrow Nasir if they could. Significantly, they turned to Israel as an accomplice.

ISRAEL'S EARLY YEARS

Although the Arabs viewed Israel as an agent of Western imperialism, the Israelis saw themselves as an embattled nation seeking to ensure the survival of the Jewish people in the wake of the Holocaust. They regarded their war for independence as a struggle by an oppressed people for freedom from outside domination. Most of the Arab states against which Israel fought in 1948 were still influenced by British advisers and ruled by kings and landowners. Few Israelis realized they were creating another oppressed people: the Palestinian Arabs.

When revolutions later toppled the discredited regimes in Syria and Egypt, the Israelis were disappointed that the new leaders made no peace overtures to them. But the Israelis were busy rebuilding a war-torn country. In addition, they absorbed the thousands of Jewish refugees who had survived the war and the death camps of Europe. They also had to cope with the influx of even greater numbers of Jewish refugees from Arab countries. Absorbing these new Israelis, viewed as alien in language and culture by the earlier settlers (who had come from Europe), placed severe strains on the country.

Problems of the Jewish State
Israel had economic problems. Its currency, cut loose from the British pound, plummeted in value, and the new government could not borrow enough money to pay its bills. However, large amounts of US government

and private Jewish assistance, later augmented by German restitution payments to Jewish survivors of the Hitler era (the result of an agreement between West German chancellor Konrad Adenauer and Israeli premier David Ben-Gurion), eased the economic strain. This financial aid provided capital for Israel's development and reduced its balance-of-payments deficit.

Equally crucial to the country's survival was the Israelis' conviction that the Jewish people must never again face the threat of extinction, whether by Christian fanatics, totalitarian dictators, or Arab nationalists. If any skeptics asked how the existence of tiny Israel, with 1 million Jews and as many problems, better guaranteed Jewish survival than the continued presence of 10 million Jews in the West (few of whom chose to move to Israel), the Zionists countered that Germany's Jews had prospered too, but who had rescued them from Hitler? When some accused the Israelis of creating an Arab refugee problem, they in turn blamed the Arab states for not absorbing these Palestinian victims of the 1948 war, whereas Israel did accept Jewish refugees from Arab countries. If Israel could not have peace without readmitting the Arab refugees, as the United Nations insisted, then peace would have to wait.

Because the Israelis viewed their war against the Arabs as a struggle for independence, we forget that up to 1947, few Jews in Palestine or anywhere else expected the Jewish state to be born in their lifetime. As a minority group in a mainly Arab land, the early Zionist settlers had toiled to start farms in the wilderness; to build Tel Aviv amid the sand dunes north of Jaffa; to transplant the schools, theaters, and newspapers they had known in Europe; and to found new institutions, such as Histadrut, that combined labor and capital in a collectively governed organization. They had formed political parties espousing various combinations of socialism, nationalism, and Judaism. They had revived Hebrew as a spoken language and modernized it as a medium of written communication.

But they had assumed that the Jewish national home would remain in the British Commonwealth, that most of its inhabitants would be European, and that the Arabs would either leave or accept their presence and power. World War II, the Holocaust, and the 1948 war had belied these assumptions. Now Israel was an independent state, surrounded by Arab countries implacably opposed to its existence, with Jews pouring in from all parts of the world (mainly the Middle East and North Africa), and with a small Arab minority. Despite their political inexperience and economic problems, the Israelis built a nation-state with a democratic government—at least for the Jews. Israelis constructed their government in a way that precluded significant sharing of benefits and experiences with the Palestinian Arabs, although the Arabs did have representation in the Knesset, Israel's legislature.

Politics in Israel

Israel's democracy was not an exact copy of Britain's. Political parties, some of them holdovers from Jewish movements in pre-1914 Eastern Europe, proliferated. No party could ever win the support of a majority of Israel's voters, which included doctrinaire socialists, observant Orthodox Jews, secular Zionists, and the Arab minority. Furthermore, Israel did not adopt the system of geographical constituencies familiar to Anglo-Saxons; rather, it set up a representation system by which the percentage of votes cast in a general election for each party was exactly matched by the proportion of seats it held in the following session of the Knesset. For example, if 1 million Israelis voted in an election and 300,000 supported a particular party, then, out of the 120 Knesset seats, 36 would go to the top candidates on that party's list. In other words, the first 36 candidates listed by that party on the ballot would enter the Knesset; those numbered 37 and beyond would not. Decisions on ranking the candidates were made beforehand in party caucuses, not by the voters. Following a pattern familiar to Europeans but not to Americans, executive power was vested in a council of ministers (or cabinet) responsible to the Knesset. The head of government, or prime minister, had to choose a cabinet acceptable to a majority of the Knesset members. As no party has ever won a majority of the votes (hence the Knesset seats) in any election, any leader wanting to form a government has had to combine his or her party with several others, compromising on ideological principles or policy preferences in the bargain.

In the early years of the state, Israel's leading politician was David Ben-Gurion, the leader of the socialist-oriented labor party known as *Mapai* (Israeli Workers Party). Even though Ben-Gurion came to personify Israel in the minds of most foreigners and even many Israelis, Mapai never won more than 40 percent of the vote in any general election. To form a cabinet, Ben-Gurion first had to make a coalition with other parties, usually including the National Religious Party, whose leaders were determined to make Israel a more observant Jewish state. The result was a socialist republic with no formal constitution and thus no formal endorsement of religion. Yet the IDF and all government offices kept kosher dietary laws, no buses ran on the Jewish Sabbath (from sundown Friday until sundown Saturday) except in Haifa and mainly Arab areas, and all marriages and divorces were handled by the religious courts. State school systems were set up for Israelis who followed Jewish laws and for those who wanted their children to know Hebrew but were nonobservant. A separate school system existed for Israeli Arabs who wanted their children to be educated in their own language and culture.

Israel's complex system worked because its leaders, haunted by the memory of what Hitler had tried to do, believed that no personal or ideological preference was more important than the security of the state, which they equated with the survival of the Jewish people. It was hard for a passionate Zionist like Ben-Gurion to admit that anyone could live a full Jewish life outside Israel, although experience soon proved that Israel needed the political and financial support of a strong and prosperous Jewish diaspora (see Box 16.1).

Israel's Foreign Relations
Arab hostility complicated Israeli life. All land and air transportation between Israel and its neighbors was cut. Arab states refused to trade with Israel and boycotted the products of any foreign firm doing business there. Israeli citizens, Jews from abroad, and even foreign Gentiles whose passports showed that they had visited Israel could not enter most of the Arab countries. Ships carrying goods to Israel could not pass through the Suez Canal or enter Arab ports. Egypt blockaded the Tiran Straits between the Red Sea and the Gulf of 'Aqaba, stifling the growth of Israel's port at Eilat. Arab diplomats abroad shunned their Israeli counterparts.

The force of regional hostility caused many Israelis to develop a deep fear of Arabs. Almost every part of Israel was near an Arab country, and border raids—most launched by displaced Palestinians—menaced Jewish settlements. Often Israel retaliated against Arab villages and refugee camps blamed for the raids. Deaths, injuries, and property damage mounted on both sides. The winding armistice line between Israel and Jordan posed special security problems, especially when it cut off a village from its farming or grazing lands. Israel's retaliatory raid against Gaza in 1955 convinced Nasir that Egypt had to buy Communist bloc weapons to strengthen its armed forces. Israel bought some of its arms from such friendly countries as France, but whenever possible it manufactured its own.

The growing frequency of Arab *fida'iyin* raids, plus the mounting fervor of hostile propaganda, led Israel's cabinet to take stronger military measures in 1956. When Britain and France prepared to attack Egypt, Israel quickly joined their conspiracy. All three hoped to punish the Arabs, mainly Nasir, for seizing the Suez Canal and for threatening Israel. The stated concern was for the safety of international waterways; the unstated one was Europe's growing need for Arab (and Iranian) oil.

BOX 16.1   David Ben-Gurion

Ben-Gurion (1886–1973) was born David Gruen in Plonsk, Poland. His family was ardently Zionist and gave him an ideologically influenced and secular, though Hebrew-based, education. By 1904, as a student at the University of Warsaw, he joined *Poalei Zion* (Workers of Zion), a socialist-Zionist group. His ardent Zionism caused him to leave the university after two years and immigrate to Palestine when he was but twenty years old.

Upon arriving in Palestine, Gruen changed his name to Ben-Gurion and threw himself into the Zionist project. He helped found the kibbutz movement, the Histadrut (general trade union), and a Jewish defense group called *Hashomer* (the Watchman). In 1912, envisaging future Jewish autonomy within the Ottoman Empire, he went to Istanbul to study Turkish law and government. His studies were cut short by the outbreak of World War I. Ben-Gurion was deported as a troublemaker in 1915 and ended up in New York City, where he spent most of the war years and met and married a Russian-born Zionist activist, Pauline Munweis.

In 1918 Ben-Gurion returned to Palestine as a member of the Jewish Legion attached to the British army. A man of enormous energy and drive, he soon became the leader of both the Histadrut and Mapai. In the 1930s he was elected chairman of the Zionist Executive, the highest body of international Zionism at that time, and chairman of the Jewish Agency (for Palestine, which the British had designated as the official representative of the Jewish people in its mandate). He would keep this power throughout the turbulent struggle that led to Israel's creation in 1948, when he became the country's first prime minister.

Ben-Gurion was totally dedicated to Zionism, the cause that shaped his life, and he viewed the rest of the world through its ideological premises. Single-minded and ultimately successful, he was often hard to get along with. Israeli writer Amos Oz described Ben-Gurion: "Verbal battle, not dialogue, was his habitual mode of communication. . . . He was a walking exclamation mark, a tight, craggy man with a halo of silver hair and a jawbone that projected awesome willpower and a volcanic temper." Dedication to the Zionist cause also produced a clear-minded if amoral aspect to Ben-Gurion's character and behavior. He once admitted, "If I were an Arab leader, I would never make terms with Israel. . . . We came here and stole their country."

David Ben-Gurion was in many ways the father of his country. He was a politician, administrator, and commander. He achieved what he and the Zionist movement most wanted—a Jewish state in Palestine. The Western world has glorified this accomplishment, but Ben-Gurion was always very frank about what was really happening.

MIDDLE EASTERN OIL

Middle East history since 1948 often becomes an account of the military and political struggle between the Arabs and Israel. But let us not ignore other developments taking place in the region. Oil exports were becoming the main source of income for the states bordering the Gulf. The leading Middle Eastern producer in the first half of the twentieth century was Iran, a non-Arab country. In 1951, when Britain rejected an equitable profit-sharing agreement with the Iranian government, Iran's prime minister, Mohammad Mosaddiq, amid a crescendo of nationalism, nationalized the Anglo-Iranian Oil Company. In retaliation, Britain and most of its Western allies refused to buy any oil from Iran, causing a spectacular rise in the demand for Arab oil, to the benefit of Iraq, Sa'udi Arabia, and Kuwait.

Along with skyrocketing production and sale of Arab oil (and natural gas), concessions were revised to favor the host countries. This meant that some Arab government revenues also rose dramatically. In 1950 the Arabian American Oil Company (Aramco) reached an agreement with Sa'udi Arabia's government on a fifty-fifty sharing of all revenues. Soon other oil-exporting Arab countries won comparable increases in their royalty payments from the foreign oil companies. Later, these oil-rich desert kingdoms would gain the financial power to influence the policies of the other Arab states and even the West. In Iran, Mosaddiq was overthrown in 1953 by a coup sponsored by the United States and Britain, and his democratically elected government was replaced by the dictatorial regime of the shah (a subject we will cover later). The shah then agreed to put Iran's nationalized oil company under the administration of a consortium of foreign companies, mainly US firms—a fact noted by most Iranians and ignored by most foreigners at the time. The potential power of Iranian and Arab oil producers was not realized in the 1950s or 1960s. Yet by 1956, Europeans were using more oil than coal and importing most of their petroleum and natural gas from the Middle East.

THE GREAT POWERS AND THE ARAB WORLD

Nasir's notoriety resulted from his decision in July 1956 to nationalize the Suez Canal Company amid Arab applause—and Western dismay. Britain, even though it had agreed in 1954 to give up its Suez Canal base, still viewed the canal as the imperial lifeline it had been in the two world wars. Prime Minister Anthony Eden likened Nasir to Hitler and Mussolini. Recalling his own opposition to Britain's appeasement policy in the late

1930s, Eden wanted Nasir stopped before he could undermine the West's position throughout the Arab world. France, too, wanted to stop Nasir, for Egypt was backing, with words and weapons, the Algerian revolution. Both Britain and France got most of their oil from tankers that passed through the canal; the two countries were sure the Egyptians could not administer the company or manage navigation of the canal. Though many Americans disliked Nasir for his hostility to Israel and his ties with Communist states, neither President Eisenhower nor Secretary of State Dulles sought a military showdown. Eisenhower was then seeking re-election on a slogan of "peace and prosperity." This was no time for a Suez war.

The Suez Affair

Britain and France disagreed with the United States. They prepared openly to retake the canal by force. Israel, eager to destroy the *fida'iyin* bases in Gaza and to break Egypt's blockade of the Gulf of 'Aqaba, mobilized for a planned strike against Egypt. Meanwhile, the UN Security Council debated measures to head off trouble. Egypt, which was running the canal more efficiently than anyone had expected, spurned proposals for international control and treated those military preparations as a bluff.

They were not. On 28 October 1956 Israel called up its reserves, thereby doubling the number of its citizens under arms, and invaded Egypt the following day. As the attackers cut off Gaza and drove into Sinai, Britain and France issued an ultimatum to both countries, demanding an immediate ceasefire and troop withdrawals to positions 10 miles (16 kilometers) from the Suez Canal. As Israel's forces were still in the eastern Sinai at the time, this ultimatum was really directed against Egypt. When Nasir rejected it, Britain and France bombarded Egypt's air bases, landed paratroops at Port Said, and occupied the northern half of the canal. Soviet arms did not enable Nasir's army to defend Egypt against what Egyptians called the "tripartite aggression." Soon Israel occupied all of Sinai, and only a heroic but futile civilian resistance delayed the British capture of Port Said.

But Nasir was not overthrown by either his army or his people. Instead, his military defeat became a political victory. The United States joined the Soviet Union in condemning the attack in the United Nations. The General Assembly agreed to set up a UN Emergency Force (UNEF) to occupy Egyptian lands taken by the invaders. Britain and France did not get to keep the canal, Nasir was not discredited in the eyes of Egyptians or other Arabs, and Israel could not obtain recognition and peace from the Arabs. Four months later, Israel withdrew under heavy US pressure. What it gained from the war was a vague guarantee that its ships could use the

Gulf of 'Aqaba, hitherto blockaded by Egypt. A UNEF contingent was stationed at Sharm al-Shaykh, a fortified point controlling the Tiran Straits
between the Gulf of 'Aqaba and the Red Sea. This arrangement, backed
informally by the Western maritime powers, lasted up to May 1967.

Nasir had survived the Suez Affair because the United Nations—
especially the United States—had saved him. Washington publicly justified its opposition to the tripartite attack on Egypt as its support for small
nations in the Afro-Asian bloc against imperialist aggression. After all, the
abortive Hungarian revolution was going on at the same time. How could
the Americans condemn Soviet intervention to smother a popular uprising in Budapest while condoning a Western attack on Port Said? A more
cogent reason, though, was that the crisis occurred only days before the
presidential election, hardly the time for a confrontation with the Soviet
Union. This new US policy won no lasting Arab support.

The Eisenhower Doctrine

Washington thought money might win over some Arab governments.
Thus was born the Eisenhower Doctrine, a program in which the US government offered military and economic aid to any Middle Eastern country
resisting Communist aggression, whether direct or indirect. When it was
announced in January 1957, the Eisenhower Doctrine probably helped
impress the American public with the importance of the Middle East. It
may have deterred the Soviets from a more assertive policy in the area,
but its reception in Arab capitals was decidedly cool. Arab nationalists
viewed it as a US attempt to assume Britain's role as guardian of the Middle East. To them, the Suez Affair had proved that Zionism and imperialism endangered the Arab world more than did any hypothetical threat
of Communist aggression. Nasir in Egypt and the Ba'ath Party in Syria
vehemently denounced the Eisenhower Doctrine, whereas Iraq's Nuri al-
Sa'id, a veteran Arab nationalist who usually collaborated with the British,
endorsed it.

The struggle between the neutralist and pro-Western Arabs climaxed
in Jordan. Seeking Palestinian support, Husayn had given in to Arab demands in 1955 to keep Jordan out of the Baghdad Pact. Early in 1956 he
dismissed General Glubb as head of the Arab Legion. Free elections in
October resulted in a Popular Front cabinet that included Arab nationalists and even a Communist minister. Britain began pulling its troops out
of Jordan and stopped subsidizing its government, but Egypt, Sa'udi Arabia, and Syria agreed to take up the slack. Ba'athist and pro-Nasir officers

within Jordan's army began replacing royalists; early in April 1957 they threatened to seize Husayn's palace. A few days later the Arab nationalists tried to capture a major Jordanian army base, but the king rallied loyal troops to his side and personally faced down the threat to his rule. He proceeded to dismiss the Popular Front cabinet, declare martial law, dissolve Parliament, and set up what amounted to a royal dictatorship. Dulles then declared that Jordan's territorial integrity was a vital US interest and sent ships and troops to the eastern Mediterranean. In effect, the Eisenhower Doctrine was first used to thwart an Arab nationalist takeover in Jordan.

Meanwhile, the Lebanese government of President Kamil Sham'un accepted the Eisenhower Doctrine, overriding Arab nationalist protests that this action would violate Lebanon's neutrality. Pro-Western politicians, mainly Christians, held more power than Arab nationalists, most of whom were Muslim. Some detractors accused Sham'un's government of increasing its power by rigging the 1957 parliamentary elections, in which many opposition leaders failed to get re-elected. Arab nationalists, backed by Palestinian refugees in Lebanon and by Egypt and Syria, opposed the regime's pro-Western leanings and accused Sham'un of trying to keep himself in power. The stage was being set for Lebanon's 1958 civil war.

The Contest for Control of Syria

Patrick Seale, a British journalist, wrote an analysis of Arab politics from 1945 to 1958 called *The Struggle for Syria*. As the title implies, he argues that any power, local or foreign, that seeks to dominate the Middle East must control centrally located Syria. Although geographic Syria once included Lebanon, Israel, and Jordan, even the truncated Republic of Syria was a cockpit for international rivalries. Between the two world wars, France and Britain had competed to control geographic Syria, and in the Cold War the United States and Soviet Union contended for its favor. Rivalries among the other Arab regimes have been even stronger. Amir Abdallah of Transjordan, hoping to rule a Greater Syria, had sought allies within the country. So, too, did his main rivals, Kings Faruq and Ibn Sa'ud. Geography has also dictated Iraq's interest in Syria, and Egypt has usually opposed this interest, no matter who ruled in Baghdad or Cairo.

Syrian politicians, sensitive to these rivalries, have tended to ally themselves with the outside contenders in their own power struggles in Damascus. Syrians have usually been in the vanguard of Arab nationalism. It was Syrians who had formed the Ba'ath Party, which was committed to unifying all Arabic-speaking peoples within a framework that would ensure individual freedom and build a socialist economy. The Ba'ath constitution states, "The Arab nation has an immortal mission . . . that aims at reviving human values, encouraging human development, and promoting harmony and cooperation among the nations of the world."

For the Arab nation to fulfill this mission, the Ba'athists would have to take power in as many Arab governments as possible and weld them into an organic unity. In early 1957, after the Suez War had compromised Syria's pro-Western politicians, a coalition of Ba'athists and other Arab nationalists won control of its government. Spurred by Radio Cairo broadcasts and generous Soviet loans, Syria's new rulers adopted what the West saw as a hostile stance. Scarred by previous military coups backed by outsiders, Syria accused Washington of plotting its overthrow and expelled some US Embassy officials. As Turkey massed troops on its Syrian border, the United States and Soviet Union both threatened to intervene for their client states. The crisis receded by November 1957, but it made some Americans view Syria as a Communist satellite—which is not true.

Syria's leaders were Arab nationalists, not communists. A communist takeover in Damascus would have stifled the Ba'ath or perhaps set off a conservative countercoup like that of King Husayn in Jordan. In February 1958 Syria's president, meeting with Nasir in Cairo, agreed to combine their two countries. Henceforth, Syria and Egypt would be the "northern region" and the "southern region" of a new state, the United Arab Republic (UAR). Plebiscites held later that month in both regions ratified the agreement. The people voted almost unanimously for Nasir (the ballot offered no other choice) as their president. Outsiders accused Egypt of annexing Syria, but it was the Syrians who rejoiced loudest over the new union.

Uniting with Egypt settled Syria's internal unrest, at least briefly, but it put pressure on other Arab governments to follow suit. The Hashimite kings, Jordan's Husayn and Iraq's Faysal II, reacted to the UAR by forming a rival union. Sa'udi Arabia kept aloof but may have betrayed its concern when a leading Syrian politician accused King Sa'ud of offering him a bribe to murder Nasir and rupture the union with Egypt, which led to Sa'ud's downfall. His brother and heir apparent, Faysal, took charge of Sa'udi finances and foreign affairs and stayed out of the UAR, preferring not to share Sa'udi Arabia's immense oil revenues with Egypt and Syria. Yemen's ultraconservative regime did agree to federate with the UAR, but this action did not affect its internal politics. The Palestinians rejoiced at the union between Egypt and Syria, hoping that Nasir would soon restore them to their usurped homeland.

Lebanon's First Civil War and US Intervention
Lebanon did, however, feel the winds of Arab nationalism. The lure of
Arab unity was strong in Lebanon among several groups: Palestinians, especially those living in refugee camps; Muslim Lebanese, who thought the
status quo favored Christians; young people, mainly university students,
who believed that Lebanon's aloofness from Arab nationalism benefited
imperialism and Zionism; and those Lebanese politicians who were excluded from power by the Sham'un regime. Demonstrations took place in
many cities and villages. Tension mounted during the spring. The spark
that lit the fire was the assassination of a pro-Nasir newspaper editor in
May 1958. Arab nationalists were quick to blame the government and to
accuse Sham'un of plotting to amend Lebanon's constitution to secure
himself a second term as president. A heterogeneous opposition, led by
city politicians and rural grandees, banded together as a national front. A
few gunshots reignited ancient feuds in the countryside, the government
declared a curfew, and the first Lebanese civil war began.

In some ways, the war was like a comic opera: bombs exploded at ran-
dom, rebel leaders had access to the government phone and postal facilities, and the army did nothing. The Sham'un regime accused Nasir of
aiding the rebels by smuggling arms across the Syrian border. It appealed
to the Arab League and then to the UN Security Council to stop this threat
to Lebanon's independence. A UN observer group could not corroborate
charges of massive infiltration from Syria, but observers only traveled in
daylight hours on major roads, so they could not see much.

Lebanon's civil war might have wound down once President Sham'un
let the Parliament elect his successor. The rebel leaders did not really want
Lebanon to join the UAR, even if they welcomed Nasir's support. What
brought this war into the wider arena was a concurrent event in another
Arab state, the Iraqi revolution of 14 July 1958. In a sudden coup, an officers' secret society seized control of the police headquarters, the radio station, and the royal palace in Baghdad. They murdered King Faysal II and
his uncle, 'Abd al-Ilah; hunted down and shot Nuri al-Sa'id; and declared
Iraq a republic. Most Arabs rejoiced at the monarchy's downfall, but the
West was horrified. The new regime seemed the embodiment of Arab nationalism and communism combined, a triumph for Nasir, a harbinger of
the fate awaiting Jordan and Lebanon, and a stalking horse for Soviet imperialism in the Middle East. Despite its opposition to the tripartite attack
on Nasir in 1956, Washington now considered invading Iraq.

The US government dispatched the Marines to Lebanon, responding to
Sham'un's plea for aid under the Eisenhower Doctrine, and British troops

were flown to Jordan, where Husayn's regime seemed to be in peril. The West would have intervened in Iraq if there had been any hope of restoring the monarchy, but Hashimite rule was finished in Baghdad, and few Iraqis wanted it restored. The new military junta ensured its own popularity by instituting land reform, proclaiming its support for Arab unity, and renouncing its military ties with the West. When the junta's fiery young nationalist who was second in command, 'Abd al-Salam 'Arif, flew to Damascus to meet Nasir, it seemed only a matter of time before Iraq would join the UAR. But the supreme revolutionary leader, Colonel 'Abd al-Karim Qasim, realized that Iraq's oil revenues would go a lot further at home if they were not shared with 30 million Egyptians and 6 million Syrians. 'Arif was eased from power. Qasim started playing a risky game, balancing between Arab nationalists and communists. Iraq's new government bettered the lives of the masses, but many problems, notably a Kurdish rebellion in the oil-rich North, proved no easier for Qasim to resolve than they had been for the Hashimites.

The Ideas of Nasirism

Nasir claimed to be the ideological leader of all Arab revolutionaries, but what did he believe in? For many people in the Arab world, and some in other Asian and African lands, he stood for their wish to defy Western imperialism. Not only Egypt but also most Arab countries—indeed, most non-Western nations—felt humiliated by the way the West had treated them in the past. These feelings, and the conviction that the Arabs could build themselves a better future, led to an ideology called "Nasirism." Its main ideas were pan-Arabism, positive neutralism, and Arab socialism.

Pan-Arabism is Arab nationalism with a stress on political unification. Nasir and his supporters saw how foreign imperialism and dynastic rivalries had split up the Arabic-speaking peoples of the Middle East into a dozen or more countries. Thus divided, the Arabs had lost Palestine in 1948 and were still subject to the machinations of outsiders. For instance, even in the 1950s, the benefits of Arab oil were going to a few hereditary monarchs and foreign companies when they should have been shared by all the Arabs. Political unification would increase the wealth and power of the Arab world as a whole. Nasir's opponents equated his pan-Arabism with Egyptian imperialism. They accused him of trying to seize control of the rest of the Arab world to enrich Egypt in general and his own regime in particular.

Positive neutralism—Nasir's policy of not aligning Egypt with either the Communist bloc or the anti-Communist military alliances that the United

States promoted—invited other countries to join Egypt in a loose association of nonaligned states. Neutralism could reduce world tensions and maybe even resolve the Cold War. Critics called the policy one of working both sides of the street, a means by which Nasir could extract military and economic aid from the Communist bloc and the West at the same time.

Arab socialism evolved in reaction to the economic system prevalent up to the 1950s in most parts of the Arab world. This was a system in which "capitalism" really meant foreign ownership of major business enterprises or a more primitive system (often misnamed feudalism) in which land, buildings, and other sources of wealth belonged to a small native elite while masses of Arab workers and farmers lived in dire poverty. To bring about reform, Arab socialists called on their governments to run the major industries and public utilities so as to divide the economic pie more evenly among the people. They also argued that this pie could be enlarged by comprehensive state planning to expand manufacturing and modernize agriculture. Although they borrowed some of their ideas and rhetoric from the Marxists, most Arab socialists opposed communism for its atheism and rejected the notion of the class struggle. Instead, they tried to prove that their ideology was compatible with Islam and argued that shopkeepers and small-scale merchants ("national capitalists") could play a constructive role in Arab socialism. Critics said that Arab socialism lacked theoretical rigor, inflated Egypt's already swollen bureaucracy, and scared away foreign investors.

The Ebb of the Pan-Arab Tide

The summer of 1958 marked the zenith of pan-Arabism. Qasim's Iraq soon went its own way, as did Sa'udi Arabia under Crown Prince Faysal. The US Marines in Lebanon confronted more Coke vendors than communists. Lebanon's parliament chose the neutralist Fu'ad Shihab, the general who had kept the army out of the civil war, to replace the pro-Western Sham'un. US troops pulled out, and all factions agreed to respect Lebanon's independence and neutrality. Britain likewise withdrew its troops from Jordan, but Husayn's regime did not fall, to everyone's surprise. A military coup in the Sudan in November 1958, at first thought to be pro-Nasir, did not unify the Nile Valley. During 1959–1961 Egypt's heavy-handed bureaucracy tried to control Syria's hitherto capitalistic economy. Even the Ba'ath chafed when Nasir insisted that it, like all other Syrian parties, be absorbed by his new single party, the National Union.

By the early 1960s the Soviets were playing a growing role in the UAR economy. Nasir came to believe that he would have to institute state planning and take control of all major industries to fulfill his promise to double the national income during the 1960s. In his July (1961) Laws, he nationalized nearly all factories, financial institutions, and public utilities in Egypt and Syria; reduced to about 100 acres (42 hectares) the maximum landholding allowed an individual; and limited the salary a UAR citizen might earn. These laws angered bourgeois Syrians so much that two months later an army coup in Damascus ended Syria's union with Egypt. Soon after that, the UAR (as Egypt continued to be called, in case Syria rejoined the union) ended its federation with Yemen, after its imam had allegedly written verses satirizing the July Laws. At the end of 1961, Nasir, the leader who still aspired to unite the Arab world, stood alone.

Arab Socialism and Nasir's Comeback
The tide of Nasirism had receded. Egypt now looked inward and focused on building a new order under Arab socialism. Nasir convened the National Congress of Popular Forces to draw up what he called the National Charter, published amid great fanfare in 1962. A new single party, the Arab Socialist Union, replaced the flagging National Union, and half the seats in Egypt's National Council were earmarked for workers and peasants. Workers were put on the managing boards of some nationalized companies. For the first time in Egypt's history, a worker and a woman took charge of cabinet ministries. If his socialist experiment spurred economic growth and social equality, Nasir reasoned, other Arab countries would imitate Egypt. Defying political isolation, he adopted a new slogan: "Unity of goals, not unity of ranks."

The first sign of a change was Algeria's independence in July 1962, after a bitter eight-year struggle against France. Algeria's new leader, Ahmad Ben Bella, supported Nasir and all revolutionary Arab causes. The second sign was the revolution that broke out in Yemen that September, only a week after the old imam had died and Prince Badr had taken over. A group of military officers seized power in San'a and proclaimed Yemen a republic. Elated, Egypt's government hailed the new regime and assumed Badr had been killed. In fact, he and his followers had fled to the hills, where monarchist tribesmen were ready to fight for their imam (who, as his title implies, was a religious as well as a political leader). They were backed by the Sa'udis, who feared a subversive Nasirite republic on their southern border. Nasir sent an Egyptian force to aid Yemen's new regime, but its leaders were inexperienced. The civil war that started as a contest between followers of Imam Badr (mainly Zaydi Shi'ites in the hills) and republican officers (mainly Shafi'i Sunnis living near the Red Sea) became a five-year proxy struggle between conservative Saʿudi Arabia and revolutionary Egypt.

Nasir was encouraged in early 1963 when Baʿathist officers staged two successive coups: Qasim's ouster in Iraq by ʿAbd al-Salam ʿArif, followed by the toppling of Syria's separatist regime. Soon Iraq and Syria adopted identical flags, swore eternal Arab brotherhood, and sent delegates to Cairo to negotiate with Nasir for a new UAR. Popular enthusiasm for Arab unity reached a new peak in April 1963, when Egypt, Syria, and Iraq published plans for organic unification. However, Nasir and the Baʿath Party failed to agree on how the new state should be led.

RISING ARAB-ISRAELI TENSIONS

It was an Israeli move that reunited the Arabs. Ever since Israel's rebirth, its scientists and engineers had tried to get more fresh water to irrigate its lands. Hydrologists argued that the Jordan River could be harnessed to irrigate both Israel and Jordan. An American emissary named Eric Johnston had secured an agreement from both countries on the technical aspects of a plan to share the Jordan waters, but the Jordanian government rejected it on political grounds in 1955. For a few years, Israel hoped Jordan might relent, but then it decided to go ahead and build a national water carrier to meet its own needs, taking from the Sea of Galilee the share of Jordan River waters that the Johnston agreement would have allocated to Israel.

Israel's tapping of the Jordan waters galvanized the Arab countries into action. Jordan, Syria, and Lebanon hoped that if they could divert the main tributaries of the Jordan River, they could deter Israel from completing its national water carrier. But Israel threatened pre-emptive air strikes against any Arab diversion projects. Nasir invited the Arab kings and presidents to Cairo to discuss the issue in early 1964. Though unable to act in concert against Israel, the Arabs decided to hold further summits in 1964 and 1965. The consensus was that the Arab armies could not yet confront Israel, but that they would build up their military strength so that Syria and Jordan could divert the tributaries of the Jordan River.

The Palestine Liberation Organization

Another act of the 1964 summit meetings drew little outside attention but would prove fateful for the Arab world. Arab leaders voted to form the Palestine Liberation Organization (PLO), which was to act as an umbrella group for all organizations serving the Palestinian Arabs. Encouraged by

Nasir, Palestinian representatives met in Jerusalem's Old City in 1964, asked a veteran spokesman named Ahmad al-Shuqayri to appoint an executive board for the PLO, and adopted a national charter. Its main principles were that the Palestinian Arabs must fight to regain their homeland within what had been the British mandate borders and that they alone had the right of self-determination in Palestine, although Jews of Palestinian origin might still live in the liberated country. To replace the State of Israel, the PLO proposed a secular democratic state in which Jews, Christians, and Muslims would coexist in peace.

The PLO began assembling a conventional army, made up of refugees in Gaza, Jordan, and Syria. But a more effective force was a guerrilla movement called *Fatah* (which can be translated as "Conquest" or "Movement for the Liberation of Palestine"). Fatah signaled its existence on 1 January 1965 by trying to sabotage part of Israel's national water-carrier system. Its leader was Yasir 'Arafat, who had fought against Israel in 1948, then became the leader of the Palestinian students in Egypt, and worked for a few years in Kuwait. More than Shuqayri, 'Arafat spoke for militant younger Palestinians. Fatah's attacks, backed by Syria but generally launched from Jordan, caused some casualties and property damage in Israel. The Israeli government, headed since 1963 by Levi Eshkol, decided to intimidate the Arab armies to curb these commando operations. In late 1966 the IDF made a devastating retaliatory raid into the Jordanian West Bank, destroying much of the village of al-Samu'. Both Western and Arab governments protested, and the UN Security Council unanimously condemned Israel's raid. Even some Israelis thought they should have attacked Syria, which had aided the commandos, rather than Jordan.

Background to War

By the mid-1960s Syria had once again emerged as the most ardent Arab nationalist state. Unable to form a union with Egypt or even with Iraq in 1963, its Ba'athist government pressed harder for Arab unity and military action against Israel. It spearheaded the attempts to divert the Jordan River sources for Syria's own water needs and armed various Palestinian commando groups. An army coup in February 1966 brought to power a radical wing of the Ba'ath Party. Most of the new leaders belonged to an obscure minority, the Alawite religious sect, many of whose members had joined the Syrian officer corps to advance themselves socially. Hoping to win over the Sunni majority in Syria, these young Alawite officers strove to uphold the principles of Arabism and hence those of the struggle against Israel. By this time Nasir had realized that his army, still bogged down in Yemen's civil war, would not be ready to fight against Israel for a long time. He hoped to restrain Syria's new leaders from drawing Egypt into another war by forging a military alliance with them.

This was a serious miscalculation. In April 1967 Syrian MiG fighter planes got into a dogfight with Israeli jets invading Syria's airspace, and six were shot down. Eshkol warned Syria that Israel would retaliate further unless it stopped firing on Israeli settlements near the Golan Heights. Many Arabs believed that Israel's real aim was to discredit and possibly overthrow the extreme Ba'athist regime in Damascus. In early May the Soviets told Nasir that Israel was massing troops in its North for a preemptive attack on Syria. Egypt called up its reserves, routed tanks through Egypt's cities and into the Sinai, and made threats against Israel. Nasir may have been bluffing to impress Syria, but no one thought so at the time. For months his rival Arab leaders had taunted him for hiding behind UNEF in Gaza and Sinai. On 16 May Nasir asked the United Nations to withdraw some of its peacekeeping units. Secretary-General U Thant promptly pulled out all UN forces (to Nasir's amazement), without even consulting the Security Council. Once UNEF had evacuated all the key points in Gaza and Sinai, Egyptian military units moved in. Among the strategic points they occupied was Sharm al-Shaykh, from which they renewed the Arab blockade against Israeli shipping through the Gulf of 'Aqaba. Nasir's prestige soared again throughout the Arab world.

This blockade has come to be seen by Israel and its supporters as the main cause of the ensuing war of June 1967. Israel argued that it could not allow its trade or its growing ties with South Asia and East Africa to be cut off. As Arab newspapers and radio stations were openly calling for a war to destroy the Jewish state, the Israelis could hardly assume that the Arab governments would stop at blockading the Gulf of 'Aqaba. But what should they do? Their passage through the Tiran Straits had been guaranteed by the Western powers. The US government, mired in the Vietnam War, counseled caution. The European governments, realizing that they imported most of their oil from the Arab world, had cooled toward Israel since the Suez Crisis. Israel chose not to wait for a Western flotilla to force open the Tiran Straits or any UN Security Council resolution. Israel's leaders said they wanted peace yet were convinced they could defeat Egypt's Soviet-equipped army. Most Israelis (and their foreign backers) feared the worst, however.

After King Husayn flew to Cairo on 30 May to sign an agreement with Nasir on a joint Arab military command, Israel's cabinet assumed war was inevitable. Most reserve units were called up, the economy was put on a war footing, and Israel's political leaders buried their quarrels to form a new cabinet that would represent nearly all the nation's parties and factions. Especially significant was the appointment on 2 June of General Moshe Dayan as defense minister, despite his perennial differences with Prime Minister Eshkol. A hero in the 1948 independence war and the 1956 Sinai campaign, Dayan gave Israelis new hope in what many viewed as their hour of peril. No one knew for sure what would happen next.

CONCLUSION

The history of the Middle East after May 1967 was so dominated by the Arab-Israeli conflict that the preceding era seems serene by comparison. However, its political history was turbulent, and matters were complicated by the inclusion of outside powers. In addition, rapid changes, especially in education and technology, broke down the customary modes of life and thought. Masses of people, most poor and young, flocked to the big cities. Alien ideas and customs, first embraced in these growing urban centers, spread everywhere by transistor radio, newspapers and magazines, schools, rural health centers, movies, and (in some countries) television. Ideas of nationalism and progress increased at the expense of religion and respect for tradition.

Most people favored this change of direction at the time, but many nationalist slogans and ideologies have since proven false, and many Arabs did not understand these imported ideologies. As a blend of traditional and modern values, Nasirism now sounds like a personality cult. Positive neutralism was a natural reaction to the Cold War, but why was Egypt's rejection of both the Western and the Communist blocs deemed positive? Neutralism worked only so long as both sides were competing for Arab favor. Pan-Arabism overlooked the deep-seated differences within the Arab world, not just among leaders but also among their peoples, as well as between countries having and countries lacking oil. Arab nationalism tended to alienate religious and ethnic minorities, such as Lebanon's Maronites and Iraq's Shi'ites and Kurds. Parliamentary democracy broke down when the masses were hungry and uneducated and when army officers and newly trained technicians longed to govern. Arab socialism failed to change Arab society from its traditional individualism, clannishness, and patriarchy into a collectivist economic system serving the common good.

This book's early chapters showed you how Islam as a doctrine and a way of life inspired the Arabs and their converts to submerge their cares and desires into one collective enterprise encompassing the conquests, the High Caliphate, and Islamic civilization. There have been many articulate

Muslim thinkers, from Muhammad Abduh to Sayyid Qutb, but no new Arab leader came forth to recharge these batteries, to enlist the people's minds and muscles to rebuild the *umma*, to harness the tools and techniques of modern industry to create an egalitarian society, and to make Islam a guide for humane thoughts and actions in the modern world! What might the Arabs have achieved with stronger guidance and a more coherent set of beliefs?

Israel had problems, too. Political Zionism had achieved its goal of creating a Jewish state, but was it truly a light unto the Gentiles? One scholar wrote in 1963 that the most successful product to come out of Israel was the Uzi submachine gun. Judaism as practiced during centuries of dispersion meant little to Israel's founders. Ben-Gurion and others wondered why so few Jews came to Israel from the West. With half of Israel's people having come from elsewhere in the Middle East, were they becoming too much like their Arab neighbors? In reaction, Israelis developed cults of physical fitness and martial might, of archaeological quests to affirm their ties to the land, of redemption through planting trees. Divided on how Jewish they should be, they ranged from the ultraobservant (some refused to recognize the Jewish state until the Messiah came) to those who denied God's existence and the Torah's relevance to modern life. Jewish religious leadership was no stronger than its Muslim and Christian counterparts elsewhere. What part could the Arabs, then one-sixth of Israel's population, play in a state whose flag featured the Star of David and whose anthem expressed the Jews' longing for the land of Zion? What about the Arabs who had fled from Israel in 1948 and claimed the right to return? If Jews had remembered Zion for two thousand years, could Palestinians forget it in fewer than twenty? Amid the mists of ideological confusion and the dust of political combat brewed the storms that have raged in the Middle East since 1967.

17

War and the Quest for Peace

On 5 June 1967 Israel launched a series of pre-emptive air strikes against its hostile Arab neighbors. Its consequent victory over Egypt, Syria, and Jordan took only six days, thereby refuting the notion, common after 1956, that the Jewish state could not defeat the Arabs without Western allies. The victory also exploded the myth that "unity of goals" among the Arab states would enable them to defeat Israel and proved that the IDF had attained high levels of skill, valor, and coordination.

As a result, a new myth arose, shared by supporters and enemies of the Jewish state, that Israel was invincible. This myth lasted until October 1973, when another war, begun by Egypt and Syria, showed that an Arab army could exercise courage and skill to achieve limited success against Israel's military might. This October (or Yom Kippur) War was the most intensely fought, the costliest in lives and equipment, and the greatest threat to world peace of any war waged between the Arabs and Israel up to that time. It also set off a fourfold increase in the price of oil and nearly sparked a military showdown between the superpowers. Its aftermath enlarged the US role in trying to resolve the conflict and nudging Israel and the Arabs toward a settlement. Finally, President Anwar al-Sadat of Egypt, the only leader willing to take a real risk for peace, broke the impasse in November 1977 with a dramatic flight to Jerusalem. A flurry of peace conferences and high-level meetings ensued. The end result was the Camp David Accords, followed by an Egyptian-Israeli treaty in March 1979. But there was no comprehensive peace.

One of the overarching themes of Middle East history between 1967 and 1979 was the Arab-Israeli conflict. Many (though certainly not all) diaspora Jews turned into ardent Zionists. The Palestine question began to matter to Arab states as remote as Morocco and Kuwait. Because everyone assumed that Israel—if adequately armed by the United States—would win any conventional war, the unconventional tactics of the Palestinian *fida'iyin* became dominant in Arab strategy against Israel.

After 1967 the Soviet Union stepped up its role as arms supplier and adviser to many of the Arab states, as the United States did for Israel. This intensified superpower involvement in a conflict that threatened to escalate into World War III. As neither side wanted so drastic a confrontation, they frequently conferred together and with other powers, hoping to impose a solution to the conflict. Neither the Arabs nor the Jews wanted the wars, the threats, and the tensions to go on forever. But at what price could each party accept peace with the other? The old Arab issue about the displaced Palestinians tended to give way to two others: return of Arab lands taken by Israel in June 1967 and recognition of the Palestinians' national rights. The Israelis still demanded security and Arab recognition but argued among themselves over which of the captured lands— Jerusalem, the West Bank (which most Israelis call Judea and Samaria), the Gaza Strip, the Sinai, and the Golan Heights—they should give back in exchange for peace. Meanwhile, they defied international law by creating and expanding Jewish settlements in the occupied areas. Arms purchases claimed a growing share of every Middle Eastern government's budget, more young men in uniform risked dying before their time, and people's energies had to shift from constructive to destructive endeavors. "Ma'lesh [Never mind]," said the Arabs. "Ma la'asot? [What's to be done?]," asked the Israelis. No matter, both sides believed—survival and dignity were worth more than the highest price they (or their backers) could ever pay.

THE JUNE 1967 WAR

On the morning of 5 June 1967, Israel's air force attacked the main air bases of Egypt—followed by those of Jordan and Syria—and wiped out virtually all their war-making potential. Having gained air mastery in the first hour, Israel sent its army into Sinai and, in four days, took the whole peninsula. As he had done in 1956, Nasir ordered the Suez Canal blocked, but by taking Sharm al-Shaykh Israel broke the blockade of the Gulf of 'Aqaba.

Because King Husayn had made a pact with Nasir one week before the war that effectively put his army under Egyptian command, Jordan entered the war by firing into Israeli sections of Jerusalem. The IDF then invaded the northern part of the West Bank and also the north side of Arab Jerusalem to secure Mount Scopus (an Israeli enclave since the 1949 armistice) and to attack the Old City from its eastern side. On 7 June the Israelis took the city after fierce fighting and prayed at the Western Wall for the first time in nineteen years. Elsewhere on the West Bank, Israeli forces drove back the Jordanians, under Husayn's direct command, in extremely tough combat. The Arabs accused Israel of dropping napalm on Jordanian troops and of using scare tactics to clear out some refugee camps and West Bank villages. Some 200,000 Arabs sought refuge across the Jordan, and new tent camps ringed the hills around Amman. Many Palestinians, after hearing promises from the Arab radio stations that Israel would be wiped out and that they would be allowed to return home, asked why the Arab armies failed to work together for the desired victory.

Syria was the least helpful. Owing to recent border clashes with Jordan, the Syrians did nothing for Husayn until he was defeated. By then, Israel could storm Syria's well-fortified positions on the Golan Heights when no other Arab country could help the Damascus regime, which had already called for a ceasefire. If Israel and Syria had not finally agreed to stop fighting on 10 June, nothing would have stopped the Israelis from taking Damascus itself. A Palestinian historian concluded his *Modern History of Syria* with this: "Syria had often in history marched under the banner of Islam to victory and glory; it had yet to prove that it could do so under the banner of Arab nationalism."

One tragic incident during the war involved US military forces. On 8 June, a cloudless day, the US intelligence ship *Liberty* sustained repeated attacks by Israeli aircraft and gunboats, which killed 34 American sailors and wounded 172. Israel claimed this was a case of mistaken identity, having thought the *Liberty* was an Egyptian freighter, although the ship was clearly signed and flew an American flag. On the day of the attack, rescue aircraft sent to aid the ship were called back on the command of President Lyndon Johnson, who did not want to embarrass Israel. A subsequent naval investigation took no testimony from *Liberty* crew members, and there has never been a congressional investigation. Documents pertinent to the attack are still classified. Israel's motive for attacking the ship remains unclear, but Arab sources claim that Israel was trying to cover up the execution of Egyptian prisoners of war in al-Arish. Israel did issue an apology and pay compensation to the Americans.

Reasons for the Outcome

Before the 1967 War, the Arab forces had seemed superior on paper: Egypt alone had more men under arms than Israel, even if Israel mobilized all its reserve units; the Arabs had 2,700 tanks, compared to Israel's 800, 800 fighter planes to Israel's 190, and 217 ships to Israel's 37, and the population ratio was about 25 to 1. The Arabs enjoyed cautious support from the Communist bloc and most Asian and African nations at a time when Washington's position, to quote a State Department spokesman, was "neutral in thought, word, and deed," though the White House promptly changed "neutral" to "non-belligerent." With 500,000 troops in Vietnam, the United States could not easily have intervened even if Israel had asked it to do so.

One reason for Israel's victory is that they attacked first, destroyed most of the Arab fighter planes, and then kept complete control of the air. Another reason is that Egypt's best troops were still fighting in the Yemen civil war. The *New York Times* reported during the war that Israel had more troops on the field than its enemies, deployed better firepower, and used greater mobility in battle. Israel's military was also efficient, technologically sophisticated, and well coordinated. Arab armies were rife with factionalism, and their governments did not trust one another. These factors helped cause the 1948 Nakba (Palestinian catastrophe). In 1967, even after most anachronistic monarchies and landowning elites had fallen from power, even after some fifteen years of pan-Arabism and social reform in Egypt and Syria, and even after billions of dollars' worth of Soviet and Western arms had poured into the Arab world, the Arabs' divisiveness led to a swifter, more devastating defeat in 1967 than in 1948. Small wonder that Nasir, the Arab nationalist leader, tried to resign at the end of the war.

The War's Aftermath

By the time the guns fell silent on 10 June, Israel had expanded its land area to three times what it had been six days earlier, having occupied the Gaza Strip, the Sinai Peninsula, the West Bank, and the Golan Heights (see Map 17.1). Almost 1 million Arabs, most of them Palestinians, had come under Israeli rule. Israel had not anticipated this swell in population. Defense Minister Moshe Dayan and other Israeli officials had claimed during the war that they would defend, not expand, Israel's territory, though some Israelis viewed Gaza and the West Bank as a part of their biblical patrimony and wanted to absorb them. However, most were relieved just to find that the physical destruction and loss of Jewish lives were less than anyone had expected. Many Israelis hoped the militant Arab leaders would be overthrown by the moderates or that their governments would sue for peace.

Map 17.1   Israel and the occupied territories, 1967–1973

These hopes were not realized. The Arabs would not negotiate from weakness (some noted that Hitler could not persuade Churchill to talk peace in 1940), whereas Israel chose to hold all the occupied lands as bargaining chips in the peace talks it hoped would ensue. Its new borders (really cease-fire lines) were shorter and more defensible. Israel's haste to annex East

Jerusalem and to colonize the conquered lands fueled Arab fears of Israeli expansionism.

UN Peace Efforts

The Arabs believed that a just solution was more apt to come from the United Nations (as in 1956) than from direct negotiations. Responding to a Soviet call, the General Assembly held a special session that June, but none of the resolutions put forth by the various blocs could muster the necessary majority. After five futile weeks, the General Assembly handed the issue back to the Security Council. A summit meeting between Soviet premier Alexei Kosygin and President Johnson also failed. In August the Arab leaders held their own summit in Khartoum, Sudan, and resolved not to negotiate with Israel.

By the time the Security Council took up the question of peace, both sides had hardened their positions. While the Arabs ruled out direct talks with Israel, the Israelis were flaunting their occupation in the captured lands. Arab houses were razed in Jerusalem's Old City to expand the space in front of the Western Wall. Suspected *fida'iyin* in Gaza and the West Bank were jailed or deported, and often their houses were blown up; whole villages and towns were destroyed. Jewish settlers, with government backing, began building settlements in the Golan Heights, the environs of Hebron, and East Jerusalem, notably on the hills connecting Mount Scopus with the western half of the city. Israel's annexation of East Jerusalem, including the Old City, defied the UN General Assembly and violated international law. The Soviet Union rearmed Syria and Egypt, sending them more technicians and advisers. The danger of a new war loomed.

It was left to the Security Council to devise a peace formula acceptable to Israel and the Arabs, as well as to the superpowers. During the debates, Britain's Lord Caradon devised a formula with the necessary ambiguity—Resolution 242—to which all the permanent members could agree. It stressed "the inadmissibility of acquiring territory by war" and called for a just and lasting peace based on (1) withdrawal of Israeli armed forces from territories occupied in the recent conflict, and (2) the right of every state in the area to "live in peace within secure and recognized boundaries free from threats and acts of force." It also called for freedom of navigation through international waterways and a "just settlement to the refugee problem."

The Arabs saw Resolution 242 as calling on Israel to return, as a precondition for peace, all the lands it had taken in the June War. Israel claimed that the resolution meant withdrawal from only some of these lands, as each country was to live in peace within secure and recognized boundaries. Some Arabs interpreted the "just settlement to the refugee problem" to mean Israel's readmission of all displaced Palestinians wishing to return (the General Assembly had passed resolutions to that effect almost annually since 1948). Israel contended that the Palestinian refugees should be settled in the Arab countries as a population exchange. The Arab states, retaliating for Israel's "ethnic cleansing" of the Palestinians, had expelled their Jewish citizens, most of whom had settled in Israel.

Jordan, Israel, and Egypt agreed to abide by Resolution 242 (Syria, fearing any de facto recognition of Israel, rejected it until 1974), even though Arabs and Israelis disagreed on what it meant. Secretary General U Thant asked a mediator, Gunnar Jarring, to bring the two sides closer together. But even as he began his ultimately fruitless mission in early 1968, the resolution's shortcomings were becoming evident. One, clearly, was that each side expected the other to give in first. Another was that no limitation was put on the arms race, which was more feverish and financially debilitating than ever. Yet another was that the Arabs could still wage economic warfare against Israel and its backers—the boycott would go on. Finally, although this became clear only with the passage of time, Resolution 242 ignored the rights and interests of the Palestinian people.

THE PALESTINIANS

The emergence of the Palestinians as a separate factor in the Arab-Israeli conflict was one of the major developments in 1967. The idea that the Palestinians constitute a distinct people is novel. Never before in Middle East history had the Arabs living in Palestine sought or gained status as a separate and independent state. Quite the contrary, the Arabs of that region had usually chosen, if indeed they could exercise any choice at all, to claim an identity as Muslim, Arab, or (Greater) Syrian. Before Israel's rebirth, Jews and foreigners often used the name Palestinian to denote the inhabitants of Palestine, but rarely had Arabs themselves used that label. Between 1948 and 1967, the Arabs from Palestine, especially the refugees in neighboring countries, had been the most ardent backers of pan-Arabism. They hoped to erase all distinctions between them and the other Arabs whose aid they sought.

But Palestinians, because of their shared experiences and ideas, did come to see themselves as a people and then as a nation, just as surely as Eastern Europe's Jews had turned into Zionists in the early twentieth century. As the Palestinians saw their own past, the Jewish settlers in Palestine shunned the local Arabs before Israel attained statehood, expelled them during the 1948 war, and then refused to let them return to what had become Israel. The other Arab states would not absorb them. No country wanted them. But these refugees did not want to see themselves or to be seen by others as objects of pity, wards of UNRWA, or causes of embarrassment to other Arabs. After the 1967 War revealed the inadequacy of the Arab states' armies, the Palestinians decided it was time to declare their own nation, obtain arms, train themselves to fight, and regain their lands.

Palestinian Resistance

As a result of the war, therefore, the Palestine Liberation Organization (PLO), set up in 1964 at the behest of the Arab governments, emerged as a militant group. The older leaders, notably Shuqayri, gave way to younger ones who, though no less determined to wipe out Israel, knew better how to use the Western media to publicize their cause. It was easy to get support from the Communist bloc, but the PLO wanted to win public opinion in Western Europe and North America over to the Palestinian cause. To do this, the Palestinians could no longer call for Israel's destruction and the Jewish bloodbath or mass exodus that would most likely ensue. Rather, they proposed to redeem what had been Palestine up to 1948 from the "false ideology" of Zionism, a colonialist dogma that debased the Jewish faith and oppressed the Muslim and Christian Arabs who had formerly constituted most of Palestine's population. Israelis were likened to the white settlers of Rhodesia and South Africa. Palestinians viewed their *fida'iyin,* whom the Israelis called terrorists, as freedom fighters, like the Partisans who had fought the Nazi occupation of France. The PLO would keep the call for Israel's destruction in its charter only until it could convince a majority of the organization's members of the impossibility of that happening.

Early in 1968 the IDF, stung into retaliatory action by Palestinian raids and bombings, attacked the Jordanian village of Karama, some 25 miles (40 kilometers) west of Amman. Israel reportedly lost six jet fighters and twelve tanks in the battle before both sides accepted a new ceasefire. Many of Jordan's casualties were Palestinians from Fatah, whose role in resisting the IDF gave new luster to 'Arafat and his backers. Young men in the refugee camps and in many Arab cities and villages rallied to Fatah. Foreign journalists flocked to interview 'Arafat and to visit his training camps. Some, impressed by his zealous nationalism, extolled his vision of a liberated Palestine that would be secular and democratic, a state where Jews, Christians, and Muslims might live together in peace, in contrast to the "unholy land" of Zionism (Israel). Skeptics asked whether any existing Arab state was secular, democratic, or capable of preserving concord among the various religious groups living within its borders. The Palestinians admitted that many Arab leaders were reactionary, bigoted perhaps, and tied to landholding or bourgeois class interests, but the *fida'iyin* were young, well educated, and free from these ties to the past. Their aim of creating a secular democratic state in Palestine seemed sincere, at least so long as they had no power.

Abortive Peace Efforts

Meanwhile, Washington tried to resolve the Arab-Israeli conflict through an accord among the major outside powers: the Soviet Union, Britain, and France. The United States hoped that the Soviets might influence the leading Arab states, whereupon the Americans would use their leverage on Israel, probably by selling or withholding advanced weapons, to bring about a peace settlement based on Resolution 242. They hoped the Soviets wanted to stop pouring weapons into Egypt, Syria, and Iraq, arms that might never be paid for and that required large training missions. In truth, Moscow sold mainly defensive arms to Egypt and Syria, urging restraint on their governments. If Soviet forces used naval and air facilities in these countries, they were doing no less than what the US Sixth Fleet had long been doing in the Mediterranean.

During the war the Soviet Union had ruptured diplomatic relations with Israel, and many of the Arab states had broken ties with the United States. The superpowers were now less able to mediate in the Middle East. Israel argued that a peace settlement imposed by the superpowers would last only as long as the Arab states were too weak to defy it, as Egypt had undone the settlement imposed after the 1956 Suez War. Many Arabs argued that Israel's actions defied UN, Great Power, and Arab peace proposals. They doubted the US and Soviet governments would resolve the root issues once they had served their own Middle East interests.

Richard Nixon's victory in the 1968 presidential elections encouraged the Arabs; perhaps a new US administration might support them. Nixon sent a special envoy to the Middle East, who returned calling for a more "evenhanded" approach, implying that Johnson's administration had tilted against the Arabs. A major issue in debates over US Middle East policy has been the degree to which Washington should authorize arms sales to Israel or, indeed, to such pro-Western Arab states as Jordan. Johnson had arranged to sell Phantom jets to Israel, but Nixon delayed the deal, hoping to make the Israelis agree to give back land to the Arabs.

The War of Attrition

The Egyptians, noting the attention paid to *fida'iyin* raids and Israeli retaliations, did not wait. In March 1969 Nasir announced that Egypt would step up the shooting that had been going on across the Suez Canal intermittently since 1967, starting (or continuing) the so-called War of Attrition. This was a strategy designed to increase pressure on military targets. The Israelis responded by attacking both military and Egyptian civilian targets (using American equipment in violation of US arms export control laws). More Egyptians than Israelis were killed, and Egypt's cities west of the canal had to be evacuated. Many Egyptians feared a direct hit on the Aswan High Dam, which the Soviets had almost finished building. By 1970 Israeli troops had dug themselves in behind the Bar Lev line just east of the canal; in the meantime Egypt grew ever more vulnerable to Israel's new US-supplied Phantom jet fighters. Nasir had failed to predict how Israel would react to his decision to launch the War of Attrition; Israel equally misjudged Egypt's response to its deep-penetration bombing raids. Nasir flew to Moscow to get the Soviet Union to send Egypt more guns, tanks, planes, missiles, and advisers. By summer 1970, Israeli fighter pilots engaging in dogfights high above the Suez Canal found that some of the MiG pilots were speaking Russian.

POLITICAL CHANGES: 1967–1970

What else was happening during the War of Attrition? No Arab government was overthrown as a result of the 1967 defeat. Nevertheless, leadership changes did occur. Alignments of Arab governments remained kaleidoscopic.

The Two Yemens

During the 1967 Khartoum summit, Egypt and Sa'udi Arabia agreed to wind down the five-year-old civil war in Yemen. Soon after Nasir pulled out his troops, the republican regime he had backed fell from power. Its successor edged toward accommodation with the imam, his tribal backers, and the Sa'udis. Yemen remained a republic, but in 1970 its government became a coalition that included royalists. Farther south, the British had long tried to combine the urban and politicized citizens of Aden Colony with the tribal shaykhs and sultans of the southern Arabian Peninsula (once called the Aden Protectorate). The combination was to become the South Arabian Federation. The tribal leaders, most of them pro-British, were supposed to balance the urban nationalists, who gained strength in the 1960s among the unionized workers in Aden's port. This outpost of empire was becoming too costly to Britain, so the Labour government decided in 1966 to let it go. Once Britain had announced its intention to pull all troops out of southern Arabia, the two leading nationalist groups began competing for control of the entire area. In late 1967 Britain handed over southern Arabia to the victorious faction, the National (Liberation) Front. The new country was renamed the People's Republic of Southern Yemen. As its leaders hoped it might someday be reunited with North Yemen, it later became the People's Democratic Republic of Yemen, the sole Marxist state in the Arab world. The two states' politics gradually converged during the 1980s, and they united as the Republic of Yemen in 1990. The union has not been complete; a bitter civil war broke out between Aden (backed by Sa'udi Arabia) and the rest of the Yemen republic in 1994. Deep rifts endure in this supposedly unified country.

Iraq

In Iraq, 'Abd al-Rahman 'Arif (who in 1966 had replaced his brother, 'Abd al-Salam, killed in a plane crash) was ousted by a rightist coup in July 1968. Two weeks later another Ba'ath Party splinter group seized power in Baghdad. The new regime soon quarreled with Syria over the use of Euphrates River waters, even though both states were ruled by the Ba'ath Party. Relations with Iran were strained because both countries wanted to control the Shatt al-Arab, where the Tigris and the Euphrates meet before emptying into the Gulf. Kurds in northern Iraq went on fighting for their independence. As the Kurdish rebellion, backed by the shah of Iran, increasingly threatened Iraq's control over its oil-rich northern provinces, Baghdad tried to make a deal with Tehran. Meeting with the shah in 1975, Iraqi vice president Saddam Husayn (often spelled Hussein) conceded to Iran sovereignty over the Shatt al-Arab on the Iranian side of its deepest channel in return for Iran's ending all aid to the Kurdish rebels. Saddam dispersed 200,000 Kurds from the north to other parts of Iraq.

Libya

In 1969 military coups overthrew moderate governments in Somalia, Libya, and the Sudan. The most noteworthy was Libya's revolution, which brought to power an impetuous, articulate, and devout army colonel named Mu'ammar al-Qadhafi. This young officer emerged as the new champion of militant Arab nationalism. He pushed the Americans and the

British to evacuate their air bases in Libya, made all tourists carry travel documents written in Arabic, and volunteered his army for duty alongside Nasir's on the Suez Canal and the *fida'iyin* in Jordan and Lebanon. Nasir admired the Libyan revolutionary, who reminded him of himself as a young officer. We will soon discuss an attempt to unite Libya with Egypt under Nasir's successor.

Israel

Meanwhile, Ben-Gurion's successor as premier, Levi Eshkol, died in March 1969. His replacement was the former foreign minister and Mapai party secretary general, Golda Meir. Although she was supposed to serve only as a caretaker until the November 1969 elections, disputes among other politicians and factions within Israel's ruling Labor Alignment made her their most acceptable standard-bearer. After the elections she formed a broad coalition government. She proved to be a strong-willed, capable leader. Born in Russia and reared in Milwaukee, Wisconsin, she could make Americans view Middle Eastern events through Israeli glasses.

The Rogers Peace Plan

The State Department, among all branches of the US government, was the one least influenced by Israel. Thus it was Secretary of State William Rogers who would attempt yet another break in the Middle East impasse. The Rogers Plan envisaged a lasting peace "sustained by a sense of security on both sides," with borders that "should not reflect the weight of conquest"—meaning that Israel should give up almost all the lands it had taken in the war. He added that "there can be no lasting peace without a just settlement of the refugee problem," but he did not specify what that might be. As for Jerusalem, he opposed its annexation by Israel and proposed that it be united and accessible to all faiths and nationalities.

Nasir rejected the Rogers Plan at first, but the war's escalation during the first half of 1970 and the threat of superpower involvement may have made the Rogers Plan look better to Nasir. The Arab summit meeting held that month in Rabat, Morocco, did not offer Egypt enough military or economic aid to win its War of Attrition, and Nasir hoped the Americans might give him by diplomacy what Egypt's armed forces had failed to gain by war. In a dramatic policy shift, Egypt accepted a revised Rogers Plan on 23 July. Jordan, harassed by mounting *fida'iyin* activities on its soil, quickly followed suit. Israel distrusted the new US policy but reluctantly went along. A ninety-day ceasefire took effect, and Jarring resumed his rounds of Middle Eastern capitals (except Damascus, which still rejected Resolution 242). Israel's doubts seemed justified when Egypt moved some of its new surface-to-air missiles within range of the Suez Canal, an apparent violation of the agreement. Egypt replied that it had planned to move them before the ceasefire was arranged, because of Israel's earlier bombing raids, and noted that Israel had deployed more advanced weaponry in the area under the guise of resupplying its troops. In October 1973 Egypt would use its missiles against Israel in the Sinai, but in 1970 Washington did not want to derail the negotiations by forcing a pullback. Israel then cut off peace talks with Jarring, even though the United States had offered Jerusalem $500 million in credits, mainly to buy more Phantom jet fighters.

Clashes in Lebanon and Jordan

The Rogers Peace Plan set off a crisis in Jordan. Its root cause was the Palestinian problem. Barred from setting up bases in Israel's occupied lands, the *fida'iyin* stationed themselves in refugee camps and peasant villages in southern Lebanon and east of the Jordan River. Because guerrilla attacks led to Israeli retaliatory raids across the border, many Lebanese and Jordanians resented having the Palestinians in their countries. Several clashes took place in Lebanon in the fall of 1969. An accord reached in Cairo between the PLO and Lebanon's government limited the Palestinians' freedom to act there. In 1970 quarrels broke out between the PLO and King Husayn's troops, many of whom were Bedouin and had never liked the Palestinians.

The confrontation was sparked by a Marxist faction, the Popular Front for the Liberation of Palestine (PFLP), led by George Habash. He believed the Palestinians could reach their goals only by dramatizing their cause. Specifically, his group chose to hijack passenger airplanes, starting with an El Al jet that it diverted to Algiers in 1968. In September 1970 the PFLP climaxed its campaign by hijacking four Western planes, all filled with homeward-bound tourists, and forcing them to land in a desert airstrip near Amman. The hijackings so embarrassed the Jordanian government that Husayn's army attacked the Palestinians—civilians and *fida'iyin*—destroying whole sections of Amman and other cities and towns, an assault that came to be called "Black September." Syria sent an armored column into Jordan to help the Palestinians but pulled back when Israel (with US support) threatened to intervene. Egypt's government stepped in, as it had in Lebanon, but it took literally all Nasir's remaining strength to mediate between 'Arafat and Husayn. On the next day Nasir died of a heart attack. Considering how militant he had been, it is ironic that Nasir's last act was to rescue Husayn from the Palestinians, thus preserving a US peace plan.

Egypt After Nasir

Nasir's death set off an extraordinary wave of public mourning in Egypt. *The Guinness Book of World Records* cited his funeral for having had more participants (4 million is a conservative estimate) than any other in history. Anwar al-Sadat, Nasir's vice president and one of the last of the original Free Officers, was chosen to succeed him, but few expected him to last long in power (see Box 17.1). Other Nasirites competed against Sadat and with one another. Only on 15 May 1971 did Sadat assert full control of his government by purging his opponents. While feigning loyalty to Nasir's principles, Sadat began making far-reaching changes. Nasir's elaborate internal security apparatus was dismantled. Sadat invited Egyptian and foreign capitalists to invest in local enterprises, even though such investment meant a retreat from socialism. The country's name, which remained the United Arab Republic even after Syria's secession, was changed to the Arab Republic of Egypt. Although Egypt's Soviet ties were seemingly tightened by a fifteen-year alliance treaty signed in May 1971, they were actually unraveling because Moscow would not sell offensive weapons to Sadat for use against Israel. The next year Sadat's patience would become so frayed that he would expel from Egypt most of the Soviet advisers and technicians.

The End of the Rogers Peace Plan

What happened to the US government's efforts to bring peace to the Middle East? The temporary ceasefire was renewed several times during the fall of 1970 and winter of 1971, as Jarring shuttled between Egypt and Israel. In February he sent notes to both sides, inviting them to accept certain points as a precondition for direct negotiations. Egypt would have to sign a peace agreement with Israel embodying the final settlement. And Israel would have to pull back to what had been the frontier between Egypt and Palestine (giving Egypt control of Sinai, but not the Gaza Strip). Sadat offered to sign a contractual agreement on the terms of a peace with Israel, something Nasir had never done. But Israel refused to withdraw to the pre–June 1967 armistice line. Jarring ended his mission and thus the Rogers Plan.

The well-intentioned US efforts to mediate an Israeli-Arab settlement by indirect negotiations failed to get at the roots of the problem: Israel's fear of attack (and hence extinction) by the Arabs and the Arabs' fear of

---

| Box 17.1 | Anwar al-Sadat |

Anwar al-Sadat (1918–1981) was born into a family of thirteen children in the Egyptian village of Mit Abul Kom. He received a traditional village education and then gained admittance to the Military Academy in Cairo. In 1938, at the age of twenty, he was commissioned as a second lieutenant in the Egyptian army and was posted to the Sudan, which is where he met Gamal 'Abd al-Nasir.

Sadat and Nasir soon formed a secret "Free Officers" organization that dedicated itself to ousting the British from Egypt and ridding the country of the monarchy as well. The members of this organization proved persistent and willing to find assistance wherever they could. In the early 1940s several of them tried to open secret communication with the German army in North Africa, not because they were Nazis, but rather because Britain, not Germany, was the occupying power in Egypt. Their plot was discovered, and in 1942 Sadat was arrested for treason. He spent several years in jail before escaping. In 1950, after working for years at menial jobs, Sadat was allowed to rejoin the army at his former rank of captain.

Sadat had never lost contact with Nasir and the other Free Officers. The organization had helped support his family while he was in prison, and he felt an intense loyalty toward the group. Thus reunited, he participated in the 1952 coup that overthrew King Faruq. He initially served as the group's public relations liaison and later as speaker of the National Assembly. Some tension did arise between him and Nasir because Sadat maintained ties with the Muslim Brothers, but this ended after the group was outlawed in 1954. Sadat's position proved secure enough that in 1969 he was chosen to be vice president under Nasir. Upon Nasir's death in 1970, Sadat became interim president of Egypt.

At that point Sadat surprised almost everyone with his ability to outmaneuver his rivals and, with the army's support, to secure his place as Egypt's permanent leader. Pulling off surprises became his forte. He started a war against Israel in October 1973 by ordering a well-orchestrated crossing of the Suez Canal. Afterward, Sadat ended Egypt's alliance with the Soviets in favor of closer ties with the United States. As he explained, "The Russians can give you arms, but only the Americans can deliver peace."

However, his greatest surprise was his trip to Jerusalem in 1977 to confront the Israelis with a peace offer. This led to the famous Camp David talks under President Carter's auspices. Sadat signed a separate treaty with Israel and regained the Sinai, but he managed to get only empty promises from the Israelis when it came to the Palestinians.

The tragedy of Sadat's sincere efforts at peace, for which he deservedly received the 1978 Nobel Peace Prize, was that his partners were not as sincere as he. Partial success proved worse than failure, for Sadat's separate peace isolated Egypt within the Arab world and earned hatred for him personally. Finally, on 6 October 1981 a cabal of Egyptian army officers assassinated Sadat during a military parade honoring Egypt's "victory" in the October (Yom Kippur) War.

expansion (and hence domination) by the Israelis. Israel claimed it could not risk its security by agreeing in advance to make concessions that might be matched only by some—or possibly none—of its Arab foes. Israel's government and military establishment were confident about their military superiority over the combined Arab forces, but domestic tensions were growing. Israel's right-wing parties, which equated territorial expansion with security, had left the broad coalition government and denounced the Rogers Peace Plan. This in turn made further Labor Party concessions for the sake of peace politically impossible.

As for Egypt, Sadat had bent as far as he dared. A separate peace would have isolated Egypt from the rest of the Arab world and dissuaded the oil-exporting countries from supporting the faltering Egyptian economy. Jordan would have made peace with Israel in return for its complete withdrawal from the West Bank, including Jerusalem's Old City. In 1972 King Husayn proposed a federation between these Palestinian areas and the rest of Jordan, to be called the United Arab Kingdom. Neither Israel nor the Palestinians endorsed this idea. Syria maintained that Israel was an expansionist state that would never give back peacefully what it had taken by force. The Soviet Union, seeking détente with the West, did not block US peacemaking efforts, but it did not back them either. Instead, it went on cultivating its own Middle Eastern friends, including Syria and Iraq, as well as the chastened PLO and related guerrilla groups.

DANGER SIGNS IN THE MIDDLE EAST

The two years prior to October 1973 were the lull before the storm, but there were danger signals. Qadhafi, having planned to unite Libya with Sadat's Egypt, pressured Sadat to attack Israel. Palestinian *fida'iyin* dramatized their cause in ways offensive to both Israel and the West. Their targets included Puerto Rican pilgrims in Israel's Lod Airport, Israeli athletes at the 1972 Olympic Games in Munich, the US ambassador to the Sudan, and a trainload of Soviet Jewish emigrants entering Austria. IDF planes struck back at Palestinian strongholds, also taking innocent lives. The United Nations condemned Israel's reprisals, but not the Palestinian actions that had inspired them.

Meanwhile, the Western press and people began to worry about the future of energy supplies and the risks of overdependence on oil imports. Europe and Japan felt especially vulnerable. As Middle Eastern output skyrocketed, the oil companies had kept their prices low. They had even lowered them in 1959 and 1960 without consulting their host governments.

As the two sides had agreed by then to split oil profits fifty-fifty, the companies' unilateral actions lowered the governments' incomes. These price cuts may have reflected low production costs and a glutted oil market, but petroleum and natural gas are irreplaceable resources as well as the main source of national income for some of the exporting countries. Five of them (Iran, Iraq, Kuwait, Saʻudi Arabia, and Venezuela) met in Baghdad in 1960 and set up the Organization of Petroleum Exporting Countries (OPEC). Later they were joined by Abu Dhabi (now the United Arab Emirates), Algeria, Ecuador, Indonesia, Libya, Nigeria, and Qatar.

During the 1960s, as long as the world's oil supply kept up with demand, OPEC kept a low profile. But as its members came to know one another and learned more about oil economics, the organization became more assertive. In 1968 it recommended that its members explore for new resources on their own, buy shares in the oil companies, restrict their concession areas, and set posted (or tax reference) prices on their products (so that oil price drops would not reduce government revenues). Two years later the companies agreed to work toward uniform—and higher—posted prices and to pay higher taxes levied on their earnings. As world demand kept rising, the oil exporters started to flex their economic muscles.

What did this mean in terms of prices? One barrel (42 US gallons or 159 liters) of Iraqi crude oil sold in 1950 for US$2.41, dropping to $2.15 by 1960. The price rebounded to $2.41 by 1970, reaching $3.21 in 1971 and $3.40 in 1972 (prices have not been adjusted for currency inflation). The fourfold price hike that hit the West in late 1973 caused real anger against both the Arab oil producers and the big oil companies. It made little difference to the American worker, commuting by car, that few other raw materials or manufactured goods had kept the same prices between 1950 and 1970. What consumers wanted, then as now, was the lowest price possible for a product that underpinned their way of life.

Prelude to War

In September 1973 the Middle East seemed calm and an Arab-Israeli war improbable. The Israelis, celebrating their country's twenty-fifth birthday, were preparing for another Knesset election. The group that had ruled Israel since 1948 expected to retain power. The so-called Labor Alignment was a bloc of moderate and left-wing parties (but without the Arab and Jewish communists). Leading the Alignment was Mapai, once headed by Ben-Gurion and now by Golda Meir. The ruling Alignment was in coalition with the National Religious Party, for which many Orthodox Jews would vote. Menachem Begin, head of the right-wing nationalists, had served in coalition cabinets under Labor from 1967 to 1970, when he resigned to protest Israel's acceptance of the Rogers Plan. He then began welding Israel's conservative parties into a coalition called the *Likud* (Consolidation).

US Concerns

The United States, having pulled its forces out of Vietnam, was losing interest in foreign affairs. Most Americans were focused on the scandals involving the Nixon administration (mainly the Watergate affair, which grew out of its efforts to cover up a break-in of the Democratic Party headquarters in the Watergate office building in Washington). Those concerned with long-range issues watched the growing gap between US consumption and production of petroleum and other fossil fuels, a deficit that was being met by rising oil and natural gas imports from the Middle East. Some oil companies argued that unless Washington took a more balanced approach to the Middle East conflict, the Arabs would stop selling oil and gas to the West. Given the power of the pro-Zionist lobby in Washington, a more balanced approach was unlikely.

Although pressure by Jewish (and Gentile) groups had hastened US recognition of Israel in 1948, the Zionist lobby had been hampered in the early 1950s by the number and variety of Jewish organizations and pressure groups in Washington. The creation in 1954 of the American Israel Public Affairs Committee (AIPAC; originally called the American Zionist Committee for Public Affairs) was meant to unify the various voices for Israel to influence Congress (which tended to favor Israel) and the State Department (which did not). By 1973, AIPAC was a well-financed organization that could manipulate nearly all members of Congress, owing to its influence on their Jewish (and, in some cases, evangelical Christian) constituents. No Arab pressure group came close to matching AIPAC's power.

Nixon, hoping to deflect Watergate brickbats, had just named his national security adviser, Henry Kissinger, as his secretary of state. A few Arabs feared that Kissinger, who was Jewish, might back Israel, but he publicly reassured the Arab countries of his fairness. Eager to promote détente, Kissinger wanted the superpowers to stop the arms race and bring peace to the Middle East, where the danger of a confrontation remained high.

Arab Frustrations

Both Washington and Jerusalem underestimated the frustration of the Arab governments over Israel's prolonged and deepening occupation of the lands taken in 1967. Many pro-Israel observers knew this frustration existed, though they assumed that the Arabs were harping on the territorial issue to distract outsiders from their real aim of destroying the Jewish state, and they asserted that the Arab states lacked the will or the power to oust the Israelis. After all, the Arabs had never fought against Israel without having Egypt in their vanguard. Sadat seemingly weakened Egypt's ability to fight by ousting his Soviet advisers and technicians in 1972. However, he warned US and European journalists that Egypt might soon attack Israeli troops somewhere in the Sinai to create a crisis that would force the superpowers to intervene.

Sadat wanted both war and peace. A war with Israel would be costly to Egypt, but if his army and air force, equipped with an impressive arsenal of Soviet tanks, planes, and missiles, could regain some of the lands Nasir had lost in 1967, Egypt would be more willing and able to settle with Israel. Sadat had purged his government of any Nasirites who might have opposed his policies, but the military could have rebelled. Many officers and soldiers had been kept on alert since 1967 and were thirsting for either battle or a return to civilian life. Egypt's policy of "no war, no peace" had outlived its usefulness. The Egyptians watched Israel's election campaign, in which both the Labor Alignment and the Likud made glowing promises about Jewish settlements and development towns in the Sinai, especially near the Gaza Strip.

War Preparations

Sadat began, therefore, to confer publicly and privately with other Arab heads of state about an attack on Israel. He could no longer work with Qadhafi, who made frequent and often unannounced visits to Cairo to harangue the Egyptian people about the Arabs' duty to combat Zionism, the proper role of Muslim women, and the iniquity of Cairo's nightclubs. Egypt's projected union with Libya, due to take effect on 1 September 1973, was put off and finally forgotten.

Instead Sadat looked to Sa'udi Arabia, Egypt's main financial backer, and to the other confrontation states, Syria and Jordan. These two countries had been rivals ever since King Abdallah's Greater Syria scheme. However, Hafiz al-Assad, who became Syria's president in 1970, was more committed than his precursors to revive his country's economy and less inclined to subvert Jordan's politics. Husayn wanted to end his kingdom's isolation in the Arab world, so in early September Sadat brought together the two leaders for a minisummit, at which they agreed to revive their united front against Israel. High-level Egyptian and Syrian officers started quietly planning a coordinated surprise attack on the Israeli-occupied territories in the Golan Heights and the east bank of the Suez Canal.

Many Zionists have claimed that Syria and Egypt planned to invade and defeat Israel, presumably to liberate Palestine, but this was not Sadat's stated goal. The Arab leaders planned to catch Israel off guard. They thought that the Americans, paralyzed by the Vietnam debacle and the Watergate scandal, would not intervene. They agreed that Jordan, lacking missile defenses against Israeli aircraft, should stay out of the early phases of the war. Experts disagree on whether Syria and Egypt deliberately choose Yom Kippur (the Jewish Day of Atonement) as the date of their attack. The original plan was to initiate it just after sundown, on a day when the moon was nearly full. The Soviets had just launched a spy satellite over the Middle East to guide the Arabs' maneuvers.

THE OCTOBER (YOM KIPPUR) WAR

The war's outbreak was signaled by a massive Egyptian air and artillery assault on Israel's Bar Lev line east of the Suez Canal, together with a large-scale Syrian tank invasion of the Golan Heights. With only 600 officers and soldiers on the Bar Lev line and seventy tanks guarding the Golan, Israel could not blunt this first Arab assault. Within a few hours, thousands of Egyptians had crossed the canal. Using their surface-to-air missiles to down IDF planes, they effectively denied the enemy its accustomed control of the air; they also overran most of the Bar Lev line. The Syrians retook Mount Hermon and made inroads into the southern half of the Golan Heights; they might have invaded Israel itself.

Israel's Unpreparedness

Mobilizing Israel's reserves was quick and easy; on Yom Kippur most reservists were either at home or praying in the synagogues. Soon hundreds of units were grouping and heading to the two fronts. Nonetheless, Israel was taken by surprise. Both Israel and US intelligence had noted the massing of Egyptian and Syrian troops in the preceding week but had assumed they were on routine maneuvers. Besides, they doubted that Muslim armies would attack during Ramadan, Islam's month of fasting. Israel chose not to call up its reserves, having done so at great expense a few months earlier. By the time it realized that war was inevitable, Israel had missed the chance to bring its front line up to the level of strength needed to stop the Arab armies. In an emergency meeting on the morning of 6 October, the cabinet discussed a pre-emptive air strike, but Golda Meir ruled it out, lest Washington cut off all aid to Israel.

The Course of the Fighting

The Arab assault worked at first but then stopped. The Egyptians could have pushed deep into Sinai, and the Syrians could have moved down the Golan Heights into northern Israel. Why did they hold back? Sadat planned to push back the Israelis deep into the Sinai and then halt his advance. He did not intend to invade Israel, for he assumed that Washington would intervene and negotiations would begin while Egypt held an advantage on the ground.

During the first week of fighting, the Israelis concentrated their forces in the North, fearing a revolt if Syrian forces broke through into mainly Arab areas, such as Galilee or the occupied West Bank, for Israel's Arab policies had not created conditions that would foster loyalty to the Jewish state. They soon drove the Syrians back beyond the 1967 armistice line. Israeli units reached a town halfway between Kunaitra (the Golan's main city) and Damascus. Then they stopped, partly to avert any Soviet intervention or a massive attack by Jordan or Iraq but also because Israel's main thrust had shifted to the Egyptian front. After crossing the canal, Egypt's two armies took up positions about 6 miles (10 kilometers) deep into Sinai, but Israeli intelligence found a weak spot between them. In the second week, amid tank battles as large as those in World War II, the Israelis pierced that middle zone, reached the canal, and crossed it. Egyptian fire and bombardment killed most of Israel's advance units, but some managed to build a land bridge that enabled other troops to reach the west side of the canal. As the Israeli army headed for Suez City, Sadat began to worry.

Arms Supplies and the Oil Embargo

One major factor in turning the tide was the US resupply of arms to Israel. Washington had withheld ammunition and spare parts in the first week of the war, hoping to make Israel more accommodating. Then, under intense pressure from the pro-Israel lobby, it started a massive airlift. How could the Arabs discourage this resupply? The weapon they had long held back—an embargo on the sale of oil to the United States—now beckoned. Arab oil-exporting countries had briefly stopped sales to the West in the June 1967 War. Back then oil had glutted the world market, whereas even before October 1973 most industrialized countries feared shortages. Egypt had long urged the Gulf states to deny oil to the United States as a means of making Israel give up the occupied territories. An *al-Ahram* editorial argued that American students, if forced to attend classes in unheated lecture rooms, would demonstrate for Israeli withdrawals as they had demanded a US troop pullout from Indochina.

The day after the United States started flying arms to Israel, the Arab oil-producing states announced that they would reduce their production by 5 percent that month and that these cutbacks would continue until Israel had withdrawn from all the occupied territories and had recognized the national rights of the Palestinians. Some OPEC members suddenly raised oil prices by up to 50 percent. Then the Arab states (but not Iran) agreed to put an embargo on the United States and any European country deemed excessively pro-Israel. They singled out the Netherlands, not so much because of the Dutch government's policy but because most of the oil shipped to northern Europe came through the port of Rotterdam. The oil embargo failed to halt the airlift, but it did cause many European countries to deny landing rights to US planes carrying arms to Israel. All these countries publicly supported the Arab interpretation of Resolution 242. Even so, oil supplies dwindled. With winter coming, European governments adopted austerity measures to reduce fuel consumption and avert a crisis.

The Superpowers and the Ceasefire

By the third week of the longest war the Arabs and Israelis had fought since 1948, both Egypt and Syria faced military defeat. The Soviet Union, anxious to avert their collapse, invited Kissinger to Moscow. The US government might have exploited the Soviets' desire for Middle East stability, but it was having its own problems. Aside from its fear of the Arabs' oil weapon and the threat that more Arab states might enter the war, Washington was in chaos. Vice President Spiro Agnew had just resigned. President Nixon had fired his special Watergate prosecutor and accepted his attorney general's resignation, thus damaging his own credibility. Kissinger flew to Moscow to draft with Communist Party chairman Leonid Brezhnev a jointly acceptable Security Council resolution. There was to be a ceasefire in place, a reaffirmation of Resolution 242, and immediate negotiations among the parties to the conflict. This resolution was adopted by the UN Security Council and accepted by Egypt and Israel—but not by Syria. Fighting continued on both fronts, however, with Egypt and Israel accusing each other of bad faith. By the time the Security Council passed a new resolution two days later, Israel's forces in Egypt had surrounded Suez City and in Syria had seized more land around Mount Hermon.

Many Israelis did not want this ceasefire; Egypt's Third Army was trapped in Sinai east of Suez, and Israeli forces could have crushed it. But Kissinger reasoned that Egypt would be more apt to make peace if it could keep some of its initial gains. The ceasefire was shaky, the troop lines were intertwined, and most observers feared the fighting would resume shortly. Kissinger put US forces on red alert the next day, allegedly because Soviet ships were unloading nuclear warheads at Alexandria—a false report. The more probable reason was that Moscow was insisting that Israel accept the ceasefire. Finally, under duress, the Israelis complied.

THE WAR'S AFTERMATH

The June 1967 War had destroyed whatever influence the United States had possessed in Egypt and Syria. Surprisingly, after the October 1973 War the United States actually regained that lost influence, thanks to Kissinger's diplomacy. Even though he had never spent time in the Arab countries or shown much interest in them before becoming secretary of state, he managed to deal shrewdly with their leaders, strengthening their ties with Washington, which claimed that it alone could put real pressure on Jerusalem. He tried various means to bring the Arabs and the Israelis together; if one failed, he suggested another. In early November Egyptian and Israeli army commanders met in a tent pitched near the kilometer 101 marker on the Cairo-Suez road, to identify and unsnarl the lines separating the two sides and to arrange for food and medical supplies to Egypt's trapped Third Army. After these talks, Kissinger began organizing a general peace conference, to be held in Geneva in late December under the joint presidency of the superpowers. Syria stayed away because the PLO had not been invited, but Egypt and Israel both came. After a day of opening speeches, the conference adjourned, as a technical committee tried to disentangle the Israeli and Egyptian forces around Suez.

Shuttle Diplomacy

In January 1974 Kissinger began flying between Jerusalem and Aswan (where Sadat spent the winter) and arranged a "separation of forces" agreement by which Israel's troops were to withdraw from all lands west of the canal and to establish an armistice line about 20 miles (35 kilometers) east of Suez (see Map 17.2). A new UN Emergency Force would patrol a buffer

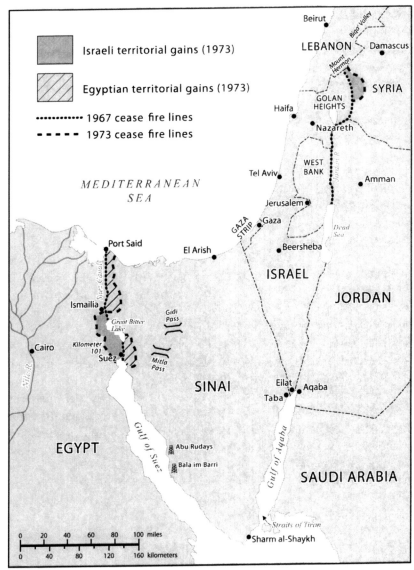

Map 17.2   The territorial situation at the end of the October 1973 War

zone east of the canal, enabling Sadat to keep the lands his forces had taken and to regain those they had lost later in the war. The Israelis benefited because they could demobilize most of their reservists. So pleased was Egypt with this agreement that Sadat helped persuade King Faysal to lift the oil embargo. Syria, too, agreed to negotiate a disengagement of forces with Israel. This deal would prove much tougher to close. It kept Kissinger in the Middle East for most of May 1974, but finally the Israelis agreed to give back to Syria what they had taken in the October War, plus the main city of the Golan Heights, Kunaitra. A UN Disengagement Observer Force was admitted into the Golan, but only for a six-month period that would have to be renewed by the consent of both sides. Despite some anxious moments at the end of each six-month period, Syria and Israel have renewed the deal ever since.

Israel's Domestic Crisis

While Kissinger was conducting his diplomacy, Israel's government underwent a severe crisis. The general election, planned for October 1973, had been put off until late December because of the war. When it was held, the conservative Likud coalition scored significant gains at the expense of the Labor Alignment and its traditional coalition partners. The voters were reacting to the mistakes made by Meir's cabinet just before the war. In early 1974 she tried to form a new government, but her efforts were stymied by disputes between secularist and Orthodox parties over the question of who is a Jew. A hoary (and unresolved) Israeli issue, it centers on whether the government may offer citizenship to any Jewish immigrant (the secularist position) or whether it may do so only for an immigrant who can prove that he or she has a Jewish mother or has been converted according to Jewish law. Orthodox Jews argue that Israel should be a truly Jewish state, not just one in which those people who call themselves Jews happen to form a majority. Meir, unable to reach a consensus on whether to include the National Religious Party (the advocate of the Orthodox stance) in her coalition and stung by criticism about the war, resigned. Once Israel's disengagement with Syria took effect in June 1974, Yitzhak Rabin became the new premier.

Effects of the Oil Embargo

The 1973–1974 crisis posed major economic and political problems for the industrialized world. Crude oil prices fluctuated wildly as countries started bidding against one another, and oil shortages challenged industries and consumers in all parts of the world.

For such countries as Saʿudi Arabia, Kuwait, and Iran, though, the sudden spurt of oil income opened new vistas for economic development and political leverage. But even they were challenged: Western entrepreneurs jammed their hotels and the waiting rooms of government officials, ships loaded with machinery and consumer goods lined up around the Gulf states' inadequate ports, and poorer countries such as Egypt (and the PLO) pestered them for economic assistance. Countries without oil, including such Arab states as Jordan, the Yemens, and Lebanon, could not pay the higher prices. India, Pakistan, Bangladesh, and other non-Western countries shelved needed development projects just to pay for oil. Europe, Japan, and the United States all suffered higher unemployment and price inflation in 1974. Such problems affected everyone who bought from these industrialized nations or tried to sell to them. US arms sales to Middle Eastern rulers, which helped pay for oil purchases, reached $9 billion in 1977. Egyptians, Yemenis, Palestinians, and Lebanese flocked to newly rich oil countries to find jobs and sent much of their earnings to their families, changing their lifestyles. Remarkably, though, AIPAC, the pro-Zionist lobby, prevented the US government from pressing Israel to withdraw from the West Bank and Gaza and make a peace compromise with the Arabs. Such a deal would probably have served American interests in the Middle East.

PLO Power at Its Zenith

Foreign countries, seeking better ties with the Arabs, backed the Palestinian cause more than they ever had before. Even though few had fought in the October 1973 War, the Palestinians were gaining leverage with the Arab governments. Many had already migrated to the oil-producing countries to make a living and now contributed heavily to the managerial elite and workforce of such countries as Kuwait, where Palestinians made up one-fourth of the whole population. The Kuwaiti government also supported the PLO financially. In October 1974 the Arab heads of state, meeting in Rabat, recognized the PLO as the "sole legitimate representative of the Palestinian people on any liberated Palestinian territory." Even King Husayn conceded to the PLO the right to negotiate for the West Bank. The UN General Assembly invited PLO chairman 'Arafat to speak. It later recognized the Palestinians' right to independence and sovereignty and granted the PLO observer status at the United Nations. Meanwhile, the UN Educational, Social, and Cultural Organization (UNESCO) cut off financial aid to Israel because of its "persistence in altering the historical features of Jerusalem." In 1975 Israel became even more isolated when the General Assembly passed by a large majority a resolution condemning Zionism as a form of racism. It later repealed this resolution.

The PLO became recognized as a movement seeking national liberation and rebutted Zionist efforts to discredit its actions as "terrorist." It justified acts of sabotage and violence against civilian Israelis as retaliation in kind. Some people argued that if the Palestinians had a state on the West Bank and the Gaza Strip, they would become more willing to accept Israel within its 1967 borders. But the Israelis did not want to take chances.

Return to Shuttle Diplomacy

In winter 1975 Kissinger launched a new series of talks with Egypt and Israel aimed at an interim Sinai agreement to keep up the momentum of the negotiations and to strengthen Sadat against rising Arab opposition. Again Kissinger tried his shuttle diplomacy, which had worked in 1974. But the talks foundered on Israel's refusal to hand back the Sinai oil fields or the strategic Gidi and Mitla Passes and on Egypt's reluctance to pledge itself to nonbelligerency as long as Israel kept parts of the Sinai. When King Faysal of Sa'udi Arabia was killed in March by his nephew, many expected new troubles in the Arab world.

Later that year, though, both Egypt and Israel became more accommodating. In June Sadat reopened the Suez Canal and allowed passage to ships with Israeli cargos. After yet another round of shuttle diplomacy, Kissinger got a new Sinai accord. Israel gave up the passes and oil fields, as a hundred US civilian technicians joined the UNEF inside the buffer zone separating the Egyptian and Israeli armies. Egypt renounced war as a means of resolving the Middle East conflict, a statement widely interpreted in other Arab capitals as a sellout, but neither the Palestinians nor any Arab leader could stop Sadat's (unacknowledged) march toward a separate peace with Israel.

LEBANON: THE ARENA FOR A NEW ARAB STRUGGLE

In Lebanon a separate but related crisis was brewing: a civil war far more lasting, costly, and bitter than that of 1958. This long conflict can be understood from several angles.

The Religious Angle

The conflict was initially seen as one between Christians and Muslims. Lebanon was a country deeply split along religious lines. The Maronites, the largest single Christian sect, had long wielded power disproportionate to their actual share of the population. Lebanon's Muslims, really the majority, sought equal rights for themselves. Not all Christians lined up on the Maronites' side, and not all Muslims had the same interests. Shi'ite Muslims were increasing, relative to the historically preponderant Sunnis, and, as the war continued, they insisted on getting recognition of their status. In later years both Christians and Muslims would split into factions at war with one another.

The Nationalist Angle

Some experts saw the war as one between Lebanese loyalists, who viewed their country as a link between the West and the Middle East, and Arab nationalists, who sought closer ties with Syria and other Arab states. This aspect of the conflict invited other Middle Eastern states to intervene. Because no Arab state would openly favor Lebanese particularism over Arab nationalism, how any one government would act depended on how much it wished to please Syria. And Syria's policy changed often. Israel's backers described the Palestinians as a foreign force that was attacking the Lebanese (meaning the Maronites, whom Israel was quietly supporting). A half million Palestinians lived in Lebanon, mainly in the south and in refugee camps around Beirut and cut off from Lebanon's political and economic life. Christian Arabs from Palestine had been assimilated, but not the Palestinian Muslims who helped to create a Muslim majority there. After 1970 the PLO, driven out of Jordan, made Lebanon its operational base. It did not want to enter the civil war, but it sided with any group that espoused Arab nationalism and wanted to liberate Palestine. It was a Maronite militia's attack on a Palestinian bus that sparked the fighting in April 1975, committing the PLO to the Arab nationalist side.

The Economic Angle

The Lebanese conflict was also a struggle between a privileged class of landowners and merchants trying to preserve the status quo and a large mass of poor people (mainly Muslim) striving for more equality. The gap between rich and poor, especially in Beirut, was immense and scandalous. High-rise apartment buildings abutted shacks built of cinder blocks and corrugated iron. Unable to tax the incomes of the rich, the government imposed high excise taxes on cigarettes and other goods consumed by the poor. Many employers did not pay the minimum wage because they could hire Palestinian refugees or newcomers from rural areas, who were desperate for jobs, for less money.

The Ideological Angle

Given such social conditions, some journalists and scholars saw the war as one between the right (guardians of the status quo) and the left (those wanting change). This was partly true. Those who were rich, well connected, and Christian tended to favor the right; those who were not generally became leftists. Some Marxists did enter the fray. The left's rifles and grenade launchers tended to be of Soviet manufacture, whereas American, European, and Israeli arms were borne by the forces of the right. Most Middle Eastern states had armed themselves heavily for years, and Lebanon had been a smugglers' haven even in peacetime. Naturally, some of its citizens possessed lots of bombs and guns.

An Attempted Synthesis

All of these angles had some truth, though none was wholly true. People fight for reasons other than religion, nationality, class interest, or ideology. Lebanese loyalties were also based on habit, family, patronage, or even region or neighborhood of habitation. Old grudges and dormant feuds were revived. Past favors or slights were paid back in kind—or worse. Lebanon had plenty of armed factions, ranging from street gangs to private militias. The two main Lebanese parties to the conflict were the Phalanges, a long-lived and largely Maronite force, and the Lebanese National Movement, which was led by members of the Jumblat family and tended to be mainly Muslim. President Sulayman Franjiyah openly backed the "Christian" side. The "Muslim" side won the support of PLO chairman 'Arafat. Savage fighting alternated with shaky ceasefires for eighteen months, especially in and around Beirut, where the hotel district, the port, and residential areas became battle zones. Approximately 70,000 Lebanese (mostly civilians) were killed, more than 500,000 people were left homeless, and property damage exceeded $1 billion in 1975–1976 alone.

Syria's Role

One puzzling aspect of this war was Syria's 1976 policy shift. Syria had deeply resented France's severance of Lebanon during the mandate period, and since independence the Syrians had wanted to reunite the two countries. Mostly Muslim and generally the bellwether of Arab nationalism, Syria had tended to side with any faction that would weaken the pro-Western Maronites in Lebanon. President Hafiz al-Assad backed the rebels morally and materially at first during the Lebanese civil war, but in

January 1976 he managed to get Franjiyah and his opponents to accept a ceasefire and a political deal that would require a slight shift in Lebanon's power balance in the Muslims' favor. The Muslim Lebanese, abetted by the PLO, rejected his proposed compromise, which angered Assad, and in response he changed sides. Syria sent tanks and troops to enforce its carefully crafted settlement, attacked Lebanese Muslims and the PLO, and battered them into submission by fall 1976.

An Arab summit meeting, held in Riyadh that October, devised a formula by which Lebanon would be occupied by an Arab League peacekeeping force, made up mainly of Syrians. President Franjiyah was succeeded by a pro-Syrian politician. Assad, a self-styled champion of Arab nationalism and socialism, protected Christian interests in Lebanon because he wanted to keep the PLO weak so that his government could control it; earlier he had quarreled with 'Arafat. Lebanon settled into an uneasy truce, but the fighting had in fact partitioned the country—and Beirut—between Christians and Muslims. Although some Christians still lived peacefully within "Muslim" zones such as west Beirut, the Maronites built a new harbor and airport north of the city and treated their area as a Christian version of Israel. Indeed, the Israelis seemed to agree. As a foretaste of larger invasions to come, Israeli forces in 1976 entered southern Lebanon to destroy Palestinian bases and warned Syria to keep its troops away from Lebanon's southern border. Christian Lebanese in the south—cut off from their coreligionists in the rest of the country—began crossing into Israel to sell their produce, seek work, or get medical care. The Arabs accused Israel of using Lebanon to prove the traditional Zionist contention that multireligious states could not last in the Middle East.

THE ROAD TO CAMP DAVID

The US government suspended its quest for Middle East peace during its 1976 presidential election. President Gerald Ford and his challenger, Jimmy Carter, pledged to back a strong and independent Israel, and both also ignored the Palestinians. The United States was not unaffected by the Lebanese civil war, as its ambassador was assassinated in 1976 and the PLO helped the embassy evacuate US civilians from Beirut. But because Kissinger had ruled out such parleys during his 1975 peace talks, Washington would not negotiate with the PLO. Most Americans opposed talking to the PLO because the US news media and politicians echoed Israel's view that 'Arafat was a murderer and his organization an umbrella for terrorist groups. After Carter's election, though, he would try a new initiative to settle the Arab-Israeli conflict, the Palestinian question, and perhaps the Lebanese civil war as well.

The key to the new administration's thinking on the Middle East lay in a report newly prepared by the Brookings Institution called *Toward Peace in the Middle East*. It urged the Arab states to recognize Israel within its pre–June 1967 boundaries (with some minor border adjustments). Israel was to turn the Gaza Strip and the West Bank over to a government of Palestinians, but not necessarily the PLO. The report also called for reconvening the Geneva Conference to reach the necessary agreements. Carter gave high priority to Middle East peace and began to talk with various heads of state, hoping to resuscitate the Geneva Conference before the end of 1977.

Policy Problems

New snags soon appeared. Israel was intensely suspicious of any conference the Soviet Union would cochair with the United States. Kissinger's shuttle diplomacy had kept Moscow out of the peace process, but now Washington seemed determined to invite the Soviets back in, embarrassing the Israelis and even Sadat. Besides, the Arab states insisted on having Palestinians at the proposed meeting. If they were left out, some Palestinian group or individual might try to block a process that was deciding their fate without consulting them. If they were included, would the PLO represent them, as the 1974 Rabat Summit had resolved? Negotiating with the PLO was totally unacceptable to Israel, which argued that Jordan was a Palestinian state and that there was no need for another, especially one whose covenant called for Israel's destruction. For their part, the Palestinians wanted the PLO to represent them. Few expected the PLO to recognize Israel, but it wanted to speak for the Palestinians at the reconvened Geneva Conference.

Political changes within Israel complicated Carter's plans. While his administration was seeking peace, Israel was holding a general election. The Labor Alignment had been hurt by internal dissension, government scandals, galloping inflation, and mounting social problems. Israel's electorate turned against Labor. Most voted for the right-wing Likud. Its head, Menachem Begin, managed to form a coalition with the National Religious Party and thus became prime minister. For the first time, the post was held by an Israeli not belonging to any of the labor parties. Begin's election seemed to be a giant step away from peace, as he hastened to assert that the West Bank (which he called Judea and Samaria) was an integral part of *Eretz Israel* (the Land of Israel) that had been liberated, not occupied, in 1967. Flouting the Fourth Geneva Convention (1949), which addressed protection of civilians in time of war and which Israel and most other countries, signed, Begin urged Jews to settle in strategic parts of that mainly Arab area. The Arabs called Begin a terrorist. As former head of the Irgun, he had carried out the 1948 Dayr Yasin massacre. It seemed unlikely that any Arab leader would talk to such a chauvinistic Israeli. Yet, amazingly, there was one.

Sadat Leads the Quest for Peace

Speaking before Egypt's Popular Assembly, Sadat declared that he was willing to go before the Israeli Knesset to argue his country's case for peace. Questioned later by American television journalists, Begin said he would receive the Egyptian president at any time. Arrangements were made hastily, and on 19 November 1977 Sadat flew to Israel. The next day he delivered before the Knesset a speech that was carried to most of the world by radio and television. He offered the Israelis peace with Egypt if they withdrew from all lands they had occupied in the 1967 War and recognized a Palestinian state. Although Israel was willing to make peace with Egypt, Sadat wanted a comprehensive settlement including Syria, Jordan, and the Palestinians. But no other Arab leader wanted the reconciliation with Israel that Sadat offered. Instead, Qadhafi and 'Arafat called him a traitor to the Arab cause.

To follow up on his Jerusalem visit, Sadat called a general conference in December 1977; however, as only Israel and the United States agreed to come to Cairo, it ended inconclusively. Yet the Egyptian people, burdened by heavy state military expenditures, saw peace with Israel as a first step toward their economic recovery. Begin met with Sadat, and they agreed on concurrent negotiations: military talks in Cairo and political ones in Jerusalem. By the time the talks began in January, though, each side was deeply and obviously suspicious of the other. Begin's insistence that Jewish settlements on the West Bank and industrial towns in the Sinai had to stay under Israeli army protection reminded Sadat of past British colonialism, so he pulled his negotiators out of Jerusalem.

Israel and Egypt also differed on how to resolve the Palestinian issue. Begin offered self-rule (with an indeterminate Israeli occupation) to the Arabs in the occupied areas. Sadat wanted self-determination for the Palestinian people. How could Begin expect Sadat to accept indefinite Israeli control over the Palestinians when the Arabs had struggled for most of the century to free themselves from foreign rule? How could Sadat expect

Begin, who believed God had promised the West Bank to the Jews, to commit his government to give that land to the Palestinians, who had not recognized Israel's right to exist? Jewish Israelis did not care to admit that Palestinian Arabs wanted freedom as much as they did, whereas Egypt (and the other Arab countries) did not realize how Israel's concern for security resulted from Jewish fears of extinction after the Holocaust and years of tension due to the Arab-Israeli conflict. Yet one could reasonably argue that retaining and settling the occupied territories, then containing more than 2 million discontented Palestinians, only increased Israel's insecurity.

Such tunnel vision was tragic, for both sides needed peace. Some Israelis were moving to other countries because they were tired of the confiscatory taxes, constant calls to military reserve duty, and ceaseless tension. Some Arabs, too, had gone abroad, especially educated young adults seeking intellectual freedom and professional opportunities. Egypt hoped to free funds earmarked for arms to rebuild its limping economy. Food riots had broken out in Cairo and the Delta cities in January 1977, drawing world attention to Egypt's economic problems.

The US government got more involved than ever in the quest for peace. Americans feared that the Soviet Union would benefit if peace talks failed; Communism would spread and Arab oil might be denied to Western buyers. Carter and his cabinet devoted a disproportionate share of their time and energy to the Arab-Israeli conflict, visits to Middle Eastern capitals, compromise formulas, balanced arms sales, and top-level meetings.

The Egyptian-Israeli Treaty

A spectacular summit, consisting of Begin, Sadat, and Carter, along with cabinet ministers and advisers from the three corresponding countries, met at Camp David (the country retreat for US presidents in Maryland) in September 1978. Twelve days of intense negotiations produced documents called "A Framework for the Conclusion of a Peace Treaty between Egypt and Israel" and "A Framework for Peace in the Middle East." The latter was intended to bring other parties into the settlement, but Jordan, Sa'udi Arabia, Syria, and the PLO refused to join in these agreements, which offered the Palestinians little hope for self-determination. After a long and bitter debate, Israel's Knesset agreed to pull its troops out of Sinai and hence its settlements and airfields from the lands it would restore to Egypt. But the Washington talks foundered on Egypt's attempt to link the establishment of diplomatic ties to Israel's loosening its control over the Gaza and West Bank Palestinians. The three-month deadline agreed upon at Camp David passed without a treaty.

Meanwhile, OPEC warned that during 1979 it would raise posted oil prices by 14.5 percent (later, after the Iranian revolution, it would boost them further and faster), increasing the West's balance-of-payments deficit. Fighting a war of nerves against each other, Egypt and Israel jockeyed for support from Carter, Congress, and the American people, and the two countries rejected compromises. The other Arab governments held a summit meeting in Baghdad in November 1978, offered Egypt inducements to quit the peace talks, and threatened reprisals if it signed a treaty. Hard-line Israelis warned that they would block any pullout from the lands Begin had offered to return to Egypt.

Concerned about the eroding US position in the Middle East, Carter decided in early March 1979 to fly to Cairo and Jerusalem to complete negotiations for the peace accord. His risky venture paid off, as Carter and his aides managed to reconcile the differences between Sadat and Begin. A complex treaty, formally ending the state of war between Egypt and Israel, was signed on the White House lawn on 26 March 1979. It would prove costly for the United States, both economically and politically. Begin reneged on promises not to add Jewish settlements on the West Bank, leaving Sadat looking as if he had sold out the Palestinians. Nearly all the other Arab governments condemned the treaty and accused Sadat of treason. The Palestinians felt betrayed, and a real chance for peace had foundered mainly because Israel was determined to keep the West Bank and Gaza (Egypt and Israel's agreement to hold autonomy talks was a diplomatic fig leaf). Washington wanted peace, but most Middle Eastern peoples rejected the terms accepted by Cairo and Jerusalem.

CONCLUSION

What do we mean by peace? Peace can be defined as the absence of conflict. But in the Middle East many conflicts smolder for years and then flare up suddenly. The Arab-Israeli conflict was muted between 1956 and 1967, and yet there was no peace. We could define peace in another way: as a condition of harmony within and between every person, every group, and every nation in the world. Two people cannot be at peace with each other unless they feel at peace with themselves. If the members of a group disagree among themselves, they cannot agree with another group. A country riven with factional, sectional, or ethnic hostility cannot make peace with another state. Such an idyllic condition rarely occurs in human life, though. Most disputes in history have just died down, enabling the parties to stop quarreling, even if they have failed to reach an accord.

When addressing the question of peace with Israel, some Arabs say they will accept *salam* but not *sulh*. What is the difference? Both words mean "peace," but in modern usage *salam* connotes a temporary cessation of hostilities and *sulh* means "reconciliation." Arabs who make this distinction may envisage an armistice with Israel, a respite from hostilities, in which they can regain their political and economic strength, but not a true reconciliation with the Jewish state. Because this distinction naturally alarms Israel and its backers, harping on it will not lead to peace.

But then is Israel just a Jewish state? It is a country inhabited by Jews and Arabs who must find a basis of coexistence that does not involve domination or repression of one side by the other. However, Arab Israelis—as well as Palestinians under Israel's occupation—do not enjoy the same rights, power, and status as Jewish Israelis. Zionists who ignore the feelings of these Arabs also impede the quest for *sulh* and maybe even *salam*. There can be no peace without security. There can be no peace without justice. For both sides. Period.

18

The Reassertion of Islamic Power

By 1979, a crucial year in Middle East history, the outlook for peace seemed about as stable as a roller-coaster ride. Most of the world wanted a just and peaceful settlement to the Arab-Israeli conflict. Yet the roller coaster of peace hopes and war fears in the Middle East swooped and sank, lurched left and right, on and on. As it veered past Camp David and the White House lawn, a new trouble spot sprang up—Iran. A country hailed by President Carter on a New Year's Day visit in 1978 as "an island of stability in one of the more troubled areas of the world" became, before the year ended, paralyzed by strikes and demonstrations. Carter, in his New Year's toast, said to Iran's leader, Shahanshah (King of Kings) Mohammad Reza Pahlavi Aryamehr, "This is a great tribute to you, Your Majesty, and to the respect, admiration, and love which your people give to you." A year later the shah would become gravely ill and cut off from his rebellious subjects, and Carter's officials were discussing ways to ease him out of Iran.

Meanwhile, the television cameras turned to a thin, dark-eyed, white-bearded octogenarian in a black turban, brown coat, and green tunic, living a spartan existence in a Paris suburb: Ayatollah Ruhollah Khomeini. An aged Shi'ite teacher, Khomeini was winning the hearts and minds of millions of Iranians, at home and abroad. For thirty-seven years, the shah had labored to modernize Iran—or so most Westerners thought—but now forces inspired largely by Muslim fundamentalism were taking over. Suddenly, "Islam" was a force in the world, and Middle East "experts" wrote books, gave lectures, and taught courses about it. In early 1979 the shah left Iran "for an extended vacation," and the ayatollah came home to a tumultuous welcome. Soldiers gave up their arms and joined the celebrating crowds. Some upper- and middle-class Iranians fled the country. The Iranians who stayed behind voted to set up an Islamic republic. Islam, not Marxism, now seemed to be the wave of the future.

For years, the US and Iranian governments had been diplomatic, military, and economic allies. The new regime, reacting against the old shah's regime, vented its resentment against the West. Militant students, abetted by their leaders, seized control of the US Embassy in Tehran and took more than sixty Americans hostage, demanding the return of the shah, his relatives, and his property to Iran. As crowds filled the streets, shouting "Death to America," the American people, uninformed about their country's previous Iran policy, wondered what had gone wrong. Their country, the strongest nation on earth since World War II, seemed to have become a helpless giant among the newly assertive peoples of the Middle East. Its ambassadors could be killed and its embassies invaded or burned. The Soviet Union could invade Afghanistan, and the US government could not effectively strike back. Its people could, however, elect the assertive Ronald Reagan in place of the more circumspect Jimmy Carter. On the day Reagan took office, the American hostages were released, but he soon had problems of his own in dealing with Iran and other parts of the Middle East.

Several regional conflicts intensified as Middle Eastern leaders turned to aggressive tactics. The Turks stayed in Cyprus and the Syrians in Lebanon, the Soviets tightened their hold on Afghanistan, Iraq invaded Iran in 1980, and the Israelis occupied the southern half of Lebanon in 1982. The cost of aggression proved high to the aggressors, but this only slowly became clear. By the decade's end, Afghan rebels backed by volunteers from throughout the Muslim world drove out the Soviets. Iran expelled the Iraqi invaders but could not bring down the Iraqi regime. The Israelis pulled back to a narrow "security zone," leaving Lebanon in more chaos.

Many officials labored to unravel these conflicts, only to entangle themselves and their governments more than ever. Sadat, whom the West viewed as having done the most to promote Middle East peace, fell beneath a hail of machine-gun bullets in 1981. The United States sent troops to join three European powers to force the withdrawal of Syrian and Israeli forces from Lebanon and to persuade the country's warring factions to reform their government. Instead, the Western powers had to leave, unable to defend even themselves against the country's sectarian fighters. No Westerner living in Lebanon was safe from kidnappers, mainly Lebanese Shi'ites. The Iran-Iraq War blazed fiercely until August 1988, costing close to $1 trillion and 1 million lives, but its basic issues were not resolved. The Palestinians, always resisting Israeli rule, launched a massive revolt, the *Intifada* (meaning "shaking off"), in December 1987 and declared the occupied territories "independent" a year later. Washington angered the Palestinians by continuing its aid to Israel and incensed the Israelis by talking to the PLO.

THE CHANGING ROLE OF RELIGION IN POLITICS

A religious revival, or a return to transcendental values, was taking place worldwide among Christians and Jews as well as Muslims. After thirty years of rising prosperity in the industrialized world, new problems set in. Some people who had never known poverty questioned the goals and assumptions of materialism and quested after a life of the spirit. Others, denied the prosperity they could see in the mass media, revived old religious traditions as their guides. Secular-minded people took up various forms of meditation. Religion no longer retreated before the advance of science. For many oppressed peoples, such as the Catholics of Northern Ireland and the Buddhists of Tibet, asserting religious beliefs and symbols was a step toward attaining their freedom and dignity. Even though most Middle Easterners had known formal independence for a generation, old complexes about colonialism lingered. Because of the economic power of multinational corporations and the pervasive influence of American pop culture, some forms of dependence were growing stronger. By the late twentieth century, the West's influence, in addition to its political and military aid to repressive regimes, was cultural, economic, intellectual, and social. Many Muslims hailed their religious revival as a response to the "Coca-Colanization" of their way of life.

In the past, most Muslims had maintained that their only legitimate state was the *umma,* a community of Muslims who believed in God, angels, holy books, divine messengers, and the Day of Judgment and who followed in the footsteps of Muhammad and his successors. Its leaders were to rule justly and according to the Qur'an and Muhammad's example, the Shari'a, to preserve internal safety and harmony. Non-Muslims could live, work, pray, and own property within *Dar al-Islam,* or the "House of Islam," but they were not to take control. Lands not under Muslim rule were called *Dar al-Harb,* or the "House of War." For centuries many Muslims believed in expanding Dar al-Islam against Dar al-Harb, but territorial losses were occurring instead. Their rulers imported weapons, tactics, and military organization piecemeal from the West. When these stratagems failed, some adopted comprehensive westernizing reforms.

Although westernization did introduce improvement in education, transport, and commerce, certain customs got lost in the process. The old moral and intellectual leaders, the *'ulama,* were displaced but not really replaced, for the new westernized elites lacked the *'ulama*'s rapport with the people. Many artisans and traders lost their livelihoods. Government tyranny and corruption, far from vanishing, increased with the telegraph

and the railroad. Bypassing Muslim political principles, native westernizers adopted secular nationalism, but this ideology did not halt the spread
of Western rule or the exploitation of the poor and minorities. Instead,
nationalism sapped popular institutions and exalted dictators such as
Ataturk, Reza Shah, Nasir, and Qadhafi. Few Muslim states (Indonesia,
Algeria, and South Yemen are exceptions) won their independence by
revolutionary armed struggles. After independence, however, many did
not build national unity or defeat their enemies. When nationalism failed
to uphold the self-worth of modern Muslims, other imported ideologies
also proved unfit: fascism degraded the individual to exalt the state, and
communism denied the basic tenets of Islam altogether. People attain
freedom and dignity not by aping others but by affirming what is true
within themselves.

The Iranian Revolution

The religious revival touched all parts of the Muslim world and directly
affected Iran, whose language, conscious cultivation of a pre-Islamic heritage, and adherence to Twelve-Imam Shi'ism were unique. In Iran the rise
of nationalism was reinforced by the beliefs of the 'ulama and the people.
The Shi'ite 'ulama had great power and prestige. As you may recall from
Chapter 7, they were freer than their Sunni counterparts to interpret the
Shari'a. Their ideas had revolutionary potential, especially their belief that
no ruler's authority was legitimate save that of the missing twelfth imam.
Until this imam returns, the lawmakers for Shi'ite Islam were the *mujtahid*s (Islamic legal experts). Their schools and mosques worked apart
from (and often in opposition to) the secular rulers. The 'ulama, along
with the bazaar merchant guilds and the athletic clubs, opposed the Qajar shahs during the 1892 tobacco boycott and the 1906 constitutionalist
movement. They were inconsistent toward the Pahlavi dynasty, backing it
against the Soviet Union and the *Tudeh* (Workers) Party but resisting its
secularizing reforms. They opposed the shah's attempts to seize their en-
dowed lands and to ally Iran with the Western powers, notably the United
States. The Western press stressed the 'ulama's opposition to such features
of the shah's White Revolution as women's suffrage, but neither women
nor men could elect their representatives during most of the shah's reign.
Muslim observance was central in most Iranians' lives, and the 'ulama
likely knew better than the shah and his ministers the feelings of devout
Iranians.

The Monarchy

The Pahlavi dynasty, which ruled from 1925 to 1979, consisted of two shahs: Reza Khan and his son, Mohammad Reza. They (along with their burgeoning family) took over a vast share of Iran's land, houses, shops, hotels, and factories. Around them swarmed a cadre of bureaucrats, landlords, military officers, and professional people who tied their lives and fortunes to the Pahlavi star. Some were patriotic Iranians who believed the shah's policies would benefit their country; others were crafty opportunists who enriched themselves by exploiting the government. Reza Shah was a dictator who admired and emulated Ataturk, but his son, Mohammad, was more complex. He could be ruthless in his pursuit of power and in imposing his westernizing reforms against the wishes of powerful and entrenched groups in Iran, or he could court popularity. At times he shrank from wielding power. Early in his reign he left Iran's government to his ministers and let the tribal and local leaders regain powers they had lost under his father. Later he was eclipsed by a popular premier, Mohammad Mosaddiq, who nationalized the Anglo-Iranian Oil Company in 1951.

After the shah was restored to power by a Central Intelligence Agency (CIA)–backed army coup in 1953, he seemed overshadowed by his US and military advisers. Iran, located between the Soviet Union and the Gulf, played a strategic role in US efforts to contain Soviet expansionism. When the Baghdad Pact (later renamed the Central Treaty Organization, or CENTO) was formed in 1955, Iran joined. In the early 1960s Americans urged the shah to curb those groups they viewed as blocking Iran's modernization: landlords, *'ulama*, and bazaar merchants. The White Revolution, proclaimed in 1963 after a popular referendum, called for (among other things) redistributing land, nationalizing Iran's forests, privatizing state-owned enterprises, enfranchising women, sharing profits in industry, and forming a literacy corps to aid village education.

Riots against the shah's program instigated by the Shi'ite *'ulama* broke out in various parts of Iran. One of the White Revolution's fiercest critics was a teacher in Qom, Ayatollah Ruhollah Khomeini. The shah's secret police, SAVAK (largely trained by the United States and Israel), used various threats and inducements to silence him. When all else failed, Khomeini was exiled. The shah used money and patronage to reward those *'ulama* who would endorse his policies. Some did. Others quietly disapproved and subtly conveyed this attitude to their younger disciples in the *madrasas* of Qom and Mashhad. One of Khomeini's most telling points in mobilizing the *'ulama* against the shah was his attack on an agreement exempting US civilian and military personnel from Iranian jurisdiction.

BOX 18.1
Sayyid Ruhollah Musavi Khomeini

Ayatollah Khomeini (1902–1989), leader of the 1979 Iranian revolution, was born the youngest of six children in a small village, Khomein, in central Iran. The name Khomeini indicates his village origin. Khomeini received a religious education in the Shi'ite tradition, which emphasizes the historical wrongs done to the Shi'ite community against a backdrop of an ongoing struggle between good and evil. After elementary school, he received a strictly religious education, much of it in Iran's holy city of Qom. Intelligent, disciplined, and hardworking, he became a recognized *mujtahid* by the 1930s. Deferential to the country's clerical leaders, who stayed out of public life, Khomeini did not become politically active until the 1940s.

Khomeini's view of Islam underpinned his belief in the perfectibility of man and his institutions and the enlightened leader's duty to push the Muslim *umma* toward moral and social perfection. This belief brought him into conflict with the corrupt and secular Pahlavi shahs and made him critical of Iran's largely passive clerical establishment. During World War II, having achieved seniority within the Shi'ite hierarchy, he became more vocal in his opposition. He declared that "government can only be legitimate when it accepts the rule of God and the rule of God means the implementation of the Shari'a." Thus, when in 1963 Mohammad Reza Shah implemented secular reforms that included women's suffrage and land redistribution, the now-enraged *mollah*s found in the Ayatollah (a title meaning "sign of God") Khomeini their militant leader. Arrested and exiled in 1964, he ended up in Paris.

This exile did not hinder Khomeini's opposition to the shah. It actually helped him by placing him beyond the shah's reach, while still allowing him to continue to direct the revolution from a distance. Never doubting that he would eventually prevail, Khomeini simultaneously refined his notion of an Islamic state at the core of which would be a powerful Muslim guide, or *Vilayat i Faqih*.

Inevitably, Khomeini found that he had to make compromises for his ideal Islamic state and society, as was evident in Iran's poor human rights record following the establishment of the Islamic Republic. Muslim rule took on a vengeful form in Khomeini's Iran. Nevertheless, he sincerely worked for the well-being of the Iranian masses, particularly the poor. Their economic condition has improved since 1979.

Khomeini's hatred of the United States, which he once called the "Great Satan," grew out of his opposition to the shah's dictatorship. Mohammad Reza Shah had relied heavily on American support. The United States not only heavily armed the Pahlavi regime but also helped organize some of its most repressive branches, such as SAVAK. If the shah was an ungodly ruler in Khomeini's eyes, so was his main foreign backer.

Even though such exemptions are common in foreign aid agreements, they reminded Iranians of the Capitulations. Khomeini's campaign was aimed at US influence, not just at the White Revolution. (See Box 18.1.)

The shah's policies were revolutionary in their attempt to change the lifestyle of the Iranian people. Their results, in terms of dams, bridges, roads, schools, clinics, factories, and farmers' cooperatives, looked impressive. The upsurge of Iranian oil revenue, from $817 million in 1968 to $2.25 billion in 1972–1973 to more than $20 billion in 1975–1976, financed the construction boom. Iran's schools and universities proliferated and turned out thousands of graduates, who, especially in liberal arts, law, and commerce, were too numerous for the economy to absorb. These graduates, along with those pursuing science, medicine, and engineering, went abroad to earn higher degrees. Many married foreigners and never came back. Those who did return, or who never left, chose to live in Tehran rather than in the provincial cities and villages where their services were most needed. The capital city swelled from about 1 million inhabitants in 1945 to 5 million in 1977, which caused traffic congestion, smog, and high rent increases.

The potential for revolution grew as unemployed and underemployed intellectuals concentrated in Tehran. SAVAK watched dissidents, censored their writings, and imprisoned thousands. Amnesty International reported that many jailed artists, writers, and *'ulama* were tortured, mutilated, and killed. As for the peasants, the White Revolution gave few of them any share of the great estates that it broke up, and its rural cooperatives did not provide resources to the farmers who needed them. Farmers flocked to the cities to seek lucrative factory jobs. Corruption spread among government employees and contractors, who opposed the White Revolution's aims but tried to enrich themselves and their families. All envied the thousands of American advisers, who were imported by the shah's regime and rewarded with princely wages.

The shah's opponents, especially Iranian students in Western universities, often portrayed him as an authoritarian dictator or a puppet of US imperialism. His ambitions were presumptuous. He dreamed of raising Iran's industrial output to the level of Italy or France by 1990. He assembled a huge armory of guns, tanks, and planes, hardly enough to stop a hypothetical Soviet invasion of his country but adequate to placate his elite officers, to cow his civilian critics, and to make Iran the policeman of the Gulf after Britain withdrew in 1971. The shah revealed his megalomania in the elaborate ceremonies for his and his wife's coronation in 1967 and for the 2,500th anniversary of the Iranian monarchy in 1971 (at a reported cost of $200 million).

Besides the overambitious shah, there were several other reasons that the White Revolution failed: (1) Iran's bureaucratic elite had less experience with westernizing reform than did those of Turkey and Egypt, but it faced greater resistance from traditional leaders, such as the rural landlords, tribal chiefs, bazaar merchants, and *'ulama*, especially because the land reforms threatened their livelihood; (2) the burgeoning oil revenues created more wealth than the economy could absorb; (3) both the traditional elites and rising middle class that rode the oil boom to power became divided and corrupt; and (4) materialist values challenged religious belief among all social classes.

Although Western observers knew about these problems, they tended to downplay the domestic opposition to the shah. US Embassy personnel were forbidden to meet with politicians from Mosaddiq's National Front, even though they were more moderate than the shah's truly strong opponents. The vociferous ones were the Iranian students abroad; they were discounted as inexperienced, infiltrated by SAVAK agents, and often too alienated to come home. Despite their protests against the shah, many students got financial aid for their studies from the Iranian government or the Pahlavi Foundation. The shah's domestic foes, such as the supposedly red Tudeh Party, were weak. Paradoxically, Moscow backed the shah's government almost as long as Washington did. Even Middle East experts ignored the "black" opposition, the Shi'ite *'ulama*, because they followed fashionable theories (or the media) instead of leading public opinion.

Carter's concern for human rights exposed a flaw in the shah's regime that should have troubled earlier administrations, which had empowered Iran to defend the Gulf and to choose what arms it wanted to buy from US and European companies. Most American Middle East specialists tended to disregard Iran because they cared most about resolving the Arab-Israeli conflict.

Fall of the Monarchy

When 1978 began, Iran seemed to be stable and the shah's position secure, as implied by Carter's toast. Trouble started a week later when the shah's information minister planted an article in Tehran's leading newspaper attacking Khomeini. This led to a sit-in by religious students in Qom, who were attacked and killed by police. From then on, riots would break out every forty days, it being the Muslim custom to hold a memorial service on the fortieth day after a death. In response to the spreading protest, the shah replaced his SAVAK chief and his prime minister. A fire in an Abadan theater, killing 477 people, was widely blamed on SAVAK agents. In early September troops opened fire on a mass demonstration in Tehran's Jaleh Square, causing between 300 and 1,000 deaths and many injuries. At this time, the leading ayatollah in Tabriz, Shariat-Madari, told the new premier that the riots would continue until he restored parliamentary government under the 1906 constitution and let Khomeini come back from his fourteen-year exile in the Shi'ite holy city of Najaf in Iraq. Instead of readmitting the ayatollah, the Iranian government asked Iraq to expel him.

This move hurt the shah, for Khomeini moved to a Paris suburb, where other exiled opposition leaders gathered around him. Soon the ayatollah, viewed in the West as a throwback to the Middle Ages, was spreading his Islamist message by means of long-distance phone calls, cassette tapes, and Western television news broadcasts. His call for a workers' strike almost shut down Iran's oil industry. Foreign companies and customers, remembering the Arab oil embargo of 1973, feared new shortages. Oil prices shot up. As the gravity of the Iranian crisis became clear in Washington, Carter's advisers debated whether to offer the shah more military support or to replace him with a regency for his eighteen-year-old son under a liberal coalition government. The shah declared martial law in early November, named a general as his premier, and banned all demonstrations during the ten days devoted to mourning the martyrdom of Husayn (the Prophet's grandson). The oil workers' strike spread to other industries. Mobs looted and burned Tehran boutiques, liquor stores, cinemas, and other symbols of Western influence. Almost all members of the royal family, most foreigners, and many rich and educated Iranians left the country. Rallies and riots continued. Carter's special envoy urged the shah to form a coalition cabinet that would include opponents of his regime. On 6 January 1979 he asked the National Front's vice president, Shapur Bakhtiar, to head a government; ten days later the shah left Iran forever.

Joyful demonstrations followed his departure, but the crisis continued as Khomeini, still in Paris, called on Iranians to overthrow Bakhtiar's government. The ayatollah was gradually taking charge as he set up his Revolutionary Islamic Council and refused to compromise with Bakhtiar, who gave in to popular pressure to let him return. Soon after Khomeini's arrival, the Iranian army stopped protecting the government; many soldiers gave away their guns and joined the demonstrators. On 11 February the shah's imperial guard fell, and so did Bakhtiar's cabinet. At no time could the United States (or any other outside power) have intervened to save the shah's regime.

Establishment of the Republic

The first revolutionary cabinet, headed by Mehdi Bazargan, an engineer who had managed Iran's nationalized oil industry under Mosaddiq, combined moderate reformers with Muslim hard-liners. It called on the strikers to go back to work (most did) and set up a national plebiscite on Iran's future government. Held in March, the referendum showed near-unanimous support for an Islamic republic, as advocated by the ayatollah. An assembly of lawyers and 'ulama drew up a new constitution; revolutionary committees effected drastic changes throughout the country. Royal symbols were destroyed in actions that ranged from blowing up statues to cutting the shah's picture out of the paper money. The poor seized and occupied abandoned palaces, streets were renamed, textbooks were rewritten, political prisons were emptied (soon they would be refilled), and agents of the old regime were tried and executed. When Westerners deplored these often violent acts, Iranians asked why the shah's government had committed worse atrocities without being scolded by the Western media.

Tehran's new regime was soon challenged by nationalist revolts—Turks in Azerbaijan, Kurds, Arabs, Baluchis, and Khurasani Turcomans—all seeking greater autonomy. It was the old story of Iran's regional and ethnic forces battling against the central government in a time of crisis. The revolutionary regime had to restore the army and the secret police—even some of the shah's personnel—to protect itself. Under the new constitution, legislative authority would be vested in a Majlis, whose candidates would be vetted by 'ulama. 'Ulama would also dominate the courts, and in contested cases verdicts would be made by Khomeini acting as the state's leading *faqih* (judicial expert). In mid-1979 the 'ulama did not yet have full control. Premier Bazargan and other moderates were trying to maintain some ties to the West, and both the left-wing revolutionary committees and the remaining right-wing generals posed potential threats to the regime.

The Hostage Crisis

The revolution shook US-Iranian relations. It exposed the weakness of Washington's Middle East policy, which had counted on a stable, pro-Western regime in Tehran. Carter had brought Egypt and Israel together to sign a peace treaty, which aroused widespread Muslim (not just Arab) anger against Sadat. Iranians seized Israel's embassy in Tehran and gave it to the PLO, and the new regime invited 'Arafat to Iran. In February, militants broke into the US Embassy, but the government promptly drove them out. Iranians anxiously watched the deposed shah's movements, recalling how he had fled at the height of Mosaddiq's power in 1953, only to return following the CIA-backed coup. Would history repeat itself? The shah moved from Egypt to Morocco to the Caribbean to Mexico as his health grew worse. The Carter administration, concerned about Americans still in Iran, hoped the shah would not come to the United States. In October, though, his doctors advised him to go to New York for specialized treatment. Pressured by the shah's friends (among them Henry Kissinger), the US government admitted him.

In response to this provocation, a group of female students followed by armed men broke into the US Embassy compound (whose marine guards had been ordered not to resist) and took sixty-three Americans hostage. They demanded that the United States send the shah back to Iran for trial and apologize for its role in his crimes and human rights abuses against the Iranian people. The US government and people saw this act as a gross violation of international law. Popular slogans such as "Nuke Iran" articulated the people's anger, and most Americans urged Carter to punish Iran. However, attacking Iran would have enraged the whole Muslim world and endangered the hostages. Washington stopped buying oil from Iran, froze more than $11 billion in Iranian assets deposited in US banks, required 50,000 Iranians holding US student visas to register, and took various measures in other countries (and in NATO, the UN, and the World Court) to pressure Iran's government to make the militants set the hostages free from their captivity in the embassy. Nothing worked.

The US government's restraint could not stop angry mobs from storming its embassies in Pakistan and Libya. Sunni militants captured the main mosque in Mecca and held it for two weeks before the Saʿudi army and national guard took it back in a bloody struggle. Shiʿite militants demonstrated in eastern Saʿudi Arabia. In effect, the ayatollah and the militant students holding the embassy came to symbolize a new assertiveness against Western power by peoples of non-Western countries; in the eyes of the American public, they stood for their government's weakness against militant Islam. Why such different perceptions? Americans generally knew and cared little about their foreign policy and how it affected other people. Nonetheless, Iran and the United States, however hostile to each other in November 1979, would still need each other in the long run. The Soviet Union reminded them of this the next month when it sent 86,000 troops into neighboring Afghanistan.

The hostage crisis, during its 444-day duration, sparked major changes: Premier Bazargan's replacement by an avowed Khomeini supporter; the

Soviet occupation of Afghanistan in December 1979; the movement of US forces into the Indian Ocean; the military takeover in Turkey to end fighting between its Muslim and Marxist factions; Iraq's invasion of Iran in September 1980; and Reagan's decisive victory over Carter in the 1980 election. Iran could no longer sell oil to Western customers, causing domestic hardships such as unemployment and price inflation. The hostage crisis also strengthened the militant 'ulama against their rivals—secular nationalists, moderate reformers, Marxists, and separatists. When a secular nationalist won Iran's presidential election, causing Americans to hope he would release the hostages, the ayatollah made sure he was stymied by Muslim militants in the cabinet and in the new Majlis.

No Western-educated politician, no matter how strongly he had opposed the shah, could hold power in Iran's new regime, but the Iranian army regained some of its luster (and power) when the US attempt to rescue the hostages failed in April 1980. However, things began to change when Iraq invaded Iran that September. Once Iran found itself at war with Iraq, it began looking for money and military support. The shah died, and therefore Iran had no reason to continue holding the remaining fifty-two hostages (some of the captives had already been freed by this time). Following patient mediation by Algerian diplomats, Iran agreed to free the hostages in return for the release of its frozen assets, from which would be deducted an escrow fund to cover claims made against the Iranian government (the amount returned was about $8 billion), and a pro forma US promise not to meddle in its internal affairs.

Once the hostages were freed, Iran faded from Americans' minds. In 1981, political unrest intensified throughout the Middle East; bombs and bullets randomly killed ayatollahs, presidents, prime ministers, and party leaders. Iran's elected president, Abol-Hasan Bani-Sadr, won some popularity by visiting Iranian forces fighting against Iraq, but he was gradually shorn of his power. Finally forced to resign, he went into exile in France, where he joined the growing number of Iranians plotting to overthrow the ayatollah. The much-feared Soviet invasion never came, despite Iranian aid to the Afghan rebels. Rather, Moscow sent arms and advisers to the new regime, which consolidated its power but became as repressive as the late shah's government. By August 1979 the government had set up an auxiliary army, the Islamic Revolutionary Guard Corps, which trained Muslim (especially Shi'ite) militants from many countries in the techniques of insurgency. The results of these labors would be seen in various violent incidents during the 1980s, notably in Lebanon and in some of the Gulf states.

THE STRUGGLE FOR GULF SUPREMACY

During the 1970s most of the oil bought by non-Communist industrial
countries came from states surrounding the Gulf: Oman, the United
Arab Emirates, Qatar, Bahrain, Saʻudi Arabia, Kuwait, Iraq, and Iran (see
Map 18.1). Huge tankers carried the oil through the Straits of Hormuz
and the Gulf of Oman into the Arabian Sea and the Indian Ocean. Even
when Iran, OPEC's second-greatest oil producer up to 1978, cut its output during the revolution, the slack was soon taken up by Saʻudi Arabia
and its neighbors. The revolution also ended Iran's role, taken over from
Britain, as the policeman of the Gulf area. The other countries had big
oil resources and revenues, small native populations (Iraq was the exception), and many immigrant workers. Pundits feared at the time that these
workers—usually young adult males, unmarried or without their families
and often coming from countries far away—might subvert conservative
Gulf societies. They never did.

The US government feared a possible Soviet invasion across Iran, for
the Russians had long been thought to harbor designs on the Gulf and
its oil. The Soviet government, in response, noted various speeches and
articles in which Americans threatened to seize the oil fields to protect
them against revolutionaries. The local Arab rulers, hereditary monarchs
except in Iraq, feared revolutions like the one that convulsed Iran but did
not want to open their lands to US military bases. When some Americans
voiced the hope that Israel would defend their oil interests, the Arabs replied that they feared Israeli expansion more than the spread of Soviet
power.

This outlook was jolted a bit when the Soviet Union, annoyed by the
ineptitude of the Marxist regime it had helped set up in Afghanistan, invaded the country in late 1979. This sudden and massive influx of Soviet
troops into a mountainous land poor in oil resources but strategically
close to both Pakistan and Iran budged Arab perceptions slightly but galvanized Washington to act. Addressing Congress in January 1980, Carter
warned that any attempt by an outside force to gain control of the Gulf
area would be viewed as an attack on US vital national interests and could
lead to war. This Carter Doctrine, as it came to be called, was a risky declaration by the United States at a time when its embassy in Iran (the country
most apt to be invaded) was occupied by militants backed by their own
government. The United States also lacked the means to transport, deploy,
and maintain a fighting force large enough to deter Soviet aggression, if
any were contemplated. At this time no Gulf state wanted to base US naval

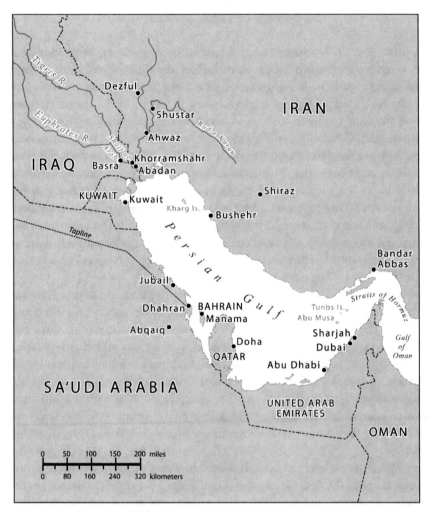

Map 18.1   The Persian Gulf area

or military personnel. The Gulf states purchased more arms, trained more troops, and coordinated their military planning, under their new Gulf Co-operation Council (GCC), formed in 1981.

No superpower confrontation occurred in the Gulf region, because neither side would risk a war to occupy it. In 1979–1980 the United States seemed perilously weak, but the Soviet Union was soon vulnerable, too, for about a fifth of its people—and a higher proportion of its youths—were Muslim. Most Soviet Muslims could be reached by Tehran radio, and some listened to Islamist and nationalist propaganda. The Soviets also found that their prolonged occupation of Afghanistan was costly in lives and equipment, insufficient to pacify the mountainous countryside, and bitterly resented in other Muslim countries, which took in about 4 million Afghan refugees. The United States and the Soviet Union thus kept each other from becoming the dominant power in the Gulf, but both committed ships and troops to the region and escorted Kuwaiti oil tankers past would-be Iranian attackers under their own flags.

The Gulf states realized that their own security depended on a balance of power: never letting one country become strong enough to control all the others. During the 1970s Iran had dominated the Gulf because of the shah's military buildup. When a rebellion, abetted by South Yemen (and indirectly by the Soviets), had threatened Oman's sultan, Iranian troops rescued him in 1973. When the Kurdish revolt against Iraq heated up in 1973–1974, Iran stopped arming the rebels only after Iraq agreed in 1975 to share its control over the Shatt al-Arab waterway, an agreement that Iraq would denounce in 1980 and revive in 1990. The Islamic Revolution eclipsed Iran's predominance, at least for a while.

Sa'udi Arabia was too sparsely populated and inadequately armed to replace Iran as guardian of the Gulf. But Iraq aspired to do so. The second largest of the eastern Arab states in both area and population, Iraq had used its abundant oil resources since the 1930s to build an economic infrastructure suited to both industrial and agricultural development. Political turbulence from 1958 to 1970 (plus the Kurdish revolt) slowed its growth, but later Iraq became more stable, under Saddam Husayn's authoritarian rule, and developed rapidly. The country was armed by and aligned with the Soviet Union (although the United States and Europe helped, too).

Yet Iraq did not live up to its potential. With two rivers, abundant oil, deserts, mountains, and fertile valleys, it could have wielded greater power but for the divisions among its people. Iraq's Muslims were more than 60 percent Shi'ite (with strong ties to Iran), and about 30 percent of its Sunni Muslims were either Kurdish or Turkish—yet the government had always been controlled by a Sunni Muslim and Arab elite. Still, Iraq aspired to unite the Arabs, as Prussia had led Germany's unification. It had laid claim to Kuwait beginning in the 1930s, tried to annex it in 1961, and occupied it in 1990. Iraq, never having made an armistice agreement with Israel, gathered all the other Arab heads of state to condemn the Egyptian-Israeli peace treaty in 1979 and block Sadat's peace efforts. When Egypt's Arab League membership was suspended, Iraq hoped to replace it as the leading Arab state. But how could Iraq prove itself?

Its answer was to attack revolutionary Iran in September 1980. President Saddam Husayn accused Iran of violating the 1975 treaty (which he had negotiated on Iraq's behalf) by not giving up a piece of its mountainous territory closest to Baghdad. Iran had also kept three Gulf islands that the shah had annexed from the United Arab Emirates in 1971 because of their proximity to the Straits of Hormuz. Iraq expected Iran's restive minorities, especially the ethnic Arabs of oil-rich Khuzistan, to rebel against Tehran and help their Iraqi liberators. Iran, by the same logic, hoped to weaken Iraq by appealing to its Shi'ite Muslim majority. Neither ploy worked. Each side tried using its air power to destroy the other's oil pipelines and refineries or to demoralize civilians. Iraq invaded the Iranian provinces of Kurdistan and Khuzistan, took Khorramshahr, and surrounded Abadan, whose oil refinery was nearly destroyed. Military and civilian casualties were higher than in any other modern Middle Eastern war, and the Iran-Iraq War lasted much longer than the Iraqis had planned. They had counted on Iran's internal instability, on its inability to buy spare parts for its inherited arsenal of US weapons, and on Western support to help thwart Iran during the American hostage crisis.

Carter's administration backed neither side at first, fearing that an Iranian defeat would enhance Soviet power. The Soviet Union sold its arms to both sides. Iraq got help from Jordan, Sa'udi Arabia, and even Egypt, whereas Iran had the support of Syria and Libya. The status quo states gravitated toward Baghdad and the revolutionary ones toward Tehran. Iran had many trained officers and soldiers, US tanks and aircraft, and three times as many people as Iraq. The two sides settled into a stalemate for more than a year, but in 1982 Iran struck back. Roused by the ayatollah's religious appeals, Iran's army (augmented by teenage volunteers) retook nearly all the lands Iraq had won earlier. Tehran demanded that Iraq admit to having started the war, pay an indemnity, and oust Saddam Husayn.

The Soviets veered toward Iran; Iraq, without renouncing its ties with Moscow, made overtures to the Reagan administration. Israel, too, entered the picture by bombing Iraq's French-built nuclear reactor in 1981 just before it was to go into operation and by selling arms and spare parts to Iran, despite Tehran's fierce anti-Zionist rhetoric, because it feared that an Iraqi victory would unleash Arab militants against the Jewish state. The United States publicly condemned this policy, but in 1986 it became known that the Reagan administration had covertly promoted the Israeli sale of missiles and spare parts to Iran in the hope of securing the release of Americans held hostage by Shi'ite militants in Lebanon. The proceeds of the sales were funneled through secret Swiss bank accounts to aid Contra rebels who were trying to oust the Sandinista regime in Nicaragua. Some reports revealed that Reagan's National Security Council had even urged Sa'udi Arabia and Egypt to help supply spare parts to Iran. To placate Iraq, Washington provided Baghdad with intelligence about Iran.

As the war dragged on, the United States and Israel hoped to prevent either side from winning decisively. However, the prolonged war threatened to impoverish both Iran and Iraq, to draw their backers into the fray, to endanger anyone shipping oil through the Gulf, and to weaken the economies of all oil-exporting states in the region. Both Iran and Iraq attacked oil tankers, not only each other's but those of neutral countries as well. The US government reflagged some Kuwaiti vessels, and its navy escorted them past Iranian mines and speedboats. By 1988 Iran could no longer buy enough arms or spare parts. Iraq was using mustard gas and other chemical weapons against Iran and its Kurdish allies (who were Iraqi citizens). When a US naval ship shot down an Iranian passenger plane and the chorus of protest was curiously muted, Tehran realized it had few friends left in the world. Nearly bankrupt, Iran accepted a 1987 Security Council resolution calling for a ceasefire. The fighting ended in August 1988.

THE RETREAT FROM CAMP DAVID

After having been enemies for thirty years and having fought five wars against each other, Egypt and Israel agreed in 1977–1978 to make peace because both needed a respite from fighting—or so they thought at the time. The protracted arms race and the destructiveness of their wars had impoverished Egypt and turned Israel into a fortress state. The prospect of an end to this cycle of war and rearmament encouraged both Egyptians and Israelis. The terms of the Egyptian-Israeli peace treaty, the Carter administration's greatest achievement, seemed to meet each side's basic needs: the phased restoration to Egypt of the Sinai Peninsula (taken by Israel in 1967); guarantees, backed by a multinational force that included Americans, that neither side would mass its troops to attack the other; mutual diplomatic recognition; and facilitation of trade, communications, tourism, cultural exchanges, and technical aid. The United States would assist ongoing talks between Israel and Egypt—plus, if possible, Jordan and the Palestinians—to arrange full autonomy for those Palestinians under Israeli administration. But this aim was soon frustrated by Begin's government.

Signing the peace treaty with Israel exposed Sadat to the wrath of the other Arab states, but he contemptuously ignored their blandishments and deflected their insults, even when the oil-rich countries cut off aid to Egypt. The Egyptian people did not like to abandon the Arab states to back Israel, but some were also tired of sacrificing their young men in every

Arab war against the Jewish state. Sadat expected the other Arab states to come around to support Egypt's peace policy. Many would do so later, but only Oman and the Sudan backed him in 1979.

If the other Arab states did not get on the peace bandwagon, part of the blame fell on Israel's government, which exploited its deal with Egypt to clamp down on the 2 million Arabs in Gaza, the West Bank, and the Golan Heights. "Full autonomy," Prime Minister Begin explained, was to be accorded to the inhabitants of these occupied areas, provided the Palestinians gained no control over defense, the police, or even the water supply on which their crops and flocks depended. Jews were encouraged by subsidized mortgage loans to settle in these areas so that no outside power (let alone the United Nations) could ever turn the lands over to the Arab majority.

Of course, the Palestinian National Council (the PLO's executive arm) thwarted the peace process, too, by its adherence to the 1964 charter calling for Arab control of all Palestine (meaning Israel's destruction). No one knew what the PLO could do to force or persuade the Israelis to hand their country, or even a part of what had been mandate Palestine, over to the Palestinians. Could Israel somehow coerce or convince the Palestinians to renounce the PLO? The two sides disagreed on how to make peace.

The Assassination of Sadat
The peace treaty with Israel raised the Egyptian people's hopes that some money earmarked for defense could now be shifted into domestic programs. The regained Sinai would become a new frontier for settlement and development. Egypt at peace would draw Western investors and tourists, another boost to economic recovery. The Arab boycott of Egypt after it signed the 1979 treaty did not stop the country's economic revival. Although foreign investment did not measure up to Egypt's hope, earnings from the sale of Egypt's oil, Suez Canal tolls, tourism revenues, and emigrants' remittances all increased after Camp David, giving Egypt a balance-of-payments surplus in 1980 for the first time in years. This surplus did not recur, nor did growth benefit most of the Egyptian people. Sadat was not interested in economic or social issues. His open-door policy benefited only a small group of newly rich entrepreneurs.

The average Egyptian, squeezed by price inflation, housing costs, and deteriorating public services, looked to move to North Africa or the Gulf states. Egypt became overpopulated in the second half of the twentieth century and has remained so ever since. Its agriculture cannot feed its own population. Birth control and family planning are on the rise, but so, too, are the housing and industry that compete with agriculture for Egypt's scarce land. Labor unemployment (or underemployment) holds down Egyptian salaries and wages, and Egypt has many bachelors in their twenties and thirties who still live with parents or other relatives until they can save enough money to move out and get married. Women marry younger, but often to men who are twice as old as they are. There are growing numbers of educated women who, if they find jobs, face sexual discrimination (including harassment) in a male-dominated work environment.

The frustration level in the early 1980s, therefore, was high. Many Egyptians believed Sadat's policies could not or would not help them. Although some Egyptians (especially the most educated) became Marxists, communism had no general appeal in a highly religious society. Religion scored major gains, among Coptic Christians as well as Muslims, after Egypt's 1967 defeat. Islamic groups permeated nearly all aspects of Egyptian life. The Muslim Brothers survived Nasir's purges, and new secret societies arose. Some resorted to terrorist acts. At first, Sadat promoted the formation of nonrevolutionary Muslim societies to counter the Marxist and Nasirite ones, especially at the universities. Muslims demanded that the Shari'a be applied to all the country's laws. The Copts, about a tenth of Egypt's population, also became more politicized, and violent communal strife broke out in a Cairo workers district in July 1981. Even before then, Sadat was clamping down on religious activists, using popular referenda to pass laws to curb opposition to his policies, including to peace with Israel. In September 1981 he banned the Muslim Brothers' popular magazine, *al-Da'wa* (Call [to Islam]); imposed censorship on mosque sermons; and locked up 1,500 alleged opponents without trial. Because the US government was spending $2 billion a year on economic, technical, and military assistance to Egypt, mainly as a result of the treaty with Israel, many Americans failed to see that Sadat had lost touch with his own people.

On 6 October, the eighth anniversary of Egypt's successful crossing of the Suez Canal to attack the Israelis occupying the Sinai, Sadat and most of his top officials were viewing a military parade in Victory City, a Cairo suburb. An army truck halted, apparently because of a mechanical failure, in front of the presidential reviewing stand. Four soldiers jumped out. Thinking they had stopped to salute him, Sadat rose to face them, whereupon they pointed their machine guns at him and opened fire, murdering the president and several of his aides. All but one of the assassins were killed. Police investigations unearthed a large conspiracy, both within the army and throughout Egypt, as well as a network of terrorist groups—the best known was *al-Takfir wa al-Hijra* (meaning, roughly, "Exposing Unbelief and Fleeing Evil"). The captured terrorists, including the surviving assassin, were put on trial. Various Arab leaders, notably Libya's Qadhafi, rejoiced at Sadat's death; only a few Egyptians mourned him. Sadat was killed for more than one reason: Egypt's deteriorating economic and social conditions, the revival of militant Islam, but also, most likely, his willingness to make a separate peace with Israel.

Vice President Husni Mubarak, who had commanded Egypt's air force during the 1973 war, was chosen by the National Assembly (followed by a popular referendum) to succeed Sadat. He declared a state of emergency, clamped tight controls on the universities and the press, and arrested more revolutionaries. But he also freed some of the political and religious leaders Sadat had jailed. He restored some public trust in the government by promising economic and social reforms and by linking himself with Nasir's legacy at the expense of Sadat's. Talks with Israel about Palestinian autonomy dragged on, and in April 1982 Egypt regained the rest of the Sinai. Israel's invasion of Lebanon six weeks later caused Mubarak to recall Egypt's ambassador in Tel Aviv, and relations between the two states turned into a "cold peace." Israel suspected Egypt of backing away from the treaty to regain its leadership of the Arab world; the Egyptian government was embarrassed by Israel's occupation of southern Lebanon and its increasingly repressive policies in the West Bank and Gaza. Egypt did resume diplomatic ties with Jordan, aid Iraq in its war against Iran, and welcome Yasir 'Arafat to Cairo in 1983. Yet at the same time it accepted billions of US aid dollars and continued its war of nerves with Qadhafi.

In 1984 Egypt held its freest parliamentary elections since 1952. Mubarak's National Democratic Party won a majority of People's Assembly seats, but opposition parties, notably the New Wafd, gained ground. Egypt's economy worsened as oil prices fell, and in 1986 security police riots frightened away foreign tourists. Relations with the United States and Israel became frayed at times, but peace prevailed, and Mubarak remained in power. The other Arab governments restored diplomatic ties with Cairo, Egypt was readmitted to the Arab League, and Mubarak led in promoting the peace process.

Israel's Rising Militancy

Peace with Egypt did not make Israel feel secure about its position as a Jewish island in an Arab sea. Increasingly, it considered the United States its only real ally. The Reagan administration had the notion that it could develop a "strategic consensus" of governments opposed to Soviet expansion in the Middle East, including Egypt, Israel, Jordan, Sa'udi Arabia, and

Pakistan. One means of building this consensus was to sell arms. Just after Sadat's assassination, the US Senate—pressured by the White House against the wishes of the AIPAC—voted by a narrow margin to approve the sale of four airborne warning and control system (AWACS) planes to Sa'udi Arabia. Washington's efforts to court pro-Western Arab governments were both a result and a cause of Israel's increasingly militant stance toward Arab governments and the PLO. Since its formation in 1977, Begin's government had followed a harsh policy against Palestinians in the occupied areas. It also backed a group of Jewish militants, *Gush Emunim* (Bloc of the Faithful), in its plans to form new settlements or to raise the Jewish population of those already set up on the West Bank.

Although Palestinians in the occupied territories and other countries viewed the PLO as their representative, Israel regarded it as a terrorist group with which it would never negotiate for peace. If Israel wished to weaken the PLO, it had to attack Lebanon, the PLO's center of operations since Black September 1970. Reluctantly at first, the PLO was drawn into the Lebanese civil war in 1975, suffering a severe defeat when Syria intervened on the Christian side and captured the fortified Palestinian "refugee camp" (really a military base) of Tel Za'tar, near Beirut. Once the Syrians settled in as an occupying army, they gradually shifted to the side of the Lebanese Muslims and the PLO, which became dominant in various parts of Lebanon, including west Beirut.

Palestinian *fida'iyin* often would launch dramatic raids against civilian targets inside Israel. Some of these were in retaliation for Israeli attacks that killed many Palestinian civilians. In March 1978 the Israeli army occupied the area up to the Litani River. The UN Security Council condemned the invasion and set up a 4,000-man, multinational buffer force to replace the Israelis and restore peace to southern Lebanon. Under US pressure, Israel's cabinet agreed to withdraw Israeli forces, provided the PLO was kept out of the buffer zone. The Israelis had no faith in any UN peacekeeping force; instead, they trusted the Christian militia of Sa'd Haddad, a renegade Lebanese colonel who in 1979 set up his "Republic of Free Lebanon" in the south. Israel absorbed the southern Lebanese Christians into its economy, thus gaining an added interest in Lebanon.

Israel went on making intermittent air raids against PLO strongholds in Lebanon, ignoring the UN presence there. These raids were sometimes reprisals or at times intended to provoke Palestinian attacks. Begin also asserted Israel's right to bombard "terrorists" in Lebanon even without prior provocation. The situation worsened in 1981 as Palestinians fired rockets into northern Israel and Israeli artillery pounded the coastal towns of

Sidon and Tyre. Both sides stepped up their attacks. Twice in July, Israeli planes bombed Beirut, killing hundreds and injuring thousands of Lebanese and Palestinian civilians. Reagan's administration sent a special negotiator, Philip Habib, to arrange a ceasefire that 'Arafat, Begin, and all the Lebanese factions accepted, but Lebanon remained tense. Syria refused to remove the surface-to-air missiles it had installed in Lebanon's Biqaʿ Valley, despite Israel's threats to bomb them as it had Iraq's nuclear reactor.

Israel was showing greater hostility toward the Arabs in other ways. On the West Bank it periodically closed Arab schools and universities, expelled elected mayors who backed the PLO, and increased the size and number of Jewish settlements. Israel tried to create "village leagues" as an alternative to the PLO, but few Palestinians came forward. Israel ascribed this attitude to PLO threats to kill would-be collaborators, ignoring the anger fueled by its own policies. According to numerous international organizations that were monitoring the Israeli occupation, Palestinian society was gradually disintegrating. Even if some Palestinians prospered, few were willing to bargain directly with Jerusalem to gain more autonomy. Even replacing the military government with a civilian one did not soften Israel's occupation policies or placate the Palestinians. Rather, they grew more sullen and militant during the 1980s.

As you know, in June 1981 Israel bombed and wiped out Iraq's nuclear reactor. Although Begin justified this belligerent act as necessary for Israel's security, others wondered how secure the Arabs could feel living next door to Israel's functioning reactors and (unacknowledged) possession of nuclear arms. In December 1981 Begin's cabinet formally extended the application of Israeli law to the Golan Heights, which amounted to the area's annexation. The UN Security Council condemned both acts, but Israel ignored the UN response.

The Begin government claimed it had carried out its treaty obligations to Egypt. Israel (with US government aid) spent vast sums to move its military equipment from the Sinai to newly constructed bases in the Negev Desert. It offered Israeli settlers generous inducements to leave their homes, factories, and gardens in the Sinai, for Egypt would not let any Israelis stay. When some resisted, the IDF removed the recalcitrant settlers and bulldozed all buildings just before the area was restored to Egypt. When Egypt got back the rest of the Sinai in April 1982, the sole contested area was a 250-acre (105-hectare) plot on the Gulf of ʿAqaba containing an Israeli hotel in the village of Taba, just on the Egyptian side of the international frontier. The Taba Affair was finally submitted to arbitration and resolved in Egypt's favor in 1989.

Israel's Invasion of Lebanon
The strife in Lebanon—Christian against Muslim, rich fighting poor, Lebanese separatist versus Arab nationalist—went on and on. By the 1980s many of the fighters were teenagers who had never known peace. In May 1982 Israel bombed a Palestinian base near Beirut, killing twenty-five people. The Palestinians shelled northern Israel, and unidentified agents killed an Israeli diplomat in Paris and badly wounded Israel's ambassador in London. This last act provided the pretext for a massive IDF invasion of southern Lebanon on 6 June. Ignoring all outside diplomatic efforts to stop the fighting, Israel thrust northward, bypassing the UN troops and pushing back both PLO and Syrian forces. The Arabs suffered many casualties. Thousands of civilians, Lebanese and Palestinian alike, lost their homes. Taking advantage of surprise and complete control over the air, the Israelis bombed Beirut heavily and destroyed many Syrian missiles in the Biqa' Valley. Extensive press and television coverage showed the efficiency of the IDF invasion—and its cost in human suffering. Israel admitted using US-made cluster bombs against "terrorists" (most of the victims were civilians).

The Arab states, including Egypt, condemned the invasion as well as the US vetoes that had blocked two Security Council resolutions against Israel. Noting that the United States kept on arming Israel, the Arabs accused the Americans of backing the invasion. No Arab state sent troops to help the Syrians and Palestinians in Lebanon, and only Iran offered to come to their aid. By mid-June the IDF had surrounded Beirut. For the first time, Israel was besieging an Arab capital, but the Arabs could not defend it. The Soviets thundered and threatened—but did not act. It was at this time that the Iranians set up their revolutionary training centers in the Biqa' Valley.

Washington was free to act, but the Reagan administration was split. Secretary of State Alexander Haig, who might have backed Israel in destroying the PLO in Lebanon, left office. Other US officials were angry at the Israeli invasion, anxious about possible Arab reprisals against American interests, and eager to pacify Lebanon. Some hoped for a general Middle East peace. The new secretary of state, George Shultz, drafted the Reagan Peace Plan, announced on 1 September 1982, calling for Israel's withdrawal from the West Bank and Gaza, free elections, and a five-year transition period to autonomy for the Palestinians and probable federation with Jordan. Israel and the PLO rejected the plan, Egypt accepted it, Jordan looked it over warily, and the Americans quietly shelved it. The Arab heads of state, meeting at Fez in Morocco one week later, produced their own plan, proposing a Palestinian state and hinting at recognizing Israel. The Americans ignored the Arab initiative.

Everyone was watching Lebanon, where Washington acted inconsistently. Vetoing UN Security Council resolutions and arming Israel's forces made the United States a de facto accomplice of the invasion. American diplomat Philip Habib shuttled among Jerusalem, Beirut, and Damascus until he reached a deal calling for a partial Israeli pullback and a complete Palestinian withdrawal from the western half of Beirut, both of which were to be supervised by US Marines and French and Italian soldiers. Negotiations would continue among the parties to set up a new government and to withdraw all foreign forces from Lebanon. In August the fighting in Beirut abated, allowing Israel's forces to pull back and the PLO to get out. Meanwhile, Lebanon's parliament—unchanged for ten years—met to elect a new president. The sole candidate was Bashir Jumayyil, a leader of the Maronite paramilitary group called the Phalanges. Owing to his ties to the Christian side in the civil war, many opposition deputies boycotted the session at which Jumayyil was elected. Elated, Begin hoped Israel could reach a lasting peace with a Christian-dominated Lebanon.

The other side did not give up. On 14 September a bomb blew up the Phalanges' headquarters in east Beirut, killing the occupants, including Bashir Jumayyil. The IDF promptly occupied west Beirut and began rooting out remaining PLO resistance fighters, who, according to Habib's peace plan, should have withdrawn. The IDF allowed the Phalanges to enter the Palestinian suburbs of Shatila and Sabra, where the Lebanese Christians massacred hundreds of Palestinian men, women, and children during a two-day rampage. Everyone was shocked, including the Israelis, who set up a commission to look into the cause of the massacres. The Israeli commission found that the IDF commander, General Ariel Sharon, had facilitated the Sabra and Shatila massacres and called for his exclusion from future cabinets. The US-French-Italian force was brought back into Beirut—for a longer stay this time—to restore peace. Lebanon's parliament elected Amin Jumayyil, Bashir's older brother, to serve as president.

If Lebanon were to have peace, the domestic factions would have to revise their government's constitution and disarm their numerous militia groups. Foreign troops—the Syrians authorized by the Arab League to occupy Lebanon, Palestinian fida'iyin, Israeli invaders, the UN buffer force, and the multinational force of France, Italy, and the United States (also joined by Britain)—would all have to leave the country. But in what order? The United States wanted a phased withdrawal, to be negotiated by all the involved parties. Syria wanted the other foreign troops to leave unconditionally. In late 1982 and early 1983, representatives of Lebanon,

Israel, and the United States carried on lengthy deliberations leading to a treaty laboriously crafted by Shultz. It soon collapsed, as the IDF would not leave unless the Syrians and the PLO simultaneously withdrew their armies from the parts of Lebanon they were occupying. Syrian president Hafiz al-Assad, opposed by Islamist Sunnis at home (he had massacred at least 20,000 of them and leveled half of Syria's conservative Muslim city, Hama, in 1982), refused to oblige the Americans by pulling out of Lebanon. Although Amin Jumayyil had signed it, the 1983 Lebanese-Israeli Treaty became a dead letter.

The emerging force in Lebanon was one that no one had ever noticed before. In the war's early years, outside observers assumed that the main religious groups were Maronite Christians and Sunni Muslims. Westerners ignored the Shi'ite Muslims, who predominated in the Biqa' Valley and parts of southern Lebanon. Gradually, though, they had become the country's largest sect, and many were flocking to Beirut's poorer districts in search of work. Many Shi'ites at first welcomed Israel's invasion, hoping it might weaken the Sunni Lebanese and the Palestinians. But when the Israeli forces refused to leave, the Shi'ites turned against them. More and more Shi'ite youths were willing to become martyrs to drive out the Israelis and their perceived allies, the US troops. A series of suicide bombings ensued, hitting the US embassies and Marine barracks and French military headquarters (partly because France was arming Iraq against Iran). US and Israeli reprisals against villages believed to be harboring Shi'ite fighters rendered many Lebanese homeless and further embittered the people against foreigners. The 241 American deaths caused by the Marine barracks blast, the threats against other US citizens in Lebanon, and the murder of President Malcolm Kerr of the American University of Beirut sapped the will of the US peacekeeping mission. Reagan decided to remove the contingent to the Sixth Fleet offshore, and the French, British, and Italian contingents also pulled out in early 1984.

The Terrorist Triumph

West Beirut fell under the control of Shi'ite and Druze militia, and the fighting raged on in the rest of Lebanon. Amin Jumayyil's government could not restore order, even though it renounced its treaty with Israel. Internal struggles split most of the sects and also the Palestinians, as Syria backed a faction opposed to 'Arafat. In the mid-1980s, US and other foreign nationals still in Lebanon were being kidnapped by shadowy Shi'ite gangs and held for ransom, which Western governments vowed never to pay (but sometimes did, secretly). The hijacking of passenger aircraft and even a cruise ship enhanced the Middle East's reputation for terrorism. The really striking development was that Lebanon's Shi'ite Muslims achieved so much more than the PLO had at the expense of the Israelis, who withdrew from most of Lebanon—without a treaty—in 1985. The Palestinian organization had the diplomatic and financial support of most of the Arab countries, but the Shi'ite groups, the largely secular *Amal* (Hope) led by Nabih Berri, the breakaway Islamic Amal, and especially the pro-Iranian *Hizballah* (Party of God), earned the credit for driving Israeli and Western troops out of Lebanon. A factor in the Shi'ites' success was their willingness to sacrifice their lives for their cause, inspired by the Ayatollah Khomeini's teachings, the success of the Iranian revolution, and, especially, the example set in 680 by Muhammad's grandson Husayn against his oppressors.

Terrorism is an old method of warfare that has been practiced around the world, oftentimes when individuals and groups cannot attain dignity, freedom, or justice against powers that rely on armies, police, and other conventional forces to maintain their control. Its basic aim is to force other individuals or groups—and their countries—to take unwanted political actions that serve the terrorists' needs. Terrorists tend to be educated youths full of zeal and determination. They believe their religion or nationality has been oppressed and must be vindicated. But governments, too, promote terrorism to demoralize their foes. Israel's bombardment of Palestinians in 1981 was a form of state-sponsored terrorism, as were Assad's massacre of Sunni Muslims in Hama in 1982 and Saddam's poison gas attacks on Iraqi Kurds in 1988.

Formerly, Middle Eastern governments and peoples had been more often victimized by terrorism than Americans and Europeans, but the terrorists now struck at the West to get vengeance. Nearly all governments condemn terrorism, but they do not agree on how to combat it, and some regimes even practice it. There are two basic schools of thought on the issue: (1) terrorism can be deterred by striking back at its perpetrators and cowing them into submission, and (2) the only way to stop terrorism is to cure the conditions that cause it. But it is hard to deter terrorists when they are backed by so many of the people around them, when punitive action fails to strike at their source, and when the lives of innocent hostages are at stake.

Reagan and his partisans attacked the Carter government for its weak handling of the American hostage crisis in Iran, but his own administration fared even worse in Lebanon and had to extricate itself from an embarrassing scandal involving the sale of US weapons to Iran. It was nearly impossible to devise policies to cure the conditions that caused terrorism, such as the ongoing Palestinian-Israeli conflict, the civil war in Lebanon, the Iran-Iraq War, urbanization, and poverty. The United Nations had tried for years to address these issues with little success, in part because the United States so often vetoed its resolutions.

WESTERN POLICY FORMATION AND ISLAMIC POLITY

Formulating policies is hard for popularly elected governments, and especially for the United States, with its power divided between the White House and Congress. In the 1980s Washington lacked a Middle East policy, and its susceptibility to both Zionist and oil lobbies made formulating one even harder. It was also a challenge for Israel, which from 1984 to 1988 was led by a shaky combination of the Labor Party, led by Shimon Peres, and the Likud, headed after 1983 by Yitzhak Shamir. The two blocs won nearly equal numbers of seats in the 1984 Knesset elections, and they agreed to form a coalition cabinet in which Peres was premier until 1986, whereupon he was succeeded by Shamir for the next two years. The two men disagreed on their Arab policies: Peres favored and Shamir opposed an international peace conference meant to restore most of the West Bank to Jordan. Shamir wanted indefinite Israeli control over the lands captured in the 1967 War. The Palestinians, too, were divided. Some called for an all-out struggle against the occupation, whereas others advocated that those who had been under Israel's administration for two decades should take an active part in Israeli politics, such as the Jerusalem elections. They also debated how far they could rely on the Arab governments to help them, but after December 1987 they chose to fight for their own cause. Policy debates on both sides did not bring peace.

Governments with a policy on a particular issue will identify its goals and choose the means most likely to reach them. As Iran in the early 1980s hoped to spread Islamic government throughout the Middle East, it formulated a policy of revolutionary subversion to undermine established governments in Muslim states by appealing to their *mostaz'afan* (literally "dispossessed," the people who felt alienated by the Middle East's westernization) and imbuing them with a zeal for self-sacrifice to combat their oppressors. This policy worked for a while in Lebanon, but it foundered on harsh economic realities in the war against Iraq, and eventually Ayatollah Khomeini had to admit that Iran could no longer afford to fight Iraq and finance revolutionary Shi'ite groups in Lebanon. Economic recovery became Iran's goal, downgrading the export of its revolution. If Israel in the 1980s wanted to ensure its survival in a hostile Arab world, the best policy seemed to be to cow enemies so thoroughly that no one would attack it. But this means could not ensure security, because the Lebanese Shi'ites and Palestinians refused to be intimidated and stepped up their attacks on Israel.

If the Reagan administration wanted a friendly Middle East, it initially thought it could build a strategic consensus of governments opposed to the Soviet Union, but this was a misguided policy, for most Middle Eastern governments feared Israel, one another, or internal revolutions more than they dreaded a Soviet invasion. Later, he would seek peace between Israel and the Arabs and among contending factions in Lebanon based on compromises that ignored the true aims of both sides. Even later, he would try to soothe the American public, condemning hostage-taking in Lebanon and other acts of terrorism yet selling arms to bargain, indirectly, with terrorist captors for the release of their hostages. Reagan used a feel-good approach; his was not a policy of ends and means.

Policymaking was defective throughout the Khomeini decade. The Islamic Republic of Iran managed to survive all attempts—internal, Iraqi, and US—to topple it and even repaid a $7 billion debt inherited from the shah; but the republic nearly ruined its economy and hastened the exodus of its richest and best-educated citizens. Iran persuaded no other country to become an Islamic republic. Khomeini and his cohorts claimed that they could re-establish the Shari'a as the law of the land, but Iranians still evaded its bans on women's cosmetics, drug addiction (opium abuse soared in Iran), and rock music. The Arab states continued to pursue policies that caused them to quarrel among themselves. Israeli policies demoralized the country and did not enhance its security. The US government did not know how to deal with Middle Eastern fundamentalism, whether Muslim, Jewish, or Christian, and its attempts at repressing terrorism by bombarding Lebanese villages in 1983 and the Libyan capital in 1986 enraged peoples who might once have supported its interests. Khomeini's Islamic Republic, Menachem Begin and Yitzhak Shamir's Greater Israel, Yasir 'Arafat's equivocation, and Ronald Reagan's patriotism all failed to illumine their policies.

The Islamic Revolution in the Middle East, as inspired by the Ayatollah Khomeini, ended with his death in June 1989. Indeed, it had been declining for several years, as Iran's revolutionary zeal waned and Iraq regained the lands it had earlier lost. Islam is a religion and a way of life; it is not a political ideology. Before 1979 Westerners underestimated Islam's power over the hearts and minds of Muslims; during the 1980s they overestimated it. Throughout history, Islamic beliefs and institutions strongly influenced the people of the Middle East, but no leader, not even Muhammad, could make Islam the sole determinant of what Muslims thought and did. The Shari'a always coexisted with other legal systems, including the edicts of kings and governors. The imperial tradition of Achaemenid Iran coexisted through the ages with the Islamic vision of Muhammad. Civil officials and military officers wielded power in an ongoing symbiosis (or rivalry) with caliphs and 'ulama.

CONCLUSION

The Islamic Revolution enabled the *mostaz'afan* to find their voice and to vent their anger on rulers and foreign advisers who exalted material wealth and power in the name of "modernization." Anger can be a powerful tool, but it does not make policy, feed the hungry, shelter the homeless, win the war, or lay the basis for peace. Religion can be a source of meaning and morality for its followers, but today's world is far more complex than the one in which the Shari'a took form. Many skills are needed to meet its challenges, whether within the lands of Islam or between Muslims and non-Muslims. All people touched by the "fundamentalist" revival are free to harness the wisdom of religion to solve economic and social problems, resolve conflicts, and create peace. It is time for Muslims and other people to work together on a basis of mutual understanding and respect. Washington should learn this lesson, too. Chapter 19 will show how, in the 1990s, the superpowers, the Middle Eastern countries, and Muslims generally ignored these exhortations.

19

The Gulf War
and the Peace Process

The Cold War ended around 1991, but we live in a world of wrenching change and rising conflict between and within nations. People are frustrated with their governments, with the conditions of their daily lives, and with the lack of the respect they believe they deserve from other people or governments. Frustration causes uprisings against entrenched regimes, religious and ethnic strife, demands for more popular participation in politics, and repressive governments. In the Middle East such problems were less visible in the 1990s than in other parts of Africa and Asia, but they lurked beneath the surface and have come back to haunt us in the new millennium. Following the Soviet Union's collapse, three Caucasian and five Central Asian states were born. Communism lost its power and allure in the Middle East.

Meanwhile, Western news media and politicians talked about the threat of "terrorism" and "Islamic fundamentalism." Middle Eastern peoples felt threatened, too. The power of the West was increasing. It had a military buildup in Saʿudi Arabia in answer to Iraq's invasion of Kuwait in August 1990. Additionally, the 1991 Gulf War, in which the coalition of American, European, and Arab forces drove the invaders back into Iraq after aerial attacks caused devastation in much of the country but did not topple its leader.

The Arab world felt divided, defenseless, and despondent about its inability to set its own course. Many Arabs who had once hoped to replicate Turkey's leap into modernity came to believe that imported ideologies and programs had divided them. Rather, Iran's Islamic Revolution pointed to a new direction to follow, but the model attracted mostly the people and not their governments. Arab leaders began open negotiations with Israel in Madrid and Washington and secret ones in Oslo and other cities. Israel broke an ancient taboo when it talked to the PLO. A laborious peace process began between the two sides, but neither was willing to offer what would most allay the other's fears. Threats of Arab violence and annihilation still haunted the Israelis, and the reality of Israel's domination and reprisals hobbled the Palestinians, who openly defied Israel's soldiers. Turkey tried to join the European Union, but it could not meet Western standards of respect for human rights when faced with a Kurdish rebellion in its southeastern provinces. Iran spoke of exporting Islamic principles to the rest of the Muslim world, but its citizens twice elected a president whose policies would moderate its revolution at home to rebuild its own society.

The period from 1990 to 2001 was one of wars, power struggles between and within Middle Eastern countries, acts of terrorism (variously defined), and the mirage of peace between Israel and the Palestinians. It was a frustrating time for all.

THE GULF CRISIS

A geological fact created a historical anomaly. Petroleum and natural gas abound in the arid lands surrounding the Gulf, where, until the 1960s, the population was sparse, mainly nomadic, and ignored by the outside world. Most of these lands remained under tribal shaykhs and amirs while army officers elsewhere in the Middle East were replacing monarchies with republics. During the middle third of the twentieth century, a motley assortment of states emerged. These ranged from Sa'udi Arabia, united by Ibn Sa'ud and enriched by oil discoveries far beyond anything he or his subjects ever could have imagined, to such minuscule emirates as Fujairah, known best for its postage stamps, and Bahrain, a fading oil producer that developed banking and tourist facilities. We call every country a "nation," but do principalities like Qatar and Dubai owe their existence to the political loyalties of their citizens? The combination of two well-armed and populous countries possessing abundant oil reserves, Iran and Iraq, with many tiny states that also had oil but no means of self-defense created a volatile situation. The perceived problem receded during the 1980–1988 Iran-Iraq War, but the potential for conflict resurfaced once the war ended.

Iraq's Complaints and Claims

Iraq arguably suffers psychological complexes about being second in the Arab world. Egypt has more influential universities, publishing houses, newspapers, and radio and television stations. Syria pioneered the development of Arab nationalism, even though Iraq became independent sooner and championed Arab unity in the 1930s and 1940s. And Sa'udi Arabia's oil, although discovered later than Iraq's, forged ahead in output and proven reserves. Iraqis think, therefore, that other Arabs (to say nothing of non-Arabs) do not respect them. Although many Arab states furnished huge loans and supplied arms to Saddam Husayn's regime during its war against Iran, Iraq spent blood and treasure purportedly to blunt the spread of Islamist militancy from Tehran to the Arab world.

A related complex is the belief of many Iraqis that Western imperialism, especially British, tried to stifle the country's development by carving out a separate emirate called Kuwait. Iraq argued that Kuwait had no right to independence. Its ruling Sabah family had recognized Ottoman suzerainty over Kuwait during the nineteenth century. In 1899, however, Shaykh Mubarak Al Sabah (r. 1896–1915) signed a treaty making the British responsible for Kuwait's defense and foreign relations, thus severing it from Ottoman control. Britain, seeking to protect its routes to India, had already made similar treaties with other tribal leaders along the Persian Gulf. During the twentieth century such pacts preserved an archaic political alignment in that area long after other Middle Eastern states had cast off monarchical rule and colonial dependency. When the British fixed the borders of their Iraqi mandate in 1921, its leaders complained that Kuwait's excision left Iraq with almost no access to the Gulf. Once Iraq gained its independence in 1932, it called for border adjustments. When British forces withdrew from Kuwait in 1961, 'Abd al-Karim Qasim tried to replace them with Iraqis, but the other Arab states and Britain sent in troops to stop Iraq's leader from annexing the emirate. Baghdad argued intermittently that Kuwait was legally Iraqi territory and that it had never formally ratified its recognition of Kuwaiti independence.

During its eight-year war with Iran, however, Iraq needed loans more than land, borrowing more than $15 billion from Kuwait—a sum it would not repay after the war. Kuwait had islands, as yet undeveloped, that could have served as loading and shipping facilities for Iraq's petroleum exports. Both Iraq and Iran needed more oil income after 1988 to rebuild their war-torn economies. To raise revenues, they had to either pump more oil or sell it for more money. Kuwait's aggressive oil sales (at cut-rate prices) helped neither Baghdad nor Tehran.

Kuwait's legendary wealth, derived from selling oil discovered and developed by foreigners, served mainly to enrich the Sabah dynasty and a few Kuwaitis who could prove that their families had long lived in the emirate, not the flood of poor immigrants from other Arab states or from lands as far away as Bangladesh and the Philippines. These guest workers, however valued they might have been for their brawn, brains, and labor, did not enjoy the rights of Kuwaitis. Seldom could foreigners get Kuwaiti citizenship, even if they had worked in the country for forty years; nor could their children, even if they had lived there all their lives. By what special merit did a few Kuwaitis amass such fortunes while most other Arabs remained poor?

Kuwaitis reply that in the eighteenth century their Bedouin ancestors settled in a sheltered inlet near the northwestern end of the Gulf and set up a small fort (*kuwayt* in Arabic) there. In 1756 the settlers chose a member of the Sabah family to manage their affairs. Although many Kuwaitis remained nomadic and national borders were fixed only in the twentieth century, they were not just "tribes with a flag." Some Kuwaitis took up trading, shipbuilding, pearl diving, and fishing. In the late 1930s, an Anglo-American firm found oil. But it was only after 1945 (when Kuwait had 150,000 inhabitants) that petroleum output became the basis for national wealth and the population skyrocketed.

Kuwaitis have shrewdly invested their oil revenues to build a modern infrastructure, educate their youths, invest billions of dollars abroad, set aside funds for a future when oil wells may dry up, and support less opulent but more populated Arab states that might protect them against aggression. Because up to 1990 a quarter of Kuwait's inhabitants were Palestinians, the regime backed the PLO and related causes economically and politically. Far from depending on the West, Kuwait was the first small Gulf state to form diplomatic ties with Communist countries. It was the only Gulf state that had a popularly elected parliament, although the amir dissolved it twice and suffrage was limited to males who could prove they descended from pre-1920 inhabitants. In 1990 Kuwait would be attacked by Iraq for not raising its oil prices or for not curtailing production to assist Iraq's redevelopment after 1988. Was it wrong to expect Iraq to pay back its loans?

Iraq's Annexation of Kuwait

The Iraqi army invaded and occupied Kuwait shortly after midnight on 2 August 1990. The Kuwaiti amir, Shaykh Jabir Al Ahmad Al Sabah; some of his relatives and high officials; and many of his subjects fled to neighboring Sa'udi Arabia. From there they called on the international community, mainly the United States, to help them win back their country. Iraqi president Saddam Husayn had accused Kuwait of pumping his country's share of oil from their jointly owned Rumayla oil field and of plotting to impoverish Iraq by overproducing oil to drive down its price on the world market. Efforts in late July by Egyptian president Husni Mubarak and Sa'udi king Fahd to mediate between Iraq and Kuwait did not satisfy the Iraqi leader. Foreign intelligence sources knew that Iraqi forces were amassing near Kuwait's border in late July, but few had expected Saddam to order an invasion. However much they quarrel, Arab states seldom invade one another.

Iraq's invasion and subsequent annexation of Kuwait ignited a diplomatic crisis. The other Arab states reacted slowly; an emergency Arab summit was called but then canceled. Did Arab leaders ignore the obvious danger? If Iraq could get away with invading another Arab country, what was to stop other strong states from seizing their most vulnerable neighbors? By contrast, the US government promptly condemned the invasion and froze all Iraqi and Kuwaiti assets in the United States. After winning the Sa'udi government's consent, George H. W. Bush's administration began airlifting troops and supplies into the desert kingdom, which had formerly barred foreign troops from Sa'udi territory—or had kept their presence as inconspicuous as possible. By the end of October 1990, more than 200,000 American men and women in uniform were encamped in northeastern Sa'udi Arabia. In the following month, Bush would double the size of that force, adding offensive units to the mainly defensive ones he had already sent, a step that marked Washington's commitment to driving the Iraqi forces from Kuwait. Many other countries, including Egypt and Syria, sent troops to join in an allied coalition with the US forces in what was officially called Operation Desert Shield.

The UN Security Council passed a series of resolutions calling on Iraq to withdraw unconditionally from Kuwait and on other member states to impose economic sanctions against Iraq until it did so. Except for small amounts of food and medicine, Iraq could not import any goods from abroad, nor could it export any oil to earn the money needed to rebuild its war-torn economy. As the sanctions tightened and Saddam did not flinch, President Bush and British prime minister Margaret Thatcher threatened military action against Iraq. The United States and its allies rebuffed mediation attempts by King Husayn of Jordan and other leaders, ordering Iraq to obey the Security Council resolutions immediately and unconditionally. To Saddam and his supporters, these demands were a direct challenge; they refused to pull out.

Iraqis looted Kuwaiti homes and despoiled schools, libraries, and businesses. Saddam's regime detained thousands of foreign nationals caught in Kuwait by the invasion, bused them to Baghdad, and housed some in

Iraqi factories or military bases as "human shields" against foreign attacks. Baghdad ordered foreign embassies to leave Kuwait, proclaimed it Iraq's nineteenth province, and tried to efface all evidence of Kuwait's existence as a separate state. Any resistance by the local inhabitants was suppressed. Thousands of Kuwaitis fled from their homes to other Arab countries.

Sadder yet was the plight of long-resident foreign workers in Kuwait and, to a lesser degree, in Iraq itself. Stripped of all the goods and money they had acquired, Egyptians, Yemenis, Pakistanis, Indians, Sri Lankans, and Filipinos straggled across the desert to Jordan, where they filled squalid, makeshift refugee camps until their countries could airlift them safely home. Most were young men and women who had come from poor households to Kuwait or Iraq to make money to send to their families. Now that they had lost everything, they and their dependents faced bleak employment prospects back home, and their countries would miss the hard-currency income once generated by their remittances.

Soaring oil prices, rising unemployment, and dislocations caused by the anti-Iraq sanctions battered the already reeling economies of the Middle East and the West. How could governments wishing to send troops and supplies to assist Operation Desert Shield find the funds to pay for them? Germany and other European countries, as well as Japan, Sa'udi Arabia, and Kuwait's government-in-exile, pledged billions of dollars. Because so many countries provided troops, tanks, planes, and money to the buildup, who would make the military decisions? How long would the allied coalition remain united?

Although the near unanimity of the United Nations against Iraq's invasion of Kuwait raised hopes that other international disputes might soon be addressed and possibly resolved by the world body, diplomacy might not settle the first issue, let alone others that might be linked with it. Saddam offered to evacuate Kuwait only if all other foreign armies (a direct dig at Israel and Syria) would withdraw from the Middle East lands they were occupying. People feared a prolonged war, marked by aerial bombing of cities and public works, burning oil wells and refineries, missile attacks, poison gas, and even germ warfare. During the fall of 1990, tensions rose in other conflicts, including the one between Israel and the Palestinians.

The Crisis of Arab Legitimacy

To many Arabs (and some non-Arab Muslims), Saddam was a folk hero who defied the West and made everyone re-examine the rules by which Middle East politics were conducted. He entranced the *mostaz'afan*. Most

Palestinians, embittered by Western neglect, Israeli oppression, and abuse from other Arabs, admired him. Pro-Saddam demonstrations spread in Jordan and in Israel's occupied territories, as well as in more remote lands, such as Tunisia, Libya, and Yemen. In countries whose regimes opposed Iraq lest it come to dominate the Arab world, notably Syria and Egypt, some people hailed Saddam in demonstrations that were promptly suppressed. However, some Arabs who had suffered indignities from the Iraqi army and had lost their livelihoods and remittances demonstrated against Saddam.

Iraq's political system, the way in which power was allocated and decisions were made, was highly dictatorial. The state controlled Iraq's major industries, all educational institutions, and the information media. Huge portraits of Saddam Husayn adorned street corners and public buildings. No one could criticize his policies. Summary executions, torture, and long jail terms without trial were common. Most of the military officers and civil officials who had belonged to his Ba'ath Party faction when it seized power in 1968 or who had helped him to become president in 1979 were later purged, exiled, or pensioned off. Saddam surrounded himself with a clique of relatives and friends from his hometown, Tikrit. His army, including the Republican Guard, "popular forces," and reservists, numbered more than 1 million and was the largest and best equipped in the Arab world. France, Germany, the Soviet Union, and even the United States had sold arms to Iraq during its war against Iran. Iraq's use of poison gas against Iranians and even Iraqi Kurds during that war enhanced its army's reputation for cruelty.

Saddam announced in August 1990 (hoping to get Iran to defy the UN sanctions) that Iraq was ready to reinstate the 1975 agreement. This action would allow Iran to share control with Iraq over the Shatt al-Arab and also return other lands Iraq had taken during eight years of war against Iran. Saddam additionally offered to give Iraqi oil to non-Western countries suffering from price hikes caused by the invasion, even after he had just complained that Kuwait was depressing oil prices that Iraq wanted to raise. Iraq's protean interests, which Saddam equated with his own, dictated these drastic policy lurches.

The Syrian and Egyptian governments, as Iraq's main Arab rivals, joined the allied coalition, ignoring their people's opposition to Sa'udi and US policies. Other governments, such as Jordan and Yemen, backed Saddam because of their economic ties with Iraq, at the risk of offending their other neighbors. Almost every Arab regime feels insecure about its own legitimacy. In a crisis, many Arab regimes will resort to some form of coercion to ensure their citizens' obedience. Without a system of collective security, all are vulnerable to invasion. If wealthy Sa'udi Arabia needed Operation Desert Shield for defense against invasion (though Iraq never threatened to occupy the Sa'udi kingdom), how was its government viewed by its own subjects, who had no constitutional means of supporting or opposing its policies? How effectively had the Sa'udis used the costly arms they had already bought from the United States and Britain? Until August 1990 the Sa'udi government could protect its own subjects and, maintaining its legitimacy, guard the holy cities of Mecca and Medina. By January 1991 the whole country was guarded by 500,000 foreign troops. Iraq, however, had no foreign troops on its soil.

OPERATION DESERT STORM

Saddam's rejection of the twelve Security Council resolutions demanding his unconditional withdrawal from Kuwait, combined with Bush's refusal to compromise with Iraq, led to the outbreak of war on 17 January 1991. Operation Desert Storm, the allied coalition's renamed campaign, began with massive aerial bombardments of Iraq's military facilities, as well as many civilian targets. Iraq launched Scud missiles against Israel (which was not part of the allied coalition), hoping to draw it into the war. Saddam calculated that if Israel retaliated against Iraq, the armies of Sa'udi Arabia, Egypt, and Syria would desert the alliance. Under heavy US pressure not to retaliate, Israel complied but threatened to strike back at some future date lest the Palestinians and other Arabs assume that Jerusalem was weak and had to hide behind a battery of Patriot missiles hastily set up by the Americans. Iraqi Scud attacks went on throughout the war, hitting Sa'udi Arabia as well as Israel, but they had no strategic value.

Some of Iraq's other ripostes to the allied air strikes, which soon numbered in the thousands, were more damaging. Saddam ordered the Kuwaiti oil taps opened, spilling millions of gallons of crude petroleum into the Gulf, threatening beaches, wildlife, and even water desalination plants, as well as deterring an amphibious assault on Kuwait City. Allied pilots shot down by Iraqis were captured, tortured, and made to confess on television to crimes against the Iraqi people. As they retreated, Iraq's troops set Kuwait's oil fields on fire. Bush and his coalition partners ordered Iraq to obey all Security Council resolutions. When it rejected their demands, the coalition began a ground offensive that within 100 hours had driven Iraqi troops out of Kuwait. The guns fell silent on 27 February 1991.

After the Storm

The Bush administration and the United States seemed to have won a great victory in a surprisingly short time. People hoped that the US government would bring all the Middle Eastern countries together to settle their political differences. To a degree, it did. Many people also feared that fighting would continue in Iraq, which it certainly did. When coalition forces occupied parts of southern Iraq, the local Shi'ites rose in rebellion against the Baghdad regime, as did the Kurds farther north. Even though the coalition leaders had encouraged these uprisings, they gave no military help either to the Shi'ites, who might have formed an Islamic republic in southern Iraq, or to the Kurds, whose formation of an autonomous Kurdistan might have sparked similar demands by Turkey's Kurds. They did not take out Saddam, who deflected all attempts, military or civilian, to oust him.

Instead, the coalition tried to destroy Iraq's presumed stash of nuclear, biological, and chemical weapons, aiming at Iraq's overall military potential. The United States and its coalition partners maintained for almost thirteen years the UN sanctions that would impoverish the Iraqi people without ever harming their leaders. Saddam believed that he had won the war because he stayed in power, whereas Bush was voted out of office in November 1992. Iraq managed to rebuild its army and the Republican Guard, menacing Kuwait again in 1993 and 1994 and defying UN weapons inspection teams in 1997 and 1998. Meanwhile, more than 1 million Iraqis died because of the sanctions, according to a UN estimate. After years of resistance, Saddam consented to a UN deal that allowed him to sell $2 billion (soon raised to an unlimited amount) worth of Iraqi oil every six months in exchange for imported food, medicine, and other necessities, starting in 1997. Much of the revenue was skimmed off by Saddam and his henchmen. Even though the UN inspectors eventually got access to most of Iraq's military installations and presidential palaces, they were ordered by Washington to leave in 1998, just before an Anglo-American bombing campaign that hurt mainly civilian Iraqis. The embargo on Iraq was increasingly resented in the Middle East. By 2001, most Arab states, Turkey, and Iran were trading with Iraq as though the sanctions had been lifted. No outsider ever found stockpiles of biological, chemical, or nuclear weapons in Iraq.

Kuwait promptly extinguished its burning oil fields, but repair of the damage Iraqi troops had done to its oil installations cost $5.5 billion. It held parliamentary elections in 1992, although women still could not vote and foreign workers still could not become citizens. Thousands of the Palestinians who had built up Kuwait's economy were exiled (without their property) and not readmitted. Their jobs were taken by Egyptians and other foreign nationals.

THE PALESTINIANS:
THEIR STRUGGLE AND AN ELUSIVE PEACE

In the 1990s the Arab-Israeli conflict became the Palestinian-Israeli conflict. Israel's backers used to blame the problem on the refusal of the Arab states to recognize the Jewish state. Well, Egypt did so in 1979, Jordan did so in 1994, and even the PLO did in 1988. The Palestinian people remained victims. Was this because certain Arab governments, notably Lebanon, refused to absorb them? Other Arab states, such as Jordan, granted the Palestinians citizenship and employment. Before the Gulf War many Palestinians found high-paying jobs in countries like Kuwait. Some Palestinians under Israeli control did thrive, but many suffered from military occupation, annexation of their lands, and discrimination. In neither case were the Palestinian people really absorbed, politically or economically. What happened and why?

The First Intifada
The story began in December 1987 with a small uprising of Gaza children and teenagers against Israel's occupying army. The discord soon spread throughout the occupied areas. The Palestinians under Israeli occupation became more coordinated in their opposition and more effective in refuting Israel's claim that most of them were happy and prosperous under its rule. The stonings and tire burnings that launched this Intifada (which literally means "shaking off") made everyone see the Palestinians' distress. They boycotted Israeli manufactures, such as soap, cigarettes, and fabrics. Some Palestinians who used to go to Israel to work for higher wages than they could earn in the Gaza Strip or the West Bank stayed home. One village refused to pay taxes to Israel's authorities. The Intifada was initially a spontaneous, homegrown protest movement, for the PLO had been in Tunis since 1983. Some of the local leaders, disillusioned with the secularist PLO, founded a Muslim resistance movement, patterned on Hizballah, called *Hamas* (meaning "Courage" or "Movement of Islamic Resistance"). It has since been proven that Israel covertly helped it emerge as a rival to the PLO.

Why did the uprising break out in December 1987? If the Palestinian Arabs had chafed under Israeli military occupation since 1967, why did it take twenty years for them to try to shake it off? Actually, there had always been resistance, both overt and covert, in the West Bank and Gaza Strip. Israel had benefited materially from its twenty-year rule, using the Palestinians as a cheap labor pool and a market for Israeli manufactures. Although some Palestinians prospered from entering the Israeli economy, all Palestinians saw more and more Jewish settlers occupying their land and using their scarce water resources. There was much tension and little integration in their relationship. No one could be sure whether Israel's gradual absorption of the occupied territories would be reversed by an exchange of land for peace, probably with Jordan and under US sponsorship, or brought to its logical conclusion by outright annexation and possibly, as some Israeli extremists proposed, by forced expulsion of all Palestinians. Many observers ascribed signs of rising Palestinian unrest to the policies of the Israeli occupying authorities and the vigilante actions of the well-armed Jewish settlers.

One key event shortly before the Intifada was the summit meeting held in Amman in November 1987, when the Arab heads of state paid lip service to the Palestinian cause but permitted one another to resume diplomatic ties with Egypt, which had been isolated from most other Arab governments since 1979 for its separate peace with Israel. Soon Sa'udi, Kuwaiti, and even Iraqi ambassadors were back in Cairo. In 1989 Egypt was readmitted into the Arab League. The unspoken message to the Palestinians was that the Arab states were not going to punish Egypt any longer and that the PLO should stop seeking their diplomatic and military support. Once the Palestinians began fighting for their own freedom, they gained respect from other Arabs, though more than 1,100 were killed by Israelis and about 1,000 by other Palestinians, whereas few Israelis died or were harmed because of the Intifada.

The PLO viewed this uprising as a means to achieve foreign recognition and international legitimacy. King Husayn validated the rebellion by renouncing Jordan's claims to the West Bank in July 1988. In November of that year, the Palestinian National Council voted to declare an independent "State of Palestine," which soon won diplomatic recognition from at least a hundred other countries. Chairman Yasir 'Arafat publicly denounced terrorism and offered to recognize Israel, to the dismay of some Palestinian revolutionaries, in order to open negotiations with Washington. The Israelis vehemently rejected any idea that the PLO might be treated as a government-in-exile, let alone as a suitable negotiating partner, but many other people and countries argued that the only way to resolve the Arab-Israeli conflict was through a "two-state solution" with a Jewish Israel and an Arab Palestine. Many Palestinians likewise opposed efforts to make peace with Israel; their violent acts soon derailed any rapprochement between Washington and the PLO. The uprising continued, as Hamas acquired firearms to fight the Israeli army and coordinated attacks in Gaza and later on the West Bank, and violence intensified throughout the occupied territories.

The End of Lebanon's Civil War

After the West had pulled out its troops from Lebanon in 1984, the government almost closed down in Beirut. No police remained to stop the abduction of US, European, and indeed Sa'udi and even Iranian hostages by the various militias. Partitioned de facto since 1976, Lebanon saw less fighting between Muslims and Christians than before 1984, but more within each religious or political grouping. As soon as one faction seemed ready to take charge and restore order, it would split into two or more competing splinter groups. The Shi'ite Muslims fought the Palestinians in 1985; by 1988 they were fighting among themselves, with the somewhat secular and Syrian-backed Amal pitted against the militantly Islamic Hizballah, supported by Iran. Only diplomatic intervention by these two outside sponsors ended the intra-Shi'ite quarrel.

Meanwhile, the Maronites, who had lost their plurality of Lebanon's population to the Shi'ite Muslims by 1980, could not agree on a leader. When Amin Jumayyil's presidential term drew to a close in the summer of 1988, the parliament could not meet in Beirut to elect his successor because the militias prevented many members from attending. The presence of 40,000 Syrian troops enabled Damascus to determine Lebanon's next president, but the loudest voice for the Maronites was Iraqi-backed General Michel 'Awn, who demanded that all Syrians leave Lebanon and even moved into the presidential palace, opposing a pro-Syrian caretaker government under Sunni prime minister Salim al-Hoss.

In October 1989, after a yearlong impasse, the Sa'udi government invited all surviving members of Lebanon's parliament (no popular election of deputies had taken place since 1972) to Taif to choose a new president. The man they elected, a moderate Christian acceptable to Syria, was assassinated after only seventeen days in power, but the parliament bravely met again to elect a replacement, Ilyas Harawi. The 'Awn and Harawi Maronite factions fought each other as bitterly in 1990 as the Shi'ite groups had among themselves in 1988. Only when Iraq became embroiled in occupying Kuwait did it stop backing 'Awn. He was soon defeated by Harawi's forces, backed by Syria, whose troops did not leave Lebanon in 1990. Lebanon and Syria signed a pact in May 1991 giving Damascus substantial control over Lebanon's foreign and military affairs.

Experts disagree on whether Syria's prolonged occupation of Lebanon, which would last until April 2005, stabilized or intimidated the country. The 1989 Taif Accords proposed a division of power among Lebanon's sects, factions, and militias that came close to matching their actual shares of the country's population. With Lebanon finally at peace, Beirut and most of the countryside returned to normal. The Lebanese people could rebuild their country. Israel's troops, having pulled back in 1985 to a security zone on the Lebanese side of its northern border, would withdraw completely in 2000 because of effective Hizballah resistance.

The Peace Process in Arab-Israeli Relations

The Gulf War changed Israel's relationship with its Arab neighbors and with the Palestinians. The Soviets altered their Middle East policy, for Mikhail Gorbachev's government did not oppose the US-led coalition. It allowed its Jewish citizens to emigrate and resumed diplomatic relations with Israel, resulting in the influx of almost 1 million Soviet Jews. It stopped arming Syria and other Arab confrontation states against Israel and Egypt. It aided US efforts to convene a general peace conference. Then it dissolved as a union at the end of 1991, leaving the United States as the sole superpower that could act independently in the Middle East. If Israel's government could trust Washington to uphold its essential interests, it could be persuaded to enter peace talks with Syria, Sa'udi Arabia, and Jordan (with an attached delegation of Palestinians, of whom none were publicly tied to the PLO). The oil-exporting Arab governments realized that their security depended on maintaining good relations with Washington and on averting any future threat to their security—a threat more apt to come from Iraq or Iran than from Israel. Syria was willing to enter peace talks if it stood a chance to regain the Golan Heights taken by Israel in the 1967 War. For Jordan and the PLO, their public support of Iraq's policies had hurt their credibility among the oil-exporting regimes that had formerly backed them financially and diplomatically. Both had suffered losses from the Gulf War. Long willing to talk peace with Israel, they confirmed their readiness to negotiate.

US secretary of state James Baker set up a general conference that opened in Madrid in October 1991. The mere fact that Arab delegates were meeting in the same room with Israeli representatives marked a step toward peace, though hard-liners on both sides ensured that the Madrid conference produced no breakthroughs. Multilateral talks on various issues concerning the Middle East as a whole, such as water rights, refugees, economic development, and arms control, went on during the following years in various locations, making marginal progress but getting little publicity. Bilateral parleys met, faltered, and resumed during 1992 and 1993, as first Israel and then the United States elected new and more liberal governments.

Many Arab groups feared that peace with Israel would do them no good. Violent resistance to Israel's occupation was carried out by Hizballah in Lebanon and Hamas in the West Bank and Gaza. Terrorist acts against Egypt's political leaders and foreigners signaled the growing power of such extreme elements as the Islamic Group. Terrorism even spread to the United States, as a group of expatriate Egyptians was arrested after planting bombs that blew up part of New York's World Trade Center in February 1993. An exiled Sa'udi millionaire, Osama bin Laden, set up terrorist cells in Sudan and then in Afghanistan. He is widely suspected of having inspired the 1993 World Trade Center bombing and attacks on the US embassies in Kenya and Tanzania in 1998. Retaliatory bombing raids on bin Laden's suspected base in Afghanistan and on a pharmaceutical factory in Khartoum (which, it turned out, had no ties to bin Laden) did nothing to blunt his appeal.

In 1993 Israel continued to bomb Lebanese villages (leaving 500,000 villagers homeless), expand its West Bank settlements, and wound or kill Palestinian demonstrators. It could also subject them to preventive detention and torture, blow up houses, draw down their water, and impose curfews on the Gaza Strip and West Bank. Hopes for peace seemed to be receding again.

The Oslo I Accord

Greater progress was made away from public notice, though, under the auspices of Norway's foreign minister and his wife, who hosted secret talks between representatives of the PLO and of Israel's new government despite their public protestations to the contrary. After the news leaked in August 1993, Oslo turned over its mediating role to Washington. On 13 September the foreign ministers of Israel and the PLO and the United States secretary of state met for a public ceremony, held on the White House lawn, to sign a formal Declaration of Principles, also called the Oslo I Accord. The ceremony included brief speeches by US president Bill Clinton, Israeli premier Yitzhak Rabin, and PLO chairman Yasir 'Arafat (see Box 19.1). The ceremony concluded with a handshake between the veteran Israeli and Palestinian leaders, symbolically ending their long enmity. Under the

Box 19.1   Yasir ʿArafat

Sources disagree on where Yasir ʿArafat (1929–2004) was born. Some say Jerusalem; others claim Cairo. His family was definitely Palestinian and, by the time he was four, was living in Jerusalem, where his father was a textile merchant. When he was eight, the family relocated to Cairo. ʿArafat was educated mainly in Egypt, eventually attending Cairo University. There he became politically active and by 1946 was smuggling weapons from Egypt into Palestine. The Arab loss in the 1948 war and the establishment of Israel discouraged him briefly, but he would soon dedicate himself to challenging this outcome.

Because his political activities often distracted him from his studies, ʿArafat did not receive his degree in civil engineering until 1956. After serving briefly in the Egyptian army during the 1956 Suez War, he left for Kuwait, where he established his own construction firm. In 1959 ʿArafat founded Fatah, for he was convinced that Palestinians had to fight to liberate their homeland and not wait for the Arab states to do it for them. By 1965 Fatah was carrying out military operations within Israel.

The Palestinians came to view ʿArafat and his companions as heroes. Their efforts inspired the formation of other resistance movements, which ʿArafat managed to unite under the umbrella of the PLO. Even though his PLO fighters could not defeat Israel militarily, ʿArafat kept the *fidaʾiyin* together at a level that demanded the world's attention. He argued always that "all options are open, including the armed struggle if necessary." ʿArafat made sure the violence and "terror" of Fatah and the other resistance groups matched Israel's destructive acts against Palestinian society as a whole. His struggle has not been understood in the West, which has consistently misrepresented ʿArafat and described Fatah's actions without any meaningful context.

This treatment obscured his positive achievements and prevented any proper response, particularly by the US government, to his initiatives. For instance, in 1988 ʿArafat convinced the PLO to accept UN Resolution 242, to recognize Israel's right to exist within its 1967 borders, and to renounce "terrorism." In 1991 he supported convening the Madrid conference, and in 1993 he accepted the Oslo Accords and shook hands with Israeli premier Yitzhak Rabin on the White House lawn. Despite all this, he was constantly called the man "who failed to grasp peace," especially because of his rejection of Clinton and Ehud Barak's offer at the 2000 Camp David Summit.

In January 1996, in the first free and fair election held in Palestine, ʿArafat was chosen president by an overwhelming 87 percent. Though he later proved to be an incompetent administrator of an occupied territory largely controlled by Israel, most Palestinians loved and respected ʿArafat, even as they became increasingly critical of his authoritarian presidential style.

declaration, Israel was to withdraw its forces from the Gaza Strip and Jericho within three months, enabling the PLO to set up a "self-governing authority" as a first step toward full autonomy for the occupied territories other than East Jerusalem (whose status would be discussed later). The Palestinians would be permitted to hold free elections for a national assembly (whose size and powers were unspecified) once Israeli troops were withdrawn from their main population centers. Jewish settlements in the West Bank and the Gaza Strip would remain under Israeli protection. Neither the Palestinians' demand for full autonomy nor the Israelis' security needs were fully met by the Declaration of Principles. But neither 'Arafat nor Rabin would benefit by abandoning the peace process.

The ensuing negotiations between Israel and the PLO did not validate Oslo I. The declaration left major issues unsettled, and both sides tended to play to their backers. Israel did pull its troops out of those parts of Gaza and Jericho not settled by Jews, allowing 'Arafat to return and to start building political institutions. At the same time, though, it expanded existing Jewish settlements, violating the spirit of Oslo I. A Palestinian police force, recruited and trained mainly in Egypt, was charged with maintaining order but gradually became a militia fighting against Israelis. Foreign governments withheld much of the $2 billion they had pledged to support the PLO's "self-governing authority" (which gradually came to be seen as a state) and to rebuild the Palestinian economy, because 'Arafat wanted full control of the money with no public accountability. His administration, hamstrung by rival authorities and security agencies, also encountered defiance from Hamas. Economic conditions in Gaza, far from improving, worsened. Conditions in the occupied lands not under the Palestinian Authority also grew tense. For instance, an armed Jewish settler entered the mosque at the Tomb of the Patriarchs in Hebron and killed or maimed more than thirty Muslim worshippers before he was overpowered and killed. Distrust on all sides intensified.

Gains and Losses in the Peace Process
Even though the Declaration of Principles brought no peace or prosperity to the Palestinians, it did open the door to political deals with Israel by other Arab countries. Jordan's King Husayn had long talked secretly with Israel about peace, but now he and his government worked openly to end their state of war. In October 1994 Clinton, Husayn, and Rabin met at the desert border between southern Israel and Jordan to sign a formal Jordanian-Israeli peace treaty. Tunisia and Morocco formed consular ties

with Israel, and several of the small Gulf states hastened to make business deals with the Jewish state. Starting in 1994 most Middle Eastern countries attended an annual economic development conference, though Arab governments critical of Israel's policies boycotted the 1997 meeting at Doha in Qatar. The United States continued to hope that Syria's government would sign a peace treaty with Israel in exchange for a phased withdrawal of Israeli troops from the Golan Heights, but even Clinton's personal visit to Assad in 1994 did not bridge the chasm between Damascus and Jerusalem. The Arab states met that year to coordinate their diplomatic strategies, for recent events showed them to be as disunited in making peace as in waging war.

In September 1995 Israel and the Palestinians signed another agreement, called Oslo II, containing an intricate plan for Israel's gradual withdrawal from the West Bank (but not any part of Jerusalem). Oslo II set up three West Bank zones. Zone A comprised eight West Bank cities, including Jericho, that Arabs already controlled. Palestinian authorities would become responsible for the zone's internal security and public order, except for the parts of Hebron containing Jewish settlers. Zone B consisted of other West Bank towns and villages where Palestinian police would eventually maintain order but Israel would retain overriding authority for security. Zone C included Jewish settlements, unpopulated areas, and lands Israel viewed as strategic. Israel retained full security authority for Zone C, pending "final status" talks. The redeployment of Israeli troops was to occur at six-month intervals. Israel and the Palestinians were to form joint patrols, and Israel would build bypass roads for its settlers. The Palestinians were empowered to elect a president and an eighty-two-member council. Jerusalem's Arab inhabitants could not run for but could cast absentee ballots in the elections, which were held in January 1996.

Israeli and Palestinian extremists combined to derail the peace process. Prime Minister Rabin was killed by a Jewish fundamentalist just after addressing a peace rally in November 1995. His successor, Shimon Peres, had less popular support, as the May 1996 general elections showed. Alarmed by two suicide bomb attacks by Hamas, the Israelis voted by a narrow margin to replace Peres and his Labor government with the Likud leader, Benjamin Netanyahu. The Likud had opposed peace talks with the PLO (and indeed the permanent-status talks were suspended) but promised to fulfill Israel's commitments under the Oslo Accords. Netanyahu even agreed to withdraw Israeli troops from most of Hebron in January 1997. But Israel put off giving back the other West Bank areas because of new anti-Israel bombings that Netanyahu blamed on 'Arafat. Clinton and his new secretary of state, Madeleine Albright, repeatedly urged Netanyahu to give up occupied lands and 'Arafat to stop acts of terrorism. 'Arafat could not do this after Israel had attacked the PLO security infrastructure in the occupied territories, making it harder to curb Hamas, a point not understood by Washington. The Palestinians grew ever more frustrated with a peace process that gave them no hope for freedom or even employment. They also resented Israel's policy of building new Jewish settlements on their lands, in violation of the Geneva Convention.

Under the 1993 Declaration of Principles, a five-year transition period was to lead to final-status talks, which were to occur in 1998, about such contentious issues as (1) the future of Jerusalem (which the Palestinians, like the Israelis, claim as their capital), (2) the dispersed Palestinians' right to return to their homes or to receive compensation from Israel, (3) the future of Jewish settlements in territories conceded to the Palestinians, (4) the configuration of final borders between Israel and the projected Palestinian state, and (5) the status of the Palestinian Authority. Israeli bullying and Palestinian terrorism combined to block the final-status talks.

Israel held general elections in May 1999, and Labor made gains at the Likud's expense and managed to form a coalition cabinet that included several splinter parties and enjoyed the tacit support of Israeli Arabs. In the first separate election ever held for the position of prime minister, Ehud Barak handily defeated Netanyahu. Clinton hoped that Barak could make peace with both the Palestinian Authority and with Syria, but neither happened. Syria's Hafiz al-Assad (who died in 2000 and was replaced by his son, Bashar) would not parley with Israel unless it promised in advance to return all the occupied Golan Heights to his country, although an inconclusive meeting did take place in Shepherdstown, West Virginia. Palestinian and Israeli representatives met at the Erez Crossing between Gaza and Israel, in an estate on the Wye River in Maryland, and finally with Bill Clinton in a three-way summit at Camp David. But there were no breakthroughs to peace. Israel would not allow the Palestinians to regain the entire West Bank and East Jerusalem, nor would it agree to readmit the Palestinian refugees (and their descendants) from the 1948 war. Palestinians promised to curb terrorism, but in practice they went on attacking Israelis, just as the IDF attacked them.

Barak's offers to 'Arafat at Camp David seemed generous to Israel's backers, but they were not, even as modified in later meetings at Taba and Sharm al-Shaykh. Israel would have given the Palestinians a truncated state that could not control its own borders, water supply, airspace, and immigration processes. They would not have been allowed arms to defend themselves against a neighbor that had often attacked them. Had such an offer been made to the Israelis, they never would have accepted it. Meanwhile, Jewish settlers continued to build new settlements and increase the size of older ones on the West Bank (at the end of 2000 the Jewish settler population in the West Bank and Gaza exceeded 200,000). They seized water resources and sometimes land belonging to the Palestinians and crisscrossed the area with new highways.

The Second Intifada

On 28 September 2000 General Ariel Sharon made a highly public visit to the Muslim shrines atop the Temple Mount, or al-Haram al-Sharif, accompanied by nearly 1,500 soldiers and police, to demonstrate Israel's sovereignty over this Muslim holy site. Sharon's act enraged the Palestinians, who began attacking Jewish settlements with rocks and sometimes firearms. The IDF struck back with massive retaliation raids, killing hundreds and maiming thousands of Palestinians, many of whom were innocent bystanders or even young children caught in the line of fire. Under the Oslo Accords, Israel and the Palestinian Authority could have carried out a joint police action. Instead, what took place was an Israeli military operation that included blowing up houses, uprooting olive and orange trees, shooting demonstrators with live ammunition, and blanketing whole villages with tear gas. The Israelis were distressed when fighting broke out between Jewish soldiers and Israeli Arab civilians in Nazareth, because they had assumed that Israeli Arabs would never rebel against them. The Palestinians suffered not only deaths and injuries but also the loss of their livelihood as Israel closed border crossings to Palestinians who had been workers in Israel.

This Palestinian uprising was soon dubbed the Intifada of al-Aqsa (referring to the large mosque on the Temple Mount). It won the support of nearly all Arabs, who called on their governments to cut diplomatic and commercial ties with Israel. Only Egypt and Jordan (whose King Husayn had died of cancer and was replaced by his son, Abdallah II) maintained formal relations with the Jewish state. The Israelis claimed their security was at risk. Angry debates took place in the Knesset because of what many politicians considered Barak's overly generous offers at Camp David. The prime minister agreed to end his term early and seek re-election. His challenger proved to be not Netanyahu (who had given up his Knesset seat and hence was ineligible to run) but, rather, Ariel Sharon. Palestinians and other Arabs were disillusioned with Barak but viewed Sharon as a war criminal for his role in supporting the 1982 Sabra and Shatila massacres and in other military actions against Arabs during his long military career. During the campaign Sharon claimed to be the one leader who was tough enough to bring the Arabs to the peace table. He defeated Barak by a 20 percent margin. Because the election did not involve the Knesset, though, the Labor Party still held its plurality of seats there, and Sharon decided to form a broad-based coalition, including Labor politicians such as Shimon Peres, who became his foreign minister. It would be hard for this cabinet to devise a unified Israeli policy or to reach a prompt settlement with the Palestinian Authority. The latter, still led by 'Arafat, was almost totally discredited among Palestinians for its corruption and ineptitude. Hizballah and Hamas seized the initiative for the Palestinians by sending suicide bombers into Israel and shooting Israelis in West Bank and Gaza settlements. Israeli troops reoccupied the Gaza Strip, bombarded Palestinian Authority buildings from the air, and interned many Palestinians without trial.

WHITHER ISLAM?

The popular catchphrase of the 1990s was "Islam is the solution," even though this fundamentalism has failed to solve problems in Iran and other countries where it has been tried. Muslim groups often deliver welfare benefits to masses of newly urbanized Middle Easterners whose needs are not well served by governments or older charitable organizations. The revival of some Muslim customs, such as the growing of beards by men and the wearing of head scarves by women, has spread throughout the Islamic world. Heightened religious observance may well be a positive development in a tense area and era. But the issue is the combination of Islam with politics.

Islamist Gains and Losses: A 1990s Scorecard

In such countries as Jordan, where some public participation in politics is encouraged, Islamist parties won votes because of economic hardship, disillusionment with the peace process, and anger at the United States. In Egypt, where political parties proliferated but those based on religion were banned, opposition to the policies of Husni Mubarak and his American backers was expressed by terrorist attacks against government officials, Copts, foreign tourists, and secularist writers. Islamists won control of the professional unions of lawyers, physicians, and engineers in the 1992 elections; later, the Mubarak government revised the unions' electoral rules. But Mubarak could not stamp out fundamentalism altogether: a judge tried in 1995 to force a woman to divorce her husband, a Cairo University professor, after he published a scholarly article that the magistrate deemed anti-Islamic. The Sudan, impoverished by years of civil strife, had an avowedly Islamist government that exported propagandists to the rest of the Arab world. Some Sudanese tried to assassinate Mubarak in 1995 during a meeting in Addis Ababa.

The Islamic revolutionaries who drove the Soviet army out of Afghanistan in 1987–1991 formed a network called al-Qa'ida, which trained activists in other Muslim countries, including Egypt and the Sudan. In Afghanistan itself the *Taliban* (Muslim students) won control of most of the country against better-armed militias in 1996 and proceeded to impose severe restrictions on women and westernized intellectuals. In Iran, President Muhammad Khatami, elected in 1997, tried to ease some Islamic restrictions and open better relations with the West, in contrast to the hard-line policies of the country's religious leader, the Ayatollah 'Ali Khamanei, who under the 1979 constitution held most of the power.

Turkey's pro-Islamist Welfare Party won enough votes in the 1995 general elections to lead a coalition government for a few months, but its diplomatic approaches to Iran and Libya, plus its threat to undo Ataturk's legacy, so incensed the army officers that its leader voluntarily resigned in 1997 and let the secularists regain power. Turkey's Islamist and the secularist governments alike strengthened military ties with Israel. The country most threatened by this alliance was Syria, where Islamist revolutionaries were not yet strong enough to threaten the Assads, either the father or the son (who were Alawites). Of Israel's neighbors, Syria continued to insist that Israel could have peace only if it returned occupied land, particularly the Golan Heights. It also got most of its irrigation water from Turkey, whose massive dams now controlled the Euphrates and Tigris rivers. Water, scarce everywhere, might cause the wars of the coming century.

During the 1990s the Islamists could only dream of someday ousting a long-entrenched Arab regime. Jordan had been ruled by the Hashimites since 1921, Syria by the Assad family since 1970, Yemen by 'Ali Abdallah Salih since 1978, Egypt by Mubarak since 1981, and Sa'udi Arabia by the family of Sa'ud since 1932. However, these countries' security forces could then thwart any Islamist revolution. A more enticing prospect might have been to take over one of the emerging Caucasian or Central Asian republics, among which Azerbaijan, Kazakhstan, and Turkmenistan had oil reserves that were just beginning to be tapped. Turkey, Sa'udi Arabia, and Iran were all contending for influence in the lands where czars and commissars formerly held sway.

CONCLUSION

Most of the Middle East's problems, such as overpopulation, scarcity of water and other resources, maldistribution of wealth, and inadequate infrastructure for industrialization, will not be solved by combining Islam with politics. Islamic leaders can set a higher moral tone for their societies, denounce leaders who fail to serve their people, and in some cases even help build democratic institutions. No king or president heading a Muslim Middle Eastern state during the 1990s enjoyed much popularity or demonstrated much vision. But the Middle Eastern states' lack of legitimacy has led their subjects to seek solutions elsewhere, possibly in some form of religious fundamentalism. In the past, state control of radio and television broadcasting could restrict what the people learned, but satellite TV stations, dish receivers, and the Internet have given Middle Easterners access to facts and ideas that would threaten their governments—and their Western backers—just a decade later.

20

The War on Terrorism

The eastern United States was basking in warm sunshine on the morning of 11 September 2001. Cars carrying men and women to their jobs were streaming into cities, factories, and shopping centers. Yellow buses bore children to their schools. Trucks, trains, ships, and airplanes were taking cargo to and from all parts of the country. Suddenly, a passenger jet flew into the North Tower of the World Trade Center in New York City. It must have been a terrible accident, people assumed, until, twenty minutes later, a second passenger plane sliced across the front and side of the South Tower. Within the hour a third plane flew into the west side of the Pentagon in Arlington, Virginia. A fourth jet crashed in a field east of Pittsburgh. It was the most horrifying attack Americans had ever experienced. How many more planes would strike? Who could have dreamed up such an atrocity? How could those in the cockpits have seized American passenger jets and flown them into major buildings? What reason could they have had for doing so?

"Why do they hate us?" was what most Americans asked. To answer that question we must review the history of the Middle East, US policies toward the region, and how they affected its peoples, especially during the past seventy years. Regrettably, few Americans have asked whether their government's policies have helped or hindered democracy, economic development, or human rights in the Middle East. Such reflection has been drowned out by misleading explanations like "Those Muslims hate our freedoms." Americans traditionally know little about foreign policy. With the public unaware of conditions abroad, special interest groups, some of which have deep pockets and little competition, have gained control over Washington's decisions about the foreign areas that concern them. Their parochial concerns come to be seen, in the White House, the halls of academe, the US Congress, and the mass media, as the national interest.

The attacker on that September morning was al-Qaʻida, a coordinating body for Muslim resistance movements operating in many countries and headed by an exiled Saʻudi businessman named Osama bin Laden (see Box 20.1). The dramatic attack began as a hijacking operation by nineteen Arab militants. It took 2,977 lives, shattered the apathy of the American people, and focused the world's attention on the terrorist threat. Within weeks, the United Nations passed a resolution condemning terrorism, US president George W. Bush declared war against terrorism, his administration arrested and detained thousands of suspects, and US warplanes began bombing Afghanistan, which harbored bin Laden and his training camps. An American-dominated coalition occupied most of Afghanistan, ousted its Taliban-led government, and pursued al-Qaʻida's fighters into the mountains near Pakistan.

Almost every government in the world, including those of the Middle East, condemned the attack on the United States and terrorism in general. However, the US response, one of repression at home and aggression in the Middle East, gradually turned sympathetic support into antagonistic opposition. The key issue for many governments and people was the unilateral US attack on Iraq that began in March 2003, purportedly to rid the country of its weapons of mass destruction and to topple Saddam Husayn's dictatorial regime. The weapons were never found, nor have freedom and a stable democracy been established in Iraq. The American occupation has stirred up bitter resistance by both Sunni and Shiʻite Muslim Iraqis, threatening to dissolve the country. It has also enabled al-Qaʻida to recruit more anti-American fighters and volunteers for terrorist attacks. Finally, it has greatly expanded Iran's influence in Iraq, which now has a Shiʻite government. Almost every US soldier left Iraq by the end of 2011, but American troops would return later to fight the Islamic State of Iraq and the Levant (ISIL) militants in 2014. Moreover, the Palestinian-Israeli conflict still simmers on, focusing mainly on Palestinians fighting Israeli rule.

Three Middle Eastern issues have dominated people's attention since 2001: the first is the so-called War on Terrorism; the second is the US war in Iraq; the third is the debilitating struggle between Israel and the Palestinians.

SURVEY OF TERRORISM

When representatives of the world's governments met at the UN General Assembly just a few days after the terrorist attacks, which came to be called

---

BOX 20.1   Osama bin Laden

Osama bin Laden (1957–2011) was born into Saʻudi Arabia's wealthy bin Laden clan, which owns one of the country's largest construction companies and is close to the Saʻudi royal family. Bin Laden was educated in Jidda and studied business management at King Abdulaziz University. Raised as a devout Muslim, he had limited experience beyond the Muslim world.

Soon after the Soviet invasion of Afghanistan, bin Laden began raising money for the resistance fighters, and in 1984 he established a "guest house" in Pakistan for Arab fighters bound for the Afghan front. This turned into a logistical center providing training and religious support, as well as funneling men and equipment into Afghanistan. By 1986 bin Laden was building his own fighting camps in Afghanistan, and he named his operation al-Qaʻida, or "the firm base." He was personally involved in at least five major battles against the Soviets. At this point, his actions were aligned with the policies of the United States, which provided him with financial and military assistance.

Bin Laden returned to Saʻudi Arabia in 1989, convinced that his efforts played a major role in ousting the Soviet army from Afghanistan. When the Iraqis invaded Kuwait, bin Laden proposed to the Saʻudi government that he mobilize the fighters he had commanded in Afghanistan to confront the Iraqis. The Saʻudis rejected his offer and instead turned to the Americans, which led to the presence of thousands of non-Muslim troops in the holy land of Arabia—a choice that appalled bin Laden.

In 1991 bin Laden left Saʻudi Arabia and eventually returned to Afghanistan, now under Taliban rule. In 1996 he issued his first *bayan* (public announcement), warning the United States to remove its troops from Arabia, or else the same fighters who had defeated the Soviet Union would wage war against America. This threat was realized in attacks on US embassies in East Africa in 1998 and on the naval vessel *Cole* in Yemen in 2000.

Bin Laden had also come to see US policies in Palestine and Iraq, and US support for dictatorships in Egypt, Jordan, and Saʻudi Arabia, as part of a Western war against Islam. From his point of view, the 9/11 attacks on the Pentagon and World Trade Center were retaliatory. In the West, he became the best-known and most wanted "terrorist mastermind." Bin Laden gave a post-9/11 interview on Al Jazeera TV, stating that "we will work to continue this battle, God permitting, until victory or until we meet God. . . . If killing those who kill our sons is terrorism, then let history be witness that we are terrorists."

Eventually, US intelligence operatives located bin Laden living in a compound in Abbottabad, Pakistan. On 21 May 2011, bin Laden's compound was raided by US Special Forces personnel, and he was killed. Although the Obama administration hailed this achievement for advancing the War on Terrorism, bin Laden's death certainly did not end al-Qaʻida terrorism against US targets. That will come only when the root causes of the animosity toward US policy in the Middle East are addressed.

9/11, nearly everyone agreed that terrorism deserved unanimous condemnation, but they did not agree on a definition. Neither do the various agencies of the US government, nor do most scholars. The CIA defines terrorism as the threat or use of violence for political purposes by individuals or groups, whether acting for, or in opposition to, established governmental authority, when such actions are intended to shock or intimidate a large group wider than the immediate victims. The United States and its allies are as likely as their enemies to use such tactics. Arguably, state terrorism is now being practiced by the United States in its use of unmanned drones in Yemen, Afghanistan, and Pakistan and by Israel in its occupied territories.

In common parlance, terrorism is carried out by individuals or by secret societies in opposition to an established government, whether elected or dictatorial. A terrorist can be any person, young or old, man or woman. Acts that have been ordered and paid for by established governments are called state-sponsored terrorism. But can a government itself commit a terrorist act? If a bomb set off in a school, marketplace, or car constitutes terrorism, what about a bomb dropped from a plane or fired by a distant launcher? Both are deliberate choices. Both have unintended consequences. Do attackers have to see their victims to be called terrorists? Can terrorist acts ever be committed by soldiers, sailors, or pilots wearing their country's uniform? Can an attack on a uniformed soldier, sailor, or pilot ever be called "terroristic"?

How do you conduct a war on terrorism, as both US and Israeli officials claim to have done for many years? In Chapter 18 we raised the choice between solving the causes of terrorism and attacking terrorists directly. Most Westerners now believe that a government cannot fight terrorism by simply educating people, eliminating poverty, or correcting injustice. But is the struggle one of law enforcement, clandestine counterterrorist measures, or traditional military confrontation? In other words, can you defeat terrorism with police, secret agents, or uniformed troops, who themselves might act like terrorists? These are not easy questions to answer.

The Middle East countries of the twenty-first century have various political, economic, and social conditions. This region also differs in the way its local and foreign governments respond to terrorists and the consequences of violence, resistance, self-sacrifice, and terrorism.

Turkey

Geographically if not culturally, Turkey is the country that can best claim to be a bridge between Europe and Asia. A pioneer in westernizing reform from above, it lives uneasily with the legacy of the Tanzimat and Kemal Ataturk. However, its government since 2002 has been a coalition led by an Islamist party and prime minister, and a growing number of Turkish citizens want to restore Islamic customs and laws. It has close cultural ties with the Arab countries, and yet up to 2009 it had a de facto strategic alliance with Israel against Syria, largely because it controls the sources of the Tigris and Euphrates rivers. It also has growing economic ties with Europe and has long sought admittance to the European Union.

One stumbling block has been its struggle with a Kurdish separatist movement. Since 1984 Turkey has faced in its southeastern provinces a Kurdish rebellion that, if successful, would threaten its territorial integrity. The Kurdish Workers Party (Partiya Karkeren Kurdistan, or PKK) fought openly for independence and committed terrorist acts in Turkey. Some observers believe the Turkish army responded with tactics that violated the rights of its Kurdish citizens and may have amounted to a form of state terrorism. Once Turkey captured Abdullah Ocalan, the PKK leader in 1999, the fighting died down. The Turkish government now lets the Kurds use their language in schools and even on state-sponsored radio, and Kurdish refugees are returning home. The PKK has changed its name and become a nonviolent pressure group, but some violent incidents still occur and Kurdish separatist forces now use northern Iraq as a base of operations against the Turkish army.

A few attacks against foreign tourists and businesses have occurred in recent years, but a strong counterterrorism agency and the police have kept terrorism in check. The country has a relatively advanced industrial economy (which has benefited from what otherwise would have been a ruinous inflation), good schools and universities, and a thriving democratic political system. In free elections held in 2002 for the Grand National Assembly, the Justice and Development Party (Islamist) got 34 percent of the popular vote, followed by the Republican People's Party (secular) with 19 percent. On 10 August 2014, the Justice and Development Party maintained its political success as Recep Tayyip Erdogan was elected president of Turkey. Commercial and diplomatic relations with Greece and other European countries are improving. Turkey still has not withdrawn its 35,000 troops from northern Cyprus, although negotiations between Greek and Turkish Cypriot leaders began in 2008 and have dragged on inconclusively.

Iran

The Islamic Revolution is now more than thirty-five years old. Most of Iran's 81 million citizens are too young to remember the shah's regime.

The Islamic Republic has become, to some and perhaps most young Iranians, a regime of old men, hardly the idealistic band of youths who ousted the shah and occupied the US Embassy in 1979. Iran's economy has benefited from new discoveries of oil and its rising price on world markets. However, the dominance of state-owned enterprises has hobbled industrialization, and increasing political tensions with the United States and Europe have hampered economic development. The government has taken steps to reduce the gap between rich and poor and correct the worst abuses of the land reform and other vestiges of the shah's regime. What terrorism does exist comes from extremist elements among Iran's ethnic minorities. The government has gradually softened its rhetoric on spreading the Islamic Revolution and has kept its distance from al-Qa'ida, but it has given material and moral support to Hizballah in Lebanon, Hamas in Palestine, and resistance fighters in Iraq under US occupation.

Many Iranians felt threatened by the American invasion of neighboring Afghanistan in 2001 and of Iraq in 2003, fearing the same fate for themselves. This fear was fueled by Bush administration rhetoric, which was similar to what it used to justify attacking Iraq and which some members of the Obama administration have adopted toward Iran. The election of Tehran's mayor, Mahmoud Ahmadinejad, as Iran's president in 2005 led to further alienation between Iran and the United States. The West is deeply worried about Iran's nuclear energy program, alleging that its aim is to produce nuclear weapons. No hard evidence supports these allegations, and Iran's nuclear program is legal under the nonproliferation treaty. Yet Iran now has the technology to enrich uranium that can be used in nuclear weapons and may soon be able to produce its own atomic bomb. Direct pressure from Western governments, now taking the form of increasing UN sanctions, seeks to forestall the yet unproven Iranian nuclear weapons program. The Iranian government insists its program is entirely peaceful, and the country's supporters ask why India, Pakistan, and Israel may have nuclear weapons, but not Iran.

Popular participation in the country's governance has gradually increased at the local and provincial levels, and the Majlis (Iran's parliament) debates, even if it does not determine, Iran's policies. All men and women over eighteen may vote. Support for the Islamic Republic runs deep, even if many Iranians have demanded further democratic reform and greater personal freedom. They argue that Ahmadinejad's re-election as president in June 2009 was rigged by the government, hence the countrywide protest demonstrations, commonly called the Green Movement, that followed the election. The government brutally suppressed these demonstrations, as well as smaller ones that took place in 2011. Popular dissatisfaction with the government does not mean that the Iranian people would support an Israeli or American attack because of the country's alleged nuclear weapons. Despite its claim that Arab uprisings are a popular Islamic expression against autocratic regimes and their alliance with the West, Iran has been vocal in its support of Assad's crackdown on Syria's opposition. This position led to Iran losing the support of Arab masses. Iran continues to argue that the defeat of Bashar al-Assad and his regime would benefit Israel and the United States. However, Hamas, which has historically benefited from the Syrian support, declined to back Assad, who has relied mostly on the political and military support of Iran and Hizballah.

Fertile Crescent Arab States

Between 2001 and 2011, Syria led the governments of the Middle East in opposing American policies. As you may recall from Chapter 14, Syria was first among the Arab countries to formulate an Arab nationalist and socialist ideology and to import Soviet arms and advisers. During and after Lebanon's civil war, Syria's troops occupied the country from 1976 until 2005.

Since 1966 Syria has been governed by a radical branch of the Ba'ath Party. After the death in 2000 of Hafiz al-Assad, its long-serving president, his son Bashar succeeded him. The government tolerates no opposition, and its heavy industries and public utilities remain under state control. Light industries are privately owned by families linked to the regime, although banks were privatized in 2004. The Israelis and the US government regarded Syria as a threat to their interests in the Middle East, mainly because it allegedly promotes terrorism. They spoke openly of replacing its dictatorial government with a more democratic regime, but in 2001 Syria aided the US government in its war on terrorists and secretly negotiated with Israel about returning the Golan Heights and ending the state of war between their countries. Syria opposed the US-led Iraq War and gave asylum to more than 1.2 million Iraqi refugees. It also withdrew its troops from Lebanon in April 2005, partly in response to a UN Security Council resolution but also because of international pressure after the car-bomb killing of Lebanon's former prime minister, Rafiq Hariri. Many people blamed the assassination on Syria's intelligence service, although the Syrian government denied any involvement and a UN commission found no proof.

Lebanon, despite the Syrian occupation (or because of it), recovered economically from its long civil war and restored its parliamentary democracy. The country's economy grew rapidly during the 1990s but has slowed since 2000. Most industries and business firms are privately owned. In 2004 a dispute arose between pro-Syrian parties centered on Hizballah and those parties supported by the West, mainly the United States and France, over who would become the country's next president. The confrontation later became violent when the Lebanese government ordered Hizballah to disarm its militia and dismantle its communications systems. In the ensuing clash, Hizballah proved stronger. The crisis was not resolved until May 2008, when the Doha Agreement led to the formation of a new government in which Hizballah and its allies (which include some Druze and Christian parties) gained more influence over Lebanon's policies. Shi'ite Muslims are now Lebanon's largest religious group, followed by the Sunnis. Christians are no longer considered the majority, although no official census has been taken since 1932.

Lebanon's periodic violence comes from foreign as well as domestic sources. After Israel unilaterally withdrew its troops from its security zone in 2000, it accused Lebanon of allowing raids and rocket attacks against Israeli territory, occasionally staging retaliatory raids into Lebanon. In July 2006 a Hizballah raid on an Israeli border patrol led to the capture of two Israeli soldiers. This incident triggered a thirty-three-day war between Hizballah forces and the Israeli army. Israeli fighter jets strafed and bombed Beirut and southern port cities. For the first time since Operation Desert Storm, Israeli cities came under missile attack. Even though Israel's technologically advanced weapons seriously damaged Lebanon's civilian infrastructure, it essentially lost the struggle to the deeply dug in, well-led, and highly motivated Hizballah fighters. Finally in mid-August a UN ceasefire was arranged, allowing Lebanese armed forces and units of a United Nations Interim Force in Lebanon (UNIFIL) to take up positions in southern Lebanon. The bodies of the captured Israeli soldiers, who had died soon after they were taken in 2006, were exchanged in August 2008 for Palestinian prisoners held by Israel. Hizballah, especially its leader, Hassan Nasrallah, enjoys enhanced prestige in Lebanon, and the Lebanese people are once again rebuilding their country. However, Nasrallah's popularity in the Arab world began to plummet as he lent political and military support to Bashar al-Assad in his attempt to suppress Syria's popular uprising. When ISIL rose to power in 2014, it threatened to attack Shi'a communities—as well as Christians and other religious groups—in Iraq and Syria; thus Hizballah and its leader Nasrallah saw a future defeat of Assad as a threat to their own existence (see Box 20.2).

Jordan has successfully evolved from a desert principality into a stable and prosperous kingdom because it has managed to retain the political and, at times, economic support of the other Arab countries. Though it is now a leader in urbanization and education, it suffered from the American

20: The War on Terrorism

Box 20.2 Hassan Nasrallah

Born in 1961, Hassan Nasrallah took over the leadership of Hizballah, the Lebanese Shiʻa paramilitary and political organization, in 1992 after Israel's assassination of ʻAbbas Musawi, Hizballah's cofounder and former secretary general. He began his political and military career within another Shiʻa political movement known as Amal; the organization was more secular than Hizballah. Nasrallah's Islamic education started in the seminary of Baʻalbek, which followed the teachings of Mohammed Baqir al-Sadr, who came from a very famous religious family with origins in Lebanon. After Israel's invasion of Lebanon, Nasrallah left Amal and joined Hizballah. Many Lebanese Shiʻa believed that, despite the role of Amal during the civil war, there was a need for a more activist and religious organization. A civil war erupted between two Shiʻa camps, leading to the emergence of Hizballah as the leading Shiʻa representative in Lebanese politics. In the late 1980s, Nasrallah moved back and forth between Iran and Lebanon as he pursued his studies in the city of Qom—his allegiance to Iran was established in these days.

Under Nasrallah's leadership, Hizballah intensified its military operations against Israel. Nasrallah instituted a new military program improving the range of their rockets with the support of Iran and Syria. Despite Israel's destruction of Lebanese infrastructure, he led many military clashes with Israel that ended with short truces since 1992. With the rise of Israel's casualties in the 1990s, Israeli politicians called for withdrawal from southern Lebanon, and Ehud Barak approved their exit in 2000. This was seen as a huge success for Hizballah's resistance and turned Nasrallah into a political celebrity in the Arab world. In 2004, he was credited for arranging an exchange of Palestinian prisoners with Israel.

In July 2006, Hizballah fighters killed and abducted Israeli soldiers in an effort to force Israel to release three Lebanese prisoners. Israel launched a major military operation that resulted in the death of more than one thousand Lebanese and the displacement of hundreds of families. Nasrallah gained even more support in the Arab world, especially after his paramilitary forces were able to hit many Israeli targets in Haifa and other cities.

Despite the indictment of members of Hizballah in the assassination of former Lebanese prime minister Rafiq Hariri, Nasrallah managed to maintain a peaceful coexistence between Hizballah and other political parties in Lebanon. In May 2013, Nasrallah declared his support for the regime of Bashar al-Assad against Assad's growing Islamic opposition, and Nasrallah's paramilitary forces joined the fighting alongside the Syrian army. Nasrallah argued that ISIL's success in Iraq and Syria poses a danger to Lebanon, Jordan, Saʻudi Arabia, and the other Gulf states.

invasion of Iraq in 2003, however, because of the loss of its oil and the influx of about 750,000 Iraqi refugees, leading to unemployment approaching 30 percent. In addition, the government has faced the challenge of balancing social and political relations between Jordanian-Jordanians and Jordanian-Palestinians.

About 1.8 million registered Palestinian refugees live in Jordan. Most have been absorbed into Jordan's political, social, and economic system. Many Jordanians are wary of America's motives and strongly oppose Israel. The Jordanian government walks a fine line among economic dependence on the United States, the need to keep on friendly terms with Israel, and citizens who tend to resent both situations. Terrorists, possibly connected with al-Qa'ida, struck Jordan in 2005 with coordinated bomb attacks on three Western-owned hotels in Amman, killing 60 and injuring 115 Jordanians and Palestinians. King Abdallah, who succeeded his late father, Husayn, in 1999, still appoints the prime minister and other ministers, as well as half the senators, and can dissolve parliament or delay its elections, but he has not abused his powers.

Iraq was the Arab state at the vortex of the Middle East crisis in the first decade of the new century. Despite the Ba'ath Party's despotic rule from 1968 to 2003, the country was, until the US invasion, among the most modern in the Arab world. Its population was well educated, and it had a large professional middle class. Because Iraq was also well armed, many other Arabs viewed it as the country most likely to stand up to Israel or the United States. Meanwhile, Iraq was condemned by the Americans and some Europeans as a military dictatorship that invaded its neighbors, murdered its Kurdish citizens with poison gas, trampled on human rights, and hoped to retain or to develop weapons of mass destruction. Prior to the 1990 invasion of Kuwait, the United States, Soviet Union, and some European countries sold arms to Saddam's Iraq. The seed stock for Saddam's biological weapons program came from the United States under government license, and American satellite technology helped provide the targeting information for conventional and poison gas attacks against the Iranians during the Iran-Iraq War.

After the 1991 Gulf War, though, both the Clinton and George W. Bush administrations maintained the UN-imposed sanctions against Iraq, which crippled its economy and cost more than 1 million lives. They sought to isolate the country, accusing Saddam of encouraging acts of terrorism against Israel and the United States, for he boasted of his ability to strike at Israel with Scud missiles and publicly gave money to the families of Palestinian suicide bombers. Americans accused Iraq of harboring terrorists tied to al-Qa'ida and of facilitating the 9/11 attacks. The outcome of these accusations, which remain unproven, was the Iraq War. The other Arab countries, as well as France, Germany, and Russia, defied the sanctions and opposed any military action.

Sa'udi Arabia and the Other Gulf States

The Sa'udi kingdom is often singled out by both friends and foes as a major US ally and trading partner. Strictly speaking, the two countries have no formal alliance, but thousands of US troops were stationed in Sa'udi Arabia from 1990 to 2003, and many Sa'udis have received advanced military training in the United States. Direct US participation in the management of Sa'udi oil has decreased since the Sa'udi government bought out Aramco between 1972 and 1980. More than half of Sa'udi crude oil exports go to Asian countries, but in 2011 the country was second only to Canada in exporting petroleum to the United States. Sa'udi Arabia has played an important role in stabilizing crude oil prices by raising or lowering its production according to market conditions, but a growing share is consumed by the Sa'udis themselves. Although oil prices fell in the 1980s and remained low for most of the 1990s, they rose to $140 per barrel in 2008, fell back, then rose again in 2011–2012.

The Sa'udi government remains an absolute monarchy. Sa'udi Arabia has a Consultative Council (Majlis al-Shura); all 150 members (6 of them women) were appointed by the king. Another appointed body, the Allegiance Commission, is charged with selecting the king's successor. Upon King Abdullah's death in January 2015, the Sa'udi royal family chose Salman, Abdullah's half brother, to succeed him, as Nayif ibn 'Abd al-'Aziz al-Sa'ud, who was crown prince, died in 2012. A growing number of Sa'udi young people are completing higher education degrees or technical training requirements. The Sa'udi government bases much of its legitimacy on its strict adherence to the rules and laws of Islam, as interpreted by the Hanbali rite, and the Wahhabi movement remains influential among many Sa'udis, especially the *'ulama* and graduates of Islamic *madrasas*. Riyadh has long exercised influence over other Arab countries because it is the guardian of Mecca and Medina and because so many Arabs from outside Sa'udi Arabia have worked in the kingdom's oil industry. Sa'udi Arabia faces challenges from neighboring states that also export oil and have less restrictive laws against alcohol consumption and nightclubs.

It has also been challenged directly by Islamic militants who have accused the kingdom's leaders of moral laxity and excessive deference to the Americans, leading to attacks on US military personnel in the Khobar

Towers in 1996, terrorist incidents in Riyadh in 2003 and 2004, and an assault on the US consulate in Jidda in December 2004. In response, the Sa'udi government has stepped up its own security forces. It has also instituted political and educational reforms and hired more Sa'udi nationals to replace foreign workers (who still compose more than a quarter of the kingdom's population). But critics claim that it still harbors militant groups attached to al-Qa'ida, and it is well known that Osama bin Laden came from Sa'udi Arabia, as did fifteen hijackers of the planes that attacked the United States on 9/11.

Yemen has traditionally had a tense relationship with Sa'udi Arabia, partly because many Yemeni people and their leaders are Shi'ites known as the Houthis. Yemen is the poorest state in the Arab world, has few known resources, and has long depended on Sa'udi Arabia for the employment of its workers and for economic aid. The union of the Yemen Arab Republic (North Yemen) with the People's Democratic Republic of Yemen (South Yemen) has lasted since 1990, weathering a civil war in 1994. Oil discoveries modestly aided Yemen's economy during the 1990s. Elections for president and a representative assembly were held in 1997, but Yemen has hardly progressed toward democracy. Terrorists attacked Yemeni socialists in 1992, foreign tourists in 1998, a US naval destroyer in Aden's harbor in 2000, and the US Embassy in 2008. More recently, al-Qa'ida has been heavily involved in Yemen's internal struggles. The country is not, therefore, regarded as stable or free from terrorism.

All the other Gulf states are members of the Gulf Cooperation Council and are major oil producers. Oman has a high per capita income, a small population, no current disputes with its neighbors, and, despite recent rumors of al-Qa'ida activity, no terrorist threat. It remains a monarchy with an appointed cabinet and senate and a lower house elected by about a quarter of Oman's adult population. About one-seventh of the country's residents come from India and Pakistan, and its historic ties have been more eastward and southward (across the Arabian Sea) than westward (across the desert).

The United Arab Emirates is a federation of seven Gulf principalities with abundant petroleum and natural gas revenues, which give the country substantial political influence among the other Arab states. Its native-born (or Emirati) citizens make up less than 25 percent of the country's population. The king appoints the prime minister and the cabinet, and the constituent emirates have a Federal State Council (also appointed). Though popular participation in government is negligible, no terrorist threat currently exists. The aged king died in October 2004, and his son succeeded him without opposition.

Qatar, a peninsula on the eastern side of the Arabian Peninsula, enjoys a high per capita income due to oil and natural gas revenues. Its native-born Arab population is roughly equal to its immigrants, mostly Indians, Pakistanis, and Iranians. It has served since 2003 as the main staging area for US troops in the Gulf region and, paradoxically, hosts the satellite television station Al Jazeera, which often criticizes American policies and is widely approved by Arabs, if not always their rulers. Qatar is also a popular resort for Sa'udis seeking an escape from their country's restrictions on alcohol and sexual license. Having had a constitution since 1999, this small state held municipal elections in April 2007. All adult citizens (less than half the population), including women, are eligible to vote. A suicide bomber managed to blow up the Players Theatre in Doha in 2005, killing a British citizen and injuring fifteen other people, and there have been failed attacks on US military installations in Qatar. Americans and Russians have both accused Qatar's government of funding terrorist groups in other countries. However, Qatar has been chosen to host the World Cup in 2022, the first Arab country to do so.

Bahrain is a kingdom made up of one large and several small islands strategically located in the Gulf. Although it enjoys high living standards, its oil reserves are relatively depleted, so it has developed financial and other services that will gradually fill in for an anticipated decline in oil revenues. Its ruling family is Sunni, but two-thirds of its people are Shi'ite, and about 10 percent are Iranian. The country has had a constitution since 1999 and held its first elections for a representative chamber in 2002. Iran has not recently pressed its historic claim to Bahrain, and the terrorist threat and social uprisings of the early 1980s receded for a generation, but now one of the Arab civil wars is raging there.

Kuwait has recovered from the 1990–1991 Iraqi occupation. Its thriving economy continues to attract immigrants from abroad. Kuwaiti Arabs make up less than half the population, which includes Egyptians, Lebanese, Turks, Palestinians (fewer than before 1991), Pakistanis, and Indians. Although under monarchical rule, Kuwait has had a constitution since 1963. In its parliamentary elections, held in 2003, most of the delegates chosen were Islamists. Voting rights, formerly limited to descendants of Kuwaiti subjects as of 1920, have been extended to males who have been naturalized for thirty years, but not yet to women. The population is about 25 percent Shi'ite. The current terrorist risk is small. Although some Kuwaiti youths crossed over to Iraq to join in the jihad against the US occupation and a few older people have given money to al-Qa'ida in Iraq or the Taliban in Afghanistan, the common saying is that "there is no terrorism in Kuwait."

Egypt

The lower valley and delta of the Nile was led by Husni Mubarak from 1981, when he succeeded Anwar al-Sadat as president, until 2011 when he stepped down during the Arab uprisings. He was re-elected four times without opposition; on his fifth try in 2005 he had several challengers, the most prominent of whom was tried and imprisoned after the election. Under its 1971 constitution Egypt had a bicameral legislature consisting of an elected People's Assembly and a partly appointed Consultative Assembly. In all parliamentary elections the National Democratic Party won the majority of seats in both houses; increasingly, the polling was rigged, and voters were coerced into supporting its candidates. Although economic conditions improved during the 1990s, aggregate growth stagnated after 2000, and Egyptians tried to find higher-paying jobs abroad. Opposition to Mubarak came from Islamist groups, especially the Society of the Muslim Brothers, which had renounced terrorism and sometimes ran candidates for public office. More clandestine and terrorist societies included al-Jihad, which had assassinated Sadat and had ties with al-Qaʻida, and the Islamic Group. Between 1990 and 1997 these two extremist groups attacked political leaders, Copts, foreign residents, and tourists. But an attack in 1997 that took the lives of some sixty European tourists in Luxor discredited the militants in the eyes of the Egyptian public, many of whom depend on tourism for their livelihood. Mubarak's regime took stern measures to suppress terrorist cells. However, many Egyptians did not conceal their delight at the 2001 attack on the World Trade Center (four of the hijackers were Egyptians), many expatriates worked for al-Qaʻida, and anti-US feeling intensified during the Iraq War, despite Washington's ongoing commitment to providing military and economic aid totaling almost $2 billion annually.

Summation on Terrorism

From 2001 to 2010, internal violence, including some attacks of a terrorist nature, threatened mainly Iraq, Saʻudi Arabia, Yemen, Israel, and the Palestinian territories. Counterterrorist efforts by some Middle Eastern and foreign governments threaten civilians and public figures alike far more than al-Qaʻida and its affiliates do. The leading practitioners of counterterrorism are the United States, Britain, Israel, Pakistan, and the governments that have been set up as a result of the invasions of Afghanistan in 2001 and Iraq in 2003. Their efforts have not stopped terrorism; in a few cases they have slowed it down, and in many others the influx of European and American troops have stirred up more violent resistance. Counterterrorism is becoming more subtle and targeted, and it must continue to develop along these lines to defeat terrorism. Meanwhile, popular opinion in the Arab countries of Turkey, Iran, Afghanistan, and Pakistan has turned against the massive invasions and bombing raids that have been called the "War on Terrorism." Many locals call it a "War on Militant Muslims."

Islam is a way of life—often a political and social system, too—and popular resistance, usually called nationalism or Islamism, flares up when non-Muslims invade and dominate Muslims. Why should Arabs, Iranians, Turks, Afghans, and Pakistanis join in a war against what they believe in? Why should they conflate this war with "liberation"? American and British leaders may think that Middle Eastern terrorism will fade away if they replace repressive autocracies with pro-Western "democracies." But fully independent Middle Eastern governments, democratically elected, will thwart Western countries that have tried to manipulate them and will support peoples who openly defy the West. The invasion of Afghanistan did eventuate in the formal election of Hamid Karzai in October 2004, but the country remained deeply split along ethnic, tribal, and sectarian lines. It is questionable whether the US-sponsored elections in occupied Iraq could be called free and fair, because it is unlikely that the US occupation authorities would have tolerated a government that opposed their presence in the country. As we will discuss in Chapter 21, the civil war in Syria since 2011, and the rise of ISIL and its success in attracting Western Muslim converts demonstrates the failure of American and European counterterrorism.

THE IRAQ WAR

After the Allied coalition drove Iraqi troops from Kuwait in 1991, some Americans maintained that it should have continued the war, invaded Iraq, and ousted Saddam Husayn. The first President Bush refused to do so, arguing that it would lead the United States into a deadly quagmire. Instead, America and its allies agreed to a ceasefire, allowed Iraq's army to operate helicopters and other light weapons, refrained from aiding the Kurds and Shi'ite Arabs who revolted against Baghdad (expecting outside assistance), and maintained the UN Security Council's sanctions on trade with Iraq until the world body's inspectors could ascertain that the Iraqi government possessed no nuclear, biological, or chemical arms (i.e., weapons of mass destruction). Iraq's powers were further limited by two no-fly zones that barred Iraqi aircraft from the country's northern and southern thirds, although the United Nations had never authorized such a restriction. US planes and long-range missiles struck Iraq in 1993, 1996, and 1998, and there were also occasional defections and efforts to subvert Iraq's military forces. The sanctions alone kept vital supplies from the Iraqi people, at a cost of between 250,000 and 1.7 million lives due to malnutrition and disease. Eventually, the United Nations and Iraq worked out a deal by which Iraq was allowed to sell oil in exchange for food and medicines, but this "oil for food" deal did little good for most Iraqis and probably lined the pockets of high officials on both sides. The Clinton administration and the Republican-dominated Congress drew up plans for invading Iraq and overthrowing Saddam, but internal problems in Washington distracted the US government from any such action.

Bush and the Neoconservatives
The election of George W. Bush in 2000 raised new possibilities for US action. Among those entering his administration was an influential group known as "neoconservatives": Paul Wolfowitz, Richard Perle, and Douglas Feith, among others. Wolfowitz, who became deputy secretary of defense, had in 1992 authored the "Defense Planning Guidance," which proposed military guidelines for the Pentagon: (1) US policy should strive to prevent the emergence of a rival superpower, (2) policy should safeguard US interests and promote American values, and (3) the United States should be prepared to take unilateral [military] action when collective action cannot be orchestrated. In a similar spirit, Perle, aided by Feith and others, wrote a policy brief in 1996 for Israel's Likud called "A Clean Break: A New Strategy for Securing the Realm." It advised Israel to work with Turkey and Jordan to contain, destabilize, and roll back threats to its existence, especially Syria. Israel should uphold the right of hot pursuit of terrorists in Palestinian areas and promote alternatives to Yasir 'Arafat as a leader. The country should forge a new relationship with the US government, abandon its pursuit of a comprehensive peace with the Arabs, and possibly aid Jordan in restoring the Hashimite monarchy in Iraq, thus weakening both Syria and Iran. Israel under Prime Minister Netanyahu did not adopt the "new strategy." Israel did not consult regularly with Turkey and Jordan, but it did cease to regard 'Arafat as a peace partner and came to reject any peace process that might lead to an independent Palestinian state.

As you can see, the neoconservatives have little use for diplomacy. For a long time, and in many countries, statesmen and scholars have formulated two contrasting approaches to international relations. One favors diplomacy and mediation as the first resort when an international conflict arises. This approach would uphold and strengthen international law and keep the United Nations viable, hoping to promote human rights and dignity throughout the world. In the United States, most leading Democrats and Republicans promoted this position just after World War II, though some did not. The opposing approach sees diplomacy as a façade, behind which force, meaning military power and the will to use it, settles international disputes. Its advocates, including the neoconservatives, scorn international law and view the United Nations as a nuisance. They argue that the United States can win any struggle when it really wants to do so, blaming its Vietnam defeat on a failure of willpower. They admire Israel's assertiveness and efforts to maintain control over the territories it has occupied since 1967. Consequently, they have aligned themselves with Israel's right-wing parties, notably the Likud.

The neoconservatives, promoting what they called the Project for the New American Century, wrote an open letter to Bill Clinton in 1998 advising him to remove Saddam Husayn from power. Allied with these three men were the Jewish Institute for National Security Affairs; the Washington Institute for Near East Policy and its parent organization, AIPAC; *Commentary;* the *National Review;* the *New Republic;* and Sun Myung Moon's *Washington Times.* Many evangelical Christians support these groups because of their belief that all Jews must be gathered in Israel before the Final Day of Judgment.

Most Americans agreed that Washington should promote American values and defend US interests. They probably did not favor unilaterally toppling Syria's government or invading Iraq as part of a neoconservative drive to spread democracy throughout the Middle East. Prior to the 2000 election, George W. Bush and Dick Cheney had been oil company executives eager to preserve access to Middle Eastern oil, an ongoing US interest. Both were susceptible to neoconservative appeals to fight terrorism by spreading American influence and dominance, which they called freedom and democracy. Upon his election, Bush ignored outgoing President Clinton's warning about the threat from al-Qa'ida and focused instead on Saddam's Iraq with its alleged weapons of mass destruction. Their imagined threat to the United States could easily be impressed on the Americans; the neoconservatives' desire to strengthen the alliance with Israel was a tougher sell.

Right after the terrorist attacks on the World Trade Center and the Pentagon, the US government began preparing for an invasion of Afghanistan to capture Osama bin Laden and destroy al-Qa'ida's training camps. Many other countries offered to aid the Bush administration against this terrorist threat, which was palpable to European and Asian governments, and the invasion and occupation of Afghanistan were carried out by a coalition of countries, notably including Pakistan, which had formerly backed the Taliban. The Taliban regime fled Kabul, and a new regime was cobbled together in Pakistan with Hamid Karzai as prime minister. Although the country has not been truly united, it did manage to convene a tribal conclave (*loya jirga*) in 2003 and hold elections in 2004.

The Bush administration allied itself with many Asian and African governments against insurgent groups linked to or inspired by al-Qa'ida. These military and diplomatic efforts constitute the War on Terrorism. This slogan or policy has been accepted by many Americans and Europeans, though terrorism cannot be defeated by bombing cities and sending in troops. Arguably, true counterterrorism would include strengthening police, covertly arming the terrorists' local rivals, practicing quiet diplomacy, promoting cultural exchanges, and removing the conditions that cause terrorism to flourish as a method or as a doctrine.

Acts of resistance to US political ambitions do not necessarily constitute terrorism. For the past half century, America's Middle East policies have angered peoples and governments and stirred up anti-Americanism and violence against the United States and its allies. If Washington truly wants to combat terrorism, it must change its own attitude and policies. This did not occur during the Bush administration. Many hoped President Barack Obama would reassess US actions in the Middle East. He delivered a stirring speech in Cairo in June 2009 supporting improved Muslim-US relations, but he has failed to follow through.

The Invasion of Iraq

Even as Washington was gearing up to fight in Afghanistan, its most prominent neoconservative, Paul Wolfowitz, called for invading Iraq, possibly as a first step toward changing all Arab governments opposing the United States and Israel. Controlling Iraq's oil was another US goal. He quickly won over Defense Secretary Donald Rumsfeld and Vice President Cheney. President Bush soon agreed, redirecting resources that could have been used against al-Qa'ida in Afghanistan to invade Iraq, whose connection with the terrorist network was often asserted but never proved. In October 2002 both houses of Congress passed by overwhelming margins a resolution authorizing Bush to send troops into Iraq. They accepted the Bush administration's insistence that Iraq possessed, and was about to use, weapons of mass destruction. Under US pressure, the UN Security Council also passed a resolution demanding that Iraq account for and surrender its nuclear, biological, and chemical weapons or "face serious consequences." The UN inspection teams, which had been hastily withdrawn in 1998 under orders from the Clinton administration, were sent back into Iraq to find its weapons of mass destruction. None were found. The Bush administration argued that the UN teams were being tricked by the Iraqi regime and would never succeed. Washington stepped up its propaganda, diplomatic pressure, and military preparations.

Future historians will debate the rationale for the Iraq War, which began with aerial attacks and an Anglo-American invasion on 20 March 2003. One motive was to secure Iraq's oil fields and installations. Another stated reason was to oust Saddam's dictatorship and replace it with a democratic government, along with promoting freedom and human rights. Finding and removing Iraq's weapons of mass destruction were what the public was told. They never were found, and a subsequent US report admitted that they no longer existed in 2003. The neoconservatives wanted to overthrow or at least neutralize the governments of Iraq, Iran, and Syria and to promote Israel's power and security. The Americans expected a brief war. An exiled Iraqi who led the US-backed Iraqi National Congress, Ahmad Chalabi, convinced US politicians that American invaders would be greeted as liberators and that he could even broker a peace between Iraq and Israel. The Bush administration believed the American people would support the war and consequently vote to re-elect Bush in 2004.

In the short run, this was true. The invaders quickly defeated Iraq's army and drove Saddam Husayn and the Ba'athists from power. Aerial attacks and guided missiles destroyed many strongholds, as well as Iraqi homes, shops, schools, and roads, in a "shock and awe" campaign. Although France, Germany, Russia, and even Canada opposed the war, the Americans assembled a "coalition of the willing" that included at least token forces from forty countries. The coalition's casualties were light. No one reported on how many Iraqi soldiers—or civilians—were killed, maimed, or missing. A statue of Saddam was pulled down in a major Baghdad square, and images were broadcast to demonstrate popular revulsion against the deposed dictator, though in fact the demolition was largely carried out by the invaders. The coalition set up an occupation government in one of Saddam's palaces, and ambitious reconstruction plans were announced. The remnants of the army and police force were dissolved, and all Ba'ath Party members were dismissed from their jobs. These were foolish mistakes: instead of co-opting Iraqi forces to side with the invaders, the Americans rendered them unemployed, destitute, and eager to join a militant resistance. In 2014, many former Ba'athists were fighting for ISIL.

It soon turned out that the coalition, especially the Americans, had no idea how to restore order in the country (see Map 20.1), or even in

Map 20.1   Iraq

Baghdad, with its 6 million inhabitants. Looters broke into the Iraqi National Museum, the National Library and Archives, and most government
offices (US troops stood by, protecting only the Oil Ministry). Schools
remained closed. Electric power was cut off and only slowly and partially
restored in Baghdad. Clinics and hospitals lacked basic medical supplies.

Raw sewage flowed into the Tigris, as the treatment plants were wrecked. Without police protection, gangs of thugs broke into people's houses, kidnapped civilians, stole cars, and dishonored women and girls if they ventured into the streets. No one guarded the storehouses of Iraqi munitions. With Iraq's borders not secured, volunteers from other countries flocked to join the Iraqis who wanted to liberate their own nation from foreign troops.

Although Bush proclaimed an end to the fighting on 1 May 2003, the insurgents stepped up their resistance, and growing numbers of US and British troops were killed. The Sunni Triangle, a complex of towns northwest of Baghdad that had enjoyed power under Saddam, became a major center of resistance, and the coalition forces went in with helicopters, tanks, and mortars. Predominantly Shi'ite cities, such as Basra, Kufa, Najaf, and Sadr (formerly Saddam) City, also rebelled. Suicide bombers and car bombs proliferated as coalition troop morale plummeted. A great number of Iraqi civilians were killed or maimed, died from disease due to poor sanitation or malnutrition, or saw their houses broken into, looted, or destroyed. At least 4 million fled to safer areas in Iraq or refuge in neighboring countries. Thousands more Iraqis were jailed without charges. In Abu Ghraib (one of the largest and most feared of Saddam's prisons), US troops tortured and humiliated some of the detainees. The Sunni Triangle became an insurgent stronghold. After a failed attack in May, coalition forces invaded Falluja in November 2004, expelling most of its civilian inhabitants and killing thousands of insurgents amid heavy destruction of hospitals, schools, mosques, shops, and homes. Saddam was captured, imprisoned, tried in an Iraqi court, and finally hanged, but popular resistance was growing among both Sunnis (particularly al-Qa'ida in Iraq) and a variety of Shi'ite militias.

Many military strategists had argued before the war, and during its early stages, that the coalition troops that invaded Iraq were too few to occupy, pacify, and rebuild the country. Secretary Rumsfeld had insisted that a small, highly mobile force would suffice. But as insurgent attacks mounted and some coalition partners withdrew, the neoconservatives and then Rumsfeld left the US government, and the Republicans lost control of both the Senate and the House of Representatives in the 2006 elections, Bush had to adopt a new strategy. Finally, in January 2007, he announced a surge in US forces to defeat the insurgency in Iraq at least to the point where the largely Shi'ite Iraqi government could make peace with Sunni leaders and negotiate an oil revenue–sharing deal with the Sunnis and the Kurds. To implement this strategy, he ordered an additional 28,500 American soldiers to go to Iraq, some for the third or fourth time.

Indeed, the violence did subside, and US casualties declined. However, the reduction in violence was caused less by increased troop strength than by three other factors: (1) the complete removal of Sunnis from religiously mixed neighborhoods and provinces, reducing the number of sectarian killings; (2) US payments to Sunni tribal leaders to reorient their efforts from resisting Iraq's government to fighting al-Qa'ida terrorism, probably a temporary arrangement at best; and (3) the Iranian government's decision to promote stability in Iraq, given its rising influence on the country's Shi'ite government and hence its restraining influence on the most prominent Shi'ite militia, Muqtada al-Sadr's Mahdi Army. The US government, political leaders, and media claimed that "the surge worked." In reality though, only the Iraqis could have won the Iraq War by achieving peace and democracy.

At the end of 2008 the UN mandate under which US troops operated in Iraq expired. After long negotiations, the United States and Iraqi president Nuri al-Maliki drafted a Status of Forces Agreement, which was endorsed by the Iraqi Parliament. This new bilateral agreement set a deadline of 31 December 2011 for the complete withdrawal of American forces. They did indeed leave by that date. Iraq ended up with a Shi'ite government with a religious fundamentalist coloring and under the partial influence of Iran. Such results were not among the goals of President Bush and his neoconservative advisers. We will leave it to you, our readers, having learned some Middle East history, to judge whether the Iraq War was worth what it has cost American taxpayers and soldiers and, of course, the Iraqi people.

Nearly all Arab peoples opposed the Anglo-American occupation of Iraq, even if some of their governments continued to facilitate troop movements and overflights. The Iraq War had no effect on Syria's withdrawal from Lebanon or the holding of Egypt's first contested presidential election in 2005. Many educated young men and women in the oil-rich countries wanted to have a greater voice in their governments, too, but promises were not matched by political reforms. In Chapter 21, we will discuss how frustrated political hopes led to a wave of revolutions in 2011.

THE CONTEST FOR PALESTINE (REDUX)

Although the 1990s marked a time when many outsiders and some Middle Easterners hoped for a settlement to the century-long Jewish-Arab contest for Palestine, events of the early twenty-first century dashed these hopes. Both Israelis and Palestinians suffered from the ongoing violent flare-ups interspersed with periodic ceasefires.

Breakdown of the "Peace Process"

The widely-used term *peace process* is a hard concept to define. Conflicts may be overt and violent or covert and subtle. They may involve physical fighting or just verbal argument. Some are resolved by mediation, arbitration, or patient diplomacy. But resolution does not occur unless all the parties in some degree seek an end to the conflict and are willing to compromise and possibly make some sacrifices. They must also expect to benefit from its resolution. If making peace is to occur in phases, as between Egypt and Israel between 1977 and 1982, both parties need to see benefits from each phase and expect that these benefits will continue. If negotiations are conducted publicly by heads of state or government, all parties must prepare with quiet parleys by lower-level diplomats who know the contestants' needs and can propose compromises that do not jeopardize any party's national security.

During the Clinton administration, the US government played a major role in the talks between Israel and the Arab governments, including the Palestinian Authority, led by Yasir 'Arafat. American-brokered negotiations, which may be viewed as partial successes, included the peace treaty between Jordan and Israel in 1995 and the 1997 Hebron agreement between Israel and the Palestinian Authority. The Oslo I and II Accords, attempts to resolve the ongoing Palestinian-Israeli conflict with the first face-to-face agreement between the two countries, were intended to be the one framework for future negotiations and relations between the Israeli government and Palestinians. The success of the accords is debatable. They can be viewed as progressive steps frustrated by later events. However, they can also be interpreted as having inherent flaws doomed from the start because the United States refused to pressure Israel when, just after the accords were signed, that country proceeded to expand its established settlements in the occupied territories. Each side committed terrorist acts against the other's civilians.

Failures included the Syrian-Israeli talks that broke down in January 2000 over the definition of their future border and, most conspicuously, the Camp David Summit between Yasir 'Arafat and Ehud Barak, hosted by Bill Clinton, in July of the same year. Most Americans thought that 'Arafat should have accepted Barak's seemingly generous offer, which would have provided for an Israeli withdrawal from almost all of the West Bank and Gaza Strip and given the Palestinians control over Christian and Muslim holy places in Jerusalem's Old City. However, Barak's offer would have created several "Bantustans" (which were small areas formerly set aside by the South African white-dominated regime for black African tribes), not a viable and independent Palestinian state. 'Arafat was blamed for insisting on the Palestinians' "right of return," a claim that has been repeated in resolutions passed by the UN General Assembly ever since 1948.

Arguably, it is doubtful that many Palestinians alive now would exercise such a claim to become, in effect, like the Israeli Arabs, but 'Arafat was a politician who had to heed his constituents. He could not negate the rights of millions of Palestinian refugees based on international law as well as the United Nations. Nevertheless, one can understand why most Israelis want to maintain the predominantly Jewish character of their state and why many Israelis and Americans became exasperated with 'Arafat's intransigent negotiating style at Camp David. Israeli and Palestinian negotiators subsequently met in Sharm al-Shaykh and Taba, making further progress on the details of a settlement (sweetening the terms for Palestinians), aided by Clinton's "Bridging Document." Both Clinton and his chief negotiator, Dennis Ross, stated that the two sides came closer to a peace settlement in 2000 than they had before or ever have since.

Intensification of the Conflict
Regrettably for the negotiators, time ran out on Clinton, and George W. Bush entered the White House with a different agenda that reflected his evangelical Christian commitment to a Greater Israel. Influenced by neoconservatives like Paul Wolfowitz and self-styled realists like Condoleezza Rice, Bush sought to weaken 'Arafat, whom he blamed for the renewed violence that followed the failure of the Camp David Summit, leading to fierce Israeli reprisals and the election of hard-liner Ariel Sharon as Israel's new prime minister. Sharon became a frequent visitor to the White House. 'Arafat, deemed a supporter of terrorism, was no longer welcome. The "Bridging Document" was shelved. Later on, a "Road Map" to peace, drafted by the United States in consultation with Russia, the Europeans, and the United Nations, foundered on Israel's refusal to stop expanding its West Bank settlements, even though the proposals would have favored its interests more than Clinton's plan had. The US government no longer claimed to be an honest broker between Israelis and Palestinians.

The effect of the 9/11 attacks was to bring together the United States and Israel in what Bush at first called a "crusade" (later, when told that Muslims hated the term, he renamed it a "war") on terrorism. Americans shared the Israelis' horror when some Palestinians strapped bombs to their bodies and blew themselves up amid Israeli teenagers waiting to enter a popular discotheque, passengers on a Jerusalem bus, and diners in a Haifa restaurant liked by both Arabs and Jews. Various conditions arguably led to these attacks. During its prolonged occupation of the West

Bank, Israel has confiscated Arab land and water, flattened homes, and torn up farmlands to make room for Jewish settlements. It has imposed prolonged curfews on whole towns and placed hundreds of checkpoints and roadblocks that impeded commerce and travel for Arabs in the occupied territories. A state should protect its borders and defend its citizens from terrorism, but these policies aim at permanent colonization and ultimate absorption of land.

Palestinians committed violent as well as nonviolent acts of resistance to the Israeli occupation, but no suicide bombings took place until after an American Jewish fundamentalist living in the occupied West Bank walked into a Hebron mosque in 1994 and killed twenty-nine worshippers in cold blood. Since then he has come to be seen as a martyr and hero by the Orthodox Jewish settlers in the occupied territories. As Palestinian violence intensified, especially after negotiations broke down in 2000, Israel adopted policies of mass arrests, targeted assassinations, and the demolition of homes of relatives of Palestinian suicide bombers.

The Israelis also began to build a wall as a barrier to terrorism (see Map 20.2). The Wall, which Israelis call a "security fence," is a series of electronically monitored fences, barbed wire, and concrete barriers up to 9 meters (28 feet) high. Most Israeli parties (and their supporters abroad) favored its construction. At first some Palestinians supported it on the mistaken assumption that it would be placed along the pre-1967 borders. In fact, however, the Israelis have placed it deep within occupied territory, taking land internationally recognized as belonging to a future Palestinian state. The International Court of Justice in the Hague declared the Wall in violation of international law in 2004, a ruling ignored by Sharon's government.

The Wall created a physical barrier that divided West Bank cities and villages into virtual cantons, or small and separated provinces (see Figure 20.1). It compressed 4.3 million Palestinians into ghettos with the world's highest unemployment figures (25 percent in the West Bank and 45 percent in Gaza), few resources for development, and indefinite poverty. Palestinians are often harassed not only by Israeli soldiers but also by well-armed settlers. Israelis believe that the Wall has diminished suicide bombings, but their periodic cessation reflects more the changing strategies of such groups as Hamas. Other forms of violent resistance, such as the shelling of Israeli cities and towns, remain viable options, making Israelis feel even less secure. Israel's supreme court ruled that parts of the Wall must be moved, but its construction has continued.

If Americans and Israelis were horrified by scenes of the aftermath of suicide bombings, Arabs shared the Palestinians' rage and revulsion

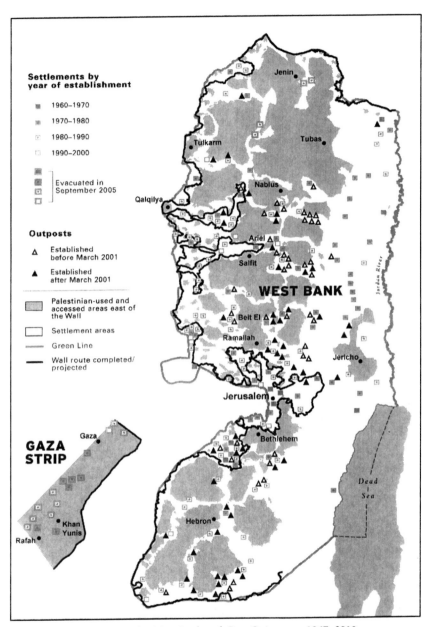

Settlements by year of establishment

- 1960–1970
- 1970–1980
- 1980–1990
- 1990–2000

Evacuated in September 2005

Outposts

△ Established before March 2001

▲ Established after March 2001

Palestinian-used and accessed areas east of the Wall

☐ Settlement areas

Green Line

Wall route completed/ projected

GAZA STRIP

Gaza
Khan Yunis
Rafah

WEST BANK

Jenin
Tulkarm
Tubas
Nablus
Qalqilya
Ariel
Salfit
Beit El
Ramallah
Jericho
Jerusalem
Bethlehem
Hebron

Jordan River

Dead Sea

Map 20.2   Settlements in the West Bank and Gaza Strip areas, 1967–2010

Figure 20.1   The separation wall

when they saw televised pictures of Israeli tanks rumbling into the streets of Jenin and Nablus, bulldozers wrecking the homes of terrorist suspects in Gaza, helicopters firing missiles into crowded urban centers, and troops besieging the Church of the Nativity in Bethlehem. Zionist propaganda counted how many innocent Israelis were killed or maimed by Palestinian suicide bombers, while Arab satellite television stations like Al Jazeera drove home the point that at least three times as many Palestinians, including many women and children, died at the hands of Israeli soldiers. Almost concurrently, the Palestinians captured two young Israeli reservists, took them to the Jenin police station, killed them, and threw their bodies out among celebrating crowds.

The economy of Israel suffered from the consequent loss of investment and tourism revenues. That of the Palestinians plummeted as an Israeli blockade cut off their trade with the outside world and barred many from going to their jobs in Israel. 'Arafat, the only Palestinian leader who could have delivered a meaningful peace, became a prisoner in his Ramallah presidential compound. At US insistence, he named first Mahmoud 'Abbas and then Ahmad Quray' his prime minister. But the Israelis refused to talk to anyone in the Palestinian Authority as long as terrorism continued. Increasingly, attacks on Israelis were carried out by Hamas (the

Palestinians' leading Muslim resistance group) or Hizballah (backed by Syria and Iran), neither of which answered to the Palestinian Authority.

On 11 November 2004 'Arafat died of an undisclosed illness. Some Westerners and Israelis hoped his death would shake things up and revitalize the "peace process." This hope was based on the questionable assumption that 'Arafat was the main obstacle to peace. The Palestinians did proceed to elect a new president. The Western press viewed these elections as a great move forward, and indeed direct elections in the Arab world are rare. But how meaningful was this vote in Palestine? First and foremost, the elections took place in an environment of Israel's ongoing occupation. With the exception of Mahmoud 'Abbas, the West's favored candidate, the Israeli authorities restricted the campaign mobility of those running for office. A significant minority of Palestinian voters, answering the call of Hamas and Islamic Jihad, chose to boycott the polls. Besides, most Palestinians do not live in the occupied territories; rather, they are refugees in the Palestinian diaspora. They could not vote, even though the winners would be negotiating with Israel over their rights. The winner of the election was 'Abbas, the head of Fatah. He has pursued peace with Israel, as the PLO has done since 1988. He and his backers have renounced armed resistance, hoping that negotiations with Israel would lead to a just two-state solution.

In January 2006 the Palestinians living in the West Bank and Gaza Strip, having chosen their president in 2005, went to the polls in an internationally supervised election for the 132-member Palestinian Legislative Council. Three-quarters of all eligible voters voted. The result shocked everyone: the Israelis, their supporters, 'Abbas, and even the winners. The Change and Reform list, whose members were associated with Hamas, took 74 seats. 'Abbas's Fatah movement won only 45, with the other 13 going to small, mostly secular parties. This outcome upset the plans of the Bush administration, Israel, and the Palestinian Authority, all of whom were pursuing a two-state solution more or less on Israel's terms. Although Hamas said it would negotiate with Israel, it wanted no more than a ten-year truce. The immediate reaction of the Bush administration, the Israeli government, and the Palestinian Authority was to reject the election results. This decision had dire consequences for the Gaza Strip Palestinians.

Outsiders' Involvement

Both Israelis and Palestinians have influential outside supporters. The US government has stepped up arms supplies to Israel and increasingly coordinated strategy with the Jewish state in the war against terrorism. The coordination has reached a point where the boundaries between Israel's and America's interests have seemingly vanished. A Defense Department analyst was accused in September 2004 of passing to Israel, via AIPAC, classified US documents on Iran. Zionists cooperate with neoconservatives to reinforce American popular support for Israel. This one-sidedness has not only undermined America's role as an "honest broker," but it has also made the US government contradict its claim to promote democracy in the Middle East.

Arab governments have vocally (but not militarily) supported the Palestinian resistance and attacked the repressive aspects of American and Israeli policies. They have not, however, effectively used their control of oil to influence American and European policies and behavior. Sa'udi Arabia took an important step when it proposed in an Arab League meeting in March 2002 a comprehensive plan that would have offered Israel peace and diplomatic recognition in exchange for Israel's withdrawal from the lands it captured in 1967. The offer was repeated at an Arab summit meeting in March 2007. Israel ignored it both times, leading others to question its real desire for peace. Commercial ties were formed between Israel and some North African countries, and Israel's foreign minister did visit Qatar in April 2008, but diplomatic relations between Israel and Egypt were frosty. Relations between Israel and Jordan were warmer at the governmental, but not the popular, level. Arabs generally believed that Israel trained Americans to interrogate, torture, and torment Iraqi prisoners. Israel supported the Kurds in Iraq and Turkey and was deeply (but secretly) involved in the Iraq War. Israelis pointed to Iran as a growing factor in the struggle and have expressed alarm at its nuclear program, the growing range and accuracy of its missiles, and threats by Iran's leaders to destroy the Jewish state. In recent times Israel has repeatedly threatened to attack Iran's nuclear development sites. The struggle has increasingly become a Muslim-Jewish one, which is drawing in peoples hitherto uninvolved in what used to be the Palestinian- or Arab-Israeli conflict. A struggle between religions is apt to be more emotional and harder to resolve than a clash of nationalisms.

The Palestinians want to have an independent and viable state on the West Bank and Gaza Strip. They will give up their claim to 78 percent of their historic homeland. Should they have to haggle over the remaining 22 percent? The Israelis claim to seek recognition by their Arab neighbors and security for their people. Yet their actions—clinging to the occupied territories (arguably the main source of their insecurity), the ongoing colonization of this land, and parallel destruction of Palestinian civil society—arguably suggest that their true goal is a "Greater Israel" rather than a peaceful and secure Israel. A policy based on fear begets conditions that increase fear. If Israel really wants peace, it should adopt the compromises needed to achieve it. What are the actual motives of the US government, American Jews, and evangelical Christians for backing Israel so unreservedly? Does this policy promote Israel's long-term security?

Both Palestinians and Israelis have made policy mistakes that render them less secure. Acts of force and terrorism by one side beget reprisals by the other. Unilateral concessions, whether by Israelis or Palestinians, are viewed as weakness and often lead to renewed violence. Any concession toward a peace settlement must be reciprocal and related to the unspoken as well as the stated concerns of one's negotiating partner. Israel's preoccupation with security emanates from the Jewish preoccupation with survival, always present but intensified since the Holocaust. The Israelis say the Palestine National Charter calls for their destruction, although the Palestinians began the process of annulling this part of the charter in 1996 and 'Arafat announced in 1997 that it had been abrogated. The Palestinians' fear of Israeli colonization is perhaps part of a greater Arab anxiety about Western imperialism, now enhanced by the American invasion and occupation of Iraq. If a series of concessions by both Israelis and Palestinians occur, peace may happen. If both sides come to realize the crushing costs and horrible consequences of a protracted and unrestricted war, they may stay their extremist tendencies.

Since 2007 the democratically elected Hamas government has been isolated within the Gaza Strip. President 'Abbas asserted unilateral control over those small parts of the West Bank still governed by Palestinians. Pressured by the United States and Israel, he has tried to nullify the Hamas victory. In the meantime, Hamas and allied Islamist militias stepped up attacks on southern Israeli communities, using missiles made in Gaza. These attacks were launched in response to the siege conditions, illegal under international law, described above. They caused minimal damage, death, and injury but did bring a sense of fear and terror to southern Israel. Israel retaliated in 2009 with attacks on Gaza's population and efforts to economically stifle the 1.8 million people living in the Gaza Strip. Finally, a ceasefire was arranged through Egyptian mediation.

CONCLUSION

The 9/11 attacks on the United States led to a widening chasm of distrust and anger between Americans and most of the peoples of the Middle East.

This alienation was evident at both the level of governments and among the peoples of both sides. The attacks were evil, for they killed, injured, or otherwise harmed many innocent Americans. The responses by the US government were maladroit and incompetent, and they also killed, injured, or harmed many innocent Middle Easterners. The military invasions of Afghanistan and Iraq protected no one from terrorism, and their costs have exceeded $1 trillion to the US government and are likely to rise further in the years to come. The costs to the Afghan and Iraqi people are beyond calculation. Two wrongs, indeed a million wrongs, cannot make a right.

21

In the Season of Arab Discontent

Beginning in 2010 the Arab world entered a new phase popularly called the Arab Spring. We may compare this phase to a person who has long lived under stress. Finally he or she reaches a point where the frustrations are unbearable and explodes in anger. No one can predict when the explosion will come, but when it does, that person will never go back to his or her stressful life unless forced to do so. Uprisings, major or minor, occurred in nearly every Arab country during this time. Most were initiated by workers or students. At first they drew support both at home and abroad. But outbursts of anger, even if they relieve some frustration, often collide with forces of reaction. Demonstrations turn into scuffles, fights, clouds of tear gas, spraying water cannons, gunshots, and bomb blasts. Entrenched regimes may resist bitterly, with lockups, torture, and unexplained mutilations and killing. In the Arab states where uprisings have succeeded in changing leadership, such as Tunisia, Egypt, and Libya, the forces of authoritarianism, militarism, and tribalism persist and may negate the democratic demands of some of the demonstrators. It is too early to speak of a revolution, and the Arab Spring has turned to bitter winter in countries like Bahrain, Syria, Libya, and Yemen.

Any historian writing a textbook that includes the recent past walks on eggshells. Events occur suddenly in the Middle East. Projections are hazardous. Who knows what a future reader will see as having been the major Middle Eastern events from 2008 to 2015? Let us give you an example by looking backward. At the dawn of the twentieth century, a burning issue was the building of a Berlin-to-Baghdad railway by a German company. Our forebears believed this railway would enhance German power in the Ottoman Empire and harm the interests of Britain, France, and Russia. In contrast, few noticed that a British subject obtained from the Persian government a concession that led to the first big oil discovery in the Middle

East. Yet today we see Middle East oil as much more important than a railroad that was never completed. By the same token, will an incident that we now view as a major event seem trivial by 2020?

SOME BACKGROUND

The Arab World has experienced large-scale popular uprisings from North Africa to the Persian Gulf. They began in December 2010 in Tunisia and spread the next month to Egypt. Since then, popular protests have broken out in Syria, Jordan, Yemen, Bahrain, Libya, Iran, and elsewhere. Not all of these revolts are harbingers of spring. As of this writing, that prospect seems confined to Tunisia and Egypt, and those revolts are likely to be short lived. In Egypt, tensions between the army and the first democratically elected president, Mohamed Morsi, ultimately led to his removal and the reinstatement of the army to power in 2013, which arguably nullified the demands of the demonstrators. Elsewhere, suppression of popular aspirations for a more equitable and democratic political environment has brought misery and disillusionment.

We know the conditions that lead to outbreaks of unrest: economic problems such as high unemployment, price inflation, and erosion of local enterprise caused by competition from abroad due to "free-trade" policies; rampant corruption that concentrates wealth in the ruling clique; and entrenched power that uses harsh, even criminal, repression by the "state security services" to protect criminal regimes. In all the Arab countries some or all of these problems have persisted for decades. Against this backdrop we can outline a general evolution of the protests that we now witness:

1. The default positions of people living under dictatorships are fear and passivity. The security services create an atmosphere of fear that reinforces the natural inclination of most people to be apolitical, to mind their own business, to remain uninvolved.

2. Against this background, some outrageous or inspiring incident may occur. In Tunisia it was the self-immolation of Mohamed Bouazizi; in Egypt it was a brutal murder of a young businessman, Khalid Sa'id, by the police. Such an atrocity is enough to overcome people's fear and passivity and bring them into the streets.

3. At this point, the regime in question often attacks the protesters. This may mean killing some of them, as happened during the June 2009 Green Movement in Iran. Here the trigger was the contested presidential re-election of Mahmoud Ahmadinejad. This usually ends the

protests, at least for a while. The population may return to its previous sullen passivity, or an underground movement may arise, possibly leading to civil war.

4. If, however, the regime hesitates, as happened in Tunisia and Egypt, or acquiesces in some of the people's demands, or if important elements of the security services or the army refuse orders, more people forsake their usual apathy, fear, and passivity. All the discontent and hatred that have built up over decades come pouring out in what Arabs called "days of rage."

5. If and when the small crowds become huge, the regime may offer half measures such as cabinet shuffles, "dialogue" committees, and vague promises, hoping to sap the protests, as happened in Morocco and Oman.

6. If the populace distrusts the half measures and the protests persist, the dictatorial regimes may fall, or a brutal civil war may ensue, as is happening in Syria.

REBELLIONS ACROSS THE REGION

Most of the major events in the Arab Middle East from December 2010 up to the time these lines are being written focus on the uprisings that we call the Arab Spring and on the repercussions and reactions that we might call the Arab Fall and Winter.

Tunisia

Zayn al-'Abidin ben 'Ali wielded dictatorial power in Tunisia for almost a quarter century. Unemployment had hovered around 14 percent for much of that time, but university graduates fared even worse: 25 percent failed to find work. Many Tunisians saw no future for themselves or their children. Corruption thrived among those close to the dictator's circle as well as within the police. The police force was a privileged element that both protected and was protected by the regime. Its interests were thus isolated from those of the larger Tunisian population.

This was the situation when, on 17 December 2010, Mohamed Bouazizi, twenty-six years old, had a confrontation with the police in the town of Sidi Bouzid. Bouazizi's sole means of support was a cart from which he sold fruits and vegetables. A policewoman confiscated his cart despite his protest. The authorities refused to hear his subsequent appeal. This toxic mix of economic despair, police brutality, and bureaucratic indifference to his plight led Bouazizi to set himself on fire in front of the Sidi Bouzid municipal building. This was the atrocity that set off mass protests in Tunisia, although other cases of self-immolation had taken place in other places in previous years in Tunisia and Morocco, and, indirectly, the rest of the Arab world.

By the end of 2010, confrontations were occurring daily throughout Tunisia. Police violence escalated, but not rapidly or harshly enough to quell the protests. On the eleventh day of the disturbances, President Ben 'Ali went on TV to tell the population that the protests would harm the economy and warned that demonstrators would be firmly punished. His speech had little impact. Soon, the poor and unemployed were joined by large numbers of lawyers and students who demonstrated in solidarity with those who had been arrested, injured, and killed by the police. Early in 2011 an anonymous cyberactivist organization proclaimed Operation Tunisia, attacking government websites and temporarily shutting some of them down. Then, in the second week of January, the regime escalated the violence by ordering snipers to shoot randomly into the crowds. Instead of quelling the protests, this action shocked most Tunisians and earned the protesters nationwide support.

At this point, 13 January, the regime tried to save itself by offering concessions. Abandoned by other members of his regime, Ben 'Ali fled the country the next day, whereupon the police proceeded to arrest those members of his family and allies who remained. This was the period when the regime tried to placate the protesters by changing the faces of those in charge. Cabinet ministers were shuffled around, as surviving elements of the ruling elite clung to power. The population continued to protest, insisting that any new government had to be free from the old ruling elite. In a parallel development, internal order melted away along with the regime's police force. Only then did the Tunisian army take charge.

Most Tunisians were willing to tolerate temporary army control, which probably saved the country from civil war. The army was acceptable because, unlike the police, the army rejected orders to shoot at the protesting crowds. The Tunisian army is a conscript force, and a relatively small one at that, drawn from the whole population. Many of the soldiers would have defied an order to fire on people just like themselves. It was probably the Tunisian army's chief of staff, General Rashid Ammar, who told Ben 'Ali that his position was no longer tenable. Once Ben 'Ali left the country, the dictatorship began to collapse. The army is also credited with maintaining order during the ensuing political vacuum, which might otherwise have led to chaos.

Later in the year, on 23 October, elections were held for a 217-member Constituent Assembly. The victor in these elections was the moderate

Islamist *al-Nahda* (Awakening) Party led by Hamadi Jebali, taking 41.4 percent of the vote. Second place was taken by the secular Congress for the Republic Party, whose leader, Moncef Marzouki, is a noted human rights activist. The new assembly had to draft a new constitution for Tunisia that reflected a workable balance between Islamist and secular ideologies. In January 2014, the Tunisian Assembly adopted one of the most progressive constitutions in the Arab world by 200 votes out of 216. Beji Caid Essebsi, who served during Ben 'Ali's rule as foreign minister, was elected in the recent presidential election. After the Arab Spring, Essebsi reinvented himself a technocrat. His secular *Nida' Tunis* (Call for Tunisia) Party benefited from the popular backlash against al-Nahda and other Islamic voices. In October 2014, Essebsi's party defeated al-Nahda in the legislative elections, allowing secular control of the government.

Egypt

The Egyptians had long borne the dictatorship of Husni Mubarak, an air force officer who took charge after the 1981 assassination of Anwar al-Sadat. Egypt's economic growth was impressive, but the gap had widened between rich and poor and the country's mood was sullen. A strike by textile workers in the industrial city of al-Mahalla al-Kubra inspired a student group to found the 6 April Movement to support them. In 2010 the brutal police murder of a young Alexandria businessman, Khalid Sa'id, and the ensuing cover-up angered many Egyptians. Some of this anger was vented in demonstrations organized via the Internet, notably on a Facebook page called "We Are All Khalid Sa'id." Though electronic social networking certainly facilitated Egypt's protest movement, it is an exaggeration to say that it caused these protests. It was high prices of food and fuel, unemployment, economic despair, repression, and corruption that sparked them.

Wikileaks released US government cables revealing the depth of Egyptian corruption in January 2011. This only increased popular anger in Egypt. To quote Mohamed Elbaradei, the former director of the International Atomic Energy Agency, who had returned to his native Egypt in 2010, "When you have half of the Cairenes in slums, when you don't have clean water, when you don't have a sewer system, when you don't have electricity, and on top of that you live under one of the most repressive regimes right now . . . well, put all that together, and it's a ticking bomb. It's not a question of *threat*; it is [a] question of looking around at the present environment and making a rational prognosis."

It is against this background that Egyptian activists, some of them adept users of social networking on the Internet, were inspired by events in

Tunisia. On 25 January, a day Mubarak had set aside to honor the police, many citizens took to the streets in what they labeled a Day of Rage, protesting abuses ascribed to some of the police. Soon demonstrations were taking place daily in Cairo (centered at the famous Tahrir Square), Alexandria, Suez, Ismailia, and elsewhere. As in Tunisia, large numbers of lawyers and students joined the protests.

The Mubarak regime initially responded with tear gas and water cannons to control the crowds. Then the authorities tried to block the Internet and cell phone communications. The regime targeted journalists, both foreign and domestic, for physical abuse and arrest. As time went on, police violence escalated. Finally, the Egyptian army was ordered onto the streets of Cairo, Alexandria, and Suez as a show of force, but the soldiers refused to stifle the protests. None of these moves deterred the protesters.

At this point, Mubarak began to dismiss and replace members of his regime in the hope that superficial changes would placate the public. He fired his cabinet on 29 January and appointed Omar Suleiman, his intelligence chief, vice president with orders to manage the emergency. On 1 February he promised not to run for re-election and to revise the Constitution. He also reduced food prices. But the situation had already gone too far. Elbaradei, hailed by many Egyptians as a possible candidate for the presidency, told the protesters amassed in Tahrir Square that they "have taken back [their] rights" and that they could not go back. By then the people were demanding Mubarak's resignation and an end to his dictatorship. Cosmetic changes would not work.

By 2 February, the regime was attacking protesters with live ammunition and army tanks now rumbled onto the streets, as well as Mubarak's thugs riding horses and camels. It was during the following week that Egyptian army leaders decided that they could not order the troops to attack the protesting crowds. As in Tunisia, Egypt's army is a conscript one. The troops came from the same general background as the protesters. This decision probably precipitated Mubarak's 11 February announcement that he would resign and turn power over to the Supreme Council of the Armed Forces (SCAF). The army commanders promised a speedy process that would lead to a democratic government.

Egypt held staggered elections for a lower house of Parliament at the end of 2011 and the beginning of 2012. The results, even more so than in Tunisia, favored the Islamists. Egypt's Freedom and Justice Party (Hizb al-Hurriya wa al-Adala), affiliated with the country's Muslim Brothers, got 47 percent of the votes, while the hard-line Salafis' *Nour* (Light) Party got 29 percent. The Salafis are ultraconservative Islamists who share an Islamic background with the Muslim Brothers, which they supported after

Mubarak; yet they espouse a stricter version of Islam. The Salafis later supported the military coup against Morsi. The liberal Egyptian Bloc Coalition (al-Kutla al-Misriya), a coalition of three small liberal parties, only managed 8.9 percent of the vote. The elections for the Shura Council, or upper house of Egypt's Parliament, held in February 2012, produced similar results. Presidential elections took place in May and June 2012. Mohamed Morsi, the candidate of the Muslim Brothers, narrowly defeated Ahmed Shafik, who was favored by SCAF, but the ruling military had already blunted Morsi's triumph by dissolving Parliament, issuing an interim constitution, and limiting the president's powers.

These elections did not end the Egyptian revolt. Since February 2011 mass demonstrations have occurred many times in Tahrir Square, and the troops have killed and injured some protesters and detained and tortured others. The military, led by SCAF, stubbornly refused to submit to any civilian government. Ever since the Egyptian military deposed King Faruq in 1952, its officers have seen themselves as the heart and soul of modern Egypt. Gamal 'Abd al-Nasir, who led the military coup against the king and later became the country's president, was arguably modern Egypt's most popular leader. The officers' self-perception, plus their considerable stake in the Egyptian economy, sets them at the top of the nation's social order. This attitude did not change with the fall of Mubarak, who was imprisoned, tried, and convicted for ordering the use of lethal force against the demonstrators, causing some 880 deaths. In 2014, Mubarak and his sons were retried and acquitted of this charge.

It seemed likely that the newly elected Islamist government would be overshadowed by SCAF's military officers. However, the power balance shifted after mysterious attackers killed sixteen Egyptian soldiers in northern Sinai in early August 2012. Within days President Morsi managed to pressure the SCAF chairman, Muhammad Husayn al-Tantawi, who was also his defense minister and had been acting president from Mubarak's resignation to Morsi's inauguration, to retire, along with the army's chief of staff. In the early stages of the revolution, the military cooperated with the Muslim Brothers, whom millions of Egyptians voted into power. However, the Muslim Brothers' political aspirations were aborted after a year of inept government, leaving Egypt weaker, more disorganized, and less prosperous than before the Arab Spring.

In June 2013, Tamarod (or Tamarrud), a popular movement opposing the Muslim Brothers, working with many other political and civil society groups, collected more than 20 million signatures calling for early presidential elections. Tamarod went so far as to support a military coup against Morsi. On 30 June, after a wave of demonstrations that resulted in clashes between supporters of Islamists and Tamarod, the military, led by Abdel Fattah al-Sisi, himself appointed by Morsi, issued an ultimatum that gave Egyptian political leadership until 3 July to meet the demands of the demonstrators, especially the resignation of President Morsi, new presidential and parliament elections, and the drafting of a new constitution. When Morsi refused to step down, the Egyptian army overthrew him, appointed Adly Mansour interim head of Egypt, and began jailing Muslim Brothers leaders and supporters. A wave of violence followed, and the Muslim Brothers was banned. The army increased its control over Egyptian politics once Sisi became president on 8 June 2014, following an election in which no Islamist was allowed to run. The army was back in power. The Egyptian old guard maintains political and economic control over the government's domestic and foreign policies. And the people no longer rally in Tahrir Square.

Syria

For almost half a century Syria has had a dictatorship under the secular Ba'ath Party, which has been controlled by the Assad family since 1970. The Assads belong to Syria's minority Alawite sect. An offshoot of Shi'ite Islam, the Alawites make up about 12 percent of the country's population. Viewed by Sunnis as not even Muslim, the Alawites' best hope for advancement was in the military. Over time they came to dominate Syria's armed forces and eventually also to control its state security services.

Syria shares the same domestic problems as other Arab countries under authoritarian regimes, including economic issues. Over the past forty years, the regime has moved from socialism toward a free-market economy, which has resulted in a cutting of state subsidies for basic goods, leading to a harder life for the poor. Freer trade has put local industries and crafts out of business, raising the unemployment rate. Ethno-religious tensions have also persisted. Alawite control of the government is resented by the Sunni majority, a growing number of whom have turned to Islamic fundamentalism. About 9 percent of the Syrian population is Kurdish, and they have rebelled several times. The regime kept a lid on these problems through widespread repression. For fifty years the Ba'ath Party ruled under the Emergency Law, which denied any constitutional protection to the poor. Syria's police and army have used their unlimited power of arrest and detention to silence all opposition.

As in other Arab countries, the events of 2011 were preceded by sporadic protests and recent rebellions. For Syria, the famous atrocity, one that unfortunately serves as a precedent for the present actions of its security services, was the government attack on the city of Hama. Hama was the stronghold of a conservative Sunni movement that launched a rebellion against the secular Ba'ath dictatorship in 1976. Resistance to the regime lasted until 1982, when the Syrian army surrounded Hama and, using tanks and artillery, shelled the city indiscriminately. As many as 25,000 citizens were killed. Kurdish and Arab riots that erupted in 2004 and 2010 were also brutally suppressed. This history helps explain the regime's willingness to resort to violence to defend its dictatorship.

Small protests began in Syria in late January 2011. Because they drew little attention, in early February Al Jazeera dubbed Syria "a kingdom of silence." Only in mid-March did the protests spread. On 15 March simultaneous demonstrations, obviously coordinated, erupted in various Syrian cities. Three days later, following communal Friday prayers, thousands of demonstrators took to the streets across the country to demand an end to corruption. This protest was centered in Dar'a, a provincial capital in southern Syria near its Jordanian border. By 20 March, protesters in Dar'a were setting fire to government buildings and the local Ba'ath Party headquarters. Protests against corruption were now joined by demands for an end to the Emergency Law and the release of political prisoners. These coordinated demonstrations usually broke out on Fridays, pointing to Syria's Muslim Brothers as the instigators. The regime was quick to blame fundamentalists and "terrorists."

The government promptly called on the army to suppress the dissidents, relying most on those divisions whose officers and soldiers were mainly Alawite. Recalling the 1982 Hama precedent, the regime began to use artillery, mortar rounds, and tank fire, as well as rooftop snipers, in Dar'a and elsewhere. At the same time, though, the regime offered concessions. It released two hundred political prisoners on 26 March and promised to end the Emergency Law, which it did, at least in name, three weeks later. The cabinet was reshuffled. Neither the pace nor the size of the demonstrations abated. But the Assad regime managed to mount large counterdemonstrations throughout Syria in support of the government.

It was also in March that the demonstrations against the regime took on a new character. Some of the antigovernment protesters were armed with weapons that had been smuggled across the Lebanese border. Some soldiers began to desert from the Syrian army. By June 2011 hundreds of Syrian security police had been killed in the uprising. Simultaneously, anger at Syrian minorities, particularly Christians who supported the regime, grew among some protesters. Rising sectarian violence in Syria became a real concern.

By October protest leaders had formed the Syrian National Council to coordinate the activities of both internal and external antigovernment groups. The council quickly won support from the United States, as President Obama called on Assad to relinquish power, and from the Arab League, which suspended Syria's membership in November, allegedly for not complying with a peace plan it had suggested.

In December the Arab League sent observers into Syria, but the government stymied their efforts. They focused on the city of Homs, which has both Sunni and Alawite neighborhoods. Here Syrian army deserters had clashed with government forces, and the situation had deteriorated into a government siege of the city. Simultaneously, car bombs exploded in Damascus, killing at least forty-four people. The rising violence caused the Arab League observers to withdraw.

The Syrian army attacked Homs in February 2012. This in turn triggered a UN Security Council resolution, proposed by the United States and European Union, calling for draconian economic sanctions on Syria. But this resolution was vetoed by Russia and China. When a humanitarian mission was finally let into Homs, having been blocked for more than a week, it found large-scale devastation. The UN estimated Syrian deaths at 23,375–30,850 as of August 2012. About half were civilians. Many were injured or imprisoned. There were 200,000 refugees and 1.5 million displaced within Syria as of August 2012.

And the civil war in Syria continues. In July and August 2012 Aleppo experienced the same violence as in Homs. In August 2013, the Syrian army was accused of using chemical weapons against civilians in the Damascus suburbs. In early 2014, the United Nations sponsored peace talks between the Syrian government and the Syrian National Coalition in Geneva. Representatives of both camps failed to agree on an agenda and UN special envoy Lakhdar Brahimi resigned. In June 2014, the Syrian regime held elections in government-controlled areas. Assad, predictably, was re-elected.

The regime lost much of its northeastern territory to Islamist factions of what came to be known as the Islamic State of Iraq and the Levant (ISIL, also known as Islamic State of Iraq and Syria, or ISIS). Mostly composed of Sunni extremist fighters, backed by Iraqi army officers who had formerly supported Saddam Husayn, ISIL took power in the Syrian governorate of Raqqa, which became their capital. This military defeat by ISIL raised fear among Alawites, especially after ISIL fighters captured military bases and government troops (see Map 21.1). Under the leadership of their caliph, Abu Bakr al-Baghdadi, ISIL invaded Iraq and managed to capture Mosul and threatened other Iraqi areas.

As a splinter of al-Qa'ida in Iraq, ISIL became a key player in the Syrian civil war after fighters from the Islamic State in Iraq (ISI) and a few al-Qa'ida-backed militants in Syria known as al-Nusra Front joined forces

427

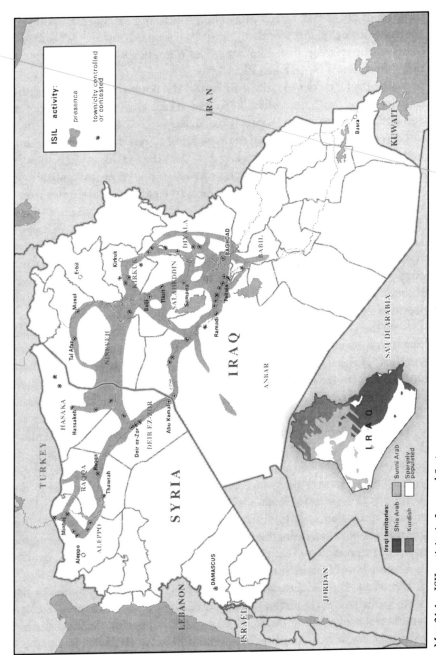

Map 21.1   ISIL activity in Iraq and Syria

in April 2013, despite the opposition of al-Nusra Front's leader. By the summer of 2014, ISIL seized Mosul and Tikrit and extended its political control over the majority of Sunni Iraq. On 29 June 2014, al-Baghdadi announced the creation of a caliphate under his authority, and ISIL became the Islamic State (IS) (see Box 21.1).

Using brutal tactics to strike fear among the population, IS fighters rely on religious cleansing, public killing, and sexual violence against women and children. They force Yazidis, Christians, and Jews to convert to their interpretation of Islam, the alternatives being to pay a high tax, abandon their homes and property, or be killed. IS uses the Syrian city of Raqqa as its headquarters to launch its purportedly Islamic government institutions and social and economic services. Based on rigid and literal interpretations of Islam, IS rejects other Islamic views as deviations from pure Islam. They proselytize and use violence to restore the early Islamic caliphate and its religious foundations. After they threatened the Kurdish region of Iraq, the Obama administration sent American troops to join with Arab supporters and Western allies to limit their growing influence. However, thousands of foreign fighters continue to join them from all over the Arab world as well as the European Union. When Americans bombed IS troops, they retaliated by beheading foreign journalists and prisoners. The United States and its allies also tried to cut off their funding and humanitarian support. However, the Islamic State has survived and grown in 2014–2015, thanks to the porous borders of the European countries and Turkey.

In spite of so much opposition, Syria's regime has as many supporters as enemies and could stay in power for a long time. In addition, the regime held a referendum on a new constitution that it claims will liberalize Syrian politics and government. Such reforms will be hard to implement as long as violence continues. But if the violence ends, the regime might feel no need to carry them out. Support from outsiders, particularly the United States, Sa'udi Arabia, and Qatar, may well sustain the rebellion against the Assad regime. Indeed, as of this writing it appears that this outside support has strengthened rebel forces to the point that the regime cannot suppress them. Yet the rebels, divided into many factions, cannot defeat the government. The Syrian civil war seems endless.

Of all the Middle Eastern countries now challenged by popular uprisings, we believe Syria matters most. Bordering on Iran, Lebanon, Turkey, and Israel, it plays a leading role historically in opposing the Zionist state. As Iran's ally, it facilitates Iran's material support to Hizballah in Lebanon. If Assad's regime falls, the power balance in the region will change, probably weakening Iran and Hizballah and also reducing the influence of Russia, which has strong political and economic reasons to keep Assad in power.

Box 21.1   Abu Bakr al-Baghdadi

Born in 1971 as Ibrahim Ibn Awwad al-Badri al-Samarrai, Abu Bakr al-Baghdadi is the self-proclaimed caliph of the Islamic State. Interestingly, Abu Bakr was the name of Islam's first caliph, and Baghdad is generally recognized as the capital in which the caliphate and Islam in general were most respected and powerful. Before he declared himself a caliph, the Islamic world had not known such a position since Kemal Ataturk abolished the caliphate in 1924.

The American forces captured and detained al-Baghdadi in February 2004 because he had established a Sunni rebel militia in Falluja. In the early years of the American occupation of Iraq, the United States army set up a number of prison camps around Baghdad, such as the infamous Abu Ghraib. Al-Baghdadi was moved to Bucca prison, where more than 20,000 Iraqi prisoners, mostly Sunnis, were held in twenty-four camps. There he came to know many members of the militant group al-Qa'ida.

Feeling politically and economically marginalized by the Americans and the Shi'a of Iraq after the fall of Saddam Hussein, Iraqi Sunnis launched an insurgency against the United States in central and western parts of their country. The Sunni revolt was led by remnants of the Ba'ath Party and a new group of fighters known as al-Qa'ida in Iraq. Al-Baghdadi was one of their first recruits. During his stay in Bucca, al-Baghdadi was a disciple of Abu Mus'ab al-Zarqawi. Yet al-Baghdadi was independently respected by many prisoners for his Islamic knowledge and lineage. He holds a PhD in Islamic Studies from the Islamic University of Baghdad, and he claims descent from the prophet's family. In addition to his charismatic leadership, these attributes would legitimize his claim to be the new caliph of the Islamic State in July 2014.

In December 2004, al-Baghdadi was released after a short period in Bucca. His good behavior in prison convinced the Americans that he did not pose any threat to their control. Prison camps like Bucca, Abu Ghraib, and Camp Cropper enabled many Sunni prisoners in the early years of the US occupation to form a communications network that would serve them after their release to launch an insurgency against the Americans and the Shi'ites who sided with them.

The Iraqi Sunni insurgency against the United States and the Shi'a began under al-Zarqawi, who had contacts with bin Laden and Ayman al-Zawahiri of al-Qa'ida. In 2006 the US Army managed to kill al-Zarqawi. Even though the Americans and their allies bomb its civil and military positions in Iraq and Syria daily, the IS continues, as of this writing, to control a large part of both countries, and al-Baghdadi is still drawing more fighters from the Islamic world and Europe.

Jordan

The Hashimite kingdom, too, has been affected by the popular unrest sweeping the Arab world. Jordan's economic condition has weakened. About 12 percent of its workers are unemployed, while 25 percent of the population lives in poverty. Inflated food and fuel prices, stagnant salaries, and regressive taxes make life worse for the people. Corruption is rampant, at least at higher levels of government. Until recently, freedom of speech and the right to demonstrate were limited. Dissidents were arrested, held without due process, and usually tortured into giving confessions.

Taking their cue from the uprisings in Tunisia and Egypt, Jordanians began peaceful protests in late January 2011. These protests came not only from the local Muslim Brothers, which, as in Egypt, is the organization that can best fill the streets, but also from trade unions and student groups. At least when mounting protests, Jordan's opposition groups have shown that they can work together. The initial demonstration occurred on 26 January, and its demands were both economic and political. The protesters blamed rising food prices on the policies of the prime minister, Samir Rifai, and demanded his resignation. They did not challenge the authority of King Abdallah II.

As one demonstration followed another and spread from Amman to other towns in the kingdom, the demands escalated. Soon the protesters not only sought the prime minister's resignation but also demanded that the office become an elected one (not appointed by the king). Another demand was that the country restore its original 1952 constitution, which had limited the king's powers. What most worried the Jordanian authorities were the demands for change from groups traditionally identified with the monarchy, such as army officers and Bedouin tribes.

The king responded not with repression but with compromise. Abdallah II fired his prime minister and took steps to replace the rest of his cabinet as well. He simultaneously announced a $650 million package of subsidies to reduce the impact of high food and fuel prices. He also liberalized the laws that restricted demonstrations and use of the Internet, and he restricted contact between protesters and his own progovernment supporters. Although these moves defused some of the anger behind the protests, they could not solve Jordan's problems in the long run. The national budget deficit, already quite high, will be raised by the king's package of subsidies. Because the country is enmeshed in a free-market international economic network, this program is unsustainable.

The king then appointed a fifty-three-member dialogue committee made up of government members and opposition leaders to draft proposals for democratic reform and greater civil liberties. The committee is said to be making progress, but the king has the power to accept or reject these reforms. The Islamic Action Front (*Jabhat al-Amal al-Islami*), the largest of the protest groups and the political wing of the Muslim Brothers in Jordan, has not backed the committee so far. If the committee manages to come up with acceptable reforms, its success will probably blunt Jordan's protest movement.

Two fear factors subdue the Jordanian protests. Jordan is next to Syria. Jordanian citizens can see the Syrian violence nightly on their TV news, and few want to experience the same thing. Jordan is also afraid of upsetting the delicate balance between its Palestinians and the Jordanians of Bedouin heritage (the so-called East Bankers). If this balance fails, Israel might counter Palestinian claims to the West Bank by labelling Jordan as the Palestinian state. Structural reforms promised by the king, such as making the prime minister's office an elected one and forming the cabinet from members of parliament, have been slow in coming. Sporadic protests have continued. If the king delays his reforms, people will conclude that his promises are false, causing Jordanian protests to spin out of control.

Despite having taken in more than a million refugees from neighboring Syria and Iraq, Jordan's government has skillfully managed its political and economic crisis. It has avoided becoming involved in the politics of its Arab neighbors, at least publicly, and continues to silently suppress political dissent.

Yemen
The Republic of Yemen is the poorest Arab country and one of the most unstable. Its population is organized into tribal factions and these are in turn divided between tribes of the North and those of the South. These two regions have been united only since 1990. Until recently Yemen was ruled by a strongman, 'Ali Abdallah Salih. A field marshal in the Yemeni army, Salih had also been president of North Yemen from 1978 to 1990.

On 28 January 2011 protests broke out in Yemen. Although initially focused on economic issues, the Yemeni protests soon centered on President Salih. His supporters in the Parliament wanted to amend the Constitution to permit Salih to serve as president for life. This effort led to the unraveling of the factional coalition that had long supported Salih's rule. Soon desertions from the government, as well as from the armed forces, swelled the protest movement and pushed the country toward possible civil war.

Demonstrations erupted in San'a, the country's capital, and in its major provincial cities. They drew tens of thousands of people and were organized under such colorful names as a Day of Rage, a Friday of Anger, and a Friday of No Return. Forces loyal to the president often suppressed the protestors with lethal weapons, and hundreds died.

In late April the Gulf Cooperation Council (to which Yemen does not belong) issued a proposal that called on Salih to resign in favor of his vice president in exchange for immunity from prosecution. Salih agreed to the GCC proposal three times, only to back out at the last moment. This devious behavior cost the president some of his remaining allies. For instance, Shaykh Sadiq al-Ahmar, head of the powerful Hashid tribal federation, broke with the government and joined the opposition.

Heavy street fighting disrupted life in San'a throughout May. On 3 June a bomb exploded in the palace mosque while Salih and other officials were praying. Saleh was seriously injured and subsequently taken to Sa'udi Arabia for medical treatment. The fighting died down in his absence; many Yemenis hoped he would never return.

It was not until November that a partially recovered Salih was finally induced to sign a power-transfer agreement that was once again a product of GCC mediation. Although this would finally remove Salih from power, it did not satisfy most of those who had spent the last year protesting in the streets. They particularly resented granting Salih immunity from prosecution for killing some of the protesters.

The turmoil that characterized Yemen in 2011 and 2012 had additional consequences. As law and order broke down, local groups affiliated with al-Qa'ida became active. This in turn drew covert US agents to Yemen, making it a front in the War on Terrorism and causing the death and injury not only of alleged terrorists but also of innocent Yemeni civilians. Even many Americans were shocked when a pilotless drone killed a suspected terrorist, Anwar al-Awlaki, who was a US citizen.

Following Salih's fall from power, presidential elections were held in February 2012, but 'Abd Rabbuh Mansur Hadi, who had been Salih's vice president, was the only candidate on the ballot. This sparked new protests, particularly in southern Yemen, where the people, more urban and sophisticated than those of the North, want democratic government, autonomy, and possibly independence.

Hadi fell from power in January 2015. Despite the effort of the GCC to control the political turmoil in Yemen in the wake of the Arab uprisings, the rise of the Houthis, a Shi'a group (also known as Ansar Allah) created anxiety in its Sa'udi neighbor, which presumed that Iran controls this group. The Houthis recently captured the capital San'a and main northern port of Hodeida, expanding their political dominance beyond the province of Saada, their traditional capital. The only benefit that the Sa'udis and the West could see in the rise of the Houthis is their opposition to al-Qa'ida in

Yemen. However, their political control is apt to intensify the Sunni-Shiʻa divide and have larger ideological consequences for the region.

Arabs believe that many issues remain unresolved: democratic reform, justice for those who were killed in protests, and the gap between rich and poor. Many Yemenis will, therefore, remain restive. As, indeed, will many Tunisians, Egyptians, Syrians, and Jordanians.

Bahrain

The small island kingdom of Bahrain in the Persian Gulf, once ruled by Persia, has since 1786 been ruled by the Khalifa family, and the current king is Hamad ibn Isa Al Khalifa. Many of the kingdom's troubles stem from the fact that, although the Khalifas are Sunni, almost two-thirds of Bahrain's citizens are Shiʻite. For generations, the Shiʻa have suffered religious, political, and economic discrimination from their Sunni masters, who control the government, major businesses, and the army and other security forces.

Inspired by the uprisings in Tunisia and Egypt, protests began in Bahrain on 14 February 2011. The date was the tenth anniversary of the nation's initial, if inadequate, constitution, more popularly known as the National Action Charter. The initial protests, mainly by young people, were peaceful and orderly and called for steps toward a more just government and the investigation of widespread corruption in the existing regime.

These demonstrations were met with massive repressive force. The heart of the protests, a central intersection in Manama, its capital, was attacked by the police, resulting in many injuries and some deaths. Its landmark statue, known as "The Pearl Roundabout," was then dismantled by government order to prevent it from serving as a future rallying point. Despite the repression, mass protests continued, sometimes drawing hundreds of thousands of citizens. The government responded by dismissing a few minor officials and releasing some political prisoners, but it offered no substantial reforms to the people.

Consequently, the protesters escalated their demands. By March they called for replacing the monarchy with a democratic republic. It was at that point that the Bahraini authorities declared martial law and called in outside help. By mid-March troops from Saʻudi Arabia and some of the Gulf emirates were pouring into Manama at the request of the Bahraini government, as the government stepped up its violence and arrested thousands of Bahrainis.

One of the more unsettling features of the violent repression was reported by Physicians for Human Rights and Doctors Without Borders. These two respected humanitarian groups stated that the government was systematically detaining, torturing, and charging with crimes medical personnel who treated protesters. This action stands out as an extreme example of the repressive tactics used against Arab Spring demonstrators throughout the region and may lead to future charges of war crimes or crimes against humanity before the International Criminal Court. In early April 2011 the government shut down the country's only independent newspaper, *al-Wasat* (Center), and systematically tore down Shi'ite historical sites, including thirty ancient mosques.

By the end of May, when King Hamad thought that his regime had sufficiently cowed the Shi'ites, he called for "a national dialogue." This turned out to be a very superficial process dismissed by most opposition groups. The king also commissioned an independent investigation of police and army behavior during the protests. Predictably, this report showed that government agents had consistently used excessive force, including torture. Little has come from this report except that the kingdom hired some notorious "hard-line" police chiefs from the United States and Europe to advise the Bahraini police.

Bahrain remains tense, and its regime precarious. In February 2012 new demonstrations broke out, marking the anniversary of the original protests. They, too, were violently suppressed, but more protests were reported in March. Some Sa'udi and United Arab Emirates forces remain in Bahrain, and the island kingdom also continues to host the US Fifth Fleet, which naturally causes Washington to support the existing regime. Despite intermittent incidents of violence against the regime, Bahrain has succeeded until now in suppressing its opposition. The crackdown enlarged the gap between Sunni and Shi'a populations, as the protests were largely led by Shi'a Muslims demanding political participation. The government responded to these calls by arresting activists, religious leaders, and human rights advocates on the grounds of national security.

Libya

Like Bahrain, Libya's experience of protest was skewed by foreign intervention. However, unlike Bahrain, the intervention in Libya came on the side of the protesters. The protests began in the eastern city of Benghazi, which complained that Libya's government favored the western provinces. The early stages of Libya's revolt had strong sectional and tribal overtones, not unlike what happened in Yemen.

Protests against Qadhafi's repressive regime erupted on 18 February 2011 in Benghazi and also in Bayda, where clashes with the police soon turned violent. Unlike the experience in other Middle Eastern countries, however, Libyan protesters often overwhelmed the security forces, capturing some, who were often savagely killed. Other elements of the security forces defected to the protesters. Within days, the entire eastern region of Libya was in open rebellion, and new protests were cropping up closer to the capital, Tripoli.

The government launched a counteroffensive in early March. Although the fighting was often heavy, the regime's army made steady progress, and by the middle of the month loyalist forces were approaching Benghazi. It was then, on 17 March, that the UN Security Council imposed a no-fly zone in Libyan airspace—purportedly to prevent widespread civilian casualties—and a few days later imposed a naval blockade on the Libyan coast. Nevertheless, government forces entered Benghazi on 19 March. In resisting the government assault, Libyan rebels used captured government aircraft, but this violation of the no-fly zone resolution was ignored by UN representatives. Instead, NATO warplanes, aided by planes from the Gulf emirate of Qatar, entered the fray on the side of the rebels.

NATO intervention in Libya may well have been opportunistic. In the West Mu'ammar al-Qadhafi was one of the most vilified Arab leaders. He was best known and most hated in the West for his alleged role in the 1988 destruction of Pan Am flight 103 over Lockerbie, Scotland. Whatever the motivation behind the rapid rallying of Western countries to press for a UN resolution, their arguments in its favor were suspect. The rationale for both the no-fly zone and the intervention by NATO warplanes was that these actions would prevent a mass slaughter of noncombatants by vengeful government troops. Yet the fighting had been going on for a month, and both sides had killed or wounded many civilians. Indeed, the introduction of high-speed jet fighters into often urban-based battles could only raise the rate of "collateral damage." When this inevitably occurred, Russia and China, both having backed the original UN resolution, balked and complained that the NATO command had overstepped the bounds of the resolution and was now bent on regime change, not protection of civilians. Clearly, regime change had always been what the West sought in Libya, and when it appeared that Qadhafi's forces would win, the resolution was introduced so that NATO could go in. But we must note that the Arab League also backed the rebels, for few of the Arab heads of state liked Qadhafi.

At any rate, NATO intervention, under cover of the UN resolution, changed the fortunes of war in Libya. Very quickly, both the Libyan air force and its air defense systems were destroyed, and the advancing government forces began to retreat. From late March on into the summer of 2011, rebel forces, consistently supported by NATO aircraft and naval vessels, slowly wore down the dwindling troops loyal to the regime. By mid-August Tripoli was surrounded. NATO helicopter gunships were active in the fighting.

By early September the regime had fallen. Qadhafi himself was captured and murdered in the streets. The Western countries involved in the assault on Libya had helped realize the defeat of a dictator. Unfortunately, this did not make Libya a stable democratic nation. Lacking a strong central government, the centrifugal forces inherent in the nation's tribal makeup became evident. After Qadhafi's remaining troops withdrew to Misrata, rebel fighters entered Tripoli on 21 August 2011. Mustafa Abdeljalil, the National Transitional Council (NTC) leader, declared the end of Qadhafi's rule in October 2011. It was not until July 2012 that Libya's transitional government could gain sufficient control over the country to hold elections for a national congress to replace the NTC. In August the transitional government officially handed power over to the new congress. Liberal secularists won the election, and Mohammed Yousef al-Magariaf of the Liberal National Front Party was chosen as interim head of state on 8 August 2012. Nonetheless, Libya remained unstable, as the tribes were still armed and fought one another for control over territory and resources.

On 8 September 2012, rebels attacked the US mission in Benghazi, killing Ambassador Christopher Stevens and three other Americans. After he failed to form a government, Magariaf resigned, and 'Ali Zeidan took over and his government was sworn in on 15 October 2012. Yet, amid security concerns Western countries began withdrawing their diplomatic staff from Libya. 'Ali Zeidan was kidnapped for a short time, before his release on 10 October 2013. In 2014, Ansar al-Shari'a, an Islamic group, began a series of military clashes with the army. On 17 February 2014 as Libya marked the third anniversary of its uprisings against Qadhafi, Libyans went to the polls to vote for a new constitution. Fighting erupted between Islamic groups and the army, the Parliament was burned to the ground, and the airport was attacked. Foreign workers began to flee Libya to Egypt and Tunisia. Political factions with military wings emerged. Groups close to ISIL drew support from members of al-Qa'ida in the Islamic Maghreb (AQIM) and attacked institutions of the government in Derna and Tripoli. Only time will tell if all violence and death that followed the defeat of the Qadhafi regime was worth it.

Palestinians

If the Palestinians under occupation drew hope and energy from the popular revolts in Tunisia, Egypt, and elsewhere, it is partly because they had actually pioneered such uprisings. Years earlier, specifically in 1987 and 2000, the Palestinians had started the Intifadas, which were popular protests against the Israeli occupation. In both of these uprisings, protests were crushed by a regime that was quite willing to use repressive tactics over an extended period. Unlike present circumstances in the Arab countries, violent repression by Israel's government draws less outside condemnation than does that applied by Arab regimes.

The Palestinians under Israeli rule acknowledge that the Palestinian (Self-Governing) Authority is corrupt, but the main issues that goad them into revolt are Israel's policies of economic deprivation and severe repression. Israel maintains large police and military forces, which have no ties to the Palestinian people and whose members have been trained from childhood to view them as deadly enemies and ethnic inferiors. The oppressors get significant support from the United States and other outside governments, which supply Israel with both financial and military assistance and diplomatic support. In short, Palestinian conditions in the occupied territories are different from and harsher than those of the protesters in Tunisia, Egypt, Syria, or Jordan.

Nevertheless, the Palestinians were encouraged by recent events beyond the occupied territories. As a result of the general upheaval in the Arab world, Palestinian youths came together in an organization called the 15 March Movement. Named for the day in 2011 when Palestinian youths mounted demonstrations throughout the occupied territories to force a reconciliation between Hamas and Fatah, the movement succeeded, but only temporarily.

Like their Tunisian and Egyptian counterparts, Palestinian protest groups demanded democratic government. They protested against not just Israel's policies but also the authoritarian behavior in the West Bank of the Palestinian Authority, which, unlike Hamas in Gaza, has no electoral legitimacy. The 15 March Movement also demanded the right of Palestinians scattered throughout the world to elect representatives to the Palestine National Council.

Morale was high, particularly among young Palestinians who expected to play a decisive role in their own future. A recent poll, reported in the *Jerusalem Post*, revealed that more Palestinians under Israeli control supported Marwan Barghuti, now in an Israeli prison, than either the Palestinian Authority or Hamas. Spreading worldwide is an energetic and growing Boycott, Divestment, and Sanctions movement, a willing and able resource for Palestine's version of popular protest.

Israel mobilized its forces to attack, reacting to rockets fired from Gaza into Israel's nearby population centers. In July 2014 the IDF launched

Operation Protective Edge against Hamas in Gaza. More than 2,000 Palestinians and 60 Israelis were killed in this Gaza-Israel conflict. The operation proved to be a public relations disaster for Israel in the eyes of the international community despite the military losses of Hamas and the destruction of much of Gaza's infrastructure. After Sweden's decision to recognize Palestine, the parliaments of Ireland, France, Spain, and England passed nonbinding resolutions calling for the recognition of a Palestinian state.

REPERCUSSIONS IN THE NON-ARAB MIDDLE EAST

There were echoes of the Arab Spring elsewhere in the region, notably in Israel, Iran, and Turkey.

Israel

To what extent did the Arab popular uprisings, especially among the Palestinians, affect Israel? The potential impact is evident in Israeli demographics. Studies originating in Israel as well as abroad show that up to half of the country's Jewish citizens are considering emigration if current political and social conditions persist. Already, *yerida* (emigration from Israel) has for years exceeded *aliya* (immigration into the country). As of 2005, according to the Israel Central Bureau of Statistics, some 650,000 Israelis, most of them Jewish, have left the country since 1948. Moreover, polls show that at least 60 percent of Jews who remain "sympathize with those who leave the country." Among those who stay, many feel safer having a second passport issued by the United States or a European country. As of 2012 the United States has issued more than 500,000 passports to Israelis over the lifetime of the Jewish state, and 250,000 additional applications are pending. Ironically, Germany runs second, having given 100,000 passports to Israeli Jews, with 7,000 new ones issued yearly. Of course, emigration from some of the rebellious Arab countries has risen apace. Yet, the rise of anti-Jewish incidents in Europe has led to a recent rise of *aliya*, as a large number of European Jews have sought refuge in Israel.

The recent Arab revolts may hasten Israeli emigration. In those Arab countries under new regimes, now more responsive to popular pressure, ties with Israel will likely deteriorate. Even where the revolts fail, Arab dictators will probably heed popular opinion more than before. Also, protests on the Israeli borders have clearly shown that many Palestinians still maintain that they should have the right of return.

Israel held national elections in March 2015, and Netanyahu was re-elected as Prime Minister. Israeli politics is generally trending toward increased concern for security, more power to the Orthodox Jewish parties, and greater hostility toward the Palestinians. The Boycott, Divestment, and Sanctions movement abroad is not likely to sway Israeli policies. But the Arab Spring has increased the sense of fear and danger felt by the average Israeli. Some of this was evident when 450,000 Israelis demonstrated in Tel Aviv on 3 September 2011 against the high cost of food and housing. Popular changes in the Arab world will not necessarily lead to positive change in Israel, even if its economy continues to grow and US support remains strong.

Israel's accomplishments are, of course, impressive. A state with 7.5 million people, of whom slightly less than 6 million are Jewish, achieved a gross domestic product (GDP) of $286 billion in 2014, slightly more than $35,000 per capita. Israelis have a life expectancy at birth of eighty-one years (compared with seventy-eight in the United States), and everyone has access to clean drinking water and sanitation. Adult literacy is 97 percent. A boy can expect, on average, to get fifteen years of schooling, and a girl sixteen. Twelve Israelis have won Nobel Prizes, more than the citizens of any other Middle Eastern country. However, taxes took 40.2 percent of the GDP in 2013, the state budget is almost always in deficit (3 percent currently), and in 2012 military expenditures amounted to 5.6 percent of GDP (compared to 2.8 for Iraq and 1.7 for Egypt). Most Israelis see themselves as highly vulnerable with so many hostile countries nearby. In recent years they view Iran as bent on the destruction of their country, and they are especially anxious about its nuclear development program, even though Iranian leaders repeatedly deny that they are making nuclear weapons and it is widely known, though never publicly acknowledged, that Israel has between seventy-five and four hundred nuclear weapons.

Iran

Iran is a non-Arab Muslim country with a majority Shi'ite population. Its own 1979 uprising against the shah's dictatorship had much in common with the recent Arab revolts. Both were truly popular events aimed at overthrowing unpopular governments. Like the Iranian revolution, the Arab uprisings are so far leading to the formation of new Islamist governments.

The Iranians point to their 1979 experience as the model for the Arab events that came later. The precedent set by the founding of the Islamic Republic inspired many Islamists in the Arab world. Yet, as recently as 2011, Iran's regime violently put down popular protests and thus set itself

up as a model of repression as well as of revolt. You can draw two opposing messages from what the ayatollahs do in Tehran. After a high electoral turnout, Iranians elected Hassan Rouhani in June 2013 as their new
president on a platform based on tradition, reform, and dialogue with the
West, especially nuclear negotiations. Despite the backing of Supreme
Leader Ayatollah 'Ali Khamanei, Rouhani's government has been slow
to act on the demands of the voters. It faces a potential challenge from
the supreme religious leader, 'Ali Khamanei, the Revolutionary Guard, a
weak economy, and international economic sanctions. Falling oil prices
have also hurt Iran, despite the support of China and Russia. Finally, the
ideological clash between Iran and Sa'udi Arabia over Iraq, Syria, Yemen,
and Bahrain and the continuing Sunni-Shi'a divide form another obstacle
to any future stability in Iran and the Persian Gulf.

There are other restraints on Iranian influence when it comes to the
Arab Spring. The Iranians have hesitated to get involved in Arab uprisings
that involve Shi'ites. Some have occurred in the Persian Gulf and Arabian
Peninsula region. As you know, Shi'ites dominated the uprising in Bahrain.
Some unrest has occurred among the Shi'ite population in eastern Sa'udi
Arabia. Because these are areas where the United States has strategic interests, especially regarding oil, any overt Iranian intervention there would
risk a confrontation with the Americans. In Alawite-controlled Syria,
though, Iran actively arms the beleaguered regime of Bashar al-Assad, because Syria remains Iran's main Middle Eastern ally. In early 2015, though,
the Iranian government has aided Iraq's predominantly Shi'ite government in its fight against the Islamic State and may also have supported the
Houthis' seizure of power in Yemen.

In fact, the main force influencing events now moves from the Arab
world to Iran. Since 2009 Iran has had a Green Movement that demands
political and social reforms from the Islamic Republic. Even though its
leaders have been arrested and its activists suppressed, demonstrations
organized in Iran to support uprisings in countries like Egypt have, on
occasion, metamorphosed into Green Movement protests against the government in Tehran. Although the authorities in Iran claim that the Arab
uprisings were inspired by the 1979 revolt against the shah, Iran's current
opposition can prove more forcefully that they are inspired by the Arab
Spring.

Finally, Iran also faces outside pressure and interference. It is subject
to broadening international sanctions due to the hostility of the United
States, the European Union, and Israel. These sanctions are motivated by
distrust of Iran's civilian nuclear power program as well as its support for

the Syrian government. As was the case with Iraq before the 2003 invasion, the sanctions regime is hurting the civilian population most. Israeli officials, echoed by members of the US Congress, make public pronouncements about the danger of a nuclear-armed Iran and say they are willing to attack that country to prevent it from "getting the bomb," despite the absence of credible evidence that Tehran has a nuclear weapons research program. At the time of this writing, Iran was negotiating with the five major nuclear powers (plus Germany) to get an agreement that would lift the sanctions on its economy in exchange for definite limitations on its nuclear program. Thus, Iran's future is just as cloudy as the rest of the Middle East region.

Turkey

As the Arab world was reeling from the aftermath of their uprisings, government bulldozers began demolishing Taksim Square's Gezi Park to set up a development project—a shopping mall and a replica of the Ottoman army barracks in Istanbul—on 27 May 2013. Local citizens began to occupy the park as a protest against the project. Prime Minister Recep Tayyib Erdogan rejected the protestors' demands to stop the demolition, and his government cracked down on the demonstrators with water cannons and tear gas and sometimes rubber bullets. Despite heavy international criticism, Erdogan defined the protestors as looters and terrorists and alleged that they are part of a foreign plot to destabilize Turkey. Many people were injured during the clashes with the security forces, and people died. As the demonstrations escalated and persisted, President Abdullah Gül announced the suspension of the development project in Gezi Park. Although intermittent protests and sit-ins continued, Erdogan and his Islamic party still managed to win the next local and presidential elections in 2014. Turkey is veering away from Ataturk's secularism.

CONCLUSION

Spring has not lasted in the Arab world. Most of the Arab revolts have been suppressed and co-opted, though they could well set the scene for recurring uprisings in the near future. The conditions of the Palestinians under Israeli occupation will not ameliorate because of the Arab revolts. They may even get worse in the long run. However, what positive changes we do find in Arab politics will serve as a model for the future. Many of these events are works in progress. The last word is yet to be spoken. We will have to watch closely the progressive elements whose voices will be louder and more recurrent as time goes by. They will compete with the voices of the Muslim Brothers, Hamas, and other Islamist groups for mastery in the Middle East. We cannot be sure who will finally wield power in those countries. In Libya and Yemen, tribal and family loyalties also compete for regional political power, which can also happen elsewhere in the Middle East.

22

◈

Changing Middle Eastern
Environments

Before the discovery of oil and natural gas, international and underground
water systems largely shaped the majority of Middle Eastern environmental landscapes. Middle Eastern inhabitants succeeded in controlling
the flow of rivers such as the Nile, Euphrates, Tigris, and Jordan, through
dams and canals. In the 1228 *Mu'jam al-buldan* (Dictionary of Countries), the medieval Arab geographer Yaqut al-Hamawi gives a detailed
description of the earthen dam of Ma'rib in today's Yemen: "the water
from springs gathers . . . collecting behind the dam like a sea. Whenever
they wanted to they could irrigate their crops from it, by just letting out
however much water they needed from sluice gates; once they had used
enough they would close the gates again as they pleased." The Ma'rib dam
is located near San'a, today's capital of Yemen. Known as the oldest dam
in the world, it was built by the Sabaeans to capture seasonal monsoon
rainfall needed for agricultural irrigation. By the time Muhammad was
born, Yemen and southern Arabia, unlike many parts of the Arabian Peninsula, boasted a developed agriculture supported by irrigation canals fed
by the dam and its networks of canals.

Today the 25 million–strong population of Yemen and the inhabitants of San'a are faced with the haunting specter of losing their water
supply. Oman has faced a similar prospect, but its conservation policies
and environmental programs have helped the Sultanate avoid Yemen's
crisis. In these arid countries and other regions throughout the Middle
East, scarcity of water, soil salinity, watercourse pollution, and lasting periodic droughts are bound to be the cause of wars, famine, and population
displacement in the coming decades. Now that you have read detailed accounts of early Islamic history and the development of Islamic societies

from the *hijra* until the twenty-first century, let us now turn to one of the new and significant challenges of the Middle East—the rising environmental and ecological risks to sustainable livelihoods. Droughts and water shortages continue to affect not only agricultural production but political security throughout the region. For instance, the rising costs of bread and food prices in the last decades in Egypt and other Middle Eastern countries have led to riots and revolutions. States with large oil and natural gas reserves, such as Sa'udi Arabia and other Gulf countries, can for the moment subsidize these goods. However, regimes lacking oil or natural gas will continue to feel these pressures.

In this chapter we cover some of the environmental issues and risks that face Middle Eastern societies. These ecological questions will affect their future political and social stability. First, we introduce the significance of water and the environment in Islam and provide a short account of water management in traditional Middle Eastern societies. Next, we note how Middle Eastern cities have grown dramatically in population and in urbanized areas, and we look at the various environmental challenges facing these cities. Finally, we examine the relationship between water use and conservation and the likelihood of future water conflicts between Middle Eastern countries.

WATER AND GARDENS

The Qur'an is full of references and parables of the garden (*al-janna*). In stark contrast to the extreme desert and harsh environmental conditions of the Middle East, scenes of green oases, gardens, and flowing water dominate Islamic art, architectural forms, and urban spaces. The courtyards of mosques and houses generally include gardens or architectural forms representing gardens as a metaphor for the paradise that awaits every faithful Muslim. Water and the garden, therefore, are imbued with spiritual dimensions. In Islam, water is not only essential for survival but is also necessary for ablution, ritual, and worship. There are many statements about its use, legal ownership, and transfer. Given its importance, Islamic teachings also stress its conservation. Water is a divine gift that should be shared among humans, made accessible to animals, and distributed for farming.

These spiritual attributes make water conservation a moral obligation in Islam. Without water there is no garden. The religious idea of the garden highlights an Islamic attitude toward the environment in general. In the early stages of Islam's development, Muslims were able to re-create this Qur'anic concept in their own urban space. Although for Muslims images and notions of the garden were a reminder of future life after death, Europeans, especially travelers, largely saw it as an exotic dimension of the Orient and its traditional cities. In their eyes, the Islamic garden and its Moorish decorations and ornaments came to represent the exoticism of the East in the fantasies of the West.

Contrary to the colonial perceptions of Islamic cities, the notion of Middle Eastern environment is tied to a cultural definition of space. The traditional Islamic city has always been a space where the environment and humans interacted. The relatively low urban density of Islamic cities made room for vegetation and green space near people's houses and workplaces. Green space has always been part of the internal structure of a compound. Called *riyad* (singular *rawd*), the garden is at the center of the courtyard and always attached to the fountain. Within the built environment, Muslims maintained orchards and small plots that supplied food for daily subsistence. Flowers and trees not only formed a green belt between the walls of the city and its bustling center but also served as the green lung of the Islamic city's residential neighborhoods, mosques, and palaces. Accordingly, even as Muslims built new cities that attracted many people from neighboring farming oases and villages, the city reproduced many elements of the environment to which country dwellers were accustomed.

In Iran, for instance, Michael Bonine, a geographer, shows how the city of Yazd was rationally built as an urban grid connected through water canals in the neighboring southeast hills. Like Yazd, many Islamic settlements such as Marrakesh have developed within an irrigated network of agricultural lands. Therefore, environmental principles and concepts were at the core of the emergence and development of Islamic city and town planning. Residential neighborhoods and public spaces, including mosques, fountains, caravansaries, and *hammams* (public baths), were all designed to channel in drinkable and gray water through canals without endangering the population's health. In addition, and as an aesthetic aspect of the house, the palace mosque, and the urban public space, the Islamic garden represents the essence of a society and civilization that relied on agriculture for its survival.

Water Management:
Traditional Systems and Modern Technologies
The West tends to perceive the Middle East as a stretch of sand dunes and deserts with few scattered oases supported by springs, underground water systems (known as *qanats*), or wells. In these mental and written images,

the camel is the only animal that could survive the unbearable heat. Although this might be true for many parts of the region, the Middle East supports a complex ecosystem where population, flora, and fauna have adjusted to climate changes and droughts and have survived protracted ecological crises. Rivers such as the Nile, Tigris, and Euphrates as well as underground water channels could provide the basis for a well-developed agricultural system in the region. However, a rising urban population and increasing demand for potable and irrigation water threaten the future security of Middle East states just as much as urban violence, religious radicalization, and youth unemployment.

The Middle East was one of the first regions where humans shifted their survival strategies from hunting and gathering to subsistence farming and settlement. The ancient civilization of Sumer in southern Mesopotamia provided one of the earliest examples of irrigated farming that led to rising population. At the same time, many argue that the population density and overuse of land increased soil salinization, which led to Sumer's downfall. At the center of the Sumerian and other Middle Eastern environmental approaches was the development of irrigation canals that sustained large settled communities. These systems of irrigated farming contained the potential for prosperity as well as for the demise of these civilizations.

In the last decade of the nineteenth century, the British built the first Aswan Dam, and it opened in 1902. Later, Middle East colonial and postcolonial societies began to abandon their traditional systems of water management in favor of building dams, digging wells, and introducing modern pumping technologies. Even though these new systems of water supply increased agricultural productivity, they increased the environmental risks in the region, especially with the overdraft of aquifers (underground water resources). Before we discuss the dramatic shift in water use since the second half of the twentieth century, let us first look more closely at the *qanats*, one of the most prominent traditional methods of irrigation and water use in the Middle East.

Qanat: *Underground Water Systems*

Known as *khattara* in Morocco, *feggara* in Algeria, *falaj* in Oman, and *kariz* in Afghanistan, the *qanat* is a series of wells connected by a subterranean tunnel that channels water to the surface (see Figure 22.1). Water flows from the original high mountain well that connects to the aquifer down the gentle slope of a series of wells that ends in a spring at the level of the village or farms. The wells or shafts allow for easy access and the removal of soil from the *qanat* tunnels. As a system of irrigation and water

Figure 22.1   *Qanats*

collection, *qanats* were developed in Iran during the first millennium BCE and spread to western and eastern parts of the Middle East. The Assyrians relied on the *qanats* as a source of drinkable water. The capital city of Persepolis was mostly irrigated by *qanats*. By the year 331 BC, the technology of *qanats* spread into places outside the Iranian Plateau, especially during the rule of the Achaemenids, who allowed diggers to profit from its revenues. New settlements emerged as additional *qanats* were dug throughout the region, including the southern shores of the Mediterranean, the Arabian Peninsula, Syria, and Oman. Eastward, the system was diffused through the Central Asian oases on the Silk Road and as far as the Chinese settlement of Xinjiang. With the emergence and spread of Islam in the Middle East, *qanats* were introduced into North African oases and Spain, the Canary Islands, and Cyprus.

The arid nature of the Middle East made the *qanat* a primary choice of water management during the pre-Islamic period. Unlike pumping technologies, the *qanat* is a very reliable and sustainable system of water management because it allows continuous flow without draining the aquifer. A hereditary class of skilled diggers called *muqannis* maintained the *qanats*, moving from one place to another to build new *qanats*. In the absence of flowing river water, these systems of water management and distribution facilitated settlement in Iran and other areas of the Middle East. By the middle of the twentieth century, settlements throughout the Middle East began to introduce modern technology to expand their irrigation capacities, especially as farmers began to move from subsistence farming to cash-crop products. These technologies led to the demise of *qanats*, as communal management of resources including water was replaced by private ownership.

ENVIRONMENTAL CHALLENGES
IN THE MODERN MIDDLE EAST

The sustainability of the Middle Eastern city has been challenged since the last decades of the twentieth century as the rural population drastically decreased relative to urban population. As Middle Eastern societies struggle for internal political compromise, lasting social contracts, and the dream of democratic representation, the Middle East remains by far one of the most environmentally stressed regions of the world. Cities must find a way to maintain a balance between the economic needs of their growing populations and the protection of the ecological system. Water is becoming increasingly scarce partly because of poor government water management, global warming, and the rising needs of a growing population. The shortage of water and its effect on farming and subsistence economies does not get the same media coverage as do wars and revolutions. However, water shortage presents serious geopolitical risks for future governments, many of which share transboundary water resources along rivers such as the Nile, Euphrates, Tigris, and Jordan. Water shortages and intermittent droughts have also decreased the labor force in the agriculture sector. Middle Eastern societies have been largely transformed from rural to urban at a rate such that cities themselves have not been able to sustain the waves of internal seasonal and long-term migrants.

Middle Eastern oil revenues have changed many traditional cultural patterns and political dynamics regarding how to deal with droughts and water shortage, conservation and management. Although a few countries like Turkey and Egypt have relied on dams to supply water, most oil-producing countries such as Sa'udi Arabia, Qatar, Kuwait, and the United Arab Emirates have used desalination plants to satisfy their water needs. By producing their food in places outside the geographic boundaries of the Middle East, these states not only make themselves more vulnerable politically, but they also make themselves less able to devise new measures to conserve natural resources.

War, Oil, and the Marine Environment

The Middle East is a major producer of oil and natural gas. It supplies almost 30 percent of the world's energy and holds more than 50 percent of the world's petroleum reserves. Large amounts of crude oil are shipped daily through the Arabian Gulf and the Gulf of Oman. This maritime transport has damaged the marine ecosystem of the Gulf and the Mediterranean through pipeline leaks, fuel spills, platform failures, and tanker collisions. This pollution has led to water contamination and the decline of fisheries. For instance, on 30 March 1994, the tankers *Seki* and *Baynuna* collided in the coastal waters of Fujairah, one of the principalities of the United Arab Emirates, and released about 16,000 metric tons of Iranian crude oil. Winds drove the light oil northward, polluting additional shoreline along the Musandam Peninsula of Oman. It took months to clean up the spill, as oil penetrated sandy shoreline sediments.

The *Seki* oil spill is an example of environmental disasters that have destroyed many local economies in the Middle East. It caused significant harm to the natural resources of the United Arab Emirates' eastern coastlines. The spill impoverished the subsistence economies of fishermen who traditionally fished along the entire UAE east coast, as the fish stock declined. Although the government provided financial support to the affected fishermen, its environmental assessment ignored the maritime ecosystem itself, as it did not include the damage caused to natural resources by spilled oil. Similar issues have harmed fishing communities in Kuwait, Qatar, Gaza, and Bahrain.

In addition to oil spills that have damaged rivers and coastlines, the frequent wars in the Middle East since the beginning of the Iran-Iraq War in 1980 have caused some of the most damaging environmental disasters in history. In addition to causing more soil, water, and air pollution, the burning of oil wells during the second Gulf War and the release of oil into the Gulf waters and the desert by Iraqi soldiers led to the deaths of many aquatic birds and animals and desert fauna and flora. A lot of desert plants died, and the polluted dunes negatively impacted the Arabian wildlife. The American troops' use of depleted uranium caused unusual respiratory problems, and lung, kidney, and liver cancers among the local Bedouin and urban populations. Environmental studies continue to trace the effects of the Gulf Wars, and their findings show an unprecedented damage to local soil and water.

Water Access and Pricing

Many regions of the Middle East have no or only occasional access to potable water. The rising cost of water supplies has led many experts in the area to promote a new culture of pricing water based on consumption. This conflict between domestic and agricultural water needs is today one of the key environmental challenges facing many Middle Eastern countries. As water availability decreases, many governments must choose between urban water supply and farming. In the end, and in cases of severe drought, many Middle Eastern governments have opted to supply their cities even as they struggle to provide food for their populations. Unlike past centuries when famine destroyed many communities as a result of this conundrum, Middle Eastern societies have relied on international support to provide food that they were not able to grow during periods of drought. These governmental policies reflect the need to rethink water policies and programs. Israel, for example, has reduced water allocation to farming from more than 80 percent during the 1960s to only 50 percent through the introduction of drip irrigation and recycled waste water. Farmers in other countries are producing less, largely because they lack access to the technology of water conservation or the financial resources to subsidize it.

Sa'udi Arabia and other Gulf states have been able to shift their water policies through leasing or buying farming lands in other countries in Africa, Asia, and Latin America. Food imports have skyrocketed since 2000. In the 1960s Sa'udi Arabia was one of the larger exporters of wheat in the global market. Given its water shortages, it began allocating most of its water to urban consumption while it purchased overseas farms to produce rice and other crops in Indonesia and other countries. Similar holding companies were established in Qatar, Kuwait, and the United Arab Emirates to finance dams, lease farmlands, or buy lands and water rights from small farmers or governments. Although this trend continues to satisfy the growing needs of these governments and their expanding populations, it remains a political liability. For instance, Egypt was one of the first Middle Eastern governments that explored implementing agricultural projects in Uganda and Sudan, but fierce local opposition and political turmoil blocked the implementation of these projects. Moreover, although most of the Gulf states are still rich enough to cope with water shortages, Jordan, Lebanon, Egypt, Syria, and others continue to look for alternative water management programs and approaches.

Water Waste and Recycling

One of the modern challenges of urban cities is the management of human waste and its negative environmental consequences. According to a report by the Arab Foundation for Environment and Development (AFED), the

Middle East produces more than 250,000 tons of waste daily. Unlike many cities elsewhere with recycling programs, Middle Eastern cities still rely on makeshift landfills to dump waste. Before urban development and rising income levels, Middle Eastern populations were one of the lowest waste producers in the world. They relied on traditional mechanisms of recycling. Few plastic bags and bottles were circulated, and food waste was fed to animals, whose manure was used as an organic fertilizer in local farm plots. This traditional concept of waste management was largely influenced by Islamic teachings that call for limiting waste. The expansion of cities and the lack of public and social awareness about the environmental consequences of waste created a different culture, where dumping waste in open public spaces is what people expect to do. There are many reasons that complicate trash management in the Middle East, including the absence of a strategy for waste management, an indifferent public, a weak legislature, a lack of bureaucratic coordination, and a lack of waste collection and disposal facilities.

Unlike Cairo and other cities lacking the financial resources to manage their waste, Dubai is one of the fast-growing urban centers of the Middle East that has been trying to manage its rising horticultural, construction, solid, and liquid wastes. In addition to laws prohibiting littering and illegal disposal of trash, in 2014 Dubai imposed a fee on commercial and industrial waste as part of a strategic plan for national waste management. Despite the modern expansion of Dubai and other Middle Eastern cities, their infrastructure has failed to keep up with the amount of daily human waste. And despite all of the measures mentioned above, Dubai is a modern city that lacks a sewer system. Raw sewage flows into the sea close to tourist beaches. Truck drivers who collect waste from septic tanks wait in long lines at the sewage treatment plants of Al Awir and Jebel 'Ali. Many illegally dump their cargo behind dunes in the open desert. In addition to the contamination of beaches, the quality of the air is also affected.

Many Gulf states, especially Sa'udi Arabia and the United Arab Emirates, have launched projects to build new wastewater treatment plants. Reliance on desalinated water requires a lot of energy, as well as financial resources, to produce. Although most of the Gulf states have the resources to do so, public officials have only begun to advocate the reuse of treated waste waters, especially in irrigation. In the United Arab Emirates and Sa'udi Arabia, however, a large percentage of treated waters are released into the sea. Some ascribe this phenomenon to the lack of infrastructure to rechannel water back to the urban environment for reuse. However, the social and cultural resistance to treated wastewater is still the primary cause of people's resistance to its use in irrigation and other purposes. This resistance prompted Middle Eastern governments and the Gulf states, in particular Oman and Saʿudi Arabia, to seek the support of religious scholars. For instance in 1978, the Council of Leading Islamic Scholars addressed this issue in a *fatwa* that claimed, "Impure wastewater can be considered as pure water, if its treatment using advanced technical procedures is capable of removing its impurities with regard to taste, color, and smell, as witnessed by honest, specialized, and knowledgeable experts. Then it can be used to remove body impurities and for purifying, even for drinking." In Oman and Jordan, these Islamic rulings encouraged local farmers to use treated water in irrigation and farming. In contrast to many Gulf States, Israel has relied on treated wastewater for its agricultural development; in 2008 more than 30 percent of water used in agriculture was treated wastewater.

Vehicle Pollution, Declining Air Quality, and Human Health
Vehicle pollution degrades the quality of air and lifestyle in today's Middle Eastern cities and towns. In Cairo, Tehran, Istanbul, and other major cities, traffic jams are a normal aspect of daily life. Tehran's air pollution is one of the highest in the world; more than 60 percent is caused by transportation vehicles. Unlike in Western countries, the majority of cars and commercial buses are old. Their exhaust emissions are high and unregulated. In addition, the type of gasoline commonly available has a high level of toxicity and causes harmful pollution. And as the population grows, many middle-class families have more than one car. Few hybrid and electric cars are in circulation, and electric train lines are not widespread. The unprecedented level of urbanization and activity of the international airports of Doha and Abu Dhabi are also blamed for degrading air quality.

Declining air quality poses major health risks in these nations. Car pollutants usually affect the lungs and compromise immunity to infections. Iran's Health Ministry reports that each year more than 4,400 people die because of air pollution in Tehran. In fact, Middle Eastern urban populations, especially in Tehran and Cairo, have seen a rise in asthma and interstitial lung disease. Airborne soot, dust, and smoke have also exacerbated heart disease and other health conditions. Local environmental protection agencies in Qatar and United Arab Emirates continue to register rising air pollution throughout the Gulf states, using wireless sensor networks to monitor air quality. Middle Eastern countries are also struggling with balancing economic development and limiting air pollution. Despite their attempts to limit the level of air pollutants, many Middle Eastern countries still lack the technologies and control programs to change the course of pollution. To curb these dangerous trends and their potential negative effects on the population's health, Middle Eastern countries have begun to introduce modest legislative regulations of air pollution.

WATER RIGHTS AND POTENTIAL POLITICAL CONFLICTS

As was mentioned earlier, water could be one of the leading causes of future conflicts in the Middle East, largely because many states share flowing water sources such as the Tigris, the Euphrates, and the Nile. The Nile has always been the lifeblood of Egypt. Egypt has negotiated a number of diplomatic treaties with other African countries, especially Sudan. However, the independence of South Sudan could threaten this more than fifty-five-year-old water treaty (it was signed in 1959 before construction began on the Aswan High Dam). Even though more than 80 percent of the Nile's water originates in Ethiopia, Egypt, at the lower end of the stream, claims that it has equal rights to the water as the rest of the countries using this water. However, traditional Islamic legal principle grants upstream communities more rights to water shares than those at the lower ends of the stream. In 1970, Egypt threatened Ethiopia after reports of a proposed dam on Lake Tana on the Nile. In 1979, Anwar al-Sadat declared that the only thing that "could take Egypt to war is water." This issue has become more acute since 2013, as Ethiopia is again trying to build dams on the Nile. Members of the Egyptian army make periodic statements about Egypt's right to defend its shares of the Nile. Given the fact that Egypt receives little annual rainfall, its agricultural and drinking water comes largely from the Nile. The strategic importance of the Nile for Egypt's survival led its leadership to negotiate the Nile Basin Initiative treaty with the countries that share the Nile basin resources.

The construction of the Aswan High Dam has given Egypt needed water security to cope with intermittent drought, though it has also indirectly led to serious environmental degradation in the Nile Delta. Lake Nasser continues to entrap large quantities of sediments that used to replenish the delta. Sea currents further erode the inadequate annual sedimentation, contributing to the destruction of the delta. This is significant given the likelihood that global warming will cause the sea level to rise. In such circumstances, the delta and its concentrated urban centers, including Alexandria, Port Said, Mansura, and Damietta, could be vulnerable to flooding. A higher water table is also a big problem for Egypt, as it can lead to increased risk of flooding, which could undermine both ancient monuments and modern buildings.

The Euphrates and Tigris pose a different political challenge to Iraq and Syria. Since the late 1950s, Turkey began a program of water conservation that involved building a series of dams on the river to support its farming industries and energy production. In 1980, the Southwestern Anatolia Project was finally launched as a national program to revitalize the poverty-stricken Kurdish region and limit its political turmoil. Syria and Iraq saw Turkey's twenty-two dams as a major threat to their water security. In fact, in 1990 Turkey completely cut off the flow of the Euphrates from Syrian towns for almost three weeks in retaliation for Syria's support of the Kurdish Workers Party. Turkey does not shy away from claiming its primary rights to the waters of the Tigris and Euphrates. In fact, after the opening of the Ataturk Dam, former prime minister Suleyman Demirel noted, "Neither Syria nor Iraq can lay claim to Turkey's rivers any more than Ankara could claim their oil. This is a matter of sovereignty. We have a right to do anything we like. The water resources are Turkey's, the oil resources are theirs. We don't say we share their oil resources, and they cannot say they share our water resources."

Iraq and Syria have also quarreled with each other over the Tigris and Euphrates. In the 1970s, Iraq complained to the Arab League over Syria's diversion of the rivers' flow to no avail. Both countries almost went to war before Sa'udi Arabia negotiated an agreement that guaranteed 60 percent of the Euphrates flow downstream to Iraqi provinces. In the past two decades, the flows of the Tigris and Euphrates have been very low. The rerouting of the rivers' flows destroyed the marshlands of Iraq and the communities that lived on the banks of the Tigris. Baghdad's water and sewage infrastructure is in bad shape owing to years of neglect, economic embargos, and war. Despite its proclaimed rights over the water sources upstream, Turkey has not yet cut the total flow of water to Iraq and Syria. Turkey realizes that disrupting the flow of the Tigris and Euphrates would inflame social unrest in these nations and trigger unwanted migration that might affect its own relative political stability. Still, the dams upstream have already created an environmental crisis, as fertile Iraqi lands on both banks of the rivers are parched. Iraq's water shortage and desertification are thought to have caused the clouds of dust that have traveled down the Arabian Gulf in recent summers. Struggling Iraqi and Syrian governments have also exacerbated the crisis, as more water is wasted due to the inefficiency of their water programs and policies.

The recent emergence of the Islamic State has shown the importance of water as a tactical weapon. Canals, dams, and sewage systems have been badly affected by the continuous civil war in Syria. Islamic rebels have also captured dams and cut off water supplies to Shi'a communities in southern Iraq. At the same time, they diverted dam waters to drown Iraqi forces or their supporters' villages. Already harmed by the drought and dams in Turkey, the Iraqi water crisis has worsened, as the Islamic State controls most of the wheat farms and the water resources and threatens to destroy the farms and flood the cities downstream, including Baghdad.

CONCLUSION

Future projections show that Middle Eastern water resources will be scarce, especially if global warming continues. Annual precipitation is also expected to decrease. These changes have already affected one of the world's most water-stressed and populated places, Gaza, where access to drinking water is very limited. In Lebanon and the mountains of Oman, precipitation will determine not only the flow of rivers but also the replenishment of underground aquifers. As water scarcity increases, there will be more disputes between governments over how much of the Nile, Tigris, and Euphrates waters each riparian country may use.

A PARTING MESSAGE

In reading the Middle East's history from the rise of Islam to the present, you may have noticed how much of your attention has been focused on confrontations, especially on wars. When you survey the history of any region or country, you risk getting bogged down in its struggles and ignoring its cultural achievements or the everyday lives of its people. In this book the closer we have moved toward current events, the more we have discussed Middle East conflicts: the United States versus the Soviet Union, oil producers versus consumers, Islamist versus secularist, Christian versus Muslim, Shi'ite versus Sunni, and Palestinian versus Israeli.

Textbook writers often make lists to condense their ideas, and this last one sums up what we see as the main causes of Middle Eastern conflict: (1) the incomplete transition from communities based on religion and obedience to divine law to nation-states enforcing human-made laws to increase their security and well-being in this world; (2) the resulting belief on the part of many Middle Eastern peoples that their governments are illegitimate and not to be willingly obeyed; (3) the quest for dignity and freedom by highly articulate peoples (or nations) who have endured centuries of subjection and are determined never again to lose their independence; (4) the involvement of outside governments and individuals who do not recognize the hopes and fears of Middle Eastern peoples and, in the worst case, play on them to serve their own needs (as can be seen in the Iraq War); (5) the growing concentration of highly destructive weapons in countries that are both volatile and vulnerable; (6) the rising need for food, water, and fossil fuels throughout the world as the amounts available for consumption decline, as we have seen in this chapter; (7) overpopulation of some countries and the widening gap between a few very rich people and the many poor; and (8) the failure to contain or resolve the Palestinian-Israeli conflict.

The Middle East is the most troubled region of a turbulent world. Its people are not at peace with one another or with themselves. They suspect that outsiders do not understand them. We hope that you will know them better and continue to learn about their cultures—not with a childish desire to prove "We're right and you're wrong" but, rather, with a mature hope of promoting true dialogue between Middle Eastern and Western ways of life. There is much to be learned from the people of the Middle East: hospitality, generosity, strong family ties, and true empathy for the needs and feelings of others. However, clashes are expected to continue, and there are no easy solutions. The Middle East is an area that has always been vulnerable to invasion and exploitation, that could not escape the ambitions of local and foreign rulers, and that has been prized for its natural resources or its strategic location. It has produced more than its share of scholars and poets, artists and architects, philosophers and prophets. This region is often called "the cradle of human civilization." Let us hope it will not become its grave.

CHRONOLOGY

570	Muhammad born; Ethiopians invade western Arabia
603–628	War between Byzantine Empire and Sassanid Persia
610	First revelations of the Qur'an to Muhammad
619	Deaths of Khadija and Abu-Talib
622	*Hijra* of Muhammad and his associates from Mecca to Medina; first Muslim *umma* is formed
624	Muslims defeat pagan Meccans at Battle of Badr
625	Meccan revenge at Battle of Uhud
627	Muslims foil Meccan attack at Battle of the Trench
628	Hudaybiyya truce between Muhammad and Meccan pagans
630	Mecca's pagan leaders accept Islam
630–632	Arab tribal delegations accept Muhammad as their leader
632	Muhammad dies; associates choose Abu-Bakr as first caliph; Arab tribal rebellion (*ridda*)
633	Muslim armies crush *ridda* and finish conquering Arabian Peninsula
634	Muslims defeat Byzantine army and start conquests outside Arabia; 'Umar succeeds Abu-Bakr as caliph
636	Arab victory over Byzantines in Battle of Yarmuk River
637	Battle of al-Qadisiyya enables Arabs to take Ctesiphon and western Persia from the Sassanids
639–642	Arabs take Egypt from Byzantine Empire
640	Arab garrison towns set up at Basra and Kufa
644	'Umar murdered; *shura* elects 'Uthman as caliph
651	Death of last Sassanid shah completes Arab conquest of Persia
653	'Uthman establishes standard version of the Qur'an

656	Rebels murder 'Uthman; 'Ali becomes caliph; Battle of the Camel opens first civil war (*fitna*)
657	Mu'awiya challenges 'Ali at Battle of Siffin; issues later submitted to arbitration
659	Arbitration goes against 'Ali, who is challenged by Kharijites
661	Kharijite kills 'Ali, whose son, Hasan, abdicates to Mu'awiya
661–750	Umayyad caliphate in Damascus
669–678	First Arab siege of Constantinople
680	Mu'awiya designates son Yazid as his successor, then dies; Husayn challenges Umayyad rule and is killed at Karbala
682–692	Second *fitna*, as Abdallah ibn al-Zubayr founds rival caliphate in Mecca; northern and southern Arab tribes quarrel
684	Pro-Umayyad southern Arabs defeat northern Arabs
685–687	*Mawali* revolt in Kufa
685–705	Caliph 'Abd al-Malik restores order, resumes conquests, and later Arabizes his bureaucracy and coinage
708–715	Arabs conquer Sind, Transoxiana, and Spain
717–720	Caliph 'Umar II equalizes status of Arabs and *mawali*
720–759	Arabs conquer and occupy southern France
724–743	Caliph Hisham reorganizes fiscal system
732	Europeans defeat Arabs in Battle of Tours
747	Abu-Muslim, backed by Shi'ite *mawali*, starts 'Abbasid revolt in Khurasan
749	'Abbasids take Kufa and proclaim Abu al-'Abbas caliph
750	'Abbasids defeat and murder Umayyads of Damascus
750–1258	'Abbasid caliphate in Iraq
751	Arabs defeat Chinese; paper introduced into Middle East
762	Baghdad founded as new 'Abbasid capital
786–809	Caliphate of Harun al-Rashid
809–813	Succession struggle between Amin and al-Ma'mun
833–842	Caliph al-Mu'tasim increases importation of Turkish slaves
874	Disappearance of Muhammad, twelfth Shi'ite imam
874–999	Samanid dynasty in Transoxiana and Khurasan
901–906	Qarmatians ravage Syria and Iraq; later sack Mecca
909	Fatimids seize power in Tunis and found Shi'ite caliphate
932–1062	Buyid dynasty in western Persia and Iraq
945	Buyids occupy Baghdad
956	Turkic leader Seljuk converts to Islam

960–1302	Seljuk dynasty in Transoxiana, spreading to Persia, Iraq, and Anatolia
962–1186	Ghaznavid dynasty in Khurasan, spreading to India
969–1171	Fatimid dynasty in Egypt, sometimes also Syria and Hijaz
971	Al-Azhar University founded in Cairo
996–1021	Reign of Fatimid Caliph al-Hakim, venerated by the Druze
998–1030	Reign of Ghaznavid amir Mahmud, conqueror of India
1055	Seljuks take control of Baghdad
1071	Seljuks defeat Byzantines at Manzikert and enter Anatolia
1092	Malikshah's death ends Seljuk unity
1096	First Crusade starts
1097–1098	Crusaders take Antioch after long siege
1099	Crusaders found Latin Kingdom of Jerusalem
1127	Zengi, former Seljuk officer, takes over Mosul
1144	Zengi leads Muslim capture of Crusader county of Edessa
1146–1174	Reign of Zengi's son Nur al-Din in Syria
1147–1149	Second Crusade fails to recapture Edessa
1171–1193	Reign of Salah al-Din ("Saladin") in Cairo
1171–1250	Ayyubid dynasty in Egypt (1174–1260 in Syria)
1187	Salah al-Din defeats Crusaders and takes Jerusalem
1189–1193	Third Crusade takes Acre, but not Jerusalem
1202–1204	Fourth Crusade takes Constantinople
1206–1227	Reign of Genghis Khan, Mongol conqueror
1218–1221	Fifth Crusade, directed against Egypt
1220	Genghis Khan defeats Khwarizm Turks, enters Khurasan
1228–1229	Sixth Crusade leads to treaty letting Christians rule Jerusalem and other Holy Land cities for a ten-year period
1243	Mongols defeat Seljuks
1248–1254	Seventh Crusade, directed against Egypt, is repelled by Mamluks
1250–1517	Mamluk sultanate in Egypt (1260–1516 in Syria and Hijaz)
1256	Mongols, led by Hulegu, capture Assassin stronghold in Persia
1256–1349	Il-Khanid dynasty in Persia
1258	Hulegu's forces sack Baghdad, ending 'Abbasid caliphate
1260	Mamluks defeat Mongols in Battle of 'Ayn Jalut
1270	Eighth Crusade, directed against Tunis
1291	Acre taken by Mamluks
1295–1304	Reign of Ghazan Khan, Il-Khanid convert to Islam

1299–1922	Ottoman Empire
1326	After long siege, Ottomans take Bursa, which becomes their capital
1354	Ottomans cross Dardanelles, also take Ankara
1369–1405	Reign of Timur Leng (Tamerlane), who takes Central and southwest Asia and founds Timurid dynasty
1389	Ottomans defeat Serbs at Kosovo
1389–1402	Reign of Ottoman sultan Bayezid I
1391–1398	First Ottoman siege of Constantinople
1396	Ottomans defeat Crusaders at Nicopolis
1397–1398	Bayezid takes Konya and rest of Muslim Anatolia
1400–1401	Timur ravages Syria and invades Anatolia
1402	Timur defeats Ottomans at Ankara and captures Bayezid I
1402–1413	Interregnum and civil war in the Ottoman Empire
1444	Crusaders invade Balkans but are repelled by Ottomans at Varna
1451–1481	Reign of Ottoman sultan Mehmet II, the Conqueror
1453	Ottoman capture of Constantinople ends Byzantine Empire
1501–1736	Safavid dynasty in Persia and parts of Iraq
1514	Ottomans defeat Safavids at Chaldiran
1516	Ottomans defeat Mamluks and capture Syria
1517	Ottomans take Egypt, then Medina and Mecca
1520–1566	Reign of Ottoman sultan Suleyman the Magnificent
1529	First Ottoman siege of Vienna
1535	First Capitulations treaty between Ottoman Empire and France
1571	Christians defeat Ottoman navy at Lepanto; Turks take Cyprus
1578–1639	Ottoman-Safavid war over Iraq and Azerbaijan
1587–1629	Reign of Safavid shah 'Abbas I
1606	Ottomans first recognize Habsburgs as equals in treaty
1645–1670	Ottoman-Venetian War in eastern Mediterranean
1656–1678	Koprulu viziers begin Ottoman reforms
1682–1699	Ottoman Empire at war against Habsburg Austria
1683	Second Ottoman siege of Vienna
1699	Karlowitz treaty; Ottomans cede Hungary to Habsburgs
1703–1730	Reign of Ottoman Sultan Ahmed III, the "Tulip Era"
1718	Passarowitz treaty; Ottomans cede some Balkan lands
1722	Afghans invade Persia, weakening Safavid dynasty
1729	Turkish printing press introduced into Ottoman Empire
1736	Nadir expels Afghans from Persia, becoming shah

1739	Nadir Shah takes Delhi from Mughals; Belgrade treaty restores some Balkan lands to Ottomans
1747	Assassination of Nadir Shah leads to anarchy in Persia
1768–1774	First Russo-Turkish War
1774	Kuchuk-Kainarji treaty strengthens Russia on Black Sea and in Balkans and lays basis for Russian claim to protect Orthodox Christians
1789–1807	Reign of Ottoman sultan Selim III, who starts *nizam-i-jedid*
1794–1925	Qajar dynasty in Persia
1798	Napoleon occupies Egypt
1799	Failing to take Acre, Napoleon returns to France; Montenegro declares independence from Ottoman Empire
1802	Amiens treaty restores Ottoman control of Egypt
1804	First Serbian nationalist revolt
1805–1849	Reign of Mehmet 'Ali in Egypt
1806–1812	Ottoman Empire resumes war against Russia
1807–1808	Janissaries depose Selim
1808–1839	Reign of Ottoman sultan Mahmud II
1811	Mehmet 'Ali destroys Mamluks, attacks Arabian Wahhabis
1812	Bucharest treaty gives Bessarabia to Russia
1820	Mehmet 'Ali starts conquest of Sudan; first British pacts with Arab shaykhs in the Gulf region
1821–1829	Greek war for independence
1826	Mahmud II massacres janissaries
1827	Europeans destroy Ottoman-Egyptian fleet
1827–1829	Fourth Russo-Turkish War
1829	Adrianople treaty grants Serbian autonomy, Greek independence, and Balkan gains for Russia
1831	Ibrahim, son of Mehmet 'Ali, invades Syria
1833	Hunkar-Iskelesi treaty lets Russian warships pass through Straits in return for guarantee of Ottoman territorial integrity
1838	Anglo-Ottoman commercial convention lowers Ottoman import tariffs
1839	Ibrahim again defeats Ottomans; Sultan Abdulmejid issues Noble Rescript of the Rose Chamber; British occupy Aden
1840	European powers confirm Mehmet 'Ali's autonomy in Egypt
1841	European powers sign Straits navigation convention
1848–1896	Reign of Nasiruddin Shah in Persia

1851–1857	Cairo-Alexandria-Suez railway built
1853–1856	Crimean War, in which France and Britain help Ottomans defeat Russia
1854	Egyptian viceroy Sa'id grants concession to French entrepreneur to build Suez Canal
1856	Paris treaty restores Bessarabia to Ottomans and demilitarizes Black Sea; Ottoman Imperial Rescript grants equality to Muslims, Christians, and Jews
1863–1879	Reign of Khedive Isma'il in Egypt
1865	Ottoman public debt administration established
1866	Syrian Protestant College (American University of Beirut) founded; first Egyptian representative assembly; rebellion in Crete
1869	Suez Canal opened
1873	Shah offers (but later revokes) Reuter concession to British company for railway and mining enterprises in Persia
1875	Isma'il sells Egypt's Suez Canal shares to Britain; Bosnia and Herzegovina rebel; Serbia and Montenegro declare war on Ottoman Empire
1876	New Ottomans seize power; Bulgarian revolt crushed; Ottoman constitution issued; Egyptian debt commission established, followed by Dual Control
1876–1909	Reign of Ottoman sultan Abdulhamid II
1877–1878	Sixth Russo-Turkish War, in which Russians take Romania, Bulgaria, Thrace, and parts of eastern Anatolia
1878	San Stefano treaty sets up large Bulgaria; Ottoman constitution suspended; Berlin treaty shrinks Bulgaria and limits Russian power in Balkans; European cabinet in Egypt
1879	Egyptian officers' uprising undermines Dual Control; Europeans press sultan to replace Isma'il with Tawfiq
1881	Europeans control Ottoman public debt administration; Egyptian nationalist officers take over government; France occupies Tunis
1881–1885	*Mahdi* leads revolt in Sudan
1882	British occupy Egypt and suppress nationalist movement
1883–1907	British consul in Cairo, Lord Cromer, reforms finances and irrigation, strengthening Britain's control over Egypt
1885	*Mahdi* takes complete control of Sudan
1888	Constantinople convention opens Suez Canal to all ships
1890	Persian shah sells tobacco concession to British company
1892	Nationwide tobacco boycott obliges shah to buy back concession

1896   Nasiruddin Shah assassinated; Young Turk coup against Abdulhamid fails; Herzl publishes *Der Judenstaat*

1897   First Zionist congress in Basel; Ottomans defeat Greeks

1898   Anglo-Egyptian army recaptures Sudan from *mahdi*'s successors

1899–1956   Sudan condominium (joint rule) under Britain and Egypt

1901   British firm (later called the Anglo-Iranian Oil Company) given concession to explore southwest Persia for oil deposits

1901–1953   Reign of Ibn Sa'ud, initially in Najd, later in all Sa'udi Arabia

1902   Ottoman Empire engages German firm to build Baghdad railway

1904   Anglo-French entente ends rivalry over Egypt

1906   Persian revolution forces shah to grant constitution

1907   Anglo-Russian agreement creates spheres of influence in Persia; new shah tries to revoke constitution

1908   Committee of Union and Progress leads revolution to restore Ottoman constitution; Austria annexes Bosnia; Bulgaria declares independence; first major oil strike in Persia

1909   Ottoman counterrevolution quashed; Abdulhamid deposed; Russian troops occupy Tabriz and Tehran, but Persian constitution prevails

1911   Russian pressure foils financial reforms in Persia; Italians invade Libya; Kitchener becomes British consul, exercising power in Egypt

1912   Ottomans surrender Libya; Serbia and Bulgaria take most remaining European territories of the Ottoman Empire in First Balkan War

1913   CUP seizes Ottoman government; Ottomans defeat Bulgaria in Second Balkan War; Albania independent; Germans send military mission to Istanbul

1914   Ottomans enter World War I on Germany's side; Britain annexes Cyprus, invades lower Iraq, and declares protectorate over Egypt

1915   Ottomans attack Suez Canal; McMahon offers British support for Arabs' independence if Hashimites rebel against Ottoman rule; Allied troops land at Gallipoli but fail to capture Dardanelles

1916   Sykes-Picot Agreement; Arabs declare revolt against Ottoman Empire

1917   Britain conquers Iraq, issues Balfour Declaration, and takes Palestine

1918   Arabs occupy Damascus, set up provisional government under Faysal; Ottomans surrender; Allies occupy strategic Ottoman areas

1919   Proposed Anglo-Persian treaty stirs national opposition; Egyptians rebel against British; Paris Peace Conference sends King-Crane Commission; Kemal (Ataturk) resists Greek invasion of Turkey

1920   San Remo agreement assigns Palestine and Iraq to Britain, and Syria to France; Ottomans sign Sèvres treaty, which Kemal rejects; Faysal ousted; Iraqis rebel against British occupation

1921   Reza Khan seizes power in Persia; British name Faysal king of Iraq and Abdallah amir of Transjordan

1922   Britain ends Egypt protectorate, subject to Four Reserved Points; Kemalist Turks expel Greek invaders

1923   Kemal abolishes Ottoman sultanate and declares Turkish Republic; Lausanne treaty ends Capitulations and Allied occupation of Turkey; Egypt drafts constitution and holds elections

1923-1938   Presidency of Kemal Ataturk in Turkey

1924   Kemal ends caliphate; Ibn Sa'ud takes Hijaz from Hashimites

1925-1927   Great nationalist rebellion in Syria

1925-1941   Reign of Reza Shah Pahlavi in Persia (renamed Iran in 1935)

1928-1929   Wailing Wall incident sparks Arab uprising in Palestine

1930   Passfield White Paper blames Jewish immigration and land purchases in Palestine for Arab uprising

1932   Iraq given independence, but Britain keeps bases and oil interests; Kingdom of Sa'udi Arabia established

1936   Montreux Convention gives Turkey control of Straits; Arab rebellion in Palestine; Anglo-Egyptian Treaty signed

1937   Peel Commission calls for Palestine partition, opposed by Arabs

1939   British White Paper limits Jewish immigration into Palestine; World War II starts

1941   British troops crush nationalist revolt in Iraq, occupy Syria and Lebanon; Britain and Soviet Union invade Iran, and Reza Shah abdicates

1941-1979   Reign of Mohammad Reza Shah Pahlavi in Iran

1942   British make Egypt's Faruq appoint pro-Allied cabinet; Allies halt German advance at al-Alamain, Egypt; Zionists issue Biltmore Program

1943   Lebanese Christians and Muslims adopt National Pact

1945   Arab League formed; United Nations formed; Jewish resistance mounts against British in Palestine; French quit Syria and Lebanon

1946   Anglo-American Committee of Inquiry visits Palestine; Transjordan becomes independent

1947   Truman Doctrine pledges aid to Greece and Turkey against Soviet Union; Britain submits Palestine mandate to UN, which sets up Special Committee on Palestine; UN General Assembly accepts Palestine Partition Plan

1948 Israel declares independence; Arab armies attack Israel but are defeated; most Palestinian Arabs flee

1949 Arab states and Israel sign armistice agreements; Abdallah annexes West Bank, creating Hashimite Kingdom of Jordan

1950 Turkey's Demokrat Party defeats Republican People's Party

1951 Mosaddiq nationalizes Anglo-Iranian Oil Company; Abdallah is murdered; Egypt renounces its 1936 treaty with Britain

1952 Egyptian mobs burn Cairo; Nasir leads military coup, ousts Faruq and institutes land reform in Egypt

1952–1999 Reign of King Husayn in Jordan

1953 Shah's partisans, aided by US, overthrow Mosaddiq

1954 Foreign consortium set up to manage Iran's oil; Anglo-Egyptian agreement calls for British evacuation of Suez Canal by 1956

1954–1970 Presidency of Gamal 'Abd al-Nasir in Egypt

1955 Baghdad Pact formed; Israel raids Gaza; Egypt buys Soviet arms; US offers Egypt loan to build Aswan High Dam

1956 US retracts Aswan offer; Nasir nationalizes Suez Canal Company; Britain, France, and Israel attack Egypt, but UN demands they withdraw from Suez Canal and Sinai

1957 US issues Eisenhower Doctrine; Husayn dismisses Arab nationalist government in Jordan

1958 Egypt and Syria form United Arab Republic; military coup ousts Iraq's monarchy; US intervenes in Lebanese civil war

1960 Military coup in Turkey; Organization of Petroleum Exporting Countries formed in Baghdad

1961 Kuwait independent; new republican constitution enacted in Turkey; Syria withdraws from United Arab Republic

1962 Yemeni army coup deposes imam, leading to Egyptian military intervention and civil war

1963 Shah proclaims White Revolution in Iran

1964 Jordan River water dispute between Arabs and Israel; Palestine Liberation Organization formed in Cairo

1964–1975 Reign of King Faysal in Sa'udi Arabia

1965–1966 Syrian-backed Palestinians raid Israel, which attacks Jordan

1967 Soviet Union falsely reports Israeli buildup near Syria; Nasir demands UN withdraw its force from Sinai and blockades Gulf of 'Aqaba to Israeli ships; Israel attacks and defeats Arab states in lightning war, taking Sinai, Jordan's West Bank, and Syria's Golan Heights; UN calls for peace settlement, mutual recognition, and Israel's withdrawal from occupied lands; British troops withdraw from Aden and South Arabia; Egyptian troops withdraw from Yemen

1969   Yasir 'Arafat elected PLO head; Nasir declares War of Attrition against Israel; Qadhafi leads coup in Libya

1970   Soviet arms buildup in Egypt; Rogers Plan for temporary ceasefire accepted by Egypt, Israel, and Jordan; indirect peace talks fail; Jordan crushes Palestinian rebellion; Nasir dies

1970–2000   Presidency of Hafiz al-Assad in Syria

1970–1981   Presidency of Anwar al-Sadat in Egypt

1971   Last British forces leave Gulf region

1972   Sadat orders most Soviet military advisers out of Egypt

1973   Surprise attack by Egypt and Syria against Israelis in Sinai and Golan; Israelis penetrate Syria and cross Suez Canal; US and Soviet Union impose ceasefire; Arab oil boycott, price hikes, and production cutbacks pressure Israel; Geneva Peace Conference

1974   Kissinger arranges separation-of-forces agreements among Israel, Egypt, and Syria; Arab states affirm PLO as sole spokesman for Palestinians; UN General Assembly invites 'Arafat to speak

1975   Sa'udi King Faysal is assassinated and succeeded by Khalid; civil war starts in Lebanon; Egypt and Israel sign interim Sinai agreement; UN General Assembly calls Zionism a form of racism

1976   Arab summit at Riyadh tries to end Lebanese civil war, appointing Syrian troops as peacekeepers

1977   Begin elected Israeli premier; Sadat addresses Knesset in Jerusalem; Egypt and Israel start peace negotiations in Cairo

1978   Southern Lebanon invaded by Israelis, later replaced by UN force; Carter calls Begin and Sadat to summit at Camp David, where they draft tentative peace treaty; successive coups in the two Yemens; exiled Khomeini inspires mass demonstrations against shah

1979   Shah names Bakhtiar premier and leaves Iran; Khomeini returns and proclaims Islamic Republic; Egypt and Israel sign peace treaty, causing other Arab states to break ties with Egypt; Saddam Husayn officially takes power in Iraq; Iranian militant students seize US Embassy, holding Americans hostage; Muslim revolutionaries occupy Mecca mosque; Soviet Union invades Afghanistan

1980   US attempts to release American hostages in Iran fail; shah dies in exile; military coup in Turkey; Iraq invades Iran, causing further oil price hikes

1981   Algeria mediates US-Iranian agreement, releasing frozen Iranian assets in return for hostages; Begin re-elected; Israel bombs Iraqi nuclear reactor; Sadat assassinated and succeeded by Husni Mubarak; US Senate authorizes AWACS aircraft sale to Sa'udi Arabia; Israel annexes Golan Heights

1982   Iran drives back Iraqi forces; Israel returns Sinai to Egypt; Sa'udi
        King Khalid dies and is succeeded by Fahd; Israel invades Lebanon,
        drives back Syrian and PLO forces, and besieges Beirut; PLO
        troops withdraw; Lebanon president-elect Bashir Jumayyil killed in
        bomb blast; Israeli troops enter west Beirut as Lebanese Christians
        massacre Palestinians in camps; Israel-Lebanon peace talks begin

1983   Peace treaty between Israel and Lebanon calls for all foreign troops
        to leave Lebanon, but Syria refuses to pull out, voiding treaty;
        Israeli forces withdraw to Awali River in Lebanon; Yitzhak Shamir
        replaces Begin as Israel's premier

1984   Western peacekeeping forces leave west Beirut as Shi'ite extremists
        take control; inconclusive Knesset election in Israel produces broad
        coalition government, headed first by Shimon Peres and then by
        Shamir

1985   Israel withdraws from Lebanon, except for self-defined security
        zone on southern border; militant Shi'ites hijack passenger plane
        and demand Israel release its Lebanese prisoners; Israel bombs
        PLO headquarters in Tunis, following Palestinian attack on Israelis
        in Cyprus

1986   Reagan orders bombing of Tripoli; US and British hostages slain
        in Lebanon

1987   Iranian troops besiege Basra; presidential commission confirms US
        arms sales to Iran via Israel; US agrees to protect Kuwaiti shipping
        in Gulf as Iran-Iraq War intensifies; UN passes Security Council
        Resolution 598, demanding end to Iran-Iraq War; Palestinian
        Intifada breaks out in Gaza and West Bank, protesting Israeli
        occupation

1988   US Navy involved in heavy Gulf fighting; Iraq and Iran accept
        Resolution 598; Lebanese Parliament fails to agree on a new
        president, leaving Lebanon ruled by two separate governments;
        King Husayn disclaims Jordanian interest in West Bank as Intifada
        continues; inconclusive Israeli elections lead to broad cabinet
        with Likud and Labor ministers; Palestinian National Council
        declares independent state of Palestine; 'Arafat formally renounces
        terrorism and recognizes Israel; US opens direct talks with PLO
        representatives

1989   Shamir calls for West Bank and Gaza elections to choose
        Palestinian negotiators with Israel but excludes PLO; Mubarak
        and US secretary of state Baker propose peace plan; Ayatollah
        Khomeini dies and is succeeded by 'Ali Khamanei as Iran's *faqih;*
        Majlis speaker Hashimi Rafsanjani becomes president; Sa'udi
        Arabia hosts meeting of Lebanon's parliament, leading to
        Taif Accords

1990   Arab leaders hold emergency summit as numerous Jewish
       emigrants from Soviet Union enter Israel; two Yemens unite;
       Shamir's broad coalition government falls; Israel's religious parties
       enter right-wing coalition led by Shamir; Iraqi forces invade and
       occupy Kuwait; UN Security Council condemns Iraq and imposes
       economic sanctions; US-led coalition sends forces and supplies to
       Sa'udi Arabia in Operation Desert Shield

1991   Operation Desert Storm begins and US-led coalition's massive
       ground assault hastens Iraqi withdrawal from Kuwait; abortive
       rebellions by Iraqi Kurds and Shi'ites; UN demands removal of
       nuclear, biological, and chemical weapons from Iraq; Israel and
       Arab states begin peace negotiations in Madrid

1992   Israeli labor parties regain power in general elections; Yitzhak
       Rabin forms narrow coalition and authorizes secret contacts with
       PLO envoys in Oslo

1993   PLO and Israeli representatives sign Declaration of Principles

1994   PLO-Israel talks on troop withdrawals, elections, and Jewish
       settlements in occupied lands; 'Arafat returns to Gaza; Jordan and
       Israel sign peace treaty; US seeks Syrian-Israeli treaty; other Arab
       states seek peace accords with Israel

1995   PLO and Israel reach new agreement on phased Israeli troop
       withdrawals; Israeli extremist assassinates Rabin; Islamist party
       wins plurality in Turkish elections and forms government

1996   Palestinian Authority elections in West Bank and Gaza; Israeli
       elections restore Likud to power, making Benjamin Netanyahu
       premier; Israel-PLO peace talks stall; Taliban forces take over most
       of Afghanistan

1997   Israel cedes control over most of Hebron; Turkish officers demand
       end to Islamist government; Iraq tries to bar UN arms inspectors
       from key sites; Iranians elect Khatami president; terrorist attacks in
       Jerusalem and Luxor

1998   Iraq continues to thwart UN arms inspections; inspectors withdraw
       as US and UK bomb Iraqi sites

1999   Likud loses general election, and Ehud Barak forms Labor coalition
       with small parties in Knesset in Israel; Abdallah II succeeds Husayn
       as king of Jordan

2000   Hafiz al-Assad dies and is succeeded by his son, Bashar, as
       president of Syria; Israeli-Palestinian negotiations lead to Camp
       David summit, where Ehud Barak and Yasir 'Arafat fail to reach
       final peace settlement; Ariel Sharon's visit to Temple Mount sparks
       new Palestinian uprising

2001   Ariel Sharon elected Israel premier; fighting intensifies between
       Israelis and Palestinians; 9/11 attacks occur—Islamist militants

hijack four American passenger jets and fly two of them into the World Trade Center and another into the Pentagon; US-led coalition invades Afghanistan

2002   President George W. Bush broadens his "War on Terrorism"; Palestinian uprising continues, and Israeli tanks invade West Bank; Sa'udi Arabia proposes full recognition of Israel in exchange for Israeli withdrawal from all lands captured in 1967 War, but Israel spurns proposal; Palestinian suicide bombers attack Israeli civilians, and Israel begins to build its separation wall; al-Qa'ida bombs synagogue in Tunisia and hotel in Kenya; UN inspectors resume search for weapons of mass destruction in Iraq

2003   UN inspectors find no WMDs, despite Iraq's cooperation; Yasir 'Arafat agrees to appoint Mahmoud 'Abbas, then Ahmad Quray', as his prime minister; US and UK launch massive aerial attacks and invasion of Iraq; after conferring with European Union, Russia, and UN, Bush announces Road Map for resuming Israeli-Palestinian negotiations; US-led coalition forms temporary Iraqi governing council in Baghdad; Iraqis resist US and UK invaders; terrorists attack foreigners in Riyadh and synagogues in Istanbul; Libya admits responsibility for 1988 Lockerbie bombing and agrees to end its nuclear weapons program if US lifts sanctions; US troops in Iraq capture Saddam Husayn

2004   Sharon announces plan to withdraw troops from Gaza Strip; Israel assassinates Hamas leader in March and successor in April; US transfers sovereignty to Iraq's interim government; Israeli wall condemned by International Court of Justice; FBI investigates Israeli spies in Defense Department and possible AIPAC connection; Israel announces expansion of West Bank settlements, violating US Road Map; 'Arafat dies

2005   Palestinians elect Mahmoud 'Abbas as president; rising attacks on US troops and Iraqi police in Iraq; elections for temporary Iraqi government held; Palestinian resistance groups announce a temporary lull in fighting, and Hamas announces it will take part in upcoming Palestinian Legislative Council elections; Israel withdraws its soldiers and settlers from Gaza Strip, ending thirty-eight years of occupation; Mahmoud Ahmadinejad elected Iran's president

2006   Ariel Sharon suffers massive stroke and is replaced by Ehud Olmert; Hamas wins surprise electoral victory and takes control of the Palestinian Legislative Council, ending forty years of Fatah-PLO dominance; Israel and US denounce victory and put draconian economic sanctions on Gaza Strip; factional fighting starts between Hamas and Fatah forces; Hamas soldiers in June capture Israeli soldier and demand the release of Palestinian prisoners in exchange for his freedom, but Israel refuses; Hizballah soldiers capture two Israeli soldiers on Israel-Lebanon border, sparking thirty-four days of heavy fighting and ending in ceasefire based on UN Resolution 1701; US Select Committee on Intelligence releases post-Iraq War report, stating that no WMDs were found in Iraq; Israeli warplanes bomb Syrian facility believed to be nuclear research site; Israel and Hamas agree to truce in November; Iraqi court finds Saddam Husayn guilty of crimes against humanity, and he is hanged 30 December 2006; President Bush announces surge of US troop commitments in Iraq; Palestinians' attempt to form unity government fails; Arab summit meeting renews Sa'udi offer to Israel for recognition and peace in exchange for Israeli withdrawal to its 1967 borders, but Israel spurns offer; Hamas forces evict Fatah from Gaza Strip; President 'Abbas nullifies Hamas electoral victory and appoints Fatah government in parts of West Bank under Palestinian control; Bush administration hosts peace conference at Annapolis, Maryland, where President 'Abbas and Prime Minister Olmert agree to resume peace talks; Israel announces plans to expand settlements in East Jerusalem

2008   Palestinians fire rockets from Gaza Strip into southern Israel, Israel retaliates by raiding Gaza; Egypt's government detains leading Muslim Brothers to block their participation in upcoming elections; Doha Agreement ends conflict between Sunni-controlled Lebanese government and Shi'ite Hizballah and Amal forces; Clash between US and allied troops with Muqtada al-Sadr's forces end with Iran's mediation; Israel and Hamas accept, through Egyptian mediation, six-month ceasefire; Israel's cabinet approves prisoner swap with Hizballah; UK prime minister Gordon Brown announces plans to withdraw troops from Iraq in early 2009; Israeli troops raid Gaza and Hamas resumes rocket attacks on southern Israel as six-month ceasefire ends, leading to Israeli invasion

2009   Israeli invasion of Gaza continues; UN Security Council passes Resolution 1860 demanding ceasefire, which is ignored by both Israel and Hamas, but Egypt brokers another ceasefire in June; Speaking in Cairo, US president Obama calls for "a new beginning between the US and the Muslim world"; Iranian president Ahmadinejad is re-elected, sparking major protests; mediation talks between Hamas and Palestinian Authority begin under Egyptian auspices

2010   Obama administration sponsors direct talks between Palestinian Authority and Israel, but Israel's renewed settlement construction leads to Palestinian withdrawal; Egyptian police torture and kill Khalid Sa'id in Alexandria, causing widespread protests; Mohamed Bouazizi, a Tunisian peddler, self-immolates to protest police confiscation of his cart, sparking demonstrations throughout Tunisia

2011   Tunisian protests lead to President Zayn al-'Abidin ben 'Ali's
        resignation; growing demonstrations occur in Cairo and other
        Egyptian cities until Mubarak resigns presidency in favor of
        Supreme Council of the Armed Forces; protests break out in Dar'a
        and spread throughout Syria, becoming an armed insurrection in
        April; protests break out in Bahrain against King Hamad ibn Isa
        Al Khalifa, seeking reforms and justice for its Shi'ite majority, and
        police respond with tear gas, sound grenades, and gunfire; Yemen's
        president 'Ali Abdallah Salih rejects demands for his resignation
        and orders army to suppress ongoing protests; Gulf Cooperation
        Council sends troops to bolster Bahrain's government; protests
        against Qadhafi break out in Benghazi, UN Security Council
        authorizes no-fly zone over Libya, spurring NATO air attacks
        on Libyan troops; Syrian president Bashar al-Assad orders his
        troops to besiege rebel-held areas, leading to US and EU freeze
        on Syrian government assets; Yemeni president Salih injured
        in bomb explosion and Vice President 'Abd Rabbuh Mansur
        Hadi takes power; Syrian National Council is formed to oppose
        Assad regime but is soon factionalized; pro-Assad demonstrators
        attack US and French embassies in Damascus, Arab League
        condemns Syria's government, Sa'udi government demands Syrian
        reforms, and Assad warns against foreign interference; Libyan
        rebels enter Tripoli and capture and kill Qadhafi; US veto threat
        thwarts Palestinian Authority bid for UN membership; Tunisian
        parliamentary elections give plurality to moderate Islamist
        al-Nahda Party, with liberals and secularists a close second; Salih
        accepts GCC plan for Yemen, transferring power to Hadi in
        exchange for immunity from prosecution; elections for Egyptian
        People's Assembly gain 40 percent of seats for Freedom and Justice
        Party (allied to Muslim Brothers) and 25 percent for Nour Party

2012   Assad announces a referendum for a new constitution; Russia
        and China veto Security Council resolution backed by the Arab
        League, and US demands Assad's resignation and sanctions against
        Syria; armed rebels in several Syrian cities attack government
        troops, who retaliate by shelling Homs; al-Qa'ida leader Ayman
        al-Zawahiri calls on all Muslims to support Syrian rebels; Hadi,
        unopposed, wins presidential election in Yemen; after Arab
        League's unsuccessful observer mission to Syria, former UN
        secretary-general Kofi Annan meets with Assad to formulate a
        peace plan, which is flouted by both sides; Mohamed Morsi wins
        Egyptian presidential elections, as Supreme Council of the Armed
        Forces dissolves Parliament, issues interim constitution, and limits
        presidential powers

2013   Tamarod calls for President Morsi's resignation, and Morsi is
        deposed in a military coup d'état; Nasrallah declares his support for
        the Assad regime as Hizballah intervenes against Syrian rebels

2014   IDF launches a military attack against Gaza; Former al-Qaʻida
        members form the Islamic State of Iraq and the Levant (ISIL); ISIL
        launches a military offensive through northern Iraq; Nuri al-Maliki
        forced to resign; US begins an air campaign to stop the advance
        of ISIL in Kurdish territories; Tunisian Assembly adopts a new
        constitution; Recep Tayyip Erdogan is elected president of Turkey
        as Justice and Development Party maintains political success

2015   Saʻudi Arabia's King ʻAbdullah ibn ʻAbdulaziz dies and is
        succeeded by Salman; Houthis take control of Yemen's capital

GLOSSARY

Abadan: Iran's main oil refinery
'Abbas, Mahmoud: Palestinian prime minister (2003) and president of the Palestinian Authority (2005-)
'Abbas I, Shah: Safavid ruler (1587-1629)
'Abbas, Khedive: Egypt's viceroy (1892-1914)
'Abbasid dynasty: Arab family descended from 'Abbas, Muhammad's uncle, who ruled from Baghdad over parts of the Muslim world (750-1258)
'Abd al-Malik: Umayyad caliph (685-705) who ended the second *fitna*
'Abd Rabbuh Mansur Hadi: Yemen's president (2012-2015)
'Abdallah: Son of Amir Husayn of Mecca, participant in Arab Revolt, and amir of Transjordan (1921-1951)
'Abdallah: Sa'udi Arabia's king (2005-2015)
'Abdallah II: Jordan's king (1999-)
'Abdallah ibn al-Zubayr: Mecca-based challenger to the Umayyads from 683 to 692, when he was killed
'Abduh, Muhammad: Egyptian Muslim reformer (d. 1905)
Abdulhamid II: Ottoman sultan (1876-1909) who promoted pan-Islam and opposed constitutional government
Abdulmejid I: Ottoman sultan (1839-1861) who favored westernizing reform
Abu-Bakr: First caliph (632-634), who put down tribal revolts and began conquests outside Arabian Peninsula
Abu Ghraib: Large prison near Baghdad, site of atrocities by US troops against Iraqi detainees
Abu-Muslim: Persian leader of the 'Abbasid revolt (d. 754)
Abu-Talib: Muhammad's uncle and protector (d. 619)
Achaemenid dynasty: Persian ruling family (550-330 BCE)
Acre: Strategic Mediterranean port city in northern Israel, captured by Salah al-Din, Crusaders, Mamluks, Ottomans, and Mehmet 'Ali, among others
Aden: Port city between the Red and Arabian Seas, ruled by Britain (1839-1967), now united with the Republic of Yemen
al-Afghani, Jamal al-Din: Influential pan-Islamic agitator and reformer (d. 1897)
Aghlabid dynasty: Arab family ruling Tunisia (800-909)

al-'Ahd: Nationalist secret society of Arab officers in the Ottoman army before and during World War I
Ahmad ibn Hanbal: Muslim jurist and theologian (d. 855)
Ahmad ibn Tulun: Turkish founder of the Tulunid dynasty of Egypt (868–908)
Ahmad Shah: Persia's last Qajar ruler (1909–1925)
Ahmadinejad, Mahmoud: Iran's president (2005–2013)
Ahmed III: Ottoman sultan (1703–1730) during Tulip Era
al-Ahram: Influential Cairo daily newspaper
'Aisha: Abu-Bakr's daughter, one of Muhammad's wives, and opponent of 'Ali at the Battle of the Camel (656)
Alawite: Offshoot of Shi'ite Islam prevalent in part of northern Syria
Aleppo: City in northern Syria
Alexandretta: Mediterranean seaport and its hinterland, now called Iskenderun, held by Turkey since 1939 but claimed by Syria
Alexandria: Egyptian city on the Mediterranean coast
'Ali: Fourth of the early caliphs (656–661), regarded by Shi'ite Muslims as the first imam (leader) after Muhammad
Alid: Pertaining to 'Ali, his descendants, or partisans of their role as Muslim imams
aliya: Jewish immigration to Israel
Allenby, Edmund: Commander of Egyptian Expeditionary Force in World War I, conqueror of Palestine, later high commissioner for Egypt and the Sudan (1919–1925)
Amal: Lebanese Shi'ite movement, led by Nabih Berri and backed by Syria
American Israel Public Affairs Committee (AIPAC): Influential pro-Israel lobby
Amin: 'Abbasid caliph (809–813)
amir: Muslim ruler or prince, sometimes written *emir*
amir al-muminin: Commander of the true believers, a title given to the caliph
Amman: Capital of Jordan
'Amr ibn al-'As: Early Arab general, conqueror of Egypt, and Mu'awiya's representative in the arbitration (d. 663)
Anatolia: Peninsula between the Mediterranean, Black, and Aegean Seas
Anbar: Province in western Iraq, area of Sunni resistance to US invasion in 2003–2004 and reconciliation during the surge (2007–2008)
Anglo-American Committee of Inquiry: Delegation that visited Palestine in 1946, urging continuation of mandate and admission of 100,000 Jews
Anglo-Egyptian Treaty: 1936 pact defining Britain's military position in Egypt, denounced by Egypt in 1951, and officially terminated in 1954
Anglo-Ottoman commercial convention: 1838 agreement limiting Ottoman import tariffs
Anglo-Persian Oil Company: Firm holding petroleum exploration, drilling, and refining rights in Iran; renamed Anglo-Iranian Oil Company; nationalized by Mosaddiq in 1951
Ankara: (1) Site of Timur's victory over Bayezid I in 1402, (2) capital of Turkey since 1923

Annapolis, Maryland: Site of US-brokered agreement in 2007 between Israel and Palestinian Authority (but not Hamas)
ansar: Medinan Muslim converts
Antioch: Ancient city in southern Anatolia; important early Christian center
anti-Semitism: Popular term for prejudice against or persecution of Jews
'Aqaba: (1) Inlet from the Red Sea, (2) city in southern Jordan
al-Aqsa: Important Jerusalem mosque
Arab: (1) Native speaker of Arabic, (2) person who identifies with Arabic cultural tradition, (3) inhabitant of Arabia, (4) citizen of a country in which the predominant language and culture are Arabic, (5) camel nomad
Arab Higher Committee: Palestinian nationalist organization of the 1930s
Arab League: Arab states' political association, founded in 1945
Arab Legion: Former name of the army of Transjordan (or Jordan)
Arab Liberation Army: Syrian-Palestinian group fighting against Israel in 1948
Arab nationalism: Movement seeking unification of all Arab countries and their independence from non-Arab control
Arab Revolt: British-backed rebellion of Arabs, mainly in the Hijaz, against Ottoman rule (1916–1918)
Arab socialism: Ideology advocating state control of Arab economies
Arab Socialist Union: Egyptian political party (1962–1977)
Arab Spring: Popular name for revolutionary demonstrations that began in Tunisia in December 2010 and spread to most other Arab states; also called Arab uprisings
Arabia: Original Arab homeland, a peninsula bounded by the Red Sea, the Arabian Sea, the Gulf, and the Fertile Crescent
Arabic: (1) Semitic language spoken by Arabs, (2) pertaining to the culture of Arabs
'Arafat: Plain near Mecca
'Arafat, Yasir: Palestinian Arab nationalist, founder of al-Fatah, PLO chairman, and Palestinian Authority's president (1996–2004)
Aramaic: Ancient Semitic language
Aramco: Arabian American Oil Company, which developed the petroleum industry in Sa'udi Arabia
Aramean: Native speaker of Aramaic
Arian: Pertaining to the belief of some early Christians that Jesus was human, not of the same substance as God the Father
'Arif, 'Abd al-Salam: Arab nationalist leader of Iraq (1958, 1963–1966)
Armenia: (1) Mountainous region of eastern Anatolia; (2) kingdom of the Armenians, conquered by the Turks in the eleventh century; (3) the Republic of Armenia
Armenian: (1) Native speaker of the Armenian language, (2) citizen of Armenia, (3) a person who identifies with Armenian culture or with an Armenian sect of Christianity
Aryan: Pertaining to the Indo-European language family (often used in juxtaposition with the term Semitic)
'asabiya: Feeling of group solidarity

al-Ash'ari: Muslim theologian (d. 935) who opposed the Mu'tazila
Ashkenazim: Jews whose recent ancestors came from Eastern or Central Europe
al-Assad, Bashar: Syria's president (2000–)
al-Assad, Hafiz: Syria's president (1970–2000)
Assassin: Member of a militant group of Isma'ili Shi'ites who fought against
  Seljuks and other Sunni rulers (1092–1256)
Assyrian: Pertaining to Nestorian Christians in Syria, Iraq, and Iran
Aswan: (1) City in Upper Egypt, (2) site of dam built by the British in Egypt (1902),
  (3) site of the High Dam, built for Egypt by the Soviet Union (1958–1970)
Attrition, War of: Artillery and air struggle between Egypt and Israel
  (1969–1970)
'Awn, Michel: Maronite general who claimed Lebanon's presidency (1988–1990)
Ayatollah: Title given by *'ulama* to respected Shi'ite legal experts
'Ayn Jalut: Crucial Mamluk victory over Mongols in 1260
Ayyubid dynasty: Salah al-Din and his descendants, who ruled in Egypt
  (1171–1250) and Syria (1174–1260)
Azerbaijan: Mountainous region of northwestern Iran
al-Azhar: Muslim mosque-university in Cairo
Ba'ath: Arab nationalist and socialist party ruling Syria since the 1960s and Iraq
  (1968–2003)
Badr, Battle of: Muhammad's first victory over the Meccans (624)
Baghdad: Iraq's capital; seat of the 'Abbasids (762–1258)
al-Baghdadi, Abu Bakr: Self-proclaimed first caliph of the Islamic State (IS)
  (2014–)
Baghdad Pact: Anti-Communist military alliance formed in 1955, renamed
  Central Treaty Organization (CENTO)
Bahrain: (1) Island country in the Gulf, (2) eastern Arabia during the caliphal
  period
bakhshish: Gift, tip, bribe, or payment for services
Bakhtiar, Shapur: Iran's last shah-appointed prime minister (1979)
Balfour Declaration: Official British statement in 1917 supporting Jewish
  national home in Palestine
Balkan Wars: Two conflicts among the Ottoman Empire and several
  southeastern European states in 1912 and 1913
Balkans: Mountainous region of southeastern Europe
Bar Lev line: Israel's defense line east of the Suez Canal breached by Egypt in
  October 1973
Barak, Ehud: Israel's prime minister (1999–2001)
Barmakid: Persian family of viziers under the early 'Abbasids
al-Barudi, Mahmud Sami: Egyptian nationalist prime minister (1882)
Basra: City in southern Iraq, founded by 'Umar to garrison troops
bast: Individual or group act of taking refuge in a mosque or other public place
  to evade arrest, a Persian custom
Baybars: Mamluk general and sultan (1260–1277)
Bayezid I: Ottoman sultan (1389–1402), who spread control in Balkans and
  Anatolia

Bayezid II: Ottoman sultan (1481–1512)

Bayt al-Hikma: Muslim center of learning under the 'Abbasids

bazaar: (1) Large trading and manufacturing center, (2) urban merchants as a corporate body, especially in Iranian cities

Bazargan, Mehdi: Iran's first prime minister (1979) after the Islamic Revolution

Bedouin: Arab camel nomad(s)

Begin, Menachem: Leader of Israel's right-wing Likud coalition and prime minister (1977–1983)

Beirut: Port city, commercial center, and Lebanon's capital

Bektashi: Sufi order, popular among Ottoman janissaries

Benghazi: Main city in eastern Libya, where the revolt against the Qadhafi regime began in February 2011

Ben-Gurion, David: Zionist pioneer, writer, politician, and Israel's defense and prime minister (1948–1953 and 1955–1963)

Berber: Native inhabitant of parts of North Africa

Berlin, Treaty of: Definitive peace settlement of the Russo-Turkish War, signed in August 1878 and replacing the San Stefano treaty

Berlin-to-Baghdad Railway: Proposed rail line that, if completed, would have enhanced Germany's power in the Ottoman Empire before World War I

Bernadotte, Folke: Swedish UN mediator, murdered during the 1948 Palestine War

Biltmore Program: American Zionist resolution in 1942 openly demanding a Jewish state in Palestine

BILU: Early Zionist movement in Russia (an acronym from the Hebrew Beit Ya'cov lchu Vnelcha, meaning "To the house of Jacob go and we will follow")

bin Laden, Osama: Leader of al-Qa'ida, originally from Sa'udi Arabia, operating in Afghanistan until 2001, and killed by US forces in 2011

Biqa': Predominantly Shi'ite valley in eastern Lebanon

Black Sheep Turcomans: Shi'ite Turkic dynasty ruling in Persia (1378–1469)

Bosporus: Straits connecting the Black Sea and the Sea of Marmara

Bouazizi, Mohamed: Tunisian street peddler who set himself on fire in December 2010, launching the revolution in Tunisia and the Arab Spring

Boycott, Divestment, and Sanctions: Movement supporting Palestinians resisting Israeli occupation

Bridging Document: President Clinton's draft compromise, presented to Israel and Palestinians during Taba peace talks in 2001

British Agency: Offices and residence of Britain's chief political and diplomatic officer in Cairo to 1914; later called the Residency and now the British Embassy

Bunche, Ralph: US diplomat and UN mediator in Palestine (1948–1949)

Bursa: City in northwestern Anatolia, early Ottoman capital

Buyid dynasty: Family of Shi'ite Persians who settled south of the Caspian, then conquered and ruled Persia and Iraq (932–1062); also called Buwayhid

Byzantine Empire: Eastern Roman Empire (330–1453), which ruled from Constantinople and professed Greek Orthodox Christianity

Cairo: Egypt's capital, founded by the Fatimids (969); seat of the Ayyubids and Mamluks

Caliph: Successor to Muhammad as head of the *umma*

Caliphate: Political institution led by the caliph

Camel, Battle of the: First clash between Muslim armies (656), in which 'Ali defeated Talha, Zubayr, and 'Aisha

Camp David: (1) US president's vacation home in northern Maryland, (2) site of intensive peace talks by Begin, Carter, and Sadat in September 1978, (3) adjective applied to the Egyptian-Israeli accords or to the 1979 peace treaty, (4) site of abortive peace talks among 'Arafat, Barak, and Clinton in July 2000

Capitulations: System by which Muslim states granted extraterritorial immunity from local laws and taxes to subjects of Western countries

Caradon, Lord: British diplomat who drafted Security Council Resolution 242

Carter Doctrine: US policy statement declaring any foreign invasion of the Gulf to be an attack on vital American interests

Caucasus: Mountain range between the Black and Caspian seas

Central Treaty Organization (CENTO): See *Baghdad Pact*

Chalabi, Ahmad: Iraqi National Congress leader, who called for US invasion

Chalcedon: Site of 451 Christian council at which the Orthodox bishops condemned the Monophysite view of Christ's nature

Chaldiran, Battle of: Major Ottoman victory over Safavid Persia (1514)

Chovevei Tzion: Early Russian Zionist group

Churchill white paper: 1922 official statement of British Palestine policy limiting Jewish immigration to the country's absorptive capacity

Cilicia: Southwest Anatolian region, formerly called Little Armenia

Circassian: Native (or descendant of a native) of the Caucasus region east of the Black Sea

Constantine: Roman emperor (306–337) who converted to Christianity

Constantinople: City on the Bosporus and Sea of Marmara, originally named Byzantium, which became capital of the Byzantine Empire (330–1204 and 1262–1453) and of the Ottoman Empire (1453–1922); called Istanbul since 1923

Constitutionalists: Persons who believe that governments should uphold a set of basic laws limiting the rulers' powers; more specifically, Persian nationalists around 1906

Copt: Egyptian (or Ethiopian) Monophysite Christian

Cordoba: Spanish city, capital of the later Umayyads (756–1030)

Cossack: (1) Horse soldier of southern Russia, (2) member of a Persian brigade trained and chiefly officered by Russian Cossacks up to 1921

Crane, Charles: American manufacturer and philanthropist, member of the King-Crane Commission (1919), and adviser to Ibn Sa'ud (1931)

Crimea: Former Turkic, later Russian, now Ukrainian peninsula north of the Black Sea

Crimean War: Conflict among powers with imperial interests in the Middle East (1853–1856), in which Britain, France, and the Ottoman Empire defeated Russia

Cromer, Lord: British consul in Egypt (1883–1907), a financial reformer, who was resented by Egyptian nationalists

Crusades: European Christian military expeditions against Muslims (and sometimes Greek Orthodox Christians) between the eleventh and fifteenth centuries

Ctesiphon: Sassanid capital, south of modern Baghdad

Curzon, Lord: Britain's main representative at the 1923 Lausanne Conference

Cyprus: Mediterranean island near Anatolia and Syria

Cyrenaica: Eastern Libya

Damascus: Syria's capital; seat of the early Umayyads (661–750)

Dar al-Islam: Lands where Islam prevails

Dar'a: South Syrian city where the uprising against Bashar al-Assad began in March 2011

Darazi, Shaykh: Syrian founder of the Druze religion

Dardanelles: Straits connecting the Aegean to the Sea of Marmara

Dayan, Moshe: Israeli general and political leader (1915–1981)

Dayr Yasin: Palestinian village near Jerusalem where the Irgun massacred Arab civilians (1948)

Declaration of Principles: Formal name of the statement signed by Palestinian, Israeli, and US representatives in 1993

Demirel, Suleyman: Turkey's president (1993–2000)

Demokrat Party: Turkish political party in the 1950s

Desert Shield: US name for the multinational military buildup in Sa'udi Arabia opposing Iraq's occupation of Kuwait in 1990

Desert Storm: US name for the multinational military attack on Iraq, driving its troops from Kuwait in 1991

devshirme: Ottoman system of taking Christian boys, converting them to Islam, and training them for military or administrative service

Dhahran: East Arabian city, site of first Sa'udi oil strike in 1938

diaspora: Group of people, usually Jews but sometimes Armenians, Palestinians, or Africans, who have been dispersed from their homeland to various parts of the world

Dinshaway Incident: British atrocity against Egyptian peasants (1906)

divan: Ottoman council of ministers; *diwan* in Arabic

Doha Agreement: Settlement, mediated in 2008 by Qatar, that allowed greater participation by Hizballah and its allies in Lebanon's government

Dome of the Rock: Muslim shrine in Jerusalem, built in 692 on site of Jewish Temple; site of Abraham's sacrifice and of Muhammad's miraculous night journey

drone: Unmanned aircraft, often controlled remotely from a ground station, used to kill presumed terrorists

Druze: Pertaining to the secret religion practiced by some Arabs in Syria, Lebanon, and Israel, and founded by Shaykh Darazi, who preached that the Fatimid caliph al-Hakim was the last of a series of emanations from God

Dual Financial Control: Joint Anglo-French economic administration in Egypt (1876–1882)

Dubai: City in the United Arab Emirates

Eden, Anthony: British prime minister during 1956 Suez Affair

Edessa: Northwest Mesopotamian town and Crusader state (1098–1144)

Egyptian Bloc Coalition: Combination of several liberal political parties that ran candidates in Egypt's parliamentary elections in 2011

Eilat: Israel's port on the Gulf of 'Aqaba

Eisenhower Doctrine: Official US policy statement opposing spread of Communism in the Middle East (1957)

Elbaradei, Mohamed: Egyptian statesman, former head of International Atomic Energy Agency, and early critic of Mubarak's regime

Elburz: Mountain range in northern Iran

Emergency Law: Term used for various edicts that suspended human rights in Egypt, Syria, and several other Arab states, inspiring protest demonstrations during the Arab Spring

emirate: State ruled by an amir

Enver: Young Turk revolutionary leader (d. 1922)

Erdogan, Recep Tayyip: Turkey's prime minister (2003–2014) and president (2014–)

Ertugrul: Turkish *ghazi* leader (d. ca. 1280), father of Osman I

Erzurum: East Anatolian city; site of 1919 Turkish nationalist congress

Eshkol, Levi: Israel's prime minister (1963–1969)

Ethiopia: East African country, mainly Christian since the fourth century, involved in Arabian politics up to Muhammad's time

Euphrates: The more western of Iraq's two rivers

Evren, Kenan: Leader of 1980 coup that restored order to Turkey

Fahd: Sa'udi Arabia's king (1982–2005)

faqih: (1) Muslim legal expert, (2) under Iran's 1979 constitution, the final lawmaking authority, (3) official title of Ayatollahs Khomeini and Khamanei

Abu Nasr al-Farabi: Muslim philosopher and theologian (d. 950)

Faruq: Egypt's last king (1936–1952)

Fatah: Palestinian guerrilla group founded by Yasir 'Arafat

al-Fatat: Early Arab nationalist student group

Fatima: Muhammad's daughter who married 'Ali

Fatimid dynasty: Arab family of Isma'ili Shi'ites claiming descent from 'Ali and Fatima, ruling North Africa (909–972) and Egypt (969–1171), and claiming control of Syria, Hijaz, and Yemen

Faysal: King of Sa'udi Arabia (1964–1975)

Faysal: Son of Husayn of Mecca, Arab Revolt leader, who headed provisional Arab government in Damascus (1918–1920); ousted by France, later became king of Iraq (1921–1933)

Faysal II: Iraq's last king (1939–1958)

Ferid, Damad: Ottoman prime minister backed by the sultan and the Western powers (1919–1920)

Fertile Crescent: Modern term for the lands extending from the eastern Mediterranean, via Syria and Mesopotamia, to the Gulf

fez: Crimson brimless head covering worn by male officials in the later Ottoman Empire and in some successor states; outlawed in Turkey by Kemal Ataturk

fida'iyin: Commandos, or people who sacrifice themselves for a cause, often applied to Palestinians fighting against Israel or to militant Shi'ites

15 March Movement: Social network for young Palestinians fighting Israeli occupation

fiqh: The science of Islamic law (jurisprudence)

fitna: Term applied to several civil wars in early Islamic history

Four Reserved Points: Britain's limitations on its unilateral declaration of Egypt's independence (1922)

Fourteen Points: President Wilson's plan to settle issues that had caused World War I, calling for self-determination of all peoples

Franjiyah, Sulayman: Lebanon's president (1970–1976)

free will: Religious doctrine that God has created human beings who can choose their actions; the opposite of predestination

Freedom and Justice Party: Egypt's leading Islamic party, linked to the Muslim Brothers

Fu'ad: Egypt's sultan and king (1917–1936)

Fustat: Egyptian garrison town in early Islamic times; later an administrative center, near modern Cairo

Gabriel: Angel, in Muslim belief, who transmitted the Qur'an to Muhammad

Galilee: Mountainous area of northern Israel, containing many Arab villages

Gallipoli: Strategic peninsula on the Dardanelles, disputed by Byzantines and early Ottomans, and the site of an unsuccessful Allied assault on Turkey in 1915–1916

garrison town: City, such as Basra, Kufa, or Fustat, set up by the early caliphs to house Arab soldiers

al-Gaylani, Rashid 'Ali: Leader of the 1941 Arab nationalist government in Iraq, overthrown by the British

Gaza Strip: Small part of southwest Palestine held by Egyptian forces in 1948 and inhabited by Arabs, administered by Egypt (1948–1956 and 1957–1967), captured by Israel in 1956 and 1967, and governed by Israel (1967–1994) and by the PLO (1994–2006) and by Hamas (2006–); evacuated by Israel in 2005, but attacked and invaded by Israel (2008–2009 and 2014)

Geneva Conference: December 1973 meeting of Israel, Egypt, and Jordan, cochaired by the US and the Soviet Union

Genghis Khan: Mongol warrior, conqueror, and ruler of most of Asia (d. 1227)

al-Ghazali, Abu-Hamid: Major Muslim theologian (d. 1111)

ghazi: Muslim border warrior

Ghazi: Iraq's king (1933–1939)

Ghazna: Afghan city, where the Ghaznavid Empire began

Ghaznavid: Turkic empire, comprising Afghanistan and parts of Iran and Central Asia, that conquered much of India (977–1186)

ghulam: Male slave, usually military or administrative, especially in Safavid Empire

Gibraltar: (1) Mountain in southern Spain, (2) straits between the Atlantic
   and the Mediterranean (originally Jebel Tariq, named after the Berber who
   commanded the Muslim conquest of Spain)
Gidi Pass: Strategic point in western Sinai, captured by Israel in 1956 and 1967,
   relinquished to a UN force in 1975, and restored to Egypt in 1982
Glubb, John Bagot: British commander of Jordan Arab Legion, dismissed in
   1956
Golan Heights: Mountainous area of southwestern Syria, occupied by Israel
   since 1967 and scene of intense fighting in 1973
Golden Horde: Group of Islamized Mongols with a Turkic majority that ruled
   Russia from the thirteenth to the fifteenth centuries
Granada: Capital of the last Muslim state in Spain
Grand National Assembly: Representative legislature of the Turkish republic
Great Khan: Title of Mongol emperor during the thirteenth century
Great Silk Route: Trade route connecting Iran with China, crossing the steppes
   and mountain passes of Central Asia
Greek fire: A liquid substance that ignited upon contact with water, used by
   Byzantine and later by Muslim sailors to destroy enemy ships
Greek Orthodox: Pertaining to the branch of Christianity that accepts the
   spiritual authority of the Constantinople patriarch and espouses the
   Christological doctrines adopted at the Nicaea (325) and Chalcedon (451)
   church councils
Green Movement: Iranian protest movement following the re-election, possibly
   rigged, of Ahmadinejad in 2009, and violently suppressed by government
   troops
Guantanamo: Cuban site of US naval base, site of prison built for enemy
   combatants captured during US-led invasions of Afghanistan and Iraq
Gulf Cooperation Council (GCC): Influential political, economic, and military
   organization, consisting of Sa'udi Arabia, Kuwait, Bahrain, Qatar, Oman, and
   the United Arab Emirates, created in 1981
Gulf War: (1) Iran-Iraq War (1980–1988), (2) campaign of US-led coalition to
   make Iraq withdraw from Kuwait (1991)
Gush Emunim: Group of religiously observant Israeli settlers on the West Bank
Habash, George: Leader of the Popular Front for the Liberation of Palestine, a
   Marxist Palestinian Arab group (1926–2008)
Habib, Philip: US negotiator among Syria, Lebanon, and Israel (1981–1982)
Habsburg: German family who ruled over the Holy Roman Empire (1273–1806)
   and Austria (up to 1918)
hadith: A statement, documented by a chain of reliable witnesses, concerning a
   saying or action of Muhammad, or an action by one of his companions that
   he approved; hence, an authoritative source of the Shari'a
Haganah: Jewish Agency's army in Palestine (1920–1948)
Hagar: Abraham's second wife, mother of Ishmael, ancestor of the Arabs
Haifa: Israel's main port city
hajj: Muslim rite of pilgrimage to Mecca, or (with a lengthened vowel) a Muslim
   who has completed the pilgrimage rites

al-Hajjaj: Authoritarian governor of Iraq (d. 714)
al-Hakim: Fatimid caliph (996–1021), venerated by the Druze
Hama: Syrian city, site of massacre by Hafiz al-Assad's troops in 1982
Hamad ibn Isa Al Khalifa: Bahrain's king (2002–), opposed by many Shi'ites
Hamas: Palestinian Islamist group
Hamdanid dynasty: Arab family whose branches ruled Aleppo and Mosul (892–1004)
Hanafi: Most widespread rite of Sunni Muslim jurisprudence, originating in Iraq, stressing communal consensus as a source of the Shari'a
Hanbali: Rite of Sunni Muslim jurisprudence that based all rules of conduct on the Qur'an and *hadiths*
Hanif: Arab true believer in God before rise of Islam
Haniya, Isma'il: Hamas leader governing Gaza (2006–2014)
Harawi, Ilyas: Lebanon's president (1989–1995)
harem: The portion of a Muslim house used by women and young children, not open to unrelated males
Hariri, Rafiq: Lebanon's prime minister (1992–1998 and 2000–2004), assassinated in 2005
Harun al-Rashid: 'Abbasid caliph (786–809)
Hasan: Older son of 'Ali and Fatima, named by 'Ali as his successor but pensioned off by Mu'awiya; recognized as second Shi'ite imam (d. 669)
Hashimite: (1) Member of the family descended from Hashim, (2) supporter of an extremist *mawali* Shi'ite sect in late Umayyad times, (3) member of the dynasty ruling the Hijaz (1916–1925), Syria (1918–1920), Iraq (1921–1958), and Jordan (1921–)
Haskala: Era of Jewish enlightenment during the eighteenth and nineteenth centuries
Hebrew: Semitic language of ancient and modern Israel
Hebron: Town in Judea (the West Bank), revered by Jews and Muslims, site of a massacre by a Jewish settler of Palestinians in 1994
Hellenistic: Pertaining to the society and culture of the Mediterranean area that used Greek as its main literary and administrative language
Heraclius: Byzantine emperor (610–641) who repulsed Sassanids but later lost Syria and Egypt to the Arabs
Hermon: Mountain in southwestern Syria, partly occupied by Israel since 1967
Herut: Israel's right-wing party, led by Begin up to 1983; now part of the Likud coalition
Herzl, Theodor: Writer and founder of political Zionism (d. 1904)
Hess, Moses: Early German socialist and advocate of a Jewish state (d. 1875)
Hijaz: Mountainous area of western Arabia
hijra: Emigration of Muhammad and his followers from Mecca to Medina in 622 (year 1 of the Muslim calendar)
Hisham: Umayyad caliph (724–743)
Histadrut: Israel's major labor union, owner of many business enterprises, and manager of health insurance plan
Hizballah: Shi'ite commando group based in Lebanon

Holy Sepulcher: Jesus's reputed burial place and a major church in Jerusalem
Homs: Syrian city, site of intense fighting in 2012
Houthis: Yemeni tribal Shi'ites who overthrew 'Abd Rabbuh Mansur Hadi in 2015; also called Ansar Allah
Hudaybiyya: Treaty made by Muhammad with the Meccans in 628, enabling Muslim emigrants to make the *hajj*
Hulegu: Mongol ruler (d. 1265), Genghis Khan's grandson, who extended Mongol conquest of Persia and Iraq and founded the Il-Khanid dynasty
Hunkar-Iskelesi: Treaty (1833) in which Russia guaranteed Ottoman Empire's territorial integrity
Husayn: Younger son of 'Ali and Fatima, killed in an anti-Umayyad revolt at Karbala (680), hence a martyr for Shi'ite Muslims and their third imam; also spelled Hussein
Husayn: Amir and sharif of Mecca (1908–1924), king of the Hijaz (1916–1924), and leader of the 1916–1918 Arab Revolt against the Ottomans
Husayn: Jordan's king (1952–1999)
Husayn, Saddam: Iraq's president (1979–2003), who began the Iran-Iraq War (1980–1988) and invaded Kuwait in 1990, leading to Operation Desert Storm; overthrown by US invasion in 2003, captured, tried, and executed in 2006; also spelled Hussein
Husayn, Taha: Egyptian writer (1889–1973)
Husayn Kamil: Egypt's sultan (1914–1917)
Husayn-McMahon Correspondence: Letters exchanged by Amir Husayn and Britain's high commissioner in Cairo (1915–1916), offering British aid for the Arabs' independence in exchange for Arab support against the Ottoman Empire
al-Husayni, Hajj Amin: Mufti of Jerusalem and early Palestinian nationalist leader (d. 1974)
ibn: Son of, often used in Arabic names; sometimes spelled bin
Ibn Khaldun: Noted historian and social thinker (d. 1406)
Ibn Rushd: Muslim philosopher, known as Averroës in Latin (d. 1198)
Ibn Sa'ud: Arab leader who conquered most of the Arabian Peninsula between 1902 and 1930 and ruler of Sa'udi Arabia (1932–1953); also called 'Abd al-'Aziz ibn 'Abd al-Rahman
Ibn Sina: Muslim philosopher, theologian, and scientist (d. 1037); known as Avicenna in Latin
Ibrahim: Mehmet 'Ali's son, conqueror and governor of Syria (1832–1840) and viceroy of Egypt (1848)
'Id al-Adha: Arabic term for Feast of the Sacrifice, annual Muslim holiday commemorating Abraham's obedience to God's command by offering to sacrifice his son Ishmael (Isma'il); tenth day of the pilgrimage month
'Id al-Fitr: Arabic term for Feast of Fast-Breaking, annual Muslim holiday following the Ramadan fast
ijtihad: Use of reasoning to determine a specific rule in Islamic law
Ikhwan: (1) Sedentarized Bedouin soldiers for Ibn Sa'ud, (2) members of the Society of the Muslim Brothers

Il-Khanid: Mongol successor dynasty in Persia (1256–1349)
imam: (1) Muslim religious or political leader, (2) one of the succession of
leaders, beginning with 'Ali, viewed by Shi'ites as legitimate, (3) leader of
Muslim congregational worship
Imperial Rescript: Ottoman decree (1856) giving equal rights and status to all
subjects regardless of religion; sometimes called the *Hatt-i-Humayun*
Inonu: (1) Site of two Turkish victories over Greeks in western Anatolia (1921),
(2) surname taken by Ismet, Turkish leader in those battles
Intifada: (1) Palestinian uprising against Israeli occupation (1987–1990),
(2) Palestinian rebellion that followed Ariel Sharon's visit to al-Aqsa
Mosque in 2000
Intifada of al-Aqsa: Palestinian revolt against Israeli rule (2000–2005)
iqta': Land grant from a ruler for military or administrative services by a client
Iran: Preferred name since 1935 for what was Persia
Iran-Contra Affair: Reagan administration's arms sales to Iran to secure release
of American hostages in Lebanon and donation of the proceeds to aid Contra
insurgents in Nicaragua (1986)
Iran-Iraq War: Ideological and territorial conflict between Iran and Iraq
(1980–1988)
Iraq: Arabic name for Mesopotamia
Iraqi National Congress: Organization, led by Ahmad Chalabi, that advocated
US invasion of Iraq in 2003 to overthrow Saddam Husayn's government
Irgun Tzvei Le'umi: Right-wing Zionist guerrilla group, commanded by Begin
and active up to 1948
Isfahan: City in central Iran and Safavid capital (1597–1736)
Ishmael: Mythic ancestor of the Arabs; Isma'il in Arabic
Islam: The religion, now prevalent in the Middle East and many other parts of
Asia and Africa, believing in one God revealed to a series of prophets, ending
with Muhammad, to whom the Qur'an was entrusted
Islamic Action Front: Jordan's branch of the Muslim Brothers
Islamic Group: Egyptian underground Islamist movement
Islamic Republican Party: Revolutionary Iran's main political movement
(1979–1987)
Islamic State of Iraq and the Levant (ISIL): An Islamist rebel group, mostly
composed of Sunni extremist fighters, that controls territory in Iraq and Syria;
also known as Islamic State of Iraq and Syria (ISIS); renamed itself Islamic
State (IS) in 2014, with Abu Bakr al-Baghdadi as its first caliph
Islamist: Pertaining to any person or group advocating government according to
strict Muslim principles
Isma'il: Final legitimate imam for Seven-Imam Shi'ites
Isma'il, Khedive: Egypt's viceroy (1863–1879)
Isma'il Shah: Founder (1501–1524) of the Safavid dynasty
Isma'ili: Pertaining to Seven-Imam Shi'ism
Ismet: Turkish general, Turkey's representative at the Lausanne Conference
(1923), and president of the republic (1938–1950 and 1961–1965); surnamed
Inonu

isnad: Chain of witnesses verifying a *hadith*

Israel: (1) Surname of Jacob and his descendants, (2) ancient northern Jewish kingdom, (3) modern Jewish state, located in what used to be Palestine

Israelis: Citizens of modern Israel

Israelites: Descendants of Jacob; often the term for the Jewish people as a whole

Istanbul: Modern name for Constantinople

Izmir: West Anatolian city, formerly called Smyrna

Jabotinsky, Vladimir: Founder of the Revisionist (right-wing Zionist) Party (1880–1940)

Jacobite: Syrian Monophysite Christian

Jaffa: Port city in Palestine/Israel, now part of Tel Aviv

janissary: Christian conscript foot soldier in the Ottoman army converted to Islam and trained to use firearms

Jarring, Gunnar: UN mediator between Israel and the Arab states (1967–1971)

Al Jazeera: Influential television station, based in Qatar, but heard throughout the Middle East

Jemal: Young Turk leader and Syria's governor (d. 1922)

Jerusalem: Judea's main city; major religious center for Jews, Christians, and Muslims; proclaimed by Israel as its capital

Jewish Agency: Organization set up under the Palestine mandate to work with Britain toward the Jewish national home; later charged with aiding Jewish immigration and absorption into Israel

Jewish National Fund: Zionist land-purchasing and development agency in Palestine/Israel, founded in 1901

jihad: (1) Defense of Islam against attackers, (2) Muslim struggle against evil within oneself, one's associates, and the *umma,* (3) name of several Islamist groups

jinn: In Muslim belief, invisible creatures living on earth, capable of doing good or harm

jizya: Per capita tax formerly paid by non-Muslim males living under Muslim rule

Jordan, Hashimite Kingdom of: State formed from the Emirate of Transjordan and parts of Arab Palestine (commonly called the West Bank) annexed by Abdallah in 1948

Jordan River: River flowing through Syria, Jordan, and Israel

Judea: Mountainous area of eastern Palestine/Israel

Jumayyil, Amin: Lebanon's president (1982–1988); also spelled Gemayel

Jumayyil, Bashir: Prominent Phalangist leader, elected Lebanon's president in 1982 but killed before he could take office

Jumblat, Kamal: Lebanese Druze leader (d. 1977)

Junayd, Shaykh: Turcoman Shi'ite Sufi leader of the Safavids in Azerbaijan (d. 1460), grandfather of Shah Isma'il

Jundishapur: Sassanid and Muslim center of learning

Justice and Development Party: Turkey's moderate Islamist party, ruling since 2002, called AK Parti in Turkish

Justice Party: Turkey's conservative party (1961–1980)

Ka'ba: Muslim shrine in Mecca housing the Black Stone, serving as the focal point for the *hajj* and setting the direction for Muslim worship

Kabul: Capital of Afghanistan

Kadima Party: Israeli liberal-centrist party, formed in 2005, to support Sharon's disengagement plan; part of ruling coalition (2006, 2009, and 2012–)

Kalb: Southern Arab tribe important in early Islam

Kamil, Mustafa: Egyptian nationalist (1874–1908)

Karbala: Iraqi city, site of Husayn's uprising and martyrdom (680); since then a Shi'ite pilgrimage center

Karlowitz: Treaty (1699) in which Ottomans ceded Hungary to Austria

Karzai, Hamid: Afghan leader since 2001, elected president in 2004

al-Kawakibi, 'Abd al-Rahman: Arab nationalist writer (d. 1902)

Kemal, Mustafa (Ataturk): Turkish general, nationalist leader, and westernizing president (1923–1938)

Kemalism: Kemal's principles of Turkish nationalism and westernizing reform

Khadija: Muhammad's first wife (d. 619)

Khalid ibn al-Walid: Arab general; conqueror of Arabia, Syria, Iraq, and Persia

Khamanei, Ayatollah 'Ali: Iran's *faqih* (1989–)

kharaj: Land tax paid by peasants on produce

Kharijite: "Seceder" who opposed 'Ali after he accepted arbitration of the Battle of Siffin (657) and killed him (661); later an anarchist group believing that any sinless Muslim could be caliph

Khartoum: (1) Sudan's capital, (2) site of 1967 Arab summit opposing peace negotiations with Israel

Khatami, Muhammad: Iran's president (1997–2005)

Khazar: Turkic tribe north of the Caspian, converted to Judaism in the eighth century

khedive: Title of Egypt's viceroy (1867–1914)

Khomeini, Ayatollah Ruhollah: Leader of Islamic Revolution in Iran (1978–1979) and *faqih* (1979–1989)

Khurasan: Persian province east of Caspian Sea; center of many dissident movements in early Islamic history

Khuzistan: Oil-rich province of southwestern Iran

Khwarizm: Region south of the Aral Sea

Khwarizm-Shah: Central Asian Turkic dynasty (1077–1231) defeated by Genghis Khan

kibbutz (pl. kibbutzim): Jewish settlement in Israel, initially agricultural, now mainly industrial, in which most property is collectively owned

al-Kindi: Muslim philosopher and scientist (d. 873)

King-Crane Commission: US committee sent by 1919 Paris Peace Conference to ascertain Syrian and Palestinian aspirations, but its report, sympathetic to Arab nationalism, was not acted upon

Kitchener, Lord: Commander of Anglo-Egyptian army that retook Sudan (1896–1898), later the British consul general in Egypt (1911–1914)

kizilbash: Shi'ite Turks, especially Safavid horse soldiers

Knesset: Israel's unicameral legislature

Konya: Southern Anatolian city, capital of the Rum Seljuk state (1077–1300)

Koprulu: Family of Ottoman viziers

Kosovo, Battle of: Site of 1389 Ottoman victory over Serbia

Kuchuk-Kainarji: Treaty (1774) in which Russia claimed the right to protect the sultan's Orthodox Christian subjects

Kufa: Iraqi garrison town founded by 'Umar; later a major commercial and intellectual center

kufiya: White or colored headcloth worn by men in Arabia and parts of the Fertile Crescent; often spelled *kaffiyeh*

Kunaitra: Main city in the Golan Heights, captured by Israel in 1967, fought over in 1973, and returned to Syria in 1974

Kurd: Member of linguistic-cultural group concentrated in southeastern Turkey, northern Iraq, northwestern Iran, and parts of Syria

Kurdish Workers Party: Kurdish independence movement that rebelled in southeast Turkey (1984–1999); also called PKK (Partiya Karkeren Kurdistan)

Kurdistan: (1) Autonomous state projected by Treaty of Sèvres (1920) and still desired by many Kurdish nationalists, (2) province in Iran

Kuwait: Oil-rich principality on the Gulf, occupied by Iraq (August 1990–February 1991)

Labor Alignment: Coalition of Israel's labor parties, ruling up to 1977, governing jointly with the Likud (1984–1990), and in power from 1992 to 1996 and 1999 to 2001

Lahud, Emile: Lebanon's president (1998–2007)

Lampson, Sir Miles: British high commissioner and ambassador in Egypt (1934–1946)

Lausanne: (1) 1923 conference and treaty between Turkey and the World War I Allies, replacing the Treaty of Sèvres, (2) 1949 peace conference between Israel and the Arab states

Lawrence, T. E.: British intelligence officer who aided the Arab Revolt; gifted writer and advocate of Arab nationalism (d. 1935)

Lebanon War: 2006 conflict between Israel and Hizballah, also called "Second Lebanon War" in Israel and "July War" in Lebanon, marked by heavy destruction in Beirut and southern Lebanon, ended by Security Council Resolution 1701

Lepanto, Battle of: European naval victory over Ottomans (1571)

Levantine: Pertaining to the Levant or the eastern shores of the Mediterranean, or to its inhabitants, especially non-Muslims

Likud: Coalition of Israel's right-wing parties, in power from 1977 to 1984, in coalition with Labor (1984–1990 and 2001–2003), with the religious parties (1990–1992, 1996–1999, 2003–2004, and 2009–2012), and with the Kadima Party (2012–2015)

loya jirga: Meeting of Afghan tribes, notably in 2003

madrasa: Muslim school, especially for law

mahdi: Rightly guided one, precursor of the Judgment Day

al-Mahdi: Leader of Sudan's successful rebellion against Egyptian rule (d. 1885)

Mahdi Army: Iraqi Shi'ite militia founded by Muqtada al-Sadr in 2003
Mahmud: Ghaznavid ruler (998–1030); conqueror of India
Mahmud II: Ottoman sultan (1808–1839) and westernizing reformer
Majlis: Iran's bicameral legislature
Maliki: Rite of Sunni Muslim jurisprudence that originated in Medina and
  stresses use of *hadiths* as authoritative legal sources
al-Maliki, Nuri: Iraq's prime minister (2006– 2014)
Malikshah: Seljuk sultan (1072–1092)
mamluk: (1) Turkish or Circassian slave soldier, (2) (cap.) member of a military
  oligarchy ruling Egypt (1250–1517) and Syria (1260–1516) and dominant in
  some areas up to the nineteenth century
al-Ma'mun: 'Abbasid caliph (813–833)
mandate: (1) Commission given by the League of Nations to a Western power to
  prepare a former territory of Germany or the Ottoman Empire for eventual
  self-rule, (2) a country governed under this tutelary relationship
Manichaeism: Dualistic religion formulated by Mani, a third-century Persian,
  calling for the liberation of the body from the soul by various ascetic spiritual
  exercises, strong formerly in Iraq, Persia, and some parts of Central and
  East Asia
al-Mansur, Abu-Ja'far: 'Abbasid caliph (754–775) who began the construction
  of Baghdad
Manzikert, Battle of: Seljuk victory over the Byzantines (1071)
Mapai: Israel's moderate labor party
marches: Frontier areas between two countries or cultures
Ma'rib: (1) Ancient Sabaean capital, (2) site of dam built in eighth century BCE,
  (3) dam in modern Yemen
Maronite: Pertaining to a Christian sect, mainly in northern Lebanon, whose
  distinguishing belief is that Christ contained two natures within one will and
  which has been in communion with the Roman Catholic Church since the
  Crusades
Marwan : Umayyad caliph (684–685)
Marxism: System of socialist thought, founded by Karl Marx and others, that
  teaches that capitalism must be overthrown by a revolution leading to a
  workers' state, which will later give way to a classless and harmonious society;
  accepted by some Middle Eastern leaders at various times
mawla (pl. *mawali*): (1) Client member of Arab tribe, entitled to protection but
  not all membership privileges, (2) non-Arab convert to Islam during the early
  Arab conquests
McMahon, Henry: British high commissioner in Egypt (1914–1916) who
  initiated the Husayn-McMahon Correspondence
Mecca: Birthplace of the Prophet Muhammad and main commercial and
  pilgrimage center in western Arabia
Medina: Northwest Arabian farming oasis, formerly Yathrib, to which
  Muhammad and his followers went in 622
Mehmet I: Ottoman sultan (1413–1421)

Mehmet II: Ottoman sultan (1451–1481), conqueror of Constantinople

Mehmet 'Ali: Albanian adventurer who took control of Egypt and instituted many westernizing reforms (1805–1849); also called Muhammad 'Ali

Meir, Golda: Israel's prime minister (1969–1974)

Mesopotamia: Greek name for the land between the Tigris and Euphrates rivers, especially Iraq

Messiah: According to the Bible, the expected deliverer of the Jewish people and, according to Christians, Jesus Christ

Middle East Supply Centre: Cairo-based British organization that coordinated manufacturing and distribution in Arab states and Iran during World War II

Midhat: Ottoman liberal reformer (1822–1883)

millet: Ottoman political-social community based on religious membership and whose leaders were named by the sultan

Milner, Lord: British statesman who headed 1919 commission of inquiry to Egypt and later negotiated unsuccessfully with Sa'd Zaghlul

minaret: Turkish name for the mosque tower from which a muezzin calls Muslims to worship five times daily

Mitla Pass: Strategic point in the western Sinai, captured by Israel in 1956 and 1967, ceded to a UN buffer force in 1975, and restored to Egypt in 1982

Mixed Courts: Egyptian tribunals for civil cases involving foreign nationals (1876–1949)

Mizrachim: Jews whose ancestors came from Spain, Portugal, or the Muslim world; sometimes called Sephardim

Mohammad Reza Shah Pahlavi: Iran's shah (1941–1979)

mollah: Persian Muslim teacher

Mongol: Nomadic horseman from northeastern Asia; member of a tribal coalition that under Genghis Khan and his descendants overran most of Asia in the thirteenth century

Monophysite: Pertaining to (mainly Middle Eastern) Christians who believe that Christ had only one nature, wholly divine; view condemned by the Council of Chalcedon in 451

monotheistic: Pertaining to belief in one god, as in Judaism, Christianity, and Islam

Morea: The Peloponnesus, or southern Greece

Morsi, Mohamed: Egypt's president (2012–2013)

Mosaddiq, Mohammad: Iran's prime minister (1951–1953), who nationalized the Anglo-Iranian Oil Company and was later ousted in a coup engineered by the shah, the British, and the CIA (d. 1967)

mosque: Place of communal worship for Muslims

mostaz'afan: People who have been dispossessed because of westernizing policies

Mosul: City in northern Iraq

Mu'awiya: Umayyad caliph (661–680)

Mubarak, Husni: Egypt's president (1981–2011)

Mudros: Aegean island on which the Ottoman Empire surrendered to the World War I Allies in 1918

muezzin: Man who calls other Muslims to communal worship, usually from a mosque roof or minaret balcony

mufti: (1) Sunni Muslim legal consultant, (2) in modern times, *'ulama* leader in a Sunni Muslim state

Mughals: See *Timurid dynasty*

Muhammad: Arab religious leader, born in Mecca and founder of the Islamic *umma*, viewed by Muslims as God's messenger, whose revelations were recorded in the Qur'an

Muhammad: Khwarizm-Shah leader defeated by Genghis Khan

Muhammad al-Muntazar: Last of the twelve legitimate imams, who vanished around 878 but is expected by Twelve-Imam Shi'ites to return someday

Muhammad ibn 'Abd al-Wahhab: Founder of the Wahhabi movement in the eighteenth century

muhtasib: Muslim market inspector

mujtahid: Learned Muslim who interprets the Shari'a, especially in Shi'ite jurisprudence

multezim: Ottoman tax collector allowed by the government to keep a share of what he collected

muqannis: hereditary class of skilled diggers who maintained *qanats*

Murad I: Ottoman sultan (1360–1389)

Murad II: Ottoman sultan (1421–1451)

Murad IV: Ottoman sultan (1623–1640)

muruwwa: Pre-Islamic code of Arab virtues

Musandam: Peninsula jutting into Hormuz Strait, a province of Oman

Muslim: (1) A person who submits to God's will, (2) anyone who believes that God revealed the Qur'an to Muhammad

Muslim Brothers, Society of the: Political group, strong in Egypt (1930–1952, 1978–) and in several other Arab countries, calling for an Islamic political and social system and opposing Western power and cultural influence; sometimes called Muslim Brotherhood

Mu'tazila: Rationalist formulation of Islamic theology, stressing that God created the Qur'an

Nadir Afshar: Military leader who became shah of Persia (1736–1747), expelled Afghan invaders, and conquered part of India

Nagib, Muhammad: Titular leader of 1952 Egyptian revolution

al-Nahda Party: Tunisia's moderate Islamist party, which won plurality of seats in 2011 elections; also known as Ennahda

al-Nahhas, Mustafa: Leader of Egypt's Wafd Party (1927–1952)

Najaf: Iraqi city where 'Ali was assassinated (661); hence a Shi'ite pilgrimage center

Nakba: Arabic term for the Arab defeat in Palestine War (1948–1949), commemorated on 15 May

Naksa: Arabic term for Arab defeat in June 1967 War; date observed is 5 June

al-Nasir, Gamal 'Abd: Leader of the 1952 military coup that ousted Egypt's monarchy; later prime minister, then president (1954–1970); also written Gamal Abdel Nasser

Nasirism: Western term for Nasir's political philosophy and program, including nationalism, neutralism, and Arab socialism

Nasiruddin Shah: Qajar ruler (1848–1896)

Nasrallah, Hassan: Islamist leader of Lebanon's Hizballah since 1992

National Bloc: Syria's independence movement from 1931; see also *Nationalist Party*

National Charter: 1962 Egyptian document describing the goals of Arab socialism

National (Liberation) Front: Aden's successful independence movement in 1967

National Pact: 1943 power-sharing agreement among Lebanon's religious and political groups

National Party: Egyptian movement seeking independence from foreign control, led by 'Urabi in 1881–1882 and by Mustafa Kamil in 1895–1908

National Religious Party: Party of observant Jews in Israel

National Transitional Council: Libyan organization that led rebellion, aided by NATO, against Qadhafi and that took control of Libya's government in August 2011

Nationalism: (1) Desire of a group of people to preserve or obtain common statehood, (2) ideology stressing loyalty to the nation-state or seeking independence of a national group

Nationalist Party: Syria's main party after World War II

Negev: Desert in southern Israel

neoconservative: Member of a political group, mainly American, that advocates a militantly pro-US policy in the Middle East and favors supporting Israel and weakening its enemies

Neoplatonist: Supporter of a philosophical system, founded in the third century, based on Plato's ideas and common in the Middle East up to the Arab conquests

Nestorian: Pertaining to Christians who believe in Christ's separate divine and human natures, condemned at the 430 Council of Ephesus

Netanyahu, Benjamin: Israel's prime minister (1996–1999 and 2009–)

New Ottomans: Turkish political movement in the 1870s demanding a constitution, parliamentary government, and other westernizing reforms

Nicaea: Northwest Anatolian city, site of the Christian church council in 325 that accepted the trinitarian view of the nature of God: Father, Son, and Holy Spirit

9/11 or Nine-Eleven: Coordinated attack by Arab militants who hijacked American passenger jets and flew them into New York's World Trade Center and Washington's Pentagon, so named for September 11 (2001), the date of the attacks

nizam-i-jedid: Military reform program promulgated by Selim III but crushed by the janissaries in 1807

Noble Rescript of the Rose Chamber: 1839 Ottoman promise of judicial and administrative reforms; sometimes called the *Hatt-i-Sherif* of Gulhane, ushering in the Tanzimat era

no-fly zones: (1) Iraqi areas in which Iraq was forbidden by the US to fly military planes (1991–2003), (2) Libyan areas in which Libya was forbidden by NATO to fly its planes in 2011

Nour Party: Egyptian ultra-Islamist group that challenges the Freedom and Justice Party

Nur al-Din: Zengid sultan of Mosul and Damascus (1146–1174)

Nuri al-Sa'id : Pro-Western Iraqi leader, killed in 1958 revolution

al-Nusra Front: Branch of al-Qa'ida operating in Syria

October War: War started by Egypt and Syria in 1973 to regain lands occupied by Israel since 1967; also called the Yom Kippur War or Ramadan War

olim: Jewish immigrants to Israel

Olmert, Ehud: Israel's prime minister (2006–2009)

Organization of Petroleum Exporting Countries (OPEC): A group formed in 1960 to maintain a minimum price for oil

Orhan: Ottoman sultan (1326–1360)

Oslo: (1) Site of secret Israeli-PLO negotiations (1992–1993), (2) term applied to 1993 Declaration of Principles, (3) term applied to 1995 Israeli-PLO agreement

Osman I: First Ottoman sultan (ca. 1280–1326)

Osmanli: Pertaining to descendants of Osman I, their soldiers and administrators, or their language

Ottoman Decentralization Party: Liberal political movement favored by moderate Arab nationalists before World War I

Ottoman Empire: Multinational Islamic state (1299–1922) that began in northwestern Anatolia and spread through the Balkans, most of southwest Asia, Egypt, and coastal North Africa

Ottomanism: Identification with the Ottoman Empire (as opposed to separatist nationalism), encouraged by early westernizers

Oxus River: Roman name for the Amu Darya, a Central Asian river flowing from the Pamir Mountains northwest to the Aral Sea

Ozal, Turgut: Turkey's prime minister (1983–1989) and president (1989–1993)

Pahlavi: (1) Pre-Islamic Persian language, (2) ruling family of Iran (1925–1979)

Palestine: (1) Geographical term for southern Syria, (2) name of the British mandate from 1922 to 1948, (3) term preferred by many Arabs for some or all of the lands currently governed by the State of Israel, (4) areas of the West Bank governed since 1994 by the Palestinian Authority

Palestine Liberation Organization (PLO): Group formed in 1964 by Arab heads of state, now the umbrella for most Palestinian military, political, economic, and social organizations

Palestinian: Inhabitant of Palestine; now the term used for Arabs who live in Palestine, came from there, or descend from emigrants from that land

Palestinian Legislative Council: The elected parliament for the Palestinians in the West Bank and Gaza, suspended since 2007

Palestinian National Council: The representative assembly for the Palestine Liberation Organization, created in 1964 and meeting every other year; elects an executive group called the Palestinian Central Council, currently headed by Mahmoud 'Abbas

Palestinian (Self-Governing) Authority: Political organization set up by Oslo I agreement to administer areas relinquished by Israel to the Palestinians; since 2007 its control limited to the West Bank

pan-Arabism: Movement to unite all Arabs in one state

pan-Islam: Idea or movement calling for unity of all Muslims, promoted by some Ottoman sultans and some popular leaders

pan-Slavism: Movement to unite all Slavs, especially under Russian leadership

pan-Turanism: Movement to unite all peoples speaking Turkic languages

Paris Peace Conference: Meeting of the victorious Allies after World War I to establish peace in Europe and the Middle East

Parthian: Persian dynasty (248 BCE–CE 227) preceding the Sassanids

Partition Plan for Palestine: Proposed division of the Palestine mandate into Jewish and Arab states, approved by the UN General Assembly in 1947

Passfield White Paper: British official report blaming both Jews and Arabs for the 1929 Wailing Wall riots in Palestine

Pearl Roundabout: Manama traffic circle, the scene of Bahraini antiregime protests in 2011

Peel Commission: British committee that visited Palestine in 1937 and first recommended partition into Jewish and Arab states

People's Assembly: Popularly elected lower chamber of Egypt's parliament since 1971

People's Democratic Republic of Yemen: Name used (1969–1990) for what used to be called Aden and the Aden Protectorate, then South Arabian Federation, then South Yemen

People's Party: Syrian independence movement from 1925 and pro-Iraqi party after World War II

Peres, Shimon: Israel's prime minister (1984–1986), Labor Party leader (1977–1992), foreign minister (1992–1996), acting prime minister (1995–1996), and president (2007–2014)

Permanent Mandates Commission: League of Nations body supervising mandates' administration

Persia: Name used for Iran until 1935

Persian Gulf: Body of water separating Iran from the Arabian Peninsula and connecting the Shatt al-Arab to the Arabian Sea; also called the Gulf or Arabian Gulf

Phalanges: Paramilitary organization dedicated to preserving Maronite Christian dominance in Lebanon

Pinsker, Leon: Russian Zionist (1821–1891), author of *Auto-Emancipation* (1882)

pogrom: Organized massacre of Jews

Popular Front for the Liberation of Palestine: Marxist Palestinian group, noted for its airplane hijackings and led by George Habash

Port Said: Egyptian city at which the Suez Canal meets the Mediterranean

Portsmouth Agreement: Abortive 1948 pact between Britain and Iraq regarding military bases, strongly opposed by Iraqi Arab nationalists and never ratified

positive neutralism: Nasir's policy of not siding with either the Communist countries or the West but seeking to reconcile the two blocs

predestination: The belief that God has determined what will happen to every living person; the opposite of free will

Punjab: A region of northwestern India, now partly in Pakistan

al-Qadhafi, Mu'ammar: Libya's leader (1969–2011)

qadi: Muslim judge

al-Qadisiyya: Central Iraqi region and site of 637 battle in which the Arabs defeated the Sassanid Persians

al-Qa'ida: Network of militant Islamist organizations, led by Osama bin Laden and then by Ayman al-Zawahiri; often spelled Al Qaeda

Qajar dynasty: Family of Turkic origin ruling Persia (1794–1925)

qanat: Underground channel carrying irrigation water

qanun: A ruler's edict, as opposed to the rules or laws contained in the Shari'a

Qarmatian: Member of an Isma'ili Shi'ite group that established a republic, allegedly practicing communism of property and spouses, in tenth-century Bahrain and Arabia

Qasim, 'Abd al-Karim: Iraq's president (1958–1963)

Qays: Northern Arabian tribe, Kalb's rival in early Muslim times

Qom: Shi'ite religious and educational center in Iran

Qur'an: The collection of revelations that Muslims believe God vouchsafed to Muhammad via Gabriel, and one of the main sources of Islamic law, literature, and culture; also called the Koran

Quray', Ahmad: Palestinian Authority prime minister (2003–2004)

Quraysh: Leading tribe of northwest Arabia, especially Mecca

al-Quwatli, Shukri: Syria's president (1943–1949 and 1955–1958)

Rabat Summit: 1974 meeting of Arab heads of state, recognizing the PLO as the sole Palestinian representative

Rabin, Yitzhak: Israel's prime minister (1974–1977 and 1992–1995)

Rafsanjani, 'Ali Akbar Hashimi: Iran's president (1989–1997)

Ramadan: Month of the Arabic calendar during which Muslims refrain from eating, drinking, and sexual intercourse from daybreak to sunset, commemorating first revelations of the Qur'an to Muhammad

Ramallah: West Bank Palestinian city north of Jerusalem

Rashid dynasty: Ruling family in northeastern Arabia, rival of the Sa'udis in the early twentieth century

Rashidun caliphs: For Sunni Muslims, Muhammad's successors as *umma* leaders: Abu-Bakr, 'Umar, 'Uthman, and 'Ali

ra'iya: Member(s) of the Ottoman subject class

refugees, Palestinian: Arabs who fled or were driven from areas now part of Israel during the 1948 or 1967 wars

Republican People's Party: Liberal Turkish party founded by Kemal Ataturk in 1923

Reshid, Mustafa: Westernizing Ottoman reformer in the early Tanzimat era (d. 1858)

Revisionist Party: Right-wing Zionist movement founded by Jabotinsky

Revolutionary Guards: Iranian-organized Islamic guerrilla movement active in various Muslim countries

Reza Shah Pahlavi: Iran's ruler (1925–1941)

Rhodes: Mediterranean island; site of the 1949 "proximity talks" between Arab states and Israel, mediated by Ralph Bunche

ridda: Rebellion of the Arab tribes against rule from Medina after Muhammad's death, quelled under Caliph Abu-Bakr

riparian: Land situated along a river

riyad (singular *rawd*): garden

Riyadh: Saʻudi Arabia's capital; site of 1976 Arab summit meeting that tried to end Lebanon's civil war

Road Map: Plan for Israeli-Palestinian peace, to be achieved in stages, prepared in 2002 by George W. Bush with European Union, Russia, and the UN, but not accepted by Israel

Rogers Peace Plan: US proposal in 1969–1970 to end the War of Attrition, calling on Israel to give back lands occupied since 1967 and on Arabs to recognize Israel

Rum: (1) Arabic, Persian, and Turkish word for Anatolia, (2) collective term for Greek Orthodox Christians

Rumayla: Large oil field shared by Iraq and Kuwait

Rushdi, Husayn: Egypt's prime minister (1914–1919)

Russo-Turkish War: Conflict (1877–1878) between Russia and the Ottoman Empire in which the latter lost land in Anatolia and the Balkans

Saba: Ancient Arab kingdom in Yemen, inhabitants of which were called Sabaeans

al Sabah: Ruling family of Kuwait

Sabra: (1) Jewish native of Israel, (2) Beirut refugee camp, site of Palestinian massacre in 1982

al-Sadat, Anwar: Egypt's president (1970–1981)

al-Sadr, Muqtada: Iraqi Shiʻite theologian and leader of Mahdi Army

Safavid dynasty: Azerbaijani Turkish family, Sufi at first, that ruled Persia (1501–1736) and upheld Twelve-Imam Shiʻism and promoted Persian culture

Saʻid: Egypt's viceroy (1854–1863)

Saʻid, Khalid: Young Egyptian businessman, tortured and killed in 2010 by Egyptian security police; the subject of a Facebook page that enraged many Egyptians against the Mubarak regime

Salafis: Muslims who model their behavior on the practices of the early Muslim community, often applied to extremely traditional Muslims, such as members of the Nour Party

Salah al-Din: Arabic name for a Kurdish military adventurer who took over Egypt from the Fatimids and Syria from the Zengids, defeated the Crusaders in 1187, and regained Jerusalem for Islam but failed to expel the Crusaders from Acre (1171–1192); also known as Saladin

salam: Arabic word for "peace," sometimes meaning "truce"; also a Muslim greeting

salat: Ritual prayer, or worship, in Islam

Salih, 'Ali Abdallah: Yemen's president (1978–2011), obliged to resign by Arab Spring revolutionaries

Samanid dynasty: Persian family that took over Khurasan and Transoxiana in the late ninth century and later imported Turkic nomads, such as the Ghaznavids and the Seljuks, to serve as border guards

Samaria: Biblical name used by some Israelis for the northern part of the West Bank

Samarqand: Major city in Transoxiana and early Timurid capital

al-Samu': Arab village subjected to harsh Israeli reprisal following Palestinian border raids in 1966

Samuel, Sir Herbert: British high commissioner in Palestine (1920–1925)

San Remo: 1920 conference in which Britain and France determined the mandate borders

San Stefano: Village near Istanbul; site of abortive Russo-Turkish treaty in February 1878 that would have strengthened Russia's position in the Balkans

San'a: Capital of Yemen

Sanskrit: The classical language of India

Sassanid dynasty: Persian ruling family (227–651)

Sa'ud dynasty: Arab family of Najd supporting Wahhabi doctrines since the reign of Muhammad ibn Sa'ud (1746–1765); rulers of most of the Arabian Peninsula during the twentieth century

Sa'ud ibn 'Abd al-'Aziz: Sa'udi Arabia's king (1953–1964)

Sa'udi Arabia: Kingdom in the Arabian Peninsula ruled by the Sa'ud dynasty

SAVAK: Iran's secret police under Mohammad Reza Shah Pahlavi

Scopus, Mount: Hill northeast of Jerusalem, site of first Hebrew University campus and Hadassah Hospital, surrounded by Jordanian-held land (1949–1967)

Security Council Resolution 242: November 1967 statement of principles for achieving peace between the Arabs and Israel, accepted by both sides but with differing interpretations

Security Council Resolution 338: Ceasefire resolution ending the October 1973 War, calling for direct Israeli-Arab talks

Security Council Resolution 598: Resolution calling for an end to the Iran-Iraq War, accepted by Iraq in 1987 and by Iran in 1988

Security Council Resolution 1701: Resolution calling for an end to the Lebanon War of 2006

Security Council Resolution 1860: Resolution calling for ceasefire in Israeli-Hamas war (2009)

security zone: Israeli term for area of southern Lebanon occupied by Israeli army (1982–2000)

Selim I: Ottoman sultan (1512–1520) who conquered Syria, Egypt, and the Hijaz

Selim II: Ottoman sultan (1566–1574)

Selim III: Ottoman reforming sultan (1789–1807)

Seljuk: (1) Central Asian Turkic tribal leader who adopted Islam in 956, (2) ruling family descended from Seljuk

Semitic: Pertaining to a subgroup of Asian languages, including Arabic and Hebrew, having consonantal writing systems, inflected grammars, and structured morphologies; a speaker of one of these languages

separation-of-forces agreement: Kissinger's formula to secure Israel's withdrawal from some Egyptian and Syrian lands taken in the October War

Serbia: Ancient Balkan kingdom, part of Yugoslavia (1918–1991); now an independent republic

Seven-Imam Shi'ite: Any Muslim who believes that the true leadership of the *umma* was passed from 'Ali through a line of heirs ending in Isma'il; also called Isma'ilis or Seveners

Sèvres: Abortive treaty imposed by the World War I Allies on the Ottoman Empire in 1920; later replaced by the Treaty of Lausanne

Shafi'i: Rite of Sunni Muslim jurisprudence, originating in Cairo, that makes considerable use of analogy

shahid: Professional witness in Muslim law

Shajar al-Durr: Woman ruler of Egypt in 1250; sometimes called Shajarat al-Durr

shaman: Pre-Islamic Turkish wizard or soothsayer believed capable of communicating with the dead, healing the sick, and preserving tribal lore

Shamir, Yitzhak: Israel's prime minister (1983–1984 and 1986–1992), head of the Likud coalition, and former Stern Gang leader

Sham'un, Kamil: Lebanon's president (1952–1958)

Shari'a: The highly articulated code of approved Muslim behavior, based primarily on the Qur'an and *sunna* and secondarily on analogy, consensus, and judicial opinion

sharif: Descendant of Muhammad

Sharm al-Shaykh: Fortified point in southern Sinai near the Straits of Tiran

Sharon, Ariel: Israeli general, defense minister during Israel's 1982 invasion of Lebanon, and alleged facilitator of Sabra and Shatila killings; prime minister (2001–2006)

Shatila: Beirut refugee camp, site of 1982 massacre of Palestinians

Shatt al-Arab: Confluence of Tigris and Euphrates rivers, contested in Iran-Iraq War

shaykh: (1) Arab tribal leader, (2) ruler, (3) learned Muslim

shaykh al-Islam: Chief Ottoman legal and religious officer, appointed by the sultan

al-Shaytan: Satan, or the devil, in Muslim belief

Shepherdstown: Site of abortive Syrian-Israeli 2000 peace talks, mediated by President Bill Clinton

Shi'ite: Muslim who believes that Muhammad's leadership of the *umma* was bequeathed to 'Ali, to whom special legislative powers and spiritual knowledge were vouchsafed

Shishakli, Adib: Syria's president (1949–1954)

al-Shuqayri, Ahmad: First PLO leader (1964–1968)

Shura: Council chosen by 'Umar in 644 to elect his successor

shuttle diplomacy: Kissinger's method of mediating between the Arab states and Israel in 1974–1975
Shu'ubiya: Ninth-century literary movement in which Persians sought equal power and status with Arabs
Sidi Bouzid: Tunisian town where Mohamed Bouazizi confronted the local police, leading to his self-immolation and, eventually, the fall of Tunisia's government; hence the Arab Spring
Sidon: City in southern Lebanon
Siffin, Battle of: Indecisive clash in 657 between partisans of 'Ali and those of Mu'awiya, who wished to avenge 'Uthman's death
Sind: Lower Indus Valley region, now part of Pakistan
sipahi: Ottoman horse soldier supported by a *timar*
al-Sisi, Abdel Fattah: Egypt's President (2014–)
6 April Movement: Egyptian group, composed mainly of educated young adults, that opposed Mubarak's regime (2008–2011)
Smyrna: See *Izmir*
Sogut: Northwest Anatolian town where Ottoman Empire started
Stern Gang: Zionist group, also called Lehi, that broke with the Irgun and committed guerrilla acts in Palestine up to 1949
Suez Affair: 1956 British, French, and Israeli attack on Egypt, following Nasir's nationalization of the Suez Canal Company
Suez Canal: Human-made channel between the Mediterranean and Red Seas
Sufi: Pertaining to Muslim mystics or to their beliefs, practices, or organizations
Sufism: Organized Muslim mysticism
Suleyman the Magnificent: Ottoman sultan (1520–1566)
sulh: Comprehensive peace settlement
sultan: Title for ruler of various Muslim states, including the Seljuk and Ottoman empires
sunna: The sayings and actions of Muhammad regarding correct Muslim belief or behavior; hence, next to the Qur'an, the most important source of Muslim law
Sunni: (1) A Muslim who accepts the legitimacy of the caliphs who succeeded Muhammad and adheres to one of the legal rites developed in the early Caliphal period, (2) careful adherent to Muhammad's *sunna*
Supreme Council of the Armed Forces (SCAF): Military committee, appointed by Husni Mubarak, that took control of Egypt after his resignation in February 2011
Sykes-Picot Agreement: Secret pact (1916) among Britain, France, and Russia outlining their plan to partition the Ottoman Empire
Syria: (1) Region east of the Mediterranean, including parts of southern Turkey, the Republic of Syria, Lebanon, Israel, Jordan, and the northern Sinai, also called the Levant, (2) the Republic of Syria
Syrian National Council: Coalition of groups (formed in 2011) opposed to Bashar al-Assad's regime in Syria
Syrian Protestant College: American University of Beirut, up to 1920

Tabriz: City in Azerbaijan and early Safavid capital

Tahrir Square: Large open area in central Cairo, site of many political demonstrations, notably the eighteen-day mass protest in 2011 that led to Husni Mubarak's resignation

Taif: Mountain city in western Arabia, near Mecca; site of 1989 conference that restructured Lebanese politics

Talat: Influential Young Turk leader (d. 1921)

Taliban: Islamist group that controlled most of Afghanistan (1996–2001)

al-Tantawi, Muhammad Husayn: Chairman of Egypt's Supreme Council of the Armed Forces and acting head of state (2011–2012)

Tanzimat: Program of intensive westernizing reforms by the Ottoman government, especially from 1839 to 1876

Tawfiq: Egypt's viceroy (1879–1892)

Tehran: Capital of Persia/Iran since 1794

Tel Aviv: Coastal city and commercial center in Israel

Temple: When capitalized, one of several edifices built in Jerusalem as the main centers of Jewish worship in biblical times

Temple Mount: Jerusalem area containing Dome of the Rock and al-Aqsa Mosque and believed to be site of the ancient Jewish Temple; called al-Haram al-Sharif in Arabic

Terrorism: Threat or use of violence by individuals, groups, or governments to shock or intimidate a group larger than the immediate victims; often used as a propaganda term

Thrace: Area on the northern shore of the Aegean Sea

Tigris: The more eastern of Iraq's two rivers

timar: Land grant by Ottoman sultans to cavalry for military service

Timur Leng: Central Asian Turkish conqueror of Khurasan, Persia, Iraq, and Syria (1369–1405); also known as Tamerlane

Timurid dynasty: Family descended from Timur, ruling Central Asia (1370–1506) and India, where they were called Mughals (1526–1857)

Tiran: Straits linking the Gulf of 'Aqaba to the Red Sea

tobacco boycott: Organized Persian refusal to buy tobacco in 1891–1892 after Nasiruddin Shah had sold to a British company the concession to process and market the product

Trans-Iranian Railway: Line linking the Caspian Sea and the Gulf, built under Reza Shah

Transjordan: Emirate or principality east of the Jordan River excised by the British from their Palestine mandate in 1921; became independent in 1946 and renamed Hashimite Kingdom of Jordan in 1951

Transoxiana: Land northeast of the Oxus River, conquered by the Arabs in the eighth century and later invaded successively by Turks and Mongols

Trench, Battle of the: Unsuccessful pagan Meccan siege of the Medinan Muslims in 627

tribe: Group of people (often nomadic) sharing real or fictitious descent from a common ancestor, as well as common traditions, customs, and leaders

Tripoli: (1) City in northern Lebanon, (2) twelfth-century Crusader state, (3) Libya's capital city

Truman Doctrine: US policy statement (1947) promising aid to Greece and Turkey against Communists

Tudeh: Pro-Communist worker's party of Iran

Turk: (1) Speaker of a Turkic language, (2) citizen of Turkey

Turkish: Pertaining to the language and culture of the Turks

Twelve-Imam Shi'ite: Any Muslim who believes that the *umma* should have been led by 'Ali and his descendants, of whom the twelfth is hidden but will someday return to restore righteousness; also known as Imami, Ja'fari, or Twelver

Ubaydallah: Founder (909–934) of the Fatimid dynasty, having his capital at Mahdiya, near modern Tunis; called the al-Mahdi (Rightly Guided One) by his followers

Uhud, Battle of: Meccan defeat of Muslims in 625

Uighur: Turkic people of northwestern China who ruled a large kingdom in the eighth and ninth centuries

'ulama: Muslim scholars and jurists

'Umar I: Second of the Rashidun caliphs (634–644); leader of the early Arab conquests

'Umar II: Umayyad caliph (717–720) who reduced discrimination against non-Arab converts to Islam

Umayyad dynasty: Clan of the Quraysh tribe who ruled in Damascus (661–750) and in Cordoba (756–1030)

umma: The political, social, and spiritual community of Muslims

Uniate Catholics: Christians of various Middle Eastern rites who are in communion with the Roman Catholic Church

United Arab Emirates: Federation of Gulf principalities, formed in 1971

United Arab Republic: Union of Egypt and Syria (1958–1961)

United Nations Disengagement Observer Force: International army stationed between Syria and Israel (1974–)

United Nations Emergency Force (UNEF): International army between Egypt and Israel (1957–1967 and 1974–1979)

United Nations Relief and Works Agency (UNRWA): International organization providing aid and education to Palestinian refugees since 1949

'Urabi, Ahmad: Egyptian army officer and nationalist who led a popular uprising against the Dual Control in 1881–1882

'Uthman: Third of the Rashidun caliphs (644–656)

Uzbeks: Central Asian Turks, sixteenth-century rivals to the Safavids

Venizelos, Eleftherios: Greek prime minister during invasion of Anatolia (1919–1922) and strong advocate of a greater Greece

vizier: Government minister in a Muslim state; *wazir* in Arabic

Wafd: (1) Unofficial Egyptian delegation to the 1919 Paris Peace Conference, (2) Egypt's main nationalist party from 1923 to 1952, revived in 1978

Wahhabi: Puritanical Muslim sect founded by Muhammad ibn 'Abd al-Wahhab; now dominant in Sa'udi Arabia

Wailing Wall incident: Fracas in Jerusalem (1929) leading to widespread Arab attacks against Jews in Palestine

Wall, the: Israel's "security fence," constructed since 2002 to separate predominantly Palestinian areas from Israel and from Jewish settlements in the West Bank

waqf (pl. *awqaf*): Muslim endowment of land or other property, usually established for a beneficent or pious purpose

weapons of mass destruction (WMDs): Biological, chemical, or nuclear weapons, especially applied to those ascribed (incorrectly) to Iraq prior to the US invasion in 2003

Weizmann, Chaim: British Zionist leader who helped to obtain the Balfour Declaration; Israel's first president (1948–1952)

Welfare Party: Islamist party that won a plurality of seats in Turkey's 1995 elections and led a coalition government until 1997

West Bank: Area of Arab Palestine annexed by Jordan in 1948 and captured by Israel in 1967, called Judea and Samaria by some Israelis; partly governed by the Palestinian Authority since 1996

Western Wall: Remnant in Jerusalem of the last Temple, revered by Jews

White Paper: British policy statement (1939) limiting Jewish immigration and land purchase rights within the Palestine mandate, assailed by Zionists

White Revolution: Broad reform program proclaimed by Iran's shah in 1963

White Sheep Turcomans: Shi'ite Turkic dynasty ruling Persia, eastern Anatolia, and Iraq (1378–1508)

Wingate, Sir Reginald: British high commissioner in Egypt (1916–1919)

Yarmuk River: Tributary of Jordan River, site of Arab victory in 636

Yathrib: Original name of Medina

Yazd: City in Iran noted for its architecture

Yazid I: Umayyad caliph (680–683)

Yemen: (1) Mountainous region of southwestern Arabia, (2) common name for the Yemen Arab Republic or North Yemen, (3) the People's Democratic Republic of Yemen (PDRY) or South Yemen, (4) republic formed by the union in 1990 of the Yemen Arab Republic and the PDRY

Yom Kippur War: See *October War*

Young Egypt: Egyptian nationalist movement in the 1930s

Young Turks: Group of Turkish nationalists who took control of the Ottoman government in 1908, restored its constitution, and instituted westernizing reforms; their main organization was the Committee of Union and Progress

Zaghlul, Sa'd: Egyptian nationalist leader (d. 1927)

zakat: Fixed share of income or property that all Muslims must pay as tax or charity for the welfare of the needy

Zayd: Fifth Shi'ite imam, leader of an abortive revolt in the early eighth century, and founder of the Zaydi branch of Shi'ism

Zayd ibn Haritha: Muhammad's adopted son

Zaydi Shi'ite: Muslim who believes that Zayd bequeathed his *umma* leadership to designated successors

Zayn al-'Abidin ben 'Ali: Tunisia's president (1987–2011), whose overthrow sparked the Arab Spring

Zaynab: Wife of Muhammad's adopted son, Zayd ibn Haritha, who divorced her so that Muhammad might marry her

Zengi: Turkic general who founded a state in Mosul (1127–1146)

zindiq: (1) Muslim heretic, (2) (cap.) Manichaean or adherent to any other pre-Islamic Persian religion

Zionism: (1) Nationalist ideology stressing solidarity of the Jewish people, (2) movement to create or maintain a Jewish state, especially in Palestine/Israel

Zionist: Believer in Jewish nationalism

Ziya ud-Din Tabatabai, Sayyid: Civilian leader of 1921 Persian nationalist revolt, which brought Reza to power

Ziyad: Arab governor of Iraq under Caliph Mu'awiya

Zoroastrianism: Pre-Islamic Persian religion popularized in the eleventh century BCE by Zoroaster, preaching the existence of a supreme deity and of a cosmic struggle between Good and Evil

Zubayr: Muhammad's associate who challenged 'Ali in the 656 Battle of the Camel, in which Zubayr died; father of Abdallah ibn al-Zubayr

APPENDIX

Appendix Figure 1: Basic Statistics for Middle Eastern Countries

Name of Country	Land Area (sq. mi./km²)	Population (mid-2014 estimate)	Languages Spoken	Religion Sn=Sunni Sh=Shi'ite Ch= Christian
Bahrain	240/665	1,314,089	Arabic	56% Sh 37% Sn 7% Ch
Cyprus	3,572/9,250	1,172,458	Greek, Turkish	78% Ch 18% Sn
Egypt¹	386,900/ 1,001,450	86,895,099	Arabic	90% Sn 10% Ch
Iran	636,293/ 1,648,000	80,840,713	Persian, Azeri, Kurdish	89% Sh 9% Sn 1% Ch
Iraq	167,920/ 437,072	32,585,692	Arabic, Kurdish, Turkish	60% Sh 37% Sn 3% Ch
Israel²	8,020/20,770	7,821,850	Hebrew, Arabic	76% Jewish 16% Sn 2% Ch
Jordan³	34,573/92,300	7,930,491	Arabic	92% Sn 6% Ch
Kuwait	6,880/17,820	3,996,899	Arabic	65% Sn 25% Sh 6% Ch
Lebanon	4,015/10,400	5,882,562	Arabic, French	39% Ch 34% Sh 23% Sn 4% Druze

(continues)

(continued)

Name of Country	Land Area (sq. mi./km²)	Population (mid-2014 estimate)	Languages Spoken	Religion Sn=Sunni Sh=Shi'ite Ch= Christian
Libya	679,536/ 1,758,540	6,244,174	Arabic	97% Sn
Oman	82,030/ 212,460	3,219,775	Arabic	64% Ibadi 22% Sn 13% Hindu
Qatar	4,468/ 11,437	2,123,160	Arabic	77% Sn 8% Ch 2% Hindu
Sa'udi Arabia	865,000/ 1,960,582	27,345,968	Arabic	95% Sn 5% Sh
Sudan[4]	967,291/ 2,505,810	35,482,233	Arabic, Nubian	97% Sn 1.5% Animist 1.5% Ch
Syria	71,498/ 185,180	17,951,639	Arabic	70% Sn 10% Ch 13% Alawite 3% Druze
Turkey[5]	300,947/ 780,580	81,619,392	Turkish, Kurdish	99% Sn & Sh
United Arab Emirates	32,375/ 82,880	5,628,805	Arabic, Persian	80% Sn 15% Sh 4% Ch
Yemen	203,850/ 527,970	26,052,966	Arabic	99% Sn & Sh

NOTES

1. Area figures and population exclude the Gaza Strip, whose estimated population in 2014 was 1,816,779 in a land area of 139 sq. mi./360 km²

2. Area figures and populations for Israel and Syria are based on their boundaries as of 4 June 1967.

3. Area figures and population for Jordan exclude the West Bank, whose estimated population in 2014 was 2,731,052 in a land area of 2,263 sq. mi./5,860 km².

4. South Sudan, independent since July 2011, has a population of 11,562,695.

5. Turkey and Yemen do not enumerate Sunni and Shi'ite Muslims separately.

Appendix Figure 2: Muslim Sects: Major Schools, Notable Branches

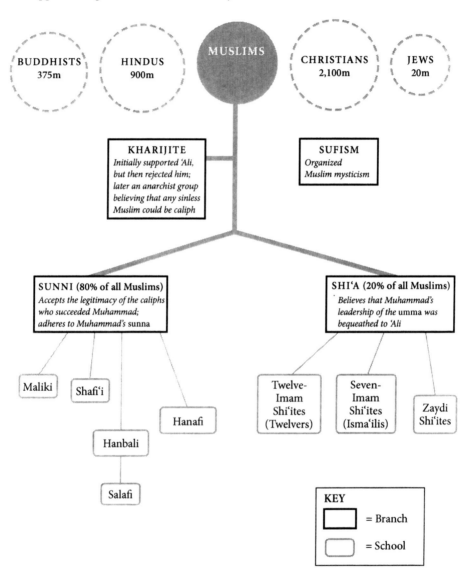

INDEX

'Abbas I, Shah, 134, 135
'Abbas, Khedive, 172, 173, 186
'Abbas, Mahmoud, 413, 415
'Abbasid caliphate
  Baghdad and, 66, 71 (box), 79, 88,
    89 (box), 90
  decline/end, 72, 85, 88, 89 (box), 90
  government/taxes, 66, 69
  Mongols and, 88, 89 (box), 90
  overview, 65–66, 67 (map), 68–70,
    71 (box), 72–73
'Abd al-Malik, 61–63
'Abd al-Rahman I, 65
Abdallah, Amir of Transjordan, 233,
    244–245, 263, 272, 273, 289
Abdallah ibn al-Zubayr, 58
Abdallah II, King of Jordan, 275–276, 318,
    382, 395, 430–431
Abdallah (son of Amir Husayn), 189,
    196–198
'Abduh, Muhammad, 169, 173
Abdulaziz, Sultan, 186
Abdulhamid II, Sultan, 174–175, 176,
    179, 200
Abdulmejid, Sultan, 157, 158 (box), 159
Abu al-'Abbas, 65, 66, 68
Abu-Bakr, 26, 28, 31, 32 (box), 34,
    45, 48
Abu Bakr al-Baghdadi, 429 (box)
Abu Ghraib, 406
Abu-Hamid, Ghazali al-, 108
Abu-Muslim, 65, 68–69
Abu-Talib, 23, 26, 27, 28, 45, 57 (fig.)

Achaemenid dynasty, 13, 134, 177,
    363, 447
Afghani, Jamal al-Din, al-, 166–169, 175,
    178, 228
Afghanistan
  Soviet Union and, 336, 346, 348–349,
    388 (box)
  US-led invasion of, 387, 402–403, 416
Ahmadinejad, Mahmoud, 391, 418
Ahmed III, Sultan, 139
AIPAC (American Israel Public Affairs
    Committee), 317, 325, 355, 402, 414
'Aisha, 31, 32 (box), 51, 55 (box)
Alawites, 11, 196, 234, 235, 277, 296, 384,
    424, 425, 426, 440
Albright, Madeleine, 380–381
Alexander the Great, 12, 13, 119, 150, 152
Alexios I, Emperor of Byzantine, 84
'Ali
  background/descriptions, 26, 51,
    57 (fig.)
  as caliph, 51–52, 55 (box)
  challenges to, 51–52, 55 (box)
  Muhammad and, 32 (box), 51
  murder of/aftermath, 52, 55 (box),
    56–57, 61
  succession issue and, 45, 55 (box), 65,
    76, 77, 96
Allenby, Edmund, 195 (box), 229, 231, 236
Amin, 70, 71 (box)
'Amr ibn al-'As, 33, 45, 52
Aqsa, al- (mosque), 261, 261 (photo), 382
"Arab" definitions, 61, 182

Arab-Israeli conflict
  Arab border raids/bombings, 284, 307,
    309, 312
  Arab countries overview, 275–281
  Arab divisions and, 273–274
  becoming Palestinian-Israeli conflict,
    373
  beginnings, 257, 258, 259 (box),
    260–263, 264, 267–268
  blockading Israel, 297
  Britain and, 271, 272
  danger signs (1971), 315–316
  Egypt and, 270, 272, 274, 284
  Hebron mosque killings/effects, 379,
    410
  Iraq and, 272, 278
  Israel attacking PLO/locations,
    355–356, 358
  Israel creation and, 269–275
  Israeli IDF/retaliation, 264, 270, 272,
    283, 296, 307, 309, 312, 315, 356
  Israeli settlements (occupied land),
    301, 305, 318, 331, 333, 355, 356,
    374, 379, 380, 381, 382, 383, 408,
    409–410, 411 (map)
  Jordan and, 275–276, 296
  Jordan River water/attacks and, 295,
    296
  Lebanon and, 272, 277
  massacres at Shatila/Sabra, 358,
    382–383
  outsiders' involvement overview,
    270–271, 413–414
  Palestinian Arabs (overview), 274–275,
    281
  roots of problem/fears, 313, 314, 332
  separation wall and, 410, 412 (photo)
  significance/summary (1967–1979),
    300–301
  Soviet Union and, 270–271
  Syria and, 272, 276–277
  Transjordan and, 270
  US and, 270–271, 320–321
  violence descriptions (twenty-first
    century), 409–410, 412–413
  Wailing Wall incident (1929),
    260–262
  war of 1948 and, 269–275

  See also Israel; 1967 war; October (Yom
    Kippur) War (1973); Palestine/
    Palestinians; *specific individuals/
    organizations*
Arab-Israeli peace efforts
  analysis, 407–409, 414–415
  Camp David peace talks/Accords, 300,
    314 (box), 329–332
  Egyptian-Israeli treaty, 300, 332–333,
    349, 351–352, 408
  Madrid talks (1991), 376–377
  Oslo I Accord/effects, 377, 379–380
  Oslo II/effects, 380–381
  "peace" meaning and, 301, 333–334
  Resolution 242 (UN), 305–306, 308,
    378 (box)
  Rogers Plan, 311–312, 313, 314
  shuttle diplomacy, 322–324, 326, 330
  "two-state solution," 374–375, 413
  UN efforts, 271–273, 355
Arab League, 238 (box), 243, 244, 246,
    265, 273, 276, 291, 329, 349, 354,
    358, 374, 414, 426, 435, 454
Arab nationalism
  in 1962, 294–295
  American Protestant missionaries and,
    184, 185
  Arab Revolt (1916–1918), 190–191,
    195 (box), 233
  Arabic literary revival and, 185
  Ba'ath Party/Ba'athists and, 277,
    288–290, 293, 295, 296
  Christian Arab nationalists, 184–185
  definition, 182
  Eisenhower Doctrine and, 288–289
  Muslim Arab nationalists overview,
    185–186
  Ottoman rule and, 183–184
  Pan-Arabism vs., 292, 298
  Suez Affair and, 287–288
  Syria and, 184, 185, 190
  UAR (United Arab Republic) and, 290,
    291, 292, 293–294
  Western ideals and, 184, 185
  World War I events and, 187–188
  Young Turks' effects, 186–187
  See also Arab-Israeli conflict; *specific
    countries; specific individuals*

Arab Spring
  background/protests evolution,
    418–419
  summary/analysis, 417, 418,
    441–442
  See also specific countries
Arabian Nights, The, 106
'Arafat, Yasir
  Arab-Israeli conflict and, 296, 307,
    312, 328, 329–330, 344, 354, 359,
    362, 378 (box), 383, 401
  background, 296, 378 (box)
  last days/death, 412, 413
  peace talks and, 374, 377, 378 (box),
    379, 381, 408–409
Armenians, 175, 200–201, 204, 225
Art/architecture overview (early
    civilization), 106–107
Assad, Bashar al-
  opposition and, 392, 394 (box)
  Syria Arab "Spring" protests/civil war
    and, 425, 426, 428
  Syria rule, 381, 392
Assad, Hafiz al-
  Arab-Israeli conflict/peace efforts,
    380, 381
  death, 392
  massacre by, 359, 360
  rule, 318, 328–329, 359, 360, 392
Aswan High Dam, 280, 309, 453
Ataturk. *See* Kemal, Mustafa (Ataturk)
Ayyubids/dynasty, 87, 90, 113, 115,
    130, 183
Azhar, al- (mosque-university), 78, 150,
    151, 166, 168–169, 173, 228, 237,
    259 (box)

Baghdad
  'Abbasid caliphate and, 66, 71 (box),
    79, 88, 89 (box), 90
  building/rebuilding, 66, 71 (box)
Baghdad Pact (CENTO), 247–248, 278,
    280, 288, 339
Baha'i faith, 160
Balfour Declaration, 193, 195 (box),
    255–256
Balfour, Lord, 255–256
Balkan Wars (1912–1913), 143

Barak, Ehud, 378 (box), 381, 382, 383,
    394 (box), 408
Barudi, Mahmud Sami al-, 169, 170
Battle of the Camel, 32 (box), 51, 58
Bayezid I/II, 124, 125
Bazargan, Mehdi, 344, 345
Begin, Menachem
  Arab-Israeli conflict and, 270, 317,
    330–331, 331
  background/beliefs, 258, 316–317,
    330–331
  as Israeli prime minister/policies,
    330–333, 351, 352, 355, 356,
    358, 362
Ben 'Ali, Zayn al-'Abidin, 419,
    420, 421
Ben-Gurion, David, 263, 283, 285 (box),
    299, 316
Berbers, 74
Bernadotte, Folke, Count, 271, 272
Bin Laden, Osama, 377, 387, 388 (box),
    429 (box)
Black September, 312, 355
Black Sheep Turcomans, 119, 132, 232
Bolshevik Revolution/civil war, 199, 201,
    205, 212, 213, 257
Bouazizi, Mohamed, 418, 419–420
Britain
  India and, 144–145, 160, 227
  World War I/II and, 188, 189, 193–194,
    199, 227, 242, 243
Britain and the Middle East
  apogee of power, 212–213
  Husayn-McMahon Correspondence,
    189–190
  Iraq and, 191, 194, 195 (box), 196, 226,
    232–233, 240, 247–248, 366
  World War I aftermath, 191–192,
    192 (map), 196, 197, 197 (map),
    198, 199
  *See also specific agreements; specific
    countries; specific events/individuals;*
    Suez Canal/Company
Buddhism, 16, 21, 80, 117, 337
Bunche, Ralph, 272
Bush, George H. W., 368, 371, 372, 400
Bush, George W., 387, 391, 395,
    401–402, 409

Byzantine Empire
  Arabs and, 44, 45–48, 53
  descriptions, 17 (map), 21, 72,
    82, 84

Caliphs, 46, 48
Camels, 9, 18, 445–446
Capitulations, 130, 131, 145, 157, 167,
    205, 239
Carter Doctrine, 347
Carter, Jimmy
  background/elections, 329, 346, 350
  Iran/hostages, 335, 342, 343, 344,
    345, 360
  Middle East peace/Camp David talks,
    314, 330, 332–333
Cheney, Dick, 402, 403
Christianity/Christians
  doctrines/institutions development,
    13–14
  early differences/sects, 14–16, 47
  Middle East history and, 13–15
  *See also specific individuals; specific
    sects*
Churchill, Winston, 197, 233, 258, 304
Ciller, Tansu, 211
Clemenceau, Georges, 194
Clinton, Bill
  Iraq and, 395, 401, 402
  peace efforts and, 377, 378 (box),
    379–381, 408, 409
Clothing, 42, 103, 203 (box), 207, 216
  See also Veiling (of women)
Constantinople, 14, 16, 49, 63, 71, 122,
    124, 125, 141–142, 158 (box), 201
Constitution of Medina, 28, 31
Coptic language, 49, 62
Copts/Coptic Christians, 15, 21, 47, 182,
    229, 235–236, 353, 383, 399
Crane, Charles, 221
  See also King-Crane Commission
Crimean War, 142, 145, 158 (box), 159
Cromer, Lord, 172, 173, 181, 228
Crusades
  description/effects, 84–86, 88, 91,
    124, 146
  Egypt and, 113
  Jerusalem and, 85, 86, 87
  Mamluks and, 87, 91, 113

Muslim reactions, 85–87
  Saladin and, 86–87
CUP (Committee of Union and Progress),
    175–176, 187, 189, 202

Dayan, Moshe, 272, 298, 303
Dayr Yasin massacre (1948), 267,
    270, 331
Din, Jamal al-. *See* Afghani, Jamal
    al-Din, al-
Dome of the Rock, 62–63, 85, 261, 261
    (photo)
Dowleh, ʿAyn al-, 179
Druze, 78, 85, 196, 234, 235, 277, 359, 393
Dulles, John Foster, 280, 287
Durr, Shajar al-, 113
Dynasty patterns, 135–136

Eden, Sir Anthony, 237, 286–287
Egypt
  Anglo-Egyptian Treaty, 237, 241–242,
    245, 272
  Arab Spring protests/results, 418,
    421–424
  Britain and, 225–231, 235–236, 237,
    238 (box), 241–242, 243–244, 245,
    246, 280, 284
  description (nineteenth century), 166
  economic/social problems (1930s), 239
  Fatimid Caliphate and, 77–79, 86
  firearms/weaponry and, 152–153
  following World War II, 225–226
  France and, 144, 146–147, 147,
    150–151, 154, 162, 170, 246, 281,
    284, 287
  French occupation, 150–151, 154
  Muslim Brothers, 239–240, 245, 353,
    422, 423, 430
  Nile river/delta importance, 78, 152
  reforms, 146, 149–154, 155, 156, 162
  renaissance (1920s and 1930s),
    236–237
  Syria union and, 290, 293–294
  terrorism risk/conditions overview, 399
  World War I and, 227, 228
  World War II/following World War II,
    238 (box), 242, 243–244
  See also Arab-Israeli conflict; *specific
    individuals;* Suez Canal/Company

Egyptian-Israeli treaty/consequences, 300, 332–333, 349, 351–352, 374, 408
Egyptian nationalism
  Anglo-French Dual Control and, 168, 169, 170, 171 (box), 184
  army and, 168, 169, 170, 171 (box)
  before World War I (overview), 166–174
  beginnings overview, 168–169
  British/occupation and, 168, 170, 171 (box), 172–173
  Capitulations and, 167, 239
  financial problems and, 167–168, 169–170
  Four Reserved Points limitations, 231
  independence struggle, 226–227, 235–237, 238 (box), 239–240, 242, 243–244, 245–247, 248
  National Party, 169, 170, 173, 228
  Palestine issue and, 244–245
  revival of, 172–174
  revolution (1952), 236, 245–246
  revolution against Britain (1919), 228–231
  revolution against British (late 1800s), 170, 171 (box)
  Wafd/Party and, 229–231, 235–236, 238 (box), 239, 242, 243, 244
  westernizing reform and, 166–167, 168
  See also specific individuals
Eisenhower, President/Doctrine, 287, 288–289, 291–292
Elbaradei, Mohamed, 421, 422
Enver, 176–177, 187, 201
Environmental challenges
  conservation and, 448, 450, 451, 452
  oil spills/damage, 449
  outside support/problems, 448, 450
  overview, 448–455
  pollution/consequences, 449, 452–453
  wars and, 371, 449
  waste management, 450–451
  See also Water
Erdogan, Recep Tayyip, 211, 390, 441
Eshkol, Levi, 296, 297, 298, 311
Europe
  balance of power, 143–144, 145, 146
  power rise/effects, 148
  See also specific countries
Evren, Kenan, 211

Farabi, Abu Nasr al-, 104
Faruq, King of Egypt
  background, 237, 238 (box)
  overthrow, 226, 245–246, 314, 423
  rule, 238 (box), 242, 243–244, 245, 273–274, 280, 289
Fatah, 296, 307, 378 (box), 413, 437
Fatima, 26, 77
Fatimid Caliphate, 76–79, 83 (map), 85, 86
Faysal I, king of Iraq, 190, 195 (box), 196
Faysal II, king of Iraq, 240–241, 291
Faysal, King of Saudi Arabia, 223, 290, 293, 323
Ferid, Damad, 201, 204
Fida'iyin, 280, 284, 287, 300–301, 305, 307, 308, 311, 312, 315, 355, 358, 378 (box)
Firearms/gunpowder, 112, 116, 119–120
Fitna, 51, 56, 59, 61, 63
Fourteen Points, 193, 225
France and the Middle East
  background, 143
  Egypt/Suez Canal and, 144, 146–147, 147, 150–151, 154, 162, 170, 246, 281, 284, 287
  following World War I, 147, 193–194, 196, 197 (map), 234–235
  Maronites/Lebanon and, 146
  oil and, 284, 287
  World War II and, 242, 243
  See also specific events; specific individuals
Franjiyah, Sulayman, 328–329
Frankincense, 20–21
Fu'ad, Sultan/King, 229, 230–231, 236, 237

Gabriel (Angel), 25, 34, 36, 37, 107
Genghis Khan, 87–88, 118, 119
Glubb, Sir John Bagot, 271, 276, 288
Golden Horde, 115, 118, 141
Great Silk Route/Road, 80, 87, 116–117, 447
Greek independence, 142, 156–157
Gulf supremacy struggle, 347–351, 348 (map)
Gunpowder/firearms, 112, 116, 119–120

Hajj, 34, 40–41, 97
Hamad ibn Isa Al Khalifa, King of
    Bahrain, 433, 434
Hamas
    actions/tactics, 373, 375, 377, 379, 380,
        381, 383, 391, 392, 410, 412–413,
        437–438
    Palestinian government and, 413,
        415, 437
Hanbali rite of Sunni Islam, 95, 96, 108,
    109 (box), 149, 218, 220, 222, 396
    See also Wahhabis
Habsburg Austria/Empire, 112–113,
    141, 144
Hanbal, Ahmad Ibn, 96, 108, 109 (box)
Hariri, Rafiq, 392, 394 (box)
Hashimite clan and Muhammad, 23, 24,
    26, 27, 28, 56, 57 (fig.)
Herzl, Theodor, 253–254
Hess, Moses, 252
High Caliphate
    Byzantine Empire and, 63
    conquests/Islamic civilization growth,
        60, 61, 62, 63
    conversions to Islam, 64
    cultural/religious mix, 60, 61, 64
    definition/overview, 60–61, 72–73
    government, 61, 62, 64, 69
    mawali and, 64, 65
    See also 'Abbasid caliphate; Umayyad
        caliphate
Hisham, 64, 65, 76
History importance, 1–3
Hitler, 2, 112, 143, 180, 216, 217, 223, 239,
    242, 256, 258, 262, 263, 264, 279,
    282, 284, 304
Hizballah, 360, 373, 375, 376, 377,
    383, 391, 392, 393, 394 (box),
    413, 428
Houthis, 397, 432–433
Hulegu Khan, 88, 89 (box), 90, 91, 112,
    116–117, 118
Hunayn ibn Ishaq, 105
Husayn, King of Jordan
    Arab-Israeli conflict/peace, 297, 301,
        302, 312, 313, 325, 374, 379
    Arab nationalism and, 288, 289,
        297, 315

Iraq's invasion/occupation of Kuwait
    and, 368
    rule/death, 276, 292, 382
Husayn-McMahon Correspondence,
    189–190, 193
Husayn (Muhammad's grandson), 51, 56,
    57 (fig.), 58, 62, 77
Husayn (sharif/amir)
    Arab Revolt (1916–1918), 190–191,
        195 (box)
    background, 188–189, 219
    Husayn-McMahon Correspondence,
        189–190, 193
    Sykes-Picot Agreement and, 191–192
Husayn, Taha, 237
Husayni, Hajj Amin al-, 258, 259 (box),
    260, 273–274

Ibn Khaldun, 105–106
Ibn Rushd, 104
Ibn Sa'ud
    Arab-Israeli conflict and, 273
    oil and, 221, 222, 223
    uniting/ruling Sa'udi Arabia, 219–220,
        221, 222–223, 224
    Wahhabi Islam and, 219–220
Ibn Sina, 104, 105
Ibn Tulun, Ahmad, 72, 77
Ibrahim, 153, 157, 187
Idols, 41–42
Il-Khanid dynasty
    Mongols and, 116
    origins/beginnings, 89 (box), 91, 112,
        116–117
    Persian culture and, 117–118
    territory (1300), 114 (map)
Industrial Revolution/effects, 152–153
Inonu, Ismet , 205, 208
Iran
    American hostages and, 336, 344–346
    "Arab" Spring/protests and, 439–441
    Green Movement/Revolution,
        391–392, 418, 440
    history summary (last half of twentieth
        century), 217–218, 335–336
    Islam revival (late 1970s/1980s),
        335, 338
    Nazi Germany and, 216–217

nuclear program and, 391, 414, 441
riots/revolution (1979), 342–344, 349,
    390–391, 439
sanctions against, 440–441
terrorism risk/conditions overview,
    390–392
war with Iraq (1980–1988), 336, 346,
    349–351, 354, 359, 361, 365, 366
White Revolution, 217, 338, 339,
    341, 342
See also Persia; Reza Khan, Shah
Iran oil
Britain/Anglo-Iranian Oil Company
    and, 215, 217, 286, 339
nationalizing, 339
revenues and, 217–218
revolution and, 343, 347
Iraq, 405 (map)
Britain and, 191, 194, 195 (box), 196,
    226, 232–233, 240, 247–248, 366
ethnic/religious diversity, 233,
    240–241, 278
France and, 232, 359
historical overview, 278–279
history (prior to nineteenth century),
    46, 231–232
independence and, 240–241, 247–248
Iraqis self views, 365–366
ISIL and, 426, 427 (map), 428
Kurds and, 278, 310, 349, 360, 365,
    372, 395
nuclear program and, 350, 356
oil/effects, 232, 278, 292, 404
sanctions against, 372, 395, 400–401
terrorism risk/conditions overview,
    395–396
war with Iran (1980–1988), 336, 346,
    349–351, 354, 359, 361, 365, 366
World War I/following, 232–233
See also Saddam Husayn
Iraq/US-led war
Bush and neoconservatives, 401–402,
    403, 404, 406, 407, 409
invasion/aftermath, 387, 403–407, 416
surge and, 406–407
Iraq's invasion/occupation of Kuwait
Iraq claims on Kuwait and, 349, 366
oil and, 367–368, 370, 371, 372

Operation Desert Shield and, 368,
    369, 371
Operation Desert Storm/aftermath,
    371–373, 400
overview, 367–373
Irgun Tzvei Le'umi, 264, 270
ISIL
actions, 387, 393, 394 (box), 400,
    404, 426, 427 (map), 428, 436, 440,
    454–455
background, 393, 426, 429 (box)
Islam
duties/prohibitions summary, 38–42
gains/losses (1990s), 383–385
major sects summary, 75–77
politics and, 385, 455
principles of, 35–38
prophets/messengers, 37–38
revival (late 1970s-1980s) and, 335,
    337–338, 361–363, 364, 390–391
term meaning, 26
See also Qur'an; *specific individuals*;
    specific sects
Islamic civilization overview
intellectual/cultural life, 104–107
"Islamic" vs. "Arabic," 92
jurisprudence, 92–98
society, 98–103
theology, 107–110
Islamic government
beginnings, 48–49, 52–53, 59
founding fathers summary, 61
territory acquisition and, 48, 59
See also Jurisprudence development;
    specific eras; *specific individuals*
Islamic State (IS) *See* ISIL
Isma'il, Khedive, 162, 166–168, 169
Isma'il, Shah of Persia, 133
Isma'ilis (Seveners), 57 (fig.), 76, 77, 78
Israel
accomplishments, 254, 439
Arab Spring and, 438–439
Arab states recognizing (by mid 1990s),
    373
before 1967/occupied territories,
    304 (map)
early years/problems, 281–284
emigration from, 438

Israel (*continued*)
  foreign relations, 284
  Jewish diaspora and, 274–275, 281,
    301, 376
  Judaism and, 283–284, 299
  kibbutz life, 254–255
  Likud Party/coalition, 324, 330, 361,
    380, 401
  militancy increase, 354–356
  nuclear reactors/arms and, 356
  politics, 283–284
  Suez Affair and, 287–288
  US support and, 270–271, 281–282,
    300–301, 308, 312, 320–321, 359,
    413–414
  "who is a Jew" debate and, 324
  See also Arab-Israeli conflict; Jews;
    specific individuals; Zionism
Israel creation
  Arab/Palestine land and, 193, 197,
    198, 223, 244–245, 247, 249, 265,
    266 (map)
  Balfour Declaration, 193, 195 (box),
    255–256
  King-Crane Commission and, 194
  partition/creation, 265, 266 (map), 267

Jabotinsky, Vladimir, 258
Jacobites (Syria), 15, 47, 117, 146
Jarring, Gunnar, 306, 311–312, 313
Jemal, 176–177, 190, 201
Jerusalem
  Crusades and, 85, 86, 87
  importance, 53, 85
Jesus, 37, 47
Jews
  ancestral land and, 250–251, 252,
    253, 254, 258, 303
  anti-Semitism and, 249, 251–252,
    264
  diaspora, 251–253
  persecution/Nazis and, 251–252, 262,
    263–264, 281, 282, 284
  Russia and, 251–252, 253, 254,
    255, 257
  See also Judaism; Zionism
Jihad definition/description, 41
Johnson, Lyndon, 302, 305, 308

Jordan
  Arab Spring protests/results, 430–431
  Britain and, 288, 293
  Eisenhower Doctrine and, 288–289
  origins, 275
  terrorism risk/conditions overview,
    393, 395
  See also Arab-Israeli conflict
Judaism, 4, 21, 24, 36, 38, 80–81, 93, 98,
  165, 251, 252, 282, 299
Judgment Day
  beliefs about, 36, 37, 38, 41, 92–93
  Muhammad and, 25, 34–35, 44
Jumayyil, Amin/Bashir, 358, 359, 375
Junayd, Shaykh, 132, 133
Jurisprudence development
  administration of law, 96–97
  applicability of the law, 97–98
  early development, 92–94, 110
  law sources, 94–95
  Muhammad and, 93, 94–95, 96
  overview, 92–98
  Qur'an and, 93, 94, 95, 96
  Shiite legal systems, 95, 96
  Sunni legal systems, 95–96, 108, 109
    (box)
  ulama and, 94–95, 96, 97–98, 99
  See also Shari'a

Ka'ba shrine, 21–22, 24, 27, 28, 33, 39,
  40, 62, 68, 166
Kamil, Mustafa, 172–173
Karlowitz, Treaty of (1699), 131, 140
  (box)
Karzai, Hamid, 400, 403
Kemal, Mustafa (Ataturk)
  background, 191, 202, 203 (box),
    214–215
  rule/reforms, 203 (box), 206–209
  status/legacy, 181, 200, 209–211, 214
  Turkey's independence and, 200,
    203 (box), 204
Khadija, 23–24, 25, 28, 31
Khalid ibn al-Walid, 33, 45, 48
Kharijites
  'Ali and, 52, 55 (box), 76
  background/views of, 52, 54, 72, 75, 76
  conflict and, 58, 59, 61, 62, 65, 68, 149

Khomeini, Ayatollah Ruhollah, 335, 339, 340 (box), 360, 361, 362

Kindi, al-, 104

King-Crane Commission, 194, 221

Kissinger, Henry, 317, 321, 322, 326, 330, 345

Koprulu family of viziers, 139, 140 (box), 154

Kurds, 225, 310
  See also Iraq; Turkey

Kuwait
  Britain and, 199, 366
  foreign workers and, 367, 369, 372–373
  loans to Iraq, 366
  oil/wealth and, 366–367
  terrorism risk/conditions overview, 398
  See also Iraq's invasion/occupation of Kuwait

Lausanne conference (1923), 205–206

Law. *See* Jurisprudence development; Shari'a

Lawrence, T.E., 191–192, 194, 195 (box)

League of Nations, 193, 196, 206, 215, 226, 232, 235, 237, 240, 257

Lebanon
  civil war/causes (starting 1975), 326–329, 355, 357, 375–376
  economic/tax problems, 327
  Eisenhower Doctrine and, 289, 291–292
  ethnic/religious diversity, 234–235, 241, 277, 326–327, 358, 359
  first civil war/US intervention (1958), 291–292, 293
  France and, 241, 247, 277, 359
  independence and, 234–235, 243, 247, 278
  Israel and, 357–359, 377
  Maronite power and, 247, 277, 326–327, 329
  Syria and, 234–235, 241, 392
  terrorism risk/conditions overview, 359, 392–393
  World War II and, 243

Libya
  Arab Spring protests/results, 434–436
  Benghazi attack (2012), 436

military coup (1969), 310–311
  NATO intervention in protests, 435–436

Lloyd George, David, 194, 202, 254

McMahon, Sir Henry, 189–190

Mahmud I, sultan, 139

Mahmud II, sultan, 155–156, 157, 207

Maliki, Nuri al-, 407

Mamluks
  Crusades and, 87, 91, 113
  decline, 116, 119, 150, 151
  Egypt/Syria and, 89 (box), 90, 112, 113, 116, 150, 151
  Mongols and, 74, 89 (box), 90
  origins/background, 87, 90, 113, 115–116
  ruling system, 113, 115
  territory (1300), 114 (map), 119

Ma'mun al-, 70, 71 (box), 73, 109

Mandates of Middle East, 197 (map)

Mansur, Abu Ja'far al-, 66, 68, 69

Maronites (Lebanon), 47, 146, 182, 184, 187, 234, 241, 247, 277, 298, 326–327, 328–329, 375

Marriage traditions, 101

Marwan, 58, 61

Mathematics/science overview (early civilization), 104–106

Mawali, 49, 59, 64, 65

Mecca
  assets of, 21–22
  history, 21–22
  Muhammad and, 27, 33–34
  "Year of the Elephant," 23

Medina
  community (*umma*) survival, 28, 29–30
  emigration (*hijra*) to, 28
  Jews and, 28, 29, 31, 33
  Muhammad and, 28–30
  Muslim land expansion and, 44, 45–48

Mehmet 'Ali
  background, 186
  Egyptian reforms and, 146, 152–154, 155, 156
  treatment of Egyptians, 183–184
  Wahhabis and, 149, 153, 218

Mehmet I/II/IV, sultans, 124–125, 139

Meir, Golda, 311, 316, 320
Middle East overview
  before Muhammad, 12–16, 17 (map),
    18–22
  borders and, 200
  civilization achievements (summary),
    12, 22
  climate/effects, 8–9
  conflict causes, 455–456
  English word origins and, 4–5
  environmental challenges, 448–455
  geographic definition, 5, 8
  human diversity/conflict, 10–11
  location effects, 9
  natural resources, 10
  physical features, 6–7 (map)
  summary (1990–2001), 364–365
  tenth through thirteenth centuries,
    74–75
Mongke Khan, 89 (box), 90
Mongols, 87–88, 89 (box), 90, 112, 186
Monophysites, 15, 16, 21, 47, 117, 125,
    130, 146
  See also Copts/Coptic Christians;
    Jacobites
Monotheism
  development, 22
  See also specific religions
Montreux Convention (1936), 206
Morsi, Mohamed, 418, 423, 424
Mosaddiq, Mohammad, 286, 339
Mu'awiya, 50, 52, 53, 54, 55 (box), 56, 125
Mubarak, Husni
  background/fall, 354, 421, 422–423
  Egypt's Arab uprisings and, 399,
    422–423
  as Egypt's leader/policies, 354, 368,
    383–384, 421
Mudros Armistice (1918), 200, 201, 232
Mughals/Mughal Empire, 119, 136
Muhammad
  background/family, 23
  death/aftermath, 34, 44–45
  early life, 23–24
  emigration (*hijra*) to Medina/life in,
    28–30
  inconsistencies/traits of, 31, 33, 34–35
  Jews and, 28, 29, 31, 33

Khadija/children and, 23–24, 25, 28, 31
  marriages/women after Khadija, 28,
    30, 31
  Mecca and, 27, 33–34
  message summary, 26–27
  pagan Arab values and, 24
  revelations, 24–25, 27, 29–30, 31, 36, 37
  succession issue and, 44–45, 52, 59
Muqaddima al- (Ibn Khaldun), 105–106
Murad I, sultan, 122, 124
Murad II, sultan, 124
Murad IV, sultan, 139
Muruwwa code, 24
Muslim Brothers, 239–240, 245, 353, 422,
    423, 430
Muslim civil wars, 56
Mussolini, 180, 237, 239, 279
Mustafa II, Sultan, 139
Mu'tazila movement, 70, 71 (box),
    107–108, 109 (box)

Nadir Afshar, Shah, 135, 160
Nagib, Muhammad, 246, 280
Nahhas, Mustafa al-, 236, 237, 243–244,
    245
Napoleon Bonaparte, 138, 143, 145, 146,
    150–151, 152, 154, 155
Nasir, Gamal 'Abd al-
  Arab-Israeli conflict and, 280, 284, 287,
    296–297, 309, 311, 312, 312–313
  assassination plots against and, 223,
    290
  background, 246, 279–280, 423
  death/funeral, 312–313
  as Egyptian/Arab nationalism leader,
    246–247, 279, 280–281, 287–289,
    290, 291, 292, 293–294, 294–295,
    295, 311
  Nasirism/ideas overview, 292–293, 298
  nationalizing Suez Canal/effects,
    280–281, 284, 286–287
  positive neutralism and, 280, 292–293,
    298
  Suez Affair and, 287–288
Nasiruddin, Shah, 160, 161, 163, 178
Nasrallah, Hassan, 393, 394 (box)
Nationalism definition/components,
    164, 177

Nationalism in Middle East
 before World War I (overview),
  164–166, 180–181
 Islam and, 164, 180
 westernizing reform and, 164, 165
 See also Arab nationalism; Egyptian
  nationalism; Ottomanism; *specific
  countries*
Nazis, 216–217, 262, 263, 264
Neoconservatives (US), 401–402, 414
Nestorianism/Nestorians, 15, 16, 18, 21,
 80, 88, 89 (box), 105, 117, 146, 233
Netanyahu, Benjamin, 258, 380–381, 401
1967 war
 background to, 296–298
 description, 297, 300, 301–302
 Egypt and, 301–303, 304 (box)
 Israeli occupied territories, 303,
  304–305, 304 (map)
 Jordan/Syria and, 301–302
 outcome reasons/aftermath, 302–305,
  304 (map)
 UN peace efforts, 305–306
 US *Liberty* ship and, 302
Nixon, Richard, 308, 317, 321
Nur al-Din, 86

Obama, Barack, 388 (box), 391, 403,
 426, 428
October (Yom Kippur) War (1973)
 aftermath, 322–326, 323 (map)
 danger signs/prelude to, 315–319
 significance/description, 300, 319–321
 superpowers/ceasefire and, 321–322
 territorial situation following,
  323 (map)
Oil of Middle East
 Arab-Israeli conflict and, 271
 embargoes and, 320–321, 323,
  324–325
 Iranian revolution/1970s and, 343, 347
 oil spills/damage, 449
 OPEC, 316, 321, 333
 overview, 286, 365
 peace/relations and, 376
 prices/supplies and Western concerns,
  315–316, 317, 320–321, 333
 See also specific countries

Oman, 199, 397
Orhan, Sultan, 122, 123 (box)
Orthodox Church (Christianity), 11, 14,
 15–16, 21, 47, 74, 78, 84, 93, 122,
 125, 130, 138, 141–142, 145, 146,
 162, 174, 184, 185, 205–206, 234
Osman I/II, sultans, 120, 122, 139
Ottoman Empire
 Arabs under, 183–184
 beginnings/descriptions, 112–113,
  120–122, 127, 174, 184
 Britain and, 144–145, 157, 174
 Byzantine Empire and, 120, 121, 122,
  123 (box), 124–125, 141–142
 Capitulations, 130, 131, 145, 157, 205
 Constantinople and, 124, 125,
  141–142
 decline/causes, 130–132, 137–138,
  140 (box), 141
 expansions, 122, 123 (box), 124, 125,
  126 (map), 127
 firearms/weaponry and, 125, 128, 131,
  133–134
 France and, 145–147, 176
 janissaries and, 128–129, 131, 132, 133,
  135, 138, 139, 154, 155, 159
 political institutions, 128–130
 reform and, 138, 139
 sultans of, 121 (fig.)
 Sykes-Picot Agreement, 191–192, 192
  (map), 195 (box), 201
 taxes/collection system, 129, 130
 as "Turkey," 142, 147
 'ulama of, 129, 132, 138, 150, 155,
  162, 163
 viziers and, 127, 128, 131, 132, 138,
  139, 140 (map), 154
 westernization, 154–159
 See also specific individuals; Turkey
Ottoman Empire nationalism
 Committee of Union and Progress
  (CUP), 175–176, 187, 189, 202
 constitution and, 174, 175, 176
 pre-World War I overview, 174–177
 Young Turks and, 175–177, 181,
  186–187, 188–189, 201, 202
Ottomanism, 174–176, 177
Ozal, Turgut, 211

Pahlavi dynasty, 339
See also Reza Khan, Shah; Reza Pahlavi
Mohammad, Shah
Palestine Liberation Organization. See
PLO
Palestine mandate (1922), 257
Palestine/Palestinians
15 March Movement, 437
Arab-Jewish conflict beginnings, 258,
259 (box), 260–263, 264, 267
Arab Spring and, 436–438
Arab strike/effects (1936), 259 (box),
262–263
Britain and, 255–258, 259 (box), 260,
262–265
Britain's White Paper, 262, 263, 264,
267, 271
Hitler's rise/Jewish persecution and,
262, 263–264
independence movement, 258, 259
(box), 260
Intifada, First, 336, 373–374, 437
Intifada, Second, 382–383, 437
Jordan/Lebanon and "Black
September," 312–313
partition and, 262–263, 265, 266 (map),
273
as people/nation concept, 306–307
refugees, 274–275, 277, 282, 284, 307
See also Arab-Israeli conflict; Balfour
Declaration; Israel; *specific groups*;
Zionism
Palestinian Authority, 379, 381, 382, 383,
408, 412–413, 437
Pan-Arabism
Arab nationalism vs., 292, 298
in late 1950s/early 1960s, 293–294
Palestinian Arabs and, 306
Pan-Islam, 162, 186
Paris Peace Conference, 193–194, 202,
225, 229–230
Peace efforts. See Arab-Israeli peace
efforts
Peel, Lord/Peel Commission, 262–263
Peres, Shimon, 361, 380
Persia
after Safavid fall, 135, 159–160
before Muhammad, 13

Britain and, 160, 163, 178, 179–180,
200, 212–213
Buyid Dynasty, 73, 76–77, 79–80
cultural fusion/tolerance and, 13, 16, 18
description summary, 211–212
geographical area, 13, 16
historical recapitulation, 212
as Iran, 200, 215
nationalism, 177–180
overview, 177–178
Parthian rule, 16, 231–232
Qajar dynasty, 159–161, 177–179, 212,
213, 214
regaining power (after World War I),
199–200
Safavid dynasty, 112, 132–135, 159–160
Sassanid dynasty, 16, 17 (map), 18, 21,
44, 45–48, 68, 215
tobacco boycott (1892), 163, 178
See also Iran
Persian oil
Britain/Anglo-Persian Oil Company,
180, 212
discoveries, 180, 417–418
Pinsker, Leon, 252, 253
PLO
formation/beginnings, 295–296
move to Tunis, 373
peace talks and, 329–330, 332, 352
tactics, 307
zenith of power, 325–326
See also specific individuals
Poetry
after Muhammad, 106
before Muhammad, 20, 21, 237

Qadhafi, Mu'ammar al-
Arab-Israeli conflict, 315
capture/murder of, 436
Libya Arab Spring and, 434, 435
as Libyan/Arab nationalism leader,
310–311, 315, 318, 354, 434, 435
terrorism and, 435
Qa'ida, al-
formation, 384
terrorism and, 387, 388 (box), 391, 395,
395–396, 397, 398, 399, 402, 403,
406, 407, 426, 429 (box), 432, 436

Qajar dynasty, 159–161, 177–179, 212, 213, 214
Qanat system, 445, 446–448, 447 (photo)
Qasim, 'Abd al-Karim, 292, 293, 295, 366
Qatar, 398
Qur'an
  on Jews, 33
  language, 37, 92
  laws and, 30
  Muhammad's revelations and, 29
  Mu'tazila movement and, 70, 71 (box), 107–108, 109 (box)
  overview, 36, 37
  See also Islam; Muhammad

Rabin, Yitzhak, 324, 377, 378 (box), 379
Ramadan, 39–40, 102
Rashid, Harun al-, 68, 69, 70, 71 (box), 72, 73
Reagan, Ronald, 336, 346, 350–351, 354–355, 356, 357, 359, 360, 362
Reform definition/description, 148–149
Reforms in Middle East
  problems summary, 161–163
  See also specific countries
Religion
  revival (late 1970s-1980s), 337–338
  See also specific individuals; specific religions
Republic of Turkey. See Turkey
Reshid, Mustafa, 157–158, 158 (box)
Reza Khan, Shah, 213–216, 339, 345, 346
Reza Pahlavi Mohammad, Shah
  downfall, 217–218, 342–343
  as ruler/opposition to, 217, 335, 339, 340 (box), 341–342
Ridda wars, 45, 48
Rogers, William/Plan, 311–312, 313, 315
Roman Empire overview, 13–16
Rumsfeld, Donald, 403, 406
Russia
  Balkans and, 142–144, 154, 162, 174
  Crimean War, 142, 145, 158 (box), 159
  Greece/Greek Orthodoxy and, 141–142, 146, 156–157, 185
  Ottomans and, 141–144

pan-Slavism, 142, 186
Persia and, 163, 178, 179–180, 200, 212, 213
Sykes-Picot Agreement, 191
  See also specific events; specific individuals
Russo-Turkish War, 142, 162, 168, 175

Sa'd Zaghlul, 169, 228–229, 230–231, 235–236
Sadat, Anwar, al-
  assassination/background, 314 (box), 336, 352–354, 399, 421
  background, 313, 314 (box)
  as Egypt's leader/policies, 313, 314 (box), 453
  Nasir and, 314 (box), 318
  October War/aftermath and, 314 (box), 318–319, 323
  peace efforts/effects, 300, 314 (box), 331–333, 336, 344, 351–352
  Soviets and, 313, 314 (box), 318
Saddam Husayn
  Iran and, 310, 349, 366
  Kurds and, 360, 395
  Kuwait and, 366, 367–368, 369–370, 371
  political system of, 349, 370
  status of, 369–370
  US war in Iraq/removal from power, 387, 404
  See also Iraq
Safavid dynasty (Persia), 112, 132–135, 159–160
Sa'id, 146–147, 169
Sa'id, Khalid, 418, 421
Saladin (Salah al-Din), 86–87, 113
Salih, 'Ali Abdallah, 431, 432
Samuel, Sir Herbert, 258, 260
Sassanid dynasty (Persia), 16, 17 (map), 18, 21, 44, 45–48, 68, 215
Sa'ud family, 149, 196
Sa'ud, King, 290
Sa'udi Arabia
  emergence/rise of, 200, 218–220
  terrorism risk/conditions overview, 396–397
Wahhabis, 149, 218–219, 396

Sa'udi Arabia oil
  Aramco, 221–222, 223, 286
  conditions/economy before oil
    discoveries, 220–221
  Dhahran ("Little America"), 221, 222
  discoveries/effects, 221–223
  exports/revenues and, 221–222, 396
  those benefiting from, 292
Science/mathematics overview (early
  civilization), 104–106
Seale, Patrick, 289
Sebuktegin, 81–82
Selim I, Sultan, 125, 126 (map), 127
Selim II, Sultan, 127, 130
Selim III, Sultan, 139, 154, 181
Seljuk Empire, 82, 83 (map), 84, 85
Seljuks, Rum Seljuks, 82, 84, 88, 120, 122
Sèvres, Treaty of (1920), 196,
  204–205, 225
Shamir, Yitzhak, 258, 361, 362
Sham'un, Kamil, 289, 291
Shari'a
  description, 93, 100, 159
  development/relevance of, 94–95,
    97–98
"Sharif" defined, 188
Sharon, Ariel, 58, 258, 382–383, 409
Shi'ite Muslims
  beginnings, 56–58, 57 (fig.)
  Buyid Dynasty and, 73, 76–77, 79–80
  description/beliefs, 57–58, 76
  Fatimid Caliphate and, 76–79, 86
  Ghulat "extremes," 76
  Muhammad's succession and, 45
  revolutionary movement, 65
  sects of, 57 (fig.), 76
Shultz, George, 357, 359
Shuqayri, Ahmad al-, 296, 307
Shu'ubiya literary movement, 69–70
Social life of early Muslims, 98–103
Soil salinization, 446
Soviet Union and the Middle East
  Afghanistan and, 336, 346, 348–349,
    388 (box)
  conflict and, 293–294, 301, 303, 305,
    315, 319, 321, 347
  peace and, 305, 376
Soviet Union collapse/aftermath, 364, 376

Stern Gang, 264, 270, 272
Stevens, Christopher, 436
Sudan and Britain, 172, 229, 236, 237
Suez Affair, 287–288
Suez Canal/Company
  attempts to take from Britain, 190
  building/costs, 167
  Egyptian nationalizing/effects,
    280–281, 284, 286–287
  inauguration celebrations/costs, 167
  World War I and, 188
Sufis/Sufism, 61, 108–110, 120, 122, 124,
  129–130, 132, 134–135
Suleyman "the Magnificent", Sultan,
  126 (map), 127
Sunni Muslims
  description/beliefs, 57, 75
  early political theory, 98–99
  Ghaznavids/Seljuks, 81–82, 84
  Saladin/rise to power and, 86
Sykes-Picot Agreement, 191, 191–192,
  192, 192 (map), 195 (box), 201
Syria
  Alawite power and, 11, 424, 440
  Alexandretta and, 242
  Arab-Israeli conflict, 276–277,
    296, 297
  Assad family and, 424
  Ba'ath Party/Arab nationalism, 277,
    288–289, 289–290, 293, 296, 310,
    366, 392
  Britain and, 184, 289
  contest for controlling, 289–291
  description before 1914, 234
  Egypt union and, 290, 293–294
  ethnic/religious diversity, 234–235, 277
  famines, 190
  following World War I, 234–235
  France and, 144, 146, 184, 191, 194,
    196–197, 234–235, 241–242,
    247, 289
  Hama massacre (1982), 424–425
  historical territory, 289
  independence and, 235, 241–242, 243,
    247, 248
  nationalism and, 184
  revolution (1925–1927), 235, 241, 276
  Soviet Union and, 289, 290

terrorism risk/conditions overview, 392
World War II and, 243
Syria Arab "Spring" protests/civil war
Assad and, 425, 426, 428
background to, 424–425
description, 419, 425–426, 428
ISIL and, 426, 427 (map)
significance of, 428

Tabatabai, Sayyid Ziya, 213–214
Talat, 176–177, 201
Taliban, 384, 387, 388 (box), 398, 403
Tawfiq, Khedive, 168, 169, 170, 171 (box), 172, 228
Temple Mount, 62, 261, 261 (photo), 382
Terrorism
in 1971 (summary), 315
causes/handling, 360–361, 381, 399–400
hijacking passenger airplanes/cruise ships, 312, 359–360
Middle East risk (overview), 387, 389–393, 395–400
New York's World Trade Center bombings (1993), 377
9/11 attacks and, 386–387, 388 (box), 389, 397, 399, 402, 409, 415–416
Pan Am flight 103 and, 435
US embassies (1998), 377
See also Arab-Israeli conflict; *specific countries; specific groups/individuals*
Thant, U, 297, 306
Timur Leng conquests, 118–119, 124, 132
Transjordan, 233, 241, 242, 244–245
Truman, Harry, 223, 267, 271
Tunisia "Arab Spring," 418, 419–421
Turkey
"Arab" Spring/protests and, 441
Armenians and, 175, 200–201, 204
army takeover (1980), 210–211
Britain and, 205
Cyprus and, 210, 336, 390
Greek claims/invasion and, 202, 204, 205–206
independence, 203 (box), 204, 205–206
Kurds and, 206, 210, 365, 372, 390
Lausanne treaty/conference, 205–206

problems following World War I, 200–202
Sèvres, Treaty of (1920) and, 204–205
terrorism risk/conditions overview, 389–390
westernization, 203 (box), 207–208
See also Kemal, Mustafa (Ataturk);
Ottoman Empire
Turks, 72, 74, 80–82, 81, 83 (map), 84
Twelve-Imam (Ja'fari) Shiites, 57 (fig.), 76, 79, 96, 133, 160, 178, 211, 338
Twitchell, Karl, 221, 222

'Ubaydallah (al-Mahdi), 77
'*Ulama* beginnings/description, 61
'Umar I
background/assassination, 26, 45, 49, 61
Byzantine/Persian empires and, 45–46, 48
as caliph, 45–46, 48, 50, 55 (box)
Islamic government and, 48–49
'Umar II, 64
Umayyad caliphate
downfall/overthrow, 55 (box), 64–65
overview, 50–51, 61–64
See also specific caliphs
Umayyads, 49, 54, 55 (box), 56
United Arab Emirates, 199, 397
'Urabi, Ahmad, 169, 170, 171 (box), 184
Urban II, Pope, 84–85
'Uthman, 50–51, 52, 55 (box)

Veiling (of women), 42, 103, 207, 216
Venizelos, Eleftherios, 202, 205
Verdi, Giuseppe, 167

Wahhabis, 149, 153, 183, 218–220, 396
Water
gardens and, 444–445
importance/significance (overview), 443–445
oil/natural gas economies and, 443, 444, 448
shortages of, 443, 444, 448, 453, 454, 455
See also Environmental challenges

Water management
    access/pricing, 449–450
    conservation and, 450
    desalinated water, 448, 451
    overview, 445–446, 448
    political issues/vulnerabilities and,
        448, 450
    population density and, 446, 448
    qanat system, 445, 446–448,
        447 (photo)
    reusing treated waste water/Islam and,
        451–452
    rights/conflicts, 453–455
Watt, W. Montgomery, 26–27
Weizmann, Chaim, 194, 255
Western (Wailing) Wall, 260–261,
    261 (photo), 271, 302, 305
Westernization of the Middle East
    problems overview, 161–163
    See also specific examples
White Sheep Turcomans, 119, 132,
    133, 232
Wilson, Woodrow, 193, 194, 225, 229
Wingate, Sir Reginald, 229
Wolfowitz, Paul, 401, 403, 409
Women and Islam
    gender roles (early Muslim society),
        100
    Kemal's reforms and, 207
    restrictions/clothing, 38, 42, 100, 101,
        103, 372
    Reza's reforms and, 216
    See also Veiling (of women)
World War I and Middle East
    Arab nationalism and, 187–188
    beginnings, 144, 187–188
    independence and, 225–226
    Middle Eastern mandates, 196,
        197 (map), 198
    Ottoman Empire entering, 187–188

Paris Peace Conference, 193–194, 202,
    225, 229–230
    postwar European control (summary),
        199
    Sykes-Picot Agreement, 191–192,
        192 (map), 201
World War II and Middle East
    (overview), 242–243, 262, 263–264

Yazid, 54, 56, 58
Yemen
    Arab Spring protests/results, 431–433
    civil war/proxy war (1960s), 294–295,
        309
    Houthis and, 397, 432–433
    split/reuniting, 309–310, 397
    terrorism risk/conditions overview, 397
    water issues, 443
Yom Kippur, 29, 31
Yom Kippur War. *See* October (Yom
    Kippur) War (1973)
Young Turks, 175–177, 181, 186–187,
    188–189, 201, 202

Zaydi Shi'ites, 57 (fig.), 76, 220
Zengi, 86
Zionism
    beliefs/description, 249, 250–251,
        299
    early Palestine settlers, 253–255, 257
    political Zionism beginnings, 252–255
    Revisionists, 258
    terrorist groups, 264
    See also Arab-Israeli conflict; Balfour
        Declaration; Israel; King-Crane
        Commission; *specific individuals*
Ziyad, 53–54
Zoroaster, 13
Zoroastrianism, 13, 16, 18, 21, 47, 49, 59,
    69, 79, 92, 108, 215